Investigations in Clinical Phonetics
and Linguistics

Investigations in Clinical Phonetics and Linguistics

Edited by

Fay Windsor
Queen Margaret University College

M. Louise Kelly
University of Edinburgh

Nigel Hewlett
Queen Margaret University College

2002

LAWRENCE ERLBAUM ASSOCIATES, PUBLISHERS
Mahwah, New Jersey   London

Lawrence Erlbaum Associates, Inc., Publishers
10 Industrial Avenue
Mahwah, NJ 07430

Cover design by Kathryn Houghtaling Lacey

Library of Congress Cataloging-in-Publication Data

Investigations in clinical phonetics and linguistics / edited
by Fay Windsor, M. Louise Kelly, and Nigel Hewlett.
  p. cm.
Papers presented at the 8th meeting of the International Clinical
Phonetics and Linguistics Association which was held in summer
2000, hosted by Queen Margaret University College, Edinburgh,
Scotland.

Includes bibliographical references and index.
ISBN 0-8058-4015-X (alk. paper)
1. Language disorders—Congresses. 2. Linguistics—Congresses.
  3. Phonetics—Congresses. I. Windsor, Fay. II. Kelly, M. Louise.
  III. Hewlett, Nigel. IV. International Clinical Phonetics and Linguistics Association. Congress (8th : 2000 : Queen Margaret University College).
RC423.A1 I58 2001
616.85'5—dc21   2001040979
                                                      CIP

Books published by Lawrence Erlbaum Associates are printed
on acid-free paper, and their bindings are chosen for strength
and durability.

Printed in the United States of America
10 9 8 7 6 5 4 3 2 1

Contents

Contributors

Hermann Ackermann
Neurologische Klinik Tübingen
Tübingen, Germany

Wafaa Ammar
Department of Phonetics
University of Alexandria
Alexandria, Egypt

Raquel T. Anderson
Department of Speech
and Hearing Sciences
Indiana University
Bloomington, Indiana, USA

Shaheen N. Awan
Department of Audiology
& Speech Pathology
Bloomsburg University
Bloomsburg, Pennsylvania, USA

Luisa Barzaghi
Department of Speech Therapy
Pontificia Universidade Católica de
São Paulo, Brazil

Kirsten Meyer Bjerkan
Bredtvet Resource Center
Oslo, Norway

Tim Bressmann
Graduate Department of
Speech–Language Pathology
University of Toronto
Ontario, Canada

Joyce C. Chun
Department of Speech
and Hearing Sciences
University of Hong Kong
Hong Kong

Heather L. Clemons
Speech–Language Pathologist
Leon County (Texas) Special
Education
Centerville, Texas, USA

Paul A. Dagenais
Department of Speech Pathology
and Audiology
University of South Alabama
Mobile, Alabama, USA

Raymond Daniloff
Department of Communication
Disorders
Louisiana State University
Health Sciences Center
New Orleans, Louisiana, USA

Barbara Dodd
Department of Speech
University of Newcastle upon Tyne
Newcastle, UK

Jan van Doorn
School of Communication Sciences
and Disorders
The University of Sydney
Lidcombe, New South Wales
Australia

Jadine Doyle
Department of Communication
Sciences and Disorders
University of Texas
Austin, Texas, USA

Matthias Fröhlich
Abt. Phoniatrie & Pädaudiologie
Universität Göttingen
Germany

Fiona E. Gibbon
Department of Speech
and Language Sciences
Queen Margaret University College
Edinburgh, UK

Jacqueline Guendouzi
School of Speech
& Language Therapy
University of Central England
Birmingham, UK

Ingo Hertrich
Neurologische Klinik Tübingen
Tübingen, Germany

Barry Heselwood
Department of Linguistics
& Phonetics
University of Leeds
Leeds, UK

Lynne E. Hewitt
Department of Communication
Disorders
Bowling Green State University
Bowling Green, Ohio, USA

Nigel Hewlett
Department of Speech
and Language Sciences
Queen Margaret University College
Edinburgh, UK

Sara Howard
Department of Human
Communication Sciences
University of Sheffield
Sheffield, UK

Damir Horga
Department of Phonetics
University of Zagreb
Zagreb, Croatia

Phil Hoole
Institute of Phonetics and Speech
Communication
Ludwigs-Maximilians University
Munich, Germany

Zhu Hua
Department of Speech
University of Newcastle upon Tyne
Newcastle, UK

Marion Jaeger
Lurija-Institute – Kliniken Schmieder
Allensbach, Germany

Youngjun Jang
Department of English
Chung-Ang University
Seoul, Korea

Deborah G. H. James
Department of Speech Pathology
Flinders University of South Australia
Adelaide, South Australia
Australia

M. Louise Kelly
Department of Psychology
University of Edinburgh
Edinburgh, UK

Misuk Kim
Department of Child Welfare Study
Chung-Ang University
Seoul, Korea

Heather Knapp
Department of Psychology
University of Washington
Seattle, USA

Catherine L. Knych
John Heinz Institute
of Rehabilitative Medicine
Wilkes-Barre, Pennsylvania, USA

Sanja Krapinec
University Clinic Sestara Milosrdnica
Zagreb, Croatia

Marianne Lind
Bredtvet Resource Center
Oslo, Norway

John L. Locke
Faculty of Social and Political Sciences
University of Cambridge
Cambridge, UK

Sharynne McLeod
School of Community Health
Charles Sturt University
Albury, New South Wales
Australia

Sandra Madureira
Department of Linguistics
Pontificia Universidade Católica de
São Paulo, Brazil

Eva Magnusson
Department of Linguistics
Lund University
Lund, Sweden

Christelle Maillart
Université de Psychologie et des
Sciences de L'Education
Louvain-la-Louvain, Belgium

Thomas P. Marquardt
Department of Communication
Sciences and Disorders
University of Texas
Austin, Texas, USA

Ben Maassen
Medical Psychology/Child Neurology
Center
University Medical Center St. Radboud
Nijmegen, The Netherlands

Harald Masur
Department of Neurology
Edith-Stein-Fachklinik
Bad Bergzabern, Germany

Beatriz Mendes
Department of Speech Therapy
Pontificia Universidade Católica de
São Paulo, Brazil

Sjoeke van der Meulen
Department of Phoniatrics
Utrecht Hospital Utrecht/Wilhelmina
Children's Hospital
Utrecht, The Netherlands

Adele W. Miccio
Department of Communication
Disorders
The Pennsylvania State University
Pennsylvania, USA

Haruko Miyakoda
Tokyo University of Agriculture
and Technology
Tokyo, Japan

Nicole Müller
Department of Communication
Disorders
University of Louisiana
Louisiana, USA

Kerstin Nauclér
Department of Linguistics
Lund University
Lund, Sweden

Lian Nijland
Medical Psychology/Child Neurology
Center
Nijmegen, The Netherlands

Susan Nittrouer
Boys Town National Research Hospital
Omaha, Nebraska, USA

Judith Oxley
Department of Communication
Disorders
Louisiana State University Health
Sciences Center
New Orleans, Louisiana, USA

Zvi Penner
Fachbereich Sprachwissenschaft
Universität Konstanz
Konstanz, Germany

Mick Perkins
Department of Human Communication
Sciences
University of Sheffield
Sheffield, UK

Vicki A. Reed
School of Communication Sciences
and Disorders
The University of Sydney
Lidcombe, New South Wales
Australia

Robert Sader
Department of Oral and Maxillofacial
Surgery
University of Technology
Munich, Germany

Nabil Samman
Department of Oral and Maxillofacial
Surgery
University of Hong Kong
Hong Kong

Gabriele Scharf
Department of Neurology
Edith-Stein-Fachklinik
Bad Bergzabern, Germany

Marie-Anne Schelstraete
Université de Psychologie et des
Sciences de L'Education
Louvain-la-Louvain, Belgium

Paul-Walter Schönle
Lurija-Institute – Kliniken Schmieder
Allensbach, Germany

Petra Schulz
Fachbereich Sprachwissenschaft
Universität Konstanz
Konstanz, Germany

Hanne Gram Simonsen
Department of Linguistics
University of Oslo
Oslo, Norway

M. Helen Southwood
Division of Speech
and Hearing Sciences
University of Alabama at Birmingham
Birmingham, Alabama, USA

Smiljka Štajner-Katušic
University Clinic Sestara Milosrdnica
Zagreb, Croatia

Stavroula Stavrakaki
School of English
Aristotle University of Thessaloniki
Thessaloniki, Greece

M. Irene Stephens
Department of Communication
Disorders
Northern Illinois University
Illinois, USA

Harvey M. Sussman
Department of Linguistics and
Communication Sciences & Disorders
University of Texas
Austin, Texas, USA

Gisela Szagun
Institute für Kognitionsforschung
Universität Oldenburg
Oldenburg, Germany

Lynne Vernon-Feagans
University of North Carolina
at Chapel Hill
North Carolina, USA

Li Wei
Department of Speech
University of Newcastle upon Tyne
Newcastle, UK

Tara Whitehill
Department of Speech
and Hearing Sciences
University of Hong Kong
Hong Kong

Amy F. Wilson
Department of Speech Pathology
and Audiology
University of South Alabama
Mobile, Alabama, USA

Fay Windsor
Department of Speech
and Language Sciences
Queen Margaret University College
Edinburgh, UK

Karin Wymann
Fachbereich Sprachwissenschaft
Universität Konstanz
Konstanz, Germany

Kristine M. Yont
Harvard University Graduate School
of Education
Cambridge, Massachusetts, USA

Mehmet Yavas
Linguistics Program
Florida International University
Miami, Florida, USA

Elena Zaretsky
Department of Psychology
Boston University
Boston, Massachusetts, USA

Preface

This book could be described as the sequel to a conference which took place in Edinburgh in the summer of 2000. The eighth meeting of the International Clinical Phonetics and Linguistics Association was hosted by Queen Margaret University College, Edinburgh and attended by delegates from 26 different countries. After the conference, presenters were invited to submit their contribution as a chapter for this book. The response was excellent and, based on referees' reports and our own judgement, we were keen to publish 38 of the submissions we received, despite the fact that this would greatly exceed the maximum length previously negotiated with the publisher. Our publisher agreed, for which we are grateful.

We believe that this book reflects the *scope of the subject area* of clinical phonetics and linguistics, the *balance of input* into it with respect to the different kinds of research being carried on, and the *representation of researchers* from different parts of the world. Its scope includes the application of all levels of linguistic analysis and the chapters of the book have been ordered as far as possible according to linguistic level, beginning with pragmatics and ending with acoustics. It will be immediately apparent that a greater number of chapters are concerned with applications of phonetics and phonology than with any other levels. We believe that this loading towards the phonetic end of the process of communication faithfully mirrors the current prevailing balance of clinical research in speech and language. This unequal distribution may be due to historical reasons or it may reflect a prevalence of phonetic and phonological disorders in the population.

Perhaps the most pleasing aspect of editing this book has been the opportunity to bring together and publicize research from all over the world. Research in different parts of the globe addresses the same issues and though the language of this book, like that of its predecessors[1], is English, the analysis of disordered communication is illustrated here on a large number of different languages, including Arabic, Croatian, Dutch, French, German, Greek, Japanese, Korean, Norwegian, Spanish, Portuguese, Putonghua and Swedish.

---

[1]See: Powell, T. W. (Ed.). (1996). *Pathologies of Speech and Language: Contributions of Clinical Phonetics and Linguistics.* New Orleans, LA: ICPLA. Siegler, W., & Deger, K. (Eds.). (1998). *Clinical phonetics and linguistics.* London: Whurr. Maassen, B., & Groenen, P. (Eds.). (1999). *Pathologies of speech and language: Advances in clinical phonetics and linguistics.* London: Whurr.

1

An Emergentist Approach to Clinical Pragmatics

Mick Perkins

In this chapter I will argue that pragmatics is not a module or a behaviorally coherent entity, and that it is therefore inappropriate to regard pragmatic impairment as a diagnostic category. I propose instead that pragmatic ability and disability are emergent functions of interactions that take place both within and between human minds.

PROBLEMS IN DEFINING PRAGMATIC IMPAIRMENT

Definitions of pragmatics vary widely, and yet despite this, in most clinical studies and assessments of pragmatic impairment it is taken for granted that the nature of pragmatics is well known and straightforward, even though quite inconsistent analytical frameworks are used. To cite only one example, two widely used checklists of pragmatic impairment – Penn's *Profile of Communicative Appropriateness*, and Prutting & Kirchner's *Pragmatic Protocol* (Penn, 1988; Prutting & Kirchner, 1983), contain 30 and 51 items respectively, and yet have only about a dozen items in common (Perkins, 2000).

A classic definition of pragmatics is 'the way *language* is used', and yet we often find non-linguistic features of communication such as gesture, eye gaze, posture and social rapport described as examples of pragmatics even when they occur independently of language use, as often happens in aphasia. This is common in the language pathology literature. For example, Dronkers, Ludy and Redfern (1998) and Avent, Wertz and Auther (1998) both assume that 'pragmatic behavior' is isolable and distinct from linguistic behavior, as is clear from the titles of their articles – viz. "Pragmatics in the absence of verbal language" and "Relationship between language impairment and pragmatic behavior in aphasic adults" respectively. Neurolinguists, also, tend to distinguish pragmatic behavior from linguistic behavior to the extent that they see them as governed by different cerebral hemispheres (cf. Paradis, 1998, p. 5, "there is increasing evidence that pragmatic competence is subserved by specific areas of the RH"). Linguists, on the other hand, whose traditional focus has been almost exclusively on language, hardly ever dissociate pragmatics from language use in this way (cf. Crystal, 1997, p. 435, who defines pragmatics as "the study of the factors influencing a person's choice of *language"* [my italics]).

This apparent difference between linguists, on the one hand, and neurolinguists and language pathologists on the other arises from the fact that the latter constantly see evidence of successful communication in the face of language loss, and therefore more readily appreciate that communication is independent of language. This is also the view of semiotically-oriented – as opposed to linguistically-oriented – theories of pragmatics such as Relevance Theory (Sperber & Wilson, 1995) and Joint Action Theory (Clark, 1996) which emphasize that language is one communication 'aid' among many, albeit a uniquely complex and central one.

SOME CONSEQUENCES FOR CLINICAL PRAGMATICS

The disparity in the assumptions made about pragmatics by different disciplines is rarely acknowledged, and this has led to a great deal of inconsistency and confusion in the description and diagnosis of pragmatic impairment. In addition, given the narrow linguistic focus of most pragmatic theories, it is particularly unfortunate that in research on communication disorders they have been imported wholesale and without adaptation, despite the potentially corrective insights available from language pathology and neurolinguistics. Furthermore, although theories of pragmatics provide a means of *describing* pragmatic impairments, the level of *explanation* they afford is rarely adequate for speech and language therapists, and does not translate easily into clinical intervention. For example, in the following exchange:

> *Adult*: and what's in this picture?
> *Child*: it's a sheep – on a farm – and my uncle's farm
> and it has babies – baby lambs
> and tadpoles – frogs have baby tadpoles
> but tadpoles don't have any legs – do they?
> but frogs have legs – and it was in the pond – and
> mommy saw it …

the child could be *described* as breaking Grice's maxims of quantity ('do not make your contribution more informative than required'), relevance ('make your contribution relevant') and possibly manner ('be brief') (Grice, 1975), but such descriptive labels don't get us very far when trying to design a remedial program (Perkins, 2000). One can hardly tell the child to "stop breaking Grice's maxims"! There are many potential causes of such behavior, and it is these which we need to address.

AN EMERGENTIST APPROACH TO PRAGMATICS

Despite the differences outlined above, one assumption apparently shared by many linguists and language pathologists alike is that pragmatic capacity may be treated as a distinct entity, whether it be as a mental module (or a set of modules) (Kasher, 1991) or as some kind of behavior (e.g. discussion of dissociations between linguistic ability and pragmatic performance (Avent et al., 1998)). In this chapter I will suggest to the contrary that pragmatics is not a coherent behavioral or cognitive entity at all, but an emergent consequence of interactions between cognitive, linguistic and sensorimotor processes (Perkins, 1998a, 1998b; 2000). This approach draws on a range of insights from Joint Action Theory (Clark, 1996), Relevance Theory (Sperber & Wilson, 1995), clinical applications of Conversation Analysis (e.g. Tarplee & Barrow, 1999) and emergentist approaches to cognitive science (e.g. Bates, Wulfeck, Hernandez & Andanova, 1996; Clark, 1997; Clark, 1999; MacWhinney, 1999), and includes the following key assumptions[1]:

1. Pragmatics involves the range of choices open to us when we communicate – e.g. what is said, how it's said, why it's said, when it's said, where it's said, and who says it.

2. Such choices are involved at all 'levels' of language processing, from discourse down to phonology and phonetics.

3. The choices are not exclusively linguistic, but also involve the way communication is distributed across verbal and nonverbal channels. (Clark, 1996, for example, has shown that most communicative signals are simultaneous composites extending across several different modalities.)

4. Pragmatics is not a module, nor a distinct level of language, and does not even constitute a separate component of a theory of language[2].

---

[1] For a much fuller account of this approach, see Perkins (forthcoming).

[2] Cf. the definition of pragmatics proposed by Verschueren (Verschueren, 1999, p. 7): "a general cognitive, social, and cultural perspective on linguistic phenomena in relation to their usage in forms of behavior".

Instead, it is an emergent function of interactions between linguistic, cognitive and sensorimotor systems (which are themselves emergent functions of neurophysiological interactions).

This view is somewhat reminiscent of Wilson and Sperber's (1991, p. 583) suggestion that pragmatics is "the domain in which grammar, logic and memory interact", although as I will suggest, we need to take into account far more than just grammar, logic and memory.

5.   In order to qualify as 'pragmatic', interactions must be motivated by the requirements of interpersonal communication. However, the interactions may occur both within individuals – i.e. *intra*personal – or between individuals – i.e. *inter*personal.

Fig. 1 (for a slightly different version and more discussion see Perkins, 1998b) summarizes some of the linguistic, cognitive and sensorimotor systems whose interactions form the basis of pragmatic ability.

Pragmatic behavior is an emergent consequence of interactions within and between:

A.   The *linguistic systems* which enable us to encode and decode meaning.
B.   The *cognitive systems* which determine what to communicate, and why, when, where and how to encode and decode what is communicated.
C.   The *sensorimotor systems* which allow for distribution of encoded information across a range modalities.

PRAGMATIC ABILITY *is a function of interactions between:*		
Linguistic systems	*Cognitive systems*	*Sensorimotor input & output systems*
e.g. phonology prosody morphology syntax discourse lexis	e.g. inference social cognition theory of mind executive function memory affect conceptual knowledge	e.g. vocal-auditory gestural-visual

FIG. 1 Linguistic, cognitive and sensorimotor bases of pragmatic ability.

WHAT IS PRAGMATIC IMPAIRMENT?

Pragmatic impairment results when communicative interaction is negatively affected by a restriction in the range of choices available for encoding and decoding meaning. For clinical purposes, rather than simply describing the resulting behavior, it is important to be able to specify whether such an impairment is a result of: a) a nonlinguistic impairment; b) a linguistic impairment; or c) a combination.

Fig. 2 (from Perkins, 1988a) provides a means of classifying pragmatic impairment in terms of contributory dysfunctions.

Type of pragmatic impairment	Underlying cause
Primary Pragmatic Impairment (PPI)	*Dysfunction of*: - inferential reasoning - social cognition - theory of mind - executive function - memory - affect - conceptual knowledge
Secondary Pragmatic Impairment (SPI)	*a) Linguistic dysfunction* - phonology - prosody - morphology - syntax - lexis *b) Sensorimotor dysfunction* - auditory perception - visual perception - motor/articulatory ability
Complex Pragmatic Impairment (CPI)	*Multiple sources*

FIG. 2 A classification scheme for pragmatic impairment.

Primary Pragmatic Impairment (PPI) results from cognitive dysfunction; Secondary Pragmatic Impairment (SPI) results from either linguistic dysfunction or sensorimotor dysfunction; and Complex Pragmatic Impairment (CPI) results from dysfunction in more than one of these systems. (For more detailed discussion, see Perkins, 2000.) The term 'primary' has been applied to pragmatic impairments with cognitive causes since it is problems with inference (e.g. Dipper, Bryan & Tyson, 1997), social cognition (e.g. Cohen, Menna, Vallance, Barwick, Im & Horodezky, 1998), theory of mind (e.g. Volden, Mulcahy & Holdgrafter, 1997), executive function (e.g. Tannock & Schachar, 1996), memory (e.g. Almor, Kempler, MacDonald, Andersen & Tyler, 1999), affect (e.g. Lorch, Borod & Koff, 1998) and conceptual knowledge (e.g. Rein &

Kernan, 1989) that are most commonly noted as concomitants of pragmatic disability.

In addition, pragmatic impairment is sometimes associated with disorders of phonology (e.g. Campbell & Shriberg, 1982), prosody (e.g. Wertz, Henschel, Auther, Ashford & Kirshner, 1998), morphology (e.g. Tesak, 1994), syntax (e.g. Niemi & Hägg, 1999) and lexis (e.g. Chobor & Schweiger, 1998), on the one hand, and on the other with disorders of hearing (e.g. Dronkers, Ludy & Redfern, 1998), vision (e.g. Mills, 1993) and articulation (e.g. Crystal, 1987). However, in such cases it is more common to regard the pragmatic impairment as a secondary consequence rather than a defining feature.

Fig. 2, however, is still somewhat simplistic in that it may be taken to suggest that there is a straightforward 1:1 relationship between an underlying dysfunction and a resulting behavior (cf. the comments made by Wilson & McAnulty, 2000, p. 46). Even at a more general level, although there may be a strong link between cognitive dysfunction and pragmatic impairment, cognition is not *solely* responsible. Rather it is the *interaction* between cognitive, linguistic and sensorimotor systems that determines pragmatic behavior. Impairment in a component of an organism creates a state of disequilibrium both within the organism itself and between the organism and other organisms, and such a state typically results in attempted compensation. In other words, virtually all instances of pragmatic impairment turn out to be instances of Complex Pragmatic Impairment (CPI). The challenge, therefore, is to describe not only impaired communicative behaviors together with the specific dysfunctions which underlie them, but also the way in which the dysfunction has been compensated for within the organism as a whole.

The picture is even further complicated by the fact that in addition to interactions and compensations within the individual, interpersonal interactions and compensations also take place between individuals motivated by communicative needs. As Clark (1996, p. 388) has noted: "Many phenomena have been treated as features of language use when they are really features of the joint activities in which the language is being used". The cognitive and linguistic capacities of individuals do not exist in a vacuum. Rather, the things that we say, think and do are integral components of the larger dynamic constituted by ourselves and our interactants. ("Our cognitive profile is *essentially* the profile of an embodied and situated organism", Clark, 1999, p. 14.) Viewed in this way, pragmatics is best regarded as emergent, or epiphenomenal (Perkins, 1998b), rather than as a distinct level of language, a mental module or any other independent cognitive or behavioral entity.

Interactionist approaches to pragmatic impairment of the kind proposed here have sometimes been criticized on the grounds that the range of phenomena encompassed is so wide-ranging and heterogeneous that the term 'pragmatics' becomes meaningless (Craig, 1995, p. 632). However, if the kinds of interactions identified above – varied as they are – are indeed necessary for a more extensive understanding of human communication and its impairment, then presumably it is more important to attempt to characterize them in as much detail as we can, rather than exclude many of them in an attempt to preserve the apparently spurious integrity of the term 'pragmatics'. In the rest of this paper, I will briefly describe two very different types of communication disorder which both merit the descriptive label of 'pragmatic impairment' but whose underlying aetiology illustrates that the interactionist approach proposed above is essential in order to be able to devise an appropriate and effective intervention strategy.

PRAGMATIC IMPAIRMENT ARISING FROM COGNITIVE DYSFUNCTION AND INTRAPERSONAL COMPENSATION

Colin, a builder in his late 40s, suffered traumatic brain injury (TBI) following a fall from a roof[3]. CT scan revealed extensive fractures over the vault of the skull, an acute subdural collection on the right side and marked oedema. Psychometric testing showed particular problems with attention, memory and executive function. His communicative behavior following the incident was perceived as 'bizarre', and he was found to be difficult to interact with. To the extent that his conversational difficulties can be traced back to underlying cognitive dysfunction, he may be described as having a primary pragmatic impairment (PPI). Two key pragmatic elements of his behavior were topic drift – a tendency to change topic with excessive and inappropriate frequency (see Transcript 1 below) – and topic bias – a tendency to focus in conversation on an inappropriately restricted set of topics. In other words, his conversational behavior could appear both unfocused and yet excessively focused at the same time.

Transcript 1: Topic drift
> and did you know then what's happened to Colin now?
> fallen off a roof and fractured his skull – you know that
> I look on life as a bonus
> and just enjoy every day as it comes
> but . I would say . a bad fault of mine
> and I would say s it's happening over t last – couple of month
> I call a spade a spade a trump a trump
> and – I just said to Sarah
> because I do go to church a lot
> and I said she says what people do I love
> and I says I only love four

---

[3] For a more extensive account of this case study, see Perkins, Body and Parker (1995).

Colin's topic bias consisted of frequent reversion to two broad classes of topic: a) opinions – as in Transcript 2, which is Colin's response to the request 'How would you fill a car up with petrol?':

Transcript 2: Topic bias
right . you basically . it's just filling up a car with petrol but there's quite a few things I would say . not a motorist . well . most motorists I would say aren't too bad but people . I would say learners . who've just passed their test or getting overconfident or a lax attitude in putting petrol into the car a lot of drivers male or female actually seem to don't give two monkeys about where the petrol goes

and b) a limited set of autobiographical episodes.

Extensive analysis revealed that Colin's topic drift and topic bias were not primary deficits in themselves, but were instead the emergent consequences of a communicative strategy by which he attempted to compensate for his problems with attention, memory and executive function, and therefore an instance of complex – rather than primary – pragmatic impairment. Continually faced with being unable to remember how he had reached a particular point in a conversation, and yet wishing to continue, Colin used one of two compensatory strategies:

a)   produce an utterance with a semantic link to the immediately preceding one, as in Transcript 3. Because this process is iterative, with Colin being unable to recall, or return to, earlier reference points in the discourse, the emergent effect is that of topic drift.

Transcript 3
the digs that I've stopped in have been farms or hostels with a big <u>garden</u>

and <u>I do actually</u> like <u>gardening</u>

<u>I do actually</u> get on with people at work

b)   revert to a default a topic whose conversational import relies on its subjective significance to Colin rather than on an objective link to a previous topic, i.e. an opinion or an autobiographical episode. The emergent effect here is that of topic bias.

Once Colin's topic drift and topic bias were construed as conversational repair strategies, rather than merely pragmatically bizarre behavior, it was possible to devise an effective intervention program.

PRAGMATIC IMPAIRMENT AND INTERPERSONAL COMPENSATION

Peter was diagnosed as having Specific Language Impairment at the age of 2;6[4]. Seven years later at 9;6 a range of formal tests put him at approximately 2 years below his chronological age on production and comprehension of grammar and lexis. However, what formal tests do not reveal is that Peter's linguistic performance is very variable. Sometimes he is able to produce fluently sentences of considerable syntactic and semantic complexity. At other times, his production is full of grammatical formulation and lexical retrieval errors, and his delivery is halting and dysfluent. Conversing with Peter typically feels labored and burdensome, and to the extent that this results from his linguistic difficulties, he may be described as having a secondary pragmatic impairment (SPI). Detailed analysis showed, however, that as in the case of Colin (discussed earlier), the only way to account for his linguistic variability was in terms of a complex set of linguistic and cognitive interactions, and that once again we are dealing with a case of CPI. When factors such as task complexity and processing speed are taken into account, it turns out that Peter's problems with lexical retrieval and syntax are compensatory solutions to competing demands on a slow and limited cognitive processing capacity. Although he is not lacking in linguistic resources, he is not able to make use of them as readily and efficiently as he would wish. To cope with this he has devised a range of compensatory strategies. For example, when under pressure he will reduce the syntactic complexity of his utterances by using coordinated lists of lexically related words and phrases; fail to monitor his lexical selection retrospectively; and make use of immediate context to aid in lexical retrieval when responding to general questions. Although such strategies are clearly helpful for Peter, they sometimes produce pragmatically bizarre results (for examples, see Perkins, in press).

A further strategy that Peter uses quite successfully is to make use of the linguistic and cognitive resources of his interlocutor. One example of this is in Transcript 4, where retrieval of the word 'waiter' results from a collaborative effort between Peter and his interlocutor, Sara.

Transcript 4

Peter	last year we went to Bulgaria and it wasn't (.) er
Sara	.hhh
Peter	it was horrible
Sara	it was horrible?
Peter	but (0.8) .hh wa (.) a we did like the dinner and (.) that (0.6) but erm (1.6) there were (.) a (.) there was (.) one

---

[4] For a more extensive account of this case study, see Perkins (in press).

called Mike (1.5) one called (2.1) oh (.) erm (3.4) erm
(2.5) I don't know his name now
Sara   right
Peter   other one
Sara   right
Peter   but there was (2.0) ff oh (.) and one was called John (1.6)
        I don't know the (0.5) other one
Sara   and who were they?
Peter   (1.4) they was do you know (.) erm (.) when you (.) do
        you know when (1.6) it's a servant (0.5) [and]
Sara   [right] (0.8) yeah
Peter   and (.) and they bring the dinner in for you
Sara   a waiter?
Peter   waiter (.) yeah

Here we see linguistic and cognitive interactions extending into the interpersonal domain. Recent research in cognitive science has shown clearly how a communicative dyad or group may effectively function as an organism in the same way as an individual person, at least as far as processes such as equilibrium and compensation are concerned (e.g. Clark, 1996, Clark, 1997, 1999; Hutchins, 1995). In the conversation between Peter and Sara shown in Transcript 4, because Peter is linguistically and cognitively impaired Sara has to work far harder than she would normally in order to achieve a satisfactory conversational outcome. One could say that Sara has been 'co-opted' by Peter to do extra inferential work and to facilitate, and to some extent carry out, his lexical retrieval. Although there may be no specific *intention* to co-opt the cognitive resources of an interlocutor, nor indeed any conscious intention on the part of the interlocutor to respond, the pressure for homeostasis through compensation exerted on the communicative process by an individual's language impairment is typically irresistible. There are many attested examples of this, particularly in the aphasiology literature (e.g. Fex & Mansson, 1998; Klippi, 1996; Oelschlaeger & Damico, 1998; Simmons-Mackie & Damico, 1996).

An important clinical consequence of regarding the human dyad as an interactive cognitive and linguistic system is that communication impairments become common property, rather than the problem of an individual. In Peter's case, remediation included making interactants such as his teachers aware of the processing demands of a range of common communicative tasks, and devising ways of reducing them.

CONCLUSION

My aim in this chapter has been to show that although language pathologists have learned a great deal from the discipline of pragmatics over the last twenty years, its theoretical focus on 'normal' communication has proved something of a straightjacket as far as the development of clinically useful procedures is concerned. Cognitively oriented approaches such as Sperber and Wilson's Relevance Theory (Sperber & Wilson, 1995) and Clark's Joint Action Theory (Clark, 1996) hold out considerable promise, though their application to communication disorders has so far been minimal. We may well have reached a situation where theories of pragmatics can offer little more to the language pathologist until the theorists themselves take on board the significance of research in the area of pragmatic impairment. As Sinclair (1995, p. 530) notes: "It seems fair to predict ... that evidence about typical breakdown patterns will in future play quite an important role in the appraisal of conflicting claims about how pragmatics is represented in the mind". What such research seems to show is that pragmatics is not a module or a behaviorally coherent entity, and that the term 'pragmatic impairment' is of little diagnostic validity because of the disparate range of conditions that in encompasses. I have suggested here that pragmatic ability and disability are best regarded as the emergent consequence of interactions between linguistic, cognitive and sensorimotor systems as motivated by the requirements of interpersonal communication. In order to characterize the nature of pragmatic impairments, we need to be able to link the relative contributions of specific cognitive (PPI), linguistic and sensorimotor dysfunctions (SPI) to the atypical communicative behaviors which result. But perhaps even more importantly, we must also be aware of the complex effects of the compensatory interactions which take place within and between individuals.

REFERENCES

Almor, A., Kempler, D., MacDonald, M. C., Andersen, E. S., & Tyler, L. K. (1999). Why do Alzheimer patients have difficulty with pronouns? Working memory, semantics, and reference in comprehension and production in Alzheimer's disease. *Brain and Language, 67*, 202-227.

Avent, J. R., Wertz, R. T., & Auther, L. (1998). Relationship between language impairment and pragmatic behavior in aphasic adults. *Journal of Neurolinguistics, 11*, 207-221.

Bates, E., Wulfeck, B., Hernandez, A., & Andanova, E. (1996). The competition model: Implications for language processing, language development and language breakdown. In B. Kokinov (Ed.), *Perspectives on cognitive science, Vol 2* (pp. 7-72). Sofia: New Bulgarian University.

Campbell, T. F., & Shriberg, L. D. (1982). Associations among pragmatic functions, linguistic stress and natural phonological processes in speech-delayed children. *Journal of Speech and Hearing Research, 25*, 547-553.

Chobor, K. L., & Schweiger, A. (1998). Processing of lexical ambiguity in patients with traumatic brain injury. *Journal of Neurolinguistics, 11*, 119-136.

Clark, A. (1997). *Being there: Putting brain, body, and world together again.* Cambridge, MA: MIT Press.

Clark, A. (1999). Where brain, body, and world collide. *Journal of Cognitive Systems Research, 1*, 5-17.

Clark, H. H. (1996). *Using language.* Cambridge, UK: Cambridge University Press.

Cohen, N. J., Menna, R., Vallance, D. D., Barwick, M. A., Im, N., & Horodezky, N. B. (1998). Language, social cognitive processing, and behavioral characteriztics of prychiatrically disturbed children with previously identified and unsuspected language impairments. *Journal of Child Psychology and Psychiatry, 39*, 853-864.

Craig, H. K. (1995). Pragmatic impairments. In P. Fletcher & B. MacWhinney (Eds.), *The handbook of child language* (pp. 623-640). Oxford: Blackwell.

Crystal, D. (1987). Towards a 'bucket' theory of language disability: taking account of interaction between linguistic levels. *Clinical Linguistics and Phonetics, 1*, 7-22.

Crystal, D. (1997). *The Cambridge encyclopedia of language (2nd ed.).* Cambridge, UK: Cambridge University Press.

Dipper, L. T., Bryan, K. L., & Tyson, J. (1997). Bridging inference and Relevance Theory: an account of right hemisphere inference. *Clinical Linguistics and Phonetics, 11*, 213-228.

Dronkers, N. F., Ludy, C. A., & Redfern, B. B. (1998). Pragmatics in the absence of verbal language: descriptions of a severe aphasic and a language-deprived adult. *Journal of Neurolinguistics, 11*, 179-190.

Fex, B., & Mansson, A-C. (1998). The use of gestures as a compensatory strategy in adults with acquired aphasia compared to children with specific language impairment. *Journal of Neurolinguistics, 11*, 191-206.

Grice, H. P. (1975). Logic and conversation. In F. Cole & J. L. Morgan (Eds.), *Syntax and semantics 3: Speech acts* (pp. 41-58). New York: Academic.

Hutchins, E. (1995). *Cognition in the wild.* Cambridge, Mass: MIT Press.

Kasher, A. (1991). On the pragmatic modules: A lecture. *Journal of Pragmatics, 16*, 381-397.

Klippi, A. (1996). *Conversation as an achievement in aphasics (Vol. 6).* Helsinki: Suomalaisen Kirjallisuuden Seura.

Lorch, M. P., Borod, J. C., & Koff, E. (1998). The role of emotion in the linguistic and pragmatic aspects of aphasic performance. *Journal of Neurolinguistics, 11*, 103-118.

MacWhinney, B. (Ed.). (1999). *The emergence of language.* Mahwah, NJ: Lawrence Erlbaum Associates.

Mills, A. E. (1993). Language acquisition and development with sensory impairment: blind children. In G. Blanken, J. Dittmann, H. Grimm, J. C. Marshall, & C-W. Wallesch (Eds.), *Linguistic disorders and pathologies: An international handbook* (pp. 679-687). Berlin: Walter de Gruyter.

Niemi, J., & Hägg, M. (1999). Syntax at late stages of acquisition: Experiments with normal and SLI children. In B. Maassen & P. Groenen (Eds.), *Pathologies of speech and language: Advances in clinical phonetics and linguistics* (pp. 76-81). London: Whurr.

Oelschlaeger, M. L., & Damico, J. S. (1998). Joint productions as a conversational strategy in aphasia. *Clinical Linguistics and Phonetics, 12,* 459-480.

Paradis, M. (1998). The other side of language: pragmatic competence. *Journal of Neurolinguistics, 11,* 1-10.

Penn, C. (1988). The profiling of syntax and pragmatics in aphasia. *Clinical Linguistics and Phonetics, 2,* 179-208.

Perkins, M. R. (1998a). The cognitive basis of pragmatic disability. In W. Ziegler & K. Deger (Eds.), *Clinical phonetics and linguistics* (pp. 195-202). London: Whurr.

Perkins, M. R. (1998b). Is pragmatics epiphenomenal?: Evidence from communication disorders. *Journal of Pragmatics, 29,* 291-311.

Perkins, M. R. (2000). The scope of pragmatic disability: A cognitive approach. In N. Müller (Ed.), *Pragmatics and clinical applications* (pp. 7-28). Amsterdam: John Benjamins.

Perkins, M. R. (in press). Compensatory strategies in SLI. *Clinical Linguistics and Phonetics, 13.*

Perkins, M. R. (forthcoming). *Pragmatics and language pathology.* Cambridge, UK: Cambridge University Press.

Perkins, M. R., Body, R., & Parker, M. (1995). Closed head injury: Assessment and remediation of topic bias and repetitiveness. In M. R. Perkins & S. J. Howard (Eds.), *Case studies in clinical linguistics* (pp. 293-320). London: Whurr.

Prutting, C. A., & Kirchner, D. M. (1983). Applied pragmatics. In T. M. Gallagher & C. A. Prutting (Eds.), *Pragmatic assessment and intervention issues in language* (pp. 29-64). San Diego: College Hill Press.

Rein, R. P., & Kernan, K. T. (1989). The functional use of verbal perseverations by adults who are mentally retarded. *Education and Training in Mental Retardation, 24,* 381-389.

Simmons-Mackie, N. N., & Damico, J. S. (1996). The contribution of discourse markers to communicative competence in aphasia. *American Journal of Speech-Language Pathology, 5,* 37-43.

Sinclair, M. (1995). Fitting pragmatics into the mind: Some issues in mentalist pragmatics. *Journal of Pragmatics, 23,* 509-539.

Sperber, D., & Wilson, D. (1995). *Relevance: Communication and cognition (2nd ed.)*. Oxford: Blackwell.

Tannock, R., & Schachar, R. (1996). Executive dysfunction as an underlying mechanism of behavior and language problems in attention deficit hyperactivity disorder. In J. Beitchman, N. Cohen, M. Konstantareas, & R. Tannock (Eds.), *Language, learning and behavior disorders: Developmental, biological and clinical perspectives* (pp. 128-155). Cambridge, UK: Cambridge University Press.

Tarplee, C., & Barrow, E. (1999). Delayed echoing as an interactional resource: a case study of a 3-year-old child on the autistic spectrum. *Clinical Linguistics and Phonetics, 13*, 449-482.

Tesak, J. (1994). Cognitive load and the processing of grammatical items. *Journal of Neurolinguistics, 8*, 43-48.

Verschueren, J. (1999). *Understanding pragmatics*. London: Arnold.

Volden, J., Mulcahy, R. F., & Holdgrafter, G. (1997). Pragmatic language disorder and perspective taking in autistic speakers. *Applied Psycholinguistics, 18*, 181-198.

Wertz, R. T., Henschel, C. R., Auther, L. L., Ashford, J. R., & Kirshner, H. S. (1998). Affective prosodic disturbance subsequent to right hemisphere stroke: a clinical application. *Journal of Neurolinguistics, 11*, 89-102.

Wilson, D., & Sperber, D. (1991). Pragmatics and modularity. In S. Davis (Ed.), *Pragmatics: A reader* (pp. 583-595). Oxford: Oxford University Press. First published in A. M. Farley, P.T. Farley & K-E. McCullough, (Eds.), 1986. The Chicago Linguistic Society Parasession on Pragmatics and Grammatical Theory. Chicago: The Chicago Linguistic Society.

Wilson, J., & McAnulty, L. (2000). What do you have in mind? Beliefs knowledge and pragmatic impairment. In N. Müller (Ed.), *Pragmatics and clinical applications* (pp. 29-51). Amsterdam: John Benjamins.

2

Defining Trouble-Sources in Dementia: Repair Strategies and Conversational Satisfaction in Interactions with an Alzheimer's Patient

Jacqueline Guendouzi and Nicole Müller

Since the 1990s, there has been a growing interest in applying qualitative conversational analysis (CA) and discourse analysis (DA) methodologies to clinical discourse data. Research into dementia, for example, has examined the types of conversational strategies utilized by both individuals with dementia and their interlocutors (e.g. Bohling, 1991; Garcia & Joanette, 1994; Goldfein, 1990; Hamilton, 1994; Milroy & Perkins, 1992; Penn, Sonneberg & Schnaier, 1988; Ripich, Vertes, Whitehouse, Fulton & Ekelman, 1991). Drawing on frameworks suggested by Orange, Lubinski and Higginbotham (1996) and Watson, Chenery and Carter (1999), this chapter will examine discourse data taken from audiotaped conversations between one of the researchers and a 79-year-old woman suffering from Alzheimer's disease (AD) with non-specified stroke-damage, and a long-established hearing impairment. While examining the efficacy of the above frameworks, we also raise the issue of how we identify potential trouble-sources in relation to the perception of conversational satisfaction.

TROUBLE-SOURCES

Trouble-sources are generally thought to be those points in a conversation where one participant feels it is necessary to clarify their understanding of what has been said in order to maintain or re-establish coherence. Trouble-sources often result in speakers adopting repair strategies in order to realign a conversation to culturally acceptable 'norms'. Trouble-sources are typically signalled in the interaction by questions, reformulations or 'self' and 'other' repair and may require speakers to adopt face-saving strategies (Brown & Levinson, 1987).

Watson et al. (1999) have suggested a framework of Trouble Indicating Behaviours [TIBs] and Repair Types [RTs] that has drawn on studies adapting CA methodologies (e.g. Van Lier 1988; Brinton, Fujiki, Frome-Loeb & Winkler, 1986; Schegloff, 1992). These models of conversational interaction are based on sequential ordering of turns where TIBs are typically followed by attempted repair strategies. Orange et al. (1996) have suggested that conversational trouble-sources are often a mismatch of intent and understanding between a speaker and listener. They suggest that this incongruence may be a result of disturbances in any of the following categories of linguistic variables: phonological, syntactic, morphological, lexical-semantic, discourse (shared pragmatic knowledge), or other disturbances such as incomplete or unintelligible utterances. While these frameworks appear to provide a very useful starting point for analyzing AD discourse, both studies have confined analysis to short sequences of talk, more typically two-part turns that do not reveal how the ensuing interaction develops.

TROUBLES-RESOLUTION

Bremer, Broeder, Roberts, Simonot and Vasseur (1987) suggest that the most effective strategies, for successfully negotiating trouble-sources within conversations, show a high degree of collaboration. They suggest that conversational troubles-resolution seeks to combine:

a)   an assessment of linguistic difficulty in the speaker;
b)   an ability to assist the speaker in overcoming this difficulty;
c)   an awareness and ability to induce the best way of protecting 'face' while coping with (a) and (b).

However, in neurogenic communication disorders we cannot always assess what the sufferer may perceive as a trouble-source. It is possible that merely sustaining an ongoing conversation, regardless of the semantic content, may give interactional satisfaction to an AD individual. Also, in conversations such as those analysed here, one may encounter many passages that are unintelligible for the hearer (i.e. the non-AD interlocutor). Thus the difficulty may reside in the listener as much as in the speaker.

CONVERSATIONAL SATISFACTION

Interactions that adhere to a framework of both cooperativity (Grice, 1975) and discourse 'norms', have typically been seen to represent conversational satisfaction. Interlocutor expectations are that shared pragmatic knowledge will result in listener comprehension and appropriate reciprocal conversational moves (e.g. turn-taking, topic management and troubles-resolution). Whether an interaction matches these expectations will affect whether we experience a conversation as satisfactory or not.

However, while it is possible to obtain feedback relating to the satisfaction levels experienced by a 'normal' conversational partner, it is not always possible to accurately access how the AD individual experiences an interaction. In conversations with AD individuals, family members and carers often attempt to direct the talk into a framework of what we would consider the 'norm'. While for close family members or acquaintances there is a recognisable need to attempt to direct the AD person towards conversational behaviours associated with their prior 'self', for the AD individual the trouble sequences may not pose an interactional problem.

DATA COLLECTION

The data examined here was collected by one of the researchers during visits to a woman diagnosed as having AD. The researcher obtained permission from both the family and the Healthcare Institution to visit the woman on a regular basis and audio-taped conversations between herself and the patient. It was preferred that the researcher had no prior knowledge of the patient or her life circumstances to accurately assess how an AD sufferer manages communicative interactions with an initially unfamiliar interlocutor.

The patient (F) began to manifest signs of memory, communication and behavioral difficulty in 1992 and was subsequently diagnosed as having AD. Her physical condition and motor control deteriorated over the next five years, and she was admitted to a health-care institution in January 1997. F had suffered from a hearing impairment from early adulthood and this added to her communication difficulties.

METHODOLOGY

Although our analysis draws on the work discussed above (e.g. Watson et al, 1998) where these frameworks proved inadequate we have added other repair moves, for example semantic-cueing. The conversational moves are enclosed in [ ] brackets and represented in *italics* within the transcripts (Table 1). We also refer to a repair-move that involves a topic shift within the discourse to a safe 'phatic-topic'. We are defining phatic-topics as those topics that involve mundane details about everyday life, such as, the weather, health and family information. This is information that is either given (i.e. known), or easily recoverable from the context (i.e. directly observable), or information that provides further details concerning entities that are already known. The notion of categorizing these phatic-topics as 'safe' arose from the observation that during exchanges where F became tearful, shifting to this type of topic typically averted her distress. Furthermore, during moments of conversational confusion, a shift to a safe phatic-topic often resulted in F being able to regain a coherent role within the interaction.

TABLE 1
Transcription conventions.

(.)	minimal pause
(0.2)	timed pause, e.g. 2 seconds
((xxx))	unintelligible text
(laughing)	contextual information in ( )
[{T}]	tearful voice
[TIB/RT]	trouble indicating behavior/repair type
[italics]	commentary on sequential organization of the talk
:	vowel lengthening
bold	very clear articulation

THE DATA

Extract 1

F: my husband was very ((xxx)) when he didn't when you didn't turn up
      [TIB/RT self repair of pronoun within a turn]

Extract 1 shows an example of pronoun self-repair within the AD speaker's turn. As was often the case in this data-set it is the repair move itself that indicates a potential trouble-source. Therefore, unlike Watson et al. (1999) we feel it would be unproductive to the analysis to attempt to separate out TIB's from RTs as they overlap and are often contained within the same conversational move. F showed awareness of pronoun errors and typically self-corrected these errors immediately within her own turn, as can be seen again in Extract 2 below.

Extract 2

1	R:	your sister lives in Leeds?
2	F:	yes
3	R:	does she come down very often?
4	F:	no she's another old lady she's eighty-seven aye what did I
5		say my er your son my son was (noise of hoover) *[TIB/RT*

self-repair of pronoun within a turn, also may be a metalinguistic comment to try and re-introduce topic of her son]

6	R:	oh let's shut the door it's too noisy (.) your son (closes door)
7		was in Oxford you said *[RT researcher responds to F's perceived confusion by offering possible explanation]*
8	F:	yes *[F makes appropriate response]*
9	R:	is your sister older than you? *[R shifts back to previous topic]*
10	F:	yes *[F offers an appropriate response]*
11	R:	uh huh
12	F:	yes m:: I'm nearly eighty-two

Extract 2 shows the researcher introducing a safe phatic-topic by asking where F's sister lives. Although F responds, she shifts back to a previous topic and her self-correction of a pronoun indicates a potential trouble-source within the conversation. R attempts to address F's memory problems by offering a potential explanation to F's half-finished utterance and before shifting back to the initial topic of F's sister. It appears to be a successful strategy as F is able to offer an appropriate response.

Extract 3

1	F:	yeah (.) but you've been in this building before
2		haven't your (.) when you were a child *[off-topic comment semantic relevance unclear]*
3	R:	sorry? *[TIB request for further information]*
4	F:	when you were a child *[RT repetition]*
5	R:	m: no
6	F:	oh? *[TIB / RT possible request for information]*
7	R:	oh no
8	F:	have you always been a bit of ((xxx)) (laughs) *[off topic and unintelligible]*
9	R:	it's a nice day today (.) the sun is out for a change
10		*[TIB/RT R shifts to safe phatic-topic]*
11	F:	m: it's lovely *[F responds appropriately]*

In Extract 3 the researcher uses a repair strategy (line 9) that allows her to both shift away from the potential trouble source of F's semantically unclear, unintelligible comment (line 1), and also address the potential face-threat to F's self-esteem by avoiding any overt indication of F's confused remark. Switching to safe phatic-topics was one of the most common repair strategies that the researcher used in dealing with off-topic or semantically unclear utterances made by F. This strategy can be seen again in the following Extract 4.

Extract 4

1	F:	oh Leeds er not a very Leeds the infirm *[semantically unclear]*
2	R:	oh: the infirmiary in Cardiff ? *[TIB/RT cue explanation]*
3	F:	yeah but the newspaper in er Leeds (.) Leeds you what I mean *[semantically unclear]*
4	R:	oh the Mercury *[RT offers explanation]*
5	F:	is it?
6	R:	yeah I think so (0.5) how many sisters have you got just one? *[RT shift to safe phatic topic]*
7	F:	four there four *[again F offers appropriate response]*
8	R:	oh
9	R:	do they all live in Yorkshire *[stays with this topic line]*
10	F:	not (laughs) no (.) there's two um only ones are in er (.) Sue's
11		in Queensland and Lucy's is in no that's wrong *[TIB/RT metacognitive awareness of error – attempts self-correction]*
12	R:	Sue lives in Queensland (.) my sister lives in Queensland *[RT researcher again shifts topic to safe phatic common]*
13	F:	oh yes *[F able to respond appropriately]*
14	R:	ah

In Extract 4, F introduces a semantically unclear topic that R initially tries to repair by offering a possible explanation for F's utterance (line 2). F's response to R's attempted repair move is still semantically unclear and R again cues an explanation by suggesting the name of the newspaper in Leeds (line 4). It is not certain from the question form of F's response whether R has given an appropriate explanation. Rather than pursue this topic, R shifts to the safe phatic-topic of the weather. As is often the case in phatic sequences, F is more able to cope with appropriate routine sequential responses. When R asks F how many sisters she has, F responds with the appropriate number. However, when R attempts to extend this line of topic F becomes confused and starts talking about her daughters in Australia. Her comment (line 11) shows meta-cognitive awareness of her confusion and at this point R intervenes with a face-saving move by shifting the topic to her own sister who also lives in Queensland.

Extract 5

1	R:	oh here's the dog (.) do you know what the dog's name is?
2		(0.2) m: do you know what the dog's name is?
3	F:	**I'm trying to say** (both laugh) [{T}] I ((xxx)) *[TIB metacognitive awareness of error]*
4	R:	you're doing very well you remembered all about the people
5		damaging the little grotto out there *[RT/face-saving comment]*

6	F:	pardon? *[TIB seeking further clarification]*
7	R:	you seemed to be remembering a lot out in the garden *[RT repetition]*
8	F:	oh yeah

In Extract 5, when R requests the dog's name, F again shows meta-cognitive awareness of her communicative problems. F explains she is trying to access the appropriate name and both she and the researcher initially laugh, which appears to be an attempt by both interactants to diffuse the face-threat caused by F's public self-acknowledgement of her mental confusion. As she becomes tearful, R attempts another face-saving strategy by offering F encouragement (lines 4-5). F seeks clarification (line 6) and R reformulates her remark enabling F to acknowledge this encouragement and both interactants cooperate in diffusing a distressing situation.

Extract 6

1	R:	does he miss Ireland or does he like Cardiff now?
2	F:	does he? *[TIB seeks further information]*
3	R:	DOES HE MISS IRELAND ? *[RT repetition]*
4	F:	iron? *[TIB/RT repetition possible hearing problem or phonological error]*
5	R:	Ireland (0.1) his home *[RT repetition of question with further information]*

Extract 6 shows an example of the most common type of TIB and repair move noted in analyzing this data-set – seeking clarification through further information. Although this appears to be a trouble-source, in F's case, as for many elderly people, this may be the result of poor hearing rather than cognitive confusion. Certainly the fact that F makes an apparent phonological error (line 4) suggests that on this occasion the error may be a hearing related deficit. It was observed by the researcher that care-staff interacting with F often attributed errors of this type to her dementia rather than simply her hearing impairment. It appeared that, as F suffered from dementia, care-staff were more likely to give up on a conversation that had become troubled.

Extract 7

1	F:	(coughs) what do I have to do about this er poem
2	R:	poem? *[TIB seeks clarification]*
3	F:	is it poem or essay ((xxx)) *[RT semantic cueing – offers further information]*
4	R:	you don't have to do anything I have to write it
5	F:	(laughing) oh::: poor you

6	R:	you don't want to write an essay do you?
7	F:	no::

Many of the semantically unclear or off-topic comments that F made were managed through interlocutor recognition of the semantic association. In this sequence it is clear from R's TIB seeking clarification (line 2) that she is initially unclear what F is referring to. However, F attempts to repair her comment through repetition with further information and subsequently R is able to infer that F is referring to her research. There was evidence within the data-set to suggest that F often relied on semantic cueing, as a conversational repair strategy to elicit a target word or concept from her interlocutor.

Extract 8

1	R:	oh they're scattered about the world I should think (laughs) *[off topic semantic content unclear]*
2	R:	they're scattered about the world? *[TIB/RT repetition seeking further information]*
3	F:	well (.) no I think you'd better leave that to them to explain *[semantically unclear but also possibly a 'buckpassing' strategy showing F's awareness of being off topic.*
4	F:	are they in Australia no:: ((xxx)) for six *[TIB/RT repetition*
5		*with further information]* months at a time that's all
6	R:	only six months?

Extract 8 shows another repair move often employed by F, that of repeating the researcher's question slowly to herself (line 4). This may be a technique that F had developed to cope with her hearing impairment but it can also be seen as a strategy that allows her to gain greater processing time and perhaps allow a potential turn transition point where her interlocutor might intervene to give her conversational support.

Extract 9

1	R:	m:: it's a pity that the weather's so bad then *[safe phatic-topic]*
2	F:	yeah ((xxx))
3	R:	all the daffodils are out now *[TIB/RT further phatic-talk]*
4	F:	((xxx)) (0.8) and they let me ((xxx)) on *[semantically and phonetically unclear]*
5	R:	there's not so many people around today? *[TIB/RT phatic-comment]*
6	F:	I ((xxx)) *I like that coat* *[topic shift to compliment]*
7	R:	yeah it's really warm yes it's nice you had a nice jumper on
8		last week

9	F:	what color?
10	R:	white with little pearls on
11	F:	oh m::

In Extract 9, during a difficult conversational sequence where F is having problems with both intelligibility and semantic coherence, F also adopts the strategy of switching to a phatic-topic. After an unintelligible comment, F makes an abrupt topic shift and offers a compliment to the researcher (line 6) although it is difficult to assess whether she has consciously used this as a repair strategy or is just distracted by the researcher's jacket. However, what is noticeable is that when shifting to a phatic sequence F appears more able to offer the appropriate turn-taking moves and maintain the conversational flow.

Extracts 10 and 11 (see Appendices I and II) are extended sequences in which there are examples of F being able to revisit earlier topics without conversational prompting on behalf of the researcher. This suggests that F is able to self-monitor conversational content during lengthy exchanges. In Extract 10 (Appendix I) the initial topic is F's birthday outing and there is further evidence of F using semantic association to repair trouble-sources (line 17). There are several potential trouble-sources and the researcher typically attempts to repair these by discursively guiding F to stay on topic by asking further questions or shifting to another safe phatic-topic (e.g. line 53). As noted above, when F is directed back toward safe phatic-topics, particularly sequences that involve compliments, she seems better able to cope with conversational turn-taking moves.

Phatic communion has been seen as talk that involves routine conversational moves (Malinowski, 1923; Laver, 1987) that maintain solidarity and keep interactions going. As Malinowski (1923) commented, the content of phatic talk may not be as important as the satisfaction derived from the shared 'communion' of interaction with others. It may also be that as with claims about 'chunking' in idiomatic speech, pragmatic routines are stored in the memory as 'whole routines' and therefore are more easily managed in a conversation. Certainly for F, these pragmatic sequences do not appear to require her to process complex semantic information, therefore phatic-talk may also allow the AD individual an opportunity to "buy" more processing time and maintain the conversational flow for a longer period of time.

F also appeared aware of politeness routines and often made complimentary remarks to the researcher (lines 68, 70 and 72) with the appropriate follow up moves. Furthermore, although the non-verbal behaviors F manifested during the interaction suggest that her confusion regarding her own age (line 21) was the result of a cognitive processing difficulty, a second possible interpretation is that she was using humour and joking about her age. Certainly there seems to be an element of verbal play in F's second claim that she is 59, although her laughter may simply be a strategy for diffusing the face-threat attached to her visible memory loss. F does show she is able to discursively join in with the researcher's attempt to reduce the face threat by turning the error into a compliment (lines 20-25).

In Extract 11 (Appendix II), F appears to find it difficult to process several items of information and maintain conversational coherence. For example, calculating where her son and grandchildren live and also attempting to recount the story of how and where her husband taught them to swim results in conversational breakdown. F appears to give up on this conversational line by turning her attention to something else (R's coat zip) although it may be that, as is common in AD, F's attention span is short and she is simply distracted. Twice, F herself appears to use the conversational repair strategy (lines 11 and 29) of shifting to a safe phatic-topic, for example after the sequence in which F appears to confuse the words "singing" and "swimming" she is able to regain conversational coherence by asking R whether she goes to the swimming pool. Later, by asking where R's parents live, she succeeds in redirecting the conversation to R's life circumstances thereby avoiding having to process further information relating to her own life.

CONCLUSIONS

The most common TIBs and RTs appeared to be information-seeking moves through the use of questions and repetition of utterances. However, as noted, we often found it unproductive to attempt to discriminate between a TIB and a repair move. Although questions and repetitions were the most commonly used indicators of potential trouble-sources, particularly in terms of attempting to maintain a specific topic line it is problematic to assume that these were the most successful repair moves. Furthermore, although generally F responds appropriately when the interlocutor switches to a phatic-topic, she was not always able to return to the topic that resulted in conversational breakdown.

While the shift to a safe phatic-topic was not always successful (e.g. Extract 9), the researcher was generally able to avert the distress manifested when F became aware of her own mental confusion by switching to a safe phatic-topic rather than attempt to pursue or correct incoherent utterances. The data also suggests that F was able to manage phatic routines more easily than topic lines or questions that required complex semantic or temporal processing. After listening to all the audio-tapes (8 tapes of approximately 40 minutes duration each) we felt that the pragmatic features of F's language skills had remained relatively intact. Exchanges that involved processing complex conceptual information or use of working memory were more likely to result in conversational incoherence. Therefore, shifting to a safe phatic-topic proved a highly effective repair strategy for R, as it addressed both F's face needs and allowed her to regain active participation in the conversation.

Watson et al. (1998) have noted in their data that in order to maintain the dignity of the speaker misunderstandings were often left unresolved. However, as discussed above, if we are concerned with engaging the AD individual in satisfying conversation we have to then consider what "satisfactory" might mean to someone suffering from AD. Do we, for example, need to orient to resolving misunderstandings or should we focus on achieving interactional communion? Certainly during the conversations examined here, F manifested behaviours that suggested she obtained a great deal of satisfaction from having the opportunity to talk for lengthy periods of time: the communion of interaction appeared to give her pleasure.

In a condition such as AD, where the current prognosis is invariably progressive decline, should the AD person's interlocutors be seeking to direct the conversation toward the accepted norms of able language users? Or should we consider which features of the conversation appear to give the AD individual interactional satisfaction? For F, this appeared to be engaging in extended interactions where her interlocutor focused on keeping the conversation going rather than attempting to elicit semantically coherent utterances.

More research involving micro level analysis of extended conversational data, may prove useful in making a real impact on the conversational satisfaction of both AD individuals and their carers. Certainly, for the researcher involved in these interactions, adapting normal conversational strategies and "going with the flow" resulted in conversations that were more easily negotiated than initially expected.

REFERENCES

Brown, P., & Levinson, S. (1987). *Politeness: some universals in language usage.* Cambridge, MA: Cambridge University Press.

Bohling, H. R. (1991). Communication with Alzheimer's patients: An analysis of care-giving listening patterns. *International Journal of Ageing and Human Development, 33,* 249-267.

Bremer, K., Broeder, P., Roberts, C., Simonot, M., & Vasseur, M. (1987). Ways of achieving understanding. In C. Perdue (Ed.), *Adult language acquisition: Cross linguistic perspectives (Vol. 2).* Cambridge, MA: Cambridge University Press.

Garcia, I. J., & Joanette, Y., (1997). Analysis of conversational topic shifts: A multiple case study. *Brain and Language, 58,* 92-114.

Brinton, B., Fujiki, M., Frome-Loeb, D., & Winkler, E. (1986). Development of conversational repair strategies in response to requests for clarification. *Journal of Speech and Hearing Research, 29,* 75-81.

Grice, H. P. (1975). Logic and conversation. In P. Cole & J. Morgan (Eds.), *Speech acts: Syntax and semantics (Vol. 3).* New York: Academic.

Goldfein, S. (1990). The use of conversational repair in the presence of Alzheimer's disease. Unpublished PhD thesis, Columbia University, New York.

Hamilton, H. (1994). *Conversations with an Alzheimer's patient: An interactional sociolinguistic study.* Cambridge, UK: Cambridge University Press.

Laver, J. (1981). Linguistic routing in greeting and parting. In F. Coulmas (Ed.), *Conversational routines.* The Hague: Mouton.

Malinowski, B. (1923). The problem of meaning in primitive languages. Supplement to C. K Ogden & I. A. Richards, *The meaning of meaning.* London: Routledge.

Milroy, L., & Perkins, L. (1992). Repair strategies in aphasic discourse: Towards a collaborative model. *Clinical Linguistics & Phonetics, 6,* 27-40.

Orange, J. B., Lubinski, R. B., & Higginbotham, J. (1996). Conversational repair by individuals with dementia of the Alzheimer's type. *Journal of Speech and Hearing Research, 39,* 881-895.

Penn, C., Sonneberg, B., & Schnaier, Y. (1988). Dementia and communication pathology: Two case examples. *The South African Journal of Communication Disorder, 35,* 65-74.

Ripich, D. N., Vertes, D., Whitehouse, P., Fulton, S., & Ekelman, B. (1991). Turn-taking and speech act patterns in the discourse of senile dementia of Alzheimer's type patients. *Brain and Language, 40,* 330-343.

Schegloff, E. A. (1992). Repair after next turn: The last structurally provided defence of inter-subjectivity in conversation. *American Journal of Sociology, 5,* 1295-1345.

Scollon, R. (1985). The machine stops: Silence in the metaphor of malfunction. In D. Tanned & M. Saville-Troike (Eds.), *Perspectives on silence.* Norwood, NJ: Ablex.

Van Lier, L. (1988). The organization of repair in second-language classrooms. In L. Van Lier (Ed.), *The classroom and the language learner: Ethnography and second-language classroom research.* London: Longman.

Watson, C. M., Chenery, H. J., & Carter, M. S. (1999). An analayis of trouble and repair in natural conversations of people with dementia of the Alzheimer's type. *Aphasiology, 13,* 195-218.

APPENDIX I

Extract 10

| 1 | R: | were those for your birthday the flowers? |
| 2 | F: | will they be? *[TIB/RT request for clarification]* |

3	R:	the flowers were they for your birthday? *[RT repetition]*
4	F:	where they take out ((xxx)) *[TIB requests further clarification]*
5	R:	m: m:
6	F:	ah we drove underneath it (laughs) *[semantically unclear]*
7	R:	did Mick take you out (.) for your birthday? *[TIB/RT return to phatic-topic]*
8	F:	er me out? *[TIB/RT request for information]*
9	R:	m: m: yesterday? *[RT gives further information]*
10	F:	oh no no: ((xxx)) to my amazement **his amazement last night**
11		*[TIB/RT self-repair]* see he go out it's ages since you went out
12		and this I wouldn't be going out so *[semantically unclear]*
13	R:	did you enjoy it? *[TIB/RT maintain topic with further question]*
14	F:	yes **nothing special but my sister came with us and we met**
15		**Elaine and one or two people coming and going** (laughs)
16	R:	which sister? which sister? *[maintaining topic flow through questions]*
17	F:	er the can't tell if it's me or not *[RT semantic cueing to cope with word loss]*
18	R:	oh she looks just like you oh I see *[RT cues potential explanation of F's remark]*
19	F:	but she's um I think she's more of a looker ((xxx)) *[RT adds further information]*
20	R:	and how old were you yesterday? *[shifts to safe phatic-topic as F becomes confused]*
21	F:	twenty-nine *[F makes cognitive error or possible joke]*
22	R:	twenty-nine? *[TIB/RT other correction]*
23	F:	er fifty-nine (laughs) *[RT/face-saving use of humor]*
24	R:	oh well you look twenty-nine *[RT/face-saving compliment]*
25	F:	**thank you** (laughs) *[acceptance of compliment shows politeness strategies intact]*
26	R:	I love your flowers all orange and you know bright *[remaining on safe-phatic topic]*
27	F:	yeah yeah it's this is the one that's adopted *[possible target doctor]* (referring to sender of some flowers) an he *[TIB/ phonological error]*
28		
29	R:	Paul ? *[RT suggests name]*
30	F:	yes and he sent baskets like that ((xxx))
31	R:	so Paul's a doctor? *[attempts repair of phonological error]*
32	F:	uh huh *[F appears to give appropriate response]*
33	R:	doctor doctor of theology ? *[RT/gives further information]*
34	F:	er yes (.) it's got longest ((xxx)) one day *[semantically unclear off-topic]*

35	R:	(reading card) Paul and Ali (.) *[TIB/RT attempts to remain on*
		topic of flowers]
36	F:	yes that's it
37	R:	is Ali his wife?
38	F:	yeah hm hm and she's a er she's ((xxx)) she can't stop walking
		[semantically unclear]
39	R:	she likes walking? (.) she likes walking? *[TIB/RT request*
		further information]
40		yeah she's finished doing a thesis back in the summer we
41		thought oh she can relax now and get out with Paul m: she
42		didn't she took out some nother paper *[RT/cues explanation]*
43	R:	oh another thesis so what was her first this thesis th I can't say
44		it *[RT/repeats and reformulates F's explanation]*
45	F:	I don't know I think that was it ((xxx)) *[semantically and*
		phonetically unclear]
46	R:	so she's going to do another? *[TIB/RT attempts to stay on topic*
		by requesting further information]
47	F:	m: she's doing another one now
48	R:	takes a lot of doing to do two
49	F:	she she can't stop it she's always
50	R:	I know what you mean
51	F:	m: and she'll have a meal and doing anything cooking she
52		doesn't do it but she's got the book fro fro ((xxx))
		[semantically unclear]
53	R:	have they got any children? *[TIB/RT shift to safer topic]*
54	F:	yes two beautiful (.) look at them they're on the mantlepiece
55		behind the flowers
56	R:	oh yeah
57	F:	bu they're real blondes
58	R:	the blonde one yeah
59	R:	m:: she's pretty isn't she? (.) so did you enjoy the meal ?
		[reintroduces previous topic of birthday meal]
60	F:	yeah *[gives appropriate response]*
61	R:	what did you have?
62	F:	scampi
63	R:	scampi
64	F:	I like scampi
65	R:	what did you have with it chips?
66	F:	peas cheese *[possible phonological error]* yes but we didn't
67		have any afters because it was the middle of the day and it was
68		right full so we didn't have any I like your navy suit *[abrupt*
		topic shift]
69	R:	yeah it's my best one
70	F:	beautiful (laughs)

| 71 | R: | I bought it in Howells (.) in Howells |
| 72 | F: | oh yeah **jolly good** |

APPENDIX II

Extract 11

1	F:	er what day is it? Wednesday? *[TIB/RT request for temporal orientation and attempted self-repair]*
2	R:	er Friday it's Friday today *[RT other correction]*
3	F:	you could try but you'll not (laughs) *[semantically unclear]*
4	R:	maybe he's gone swimming maybe he's gone swimming (R makes a comment about F's husband due to the fact that F appears to be looking for him)
5	F:	maybe he's gone swim *[TIB/RT partial repetition of R's comments]*
6	R:	swimming *[RT repetition]*
7	F:	singing or *[TIB phonological error]*
8	R:	SWIMMING *[RT repetition and increased volume]*
9	F:	oh yes er no he'll ave been this morning *[TIB/RT self correction and further information]*
10	R:	m::
11	F:	but er it's not for me do you go in there regular? *[F shifts to safe phatic-topic by asking about R's life]*
12	R:	yeah with the children WITH THE CHILDREN
13	F:	oh yeah I've two grandchildren in er er (.) oh *[TIB unfinished utterance]* (F mentioned seeing her grandchildren in
14		Singapore in the researcher's first visit) Singapore *[RT cues possible explanation]*
15	F:	where the Universities are *[RT semantic association cue]*
16	R:	Oxford (Flo's son went to Oxford)
17	F:	That's it oh grandads taught them to swim there and they're
18		like two fishes ((xxx)) and then when they got that they could
19		barely sing it upset granddad they're not really interested in
20		learning now cause they can do all the tricks *[TIB possible phonological error swim – sing]*
21	R:	oh
22	F:	and er they're two and four and fives and ((xxx)) pardon me
23		and afternoon day they were **twiddle about a bit** and they
24		have a swim and something else that's a tiny ((xxx)) *[off-topic]* (Flo seems fascinated by the researcher's jacket)
25	R:	what? Oh my jacket *[TIB/RT request further information and cues explanation]*

26   F: nice tiny little key
27   R: m: it's the zip *[TIB/RT other correction]*
28   F: ah (fiddles with R's zip) well do your parents live around
29   here? *[TIB/RT? shifts to phatic-topic]*
30   R: no: they live in Australia
31   F: oh::

3

Evidence for a Direct Orthography-to-Phonology Route in Reading

M. Helen Southwood

Many reading theorists acknowledge the existence of a direct lexical reading route (Southwood & Chatterjee, 1999; Friedman & Kohn, 1990; Coslett, 1991). Information fed forward from the orthographic input lexicon (OIL) directly constrains a word in the phonological output lexicon (POL) without activating its semantic information (Sartori, Masterson & Job, 1987; Funnell, 1983). Traditionally, this route is lexical because it does not mediate nonword reading (Ellis & Young, 1988). However, the existence of this route and its role in reading remain somewhat contentious.

Evidence supporting a direct lexical route comes from studies showing some individuals with poor nonword reading read words they do not comprehend (Schwartz, Saffran & Marin, 1980; Bub, Cancelliere & Kertesz, 1985; Southwood & Chatterjee, 2000a). The presence of two impairments, semantic access from print and grapheme-to-phoneme conversion (GPC) suggest mediation of reading through a direct connection between the OIL and POL.

Traditional dual-route cognitive neuropsychological models of oral reading do not incorporate this third reading route. Theorists argue against a third route by suggesting that good reading performance in patients with impaired reading comprehension occurs via a nonlexical mechanism where the letter string is parsed into units differing in size (e.g. syllables or consonant clusters; Shallice, Warrington & McCarthy, 1983). Reading still uses GPC for different sized units. However, there is some uncertainty in this argument because many of these patients cannot pronounce individual sounds for letters, making it unlikely they could produce print-to-sound correspondences for larger sized units.

In direct contrast, analogy models of oral reading substitute a direct orthography-to-phonology reading route for GPC (Friedman & Kohn, 1990;

Friedman, 1996). Analogy theorists argue that the direct route is the principle route for both words and nonword reading (Kay & Marcel, 1981; Friedman, 1996). Nonword reading occurs by activating a series of visually or phonologically related words in the phonological lexicon directly from the OIL. Nonword pronunciation results from segmentation and recombination of words.

In analogy models poor nonword reading with relatively preserved word reading occurs when the direct lexical route is impaired (Friedman & Kohn, 1990). In this instance, nonword reading occurs via the semantic route. Nonwords are read poorly because they lack semantic representations. With an impaired direct route word reading also occurs through semantics. Therefore, semantic errors should appear in word reading with additional damage to the semantic system. Analogy theory cannot explain prudently the absence of semantic errors in oral reading in conjunction with poor nonword reading.

Alternative proposals like the Summation Hypothesis (Hillis & Caramazza, 1991) suggest interactions between semantic and nonsemantic mechanisms to account for the presence of semantic errors in reading and their absence in picture naming. The ability to read incomprehensible words and the absence of semantic errors in oral reading results from an interaction between impaired semantics and GPC (Hillis & Caramazza, 1991). Phonological information provided by GPC summates with semantic information activating the correct phonological entry in the POL. GPC must be intact for semantic errors to be absent when reading. This hypothesis cannot explain clearly relatively intact oral reading and the absence of semantic errors with both impoverished semantics and GPC.

The Simultaneous Activation Hypothesis (SAH; Southwood & Chatterjee, 1999) provides an alternative explanation of dissociations between reading and picture naming. Southwood and Chatterjee (2000a) used this hypothesis to elucidate such dissociations in patients with phonological dyslexia with impairments to both GPC and semantics. Nonword reading was severely impaired. Semantic errors were absent when reading aloud but frequent when naming pictures.

The SAH incorporates all three functionally independent reading routes. These routes activate simultaneously on encountering a letter string. Information from all routes integrates at the POL to constrain selection of the correct phonological entry (see Southwood & Chatterjee, 1999, for complete details).

When semantics and GPC are impaired, the direct lexical route provides additional information, which helps constrain the correct phonological entry in the POL, obfuscating semantic errors in reading. Picture naming can only occur via semantics, additional information from the other routes is unavailable. Therefore, errors will occur in picture naming when semantics is impaired.

In this chapter, we provide additional evidence for the existence of a direct lexical reading route and extend the notion of simultaneous activation of multiple routes when reading. Good word reading in the presence of both semantic and GPC deficits suggests that the direct orthography-to-phonology route also mediates word reading. The SAH can accommodate discrepancies between error patterns observed in oral reading and picture naming with compromised GPC and semantics. If all routes are functionally encapsulated and do not integrate at the POL dissociations between oral reading and picture naming errors would not occur. The SAH predicts relatively well-preserved word reading with impaired semantics and GPC because the direct orthography-to-phonology route effectively integrates with the information from these two routes at the POL to assist in constraining selection of the correct phonological entry.

CASE HISTORY

V.D. was a 42-year-old right-handed man with a 12th-grade education who owned a pawn-broking business. V.D. had a left posterior cerebral artery stroke on June 17, 1997. Weakness and incoordination were absent. The patient was alert and responsive to verbal stimuli. V.D. answered simple yes or no questions with 100% accuracy.

TABLE 1
Western Aphasia Battery Results for V.D.

Spontaneous Speech	
Information Content	8/10
Fluency	8/10
Comprehension	
Yes/No Questions	59/60
Word Recognition	54/60
Sequential Commands	53/80
Repetition	96/100
Naming	
Object Naming	20/60
Word Fluency	0/20
Sentence Completion	10/10
Responsive Speech	8/10
Reading	
Comprehension	4/40
Reading Commands	15/20
Word–Object Matching	5/6
Word–Picture Matching	6/6

Spontaneous speech was characteristic of anomia. Language evaluation on July 2, 1997 using the Western Aphasia Battery (WAB) (Kertesz, 1982) resulted in a clinical diagnosis of anomic aphasia. His aphasia quotient was 75.40. Fluency was 8.0, comprehension was 8.3, repetition was 9.6, and naming was 3.8. Table 1 shows V.D.'s complete results. Auditory comprehension and word recognition were relatively intact. V.D. had difficulty with sequential commands increasing in length. Repetition was good, object naming and word fluency were poor, and reading comprehension was poor.

METHOD AND RESULTS

We administered a series of tests to determine the nature and locus of V.D.'s reading deficit. We wished to know if impairment to the OIL, the semantic system, the POL or impaired GPC caused his reading deficit. We administered the *Battery of Adult Reading Function* (Gonzalez-Rothi, Coslett, & Heilman, 1984) and assessed frequency, length, GPC and letter identification.

Assessment of his orthographic, phonological, and semantic systems followed. Finally, we extensively analyzed oral reading and picture naming errors to understand the underlying mechanisms affecting reading.

Oral Reading of Single Words

We administered *The Battery of Adult Reading Function* (Gonzalez-Rothi et al., 1984) to determine the underpinnings of his reading deficit. V.D. read 30 regular (e.g. sink), 30 rule-governed (e.g. beast), 30 irregular (e.g. aisle), and 30 function words (e.g. though). Average word frequency was 43.7 per million for words and 403.3 for function words (Kucera & Francis, 1967). V.D. also read 30 phonologically plausible nonwords (Kay & Marcel, 1981). Graphemes per word averaged 5.3 (range = 4-8).

Errors were classified as 1. Semantic – a word related in meaning to the target (e.g. ankle → knee). 2. Neologism – a nonword containing randomly ordered phoneme strings (e.g. caterpillar → /lɪləpɛpə/). 3. Derivational – a word with the same free morpheme but different bound morpheme (e.g. carrot → carrots). 4. Phonological – a word phonologically similar to the target (e.g. thimble → /sɪmbəl/. 5. Unrelated word – a word with no phonological or visual similarity to the target (e.g. though → specialty), and 6. No Response.

Table 2 shows percent correct scores for nonword and word reading. Word reading scores ranged from 73 to 100%. V.D. had some difficulty reading irregular words. Nonword reading was extremely poor.

Error Responses. V.D. produced one error, a neologism (/tɪtɪfəl/ for *pitiful*) when reading regular words. When reading irregular words he produced eight errors, three were phonological (e.g. *hire* for *heir),* three were regularization (e.g. *corpse* for *corps*), one was a substitution of a visually similar word (*subtotal* for *subtle*) and one was a neologism (/baʊkʌt/ for *bouquet*).

TABLE 2
Percent Correct Word Reading Scores for V.D.

Nonwords	Regular Words	Rule-Governed Words	Irregular Words	Function Words
10	97	100	73	83

V.D. produced five errors when reading function words; four were substitutions of other function words or words and one was phonological.

V.D. read three nonwords correctly. He produced 19 word substitutions; 16 being visually similar words (e.g. *soup* for *soud*) and three unrelated words (e.g. *hemp* for *vatter*). He produced four phonological errors (e.g. *biller* for *ziller*) and one neologism. Three nonwords were not attempted.

Results of *The Battery of Adult Reading Function* (Gonzalez-Rothi et al., 1984) lead to a diagnosis of phonological dyslexia. Nonword reading was inferior to word reading. Semantic errors were absent when reading words.

Frequency and Word Length Effects

Frequency effects. V.D. read 20 high frequency words (99 to 897 per million, mean = 253) and 20 low frequency words (0 to 6 per million, mean = 2) (Snodgrass & Vanderwart, 1980) controlled in length. For both high and low frequency words, 17 were one syllable in length and three were two syllables in length. V.D. read both high and low frequency words accurately.

Word length effects. V.D. read a set of 114 one-, two-, and three-syllable words. Each set contained 38 words. Accuracy for one-syllable words was 95% and for two- and three-syllable words 90%. He produced five errors, one on one-syllable words and two each on two- and three-syllable words. Errors were word substitutions (e.g. *magnesium* for *magazine*) or non-responses.

Assessing Grapheme-to-Phoneme Conversion

Reading pseudohomophones. To assess GPC V.D. read 35 pseudohomophones (e.g. *blud* for *blood*). V.D. produced 16 errors, 12 were visually similar words (e.g. *bran* for *brane*), three were neologisms (e.g. /pɛli/ for the pseudohomophone of *police, palees*) and one was phonological (/pist/ for *beest*).

Letter-to-sound conversion. This task verified the ability to convert letters to sounds. We instructed V.D. to say the sound associated with each letter of the alphabet. Although he understood the nature of the task, V.D. could only name the letter rather than produce the associated sound.

Assessing the Integrity of Letter Identification

Cross-case letter matching. This task assessed the integrity of abstract letter identification (Coltheart, 1987). Each letter of the alphabet was printed in upper case on a single sheet of paper. Patients identified each letter from all 26 letters printed randomly in lower case below the letter. V.D. was 100% accurate.

Cross-case letter string matching. This task evaluated integration of letter strings. We gave V.D. 30 three-letter strings, each printed in upper case on a sheet of paper. He chose the letter string from a set of six lower case strings printed below. V.D. accurately matched all letter strings.

Naming letters. To confirm accurate letter identification, V.D. named the letters of the alphabet, presented in random order. Accuracy was 100%.

Assessing the Integrity of the Orthographic Input Lexicon

To determine access of orthographic lexical forms from writing, V.D. performed a non-timed visual lexical decision task. Forty nonwords and 40 words were presented in random order. There were ten regular, ten rule-governed, ten irregular and ten function words. V.D. indicated 'yes' if he thought the letter string was a word and 'no' if he thought it was a nonword. His performance was compared to that of four normal adults, aged 19 to 41 years (mean = 30.5 years), all with at least one year of college and no history of neurological, reading, speech or language problems.

V.D. had little difficulty identifying nonwords, regular words, and function words, with scores resembling the mean scores of the normal young adults (see Table 3). V.D.'s scores for rule-governed words and irregular words were slightly poorer than the scores of the young adults.

TABLE 3
Percent correct scores for V.D. and mean percent correct scores from four normal young adults on a written lexical decision task.

	Nonword	Regular	Rule-Governed	Irregular	Function
V.D.	93	90	80	60	100
Normals	86	97	97	96	98

Assessing the Integrity of the Phonological Output Lexicon

Rhyme judgments assess accessing phonological representations within the POL (Friedman & Kohn, 1990). Stored orthographic representations are accessed followed by their corresponding output phonological representations.

V.D. saw 40 word pairs, ten were visually similar rhyming (e.g. late–rate), ten were visually similar non-rhyming (e.g. rough–cough), ten were visually non-similar rhyming (e.g. soar–bore) and ten were visually nonsimilar nonrhyming (e.g. feet–jump). His performance was compared to that of the four young adults.

Rhyme judgments were relatively accurate, ranging from 70% to 100% (see Table 4). Although V.D. had some difficulty judging visually similar nonrhyming pairs his performance resembled that of the four young adults. The results show that V.D. had relatively intact access to the POL from the OIL.

TABLE 4

Percent correct written rhyme judgment scores for V.D. and mean percent correct scores for four normal individuals.

	Visually similar nonrhyming	Visually similar rhyming	Visually nonsimilar rhyming	Visually nonsimilar nonrhyming
V.D.	70	80	80	100
Normals	78	100	95	100

Assessing Semantic Integrity

Picture-picture matching, and word-word matching using the *Pyramids and Palm Trees Test* (PPTT; Howard & Patterson, 1992) assessed semantic access. The PPTT is a semantic associate test consisting of 55 triads. The top item in the triad is matched to one of two items below. V.D. performed both the word- and picture-matching tasks on two separate occasions. We assessed semantic access via the OIL with homophone-picture-matching because phonological lexical access does not aid performance. In this task, the subject was given one picture (e.g. a letter) and asked to match it to one of a pair of homophones (e.g. mail and male). Pseudohomophone-picture-matching assessed if semantic access occurred through the POL via GPC.

Picture-picture and word-word matching. Picture-picture matching accuracy was 36/55 and word-word matching accuracy was 21/55.

Homophone-picture matching. Twenty homophone pairs (e.g. pair, pear) were presented, each pair being homophonic but not homographic. The task required matching a homophone to the appropriate picture. V.D. identified 13/20 of the homophones accurately.

Pseudohomophone-picture matching. This task determined if phonological recoding of graphemes assisted lexical access. V.D. saw 18 pseudohomophones, each printed below three pictures. V.D. chose the picture matching the pseudohomophone 13/18 times correctly.

Reading and naming to definition. To determine if V.D.'s semantic problems related to semantic access or an impaired semantic system, we had V.D. read and name to definition. We developed definitions for the PPTT items (e.g. seat for riding a horse – saddle). On one occasion, we gave V.D. the definitions auditorily, and on the second, he read the definition and provided a verbal answer. For naming to definition, V.D. scored 14/55. Of his errors, 30 were semantic (e.g. *wrench* for *drill*), nine were non-responses and two were unrelated words (e.g. *poison* for *path*). For written definitions, he scored 8/55. Twenty-seven of his errors were semantic (e.g. *camper* for *tent*). Nonresponses made up 18 of his errors and two were unrelated words (e.g. *wrench* for *windmill*). He produced no phonological errors, derivational errors or neologisms.

Peabody Picture Vocabulary Test – III (PPVT; Dunn & Dunn, 1997). We administered the PPVT. V.D.'s overall raw score was 136. His standard score was 73 and his age equivalency was 10-11 years. To further evaluate the existence of a direct reading route, we had V.D. read the 32 words from the PPVT he did not comprehend. Words included *indigent*, *filtration*, *primate*, and *octagon*. He read 29/32 correctly. Two words he did not know and one error was phonological.

On all semantic tasks, V.D. performed at chance or a little above chance. Poor performance of semantic tasks in all modalities suggests impairment to the semantic system rather than semantic access.

Oral reading and picture naming from the Pyramids and Palm Trees Test (PPTT)

Oral reading PPTT. Theorists (Friedman & Kohn, 1990) argue that phonological dyslexia arises from poor phonological access. To assess phonological lexical access in the POL, V.D. read the words from the PPTT. He read all but five words correctly. Four errors were phonological (e.g. *bath* for *path*) and one was a neologism (/rɑstrɛl/ for *rooster*).

Picture naming PPTT. To establish if a general phonological deficit was responsible for his reading problems V.D. also named the pictures in the PPTT. In contrast to his oral reading, V.D.'s picture naming was poor. He scored 17/55 errors were either semantic or non-responses. Semantic errors were either a semantic associate (e.g. *drink* for *bottle*) or a vague description of the picture (e.g. for *Eskimo* he reported *"person in cold stuff"*).

Comparison of oral reading and picture naming errors. V.D. produced a marked dissociation between oral reading and picture naming errors. We computed error proportions because of the different error frequencies produced when reading and picture naming. When reading, V.D. only produced phonological errors and neologisms. The opposite occurred for picture naming, in which semantic errors and non-responses were prevalent (see Fig 1).

Semantic errors were absent in oral reading. Phonological errors were absent in picture naming. V.D. also produced unrelated word substitutions and derivational errors when picture naming but not when reading.

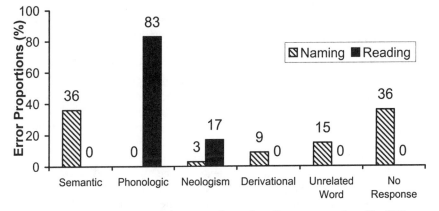

FIG. 1 The proportion of picture naming and reading errors produced by V.D.

DISCUSSION

V.D. a phonological dyslexic had disproportionately poorer nonword than word reading, indicating inefficient grapheme-to-phoneme conversion. When reading nonwords V.D. often substituted visually similar words or produced the occasional neologism. V.D. produced phonological errors and neologisms but no semantic errors when reading words. Frequency and length did not affect reading.

Cross-case letter matching tasks showed intact early visual processes. Written lexical decision showed relatively intact access to the OIL. Word-word, picture-picture matching and definition results revealed impaired semantics. Rhyme judgment results indicated intact access to the POL.

Picture naming was poor. Naming errors were more frequent and qualitatively different from reading errors. Picture naming errors were primarily semantic or nonresponses. Picture naming errors resulted from degraded semantics.

Current serial models of oral reading cannot explain the dissociation between V.D.'s reading and picture naming patterns. Traditional dual-route models of oral reading only include the lexical semantic route and GPC. Reading generally proceeds through lexical semantics. If both semantics and GPC were impaired, dual-route models would predict qualitatively and quantitatively similar reading and picture naming errors. This was not so for V.D.; reading errors were less frequent than picture naming errors. Furthermore, reading and picture naming errors differed qualitatively. Semantic errors were absent in reading but present in picture naming. Phonological errors were present in reading but absent in picture naming.

Analogy models of oral reading substitute a direct lexical route for GPC. In this model, both word reading and nonword reading occur primarily through the direct lexical route. Phonological dyslexia, like V.D.'s, arises from either impairment to the direct OIL to POL route or to disturbances to the POL. Analogy theorists argue that if the direct route is impaired readers rely on the semantic route. Nonwords are read poorly because they have no semantic representations. As readers rely on the semantic route reading errors should be semantic in nature with disruption to both the direct OIL to POL route and semantics. This pattern was not evident in V.D.'s reading. Therefore, analogy models cannot explain adequately the inability to read nonwords and the lack of semantic errors when both the direct lexical route and semantics are impaired. The absence of semantic errors in reading can only occur if the direct route is intact. If the direct route is intact and this is the route for reading nonwords, nonword reading should be accurate. V.D. could barely read any nonwords. Analogy models therefore fail to explain the presence of poor nonword reading with an intact direct lexical route.

To counter this argument, analogy theorists propose that phonological dyslexia can also arise from impairment to the phonological lexicon. In this case, analogy theorists would predict that errors in reading and picture naming should be qualitatively similar. Phonological errors should be present in both reading and picture naming. V.D. however, never produced phonological errors when picture naming but they were the most frequent reading error. Therefore, it is unlikely that impairment to the POL caused the phonological dyslexia in V.D.

To account for dissociations between linguistic tasks requiring similar cognitive processes, Hillis and Caramazza (1991) proposed an interaction between semantics and GPC. Their model does not incorporate a direct lexical route. Hillis and Caramazza postulated that the absence of semantic errors in reading when semantics is impaired occurs because intact information from the GPC route facilitates activation of the correct phonological representation.

However, if both GPC and semantics were impaired, we would predict from this model the presence of semantic errors in both reading and picture naming. Although V.D. had both a semantic and a GPC deficit semantic errors were absent from reading, a result unexplained by this interactive model.

V.D. presented with a severe semantic deficit. He was unable to comprehend many words, yet he was able to read them accurately. Reading with grapheme-to-phoneme conversion cannot explain his accurate word reading. V.D. was incapable of producing sounds associated with letters and nonword reading was extremely poor indicating a severely compromised GPC route. The presence of nearly accurate word reading in the presence of impaired GPC and degraded semantics corroborates the existence of the direct lexical route from the OIL to the POL (Schwartz et al., 1980; Sartori et al., 1987; Coslett, 1991). If V.D. relied entirely on residual semantic information we would predict that word frequency should also influence reading. However, frequency should not affect reading if mediated by the direct lexical route, because this route is assumed to be independent of semantic mediation. Frequency did not affect reading. V.D. read both high and low frequency words accurately supporting the notion that the direct lexical route also mediates word reading.

These findings provide support for the Simultaneous Activation Hypothesis (SAH; Southwood & Chatterjee, 1999). We proposed that all three reading routes are not modular and functionally encapsulated in the traditional sense (Fodor, 1983). All routes activate simultaneously when reading and information from all three routes integrates at the POL to constrain selection of the correct phonological entry. The SAH can readily explain the production of phonological errors in reading and their absence in picture naming. V.D. produced phonological errors when reading because the POL does not receive complete information from all three routes. Results showed degradation of GPC and semantics. Therefore, the POL receives some ambiguous information, which interferes with activation of a complete phonological representation. Instead, there is activation of a partial phonological representation, hence the production of phonological errors. Phonological errors were absent in picture naming because ambiguous information from the degraded routes does not interfere with selection of a phonological entry in the POL. In the absence of a general phonological deficit and the lack of ambiguous information from the other reading routes V.D. produced no phonological errors in picture naming.

The SAH can also explain the presence of semantic errors in picture naming and their absence in reading. Semantic errors are absent when reading because the POL receives additional information from the spared direct lexical route which facilitates activation of the correct phonological entry decreasing the likelihood of producing a semantic error. During picture naming the only route available is the semantic route. No additional information is available from the direct lexical route and GPC to assist in constraining selection of the correct phonological entry. Therefore, phonological selection relies solely on degraded semantic information that feeds forward to the POL, increasing the probability of selection of a semantic associate, and hence, the production of a semantic error.

Overall, this study provides additional evidence for the existence of a direct lexical route and further supports the SAH (Southwood & Chatterjee, 1999; 2000a; in press). If reading was strictly serial, relying primarily on the semantic route, reading and picture naming errors should be qualitatively and quantitatively similar, a pattern noticably absent in V.D. Our SAH provides a plausible explanation of the dissociation between semantic and phonological errors in reading and picture naming.

REFERENCES

Bub, D., Cancelliere, A., & Kertesz, A. (1985). Whole-word and analytic translation of spelling-to-sound in a non-semantic reader. In K. E. Patterson, J. C. Marshall & M. Coltheart (Eds.), *Surface dyslexia*. London: Lawrence Erlbaum Associates.

Coltheart, M. (1987). Functional architecture of the language processing system. In M. Coltheart, G. Sartori & R. Job (Eds.), *Cognitive neuropsychology of language*. Hillsdale, NJ: Lawrence Erlbaum Associates.

Coslett H. B. (1991). Read but not write "idea": Evidence for a third reading mechanism. *Brain and Language, 40,* 425-443.

Dunn, L. M., & Dunn, L. M. (1997). *Peabody Picture Vocabulary Test* (3rd ed.) Circle Pines, MN: American Guidance Service.

Ellis, A. W., & Young, A. W. (1988). *Human cognitive neuropsychology.* London: Lawrence Erlbaum Associates.

Fodor, J. A. (1983). *The modularity of mind.* Cambridge, MA: MIT Press.

Friedman, R. B., & Kohn, S. E. (1990). Impaired activation of the phonological lexicon: Effects upon oral reading. *Brain and Language, 38,* 278-297.

Friedman, R. B. (1996). Recovery from deep alexia to phonological alexia: Points on a continuum. *Brain and Language, 52,* 114-128.

Funnell, E. (1983). Phonological processes in reading: New evidence from acquired dyslexia. *British Journal of Psychology, 74,* 159-180.

Gonzalez-Rothi, L. J., Coslett, H. B., & Heilman, K. M. (1984). *Battery of adult reading function* (experimental edition).

Goodglass, H., Kaplan, E., & Weintraub, S. (1983). *The Boston naming test.* Philadelphia: Lea & Febiger.

Hillis, A. E., & Caramazza, A. (1991). Mechanisms for accessing lexical representation for output: Evidence from a category specific semantic deficit. *Brain and Language, 40,* 106-144.

Howard, D., & Patterson, K. (1992). *The pyramids and palm trees test.* Suffolk: Thames Valley Test Company.

Kay, J., & Marcel, A. J. (1981). One process, not two, in reading aloud: Lexical analogies do the work of non-lexical rules. *Quarterly Journal of Experimental Psychology, 33*, 387-413.

Kertesz, A. (1982). *The Western Aphasia Battery.* The Psychological Corporation: Harcourt Brace Jovanovich.

Kucera, H., & Francis, W. N. (1967). *Computational analysis of present-day American English.* Providence, RI: Brown University Press.

Sartori, G., Masterson, J., & Job, R. (1987). Direct route reading and the locus of lexical decision. In M. Coltheart, G. Sartori & R. Job (Eds.) *Cognitive neuropsychology of language.* London: Lawrence Erlbaum Associates.

Schwartz, M. F., Saffran, E., & Marin, O. S. M. (1980). Fractionating the reading process in dementia: Evidence for word-specific print-to-sound associations. In M. Coltheart, K. Patterson & J. C. Marshall (Eds.), *Deep dyslexia.* London: Routledge & Kegan Paul.

Shallice, T., Warrington, E. K., & McCarthy, R. (1983). Reading without semantics. *Quarterly Journal of Experimental Psychology, 35*, 111-138.

Snodgrass, J. G., & Vanderwart, M. (1980). A standardized set of 260 pictures: Norms for name agreement, image agreement, familiarity, and visual complexity. *Journal of Experimental Psychology: Human Learning and Memory, 6*, 174-215.

Southwood, M. H., & Chatterjee, A. (1999). Simultaneous activation of reading mechanisms: Evidence from a case of deep dyslexia. *Brain and Language, 67*, 1-29.

Southwood, M. H., & Chatterjee, A. (2000a). Interactions of multiple routes in oral reading: Evidence from dissociations in naming and reading in phonological dyslexia. *Brain and Language, 72*, 14-39.

Southwood, M. H., & Chatterjee, A. (in press). The Simultaneous Activation Hypothesis: Explaining recovery from deep to phonological dyslexia. *Brain and Language.*

4

Past Tense Expression in a Norwegian Man with Broca's Aphasia

Hanne Gram Simonsen and Marianne Lind

This chapter presents a case study of a Norwegian man in his mid-fifties (hereafter referred to as Aksel) who has suffered from a severe Broca-type of aphasia since 1992. Aksel's verbal production is severely limited, lexically as well as grammatically. His utterances are short and dominated by a small set of interjections and set phrases, and only a minor portion of the words he uses are content words.

Both nouns and verbs are scarce in his spontaneous production, but verbs seem to be particularly problematic, and for this reason, we will concentrate on his use (and non-use) of verbs in this paper. For instance, in a conversation which lasted for a little more than one hour, Aksel produced approximately 2000 word forms of which only 36 were verb tokens. These were distributed over 13 verb types. (In comparison, he produced 99 noun tokens from 42 noun types – excluding proper names). In the same conversation, the non-aphasic participant produced more than twice as many word forms (approximately 4400), and reached a level of 36 verb tokens after approximately 175 word forms.

Furthermore, Aksel hardly ever inflects his verbs for past tense in spoken interaction. In a data set consisting of three videorecorded conversations with a total duration of about 2.5 hours, there were only three instances in which Aksel produced a more or less correctly inflected past tense form. However, he often made reference to the past without expressing this through verbal inflection. In some of these cases he used a verb in the infinitive or in the present tense, and in other cases he managed to express past temporal displacement without using verbs at all.

This lack of verb forms in conversation – especially verb forms inflected for past tense – led us to test Aksel's performance in an experimental setting with a past tense picture elicitation task. It turned out that his performance here contrasted sharply with that of his spontaneous speech. In this paper, then, we will focus on Aksel's production of verbs, more specifically his expression of past tense with and without verbs, comparing his spontaneous speech performance with his test performance. Finally, we will discuss the possible implications of the findings in relation to what may actually be impaired in his language abilities, and what the consequences might be for assessment and therapy.

PERFORMANCE IN SPONTANEOUS CONVERSATION

We will start by reviewing some of the ways in which Aksel refers to the past in interaction, without the use of past tense inflection – and even without verbs. The spontaneous speech data are taken from the data set mentioned in the introduction: 3 videorecorded dyadic conversations between Aksel and different non-aphasic interlocutors, with a total duration of approximately 2.5 hours. (Other aspects of these conversations are analyzed in Lind, 1998, 1999, this volume, in progress.) The data were collected 5-6 years post-onset.

Expressing Temporal Displacement in the Past without Past Tense Inflection

The fact that a verb in interaction is not inflected appropriately or not inflected at all does not in itself automatically mean that the utterance is incomprehensible or that a misunderstanding arises. The following example from an interaction between Aksel and a non-aphasic participant illustrates how a verb in the infinitive is unproblematically interpreted as referring to the past tense:

1. Non-aphasic: ... (5.4) kan ikke du fortelle hva jeg var med på i går da
                    can't you tell what I did yesterday then
2. Aksel: ... (1.9) danse ... (1.2) ja
                    dance <INF> yes
3. Non-aphasic: ... hva .. hva da
                    what what then <i.e. what kind of dancing>

The prerequisite for the interpretation of the verb form here seems to be some kind of *contextual anchoring*. This means that the verb form is interpreted either in relation to a preceding utterance in which the temporal context is displayed, or in relation to some other aspect of the common ground making a past tense interpretation contextually most relevant. In the first utterance in the above example, the non-aphasic participant asks about a past event (something which took place 'yesterday'), thus creating a temporal frame referring to the past. The verb form *danse* 'dance' in Aksel's response, which is presented in the infinitive, can therefore unproblematically be interpreted as expressing the past tense.

Relying on such contextual anchoring is relatively unproblematic as long as the interaction is kept within one and the same temporal frame. When there is a shift between temporal frames – which often coincides with a topical shift – the interpretation is potentially more complex. There is often a greater need for more explicit temporal contextualization of the utterances in such cases. When explicit marking of a shift is lacking, misunderstandings often occur and repair is required.

Expressing Temporal Displacement in the Past without Verbs

Aksel may also express past tense without using a verb at all. One of his strategies is to write down a number referring to a year in the past, often accompanied by uttering the word *år* 'year'. This is then followed by an utterance saying something about what happened in the past, or how something was in the past. This utterance may consist of a verb form not inflected for past tense, or it may consist of another type of word, e.g. an adjective.

One example of this in the conversational data is an exchange where the non-aphasic participant starts by asking whether Aksel has been 'here' (referring to the university) before. Aksel confirms this, goes on to utter the word *år* 'year', and starts writing down the number *1966* on the table. Typically, when Aksel writes down a number, the non-aphasic interlocutor verbalises what he is writing. In this way, the non-aphasic participant partly makes the aphasic participant's contribution 'public' as a verbal act and partly checks on his or her own understanding of the contribution. After writing the number *1966,* Aksel utters the infinitive form *spise* 'eat'. This verb phrase is interpreted as an expression of the past tense by the co-participant as evidenced in *her* next turn, which runs as follows: *var du her og spiste* (literally: 'were you here and ate') – with past tense forms.

Another strategy used by Aksel is to present a nominal or adjectival phrase contextualizing the following contribution as temporally displaced in relation to the time of utterance. Nouns referring to the days of the week or months of the year are used in this way. In a slightly less orthodox way, he may also use an adjective like *små* meaning 'small', 'little' or 'young' (plural). In combination with a proper noun, he uses this adjective to refer to the past with the meaning 'when this particular person was a child'. Like verb forms in the infinitive, these nominal and adjectival expressions need to be interpreted by the non-aphasic interlocutor for the past tense meaning to be established.

Preliminary Conclusions: Spontaneous Speech

Summing up so far, these data show that generally, Aksel has severe problems with the use of verbs and appropriate verbal inflection in conversation. However, the data also show that Aksel knows that utterances must be contextualized temporally, and they illustrate how temporal displacement can be achieved by means other than verbal inflection, e.g. by writing numbers, by using certain nouns and adjectives, and by relying on the non-aphasic participant to provide a temporal frame. Often, the expression of past tense is established through a tripartite structure in which a) the aphasic participant presents an utterance which is incomplete in relation to temporal contextualization, b) the 'correct' form of the verb phrase is first given in the non-aphasic participant's contribution, and c) this is then either acknowledged or disclaimed by the aphasic participant in a third turn position. These data clearly display how the expression of past tense is a matter of negotiation, carried out in sequences where the non-aphasic participant primarily has a 'scaffolding' role. As such, these data add to the growing number of studies which demonstrate how interactional tasks are managed in an explicitly *collaborative* manner in interactions where one of the participants suffers from a speech or language impairment (cf. Collins & Marková, 1995; Goodwin, 1995; Klippi, 1996; Lind, 1998, in progress; Milroy & Perkins, 1992).

PROVIDING PAST TENSE FORMS
IN AN ELICITATION TASK

Turning now to the test results, we shall see that Aksel's performance here contrasts sharply with his performance in spontaneous speech.

The test used was originally developed for testing children's development of past tense inflection (Ragnarsdóttir, Simonsen & Plunkett, 1999). It is an elicitation task following the pattern from Berko (1958), and also used by Bybee and Slobin (1982), where the subject is shown a picture of someone performing an action. The experimenter says: "This is a boy who VERBS. He is VERBING. He did the same thing yesterday. What did he do yesterday?" And the subject fills in, presumably with the past tense form of the verb: "He VERBED (or, e.g. VARB)".

The test consists of 60 verbs, chosen to represent the main verb classes of Norwegian. Norwegian is similar to English in having a clear distinction between a large group of weak (or regular) verbs and a small group of strong (or irregular) verbs, but differs from English in having two classes of weak verbs, one of which is larger than the other. The verb classes also differ in other ways than size, but we do not go into these details here. (For more information about Norwegian verb classes see Endresen & Simonsen, 2001; Ragnarsdóttir et al., 1999.) This gives a three-way main distinction between verb classes: Strong verbs (S), constituting 4% of the verbs, the Smaller Weak class (WS) with 40% of the verbs, and the Larger Weak class (WL) with 56% of the verbs, as illlustrated in Fig. 1.

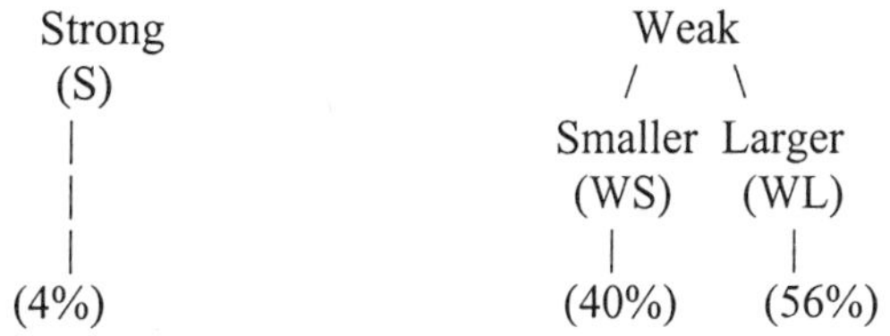

```
      Strong                        Weak
       (S)                        /      \
        |                  Smaller  Larger
        |                   (WS)     (WL)
        |                    |        |
      (4%)                  (40%)    (56%)
```

FIG. 1 Main verb classes in Norwegian.

The strong verbs may also be subclassified further; some strong subclasses are relatively large with many verbs following the same pattern, whereas some are small or idiosyncratic. In the test, the 60 verbs were distributed across the different classes in the way indicated in Table 1.

TABLE 1
Verb types included in the test.

VERB CLASS	Weak, larger (WL)	Weak, smaller (WS)	Strong, large subclass 1	Strong, large subclass 2	Strong, idio-syn-cratic	TOTAL
No. of verbs	16	17	9	9	9	60

In the test, the verbs were also matched for token frequency, with approximately the same number of high and low frequency verbs in each subclass of verbs. (For details on frequency counts, see Ragnarsdóttir et al., 1999.)

When Aksel was tested, the infinitive form of the verb was shown in writing under the picture of the action. The oral cue was given in the present tense and ample time was given for him to respond. Aksel gave a correct response (mostly directly, but sometimes after a couple of wrong trials) on 50 of the 60 verbs. For the 10 remaining verbs, he did not manage to come up with the correct response on his own, but gave an 'OK' when we provided him with the correct form, and a 'no' in the cases when we gave him an incorrect form first. The fact that he finally ended up with a correct set of verb forms indicates that his verbal inflection system is somehow intact in his lexicon.

However, the 10 verbs which Aksel did not manage to inflect correctly by himself will be considered as 'errors' in this context. In Table 2 we compare Aksel's responses to the responses of a control group of 30 normal adults who were tested on the same set of verbs, but who had to give their answers under a time constraint to induce errors (Bjerkan, 2000; Simonsen & Bjerkan, 1998). The controls had a total average of 94 % correct responses, i.e. 56.4 correct verb forms, with a SD of 5 % (3 forms).

TABLE 2
Correct responses.

	(Total :	60 verbs)
	Mean	SD
Controls	56.4 (94%)	3 (5%)
Aksel	50 (83%)	

Aksel's score of 50 correct verbs is a little more than 2 SD below this mean. However, the score is not evenly distributed across the verb classes, as indicated in Table 3.

TABLE 3
Correct responses by verb type.

	WL class (16 verbs)		WS class (17 verbs)		S class (27 verbs)	
	Mean	SD	Mean	SD	Mean	SD
Controls	14.6 (91%)	1.6 (10%)	16.5 (97%)	0.9 (5%)	25.4 (94%)	1.9 (7%)
Aksel	13 (81%)		16 (94%)		21 (78%)	

For the weak verbs, Aksel is within 1 SD of the mean of the control group for both classes, but his problem clearly lies with the strong verbs, with only 21 out of 27 verbs correctly produced. Furthermore, it is worth noting that a majority (four of six) of the problematic strong verbs were from the group of idiosyncratic strong verbs (i.e. verbs that do not belong to a family of verbs following the same pattern). Table 4 shows the types of errors he makes, compared to the normal controls.

Note that the first three error types represent overgeneralizations of each of the main past tense inflectional patterns, while the next two result from choosing a wrong inflection or a wrong verb, respectively. Aksel makes more errors than the control group, but generally, he makes the same *kinds* of errors as the control group – with one exception: in error type #4, the wrong inflections of the adult controls are all past participles, while the wrong inflections produced by Aksel may be infinitives or present tense forms as well. Besides, his error *pattern* is different in two respects:

1. He has very few overgeneralization errors, and in particular no overgeneralizations at all to the smaller weak class, the error type which is dominant in the adult controls (error type #2).

TABLE 4
Error types: Percentages across all verb groups.

	Average number of errors (max 60)	#1 GEN >WL	#2 GEN > WS	#3 GEN > S	#4 WRONG INFLEC- TION	#5 WRONG VERB
				ERROR %		
Controls	3.6	10%	47%	17%	11%	15%
Aksel	10	10%		10%	50%	30%

2. His dominant errors consist of using a wrong inflectional form – past participle, present tense or infinitive form (error type #4), or of using a wrong verb – semantically or phonologically related to the target verb (error type #5).

Sometimes both of these dominant error types occur with the same verb when he struggles to find the correct form, as illustrated with his responses concerning the verb VEKKE 'wake (someone) up':

VEKKE 'wake (someone) up' – target past tense form: *vekte*
- *vakna*   (past tense of VÅKNE 'wake up' (intransitive))
- *våkne*   (infinitive of VÅKNE)
- *vekker*   (present tense of VEKKE)
- *vakna*   (past tense of VÅKNE)
- *vekte*   (past tense of VEKKE (= target))
- *vakna*   (past tense of VÅKNE)

Successively, Aksel tried – and rejected – all of these different forms: the past tense of a semantically and phonologically related verb (*vakna*), the infinitive of this verb (*våkne*), the present tense of the target verb (*vekker*), the past tense of the related verb again (*vakna*), even passing through the target past form, but rejecting it. When we suggested the target form *vekte* again, however, he accepted it as the correct answer.

Preliminary Conclusions: Experimental Data

The experimental data indicate that Aksel's verbal inflection system is intact in his lexicon. He produces many more past tense forms than would be expected from his spontaneous speech. His performance (without a time constraint) is at 2 SD lower than that of the normal controls (with a time constraint), but this reduced performance is mainly related to the strong or irregular verbs, and predominantly to the most irregular ones among them, i.e. verbs which do not belong to a clear subpattern. His errors are generally of the same type as those of the controls, but they pattern differently. As opposed to the normal controls, he produces few overgeneralization errors. Rather, his errors are either a wrong verb which is semantically and/or phonologically related to the target verb, or a wrong form of the target verb (a past participle, present tense or infinitive form).

DISCUSSION

It is a well established fact that verbs are problematic for nonfluent and/or agrammatic aphasic speakers, both in the sense that they use few verbs in spontaneous speech, that they perform worse on action naming than on object naming tasks, and that they have problems with verb inflection (Bastiaanse & Jonkers, 1998; Bates, Chen, Tzeng, Li & Opie, 1991; Bates, Wulfeck & MacWhinney, 1991; Caramazza & Berndt, 1985; Kolk & Heeschen, 1992; Menn, O'Connor, Obler & Holland, 1995). Aksel's performance in spontaneous speech fits this pattern. We have only investigated his performance with verbs, so we do not claim that he has a selective verb deficit – other word classes (e.g. nouns may also be problematic for him).

A better performance in elicited than in spontaneous speech has also been documented for aphasic speakers (e.g. Badecker & Caramazza, 1985; Kolk & Heeschen, 1992; Martin, Wetzel, Blossom-Stach & Feher, 1989; Wilkinson, 1995), and Aksel's production pattern is in accordance with these findings, with an extreme difference in performance between the two types of tasks. However, the elicited speech in the studies mentioned has most often been the result of different picture description tasks, which are not quite comparable to our experimental task requiring the production of one single word form only, a past tense inflection of the verb.

As far as we know, no study of this kind has been done for Norwegian, so Aksel's case is a new addition to the cross-linguistic database on nonfluent aphasic speakers. We find his different performances in the use of verbs and verb inflection in spontaneous speech and in an experimental setting so striking that they are worthy of closer investigation to see what they can tell us about:

- his ability to inflect verbs for tense
- the structure of his lexicon/inflectional system
- possible consequences for assessment and therapy

The experimental data show us that the inflectional patterns must in some way be intact in Aksel's linguistic system. This indicates that his problem with verb inflection in spontaneous speech is not primarily a question of specifically impaired linguistic competence, but rather a question of problems with accessing and processing the verb form. Spontaneous linguistic interaction presents the participants with a complex set of tasks that need to be undertaken simultaneously. For persons with an impaired processing capacity – and/or an impaired memory – this may lead to an overload of cognitive demands, which then has to be reduced in some way. The fact that verbs are particularly hard for Aksel to access and process may be related to the fact that they are, in general, low in imageability (it is hard to produce a mental image of them), as suggested by Bird and Franklin (1996); Bird, Howard & Franklin (2000).

Aksel's strategies in spontaneous speech may all be viewed from the perspective of overload reduction. His main strategy of relying on the contributions of his conversational partner as a scaffold is a strategy used in interaction by all speakers, but what is unique for Aksel (and other language impaired speakers) is the extremely high degree of reliance on such scaffolding. The use of certain nouns or adjectives to set the temporal stage is also used in normal interaction, but generally this is used in combination with an inflected verb form – and this is lacking in Aksel's speech. The strategy of writing down a number to indicate a year is interesting because Aksel opts to use another modality of expression (writing instead of speaking). It is possible that in this case the written modality allows him to take a shortcut without having to process the whole number linguistically. For instance, the first two digits in a number indicating a certain year (in this case, 19) may be quite automatized.

The experimental situation reduces Aksel's cognitive load considerably. All he needs to process is one single verb form, the rest is already given through the set frame, including the choice of which verb to use. In addition, the verb form is required, so there is no way around producing a verb in this setting. In this situation, he manages to access and/or process the verb more easily. It is clear from his performance that he does not access all verb forms directly, but actually processes them (e.g. for the verb *ringe* 'ring', which is a weak verb in Norwegian) he first gave *rang* as a past tense form, but corrected it immediately to the correct form *ringte*.

The experimental situation, then, seems to tap his competence for inflecting verbs. The patterns of his responses may be informative regarding the way in which his inflectional system is organised. We noted that the verbs which are most problematic for him are the strong verbs, and in particular the most irregular ones among them. These verbs belong to classes with a low type frequency (i.e. with few other members) while they generally have a high token frequency. For acquisition, earlier studies with the same verb test (Ragnarsdóttir et al., 1999) have shown that verbs with a high type frequency are acquired earlier than those with a low type frequency. Token frequency also had a positive effect for acquisition, but this effect disappeared with age. For Aksel, too, the verbs which have the least anchorage in a pattern with other verbs, seem to be the most difficult to retrieve and process. The strategy he then resorts to is mainly to use another inflectional form of the same verb, or to use another verb which is phonologically and/or semantically related to the target verb. If we see his lexicon as a structured network of words linked together by semantic and phonological similarities, the implication may be that he tries to deal with the more difficult forms by accessing a larger portion of the network than that of the intended verb – the larger "family" to which the verb is related, phonologically and semantically.

Aksel's performance in the test differs from that of the normal controls mainly quantitatively. However, the dominant error type of the controls, overgeneralization to another class, is infrequent in Aksel's performance. This may possibly indicate that accessing forms in the system is easier for him than processing forms from the system – although there is evidence that he does both.

Finally, can we point to any possible consequences for assessment and therapy from these findings? Concerning assessment, it is evident that both spontaneous speech and controlled tests are necessary to assess a client's linguistic abilities. As for therapy, these findings present us with several possibilities. Knowing that Aksel's inflectional system is intact at some level, it might be possible to overcome the problem of cognitive overload in spontaneous interaction by training him in the use of verbs in spontaneous speech. On the other hand, this type of training may be inappropriate as long as he is able to express temporal displacement in interaction through other means. The main problem here seems to be that Aksel does not signal clearly enough when a change in temporal frame – often related to a change of topic – takes place. Possibly, a better aim in therapy would be to focus on the necessity of such signaling, instead of focusing on the actual production of verbs, which evidently is very hard for him in spontaneous interaction.

REFERENCES

Badecker, B., & Caramazza, A. (1985). On considerations of method and theory governing the use of clinical categories in neurolinguistics and cognitive neuropsychology: The case against agrammatism. *Cognition, 20,* 97-125.

Bastiaanse, R., & Jonkers, J. (1998). Verb retrieval in action naming and spontaneous speech in agrammatic and anomic aphasia. *Aphasiology, 12,* 951-969.

Bates, E., Chen, S., Tzeng, O., Li, P., & Opie, M. (1991a). The noun-verb problem in Chinese aphasia. *Brain and Language, 41,* 203-233.

Bates, E., Wulfeck, B., & MacWhinney, B. (1991b). Cross-linguistic research in aphasia: An overview. *Brain and Language, 41,* 123-148.

Berko, J. (1958). The child's learning of English morphology. *Word, 14,* 150-177.

Bird, H., & Franklin, S. (1996). Cinderella revisited: A comparison of fluent and non-fluent aphasic speech. *Journal of Neurolinguistics, 9,* 187-206.

Bird, H., Howard, D., & Franklin, S. (2000). Why is a verb like an inanimate object? Grammatical category and semantic category deficits. *Brain and Language, 72,* 246-309.

Bjerkan, K. M. (2000). *Verbal morphology in specifically language impaired children: Evidence from Norwegian.* Oslo: Unipub Forlag.

Bybee, J. L., & Slobin, D. I. (1982). Rules and schemas in the development and use of English past tense. *Language, 58,* 265-89.

Caramazza, A., & Berndt, R. (1985). A multicomponent view of agrammatic Broca's aphasia. In M-. L. Kean (Ed.), *Agrammatism* (pp. 27-63). New York: Academic.

Collins, S., & Marková, I. (1995). Complementarity in the construction of a problematic utterance in conversation. In I. Marková, C. F. Graumann & K. Foppa (Eds.), *Mutualities in dialogue* (pp. 238-263). Cambridge, MA: Cambridge University Press.

Endresen, R. T., & Simonsen, H. G. (2001). The Norwegian verb. In H. G. Simonsen & R. T. Endresen (Eds.), *A cognitive approach to the verb: Morphological and constructional perspectives* (pp. 73-94). New York and Berlin: Mouton de Gryuter.

Goodwin, C. (1995). Co-constructing meaning in conversations with an aphasic man. *Research on language and social interaction, 28,* 233-260.

Klippi, A. (1996). *Conversation as an achievement in aphasics.* Helsinki: Suomalaisen Kirjallisuuden Seura.

Kolk, H., & Heeschen, C. (1992). Agrammatism, paragrammatism and the management of language. *Language and Cognitive Processes, 7,* 89-129.

Lind, M. (1998). Hva innebærer det å delta i en samtale? Et eksempel fra en samtale mellom en afasirammet og en ikke-afasirammet deltaker. In J.T. Faarlund, B. Mæhlum & T. Nordgård (Eds.), *MONS 7. Utvalde artiklar frå det 7. Møtet om Norsk Språk i Trondheim 1997* (pp. 131-153). Oslo: Novus.

Lind, M. (1999). Deltakelsesfremmende strategier i samtale med en afasirammet taler. *Norsk Lingvistisk Tidsskrift, 17,* 109-124.

Lind, M. (this volume). The use of prosody in interaction: Observations from a case study of a Norwegian speaker with a non-fluent type of aphasia.

Lind, M. (in progress). Conversational cooperation: The establishment of reference and displacement in aphasic interaction. Doctoral thesis, University of Oslo.

Martin, R. C., Wetzel, W. F., Blossom-Stach, C., & Feher, E. (1989). Syntactic loss versus processing deficit: An assessment of two theories of agrammatism and syntactic comprehension deficits. *Cognition, 32,* 157-191.

Milroy, L., & Perkins L. (1992). Repair strategies in aphasic discourse: Towards a collaborative model. *Clinical Linguistics & Phonetics, 6,* 27-40.

Menn, L., O'Connor, M., Obler, L. K., & Holland, A. (1995). *Non-fluent aphasia in a multilingual world.* Amsterdam and Philadelphia: John Benjamins.

Ragnarsdóttir, H., Simonsen, H. G., & Plunkett, K. (1999). The acquisition of past tense morphology in Icelandic and Norwegian children: An experimental study. *Journal of Child Language, 26,* 577-618.

Simonsen, H. G., & Bjerkan, K. M. (1998). Testing past tense inflection in Norwegian: A diagnostic tool for identifying SLI children? *International Journal of Applied Linguistics, 8,* 251-270.

Wilkinson, R. (1995). Aphasia: Conversation analysis of a non-fluent aphasic person. In M. Perkins & S. Howard (Eds.), *Case studies in clinical linguistics.* London: Whurr.

5

Sentence Comprehension in Greek SLI Children

Stavroula Stavrakaki

Specific Language Impairment (SLI) has been defined as a non-acquired language disorder with language difficulties in the absence of hearing acuity impairment, mental retardation, motor-articulator impairment, frank neurological impairment, or psycho-emotional disturbance (on criteria setting, cf. Stark & Tallal, 1981). Research findings indicate that grammatical errors are a "hallmark" of SLI (Bishop, 1994). In particular, inflectional and derivational morphology is severely impaired in SLI (Clahsen, 1989, 1991; Gopnik & Crago, 1991; Gopnik & Goad, 1997; Rice, Wexler & Cleave, 1995). The impairment also extends to syntactically complex utterances involving embedded structures as shown by production and comprehension data (van der Lely, 1998). Based on empirical data, diverse explanatory models of SLI have been developed in an attempt to identify the status of the linguistic mechanism attributed to SLI children, the locus of the deficit as well as the linguistic outcome of the deficit (Rice, 1994).

A background assumption that some of those models share is that the deficit concerns the grammatical features intrinsic to lexical items[1]. Within the framework of the above approach, the syntactic–semantic features such as person, number, tense, aspect, and gender are suggested to be missing from the grammar of SLI individuals (Gopnik, 1990a, 1990b). Since SLI children lack the sub-lexical features that encode the inflectional information, they cannot construct the rules that operate on these features (Gopnik & Crago, 1991). Alternatively, it has been suggested that the deficit in SLI lies in the non-interpretable features of grammar (Tsimpli & Stavrakaki, 1999; Tsimpli, in press), that is, features irrelevant for semantic interpretation (Chomsky, 1995). Another account that looks at the deficit more narrowly argues that only the

---

[1] See van der Lely (1998, p.177) for such classification of SLI models.

optional non-interpretable θ-features of verbs are affected (Clahsen, Bartke & Gollner, 1997). In the same sense of the narrow interpretation of the deficit in SLI, Rice et al. (1995) and Rice & Wexler (1996) postulate that the feature of Tense is missing or underspecified, hence the optionality of Tense projection in SLI grammar.

Following a different line of reasoning, van der Lely (1994, 1997) suggests that the features of grammar may not be missing per se. Alternatively, she puts forth the Representational Deficit Model for Dependent Relations (henceforth, RDDR) which postulates that the deficit causing SLI lies mainly in the computational component of the language. In particular, the deficit in SLI is concerned with linguistic structural complexity. Therefore, local syntactic relations are expected to be handled correctly but a breakdown of performance will be exhibited on long-distance dependencies involving operations such as movement. In a recent and more elaborated version of the RDDR model, van der Lely (1998) suggests that the principle that forces movement of unchecked features, i.e. the Must Move principle, is missing from SLI grammar and this deficit causes optional movement.

Against the empirical and theoretical background presented above, the primary aim of this study is to present SLI comprehension data from Modern Greek. The questions raised in this study are concerned with the following issues. First, whether Greek SLI children's ability to interpret reversible syntactic constructions differs from that of their Language Age (LA) and Chronological Age (CA) peers, and if so, in what ways. Secondly, what the status of the linguistic mechanism in SLI grammar is. The final aim of this study is to contribute to the linguistic characterization of the deficit in SLI.

The overall organization of this chapter is as follows. First, some background theoretical assumptions are provided, under the framework of which the empirical data will be analyzed. Second, the experiment designed to investigate SLI children's sentence comprehension is reported and the results on group performance are presented and analyzed. Finally, the implications of my study for the theory of SLI are discussed.

THEORETICAL PRESUPPOSITIONS

Language Modularity and the Implicit/Explicit Learning Distinction

The modular approach for organization of the Language Faculty is adopted as suggested by Fodor (1983) and developed by Smith & Tsimpli (1995). According to Fodor's modularity thesis (1983), language is underpinned by modular processes. However, some aspects of language, particularly pragmatic interpretation and substantive categories, are linked to central operations. More specifically, substantive elements are assumed to be linked to a conceptual slot in the mental lexicon, which is largely universal (Sperber & Wilson, 1986). On the other hand, the elements that are parameterized across languages, that is, functional categories, constitute an independent module of UG, i.e., the Functional Module (Tsimpli & Ouhalla, 1990; Tsimpli, 1996). Under this hypothesis, the mapping of the concept onto a linguistic representation can be assumed to take place at an interface level, where the morphological realization of both functional and substantive categories takes place. In this respect, the morphological component is accessible to both functional categories and substantives. Therefore, it has a quasi-modular status (Smith & Tsimpli, 1993), which means that it is fast, automatic and mandatory on the one hand, and accessible by central operations on the other. In contrast, syntax seems to be impenetrable by central systems (i.e. it is strictly modular).

Apart from the distinction between the modular and non-modular components of the Language Faculty, a further dissociation within the Language Faculty can be provided on the basis of whether the language components reflect knowledge that has been stored implicitly or explicitly.

Implicit knowledge is acquired incidentally, stored implicitly, and used automatically (Paradis, 1994). It is also argued to be procedural on the grounds of its relation to the internalized procedures that make the performance of a particular cognitive, language or motor task automatic (Cohen, 1984). In contrast, explicit learning is fully conscious and achieved effortfully by focusing on that which is to be retained in memory. Thus, the result of this learning, that is, explicit knowledge, consists of anything that can be represented at conscious level. Hence, its characterization as declarative memory (Cohen, 1984).

As argued by Paradis (1994) and Paradis & Gopnik (1997), both the acquisition and use of morphosyntax and phonology are in accordance with the characteristics of procedural memory, while at least some aspects of the lexicon fit in with those of declarative memory.

Based on the discussion above, the following correlation could be postulated with respect to the nature of the learning process that underlie the linguistic components. The non-modular linguistic components (i.e. the mental lexicon) are subject to explicit learning, while the quasi-modular and the strictly modular components, (i.e. morphology and syntax respectively) are subject to implicit learning. However, being penetrable by central operations, the morphological component is not in principle disallowed from being subject to explicit learning. By contrast, this is disallowed for syntax by definition, due to its strictly modular nature.

Competence Versus Performance

Within the theory adopted in this study, competence is contrasted with performance, the latter being concerned with the implementation of the linguistic knowledge. In particular, it is assumed that language use is not necessarily a reflection of knowledge of language. In other words, grammar consists of the knowledge that a hearer/speaker has of a language, which guides the use of the language but does not prescribe any particular parsing algorithm for how that knowledge is put to use (Chomsky, 1968). Therefore, parsing – computing structural relations between words – can involve processes that are independent of grammar such as parsing preferences. Such preferences are as follows:

- Prefer local associations (Frazier,1987; Gibson, 1998).
- Rely on morphological contrast cues, that is, the morphological case. More specifically, nominative case is associated with agent theta-role and accusative case with patient theta-role, as shown by on-line sentence interpretation experiments in Greek (Kail & Diakogiorgi, 1994).
- Also, prefer the first NP marked for the nominative case to be the agent, as indicated by the same online experiments (Kail & Diakogorgi, 1994).

It is further assumed that the more the preferences of the parser are violated the more difficult the processing of the structures will be. Therefore, when a structure is not compatible with parsing preferences, then the interpretation of that structure can be exclusively based on syntax.

THE EXPERIMENT

Subjects

Three groups of subjects participated in the experiment. A summary of the three groups' details can be found in Table 1. The first group consisted of 8 SLI children, selected according to a set of criteria proposed by Stark and Tallal (1981). Each child in the SLI group was individually matched with two control groups on the basis of individual raw scores from the Diagnostic Verbal IQ (DVIQ) Test for Greek children (Stavrakaki & Tsimpli, 1999). Therefore, the Language Age (LA) control group consisted of 16 normally developing children, who were selected on the basis of raw scores in the Diagnostic Verbal IQ Test. Each SLI child was also matched with one normally developing child on the basis of chronological age (+/-3 months). Therefore, the Chronological Age (CA) control group consisted of 8 children.

Notice that no significance was found between the performance of the SLI children and LA controls on the raw scores from the DVIQ test [t (22) = .330 p = .744]. Interestingly, the SLI children of this study seem to be grammatical SLI children in van der Lely's (1997, 1999) terms, as they did more poorly on the part of the verbal IQ test that examined grammatical and morphological abilities than on the part testing lexical abilities [t (7) = -6.902, p < .001].

TABLE 1
Subject details: chronological ages (all groups) and raw scores from the
diagnostic verbal IQ (DVIQ) test (SLI children and LA controls).

Subject Group	Chronological Age			Raw Scores		
	Range	Mean	S.D.	Range	Mean	S.D.
SLI group N = 8	6.1–10	8.1	1.4753	64–98	82.875	12.5178
CA Controls N = 8	6.2–10	8.1	1.4160			
LA Controls N = 16	3.6–5.6	4.4	0.73	63–100	81.18	11.44

As shown by their mean chronological age in Table 1, the SLI children are
school age children. An assessment of their morphosyntactic abilities on the
basis of spontaneous speech data has been conducted. Consider now Table 2,
where we provide data showing the correct use of some grammatical categories
in obligatory contexts.

TABLE 2
The use of some grammatical categories by SLI children.

	Correct Use
Past tense	198/200 (99%)
AgrS (2ndS/P)	78/80 (97.5%)
Definite article	284/290 (97.93%)
Object clitic pronouns (3rd person)	48/50 (96%)
Prepositions	54/60 (90%)
Case (the marked form: Nom. Masculine gender)	75/75 (100%)
Interrogative words	26/26 (100%)
Complementizers	14/22 (63.64%)
The mood marker na (= to).	35/40 (87.5%)

As shown in Table 2, the grammatical profile of SLI children is far from
that described at an early stage of their linguistic development where most of the

above categories were found to be severely impaired. In particular, research findings (Stavrakaki, 1996, 1999; Tsimpli & Stavrakaki, 1999; Tsimpli, in press) indicate that Greek SLI children[2] – aged 5 – consistently omit the definite articles, the clitic object pronouns, the case marker of the masculine NPs and the interrogative pronouns. They also have problems in marking subject-verb agreement and in particular the second person singular and plural. Interestingly, Greek SLI children mark correctly the past tense in their spontaneous speech, although they are not always able to retrieve it in elicitation tasks (Dalalakis, 1994; Stavrakaki, 1999). Although the SLI children of this study produce correctly most of the above morphemes, they appear to be able to build up only simple syntactic structures and not complex ones (cf. van der Lely, 1997).

Design and Materials

The test sentences consisted of base-generated constructions, i.e. simple active sentences with SVO word order, simple active sentences with clitics, structures formed by operator movement, i.e. focus constructions[3], subject and object clefts and pseudo-clefts, subject and object long-distance wh-questions, and A-movement, i.e. actional passives[4]. All of them were reversible. Examples of the sentence types are presented below:

Simple Active Sentences With SVO Word Order   (SA)
(1) O elefantas   kiniga   ton pithiko
     the-elephant-nom-chase-3s-the-monkey-acc
     The elephant is chasing the monkey

Simple Active Sentences With Clitic   (SAcl)
(2) O elefantas   ton kiniga
     the-elephant-nom-him-chase-3s
     The elephant is chasing him

Focus Constructions   (FC)
(3) TIN TIGRI sproxni o rinokeros
     the-tiger-acc-push-3s-the-rhino-nom
     The elephant is pushing THE TIGER.

---

[2] Three out of the eight SLI children in this study participated in those studies.
[3] In Greek, focus constructions have been analyzed as involving operator movement (see Tsimpli, (1995, 1998) for a detailed discussion).
[4] For the Greek SLI children's comprehension of relative clauses, see Stavrakaki (in press).

Subject-Clefts   (SC)
(4) O skilos ine pu kinighai tin katsika
     the-dog-nom-that-chase-3s-the-goat-acc
     It is the dog that is chasing the goat

Subject Pseudo-Clefts   (SPC)
(5) Aftos pu xtipai tin kamila ine o skilos
     the-one-nom-that-hit-3s-the-camel-acc-be-3s-the-dog-nom
     The one that is hitting the camel is the dog

Object clefts   (OC)
(6) O pithikos ine pu htipai o elefantas
     the-monkey-nom-be-3s-that-hit-the-elephant-nom
     It is the monkey that the elephant is hitting

Object Pseudo–Clefts   (OPC)
(7) Aftos pu htipai o rinokeros ine o pithikos
     the-one-nom-that-hit-3s-the-rhino-nom-be-3s-the-monkey-nom
     The one that the rhino is hitting is the monkey

Long Distance (LD) Who–Subject Questions   (Wh-S)
(8) Pjios tha pi o rinokeros oti kinijise ton elefanta?
     who-nom-will-say-the-rhino-nom-chased-3s-the-elephant-nom
     Who will the rhino say chased the elephant?

Long Distance (LD) Who–Object Questions   (Wh-O)
(9) Pjon tha pi o rinokeros oti klotsise i katsika?
     who-acc-will-say-the-rhino-that-kick-the-goat-nom
     Who will the rhino say that the goat kicked?

Passive Voice   (P)
(10) O pithikos sproxtete apo tin tigri
     the-monkey-nom-push-3s-mp-by-the-tiger
     The monkey is pushed by the tiger

Four stories for each question type were invented; concerning the other structures, 14 exemplars for each sentence type were tested. The characterization of the syntactic structures was mainly based on processing criteria, that is, whether the processing properties of the testing structures are compatible or not with the parsing preferences, as sketched before. Consider Table 3, where the test constructions and their processing properties are presented.

TABLE 3
The test constructions and their processing properties.

Sentence Type	Processing Properties
Simple active (SVO)	Compatible with parsing preferences
Simple active with clitic	*Non-local association between the clitic and the referent NP
Focus constructions	*The first NP is not the agent but the morphological case is correctly associated with the theta-role
S-clefts/pseudo-clefts	Compatible with parser's preferences
O-clefts/pseudo-clefts	*Nominative case is associated with patient theta-role *The first NP is not the agent
LD who-subject questions	*Long distance association between the verb in the subordinate clause and the subject wh-pronoun The first wh-pronoun is the agent
LD who-object questions	*Long distance association between the verb in the subordinate clause and the object wh-pronoun *The first wh-pronoun is not the agent
Passive voice	*Nominative case is associated with patient theta-role *The first NP is not the agent

Note. * indicates a violation of parsing preferences.

Procedure

An acting-out task was employed for all sentences apart from long-distance wh-questions. This task requires the subject to manipulate toy animals in such a way so as to demonstrate the thematic roles of nouns in verbally presented sentences. Before beginning the task, the children were asked to identify all animals by pointing to them in turn when they were named by the experimenter. They were also encouraged to play with the toys[5] in order to be familiar with them. Finally, the children were instructed to do what the experimenter said.

A somewhat different method, which is nevertheless based on a toy manipulation task, was used for LD who-questions. The children were told that they should help the puppet to understand what was going on in the story by telling the puppet the answer. Three figurines were placed on the table. For example, one dog, one elephant and one fox. The experimenter told the child a story in which the fox was chasing the dog and after that the dog was chasing the elephant. At the same time, she showed that the fox was chasing the dog and the dog was chasing the elephant. At the end, the child should help the puppet to answer the question following:

---

[5] Apart from the toys corresponding to the nouns occurring in the sentence, some distractors were also used. Notice that in simple active sentences with a clitic, the distractor was marked with a different gender to that of the clitic.

"Who will the rhino say chased the dog?"

Results and Discussion

The three groups' correct performance on all testing constructions is presented in Table 4. A 3x10 (Group x Sentence type) way ANOVA was conducted to investigate the data. The main effects of subject group and sentence type were both significant [F (2,320) = 96.473, $p <$ .001, and F (9,320) = 38.878, $p <$ .001]. Posthoc analysis (Scheffe technique) confirmed that the scores of the SLI children were significantly lower than those of the LA controls ($p <$ .001) and the scores of the LA controls were significant lower than those of CA controls ($p <$ .001). In general terms, CA controls exhibited an overall high level of performance; LA controls exhibited lower performance than that of CA controls as they undergo the normal process of language acquisition, hence their performance is often subject to developmental matters[6]. Notice that the crucial comparison in order to draw conclusions on SLI is between the performance of SLI children and LA controls (van der Lely & Howard, 1993; Bishop, 1997).

Let us now consider the groups' performance in detail[7]. As shown in Table 4, the same level of performance on simple active sentences, subject clefts and pseudo-clefts was exhibited by all groups. The above structures are completely compatible with the parsing preferences. Notice that the difference between the performance of SLI children and LA controls on long-distance who-S questions and focus constructions failed to reach significance [t (20) = -.981, $p =$ .338 and, t (22) = -1.326, $p =$.198 respectively].

Interestingly, the above structures violate to some extent but not entirely the parser's preferences and thus some PF cues are provided for their interpretation. In particular, the association between the morphological case and theta-roles as well as the preference for the first NP to be the agent seem to be exploited in focus constructions and subject questions respectively.

---

[6] Due to reasons related to the immature status of linguistic and/or processing mechanism, the children's performance on linguistic tasks may be different that that of the adult one. In other words, the non-adult performance of children can be contributed to reduced processing capacity or to immature grammar (see Avrutin 2000; Borer & Wexler 1987; Crain & Thornton, 1998, among others).

[7] Error analysis is not provided here due to space limitations. However, it should be noted that different error types were produced by SLI children and LA controls in most cases. For example, in the obligatory contexts of LD O-questions, SLI children reversed theta-roles, while LA controls produced the correct NP marked for nominative case instead of accusative. In this respect, the two groups exhibited a qualitatively different type of performance (for a detailed error analysis and discussion, see Stavrakaki, 2001).

TABLE 4

The correct performance (%) of all groups' on the tested constructions.

	SLI children		LA Controls		CA controls	
	Mean	S.D.	Mean	S.D.	Mean	S.D.
Simple active (SVO)	100	.0	100	.0	100	.0
Simple active with clitic	56.25	17.68	91.51	5.96	100	.0
Focus constructions	62.5	25.54	77.23	25.72	100	.0
Subject clefts	100	.0	100	.0	100	.0
Subject pseudo-clefts	98.21	3.3	100	.0	100	.0
Object clefts	12.5	9.15	36.6	32.13	73.21	32.12
Object pseudo-clefts	30.35	14.16	57.14	28.21	92.85	15.27
Long distance who-S questions	87.5	13.36	92.85	11.72	100	.0
Long distance who-O questions	46.88	24.77	85.71	16.16	100	.0
Passive voice	18.75	7.81	57.59	34.45	96.43	6.61

We now turn our consideration to the structures where the performance of SLI children and LA controls was found to differ significantly. SLI children's performance drops significantly below than that of LA controls on simple active sentences with clitic [t (7.807) = -5.489, p = .001], object clefts and pseudo-clefts [t (19.180) = -2.783, p = .012 and t (12.886) = -2.355, p = .035 respectively], passive constructions [t (17.840) = -4.294, p < .001], and who-O questions [t (20) = -4.469, p < .001].

What all the above structures have in common is that they violate the parsing preferences to a certain degree and consequently their interpretation depends on a full syntactic analysis. Notice, crucially, that all of them are formed by movement except for the simple active sentences with clitic, whose interpretation requires the identification of the appropriate referent for the clitic pronoun on the basis of the clitic's morphosyntactic properties, i.e. case and phi-features.

Based on the remark that the role of syntax is crucial in the significant drop of SLI children's performance, two hypotheses can be formulated with respect to the source of the deficit in SLI (see Lukatela, Shankweller & Crain, 1995 for similar discussion on aphasia). Both hypotheses are empirically testable:

1. SLI children's lower performance on the processing demanding structures is due to a processing deficit, that is, the parser cannot have access to the underlying syntactic representations. Under this hypothesis, it is predicted that the difference between the performance of the two groups will be only quantitative, and thus the performance of LA controls and SLI children will drop on the same structures in a similar manner but to a different extent.

2. SLI children's lower performance is due to a deficit in the underlying syntactic representation. Under this hypothesis, it is predicted that the difference between the performance of the two groups will also be qualitative, and thus, the SLI children's performance will drop on structures, whereas those of LA controls will not.

Consider now the drop in CA and LA controls' performance on the testing structures compared to that in SLI children's performance, as presented in Fig. 1. Notice that the classification of structures from left to right was made on the basis of the LA controls' performance, and particularly, starting from the highest and ending with the lowest percentages.

As shown in Fig. 1, asymmetries were found between the performance of the SLI children and LA controls on 1) simple active sentences with clitics (SAcl), 2) long distance who-object questions   (Wh-O) and 3) passive voice (P).

In other words, the drop of performance of SLI children on the above structures does not follow the drop of LA controls' performance. That is, the hierarchy in the difficulty of the structures is not exactly the same for SLI children and LA controls. In this respect, the data seem to support the grammar deficit hypothesis.

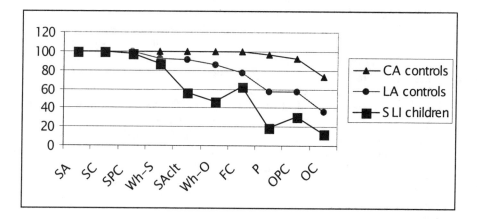

FIG.1 The drop in all groups' performance.[8]

---

[8] Key to Fig.1: SA = Simple Active, SC = Subject Cleft, SPC = Subject Pseudo-Cleft, Wh-S = Long Distance Who-Object Questions, SA-clt = Simple Active Sentences with Clitics, FC = Focus Constructions, P = Passive Voice, OPC = Object Pseudo-Clefts, OC = Object Clefts.

THEORETICAL IMPLICATIONS

If the deficit lies in grammar, then the question raised is concerned with the *locus* of the deficit in SLI grammar. Let us now consider our data against the predictions of the linguistic models of SLI. Recall that the SLI children of this study appear to be able to handle aspects of morphology in their spontaneous speech but their performance drops significantly below than that of LA controls on the interpretation of syntactic structures violating the parsing preferences.

Such findings fit well with the general prediction of the RDDR model (van der Lely, 1997), which postulates that SLI children will have problems mainly in computing complex syntactic structures. However, the outcome of the deficit cannot be described in terms of optional movement (van der Lely, 1998). If this were the case, then it would be expected that optionality would be found in all structures formed by movement, i.e. object- and subject-extracted questions, clefts, etc. Therefore, SLI children would exhibit relatively similar performance on all testing constructions formed by movement. Instead, our data seem to be conditioned by the following rule: If the structure is not at all compatible with the parsing preferences and the interpretation is purely dependent on syntactic cues, then significant drop in SLI performance is expected. Therefore, it seems that the SLI performance is rather conditioned by the parsing preferences and some movement operations (at least A-movement and A-bar movement) are missing from the grammar of SLI children.

Consider now an interpretation assuming that the grammatical features are missing per se. Neither the narrow (Clahsen et al., 1997; Rice et al., 1995) nor the broad version (Gopnik, 1990a; Tsimpli, in press) of such interpretation seem to be compatible with our data, as the features which are assumed to be impaired are correctly employed by the SLI children of this study[9]. However, as mentioned previously, this is not the case at an early stage of Greek SLI children's grammatical development, where LF non-interpretable features are severely impaired (Tsimpli & Stavrakaki, 1999; Tsimpli, in press). In particular, Greek SLI children's PF marking of case and phi-features seems not to be available, as shown by their performance on the functional categories encoding such features. Therefore, it seems that an account postulating that the deficit lies in the non-interpretable features of grammar seems to be adequate to accommodate findings from SLI children aged 5, but not from older SLI

---

[9] An exception to this conclusion may concern the strength property of a feature, which is a non-interpretable feature itself and related to movement operations. As shown by our data, SLI children have problems in some structures formed by movement. It could therefore be said that such problems are predicted by a hypothesis postulating a deficit in the non-interpretable features of grammar. However, this is not the case for all non-interpretable features. As shown by spontaneous speech data, the feature of case as well as the phi-features of verbs are correctly employed by SLI children.

children whose performance falls within the general predictions of the RDDR model.

The above finding is not as contradictory as it would seem at first sight. Non-interpretable features play a crucial role with respect to the nature of the derivation in the computational system. These features have to be checked at some point of the derivation. Therefore, feature checking is triggered by non-interpretable features and linked with movement under the principle of Last Resort (Chomsky, 1995). According to the Last Resort principle, only features needing to be checked will move. In this respect, non-interpretable features being responsible for checking operations are explicitly associated with the computational component of language (i.e. narrow syntax) in terms of Chomsky (1998, 1999).

Let us now turn to the SLI data. The SLI children of this study correctly use some non-interpretable features (e.g. case) in the simple structures they produce in their spontaneous speech, but there is no evidence that they can use them to interpret a complex structure. Thus, they seem to be able to learn the morphological aspect of the non-interpretable features; they may achieve it by means of explicit and not implicit memory (Paradis & Gopnik, 1997). Morphology is susceptible to explicit learning procedures, due to its quasi-modular status. However, syntax is impenetrable by such procedures, due to its strictly modular status. Since syntax is not subject to learning procedures, SLI children are expected to have severe difficulties with syntactic operations. In this respect, I conclude with van der Lely (1999) that the deficit in SLI appears mainly in the computational system of language (i.e. syntax). However, this deficit may result from a severe impairment in the non-interpretable features of grammar (Tsimpli & Stavrakaki, 1999) rather than from the optionality of movement in SLI grammar (van der Lely, 1998).

ACKNOWLEDGMENTS

This work was supported by the National Scholarship Foundation of Greece (IKY). I thank Heather van der Lely and an anonymous reviewer for their insightful comments.

REFERENCES

Avrutin, S. (2000). Comprehension of discourse-linked and non-discourse-linked questions by children and Broca's aphasics. In Y. Grodzinsky, L. P. Shapiro & D. Swinney (Eds.), *Language and the brain* (pp. 295–313). New York: Academic.

Bishop, D. V. M. (1994). Grammatical errors in specific language impairment: Competence or performance limitations? *Applied Psycholinguistics, 15*, 507–550.

Bishop, D. V. M. (1997). *Uncommon understanding: Comprehension in specific language impairment.* East Sussex, UK: Psychology Press.

Borer, H., & Wexler, K. (1987). The maturation of syntax. In T. Rooper & E. Williams (Eds.), *Parameter setting* (pp. 23–172). Dordrecht: Reidel.

Chomsky, N. (1968). *Language and mind.* New York: Harcourt Brace.

Chomsky, N. (1995). *The minimalist program.* Cambridge, MA: MIT Press.

Chomsky, N. (1998). Minimalist inquiries: The framework. Cambridge, MA: MIT Press.

Chomsky, N. (1999). Derivation by phase. Cambridge, MA: MIT Press.

Clahsen, H. (1989). The Grammatical characterization of developmental dysphasia. *Linguistics, 27*, 897–920.

Clahsen, H. (1991). *Child language and developmental dysphasia: Linguistic studies in the acquisition of German.* Amsterdam: John Benjamins.

Clahsen, H., Bartke S., & Gollner, S. (1997). Formal features in impaired grammars: A comparison of English and German SLI children. *Journal of Neurolinguistics, 10(2/3)*, 151–172.

Cohen, N. (1984). Preserved learning capacity in amnesia: Evidence for multiple memory systems. In L.R. Squire & N. Butters (Eds.), *The neuropsychology of human memory* (pp. 83–103). New York: Guilford.

Crain, S., & Thornton, R. (1998). *Investigations in universal grammar.* Cambridge, MA: MIT Press.

Dalalakis, J. (1994). Developmental language impairment in Greek. *McGill Working Papers in Linguistics, 10*, 216–227.

Fodor, J.A. (1983). *The modularity of mind.* Cambridge, MA: MIT Press.

Frazier, L. (1987). Sentence processing: A tutorial review. In M. Coltheart (Eds.), *Attention and performance, XII: The psychology of reading.* (pp. 559–586). Hove, UK: Lawrence Erlbaum Associates.

Gibson, E. (1998). Linguistic complexity: locality of syntactic dependencies. *Cognition, 68*, 1–76.

Gopnik, M. (1990a). Feature-blind grammar and dysphasia. *Nature, 344*, 715.

Gopnik, M. (1990b). Feature blindness: A case study. *Language Acquisition, 1*, 139–164.

Gopnik, M., & Crago, M. (1991). Familial Aggregation of the Developmental Language Disorders. *Cognition, 39*, 1–50.

Gopnik, M., & Goad, H. (1997). What underlies inflectional error patterns in genetic dysphasia? *Journal of Neurolinguistics, 10*, 109–138.

Kail, M., & Diakogiorgi, K. (1994). Morphology and word order in the processing of Greek sentences. In I. Philippaki-Warburton, K. Nikolaidis & M. Sifianou (Eds.), *Themes in Greek linguistics* (pp. 324–332). Amsterdam: John Benjamins.

Lukatela, K., Shankweller, D., & Crain, S. (1995). Syntactic processing in agrammatic aphasia by speakers of a Slavic language. *Brain and Language, 49*, 50–76.

Paradis, M. (1994). Neurolinguistic aspects of implicit and explicit memory: Implications for bilingualism. In N. Ellis (Ed.), *Explicit and implicit learning of second languages* (pp. 393–419). London: Academic Press.

Paradis, M., & Gopnik, M. (1997). Compensatory strategies in genetic dysphasia: declarative memory. *Journal of Neurolinguistics, 10*, 173–186.

Rice, M. (1994). Grammatical categories of children with specific language disorders. In R. Watkins & M. Rice (Eds.), *Specific language impairments in children* (pp. 69–76). Baltimore: Paul Brookes.

Rice, M., & Wexler, K. (1996). A phenotype of specific language impairment: Extended optional infinitives. In M. Rice (Ed.), *Towards a genetics of language* (pp. 215–238). Mahwah, NJ: Lawrence Erlbaum Associates.

Rice, M., Wexler, K., & Cleave P. (1995). Specific language impairment as a period of extended optional infinitives. *Journal of Speech and Hearing Research, 38*, 850–863.

Smith, N.V., & Tsimpli, I. M. (1993). A special intelligence: The case of a polyglot savant. *UCL Working Papers in Linguistics, 5*, 413–450.

Smith, N.V., & Tsimpli, I. M. (1995). *The mind of a savant: Language learning and modularity*. Oxford: Blackwell.

Sperber, D., & Wilson, D. (1986). *Relevance: Communication and cognition*. Oxford:Blackwell.

Stark, R., & Tallal, P. (1981). Selection of children with specific language deficits. *Journal of Speech and Hearing Disorders, 46*, 114–122.

Stavrakaki, S. (1996). SLI in Greek: Evaluation of person and number agreement, case assignment to overt subject pronouns and tense marking. MA thesis, University of Essex.

Stavrakaki, S. (1999). The case of a Greek SLI child: Evaluation of person and number agreement, case assignment to overt subject pronouns and tense marking. *AUTH Working Papers in Theoretical and Applied Linguistics, 6*, 165–188.

Stavrakaki, S. (2001). SLI in Greek: Aspects of syntactic production and comprehension. Unpublished PhD thesis, Aristotle University of Thessaloniki.

Stavrakaki, S. (in press). Comprehension of reversible relative clauses in specifically language impaired and normally developing Greek children. *Brain and Language*.

Stavrakaki, S., & Tsimpli, I. M. (1999). Diagnostic Verbal IQ Test for Greek preschool and school age children. Poster presented at the 5th European Conference on Psychological Assessment, August 25–29, University of Patras.

Tsimpli, I. M. (1995). Focusing in Modern Greek. In K. Kiss (Ed.), *Discourse configurational languages* (pp. 177–205). Oxford: Oxford University Press.

Tsimpli, I. M. (1996). *The prefunctional stage of language acquisition: A cross-linguistic study.* New York & London: Garland.

Tsimpli, I. M. (1998). Individuals and functional readings for focus, wh- and negative operators: Evidence from Greek. In B. D. Joseph, G. C. Horrocks & I. Phillippaki-Warburton (Eds.), *Themes in Greek linguistics II* (pp. 197–227). Amsterdam: John Benjamins.

Tsimpli, I. M. (in press). Morphosyntactic features in the verbal and nominal domains: a comparison between normally developing children and SLI Greek children. *Brain and Language.*

Tsimpli, I. M., & Ouhalla, J. (1990). Functional categories, UG and modularity. Ms, University College & Queen Mary & Westfield College, London.

Tsimpli, I. M., & Stavrakaki, S. (1999). The effects of a morphosyntactic deficit in the determiner system: The case of a Greek SLI child. *Lingua, 108,* 31–85.

van der Lely, H. K. J. (1994). Canonical linking rules: Forward vs. reverse linking in normally developing and specifically language impaired children. *Cognition, 51,* 29–72.

van der Lely, H. (1997). Language and cognitive development in a grammatical SLI boy: Modularity and innateness, *Journal of Neurolinguistics, 10,* 75–103.

van der Lely, H. K. J. (1998). SLI in children: Movement, economy and deficits in the computational-syntactic system. *Language Acquisition, 7,* 161–192.

van der Lely, H. K. J. (1999). Learning from grammatical SLI. *Trends in Cognitive Sciences, 3,* 286–288.

van der Lely, H. K. J., & Howard, D. (1993). Children with specific language impairment: Linguistic impairment or short-term memory deficit? *Journal of Speech and Hearing Research, 36,* 1193–1207.

6

The Importance of Input Factors for the Acquisition of Past Tense Inflection: Evidence from Specifically Language Impaired Norwegian Children

Kirsten Meyer Bjerkan

Earlier studies have shown that different input factors can influence the acquisition of past tense inflection of verbs (e.g. Ragnarsdóttir, Simonsen & Plunkett, 1999). Phonological factors and frequency factors may both play a role, therefore, in the acquisition of past tense inflection by normally developing (ND) and specifically language impaired (SLI) children. The influence of these two factors, however, may differ across the two groups of children. This study investigated past tense inflection in Norwegian SLI children and compared their behavior with ND children.

Norwegian is a Germanic language, and its verb morphology resembles, but is not identical to, that of English. One main difference is that English has two main verb classes (one regular and one irregular), whereas Norwegian has three (two regular and one irregular). The formal distinction between them is that the regular classes carry a syllabic suffix in the past tense, whereas the irregular classes do not. As in English, irregular verbs may have a vowel mutation in the past tense.

The two regular classes in Norwegian are distinguished by the suffixes they carry. The larger regular class carries a suffix starting in a vowel, *-et* or *-a*, whereas the smaller regular class carries a suffix starting in a consonant, *-te* and *-de*.

The three verb classes differ in type frequency. The larger regular class has the highest type frequency. The smaller regular class also has a fairly high type frequency, but within this class there are two distinct subclasses, one of which has a high number of members. This subclass consists of words of a latinate origin, most of which are rare in child or child-directed language. If this subclass is left out, the smaller weak class has a medium type frequency. The irregular class has a low type frequency, although there is some variation between the different subclasses.

The phonological properties of the two regular classes differ, both with respect to vowel quantity and vowel and consonant quantity (Bjerkan, 2000). These differences are tendencies only.

METHOD

A structured test was used to elicit past tense forms. The test was designed for normally developing children by Ragnarsdóttir, Simonsen and Plunkett (1999). The test consists of 60 verbs, half of which are regular and half irregular. There is an equal number of verbs from each of the two regular classes, and in each of the two regular classes, half of the verbs rhyme with irregular verbs, and half do not.

Token frequency of the verbs was varied within each verb class, so that about half of the verbs in each class had a high token frequency and half had a low token frequency.

The subject groups consisted of eight SLI children, four aged 6 and four aged 8 (see Table 1), who were compared to ND children aged 4, 6 and 8 (studied by Ragnarsdòttir et al., 1999, and Simonsen & Bjerkan, 1998), and a group of normal adults. The normal groups each consisted of approximately 30 subjects.

The SLI children had been referred to the Bredtvet Resource Centre with language impairment, and were diagnosed as specifically language impaired by the help of standardised tests of verbal and non-verbal abilities. Six children were tested using the *Reynell Developmental Language Scales* (Reynell, 1983) and two children were tested using the *Illinois Test of Psycholinguistic Abilities* (Kirk, S. A., Kirk, W. D. & McCarthy, 1968). Wechsler's scales were used to measure intelligence (the *Wechsler Preschool and Primary Scale of Intelligence* and the *Wechsler Intelligence Scale* were used with the six-year-old and eight-year-old children, respectively).

TABLE 1
SLI subjects.

Name	Age	Name	Age
Ida	6;1	Henry	8;1
Alex	6;6	Michael	8;2
Tim	6;7	Albert	8;2
Rita	6;9	Karen	8;8

The elicitation task was performed in the same manner for the SLI children and the ND children, using pictures, as in Bybee and Slobin's (1982) study. For example:

Experimenter: "Here you see that Garfield drinks. He did exactly the same thing yesterday. What did he do then?"
Child: [Preferably in the past tense] "drank" or "drinked...".

For the adults, the task was slightly different. A time constraint test was used, as for the adults in Bybee and Slobin's (1982) study. The experimenter read the infinitive form of the verb, and the subject was asked to give the past tense form as quickly as possibly.

RESULTS

Correct Performance

The results show that all of the children understood the test and were able to inflect verbs for past tense. For the ND subjects, the results are presented as group means with standard deviations. The SLI children were too few and too heterogeneous to constitute a group and they are therefore presented as individual case studies. However, a number of general tendencies emerged across the SLI children and it is these tendencies that form the basis for discussion.

The overall correct performance for the ND subjects shows a clear development with age, with a statistically significant difference between each age group. Performances on each separate verb class, as well as standard deviations, are shown in Table 2. For the 4- and 6-year-olds, the smaller regular class of verbs clusters with the irregular class, the performance on these two classes being significantly worse than on the larger regular class, though they are not significantly different from each other. The 8-year-olds perform better on the smaller regular class, and the performance on the two regular classes are significantly better than on the irregular class, though not different from each other. For the adults there is no significant difference between any of the verb classes.

The results for the SLI children are shown in Table 3. Generally, they have a lower percentage of correct inflections than their age-matched peers. Most of the SLI children, like the groups of ND children, have their highest score on the larger regular class, with the smaller regular class being second best and the irregular class the worst. Some of the individual SLI children differ from the appropriate age-matched group of ND children by having disproportionately low

TABLE 2
Correct performance on each verb class, ND children and adults.

Age	Larger regular class		Smaller regular class		Irregular class	
	Mean	SD	Mean	SD	Mean	SD
4 years	85%	20%	47%	27%	33%	24%
6 years	94%	8%	71%	18%	60%	22%
8 years	96%	5%	91%	10%	86%	14%
Adults	91%	10%	97%	5%	94%	7%

TABLE 3
Correct performance on each verb class, SLI children.

Name	Larger regular class	Smaller regular class	Irregular class
Rita, 6 yrs	88%	94%	48%
Ida, 6 yrs	88%	35%	44%
Alex, 6 yrs	63%	53%	19%
Tim, 6 yrs	75%	71%	52%
Henry, 8 yrs	88%	82%	70%
Albert, 8 yrs	88%	88%	44%
Michael, 8 yrs	94%	29%	74%
Karen, 8 yrs	100%	82%	89%

scores on one or both of the smaller regular or the irregular class. This is particularly evident in the performance of Ida, Alex and Michael.

Error Types

There were different types of errors, and the types of errors made by the children varied with age. There were also some differences between the SLI children and the ND children. The focus here will be on overgeneralization errors of which there were three types: overgeneralization to the larger regular class (Gen > LRC); overgeneralization to the smaller regular class (Gen > SRC); and overgeneralization to the irregular class (Gen > IRREG), i.e. to an irregular subclass or pattern. The total number of errors and the distribution of the overgeneralization errors are shown in Table 4. Note that the total number of errors is the mean for each age group out of a total of 60 verbs, whereas the generalizations add up to 100% overgeneralization errors. The column '% overgeneralization errors' shows the proportion of overgeneralizations relative to the total number of errors.

TABLE 4
Distribution of overgeneralization errors, ND children and adults.

	Tot. no. of errors	% overgen. errors	Gen > LRC	Gen > SRC	Gen > IRREG
ND 4-year-olds	29 (49%)	58%	76%	21%	3%
ND 6-year-olds	17 (28%)	88%	59%	31%	10%
ND 8-year-olds	6 (10%)	94%	39%	47%	14%
Adults	4 (6%)	74%	14%	60%	26%

TABLE 5
Distribution of overgeneralization errors, SLI children.

	Tot. no. of errors	% overgen. Errors	Gen > LRC	Gen > SRC	Gen > IRREG
Ida	28 (47%)	32%	89%		11%
Alex	36 (60%)	67%	67%	33%	
Tim	22 (37%)	50%	45%	55%	
Rita	17 (28%)	35%		100%	
Henry	13 (22%)	54%	71%	29%	
Michael	20 (33%)	70%	57%	14%	29%
Albert	19 (32%)	68%	38%	54%	8%
Karen	6 (10%)	100%	33%	50%	17%

With the ND children, there is a clear development with age in the range of classes or patterns they use productively. The younger children overgeneralize predominately to the larger regular class, whereas the older children overgeneralize equally often to each of the regular classes. The adults overgeneralize most frequently to the smaller regular class, and rarely to the larger regular class. Overgeneralization to the irregular class is rare for all age groups, but increases with age. The SLI children overgeneralize to both of the regular classes, and some of them even have a few overgeneralizations to the irregular class. There is vast individual variation here, both in the number of errors and in the kinds of errors made.

THE ROLE OF INPUT FACTORS

Although SLI children constitute a heterogeneous group, and no consensus exists among researchers and therapists as to definition or cause, various studies have found that they often have particular problems with morphology. Different hypotheses have been formulated to account for this morphological impairment, among them the Sparse Morphology Hypothesis, the Missing Feature Hypothesis and the Surface Hypothesis. The Sparse Morphology Hypothesis is formulated to account for cross-linguistic data, but may also be used for monolingual data, the idea being that SLI children do not have the capacity to focus on all the aspects of the morphological system they are acquiring. The hypothesis is that SLI children have a limited processing capacity, and as a result of this they are forced to focus on the most salient or important aspects of the language system they are acquiring (Leonard, 1998; Rom & Leonard, 1990). The Missing Feature Hypothesis claims that the underlying grammar of SLI children is deficient, in that it lacks features needed for both morphophonemic rules and agreement relations. Hence, rules for past tense inflection are absent (Gopnik 1990; Gopnik & Crago, 1991). The Surface Hypothesis claims that SLI children have particular problems with morphemes of low phonological salience, i.e. non-syllabic consonant segments and unstressed syllables characterized by shorter duration than adjacent morphemes and, often, lower frequency and amplitude (Leonard, 1989).

Type Frequency

The results from this investigation show that the verb classes are acquired according to their type frequency. The larger regular class, which has the highest type frequency, is acquired first. The younger ND children (4- and 6-year-olds) perform best on this class, with the smaller regular class and the irregular class lagging behind; type frequency appears to be important during the process of language acquisition. The older children (8-year-olds) and the adults perform equally well on both regular verb classes. This tendency for type frequency to be most important to the youngest children is also evident when the error types are considered. Whereas the younger children generalize the most to the larger regular class, the older children and adults use the smaller regular class productively to a much greater extent.

The majority of the SLI children resemble the younger ND children in having a higher score on the larger regular class and overgeneralizing most frequently to this class. Hence, type frequency appears to play an important role in children's acquisition of verbal inflections.

Token Frequency

The results show a clear effect of token frequency in the ND children, so that verbs with high token frequency have a higher percentage of correct performance. This effect seems to be less marked with age, and is not present in the adults. The effect is only found for the larger regular class and the irregular class, not for the smaller regular class. It is interesting to note that a token frequency effect is found for the ND children for the larger regular class. This is the class which comes closest to counting as a default class and is therefore assumed by some models not to be influenced by input factors.

The SLI children showed the same behavior as the ND children with respect to token frequency. A token frequency effect was found for the larger regular class and the irregular class, but not for the smaller regular class. In the smaller regular class the SLI children actually made more errors on high frequency verbs than on low frequency verbs. However, the frequency counts used in this investigation were based on adult language, and to a large extent on written language, which may account in part for the discrepancy between the classes. On the other hand, frequency estimates for all verb classes were based on the same sources, and some of the verbs the children made errors on in the smaller regular class were common everyday verbs like *bake* and *eat*.

Phonological Factors

The verb classes differ in segmentability and salience. The past tense of the larger regular class, with its vowel initial suffix, is easily segmentable, and also fairly salient, the suffix being syllabic. The smaller weak class also has a syllabic suffix in the past tense, and as such is fairly salient, but the suffix is not always as easily segmentable. When the root of the verb ends in *-r*, a sandhi rule will merge the *-r* and the *-t* of the suffix, and give /ʈ/, like in the verb *kjøre* 'drive': root /çøːɾ/ + suffix -/te/ becomes /çøːʈe/ and not /çøːɾte/.

The past tense of the irregular class is not segmentable, since it does not contain a suffix. Vowel mutation ('ablaut') is found in many of the irregular subclasses, and this would be a salient feature, but the problem is that there are many different subclasses with different vowel patterns; in addition, there are a number of irregular verbs with the same vowel throughout the paradigm.

Segmentability and salience follow the same hierarchy as type frequency, and, as discussed previously, this corresponds to the order in which the verb classes are acquired. It is, however, not possible from these data to determine which is the more important factor: frequency, segmentability or salience. Most likely, they all play a part in influencing the results.

The verb classes also differ in their degree of phonological openness and coherence. The larger regular class is the most phonologically open, whereas the smaller regular class has subclasses with very high phonological coherence, plus a more restricted set of phonological patterns for the rest of the verbs. However, these patterns are not clear-cut, and children may require more time to discover these particular verbs. Thus, we may have evidence for a critical mass effect here: before the child is able to generalize over these subtle patterns, a substantial number of verbs have to be acquired. This may help explain the developmental profile of the regular verbs. The larger regular class, being the most open as well as having the highest type frequency and the highest degree of segmentability, will make this class the easiest one to acquire and to generalize over. Both the youngest ND children and the SLI children show an ability to inflect verbs from the larger regular class correctly and to generalize over this pattern. The patterns of the smaller regular class and the irregular subclasses are more difficult to acquire, and as was shown by the results, both the younger ND children and most of the SLI children have some problems with these classes. Nevertheless, the children are able to generalize over the pattern of the smaller regular class to some extent, and some children even overgeneralize to one or more irregular patterns. The ND 8-year-olds and the adults perform best on the smaller regular class, and this is also their most productive class.

The main difference between the SLI children and the younger ND children on the one hand, and the older ND children and the adults on the other, is seen in their use of phonological cues for verb class membership. The two regular classes differ in their phonological patterning: verbs in the larger regular class tend to have a short stem vowel while verbs in the smaller class tend to have a long vowel. There are also differences in the vowel and consonant inventories of the two classes. These differences are not clear-cut but have obviously been discovered by the older ND children and the adults. These groups make more errors on verbs which deviate from the typical pattern in each class, and overgeneralize these verbs to the class they most closely resemble. No such tendency is seen in the younger ND children and the SLI children, who do not seem to have perceived these patterns and are therefore unable to make use of these phonological cues.

DISCUSSION

We now return to the predictions made by the hypotheses referred to earlier. According to the Missing Feature Hypothesis, SLI children lack the underlying rule for past tense formation. Thus, token frequency is predicted to play an important role for these children. Since they do not have access to the rules, or cannot form generalizations on the basis of the past tense forms they hear, they must learn all inflected forms by rote. ND children, on the other hand, only have to learn irregular forms by rote. For regular forms, they use the rule. Hence, for them, token frequency is expected to have an effect on irregular verbs only.

The results of the present study are not in accordance with this hypothesis; token frequency influenced the performance of ND and SLI children on both the regular and the irregular verb classes. Type frequency is not predicted to influence the performance of SLI children, since they do not have the ability to generalize over patterns. The data here shows that the SLI children have acquired the regularities of at least the larger regular class. This group had a fairly high percentage of the verbs from this class correct, and they were able to use the pattern productively and inflect other verbs according to this pattern. The predictions of the Missing Feature Hypothesis were not borne out.

The Surface Hypothesis holds that SLI children have particular problems with the perception of segments of low phonological salience. Our data shows that phonological properties of the verb classes played a minor role in the performance of the SLI children, with regard both to correct performance and errors made. For the ND 6- and 8-year-olds, on the other hand, phonological factors were important; this generally performed better on verbs which were typical of the verb class to which they belonged. In addition, when verbs deviated from the typical pattern, the ND 6- and 8-year-olds were more likely to overgeneralize these verbs to the class they most closely resembled. These subtle phonological features seem to be difficult for the SLI children to perceive, indicating that they may have problems with segments of low phonological salience.

According to the Sparse Morphology Hypothesis, SLI children have a limited processing capacity. In our data, the SLI children show a reduced ability to focus on available cues of verb class membership compared to ND children of the same age. The SLI children tended to master the larger regular class fairly well, whereas they often had problems with the other two verb classes. They do not use phonological cues of class membership to the same extent as their ND peers, and their performance seems to be determined more by type frequency, as is the case for the youngest ND children. Hence, it may be the case that SLI children have a limited processing capacity.

CONCLUSION

This chapter shows that input factors are important for the acquisition of past tense inflection in both ND and SLI children. Frequency factors are important to both groups of children, although their importance decreases with age for the ND children. Phonological factors are more important for ND children than for SLI children. The subtle phonological cues of the Norwegian verb classes do not seem to be available to the SLI children. Our study found no support for the Missing Feature Hypothesis, whereas the findings are compatible with the Surface Hypothesis and the Sparse Morphology Hypothesis. In order to determine which of the two latter hypotheses is correct, further studies are required of auditory perception and ability to focus on more than one aspect of a morphological system at the same time. At this stage, all that can be concluded is that SLI children appear to have a limited processing ability, which has two effects: they have difficulties in perceiving morphemes with low perceptual salience and they are only able to focus on the most prominent aspect of the morphological system they are acquiring, i.e. frequency factors in Norwegian.

REFERENCES

Bjerkan, K. M. (2000). Verbal morphology in specifically language impaired children: Evidence from Norwegian. *Acta Humaniora, 73*. Oslo: Unipub.

Bybee, J. L., & Slobin, D. I. (1982). Rules and schemas in the development and use of the English past tense. *Language, 58*, 265-289.

Gopnik, M. (1990). Feature blindness: a case study. *Language Acquisition, 1*, 139-164.

Gopnik, M., & Crago, M. (1991). Familial aggregation of a developmental language disorder. *Cognition, 39*, 1-50.

Kirk, S. A., Kirk, W. D., & McCarthy, J. D. (1968). *Illinois Test of Psycho-linguistic Abilities*. Norwegian edition by H. J. Gjessing & H. D. Nygaard, 1975. Oslo: Universitetsforlaget.

Leonard, L. B. (1989). Language learnability and specific language impairment in children. *Applied Psycholinguistics, 10*, 179-202.

Leonard, L. B. (1998). *Children with specific language impairment*. Cambridge, MA: MIT Press.

Ragnarsdóttir, H., Simonsen H. G., & Plunkett, K. (1999). The acquisition of past tense morphology in Icelandic and Norwegian children: An experimental study. *Journal of Child Language, 26*, 577-618.

Reynell, J. (1983). *Reynell Developmental Language Scales* (Rev. Ed.). England: NFER-Nelson. Norwegian standardization by B. E. Hagtvedt & R. Lillestølen, 1985. Oslo: Universitetsforlaget.

Rom, A., & Leonard, L. B. (1990). Interpreting deficits in grammatical morphology in specifically language-impaired children: Preliminary evidence from Hebrew. *Clinical Linguistics & Phonetics, 4,* 93-105.

Simonsen, H. G., & Bjerkan, K. M. (1998). Testing past tense inflection in Norwegian: A diagnostic tool for identifying SLI children? *International Journal of Applied Linguistics, 8,* 251-270.

Wechsler, D. (1967). *Wechsler preschool and primary scales of intelligence.* New York: Psychological Corporation. Norwegian standardization by M. Langseth, (1976). Oslo: Universitetsforlaget.

Wechsler, D. (1974). *Wechsler Imtelligence Scale for Children – Revised.* New York: Psychological Corporation.

7

Morphosyntactic Problems in Children with Specific Language Impairment: Grammatical SLI or Overload in Working Memory?

Christelle Maillart and Marie-Anne Schelstraete

Not all children learn language effortlessly. Between 3% and 5% of children have a significant limitation in language ability without any apparent explanation (hearing impairment, low verbal intelligence test scores, psychological problems or neurological damage) which could explain these difficulties (Stark & Tallal, 1981). This limitation in language learning, called Specific Language Impairment (SLI), is characterized by a large heterogeneity in verbal symptoms. However, relatively homogeneous subgroups of SLI children can be identified (Rapin & Allen, 1987) and several studies have focused on specific SLI subsamples: Familial SLI (Gopnik, 1990), Semantic-pragmatic SLI (Adams & Bishop, 1989) or Grammatical SLI (Van der Lely, 1993, 1994, 1997). The latter category encompasses children with disproportionate impairment in grammatical comprehension and expression of language. Although very few children qualify for the deficiencies proposed by Van der Lely to be considered as G-SLI (Bishop, Bright, James, Bishop & Van der Lely, 2000), deficits in the use and the understanding of morphosyntactic information remain a hallmark of specific language impairment.

Most studies have been interested in the morphosyntactic deficits appearing in production. Compared to age-matched controls, children with SLI consistently demonstrated difficulties with a range of grammatical morphemes such as present third-person singular inflections, regular past inflections, articles and copula forms (e.g. Leonard, Bortolini, Casseli, McGregor & Sabbadini, 1992; Leonard, Eyer, Bedore & Grela, 1997; Oetting & Horohov, 1997; Rice, Wexler & Cleave, 1995). Nevertheless, a similar report could be made for grammatical understanding: children with SLI are usually impaired for comprehension of sentences (Bishop, 1979). Their difficulties are concentrated on understanding semantically reversible sentences in which word order is particularly important but also on interpreting complex sentences such as passive and embedded sentences and even simple active transitive sentences (Bishop, 1982; Van der Lely & Dewart, 1986; Van der Lely & Harris, 1990).

The cause of the grammatical deficit in SLI is at the origin of a considerable controversy in developmental psycholinguistics. For some authors (Bishop, 1997; Leonard, 1998; Tallal et al., 1996), an input-processing deficit could account for this impairment whereas for others (Gopnik, 1990; Rice & Wexler, 1996; Van der Lely, Rosen & Mc Clelland, 1998) a grammar specific deficit has to be postulated. Moreover, partisans of a grammatical specific impairment do not agree among themselves on the nature of this specific problem: deficit in the marking of agreement (Clahsen, 1989), failure to extract hierarchical structure (Cromer, 1978), use of Extended Optional Infinitive (Wexler, 1994) or Representational Deficit for Dependent Relationships (Van der Lely & Harris, 1990) are the main hypotheses proposed to explain the linguistic profile of SLI children. However, proponents of a grammatical origin agree that the deficit has to be relevant to an all-or-none condition in which a modular grammatical system failed to develop properly. Van der Lely and Stollwerck (1997) went further by claiming that the etiology of G-SLI is strongly genetic, possibly controlled by an autosomal dominant gene. On the other hand, partisans of an input-processing deficit proposed a non-modular explanation of the poor grammatical competence observed in SLI children. The performance of a child on a given grammatical task would not depend on the development of a specific grammatical module but rather on some general processing characteristics of the cognitive system. For instance, Leonard (1989) proposed the "Surface Hypothesis" which maintained that the perceptual and articulatory characteristics of grammatical morphemes would be responsible for the observed deficit. In English, many grammatical morphemes are brief, unstressed and tend to occur in non-salient positions. These features make such morphemes hard to detect. Thus, performances on grammatical tasks could be impaired, not because of a deficit of an innate language learning module but because of inadequate perception of language input. According to the surface hypothesis, cross-linguistic differences are expected, depending on the perceptual salience of grammatical morphemes. Another non-modular interpretation deals with the burden imposed on working memory by grammatical processing. Understanding sentences implies processing grammatical cues such as word order or inflection and maintaining this information in working memory as long as necessary. If children with SLI have processing capacity limitations, they could base their understanding of the sentence on less demanding information, such as lexical information, rather than on more demanding processing of grammatical cues. Therefore, grammatical performance would depend more on the load imposed in working memory than on actual grammatical abilities.

Several studies have tried to manipulate the load on working memory to account for some developmental language difficulties. For example, Valian, Hoeffner & Aubry (1996) used an elicited imitation task to determine whether young children's inconsistent production of sentence subject was due to limitations in knowledge of English or in the ability to access and use that knowledge. The length of sentence was varied to contrast the two hypotheses: Competence-deficit hypothesis and Performance-deficit hypothesis. The latter would suggest that young children omit more subjects in long sentences than short ones, and that older children (with higher MLU) would not show any length effect. This hypothesis was confirmed, thus showing that working memory load was a critical factor in grammatical development. As noted earlier, most of the performance limitation theories to date have focused on language production and it is usually assumed that comprehension should not be affected by processing problems because it is based on less costly processes. Nevertheless, Miyake, Carpenter and Just (1994) showed that by varying the load in working memory during a comprehension task, it was possible to decrease performances of normal adult subjects to a level observed in patients with asyntactic comprehension. The overload in working memory was obtained by increasing the rate of presentation of the sentence to process. Therefore, it can be concluded that variation in working memory load does result in poorer performance in language comprehension.

The experiment reported here aimed to contrast, in a multiple, single-case approach, the grammatical deficit hypothesis and the working memory overload hypothesis in children with specific grammatical comprehension impairment. Experimental sentences were built by varying the load in working memory while keeping constant the level of syntactic complexity and the vocabulary. The following opposite predictions could be made: if the trouble was specifically syntactic, participants would have the same performance whatever the load on working memory. Conversely, if the load was the critical factor, we would expect different profiles as a function of working memory load variations. Moreover, with regard to control children matched by comprehension level, the SLI children would show a significant degradation of performance.

METHOD

Participants

Five children with SLI were selected for participation. These children had been previously diagnosed by speech therapists as having severe and persistent difficulties with language development using standardized test of language abilities. Their receptive language test score fell at least −1.5 SD below what is expected for their chronological age. A summary of the background information on participants can be found in Table 1.

TABLE 1
Background information on SLI children.

	Sex	Age	Phonological Impairment	IQP	Syntactic Impairment (production)	Ecosse[d]
J.C.	F	6; 8	Yes, severe	80[ac]	Yes, severe	29 (-2.5 SD)
A.G.	M	9; 3	Yes, severe	68[ac]	Yes, severe	33 (-5.6 SD)
F.R.	F	7; 1	Resolved	95[b]	Resolved	21 (-1.5 SD)
M.H.	M	7; 5	Yes, severe	> 85[b]	Yes, severe	33 (-4 SD)
V.M.	M	8; 10	Resolved	> 85[b]	Never	19 (-2.7 SD)

a) *Leiter intelligence non verbal scale;* b) *WISC–III*; c) two participants had an I.Q. level below 85 at the time of the data collection. However, their background showed that their non-verbal intellectual abilities had actually decreased, an observation also recently made by Bishop et al. (2000); d) Ecosse (Lecocq, 1996), French version of the T.R.O.G. (Bishop, 1983). Scores are given in number of errors.

Because the children varied in age, schooling history, severity of speech disorder and non-verbal abilities, a multiple single case design was applied. Each SLI child was matched with two groups of four or five children developing language abilities normally: one group was matched by linguistic level (AL), measured with a comprehension test (Ecosse), and the other by chronological level (AC) (see Table 2). All the children were native French speakers and had normal hearing.

Materials and Procedure

Active sentences with similar length and the same syntactic structure were recorded. A computer, using the *Metacard* software, played the sound files just before displaying pictures on the screen. Sentences were built on the model: *Push on the button... when you see a....* For instance, the child might hear *Push on the button 'house', when you see a rabbit.* There were three different response buttons identified with images of a *house*, a *sun* or a *duck* in front of the computer. The participants were asked to push on the button specified by the sentence when seeing the picture. Reaction times were recorded. The complete design involves six different experimental series of sentences (henceforth Series 1, Series 2, etc.), varying in the nature and the number of pictures shown. In Series 1, only one picture was displayed to obtain a simple measure of reaction time. For Series 2–6, several pictures were presented sequentially every 3000 ms. These trials were planned and administered to the participants in order to compare different series (within subject design). Before administering the series, training items were used to familiarize the child with the procedure. The six different series were presented to all the children following the same order of presentation. The test, lasting two hours, was divided into two sessions. The main dependent variable in this experiment was the number of correct responses (correct button at the right time). The overload in working memory was induced by changing (1) the order, (2) the number and (3) the nature of elements to be maintained in memory.

TABLE 2

Age of subjects and mean age (range in brackets) of control groups and their test scores.

Subjects	Age (months)	Ecosse (number of errors)
J.C.	80	29
AC (n = 4)	80 (76–84)	8 (3–10)
AL (n = 5)	53 (52–55)	31 (28–37)
A.G.	111	33
AC (n = 4)	112 (107–116)	5 (4–7)
AL (n = 5)	54 (52–55)	34 (28–41)
F.R.	85	21
AC (n = 4)	84 (80–90)	8 (3–10)
AL (n = 5)	53 (50–57)	21 (18–22)
M.H.	89	33
AC (n = 4)	86 (82–89)	6 (2–9)
AL (n = 5)	54 (52–55)	34 (28–41)
V.M.	106	19
AC (n = 4)	109 (103–116)	5 (4–7)
AL (n = 4)	54 (50–57)	19 (16–21)

Note: all the children in the control groups performed within normal limits on Ecosse.

Information Order. A way to increase the burden on working memory is to change the locus of branching structure (left versus right) in complex sentences made up of a main clause and a subordinate one. A subordinate clause at the beginning of the sentence (left-branching) does not create the same load as having the same clause at the end of the sentence (right-branching). Kemper (1988) suggested that left-branching structures exact high processing demands and tax the limited working memory resources of elderly subjects. In several studies, differences between performance in repetition or comprehension of center-embedded (left-branching) and right-branching sentences were reported as an indication of a reduced processing capacity in elderly adults as compared to younger subjects (Baum, 1982, 1993, Kemper, 1987, 1988). In our experiment, in all series, half of the sentences were right-branching (*Push on the button... when you see ...*) and the other half were left-branching (*When you see ..., push on the button ...*). Left-branching structures were expected to impose a greater load on working memory than right-branching ones, whereas both were assumed to require the same syntactic processes.

Number of Relevant Elements. Increasing the number of elements to be maintained in working memory is a well-known way to charge the working memory. The different series varied according to the number of elements to be memorized (from one to three) were used. Each condition except the first one contained 32 sentences. In Series 1, the easiest, the picture to detect was always the same and only the button varied: *Push on the button ..., when you see a bee.* The child had just to figure out which button (out of the three possibilities) to press. This was the neutral condition used to measure reaction time. In Series 2, the pictures were changing: *Push on the button when you see a rabbit* (or *a pig, or a mouse*). The child did not know which picture was coming first so she/he had to remember both the picture and the button, thus inducing a greater load on memory. Finally, Series 6 added another complication: the child had to pay attention to the color of the animal displayed as well (*Push on the button when you see a white* (or *black*) *cat* (or *dog*)).

Nature of Information. Children with SLI have particular problems processing morphosyntatic information. So, memorizing grammatical information would be more costly than lexical information. To test this hypothesis, a Series 3 with grammatical information was constructed: the child had to maintain two elements in memory. This series was contrasted with Series 2 (see above) where the information to be maintained was lexical (*rabbit, pig* or *mouse*). In the grammatical condition, the child had to process the information carried by the articles. In this case, pictures always represented a boy (sometimes one boy, sometimes several boys) and the child had to remember the name of the button and the article. In French oral language, there is no auditory difference between the plural and the singular form of the noun itself (*le garcon* (the boy)– *les garcons* (the boys); the final 's' of the latter is not pronounced), so the only way to know if the referent is singular or plural is to process the article. According to the surface hypothesis (Leonard, 1989), it would be expected that perceptual and articulatory characteristics of grammatical morphemes could influence performance. Another similar series, Series 4, used feminine forms, in which the singular article is more perceptually distinct from the plural (*la fille* (the girl) – *les filles* (the girls)). Finally, Series 5 was constructed to measure the effect of additional morphosyntactic cues in the noun ending (*le cheval* (the horse)- *les chevaux* (the horses)).

RESULTS

The main results for both the SLI children and the control groups, for each series, are presented in Table 3. It is noticeable that the deterioration of performance across series observed for the SLI children does not appear in the age control groups. The latter remain stable at a high level. The AC children do not seem to be affected by the variation induced in material. Conversely, younger children belonging to the control groups matched by linguistic level were mostly influenced by the overload induced in working memory.

TABLE 3

Percentage of correct responses by series, with standard deviations in brackets.

	Series 1	Series 2	Series 3	Series 4	Series 5	Series 6
J.C.	100	70	51.7	20	34.2	22.5
AC	100	86.7 (2.7)	92.9 (4.7)	91.4 (1.6)	93.7 (2.6)	87.5 (15.3)
AL	100	78.6 (13.5)	63.3 (8.9)	77.9 (8.9)	74.3 (17.5)	59.2 (15.3)
A.G.	100	60	50	34.8	38.7	30
AC	100	89.2 (1.7)	90.6(5.7)	92 (4.3)	89.8 (4.7)	90.6 (8.3)
AL	100	73 (6.1)	59.8 (9.7)	69.4 (15)	70.4 (12)	55.5 (12.5)
F.R.	100	70	51.4	59.4	51.4	57.5
AC	100	87.5 (1.7)	93.7 (4.4)	90.6 (2.6)	94.5 (3.9)	86.2 (9.7)
AL	100	82 (13.1)	81.7 (13.1)	80.2 (12.2)	81.7 (6.1)	78.5 (8.2)
M.H.	100	56.7	40	—	53	40
AC	100	85.8 (3.2)	89.8 (8.6)	90.6 (5)	92.2 (6.0)	85.6 (8.3)
AL	100	73 (6.1)	59.8 (9.7)	69.4 (15)	70.4 (12)	55.5 (12.5)
V.M.	100	80	78.1	81.2	90.6	62.5
AC	100	89 (1.7)	89.1 (4.1)	91.2 (4.1)	89.1 (4)	88.1 (5.6)
AL	100	82 (3.2)	81.9 (15.1)	80.2 (12)	81.9 (7.1)	78.2 (9.5)

Due to space limitations, the results concerning reaction time and comparisons of different groups for each series cannot be developed here. We will focus here on a comparison between the series in order to explore the effect of load on working memory.

In Series 1, ceiling effects were obtained for all children, showing that the syntactic structure of the sentence was easily understood. For some SLI children (A.G., F.R. and M.H.) performances on Series 2 were different from those of their control groups. However, this difference was mostly due to slow reaction times (pictures were changed every 3000 ms and the SLI children pushed too late on the button) rather than to errors such as forgetting the image or the button, or answering to quickly. Conversely, these latter errors were observed in all the other series, which is typical of overload in working memory.

The data collected in the present study are not all independent, so classical statistical analyses could not be carried out. To compare the performance of each of the SLI children with their control groups, confidence intervals were used with a 95% confidence limit. As a consequence, the results obtained on different series using different conditions (according to position of the subordinate clause) could not be directly compared. One can either study the effects of a condition within a given series or compare between different series without taking into account the condition.

Order of Information: Position Effect

The *position effect* was obtained by subtracting the percentage of correct responses for left-branching sentences (condition A) from the same percentage obtained for right-branching (condition B). As mentioned previously, sentences with right-branching structures were expected to be better achieved than left-branching ones. As Table 4 shows, this tendency was confirmed for all the children. Among SLI children, only three (M.H., F.R. and V.M.) showed a pattern of performance significantly different from their AL group level. These children were more affected by the position effect than children matched by comprehension level.

TABLE 4
Difference (condition A – condition B) in percentage of correct responses (SD in brackets).

	Position effect		
	SLI	*AC*	*AL*
J.C.	-9.17	-8.33 (10.47)	-18.78 (10.34)
A.G.	-1.67	-3.95 (4.48)	-18.36 (10.79)
M.H.	-38.33	-14.37 (10.03)*	-18.36 (10.79)*
F.R.	-47.5	-13.33 (5.65)**	-19.5 (4.23)*
V.M.	-40.83	-1.04 (2.68)**	-20.62 (3.93)*

$**p < 0.001$; $*p < 0.05$.

Number of Elements : Number Effect

The *number effect* was calculated by comparing Series 1 (one element), 2 (two elements) and 6 (three elements). Actually, because ceiling levels were observed for Series 1, only Series 2 and 6 were contrasted. Recall that a degradation of performance from Series 2 to Series 6 would occur if the number of elements to remember induces an overload in working memory. No child in the AC group seemed to be sensitive to this effect, as showed by the weak difference between the series. This can be explained by the high level of performance for the two series (from 80 to 100%). Conversely, some younger children and all the SLI children showed considerable deterioration in performance when the number of elements to remember increased. Two SLI subjects (J.C. & A.G.) were statistically distinguishable from their AC and AL groups.

Nature of Elements: Grammatical Effect

When comparing the performances obtained using Series 2 (lexical elements) with those of Series 3 (grammatical elements), one can observe a *grammatical effect*. In accord with the particular morphosyntactic problems shown by SLI children, a deterioration of performance according to grammatical material was postulated. Except for V.M., SLI children performed at a worse level than their chronological control groups. However, as is evident in Table 6, all the SLI children showed a difference between the two series similar to that observed in their linguistic control groups. No subjects showed a significant grammatical effect.

TABLE 5
Difference (Series 2 – Series 6) in percentage of correct responses (SD in brackets).

		Number effect	
	SLI	AC	AL
J.C.	47.5	-0.8 (8.19)**	19.09 (7.97)**
A.G.	30	-1.4 (7.65)**	17.84 (7.27)*
M.H.	16.67	0.2 (5.19)**	17.84 (7.27)
F.R.	12.5	-2.5 (6.12)**	3.5 (9.67)
V.M.	17.5	-1.04 (5.15)**	4.38 (10.96)

**$p \leq 0.001$; *$p \leq 0.05$.

TABLE 6
Difference (Series 2 – Series 3) in percentage of correct responses (SD in brackets).

		Grammatical effect	
	SLI	AC	AL
J.C.	18.33	-6.3 (3.9)**	15 (14.13)
A.G.	10	-1.4 (5.32)*	13.48 (12.24)
M.H.	16.67	-4.01 (5.51)**	13.48 (12.24)
F.R.	18.54	-6.25 (3.91)**	0.29 (11.64)
V.M.	1.875	0.10 (3.95)	0.57 (13.42)

**$p \leq 0.001$; *$p \leq 0.05$.

Phonological Effect

Because of perceptual difficulties, more salient morphemes might be expected to be better processed by the SLI children than less salient ones. In this case, a *phonological effect* should be seen in comparing Series 3 and 4, distinguished by more salient contrasts between articles in Series 4. A significant effect was observed for two of the SLI children (J.C. and A.G.), but in reverse fashion. For these children, performances on Series 4 were at random level.

Morphosyntactic Cues Effect

As with more perceptually salient forms, additional morphosyntactic cues strengthen the contrast between singular and plural forms, which should involve a less substantial burden on working memory. If this assumption is correct, Series 5 would be better performed than Series 3. Three SLI children (M.H.,

V.M. and F.R.) and all the control groups behaved in this way. On the other hand, for J.C. and A.G. processing additional morphosyntactic cues seemed to induce overload instead of relieving the working memory.

TABLE 7

Difference (Series 3 – Series 4) in percentage of correct responses (SD in brackets).

		Phonological effect	
	SLI	*AC*	*AL*
J.C.	31.67	1.56 (5.98)**	-14.65 (3.63)**
A.G.	15.63	-1.4 (8.47)*	-9.55 (9.09)*
F.R.	-7.91	3.16 (6.25)*	1.46 (5.23)
V.M.	-3.12	-2.18 (8.04)	1.72 (6.00)

$**p \leq 0.001; *p \leq 0.05.$

TABLE 8

Difference (series 3 – series 5) in percentage of correct responses (SD in brackets).

		Morphosyntactic cues effect	
	SLI	*AC*	*AL*
J.C.	17.5	-0.78 (5.33)**	-10.94 (13.64)*
A.G.	21.25	0.78 (1.56)**	-10.52 (13.14)*
M.H.	-13.33	-2.34 (8.98)	-10.52 (13.14)
F.R.	18.54	-1.56 (5.98)**	-0.04 (8.77)*
V.M.	-12.5	0 (0)**	0.05 (10.12)

$**p \leq 0.001; *p \leq 0.05.$

DISCUSSION

Our results show that, for all SLI children, there was a significant degradation of their comprehension performance when the load on working memory was increased. In this experiment, the load was increased by adding elements to be maintained in memory from one series to another, by varying the position of the subordinate clause (left- versus right-branching) and finally the nature of the elements to be maintained in working memory. The SLI children did not all behave in the same way. Two of them (J.C. and A.C.) were shown to be particularly sensitive to the amount of information, whereas for the three others (F.R., M.H. and V.M.) the relevant variable was the order of the elements.

The fact that the burden on working memory appeared to interact with the performances is contrary to what would be predicted by the partisans of a grammatical specific deficit. According to their proposals, some grammatical information would be mastered, although other grammatical information would never be used nor understood properly by SLI children. In this experiment, for some participants, the performances degraded from a high to a random level when processing sentences with an identical syntactic structure, which would imply that the comprehension of such sentences is not an all-or-none phenomenon. Our results are heading in the same direction as those of the partisans of a non-modular explanation of the poor grammatical performance observed in SLI children. Indeed, the SLI children seem more disturbed by additional cognitive demand than children matched by comprehension level.

Moreover, several profiles appeared among the SLI children in our sample despite the fact that all were selected for similar grammatical comprehension impairments. First of all, a simple augmentation of the number of relevant elements to remember puts some children into difficulties. It is worth noting that two of these children (J.C. and A.C.) also had phonological problems which could explain poor memory span. However, another child with phonological difficulties (M.H.) did not have such sensitivity to additional elements. Secondly, a change in the order of information handicapped several SLI children (F.R., M.H. and V.M.). A possible explanation for these difficulties could be the presence of a sequential deficit, which would account for the better performances observed for the last information heard. This explanation was relevant for two children (F.R. and V.M.) but not for M.H., a child with severe linguistic problems. Finally, and contrary to our expectations, the processing of articles did not tax SLI children more than normally developing children. Nevertheless, processing of grammatical elements seemed to remain costly as demonstrated by the reverse effect observed for morphosyntactic cues.

REFERENCES

Adams, C., & Bishop, D. V. M. (1989). Conversational characteristics of children with semantic-pragmatic disorder: I. Exchange structure, turn taking, repairs and cohesion. *British Journal of Disorders of Communication, 24,* 211-239.

Baum, S. (1982). Loneliness in elderly persons: A preliminary study. *Psychological Reports, 50* (3, pt. 2), 1317-1318.

Baum, S. H. (1993). Processing of center-embedded and right branching relative clause sentences by normal elderly individuals. *Applied Psycholinguistics 14,* 75-88.

Bishop, D. V. M. (1979). Comprehension in developmental language disorders. *Developmental Medicine and Child Neurology, 21,* 225-238.

Bishop, D. V. M. (1982). Comprehension of spoken, written, and signed sentences in childhood language disorders. *Journal of Child Psychology and Psychiatry, 23,* 1-20.

Bishop, D. V. M. (1983). *T.R.O.G. Test for reception of grammar.* Medical Research Council, University of Manchester: Chapel Press.

Bishop, D. V. M. (1997). *Uncommon understanding. Development and disorders of language comprehension in children.* Hove: Psychology Press.

Bishop, D. V. M., Bright, P., James, C., Bishop, S. J. & Van der Lely, H. K. J. (2000). Grammatical SLI: A distinct subtype of developmental language impairment? *Applied Psycholinguistics, 21,* 159-181.

Clahsen, H. (1989). The grammatical characterization of developmental dysphasia. *Linguistics, 27,* 897-920.

Cromer, R. F. (1978). The basis of childhood dysphasia: A linguistic approach. In M. A. Wake (Ed.), *Developmental dysphasia* (pp. 85-134). London: Academic.

Gopnik, M. (1990). Feature blindness: A case study. *Language Acquisition, 1,* 139-164.

Kemper, S. (1987). Life-span changes in syntactic complexity. *Journal of Gerontology, 42,* 323-328.

Kemper, S. (1988). Geriatric psycholinguistics: Syntactic limitations of oral and written language. In L. Light & D. Burke (Eds.) *Language, memory, and aging* (pp. 58-76). New York: Cambridge University Press.

Lecocq, P. (1996). *L'ECOSSE. Une épreuve de compréhension syntaxico-sémantique.* Lilles: Presses Universitaires du Septentrion.

Leonard, L. B. (1989). Language learnability and specific language impairment in children. *Applied Psycholinguistics, 10,* 179-202.

Leonard, L. B. (1998). *Children with specific language impairment.* London: MIT Press.

Leonard, L. B., Bortolini, U., Casseli, M. C., McGregor, K. K., & Sabbadini, L. (1992). Morphological deficits in children with specific language impairment: The status of features in the underlying grammar. *Language Acquisition, 2,* 151-179.

Leonard, L. B, Eyer, J. A., Bedore, L. M., & Grela, B. G. (1997). Three accounts of the grammatical morpheme difficulties of English-speaking children with specific language impairment. *Journal of Speech and Hearing Research 40,* 741-753.

Miyake, A., Carpenter, P. A., & Just, M. A. (1994). A capacity approach to syntactic comprehension disorders: Making normal adults perform like aphasic patients. *Cognitive Neuropsychology, 11,* 671-717.

Oetting, J. B., & Horohov, J. E. (1997). Past tense marking by children with and without specific language impairment. *Journal of Speech and Hearing Research, 40,* 62-74.

Rapin, I., & Allen, D. (1987). Developmental dysphasia and autism in pre-school children: characteristics and subtypes. *Proceedings of the first international symposium on specific speech and language disorders in children* (pp. 20-35). London: Association for Speech Impaired Children.

Rice M. L., & Wexler, K. (1996). A phenotype of specific language impairment: Extended optional infinitives. In M. L. Rice (Ed.), *Toward a genetics of language* (pp. 215-237). Mahwah, NJ: Lawrence Erlbaum Associates.

Rice, M. L., Wexler, K., & Cleave, P. L. (1995). Specific language impairment as a period of extended optional infinitive. *Journal of Speech and Hearing Research, 38*, 850-863.

Stark, R. E., & Tallal, P. (1981). Selection of children with specific language deficits. *Journal of Speech and Hearing Disorders, 46*, 114-122.

Tallal, P., Miller, S. L., Bedi, G., Byma, G., Wang, X., Najarajan, S. S., Schreiner, C., Jenkins, W. M., & Merzenich, M. M. (1996). Language comprehension in language-learning impaired children improved with acoustically modified speech. *Science, 271*, 81-84.

Valian, V., Hoeffner, J., & Aubry, S. (1996). Young children's imitation of sentence subjects: Evidence of processing limitations. *Developmental Psychology, 32*, 153-164.

Van der Lely, H. K. J. (1993). Specific language impairment in children: Research findings and their therapeutic implications. *European Journal of Disorders of Communication, 28*, 247-261.

Van der Lely, H. K. J. (1994). Canonical linking rules: Forward versus reverse linking in normally developing and specifically language-impaired children. *Cognition, 51*, 29-72.

Van der Lely, H. K. J. (1997). Language and cognitive development in a grammatical SLI boy: Modularity and innateness. *Journal of Neurolinguistics, 10,* 75-107.

Van der Lely, H. K. J., & Dewart, H. (1986). Sentence comprehension strategies in specifically language impaired children. *British Journal of Disorders of Communication, 21*, 291-306.

Van der Lely, H. K. J., & Harris, M. (1990). Comprehension of reversible sentences in specifically language impaired children. *Journal of Speech and Hearing Research, 55*, 101-117.

Van der Lely, H. K. J., Rosen, S., & McClelland, A. (1998). Evidence for a grammar-specific deficit in children. *Current Biology, 8*, 1253-1258.

Van der Lely, H. K. J., & Stollwerck, L. (1997). Binding theory and grammatical specific language impairment in children. *Cognition, 62*, 245-290.

Wexler, K. (1994). Optional infinitives. In D. Lightfoot & N. Hornstein (Eds.), *Verb movement* (pp. 305-350). New York: Cambridge University Press.

8

How do Preschool Language Problems Affect Language Abilities in Adolescence?

Kerstin Nauclér and Eva Magnusson

A question of vital importance in clinical work with language-impaired children is prognosis: Do language problems noticed in the speech of preschool children disappear during the school years or do they persist into adolescence? If they persist, in what way do they affect the adolescents?

Until recently, studies of the long term consequences of language impairments have been relatively few. Many of the earlier studies were retrospective, using data from clinical records and routinely made assessments. The results are often difficult to interpret as the studies vary both in terminology and methodology, some including only a few cases (Scarborough & Dobrich, 1990) and others having very large samples (e.g. Schery, 1985). In some studies, subjects were followed up after one or two years at school; in others not until adulthood. Despite the differences among the studies, they agree on one thing: language-impaired children's prognosis is poor. According to a review of a number of follow up studies (Scarborough & Dobrich, 1990), up to 75% of those who had language impairments in childhood still had speech and language problems as teenagers or adults and up to 95% had reading problems. In their follow-up of young adults, Hauschild and Elbro (1992) found that only 38% had attended regular schools and about half of them were either unemployed, had sheltered work or a pension.

There are exceptions to this picture. Studies of children whose problems are predominantly phonological in nature often show that these children outgrow their language problems (Silva, 1980; Bishop & Edmundson, 1987; Hall & Tomblin, 1978). However, the fact that they have solved their speech production problems does not guarantee that they acquire literacy effortlessly. Many studies report that earlier speech problems turn into problems with written language when preschool children become school children (e.g. Scarborough & Dobrich, 1990; Menuyk et al., 1991; Lewis & Freebairn, 1992). In an ongoing discussion researchers try to tie certain types of language problems or combinations of problems to reading difficulties (Haynes & Naidoo, 1991). According to Shriberg and Kwiatkowski (1988) phonological problems do not cause reading problems, while Bishop and her colleagues (e.g. Bird, Bishop & Freeman, 1995) claim that phonological problems with or without other language problems lead to reading difficulties. Catts (1993) in his longitudinal study of language-impaired children argues that phonology is related to word decoding and that other language abilities are connected to reading comprehension. In a recent follow-up, Stothard, Snowling, Bishop, Chipchase & Kaplan (1998) found that the recovery of the preschool children reported in a study by Bishop and Edmundson (1987) was illusory. At the age of 15 they performed significantly less well on tests of literacy skills than did a control group.

During the 1980s, we followed the language development of 115 language-impaired and linguistically normal children from preschool to the end of grade 4 (Magnusson & Nauclér, 1990a, 1990b, 1991). We compared their preschool data with their reading and writing development during the first four school years.

The language-impaired subjects' problems varied from the beginning of the study. They were not diagnosed as specific language-impaired (SLI), according to the definition by Leonard (1998), but had language problems or combinations of language problems affecting any linguistic level, including phonology. They were of normal intelligence, had no other known impairments, and spoke Swedish as their first language.

The language-impaired group consisted of both mildly and severely language-impaired children. The latter were matched on an individual basis for sex, age and non-verbal cognitive level with children with no known language problems. From the start, these two groups differed significantly on all language tests. Both comprehension and production were tested in a number of tasks including tests of syntax, morphology, phonology, and vocabulary (Magnusson & Nauclér, 1987). There was also a significant difference on all tests tapping linguistic awareness, especially phonological awareness, and on tests of short-term memory.

At the end of Grade 1, the group of language-impaired children scored much lower on reading and spelling tasks than the matched normal group and were inferior to the matched normal group on both linguistic awareness and short-term memory tasks. However, in both groups there were subjects who did not conform to the group pattern; in the impaired group, we found subjects who performed comparatively well and in the normal group there were subjects who performed worse than their matched subjects. The performance of the mildly impaired group was in between the severely impaired and the normal group.

In Grades 3 and 4, the gap between the two groups regarding both spelling and decoding had almost disappeared. Both groups contained equally poor spellers and equally good decoders. However, when reading comprehension was assessed, the gap between the groups remained.

Some of the linguistic and metalinguistic skills the children demonstrated in preschool were found to be more important than others for their reading and writing development through to grade 4, and more predictive of the outcome than either reading method or amount of time spent in special education (Magnusson & Nauclér, 1991).

Recently we performed a follow-up study with the same subjects, now at the age of 18 and about to leave school. With these data it will be possible to look for answers to the following questions:

1. Does a preschool child's language impairment persist into adolescence?
2. In what ways do early language problems affect adolescents who are about to finish school?
3. How does 12 years of schooling improve the language-impaired children's command of spoken and written language?

In this chapter we compare the spoken and written language abilities of adolescents with and without childhood language impairments. The focus is on nine matched pairs from the longitudinal study.

METHOD

Subjects

The longitudinal study began with 115 six-year-olds, 76 of which were language-impaired children with no other known handicap, divided into two groups:

1. 39 subjects with severe impairments who had treatment during their preschool years. They were individually matched for age, sex and non-verbal cognitive level (Raven's colored matrices; Raven, 1956) with 39 children with no known language problems constituting a control group.
2. 37 subjects with mild impairments who were checked by a speech pathologist once or twice a year, but who were not enrolled in any language intervention program before starting school.

TABLE 1
Number of subjects who participated at each grade (Q = questionnaire, T = tests) .

	Severely impaired		Normal group		Mildly impaired		
	Boys	Girls	Boys	Girls	Boys	Girls	Total
Preschool	27	12	27	12	22	15	115
Grade 1	27	12	27	12	22	15	115
Grade 3	22	9	24	10	21	12	98
Grade 4	22	9	24	10	21	12	98
Grade 12 (Q)	21	9	21	10	20	12	93
Grade 12 (T)	10	7	10	8	9	10	54

The subjects were tested one year preschool (aged 6 years) and again at the end of Grades 1 (7 years), 3 (9 years) and 4 (10 years). For the study reported here, 106 of the original subjects were identified. They were invited to take part in a fifth testing in grade 12 (18 years) and to fill out a questionnaire. This was done by 93 of the original subjects; 54 of these also took the full test battery. The number of subjects at the different test occasions is shown in Table 1.

Tests and Materials

The test battery comprised tests used in clinical practice and in assessment of reading. In addition, we used some tasks and procedures developed by us, when no standard tests were available that met the requirements of the present study. An overview of the different tests in the fifth testing with the 18-year-old subjects is presented in Fig. 1 and a description of each follows.

	6 yr.	7 yr.	9 yr.	10 yr.	18 yr.
ORAL LANGUAGE					
comprehension	x	x	x	x	x
production	x	x	x	x	x
WRITTEN LANGUAGE					
reading		x	x	x	x
spelling		x	x	x	x
writing			x	x	x
PHONOLOGICAL					
AWARENESS	x	x	x	x	x
SHORT-TERM MEMORY	x	x			x
QUESTIONNAIRE					x

FIG.1 Overview of tests administered at different ages.

Tests of Oral Language. To measure receptive vocabulary, a non-standardized Swedish translation of the Peabody Picture Vocabulary Test (PPVT; Dunn & Dunn, 1981), is used. To assess the comprehension of sentences two tests are administered: an oral version of the Token Test (de Renzi & Vignolo, 1962) and an oral version of a syntactic comprehension task (Magnusson & Nauclér, unpublished manuscript).

For the assessment of spoken language production, the subjects are engaged in conversation and are encouraged to talk as much as possible about their hobbies and other topics of interest.

Word retrieval is measured with phonological as well as semantic triggering. In the phonological task, the subjects are encouraged to say as many words as they can think of, in one minute, that start with /s/; and in the semantic task, to name as many kinds of food as possible in one minute.

Phonology is examined by two repetition tasks: repetition of long and phonologically complicated words (Magnusson & Nauclér, unpublished manuscript) and repetition of tongue twisters (Magnusson & Nauclér, unpublished manuscript).

Tests of Written Language. Decoding is assessed in four different ways: by a word chain test (Jacobson, 1993) and by a non-word loud reading task (Magnusson & Nauclér, unpublished manuscript), single word reading (Johansson, 1992) and text reading (Björkqvist & Järpsten, 1974).

Reading comprehension is examined by four different tasks: a test of single-word reading (Johansson, 1992), a written version of the Token Test (de Renzi & Vignolo, 1962), a written version of the syntactic comprehension task mentioned earlier (Magnusson & Nauclér, unpublished), and a test of text comprehension (Johansson, 1992).

Spelling is assessed by a test of single-word spelling (Magnusson & Nauclér, unpublished) and to assess written language production, subjects are asked to write about their plans for the future.

Phonological Awareness. This is assessed in two ways: by administering a phoneme metathesis task, in which the subjects identify and produce spoonerisms (Magnusson & Nauclér, 1993) and by asking them to talk backwards (Magnusson & Nauclér, unpublished manuscript).

Short-term Memory. Verbal short-term memory is measured by repeating orally presented digits and words; non-verbal short-term memory is assessed by means of a visuo–spatial task, using Corsi blocks (Corsi, 1972).

Questionnaire. Information about subjects' reading and writing habits and their evaluation of their reading and writing skills is collected through a questionnaire.

Procedure

The questionnaire was completed by the subjects at home and returned to us. Those who consented to taking part in the testing were seen on two occasions. The first occasion was an individual session that lasted for about two hours. All tasks requiring tape recording were done during this session. The second occasion included all paper and pencil tasks, given either individually or in small groups. This session also lasted approximately two hours.

RESULTS

Groups

The outcome of the Grade 12 study clearly showed that preschool children with severe language impairments do not outgrow their problems at school. Mildly impaired subjects, however, stand a much better chance. They often scored at the same or similar level as normal controls.

From the reading and writing habits reported by 93 subjects in the questionnaire it was obvious that the severely impaired group consisted of less frequent readers and writers than the mildly impaired group and the control group. The severely impaired group, who judged their own written and spoken language skills the lowest, generally scored lower on all the tasks than both the mildly impaired group and the normal controls. The results are shown in Tables 2, 3 and 4.

Oral Language. The results from tests of oral comprehension and production are shown in Table 2. Significant differences between the severely impaired group and the normal controls were found (unpaired t tests) for the three comprehension tasks, PPVT ($t(33) = -2.67$, $p < 0.02$), Token test ($t(33) = -2.92$, $p < 0.01$), and syntactic comprehension ($t(33) = -5.23$, $p < 0.0001$). For the production tasks the picture varied. There was a significant difference for word retrieval with a semantic trigger ($t(33) = -2.46$, $p < 0.02$), but not with a phonological trigger ($t(33) = -1.09$, $p = 0.2833$). Furthermore the severely language-impaired subjects were significantly slower and less accurate than the normal controls in repeating long and complicated words ($t(32) = 2.56$, $p < 0.02$ and $t(33) = -3.56$, $p < 0.001$, respectively) and slower in repeating tongue twisters ($t(32) = 2.04$, $p < 0.05$) but not significantly less accurate ($t(33) = -1.70$, $p = 0.0978$).

TABLE 2
Group results on oral language tests in grade 12.

Test task	Severely impaired		Normal		Mildly impaired	
	Mean	SD	Mean	SD	Mean	SD
Comprehension						
PPVT	141	21	156	10	148	19
Token	20	2.5	22	1.4	22	1.6
Syntactic compr.	19	3.3	24	3.2	23	3.2
Production						
Word retrieval						
semantic	16	6.3	21	6.0	18	5.5
phonological	15	6.2	17	4.6	16	4.8
Word repetition						
rate	28	7.9	22	5.5	18	5.5
no. correct	10	1.5	11	0.8	11	1.5
Phrase repetition						
rate	342	239	223	63	305	150
no. correct	3.3	1.5	4	0.8	3.6	1.5

Written Language. The results shown in Table 3 are divided into decoding, comprehension and spelling. In some of the decoding tasks the severely impaired group is faster and in some others slower, but the difference in speed is not significant, nor is the difference in accuracy (unpaired *t* tests). All four reading comprehension tasks showed significant differences between the severely impaired group and the normal controls: single words ($t(30) = -2.68$, $p < 0.02$), Token test ($t(33) = -2.78$, $p < 0.01$), syntactic comprehension ($t(30) = -2.76$, $p < 0.01$) and text ($t(30) = -2.80$, $p < 0.01$). In the spelling task the severely impaired group spelt fewer words correctly, but the difference was not significant ($t(29) = -1.62$, $p = 0.1163$).

Phonological Awareness. The results on the phoneme metathesis tasks (spoonerisms) in Table 4 show the same pattern: the severely disordered group scored lower than the other two groups, but the difference was not significant. The results from speaking backwards show no difference at all when number of correctly reversed words is considered, but interestingly enough, the severely disordered group was faster than the other two groups.

TABLE 3
Group results on written language tests in grade 12.

Test task	Severely impaired Mean	SD	Normal Mean	SD	Mildly impaired Mean	SD
Decoding						
Word chains	62	14.3	71	11.2	71	13.1
Non-words						
rate	26	6.2	28	8	28	6.6
no. correct	21	2.6	22	2	21	1.9
Single words						
rate	64	12.1	63	13.5	66	15.8
no. correct	47	2.8	48	2.3	48	2.2
Text	161	16	149	19	160	34
Comprehension						
Single words	25	8	31	5.5	30	7
Token	21	2.4	23	1.4	22	1.6
Syntactic compr.	22	3.1	25	2.7	24	2.8
Text	19	6.6	24	4.3	24	5.9
Spelling	20	5	23	4	22	4

TABLE 4
Group results on test of phonological awareness and short-term memory in grade 12.

Test task	Severely impaired Mean	SD	Normal Mean	SD	Mildly impaired Mean	SD
Phonological awareness						
Phoneme metathesis						
identification	9.2	3.2	10.7	2.3	10	2.8
production	7.4	5	8.9	3.3	8.5	3.8
Speaking backwards						
rate	160	35	173	50	170	44
no. correct	13	1.2	13	1.7	13	1.5
Short-term memory						
Verbal						
digits	38	10.7	40	14.8	37	11
words	23	7.8	30	13.2	26	10.6
Non-verbal	14	5.4	16	6.4	16	10.9

Short-Term Memory. The scores in the short-term memory tasks are also lower in the severely impaired group than in the other two groups. However, only the difference between the severely disordered group and the normal group regarding words was close to significant ($t(33) = -1.85$, $p = 0.0728$).

In summary, after 12 years of schooling, subjects with severe language impairments scored significantly lower than the matched normal subjects on both spoken and written language comprehension tasks. On other tasks, for example word and non-word decoding, oral production, and verbal and non-verbal short-term memory tasks, however, their scores are nearly at the same level as the normal controls.

Matched Pairs

The subjects in the normal and the language-impaired groups whose results we have reported ear;ier constitute less than 50% of the original 115 subjects. The reduced number of subjects makes the results less reliable. However, the subjects participating in the testing are fairly evenly distributed among the three groups, as shown in Table 1, although the ratio of boys to girls has changed dramatically. Furthermore, only nine of the original 39 matched pairs remained. In order to keep factors like sex, age and IQ under better control we restricted the analysis to those matched pairs that had taken part in all the testings. Another reason for looking more closely into individual pairs is the large variation in the group of severely impaired subjects.

A non-parametric analysis (Wilcoxon's Signed Rank Test) was used and showed no significant difference in the matched pairs regarding written language (see Table 5) when decoding of non-words and single words (rate and accuracy) was calculated. This is in accordance with the group results. The only significant difference was found for text decoding rate ($z = -2.43$, $p < 0.02$). It should be noted, however, that this was not a pure decoding task, but included forced choices of triplets of words, all contextually appropriate. The difference in spelling (accuracy) in the matched pairs was also non-significant. None of the tasks tapping phonological awareness (i.e. recognition and production of phoneme metatheses and speaking backwards; see Table 6), showed significant differences, nor did the non-verbal and the two verbal short-term memory tasks (see Table 6). This is also in accordance with the results obtained when the two groups of severely impaired and normal subjects were compared.

The results from all tasks assessing comprehension showed significant differences within the matched pairs. The difference in listening comprehension (see Table 7) measured as vocabulary (PPVT) was significant ($z = -2.52$, $p < 0.02$), as was the difference in comprehension of instructions (Token; $z = -1.96$, $p < 0.05$) and comprehension of syntactic structures ($z = -2.67$, $p < 0.01$). All tasks tapping reading comprehension (see Table 5) showed significant differences, that is comprehension of single words ($z = -2.67$, $p < 0.01$), of instructions (Token; $z = -2.52$, $p < 0.02$), of syntactic structures ($z = -2.52$, $p < 0.02$), and of texts ($z = -2.43$, $p < 0.02$). Consequently, we find the same differences in the matched pairs as we did between the severely language-impaired group and the normal group.

TABLE 5
Results on written language tests for the nine matched pairs in grade 12.

Test task	Severely impaired		Normal	
	Mean	SD	Mean	SD
Decoding				
Word chains	57	11.6	67	14
Nonwords				
rate	29	6.4	28	8.9
no. correct	21	2.7	22	2.3
Single words				
rate	68	12.2	66	15.3
no. correct	48	3.0	48	2.7
Text	167	12	148	21
Comprehension				
Single words	24	5.5	32	5.2
Token	20	2.1	23	1.0
Syntactic compr.	22	2.8	25	2.6
Text	18	5.8	25	3.3
Spelling	21	4.3	22	4.0

In a few cases of oral production (see Table 7) the difference within the matched pairs and the difference between the groups did not coincide, e.g. in the tests of word retrieval and phonology. When word retrieval was assessed by means of a phonological trigger, the difference was not significant either between the groups or in the matched pairs. However, when using a semantic trigger, the difference between the groups was significant ($t(33) = -2.46$, $p < 0.02$), but not in the matched pairs ($z = -1.66$, $p = 0.0972$). The difference in repetition rate for long and complicated words and tongue twisters was significant between the groups ($t(32) = 2.56$, $p < 0.02$ and $t(32) = 2.04$, p < 0.05 respectively), but not in the pairs ($z = -1.69$, $p = 0.0910$ and $z = 1.68$, $p = 0.0929$ respectively). Furthermore, the difference between the groups regarding correctly repeated words was significant ($t(33) = -3.56$, $p < 0.001$) but not significant in the matched pairs ($z = -1.46$, $p = 0.1441$).

Generally, the performance of language-impaired subjects varies more than that of the control group. Therefore we have analyzed the profiles of the pairs on

TABLE 6
Results on test of phonological awareness and short-term memory for the nine matched pairs in grade 12.

Test task	Severely impaired		Normal	
	Mean	SD	Mean	SD
Phonological awareness				
Phoneme metatheses				
identification	10.2	2.3	10.7	2.6
production	8.7	3.5	8.7	3.0
Talking backwards				
rate	161	28	184	59.6
no. correct	13	1.1	14	1.7
Short-term memory				
Verbal				
digits	38	10.9	42	20.1
words	23	6.6	28	12.9
Non-verbal	14	3.6	14	6.8

TABLE 7
Results on oral language tests for the nine matched pairs in grade 12.

Test task	Severely impaired		Normal	
	Mean	SD	Mean	SD
Comprehension				
PPVT	143	19	158	6
Token	20	2.3	22	1.5
Syntactic compr.	19	2.4	24	2.6
Production				
Word retrieval				
semantic	16	7.0	23	6.6
phonological	13	5.0	17	5.2
Word repetition				
rate	27	4.6	21	5.6
no. correct	10	1.1	11	0.8
Phrase repetition				
rate	370	184	222	79
no. correct	3.6	1.2	4	0.9

each separate task. As would be expected, the normal subject in a pair usually scores higher than the matched language-impaired subject. This can be seen from the profiles of listening comprehension (e.g. PPVT and syntax) in Fig. 2.

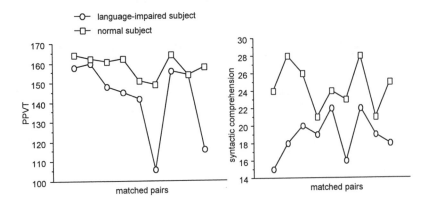

FIG. 2 Listening comprehension scores for nine matched pairs in grade 12. (The leftmost pair is pair no. 1 and the rightmost pair is pair no. 9).

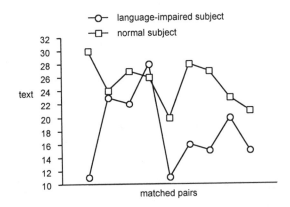

FIG. 3 Reading comprehension scores for nine matched pairs in grade 12. (The leftmost pair is pair no. 1 and the rightmost pair is pair no. 9).

Occasionally the language-impaired subject in a pair scores better on single tasks. However, in such cases the difference between the matched subjects is very small (as in pair no. 4 in the text comprehension task shown in Fig. 3) and/or the performance of the normal subject in the pair is very low, as in the decoding of single words (pairs nos. 3 through 6) and the STM task for digits (pair nos. 2, 4, 5, 9) in Fig. 4. Pair no. 4, with its reversed pattern in reading comprehension, was unique among the nine matched pairs. In none of the other pairs did the language-impaired subjects score high, or higher than the matched controls.

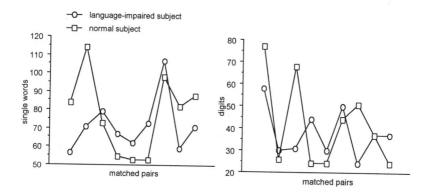

FIG. 4 Single word decoding scores (left figure) and short-term memory scores (right figure) for nine matched pairs in grade 12. (In each case, the leftmost pair is pair no. 1 and the rightmost pair is pair no. 9).

In summary, the gap that we found between the subjects in the matched pairs in preschool remains in Grade 12. Twelve years of schooling altered the prominence of the impairment from oral language production to language comprehension, both spoken and written.

CONCLUSIONS

The results obtained from testing the written and spoken language ability of adolescents, diagnosed as language-impaired in childhood, and normal controls, enable us to respond to the questions raised in the beginning of this paper: *Does preschool children's language impairment persist into adolescence and, if it does, in what way?* The results show that the language impairment of the severely impaired subjects persists but the mildly impaired subjects perform at the same or similar level as the normal controls. The earlier problems of the severely impaired group were not found in spoken language any longer, nor in the decoding of written language or spelling. Their problems remain in the domain of language comprehension, both spoken and written.

How do twelve years of schooling improve the language-impaired subjects' command of spoken and written language? The subjects who were mildly impaired in preschool have reached the same level of spoken and written language in Grade 12 as the normal controls. The severely impaired subjects are good decoders and do not spell much worse than the normal controls. However, when it comes to language comprehension, school has not had the same impact. In listening comprehension tasks and in reading comprehension, the severely impaired subjects score significantly lower than the normal controls. The fact that none of the severely impaired subjects was taking theoretical classes during the last three school years might be explained by their persisting comprehension problems.

ACKNOWLEDGMENTS

The research reported in this chapter was supported by grants from HSFR, the Swedish Council for Research in the Humanities and Social Sciences.

REFERENCES

Bird, J., Bishop, D. V. M., & Freeman, N. (1995). Phonological awareness and literacy development in children with expressive phonological impairments. *Journal of Speech and Hearing Research, 38*, 446-462.

Bishop, D. V. M., & Edmundson, A. (1987). Language-impaired 4-year-olds: Distinguishing transient from persistent impairment. *Journal of Speech and Hearing Disorders, 52*, 156-173.

Björkquist, L-M., & Järpsten, B. (1974). *Diagnostiska läs-och skrivprov.* Stockholm: Psykologiförlaget.

Catts, H. W. (1993). The relationship between speech-language and reading disabilities. *Journal of Speech and Hearing Research, 36*, 948-958.

Corsi, P. M. (1972). *Human Memory and the Medial Temporal Region of the Brain.* Unpublished doctoral dissertation, McGill University.

Dunn, L. M., & Dunn, L. M. (1981). *Peabody Picture Vocabulary Test* (Revised). Circle Pines: American Guidance Service.

Hall, P. K., & Tomblin, J. B. (1978). A follow-up study of children with articulation and language disorders. *Journal of Speech and Hearing Disorders, 43*, 227-241.

Hauschild, K-M., & Elbro, C. (1992). *Hvad blev der af dem?* Monografi nr 15, Audiologopædisk forening.

Haynes, C. P. A., & Naidoo, S. (1991). Children with specific speech and language impairment. *Clinics in Developmental Medicine, 119*. London: MacKeith Press.

Jacobson, C. (1993). *Ordkedjor. En snabb och enkel metod för ordavkodning.* Psykologiförlaget, Stockholm.

Johansson, M-G. (1992). *LS. Klassdiagnoser i läsning och skrivning för högstadiet och gymnasiet.* Stockholm: Psykologiförlaget.

Leonard, L. (1998). *Children with Specific Language Impairment.* Cambridge, MA: MIT Press.

Lewis, B. A. & Freebairn, L. (1992). Residual effects of preschool phonology disorders in grade school, adolescence and adulthood. *Journal of Speech and Hearing Research, 35,* 819-831.

Magnusson, E., & Nauclér, K. (1987). Language disordered and normally speaking children's development of spoken and written language: Preliminary results from a longitudinal study. *RUUL, Reports from Uppsala University, Department of Linguistics, 16,* 35-63.

Magnusson, E. & Nauclér, K. (1990a). Four years later - Status report from a longitudinal study of language disordered children's reading and spelling. *Proceedings from XXIst IALP Congress, Prague, 6-10 August 1989.*

Magnusson, E. & Nauclér, K. (1990b). Reading and spelling in language-disordered children – Linguistic and metalinguistic prerequisites: Report on a longitudinal study. *Clinical Linguistics and Phonetics, 4,* 49-61.

Magnusson, E. & Nauclér, K. (1991). On the development of reading in good and poor readers. *International Journal of Applied Linguistics, 1,* 174-185.

Magnusson, E. & Nauclér, K. (1993). *Bedömning av språklig medvetenhet hos förskolebarn och skolbarn.* Löddeköpinge: Pedagogisk Design.

Magnusson, E., & Nauclér, K. (Unpublished manuscript). Tests of oral and written language. Lund University, Department of Linguistics.

Menyuk, P., Chesnik, M., Liebergott, J. W., Korngold, B., D'Agostino, R. & Belanger, A. (1991). Predicting reading problems in at-risk children. *Journal of Speech and Hearing Research, 34,* 893-903.

Raven, J. C. (1956). *Coloured progressive matrices – revised order.* London, W.C.1: H. K. Lewis & Co. Ltd.

de Renzi, E. & Vignolo, L. A. (1962). The Token test: A sensitive test to detect receptive disturbances in aphasics. *Brain, 85,* 665-678.

Scarborough, H. & Dobrich, W. (1990). Development of children with early delay. *Journal of Speech and Hearing Research, 33,* 70-83.

Schery, T. (1985). Correlates of language development in language-disordered children. *Journal of Speech and Hearing Research, 50,* 73-83.

Shriberg, L. D. & Kwiatkowski, J. (1988). A follow-up study of children with phonologic disorders of unknown origin. *Journal of Speech and Hearing Disorders, 54,* 144-155.

Silva, P. A. (1980). The prevalence, stability and significance of language delay in preschool children. *Developmental Medicine and Child Neurology, 22,* 768-777.

Stothard, S. E., Snowling, M. J., Bishop, D. V. M., Chipchase, B. B. & Kaplan, C. A. (1998). Language-impaired preschoolers: A follow-up into adolescence. *Journal of Speech, Language, and Hearing Research, 41,* 407-418.

9

Comprehension of Resultative Verbs in Normally Developing and Language Impaired German Children

Petra Schulz, Zvi Penner and Karin Wymann

Between the ages of two and six, a normally developing (ND) child learns approximately 10 new words every day. The question of how children succeed in this task has long puzzled language acquisition researchers. Acquiring the labels for objects is already complex (Landau, 1994; Markman, 1994; Woodward & Markman, 1998), but learning the meaning of verbs poses even more challenges to the child. Unlike nouns, verbs do not refer to a concrete object but to events, which are typically fleeting.

Recently a number of studies have focused on verb acquisition strategies employing the distinction between manner and change-of-state components of verb meanings (for English cf. Behrend, 1990; Gentner, 1978, 1982; Gropen, Pinker, Hollander & Goldberg, 1991; Kelly & Rice, 1994; for German cf. Wittek, 1998, 1999). Findings from both comprehension and production tasks suggest that ND children up to 5 years of age and children with language impairment (LI) at an even later age prefer manner components of meaning to change-of-state components. This preference is referred to as the "manner bias" (Gentner, 1978).

In the present study, we investigate more closely children's verb comprehension in German. Our experimental evidence suggests that ND children correctly interpret resultative verbs as specifying the achieved endstate. Children with LI, however, are at chance in interpreting these verbs. Restating the notion of interpretation biases in event semantic terms, we argue that German speaking ND children possess a target-like event semantic representation of complex events, whereas LI children lack this representation.

The first section of this chapter sketches the organisation of the verb lexicon and spells out how resultative interpetations of verbs are achieved in German. In the second section we summarize our findings from longitudinal studies with ND and LI children and outline the rationale of our experimental study. The third section presents the design of our comprehension study; the results are detailed in section 4. The last section discusses the findings in light of the "manner bias" proposed for young children and offers an outlook on future research.

ORGANIZATION OF THE VERB LEXICON

The Event Structure of Verbs

Unlike referential terms such as *Edinburgh* or *house*, verbs and most relational words including *play, eat, gone, more* and particles such as *up* refer to events or parts of events. Consequently, the lexical representation of a verb contains information not only about the core meaning and the argument structure but also about the type of event designated by the verb (i.e. aspectuality). Following Pustejovsky's (1995) model of event typology, we distinguish between states (*know, sleep*), processes (*play, eat, walk*) and transitions (i.e. complex events involving a transition from one subevent to another). Verbs such as *mix* and *build* and verbs such as *open* and *close* both designate a transition and are traditionally referred to as resultative verbs. However, there is a crucial difference between these two types of verbs regarding the hierarchy of the subevents. In *mix* and *build* the process subevent is more prominent, whereas in *open* and *close* the endstate subevent is more prominent. We will call verbs of the *mix*-type 'process-oriented' and verbs of the *open*-type 'endstate-oriented'.

Endstate-Oriented Verbs in German

Languages differ as to how event types are marked in syntax and word formation. Apart from verbs with an inherently endstate-oriented event type (e.g., *ankommen,* arrive), endstate-orientation of the predicate often depends on event-semantic properties of other elements in the sentence (cf. Hollebrandse & van Hout, 1998; van Hout, 1996). In German, endstate-orientation is often marked by verb prefixation.[1] Prefixes such as *auf* or *zu* can mark the transitional events as endstate-oriented, as shown in (1):

(1) a. Er hat aufgegessen.
         'he has AUF-eaten'
         He ate up.
     b. Er hat die Tür aufgemacht/ zugemacht.
         'he has the door AUF-made/ ZU-made'
         He opened/closed the door.

Event type marking via endstate-oriented prefixes is subject to considerable variation, however, depending not least on the semantic type of the verb and its arguments. In addition to endstate-oriented prefixes there are deictic prefixes such as *runter* or *rauf*, which express the speaker's perspective on an event and which are process-oriented (cf. Penner, Wymann & Dietz, 1998; Schulz, Wymann & Penner, in press). Thus, deictic prefixation can result in a process-oriented interpretation of the predicate, as shown in (2):

(2) Er ist den Turm raufgestiegen.
     'he is the tower RAUF-climbed'
     He climbed on the tower.

Given this intricate relation between a predicate's specific event type and its marking in a particular language, the question arises of how the child succeeds in learning the meaning of verbs.

VERB ACQUISITION IN NORMALLY DEVELOPING AND LANGUAGE-IMPAIRED CHILDREN

Words referring to events not only occur very early in children's speech (for English cf. Woodward & Markmann, 1998; for German cf. Behrens, 1999), but make up a significant proportion of a normally developing child's lexicon (Kauschke, 1999). Studies comparing verb inventories of LI and ND children suggest that children with LI have fewer verbs in their lexicons and make more frequent use of general purpose verbs than either their age-matched or their language-matched peers (Rice, 1991; Rice & Bode, 1993). To date, however, no study has examined in more detail how ND and LI children log into the verb lexicon. Put differently, in which order do these children produce which types of verbal prefixes and verbs?

This question is addressed in our longitudinal studies of 5 ND and 5 LI German children, who have been recorded from the onset of word production (Penner et al., 1998) The latter children were Late Talkers, defined as children

---

[1] Depending on the verb type, endstate orientation is also marked by determiners (cf. Krifka, 1989; Verkuyl, 1972, 1993; for acquisition cf. Van Hout, 1996, 1997).

who produce less than 50 lexical items at the age of 2;0. Later they were diagnosed as language-impaired. The main results are as follows. ND children log into the verb lexicon around their first birthday. All start out with the endstate-oriented prefixes *auf* or *zu*. Several weeks later, the first verbs occur in their speech. These are typically endstate-oriented verbs such as *aufmachen* (AUF-make, open). LI children exhibit a very different acquisition pattern. In addition to being delayed with regard to the emergence of verbal items, which are first produced around the age of 2;0, LI children start out with the deictic prefixes *runter* or *rauf*. Up to a year later, endstate-oriented prefixes and the first verbs occur in their speech.

A closer look at the usage of the first words referring to events confirms these qualitative differences between ND and LI children. In an analysis of how endstate-oriented events are expressed, we found that ND children lexicalized this endstate-orientation with an appropriate relational word in 82% of the cases. LI Children, on the other hand, correctly lexicalized the endstate-orientation in only 19% of the cases (Penner, Schulz & Wymann, in prep.).

In summary, our production data suggests that German ND children pay attention to the endstate of transitions from early on, whereas German LI children lack this endstate-orientation. An analysis of their usage of relational words moreover indicates that ND children possess a target-like event semantic representation of complex events that takes into account the hierarchy of subevents in transitions. LI children, by contrast, exhibit violations of the event semantic representation of complex events. This violation may be due to a lack of an explicit event semantic representation (cf. Penner et al., 1998; Penner, Wymann & Schulz, 1999; Schulz, Wymann & Penner, 1999, in press).

According to our account of the initial stages of ND and LI children's verb acquisition, analogous differences should arise at the level of comprehension. The experimental study was therefore designed to investigate whether and how the qualitative differences between ND and LI children with regard to event representations also affect their comprehension of event structures.[2] We hypothesized that ND children, adhering to an endstate-orientation, should recognize that the endstate is a necessary property of endstate-oriented verbs. LI children, on the other hand, due to a lack of the endstate-orientation should not recognize that the endstate is entailed by endstate-oriented verbs. This contrast should be especially clear when comparing the performance of children with LI and their age-matched peers, but it should also show up with very young ND children. To avoid ambiguous responses, we concentrated on clearly endstate-oriented transitions. The endstate-oriented verb *aufmachen* was chosen for two

---

[2] This experimental study is an extension of the experiment reported on in Schulz et al. (in press). Besides enlarging the data base by including a group of 16 ND children age-matched with the LI children, the statistical analyses have been modified and extended.

reasons. First, the hierarchy of subevents is optimally transparent, because the prefix *auf* unambiguously marks the endstate as the more prominent subevent, whereas the process subevent is lexically marked by the light verb *machen* (make, do) that carries little meaning on its own. Secondly, *aufmachen* has been documented in children's speech from very early on.

METHOD

Subjects

Forty-eight children participated in this experiment: 16 young normally developing children (10 girls, 6 boys, M = 2;10, *range* = 2;00 to 3;01), 16 language-impaired children (8 boys, 8 girls, M = 3;10, *range* = 2;11 to 4;10)[3], and 16 chronologically age-matched normally developing children (7 boys, 9 girls, M = 3;10, *range* = 2;11 to 4;10). Sixteen university educated adults served as a control group (6 men, 10 women, M = 37;08, *range* = 27 to 66). All of the subjects were native German speakers, with no known history of physical, socio-emotional, or mental impairments. The normally developing children exhibited age-appropriate speech, language, social, and cognitive functioning according to preschool teacher and parent reports. The children with language impairment met the following criteria: (a) they had been diagnosed by speech therapists as suffering from receptive and expressive language deficits, (b) the cognitive functioning was reported to be within normal limits for age, and (c) there was no report of hearing impairments. The chronologically age-matched children were matched so that for each child in the group of children with language impairment there was a child in the age-matched group within 1 month of age.

An additional seven children were tested, but had to be excluded from analysis. One young ND child and three LI children failed the pretest, and three young ND children did not complete the experiment.

Materials

Thirty-two picture sequences were created, each composed of two photographs depicting different instances of opening a container, e.g. a bottle or a cardboard-box. The first photograph always depicted the closed container and a hand moving towards it. The second photograph depicted the outcome of the action: The container was either opened or still closed, while the hand was being withdrawn. Using a variant of the truth-value judgment task (Crain & McKee,

---

[3] The higher age of the LI children is because, unlike ND children, they could not be subjected to tests involving yes/no questions until about their third birthday.

1985), we designed yes/no questions asking whether the person had opened the container. A subject who knows that the meaning of *aufmachen* entails the endstate [be open] should answer *yes* in the first case and *no* in the second case. In half of the picture sequences, the container was being manipulated by using just the hands, while in the other half it was being manipulated with the help of a tool (e.g., a wrench). Consequently, each picture-sequence varied with regard to the variables ENDSTATE [+/-] and INSTRUMENT [+/-]. There were 8 different instances of opening a container. Each subject thus saw a total of 8 test trials, two each in the four conditions. An example is given in (3):

(3)   Sample item [-endstate, -instrument]

Diese Mutter wollte mit ihrem Kind spielen. Guck, da siehst du ihre Hand, und hier ist die Schachtel. Und dann.   .   .
This mother wanted to play with her child. Look, there you can see her hand, and here is the box. And then . . .

Test question: *Hat siese aufgemacht?*   *Nein*
                 'has she-her.CL AUF-made.PART'
                 Did she open it?   No

The perfect tense used in the questions is the standard form to refer to past events in colloquial (Southern) German, spoken by all participants. The four conditions were counterbalanced across the eight test items, yielding four different versions. Possible effects of order of test item were controlled for by designing two different orders, thus arriving at eight different lists to which subjects were assigned randomly.

Procedure

Each subject was tested individually. Preceding the actual experiment, a pretest was administered to ensure that both ND and LI children were able to respond to yes/no questions appropriately. While children were given the opportunity to manipulate the containers depicted in the picture sequences, they were asked simple yes/no questions about the objects (e.g., *Is that a suitcase?*). Only those children who answered all four pretest questions correctly participated in the main test. The encounters with the concrete objects moreover served the purpose of discouraging the child from basing her responses to the test trials merely on her previous world knowledge about the respective containers.
    Following four practice trials, each subject was presented with the eight test items. As in the practice trials, the experimenter narrated the event. A hand

puppet then asked the yes/no question. Interspersed with the test items, there were four control items that contained verbs other than the test verb but were also phrased in the perfect tense. These were added to counteract processing strategies and moreover to ensure that children paid attention to each item until the end.

Predictions

We predicted that the ND children would perform better overall than the LI children. More specifically, both groups of ND children should correctly reject *aufmachen* for events in which the endstate is not reached, because they are aware that endstate-oriented verbs entail their endstate. Due to the age difference, we expected that performance of the three- and four-year-olds would be even better than performance of the 2-year-olds. LI children, on the other hand, should incorrectly accept *aufmachen* for events in which the endstate is not reached. With regard to the condition [+endstate], we expected that all groups would correctly accept the endstate verb *aufmachen* if the picture depicts an event in which the endstate is reached. Performance on the controls was predicted to be high for all subjects.

Scoring and Data Analysis

Responses to the test items were coded as correct or incorrect, as described in the materials section. A correct response received a score of 1, an incorrect response received a score of 0. Then, for each subject, the total number of correct responses for each of the four conditions and for the controls was calculated. In order to compare the mean of the controls to the mean of all test items, we introduced a meta-variable 'item' with the conditions [control] and [test item].

RESULTS

Group Responses to Controls and Test Items

All responses were first analyzed by a (4) group × (4) version × (2) order × (2) item ANOVA, with the last factor as a repeated measure ($\alpha = .05$). There were no significant effects of version ($F (3,32) = .45, p = .716$) nor of order ($F (1,3) = .17, p = .683$). Therefore, the between-subject factors version and order were neglected in the further analysis. All responses were then analyzed by a 4 (group) × 2 (item) ANOVA, with the last factor as a repeated measure. The proportion of correct responses for test items and controls is presented in Table 1.

TABLE 1
Proportion of correct responses (and standard deviation)
by item type and subject group.

Item	Young ND	Age-m. ND	LI	Adults
Controls	87.50 (15.81)	98.44 (6.25)	95.31 (10.08)	100 (.0)
Test items	89.06 (13.59)	92.97 (11.15)	64.13 (11.06)	97.66 (6.80)

There was a significant effect of group, $(F\ (3,60) = 19.83, p < .001)$ and a significant effect of item $(F\ (1,60) = 13.59, p < .001)$. The interaction of group and item was also significant $(F\ (3,60) = 13.59, p < .001)$. A *post hoc* analysis using the Scheffé procedure $(p < .05)$ revealed that the means of the test items of the LI children differed significantly from the means of the test items of the young and the age-matched ND children and the adults, which formed a homogenous subset. A second *post hoc* comparison (Scheffé) indicated that the means of the controls of the LI children did not differ significantly from the three other groups.

Analysis of Test Items and Subgroup Comparisons

The responses to the four test conditions were analyzed by a 4 (group) × 2 (endstate) × 2 (instrument) ANOVA, with the last two factors as repeated measures (preserving α at .05). The analysis revealed a significant effect of group $(F\ (3,60) = 30.14, p < .001)$ and of endstate $(F\ (1,60) = 16.87, p < .001)$, but not of instrument $(F\ (1,60) = .37, p = .547)$. With regard to the two-way interactions, the interaction between group and endstate process was significant $(F\ (3,60) = 2.94, p < .05)$, as illustrated in FIG. 1.[4]

---

[4] The significant interaction between group and instrument $(F\ (3,60) = 3.36, p = .024)$ was due to the low mean in the [-instrument] condition for the LI children and is neglected in the further analysis (cf. Schulz et al., in press, for an explanation of this result).

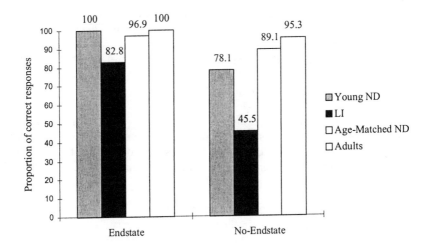

FIG. 1 Proportion of correct reponses to the test item by Endstate and subject group.

As can be inferred from Table 1 and FIG. 1, adults performed very well on all conditions. Hence only children's data was analyzed further. Weighted analyses of contrast were employed to examine possible distinctions between the three child groups. For the [-endstate] condition, there was a signifiant difference between the two groups of ND children and the LI children (T (45) = 4.256, p < .001), due to the low mean of the latter group (M = 45.5). To test whether performance of the LI children was different from chance, the means for the [-endstate] condition were compared to the proportion anticipated by chance (50.0) using the G test. It was found that if the endstate was not reached, performance was at chance level (p = .69). The contrast between the performance of the young and the age-matched ND children in the [-endstate] condition was not significant (T (45) = -1.053, p = .298). Regarding the [+endstate] condition, the contrast between ND children and LI children was significant (T (45) = 3.514, p < .001), whereas there was no contrast between the performance of the younger and the older ND children (T (45) = .609, p = .546). The G test revealed that in the [+endstate] condition, LI children performed significantly above chance (p < .01). Weighted analyses of contrast taking into account children's performance in both conditions revealed that the difference between LI children and ND children in the [-endstate] condition is significantly greater than in the [+endstate] condition (T (90) = -2.258, p < .05). A *post hoc* analysis (Scheffé) confirmed that the means of the LI children in the [-endstate] condition differed significantly from all other means, which formed a homogeneous subset.

Finally, an ANOVA with the factor endstate as repeated measures was used to assess the responses of the LI children in isolation. There was a significant effect of endstate (F (1,15) = 6.43, $p < .05$), resulting from a lower mean in the [-endstate] condition ($M = 45.31$) than in the [+endstate] condition ($M = 82.75$).

Analysis of Individual Responses

Individual responses were examined to investigate whether the observed group differences between ND and LI children in the [-endstate] condition were also found in children's individual performances. Table 2 shows the percentage of correct answers to the [-endstate] condition for each child in the three subject groups.

TABLE 2
Percentage of correct responses in the [-endstate] condition
distributed over subjects by subject group.

Percentage of correct responses *(4 correct responses possible per subject)*	*Young ND* *(N = 16)*	*Age-m. ND* *(N = 16)*	*LI* *(N = 16)*
100%	8	11	4
75%	4	4	0
50%	2	0	5
25%	2	1	3
0%	0	0	4

The endstate-orientation of the verb *aufmachen* was considered to be mastered by a child if she gave at least three correct responses in the [-endstate] condition. 12 out of 16 (75%) normally developing two-year-olds responded as though they had mastered the endstate-orientation of *aufmachen*. Among the three- and four-year-olds, 4 out of 16 (25%) LI children and 15 out of 16 (93.75%) ND children had mastered the endstate-orientation.

DISCUSSION

The high number of correct responses to the controls shows that both ND and LI children had in general no difficulty understanding yes/no questions containing a verb in the perfect tense. Thus, we can conclude that children's performance on the test items is not impeded by general problems with this question format. The analysis of the children's data confirmed that both groups of ND children performed much better on the test items than the children with LI. Both groups of ND children correctly rejected *aufmachen* for events in which the endstate is not reached in 78% and 89% of the cases, respectively. Although not reaching significance, performance of the three- and four-year-olds was better in this condition than performance of the two-year-olds, as expected. LI children's rejection of *aufmachen* for events in which the endstate is not reached, on the other hand, was at chance level (46% correct). Analysis of the individual responses confirmed this difference between ND and LI children. The majority of the ND children but only 25% of the children with LI had mastered the endstate-orientation of *aufmachen*. All groups correctly accepted the endstate verb *aufmachen* if the picture depicted an event in which the endstate is reached. The children with LI performed significantly above chance but lower than all other groups (83% correct).

In summary, our experimental data revealed that ND children between the ages of two and four, but not three- and four-year old LI children, recognize that the endstate is a necessary property of endstate-oriented verbs such as *aufmachen*. Taken together with our data from spontaneous production, these findings corroborate our assumption that ND children possess a target-like event semantic representation of complex events, whereas LI children exhibit violations of the event semantic representation of complex events.

Both production and comprehension data are not compatible with the "manner bias" suggested to hold for English speaking children. Due to their preference for manner over change-of-state components, children up to the age of five have been found to misinterpret change-of-state verbs like *fill* or *mix* as specifying the manner-of-motion instead of the achieved change-of-state (Behrend, 1990; Gentner, 1978, 1982; Gropen et al., 1991). Likewise, regarding German Wittek (1998, 1999) argues that four- and five-year-old children do not treat the endstate component as a necessary property of change-of-state verbs and thus misinterpret verbs such as *vollmachen* (fill), *aufwecken* (wake up) and *aufmachen* (open). However, many of the change-of-state verbs employed in these studies are process-oriented rather than endstate-oriented. *Fill* and *mix* as well as *wake up* refer to a gradual change, with the process subevent being the more prominent subevent. A verb-by-verb analysis of the German data confirms that the selection of the verbs considerably affected the results: Endstate-oriented verbs were in fact correctly interpreted as entailing their endstate in 80% to 100% of the cases, compared to 0% to 40% endstate-oriented interpretations for process-oriented verbs (cf. Wittek, 1999, p. 46).

Our results regarding LI children's verb interpretation are partially compatible with Kelly and Rice, (1994) findings regarding English speaking children with LI. They found that five-year-old LI children, unlike their age-matched peers, did not show any preference in applying a novel verb to either a motion or a change-of-state scene. As noted by Kelly and Rice (1994, p. 190), an account is needed of how children with LI differ from their age-matched peers in their strategies for verb acquisition and interpretation. Emphasizing the role of the verb's event structure, we advanced the hypothesis that LI children lack a target-like event semantic representation of complex events. We hypothesized that this deficit results from a learning strategy for acquiring the event structure of verbs that does not consider the hierarchy of subevents (cf. Penner et al. 1998, 1999; Schulz et al., in press). The lack of a preference for a certain event type as observed by Kelly and Rice would follow then from a lack of an explicit event-semantic representation.

It remains for future research to evaluate this account, for example, by employing a wider range of resultative verbs. Moreover, studies with older LI children will have to show how persistent the observed deficits are. Preliminary results from a study with LI children between the ages of five and eight indicate that although their performance increases the deficits still exist (cf. Penner et al., in prep.).

ACKNOWLEDGMENTS

We thank the audience at the International Clinical Phonetics and Linguistics Association Conference in Edinburgh for comments on an earlier version of this chapter. Discussions with Jill de Villiers, Tom Roeper, Jürgen Weissenborn and Angelika Wittek were especially helpful. We are grateful to the teachers and speech therapists of the day-care centers in Stuttgart, Germany, and in Bern, Switzerland, and to the children for their participation in the study. This research was supported by a grant from the Deutsche Forschungsgemeinschaft to Zvi Penner (SFB No. 471).

REFERENCES

Behrend, D. (1990). Constraints and development: A reply to Nelson. *Cognitive Development, 5,* 313–330.

Behrens, H. (1999). Was macht Verben zu einer besonderen Kategorie im Spracherwerb? In J. Meibauer & M. Rothweiler (Eds.), *Das Lexikon im Spracherwerb* (pp. 32–50). Tübingen: Francke.

Crain, S., & McKee, C. (1985). The acquisition of structural restrictions on anaphora. In S. Berman, J.-W. Choe & J. McDonough (Eds.), *Proceedings of the Sixteenth Annual North Eastern Linguistic Society* (pp. 94–110). Amherst: University of Massachusetts.

Gentner, D. (1978). On relational meaning: the acquisition of verb meaning. *Child Development, 49,* 988–998.

Gentner, D. (1982). Why nouns are learned before verbs: Linguistic relativity versus natural partitioning. In S. Kuczaj (Ed.), *Language development, Vol. 2: Language, thought, and culture* (pp. 301–334). Hillsdale, NJ: Lawrence Erlbaum Associates.

Gropen, J., Pinker, S., Hollander, M., & Goldberg, R. (1991). Syntax and semantics in the acquisition of locative verbs. *Journal of Child Language, 18,* 115–151.

Hollebrandse, B., & van Hout, A. (1998). Aspectual bootstrapping via light verbs. In N. Dittmar & Z. Penner (Eds.), *Issues in the theory of language acquisition* (pp. 113–134). Bern: Peter Lang.

Kauschke, K. (1999). Früher Wortschatzerwerb im Deutschen: Eine empirische Studie zum Entwicklungsverlauf und zur Komposition des kindlichen Lexikons. In J. Meibauer & M. Rothweiler (Eds.), *Das Lexikon im Spracherwerb* (pp. 128–156). Tübingen: Francke.

Kelly, D., & Rice, M. (1994). Preferences for verb interpretation in children with specific language impairment. *Journal of Speech and Hearing Research, 37,* 182–192.

Krifka, M. (1989). Nominal reference, temporal constitution, and quantification in event semantics. In R. Bartsch, J. van Benthem & P. van Emde Boas (Eds.), *Semantics and contextual expressions* (pp. 75–115). Dordrecht: Foris.

Landau, B. (1994). Where's what and what's where: the language of objects in space. In L. Gleitman & B. Landau (Eds.), *The acquisition of the lexicon* (pp. 259–296). Cambridge, MA: MIT Press.

Markman, E. M. (1994). Constraints on word meaning in early language acquisition. In L. Gleitman & B. Landau (Eds.), *The acquisition of the lexicon* (pp. 199–288). Cambridge, MA: MIT Press.

Penner, Z., Schulz, P., & Wymann, K. (in prep.). Learning the meaning of verbs - What distinguishes normally developing from language-impaired children? University of Konstanz.

Penner, Z., Wymann, K., & Schulz, P. (1999). Specific language impairment revisited: parallelism vs. deviance: a learning theoretical approach. Talk presented at GALA, University of Potsdam, Germany.

Penner, Z., Wymann, K., & Dietz, C. (1998). From verbal particles to complex object-verb constructions in early German. The acquisition of event structure in normally developing and language impaired children. In Z. Penner & K. Wymann (Eds.), *Normal and impaired language acquisition. Studies in lexical, syntactic, and phonological development* (Arbeitspapier No. 89, pp. 4–109). Fachgruppe Sprachwissenschaft, University of Konstanz.

Pustejovsky, J. (1995). *The generative lexicon.* Cambridge, MA: MIT Press.

Rice, M., & Bode, J. (1993). GAPS in the verb lexicon of children with specific language impairment. *First Language, 13,* 113–131.

Rice, M. (1991). Children with specific language impairment: towards a model of teachability. In N.A. Krasnegor, B. M. Rumbaugh, R. L. Schiefelbush & M. Stoddart-Kennedy (Eds.), *Biological and behavioral determinants of language development* (pp. 447–480). Hillsdale, NJ: Lawrence Erlbaum Associates.

Schulz, P., Wymann, K., & Penner, Z. (in press). The early acquisition of verb meaning in German by normally developing and language impaired children. *Brain and Language.*

Schulz, P., Wymann, K., & Penner, Z. (1999). The acquisition of event structure. An experimental study of normally developing and language impaired children in German. In Z. Penner, P. Schulz & K. Wymann (Eds.), *Normal and impaired language acquisition II. Studies in lexical, syntactic, and phonological development* (Arbeitspapier No. 105, pp. 65–81). Fachgruppe Sprachwissenschaft, University of Konstanz.

van Hout, A. (1996). Event semantics of verb frame alternation. A case study of Dutch and its acquisition. Unpublished Ph.D. thesis, University of Tilburg.

van Hout, A. (1997). Learning telicity: acquiring argument structure and the syntax-semantics of direct objects in Dutch. *Proceedings of the 21st Boston University Conference on Language Development.* Cascadilla Press.

Verkuyl, H. (1972). *On the compositional nature of the aspects.* Dordrecht: Reidel.

Verkuyl, H. (1993). A theory of aspectuality. Cambridge, MA: Cambridge University Press.

Wittek, A. (1998). Zustandsveränderungsverben im Deutschen – Wie lernt das Kind die komplexe Semantik? In J. Meibauer & M. Rothweiler (Eds.), *Das Lexikon im Spracherwerb* (pp. 278–295). Tübingen: Francke.

Wittek, A. (1999). "... and the prince woke the Sleeping Beauty again." Learning the meaning of change-of-state verbs: a case study in German. Unpublished Ph.D.thesis. MPI Nijmegen/University of Tübingen.

Woodward, A., & Markman, E. M. (1998). Early word learning. In D. Kuhn & R. S. Siegler (Eds.), *Handbook of child psychology: Vol. 2, Cognition, perception and language* (pp. 371– 420). New York: John Wiley and Sons.

10

Learning the H(e)ard Way: The Acquisition of Grammar in Young German-Speaking Children with Cochlear Implants and with Normal Hearing

Gisela Szagun

In cases of sensory hearing loss cochlear implantation provides access to audition for profoundly deaf persons. In recent years cochlear implantation has become increasingly popular for young congenitally deaf or prelingually deafened children. Studies of speech perception and speech production indicate that children implanted at a young age are capable of acquiring spoken language (Fryauf-Bertschy, Tyler, Kelsay, Gantz & Woodworth, 1997), but so far, there has been little research on these children's language development from a developmental psycholinguistic perspective. This chapter takes such a perspective; it aims to delineate the course of acquisition of grammatical structures in children with cochlear implants in comparison to normally hearing children.

An interactional approach to language learning is adopted here viewing grammar as the result of an interaction between maturational processes and language input. For normal language development it has been suggested that rapid growth in synaptic connectivity in different brain regions around 16-24 months increases children's capacity for storage and coding of information, and thus enables rapid growth in vocabulary and grammatical structures (Bates, Thal & Jankowski, 1992). Children can now pick up and store large amounts of vocabulary and they can make use of distributional information (i.e. patterns of co-occurrence of phonemes and morphemes to construct a grammar; see MacWhinney, 1987; Plunkett & Marchman, 1993). Such information functions as a cue to underlying grammatical categories. For instance, in English an -s on the verb stem functions as a cue to third person singular. The German equivalent is the suffix -t. By relating such cues to meaning and detecting recurrent structural patterns in the input language children construct the grammar of their mother tongue.

For children with normal hearing the input language offers abundant material to assimilate via the auditory channel and use for constructing grammar (Moerk, 1983). Children with cochlear implants, however, resemble mildly to moderately hearing-impaired persons. Their impaired hearing may lead them to miss elements of the spoken input language more frequently, and thus, input may effectively be reduced. Also, young deaf children who undergo cochlear implantation beyond age 2 start receiving auditory and linguistic input much later than normally hearing children and have missed the optimal starting point for setting off language. The question is whether near normal language acquisition is still possible given these conditions, and if it proceeds differently, where the differences lie.

Current viewpoints on sensitivity for language learning lead to different predictions. A "sensitive period" view suggests that, based on the brain's increased sensitivity, humans have an enhanced capacity for learning language early in life which decreases gradually up to puberty (Oyama, 1979; Johnson & Newport, 1993). An age of first decline in language learning ability is not specified, but data from second language learning suggest that it may lie around middle childhood (Johnson & Newport, 1993). A "critical period" view (Locke, 1997) is more specific about the age of first decline. According to this view, an analytic mechanism responsible for building grammar is turned on around 24 months if the child has acquired a sufficient vocabulary. During a "critical period" between 24 and 36 months, this mechanism functions optimally to set off grammatical analysis. If there is insufficient vocabulary during this time span, the mechanism will not be fully activated and grammar acquisition will be slow and less efficient.

Both views would predict slower language growth for prelingually deafened children with cochlear implants because these children start language acquisition later. Under a "critical period" view, grammatical progress at pace with that of normally hearing children should be precluded, because the children with cochlear implants are unlikely to acquire a sufficient number of words within the limits of the critical period. The "sensitive period" view, however, can accommodate slower growth as well as growth at pace with normally hearing children because it is less specific about an age of first decline in language learning ability.

It is hypothesized here that children with cochlear implants will acquire language more slowly due to age-related maturational factors. Additionally, it is suggested that quality of children's preoperative and postoperative hearing will influence their language acquisition. Better preoperative hearing is assumed to lead to faster language acquisition, because children's increased auditory experience may have contributed to building neural pathways required for acquiring language via audition. Children's postoperative hearing impairment is seen to have a selective influence on language acquisition. It may cause them to miss elements of the spoken input language which are low in perceptual salience, such as articles which are in unstressed prenominal sentence position.

It is predicted that the acquisition of articles will be particularly slow in children with cochlear implants.

In analyzing language acquisition, this analysis focuses on the global language measure of mean length of utterance (MLU) measured in morphemes, and the acquisition of inflectional morphology in the areas of verb inflections and case marking on articles. Linguistic progress in children with cochlear implants and in children with normal hearing are compared. Such a comparison would seem important for assessing the benefit children may have from cochlear implantation. Individual differences in overall grammatical development, which are well documented in normal language development (Fenson, Dale, Reznick, Bates, Thal & Pethick, 1994) are examined for both groups.

METHOD

Participants

The participants were 22 deaf children with cochlear implants and 22 children with normal hearing. There were 12 girls and 10 boys in each group. Mean implantation age was 2;5 (year;months), SD = 0;9, range 1;2 to 3;10. For 19 children, the etiology of hearing loss was from unknown congenital causes, three children were deafened as a result of meningitis at 0;1, 0;8, and 1;6 months respectively. In the deaf group, children had hearing thresholds between 50 and 100 dB SPL for frequencies of 500 Hz and 1000 Hz as assessed by preoperative audiograms under hearing aid conditions. Preoperative audiometric assessment rendered no electric responses during electric response audiometry (ERA), and children did not react to stimuli below 80 dB nHL during electrocochleography. The sample of children with cochlear implants was drawn from the youngest children (i.e. under 4 years at implantation, attending Hannover Cochlear Implant Center and starting their rehabiliation during the course of the years 1996 and 1997). Only children from monolingual environments, with no sign language, and children without a diagnosed handicap besides their hearing impairment, were included. Children's I.Q. was within the normal range, measured by Snijders-Oomen Non-verbal Intelligence Test (Snijders, Tellegen, Winkel, Laros & Wijnberg-Williams, 1996).

The 22 children with normal hearing had no diagnosed hearing problems and no diagnosed developmental delays. The children were 1;4 at the start of data collection and were at age-appropriate levels of object permanence knowledge according to the Infant Psychological Development Scales (Uzgiris & Hunt, 1975). All of the children were growing up in monolingual environments. The children were resident in Oldenburg, northern Germany, and were recruited from three pediatricians' practices and two Oldenburg daycare centers.

Design, Data Collection and Data Transcription

The study was longitudinal covering a period of 18 months. One and a half hours of spontaneous speech samples were collected in a free play situation with the child, a parent, and an investigator. Speech samples were collected about every 20 weeks, time intervals being determined by the cochlear-implanted children's rehabilitation stays at the Cochlear Implant Center Hannover. There were five data points. For the normally hearing children these were at ages 1;4, 1;8.15, 2;1, 2;5.15, and 2;10 (years;months.days). For children with cochlear implants, age was calculated from the date of first tune up, because their chronological ages vary. First tune up is the first fitting of the device to the child's level of comfortable hearing and takes place 6 weeks after implantation. Data points counted in tune up age were 0;5, 0;9.15, 1;2, 1;6.15, and 1;11.

Normally hearing children and children with cochlear implants were matched for initial language level, as measured by mean length of utterance (MLU) and number of words. Initial MLUs ranged from 1.0 to 1.20 in the normally hearing group, with a mean of 1.05, SD = 0.08; and from 1.0 to 1.23 in the cochlear-implanted group, with a mean of 1.04, SD = 0.06. Vocabulary, as assessed by parental report, was between 0 and 88 words, mean 17.5, SD 19.4 for the normally hearing group, and between 0 and 72 words, mean 20.9, SD 20.8, for the cochlear-implanted group.

Data collection took place in a playroom at the Cochlear Implant Center Hannover for the children with cochlear implants, and in a playroom at the University of Oldenburg for the normally hearing children. The situation was free play, and a parent and a female investigator were present and played with the child. Toys were similar in the two settings. Digital auditory tape recording (DAT) was carried out, using portable Sony DAT-recorders and high-sensitivity Sony or Aiwa microphones. In Oldenburg, video recordings were also made, but in Hannover, nonintrusive video-recording would not have been possible and was therefore not carried out.

Everything spoken by the child was transcribed using the CHILDES system for transcribing and analyzing child speech (MacWhinney, 1995). An adaptation to German for transcribing child speech, for coding MLU, and for morphosyntactic coding (Szagun, 1999) was used. Transcription was performed by eight trained transcribers. Reliability checks on transcription were calculated for 7.3% of the transcripts, and percentage agreements ranged between 96% and 100% for different pairs of transcribers. Coding for MLU and morphosyntax was performed by three researchers. Reliability checks on MLU were performed on 20% of the transcripts. As a measure of reliability Cohen's kappa was calculated. Kappas ranged between .94 and .98. Reliability checks for morphosyntactic coding were done on 10% of the transcripts. Percentage agreements ranged between 96% and 98%. CLAN programs were used for calculating MLU and frequencies of individual morphemes.

RESULTS

Mean Length of Utterance (MLU)

Mean length of utterance (MLU) measured in morphemes was used as a general indicator of grammatical progress. Effects of age and group were tested by two-way ANOVA with repeated measures on age (5) and group as a between subjects factor (2). There was a significant effect of age, $F(4,168) = 189.69$, $p < .000$, a significant effect of group, $F(1,42) = 18.2$, $p < .001$, and a significant age x group interaction, $F(4,168) = 28.31$, $p < .000$. MLU values were significantly lower for the CI (cochlear-implanted) group at the last two data points, Tukey, $p < .05$. For the NH (normally hearing) children, MLUs increased significantly between every adjacent age level from data point 4.15 (4 months.15 days since first data collection), and for the CI children, from data point 9.00 (Tukey's HSD for repeated measures, $p < .05$). Fig. 1 shows the means for each group of children plotted over age.

Inflectional Morphology: Verb Marking and Case Marking

Although MLU is a useful measure of general grammatical progress, it does not give any information about the acquisition of specific grammatical morphemes. Here, the acquisition of inflectional morphology in the areas of verb marking and case marking are presented. Only correctly marked forms are counted in this analysis. A criterion of initial productivity was used here. For content words, it was if a correct inflection occurred on three different lexical items; for function words it was three correct occurrences in a speech sample. As there was hardly any use of inflectional morphology at the first age level, only four age levels were included.

Verb inflectional marking on the main verb. In German, verbs are marked for person and tense. Table 1 presents the verb inflectional markings considered here. A score of 1 is assigned when a child uses a particular verb inflection on 3 different lexical items. This renders a maximum score of 9 summed up over personal endings, imperative, infinitive and past participle (see Table 1).

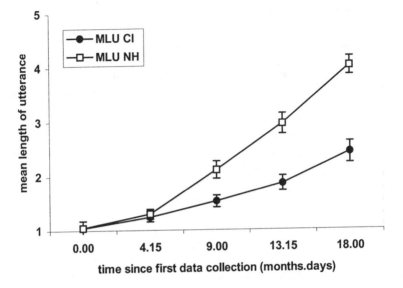

FIG. 1 Mean MLU values for cochlear-implanted (CI)
and normally hearing (NH) children plotted over age.

TABLE 1
Verb inflectional marking in German.

Verb form	Example
1st person singular -e or -∅	ich sag-(e) (I say)
2nd person singular* -st	du sag-st (you say)
3rd person singular* -t	er sag-t (he says)
1st person plural -en	wir sag-en (we say)
2nd person plural -t	ihr sag-t (you say)
3rd person plural -en	sie sag-en (they say)
imperative singular*	-e or -∅ sag-(e) (say)
infinitive -en	sag-en
past participle* -t, -en, ge-	ge-sag-t (said)

Note. *Vowel changes are possible but are not presented here.

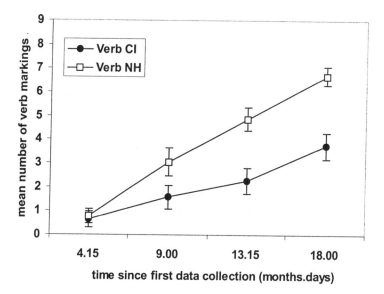

FIG. 2 Mean scores of verb inflectional marking for cochlear-implanted (CI)
and normally hearing (NH) children plotted over age.

For verbs, a two-way ANOVA with repeated measures on age (4) and group (2) as a between-subjects factor was computed. There was a significant effect of age, $F(3,126) = 118.85$, $p < .001$, and of group, $F(1,42) = 9.14$, $p < .004$, as well as a significant age x group interaction, $F(3,126) = 13.2$, $p < .001$. In both groups, verb inflectional scores increased between every adjacent age level (Tukey for repeated measures, $p < .05$). The two groups differed significantly at the two highest age levels with lower scores for CI children (Tukey, $p < .05$). Mean verb scores are shown in Fig. 2.

Case marking on the definite article. German marks for case and gender. Case marking on the definite article for nominative and accusative is considered next. The corresponding forms for the three genders are nominative: masculine *der*, feminine *die*, neuter *das*; accusative: masculine *den*, feminine *die*, neuter *das*. A score of one is assigned when a child uses a form of the definite article at least three times in a speech sample. Summing up over gender this renders a maximum score of three for each case.

For each case variable, a two-way ANOVA was computed with repeated measures on age (4) and group (2) as a between-subjects factor. For the nominative, there was a significant main effect of age, $F(3,126) = 55.64$, $p < .001$, and group $F(1,42) = 35.46$, $p < .001$, and a significant age x group interaction, $F(3,126) = 9.39$, $p < .001$. For the NH group scores between adjacent age levels increased significantly from data point 9.00, but for the CI group, only between the last two age levels (Tukey for repeated measures, $p <$ .05), indicating slower increase in this group. From data point 9.00 NH children had significantly higher scores (Tukey, $p < .05$). For the accusative there was a significant main effect of age, $F(3,126) = 39.57$, $p < .000$, and group $F(1,42) = 13.84$, $p < .000$, and a significant age x group interaction, $F(3,126) = 9.75$, $p < .001$. For the NH group, scores increased significantly from data point 9.00 (Tukey for repeated measures, $p < .05$), but for the CI group there were no significant differences between adjacent age levels. At the last two age levels NH children had significantly higher scores (Tukey, $p < .05$). Means for nominative and accusative scores are depicted in Fig. 3.

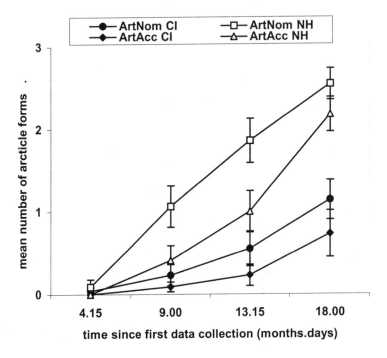

FIG. 3 Mean scores of nominatives (ArtNom) and accusatives (ArtAcc) of the definite article for cochlear-implanted (CI) and normally hearing (NH) children plotted over age.

Individual Differences

Individual differences in MLU. To explore individual differences between children, subgroups of children with very similar individual MLU curves (SDs ranging from .01 to .52) within each of the two major groups, CI and NH, were formed and compared. There were four subgroups per group. Fig. 4 shows mean

MLU values for the two most rapidly progressing subgroups of CI children, the two most rapidly progressing subgroups of NH children, and for a subgroup of NH children with moderate progress. For CI children subgroup CI1 (n = 3) contains the children with most rapid progress and subgroup CI2 (n = 7) the children with next rapid progress. For NH children subgroup NH1 (n = 9) is the group with most rapid progress, followed by NH2 (n = 4), and NH3 (n = 5) who are children with moderate progress. Figure 5 shows mean MLU values for the more slowly progressing children in both groups, subgroup CI3 (n = 6) and subgroup CI4 (n = 6), and again for subgroup NH3 (n = 5), the subgroup of normally hearing children with moderate progress, and for NH4 (n = 4) who are the normally hearing children with least rapid progress.

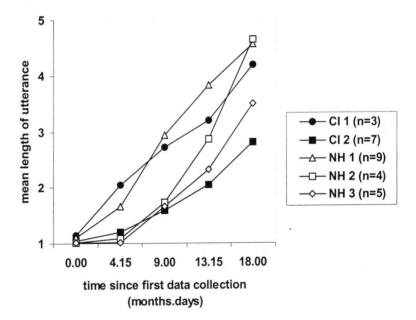

FIG. 4 MLU curves for subgroups of cochlear-implanted (CI) and normally hearing (NH) children with fast and moderate progress.

A two-way ANOVA with age as within-subjects factor (5) and subgroups as between subjects factor (8) was run. There was a significant main effect of subgroup, $F(7,36) = 68.21, p < .001$, a significant main effect of age, $F(4,144) = 489.37, p < .001$, and a significant age x subgroup interaction, $F(28,144) = 23.13, p < .001$. In terms of post-hoc comparisons, differences between NH and CI subgroups with fast progress, and between NH and CI subgroups with slow progress are of interest. There was no difference between subgroups CI1 and NH1, but subgroup CI2 had a significantly lower MLU than subgroup NH2 at the final age level (Scheffé, $p < .05$). Subgroups CI2 and NH3 did not differ significantly. Thus, across groups, the two subgroups with most rapid progress did not differ, and the CI subgroup with next rapid progress (CI2) did not differ from a subgroup of NH children with moderate progress (see Fig. 4).

The two slower CI subgroups, CI3 and CI4, had significantly lower MLUs than the moderate and slow NH subgroups NH3 and NH4 (Scheffé, $p < .05$) at the final age level (see Fig. 5).

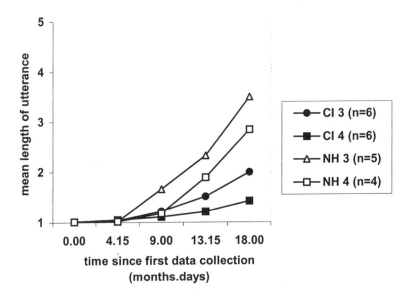

FIG. 5 MLU curves for subgroups of cochlear-implanted (CI) and normally hearing (NH) children with slow and moderate progress.

Relations between age, pre-operative hearing and linguistic progress for cochlear-implanted children. The relation between chronological age at implantation and linguistic progress, and between preoperative hearing with hearing aids and linguistic progress, was tested by correlational analysis (Pearson product-moment correlation coefficients). Preoperative hearing was measured in terms of thresholds in dB SPL at 1000 Hz (500 Hz for 6 children). Two children deafened by meningitis at 8 and 18 months were excluded from this analysis, as they were not comparable to congenitally deaf children in terms of preoperative auditory experience. To have a measure of linguistic growth rather than outcome, growth rate of MLU was calculated. Growth rates were obtained by fitting mathematical functions to each child's MLU values over time using SPSS curve estimation procedures. In most cases, there were significant linear and quadratic trends in the data. Growth rate is identical to the first derivative of a curve and was calculated per data point and child using the appropriate equation for the combined linear and quadratic trends.

Partial correlations were calculated between growth rate of MLU and chronological age at implantation controlling for preoperative hearing, and between growth in MLU and preoperative hearing controlling for age. Correlation coefficients are presented in Table 2. Preoperative hearing correlates significantly with growth in MLU at all data points. Age at implantation correlates significantly with growth in MLU at three data points. However, chronological age accounts for less of the variability (i.e. between 24% to 30%). Preoperative hearing accounts for 30% to 72% of the variability.

TABLE 2
Partial correlations between chronological age, preoperative
hearing with hearing aids, and growth rates in MLU.

Growth rate of MLU	Chronological age	Preoperative thresholds (dB SPL at 1000 Hz)[a]
MLU at 0;5	-.37	-.81***
MLU at 0;9	-.50*	-.85***
MLU at 1;2	-.55**	-.83***
MLU at 1;6	-.49*	-.75***
MLU at 1;11	-.38	-.55**

Note. [a] for six children responses are at 500 Hz
$*p < .05, **p < .01, ***p < .001$ (two-tailed)

DISCUSSION

These results show that hearing impaired children with cochlear implants who were implanted at a young age acquired spoken language spontaneously but more slowly than normally hearing children who were at a comparable initial linguistic level. At the end of the first 18 months of grammar acquisition, starting from an MLU of ≤ 1.25 in both groups, the cochlear-implanted group reached an average MLU of 2.5 as opposed to 4.0 for the normally hearing group. A closer look at specific inflectional morphology showed that children with cochlear implants acquired verb inflections and case and gender marking on the definite article more slowly than children with normal hearing. However, the magnitude of the difference was larger for articles. Although the cochlear-implanted children progressed more slowly as a group, there was considerable variability within the group. In terms of increases in MLU, 3 children with cochlear implants progressed as fast as 9 normally hearing children with most rapid progress. Another 7 children with cochlear implants did not differ from 5 normally hearing children with moderate linguistic progress. However, 12 children in the cochlear-implanted group progressed more slowly than the 4 slowest normally hearing children. Age at implantation and preoperative hearing with hearing aids were associated with subsequent grammatical growth, with preoperative hearing having the stronger relation.

The present results confirm the predictions of slower language acquisition in hearing impaired children with cochlear implants. This could be indicative of a strong maturational influence in the sense of a lessening sensitivity for building a grammar when the optimal time window for setting off the behavior has been missed. However, at least two of these findings would lead to a qualification of such an interpretation. One is that implantation age alone is a weaker predictor of children's subsequent linguistic progress than is preoperative hearing. The other is that some children with cochlear implants develop at a pace with fast and moderately progressing normally hearing children. These findings would question age as a major determinant of linguistic development, at least for children who receive their cochlear implants fairly young, and it would thus argue against the strong influence attributed to age in "critical" and "sensitive" period viewpoints of development. Furthermore, for the cochlear-implanted children who progress at pace with fast and moderately developing normally hearing children, the results would not seem in line with a "critical period" viewpoint (Locke, 1997) with its narrow age range for beginning grammar. None of these children could have acquired a vocabulary by 2 to 3 years of age which would have been large enough to turn on the analytic mechanism for grammatical learning. For the children with very slow development, however, the "critical period" view could apply. The "sensitive period" viewpoint (Oyama 1979; Johnson & Newport, 1993) can accommodate either finding because it does not preclude linguistic progress equivalent to normal for the age range studied here. However, insofar as the "sensitive period" viewpoint relies heavily on age as a determining factor, it can only partly account for the data.

It was assumed here that over and above age, for children with cochlear implants their quality of hearing might contribute to their linguistic progress. For preoperative hearing this assumption is clearly supported by the fact that pre-operative hearing predicts subsequent linguistic growth even better than age at implantation. The influence of postoperative hearing impairment is more difficult to assess because no direct measure of discrimination of different grammatical morphemes is available. It is assumed here that children's persisting postoperative hearing impairment would make articles very difficult to acquire because they lack perceptual salience and can easily be missed in incoming speech by a hearing impaired person. Indeed, the magnitude of the difference between the two groups of children was larger for articles than for verbs, the latter marking being more salient at the end of content words. This could possibly be interpreted as some evidence for a selective effect of postoperative hearing impairment making low salience elements of the language particularly hard to acquire. However, other evidence is needed to substantiate this argument. Error analysis in the different inflectional paradigms, for instance, could reveal whether children with impaired hearing have particular problems with the article system in German. Yet, even for this data, age alone does not explain outcome. It would seem that children with cochlear implants create specific developmental pathways for grammar in accordance with maturational readiness for language learning and the specific auditory processing conditions of their hearing impairment.

ACKNOWLEDGMENTS

This research was funded by Deutsche Forschungsgemeinschaft, grant no. Sz 41/5-1 to the author and Thomas Lenarz, Medizinische Hochschule Hannover.

I am most grateful to the children and their parents who so willingly participated in this study. Sonja Arnhold-Kerri, Tanja Hampf, Elfrun Klauke, Stefanie Kraft and Claudia Steinbrink assisted in data collection, data transcription and analysis. I would like to thank them and Bodo Bertram and his team at Cochlear Implant Center Hannover for giving us their friendly support.

REFERENCES

Bates, E., Thal, D., & Jankowski, J. S. (1992). Early language development and its neural correlates. In S. J. Segalowitz & J. Rapin (Eds.) *Handbook of neuropsychology, Vol. 7, Child neuropsychology* (pp. 69-110). Amsterdam: Elsevier.

Fenson, L., Dale, P., Reznick, J. S., Bates, E., Thal, D., & Pethick, S. (1994). Variability in early communicative development. *Monographs of the Society for Research in Child Development, 59*(5).

Fryauf-Bertschy, H., Tyler, R. S., Kelsay, D. M. R., Gantz, B., & Woodworth, G. G. (1997). Cochlear implant use by prelingually deafened children: The influences of age at implant and length of device use. *Journal of Speech and Hearing Research, 40*, 183-199.

Johnson, J. E., & Newport, E. (1993). Critical period effects in second language learning: the influence of maturational state on the acquisition of English as a second language. In M. J. Johnson (Ed.) *Brain development and cognition* (pp. 248-282). Oxford: Blackwell.

Locke, J. L. (1997). A theory of neurolinguistic development. *Brain and Language, 58*, 265-326.

MacWhinney, B. (1987). The competition model. In B. MacWhinney (Ed.) *Mechanisms of language learning* (pp. 249-308). Hillsdale, NJ: Lawrence Erlbaum Associates

MacWhinney, B. (1995). *The CHILDES project: Tools for analyzing talk.* Hillsdale, NJ: Lawrence Erlbaum Associates.

Moerk, E. (1993). A behavioral analysis of controversial topics in first language acquisition: Reinforcements, corrections, modeling, input frequencies, and the three-term contingency pattern. *Journal of Psycholinguistic Research, 12*, 129-155.

Oyama, S. (1979). The concept of the sensitive period in developmental studies. *Merrill-Palmer Quaterly, 25*, 83-103.

Plunkett, K., & Marchman, V. (1993). From rote learning to system building: Acquiring verb morphology in children and connectionist nets. *Cognition, 48*, 21-69.

Snijders, T., Tellegen, P. J., Winkel, M., Laros, J., & Wijnberg-Williams, B. (1996). *SON-R 2½ -7 Snijders-Oomen Non-Verbaler Intelligenz test.* Frankfurt: Swets & Zeitlinger.

Szagun, G. (1999). *Rules for transcribing and analyzing German child language.* Institut für Kognitionsforschung, University of Oldenburg, Germany.

Uzgiris, I., & Hunt, J. (1975). *Assessment in infancy: Ordinal scales of psychological development.* Champaign: University of Illinois Press.

11

Acquisition of the Novel Name–Nameless Category (N3C) Principle by Young Korean Children with Down Syndrome

Misuk Kim and Youngjun Jang

The development of expressive language in young children with Down syndrome is reported to be severely retarded in comparison with typically developing children, although comprehension is well developed (Miller, 1987). However, there seem to be some discrepancies. For example, children with Down syndrome have rather advanced lexical development in comparison with other language domains such as grammar and semantic comprehension. It is reported that 20- to 36-month-old children with Down syndrome use the Novel Name–Nameless Category (N3C) principle to learn new words (Mervis & Bertrand, 1995). The N3C principle, or heuristic, refers to the way in which children "fast map" a new word to a basic level category. For example, a mother has bought her child a new set of toy animals comprising an elephant, a lion, a monkey and a giraffe. If the child is familiar with all the animals except the giraffe, and the mother says "where's the giraffe?" the child will look for the animal for which she does not yet have a name. Mervis and Bertrand (1993, 1994, 1995) suggested that young children's use of the N3C principle mainly contributes to lexical development. According to them, children use six different heuristics to learn new words: reference, extendability, object scope, categorical scope, the N3C principle, and conventionality.

The ability to use these heuristics is developmentally constrained. Young children are found to develop the principles of reference, extendability, and object scope at an early stage of lexical development, and gain the remaining heuristics, including the N3C principle, between the ages of 16 and 18 months. For example, parents of some infants reported that their children underwent a period of rapid vocabulary acquisition at age 16 months (Mervis & Bertrand, 1994), which implies that lexical development may be directly related to the use of the N3C principle. Mervis and Bertrand (1994) also argue that emergence of the N3C principle at 16 months corresponds with children's ability to categorize. Simple categorization ability, for example, 'exhaustive touching' (when children first touch one pile of objects then another), is stabilized in children who are 16 months old (Mandler & Bauer, 1988). In addition, the ability to group objects into two higher categories begins to develop between the ages of 16 and 18 months (Gopnik & Meltzoff, 1987, 1992).

Even though Mervis and Bertrand (1993, 1994, 1995) reported that young children with Down syndrome use the N3C principle and accordingly increase the rate at which they acquire new vocabulary, their language development does not seem to be contingent on general cognitive skills (Miller, 1999). In particular, the children with Down syndrome could not fast-map in production tasks and could not infer the likely referent of novel words in story contexts (Miller, Leddy & Leavitt, 1999). These contradictory results indicate that the lexical development of children with Down syndrome might proceed differently from typically developing children. The specific aim of this study, based on young Korean children with Down syndrome, is to test Mervis and Bertrand's (1993, 1994, 1995) hypothesis regarding the use of the N3C principle and lexical development, and the relation between the use of the N3C principle and categorization ability.

METHOD

Subjects

Twelve Korean children with Down syndrome (five girls and seven boys) aged between 47 months and 73 months participated in the present study. All of the children were enrolled in a preschool or welfare institution for special children. The children were reported to be sociable and active. Their level of verbal comprehension and production varied: the ratio of verbal comprehension to production (single words) ranged between 175/165 and 14/0.

Materials

Fast-mapping task. Three types of words were included, 'familiar', 'unfamiliar' and 'nonsense' words, and the words were distributed between four categories: transportation, animals, fruit, and objects. An experimenter pre-selected all of the familiar words used in the fast-mapping task by informal assessment. For example, pictorial charts of animals and fruit were displayed on the walls of the children's classrooms. The experimenter pointed to a picture and asked what it was. Although some of the children had difficulty pronouncing the familiar words, their comprehension of these words was perfect. Four words were included in each category. Regarding the unfamiliar words, eight picture cards were used representing two words in each category. Four distractor cards of unfamiliar objects were also included. For the comprehension task, each trial included four picture cards of familiar objects[1] and a picture card of an unfamiliar object. For the generalization task, three familiar picture cards, an unfamiliar picture card, and a distractor card were used. The selected unfamiliar and nonsense words are shown in Table 1.

Categorization task. Two categories were used, cars and people. Each category had four members represented by miniature objects.

TABLE 1
Unfamiliar and nonsense words used in the comprehension and generalization tasks.

Unfamiliar words	*Nonsense words*
Comprehension task	
Hoe	Kika
Gomang	Hella
Back-pipe	Tara
Anemone	Shalla
Generalization task	
Shovel	Mae
Mangtae	Hula
Flute	Bomi
Sea Urchin	Gora

Note. The real words are translations from the original Korean.

PROCEDURE

Fast-mapping

Two tasks, comprehension and generalization, were manipulated. Each child was seen individually and the procedure was the same for each child for each of the four categories of words. For the comprehension task, four familiar words and one unfamiliar word were included. The experimenter spread the picture cards from one category in front of the child and then proceeded to ask "show me the

---

[1] The familiar words for the comprehension task were selected in the following way: First, the experimenters asked the parents of the children to keep a record of words that their children seemed to understand or produce prior to their participation in the study. Second, the experimenters observed each child on two occasions for 20 minutes and compiled a list of words that were produced.

____ ". When two pictures representing familiar objects had been identified, the experimenter asked "show me the *sella*" (an unfamiliar word representing an unfamiliar object). For the generalization task, the experimenter presented five cards, consisting of three familiar words, one unfamiliar word from the same category, and a distractor word. The experimenter then went through the same procedure as above. In total, eight trials were conducted for each subject, four trials for the comprehension task and four trials for the generalization task. After the children had completed the eight trials they moved onto the categorization task.

Categorization Task

The children were given the eight miniature objects belonging to the two higher categories and were asked to group the things that went together. If the children did not respond, the experimenter allowed them to play with the objects for approximately five minutes. The instruction was then repeated. If the children simply touched the objects, or picked up two toys belonging to one cateogry, it was scored as a failure. To be successful, the child had to sort all of the objects into two separate groups. If the child could not classify the objects into two separate groups, he or she was considered to have failed the categorization task.

Vocabulary Assessment

The experimenters compiled a vocabulary list based on a language development profiled of 3- to 5-year old children with Down syndrome. Parents of the children were then asked to identify words on the list that their child could produce and understand.

RESULTS

Fast-Mapping

The results were inconsistent. In the comprehension test, four children who were at the average level of 150/120 words of comprehension/production, successfully fast-mapped nonsense words to the pictures of unfamiliar objects. However, five children whose language level was low (i.e. a comprehension/production ratio of 14/0), failed to fast-map in all 4 trials. Three other children succeeded on 50% of the task. For the generalization task, there were various responses. Only two children who succeeded in fast-mapping passed 75% of four trials. The remaining two children were 50% successful. The children who failed to fast-map were also unable to pass all four of the generalization trials. These results indicate that the use of the N3C principle is related to lexical development. That is, young children with Down syndrome who use the N3C principle also show a high rate of lexical development, compared to others who do not use it. These results seem to confirm Mervis and Bertrand's (1993, 1994, 1995) hypothesis.

Categorization Task

In the categorization task, seven children sorted the miniature objects into two separate groups, implying that they could successfully categorize the objects. This included two children who passed the fast-mapping task. Two other children with a high vocabulary level who passed the fast-mapping task, failed in the categorization task. Five children who did not pass the fast-mapping task succeeded in the categorization task. Three other children with a low vocabulary level who did not use the N3C principle failed the task. These results indicate that use of the N3C principle and the cognitive ability of categorization may not be directly related in young children with Down syndrome, contrary to the suggestion of Mervis and Bertrand (1993, 1994, 1995).

Vocabulary Assessment

The parental checklists showed that the children's vocabularies included words in the following categories: familiar objects, family, body, movement (verbs), animals, numbers, fruit, color, cookies and toys. Each category contained 12 to 26 words. The children's mothers reported that their children usually used gesture to express themselves and used nouns more than verbs. They also reported that they did not do anything special to encourage their child's lexical development. In addition, as far as speech production is concerned, only one parent reported that she tried to correct her child's pronunciation. These findings support those of Roch, Barratt and Leavitt (1999) who concluded that parents of young children with Down syndrome may have low motivation for educating their children and do not explore every avenue in terms of enhancing their children's language development.

DISCUSSION

The study explored the relation between lexical development, the N3C principle, and the categorization ability of young Korean children with Down syndrome. The results were inconsistent. Four children fast-mapped nonsense words to unfamiliar object pictures in the comprehension task. Eight children whose language level was low failed to fast-map in all four trials. In the generalization task, only two of the children who succeeded in the fast-mapping task passed

75% of four trials. The remaining two children achieved a 50% success rate over four trials. These results are consistent with Mervis and Bertrand's (1994) findings that hypothesized that young children with Down syndrome used the N3C heuristic between the ages of 16 and 18 months when their vocabulary underwent a period of rapid expansion.

In our study, young children with Down syndrome also showed this tendency. However, in the present study, the time at which various aspects of language development emerged (e.g. vocabulary level, categorization ability, and/or comprehension versus production levels), was not found to be consistent. Despite the fact that the mental age of the children exceeded 18 months (with the exception of one child), four children used the N3C principle, while the others did not. This fact strongly suggests that there may be individual differences in exploitation of the N3C principle and vocabulary development which are worthy of further investigation. What is important at this stage, however, is the fact that in the study, the use of the N3C principle and the cognitive ability of categorization was not found to be directly related. Some children who used the N3C principle failed the categorization task, while others who succeeded in the categorization task did not use it. This result contradicts the hypothesis of Mervis and Bertrand (1993, 1994, 1995). They hypothesized that young children mapped new vocabulary on the basis of conceptual categories, and thus, the ability to categorize emerged at the same time as use of the N3C principle. However, young children may, in fact, categorize earlier than Mervis and Bertrand (1993, 1994, 1995) suggested.

Traditionally, it was believed that young children represent concepts in terms of surface features and correlations rather than deep conceptual structures. From this perspective, it has been argued that older children (i.e. children above age 18 months) and adults can classify into hierarchical categories, whereas younger children (i.e. children below age 18 months) are only able to classify into basic categories. Recently, however, this point of view has been criticized. For example, Gelman (1990) and Wellman (1990) have explored the ability of young children to represent concepts at an early age in great detail and found that even 11-month-old children can categorize hierarchically. In fact, children as young as 8 months can represent concepts such as gravity (Spelke, 1991). These results suggest that infants also represent concepts in terms of the deep/abstract essence of an object rather than only on surface features. What this implies is that a specific cognitive ability, namely categorization, is developed at an early stage of life regardless of linguistic ability, and in particular, the N3C principle. Therefore, it is highly doubtful that categorization ability and lexical development are as closely related as Mervis and Bertrand (1994) suggested. The hypothesis needs to be further explored in a more systematic and focused way.

REFERENCES

Gelman, R. (1990). Structural constraints on cognitive development. *Cognitive Science, 14,* 14-39.

Gopnik, A., & Meltzoff, A. N. (1987). The development of categorization in the second year and its relation of other cognitive and linguistic development. *Child Development, 58,* 1523-1531.

Gopnik, A., & Meltzoff, A. N. (1992). Categorization and naming: Basic level sorting in eighteen-month-old and its relation to language. *Child Development, 63,* 1091-1103.

Mandler, J. M., & Bauer, P. J. (1988). The cradle of categorization: Is the basic level basic? *Cognitive Development, 3,* 247-264.

Mervis, C. B., & Bertrand, J. (1993). Acquisition of early object labels: the roles of operating principles and input. In A. Kaiser & D. B. Gray (Eds.), *Enhancing children's communication: Research foundations for intervention.* Baltimore: Brooks.

Mervis, C. B., & Bertrand, J. (1994). Acquisition of the novel name-nameless category (N3C) principle. *Child Development, 65,* 1646-1662.

Mervis, C. B., & Bertrand, J. (1995). Acquisition of the novel name-nameless category (N3C) principle by young children who have Down syndrome. *American Journal on Mental Retardation, 100,* 231-243.

Miller, J. F. (1987). Language and communication characteristics of children with Down syndrome. In S. M. Pueschel, C. Tingly, J. E. Rynders, A. C. Crocker & D. M. Crutcher (Eds.), *New perspectives on Down syndrome.* Baltimore: Brooks.

Miller, J. F. (1999). Profiles of language development. In J. F. Miller, M. Leddy & L. Leavitt (Eds.), *Improving the communication of people with Down syndrome.* Baltimore: Brooks.

Miller, J., Leddy, M., & Leavitt, L. (Eds.). (1999). *Improving the communication of people with Down syndrome.* Baltimore: Brooks.

Roch, M. A., Barratt, M. S., & Leavitt, L. A. (1999). Individual differences in mother's communication with their young children with Down's syndrome. In J. F. Miller, M. Leddy & L. Leavitt (Eds.), *Improving the communication of people with Down's syndrome.* Baltimore: Brooks.

Spelke, K. (1991). Physical knowledge in infancy: Reflections on Piaget's theory. In S. Carey & R. Gelman (Eds.), *Epigenesis of the mind: Essays in biology and knowledge.* Hillsdale, NJ: Lawrence Erlbaum Associates.

Wellman, H. M. (1990). *The child's theory of mind.* Cambridge, MA: MIT Press.

12

Acquisition of Syllabic Structure in Egyptian Colloquial Arabic

Wafaa Ammar

THE SYLLABLE IN ARABIC PHONOLOGY

The syllable plays an important role in both colloquial and classical Arabic phonology (Bird & Blackburn, 1990; Kay, 1987; McCarthy, 1981). The importance of the syllable is deeply rooted in the history of the analysis of Arabic. Major descriptions of Arabic by Old Arab Grammarians tended to ignore stress, intonation, and tempo, while providing lengthy descriptions of the alternations of vowels and consonants (ElSaaran, 1951). The metrics of Arabic were also described in terms of successions of vowels and consonants, for example, in terms of syllables (Prince, 1989; Maling, 1973).

The syllable derives its prominent status in Arabic phonology partly because word stress is completely predictable from the syllable structure of the word (Welden, 1980) so that analysis of stress patterns must be based on an analysis of syllable structure (Abdo, 1969; Angoujard, 1990; Birkeland, 1954; Harms, 1981; Janssens, 1972; Larudee, 1973; McCarthy, 1979; and Welden, 1980). There is also evidence that intonation is predictable in terms of syllable structure. The intonation of Arabic is monotonous; there are few types of pitch accents and contours. Pitch accents are always associated with stressed syllables (Abdalla, 1960; Mitchell, 1990; Rifaat, 1991, 1994).

Description of Syllable Structure in Colloquial Egyptian Arabic (CEA)

Broselow (1976), Gaber (1972), and Mitchell (1978) provided descriptions of Arabic syllable structure. The following generalizations about CEA syllable structure can be made:

- There are five syllable types: CV, CVC, CV:, CV:C, and CVCC.
- CV and CVC are considered short (or 'light') and the rest are long (or 'heavy'). Heavy or long syllables are always stressed, that is, have the primary stress. More generally, these concepts express the prosodic weight or load of the syllables.
- There is only one heavy or long syllable per word.
- CV and CVC occur anywhere in the word (e.g. /simiʕtu/ 'you heard' (plural), and /mistaʁrab/ 'he is wondering'); CV: occurs prefinally (e.g. /tajja:ra/ 'an aeroplane'); and CV:C and CVCC occur only word finally (e.g. /kita:b/ 'a book' and /katabt/ ' I wrote').
- All syllable types are allowed in monosyllabic words, for example, /di/ 'this' (feminine), /kol/ 'eat' (imperative), /la:/ 'no', /mo:z/ 'banana', /bard/ 'cold' (noun). Nevertheless, monosyllabic words of CV, CVC, CV: are relatively infrequent.
- A word is composed of one to seven syllables (e.g. /ʃa:b/ 'he grew old', /ʔaxu:k/ 'your brother', /madrasa/ 'school', /ʕarabijja/ 'car', /ʔistalamtuhum/ 'I received them', /ʔistalamithu:lak/ 'she received it for you', and /mastalamithumluku:ʃ/ 'she did not receive it for you'). However, words with six or seven syllables are comparatively rare.

The Present Study

This study describes syllabic structure in the speech of two- to three-year-old normal Egyptian children. The parameters investigated were the types of syllables that a child acquires at this age and the combinations of syllables found in polysyllabic words. In addition, the effects of syllable processes on word prosody were examined. The results suggest that certain syllable types should be given priority in designing a therapeutic program for children with delayed language development.

METHOD

Subjects

The subjects were ten children (six boys and four girls), aged 2 to 3 years (mean age = 2;4 years), from two middle-class nurseries in Alexandria. All of the children were considered to have normal language development, based on the children's files and teachers' reports. None of the children were bilingual.

Data Collection

A speech sample was elicited from each child using five large color pictures of different situations, a word list, and by engaging them in conversation. The aim was to obtain a large, comprehensive, representative sample of speech from each child. Each speech sample contained target words of different syllabic structures representative of the lexicon for the relevant age (Karam, 1990).

The sample was transcribed 'live' using a broad transcription and also recorded on tape cassette for later verification and further analysis. The length of a session ranged between 30 and 70 minutes. The number of words elicited from each child ranged between 75 and 334, with a mean of 235.

Analysis

1. The incidence of each syllable type by each child was ascertained, and expressed as a percentage of all the syllables the child produced. Then the percentage occurrence of each syllable type was computed across all children.

2. All the different combinations, normal or abnormal, of syllabic structures in polysyllabic words were computed in the speech sample from each child, and across all children.

3. High scoring syllable combinations were noted with a view to detecting any tendencies towards the early acquisition of certain combinations.

4. Stress placement was recorded in multisyllabic words. In most cases, stress position was perceptually clear. In the few cases where it was doubtful, a wave editing program (Speech Analyzer version 1.5, test version 10.6 by JAARS-ICTS, Waxhaw, NC) was used to help locate the stress position from the acoustic record. In Arabic, stress is associated with increase in fundamental frequency, intensity, and duration, although fundamental frequency is the most important factor (Rifaat, 1987).

RESULTS AND DISCUSSION

Incidence of Syllable Types

Nine out of ten (90%) of the subjects demonstrated all syllable types in their speech, suggesting that most 2- to 3-year-old children will have acquired mastery of the full range of syllable types of CEA. All syllables, except CVCC, gained 100% correct production in the speech of all subjects. CVCC did not occur at all in the speech of one child, although it occasionally underwent simplification processes in the speech of some others. Simplification processes comprised production of CVCC either as CV:C or CVC.

Syllable Structure Combinations in Words

Number of syllables. The maximum number of syllables in a word was five (one occurrence each in the speech of two subjects). Words with four syllables occurred in the speech of nine children, although they were usually limited to one type of structure. Words with two and three syllables occurred in all children's speech, with a variety of syllable structures.

Monosyllabic words. Monosyllabic words were composed mainly of two types: CVCC and CV:C. CV:C words were the most frequent. This was because they appeared as the correct realizations of target words and as the result of simplifying processes operating on other target syllable structures.   For example, CVCCV:C structure was realized as CV:C: /mufta:ħ/ 'key' realized as [ta:ħ].

Polysyllabic words. Table 1 summarizes the syllable combinations found in disyllabic words and the percentage of subjects who produced them. These structures were realized correctly as target or as simplification for tri- and quadro-syllabic words. The syllable combinations shown in rows 9 and 11 of Table 1 are illegal in adult CEA. The structure in row 9 violates syllable position rules by realizing target CVCCV with a long vowel in the first syllable (e.g. /radjo/ 'radio' as [ra:djo]).   The structure in row 10 resulted from the addition of the definite article /ʔil/ to certain words. The structure in row 11 also violated the syllable position rules in CEA due to the prolongation of the first vowel.

There are 25 different syllable combinations among the trisyllabic words, 17 of which had an incidence of between 17% and 50%. Most of these latter structures are nonadult pronunciations resulting from various simplification processes. Table 2 shows the structures that had an incidence of over 50%. The results suggest that children prefer open-syllable structures. They also suggest that children prefer structures with long-vowel syllables.

TABLE 1
Percentage of occurrence of different syllabic structures of disyllabic words.

	Structure	Example	Percentage
1	CV: /CV	[ko:ra] 'ball'	100%
2	CV/CV:C	[siri:r] 'bed'	100%
3	CV: /CVC	[χa:jif] 'afraid'	100%
4	CV/CVC	[laban] 'milk'	100%
5	CVC/CV	[majja] 'water'	100%
6	CVC/CVC	[ʔaḥmar] 'red'	100%
7	CV/CV	[hena] 'here'	90%
8	CVC/CV:C	[mufta:ħ] 'key'	90%
9	CV:C/CV	[ra:djo]* 'radio'	70%
10	CVC/CVCC	[ʔilbent] 'the girl'	40%
11	CV:C/CVC	[je:ʁsil]* 'he washes'	40%

TABLE 2
Percentage occurrence of different syllabic structures in trisyllabic words.

	Structure	Example	Percentage
1	CV/CV:/CV	[ʕaru:sa] 'doll'	100%
2	CV/CV/CV	[waraʔa] 'paper'	90%
3	CV/CV/CV:C	[manaχi:r] 'nose'	80%
4	CV/CV:/CVC	[baṭa:ṭis] 'potatoes'	80%
5	CV/CV/CVC	[ʃarabit] 'she drank'	70%
6	CV/CVC/CV	[miṛabba] 'jam'	60%
7	CVC/CV/CV:C	[bortoʔa:n] 'oranges'	60%

There were 16 different structures in quadrosyllabic words. Only one of these scored 90%. The remaining structures had one type that scored 40% and the rest had less than 40%, with a majority of 10%. The only frequent structure was the series of open syllables CV/CV/CV:/CV, as in /ṭarabe:za/ 'a table'.

Effect of Syllable Structure Processes on Prosody

The results provide evidence to support the hypothesis that Arabic prosody is dominated by syllable structure. Without exception, whenever a child changed the syllabic structure of the word, they preserved the prosodic weight of the altered syllable to keep the stress relations unchanged. The following different strategies were observed:

1. Long syllables were altered to short ones only in monosyllabic words, never in polysyllabic words.

2. Long syllables never underwent syllable deletion processes.
3. Following syllable deletion within polysyllabic words, a short syllable would be changed to long where this was necessary to preserve the stress pattern, e.g. /tifʼtaḥu/ "you open it" was changed to [ˈtaːḥu].

Distribution and shape of pitch accents were found to be normal. All children were capable of producing all types of accents (H, L, H+L, and L+H; Pierrehumbert, 1980). As reported by Rifaat (1994), stressed syllables were always associated with a peak, for example, an H accent. Final accents were always H+L or L+H.

CONCLUSIONS

1. Most children acquire all syllable types in CEA between age 2 and 3. Children age 2 and 3 prefer short words containing a maximum of three syllables. Quadrosyllabic words tend to be limited to one type of structure. Open-syllable structures are the most frequent in polysyllabic words. Closed syllables usually contain a long vowel. Prolongation of vowels seemed to be a preferred technique to facilitate articulation.
2. Syllable structure processes always preserved the prosodic structure of the target form.

IMPLICATIONS FOR THERAPY

When designing a therapeutic program for children with delayed language development, the results of this study suggest that the following syllable types and structures should be selected on the basis that they are most immediately accessible to young children:

- For monosyllabic words, CV:C type.
- For disyllabic words, CV:C/CV, then CV/CV:C.
- For trisyllabic words, CV/CV:/CV, then CV/CV/CV:C, or CV/CV:/CVC.
- For quadrosyllabic words, CV/CV/CV:/CV.

REFERENCES

Abdo, D.A. (1969). Stress and Arabic phonolgy. Unpublished PhD thesis, University of Illinois.

Abdalla, A.G. (1960). An instrumental study of the intonation of Egyptian Colloquial Arabic. Unpublished PhD thesis, University of Michigan.

Angoujard, J-. P. (1990). *Metrical structure of Arabic.* Dordrecht: Foris Publications.

Bird, S., & Blackburn B. (1990). A logical approach to Arabic phonology. *Proceedings of the fifth conference of the European chapter of the association for computational linguistics,* (pp. 89-94).

Birkeland, H. (1954). *Stress patterns in Arabic.* Oslo: Dybwad.

Broselow, E. I. (1976). The phonology of Egyptian Arabic. Unpublished PhD thesis, University of Massachusetts.

ElSaaran, M. (1951). A critical study of the phonetic observations of the Arab Grammarians. Unpublished PhD thesis, University of London, SOAS.

Gaber, A. M. (1972). The phonology of the verbal piece in Cairo Egyptian Arabic. Unpublished PhD thesis, University of London.

Harms, R. T. (1981). A backwards metrical approach to Cairo Arabic stress. *Linguistic Analysis, 4,* 429-450.

Janssens, G. (1972). Stress in Arabic and word structure in the Modern Arabic dialects. *Orientalia Gandensia V,* 1-167.

Karam, L. (1990). *Qawa'im Al-kalimt Al-'kthar 'intashran fi Aḥdth Al-atfl min ᶜumr ᶜm ḥata sittat 'aᶜwm.* Cairo: The Egyptian National Book Institution.

Kay, M. (1987). Non-concatenative finite-state morphology. *Proceedings of the 3rd meeting of the European chapter of the association for computational linguistics,* pp. 2-10.

Larudee, F. (1973). Word stress in the spoken Arabic of Cairo. *Language Sciences, 6,* 31-34.

Maling, J. M. (1973). The theory of Classical Arabic metrics. Unpublished PhD thesis, MIT.

McCarthy, J. (1979). On stress and syllabification. *Linguistic Inquiry, 12,* 443-465.

McCarthy, J. (1981). A prosodic theory of nonconcatenative morphology. *Linguistic Inquiry, 12,* 373-413.

Mitchell, T. F. (1978). Prominence and syllabification in Arabic. In S. Al-Ani (Ed.), *Readings in Arabic linguistics* (pp. 329-355). Indiana: Indiana University Linguistics Club.

Mitchell, T. F. (1990). *Pronouncing Arabic.* Oxford: Clarendon Press.

Pierrehumbert, J. (1980). The phonology and phonetics of English intonation. Unpublished PhD thesis, MIT.

Prince, A. (1989). Metrical forms. In P. Kiparsky & G. Youmans (Eds.), *Phonetics and phonology: Vol. 1 rhythm and meter* (pp. 45-80). New York: Academic.

Rifaat K. (1987). The acoustic correlates of stress in colloquial Egyptian Arabic. Unpublished MA thesis, University of Alexandria.

Rifaat K. (1991). The intonation of Arabic: An experimental study. Unpublished PhD thesis, University of Alexandria.

Rifaat K. (1994). The pitch accents of Egyptian Arab children. *Proceedings of the colloquim on Arabic linguistics.* Bucharest: University of Bucharest, Center for Arab Studies (Vol. 1; pp. 219-232).

Welden, A. (1980). Stress in Cairo Arabic. *Studies in the Linguistic Sciences, 2,* 99-120.

13

Phonological Breakdowns in Children with Specific Language Impairment

Kristine M. Yont, Adele W. Miccio and Lynne E. Hewitt

Children with specific language impairment (SLI) have deficits in morphosyntactic, lexical, and pragmatic development that limit their communicative success (Fey, Warr-Leeper, Webber, & Disher, 1988). In addition, many children with SLI have concomitant speech disorders (Shriberg, Tomblin, & McSweeny, 1999) that further compound their communication difficulties. The phonological characteristics of children with SLI have been reported in many studies (see Leonard, 1998 for a review). Early studies found that children with SLI have errors in their production of individual consonants and vowels (Farwell, 1972; Leonard, 1973). More recent inquiries report homonymy in the productions of children with SLI (Leonard, Camarata, Schwartz, Chapman, & Messick, 1985), difficulty with certain feature contrasts such as voicing (Catts & Jenson, 1983), and unusual error patterns (Fey, 1985; Leonard & Brown, 1984; Leonard, 1985). Children with SLI also have phonological errors resulting from contextual influences within and between words (Chiat, 1989; Grunwell, 1992). For example, Leonard's (1982) description of the phonological characteristics of children with SLI revealed that almost a quarter of errors in stop consonants were attributable to harmony. In addition, Leonard (1982) reported that children with SLI experienced errors due to syllable reduplication approximately 15% of the time, and syllable reductions almost 40% of the time, during extended conversations.

Contextual paradigms used to measure the phonological abilities of children with SLI vary across studies. Phonology is frequently assessed using single-word naming tasks; however, these instruments are limited in speech sound sampling (Lowe, 1996). Recent approaches to phonological assessment advocate conversational speech sampling as the measurement procedure of choice, because speech production can be examined in real communicative contexts

(Morrison & Shriberg, 1992). Due to the complexity of the communication process, children experience instances when a conversational partner does not understand their message (Ninio & Snow, 1996), resulting in a breakdown. Breakdowns from phonological errors occur in the conversations of typically developing children (Garvey, 1977; Gallagher, 1981). Thus, children with known speech production disorders are at-risk for phonological breakdowns during extended conversations. In a recent investigation, Yont (1999) found that preschoolers with SLI experienced significantly more breakdowns than their typically developing peers during interactions with their mothers due to pragmatic, content, and phonological errors. Phonological breakdowns accounted for over one-third of the total breakdowns found in this SLI group. Analysis of phonological breakdowns offers a unique opportunity to examine types of production problems that reduce children's communication success. The current research provides a descriptive analysis of the nature of phonological breakdowns in preschoolers with SLI during conversations with familiar partners.

METHOD

Participants

Twelve children from Yont's (1999) investigation participated in this study (ages 3;5 through 5;3 years). Children were monolingual, native English speakers with histories unremarkable for neurological, social, emotional, or behavioral problems. All of the children had normal hearing sensitivity (per ASHA guidelines, 1990) based on screenings administered at the time of testing, and age-appropriate nonverbal cognitive ability as measured by the Columbia Mental Maturity Scale (CMMS; Burgmeister, Blum, & Lorge, 1972). Children scored at least one standard deviation below the mean on the Peabody Picture Vocabulary Test-3 (PPVT-3; Dunn & Dunn, 1997) and mean length of utterance in morphemes (MLU-m; Miller & Chapman, 1981). Each child had a concomitant phonological disorder as measured by the Goldman-Fristoe Test of Articulation (GFTA; Goldman & Fristoe, 1986) and Percentage of Consonants Correct (PCC; Shriberg & Kwiatkowski, 1982). Children with severe phonological disorders, defined by a PCC score < 50%, were excluded from the study because their conversations would be highly unintelligible.

Procedure

Speech and language testing was completed in each child's home. A naturalistic 30-minute caregiver–child language sample was collected, and mothers were encouraged to interact with their children as they normally would during spontaneous play.

Transcription and Coding

Mother–child interactions were orthographically transcribed using the Systematic Analysis of Language Transcripts (SALT, Miller & Chapman 1991) and analyzed for breakdowns using the Breakdown Coding System (BCS, Yont, Hewitt & Miccio, 2000). Consistent with the literature on conversational breakdowns, the BCS identifies children's breakdowns by the presence of an adult clarification request, such as neutral requests (e.g., "Huh?" or "What?") and more specific requests (e.g., "Who is Jane?"; Garvey, 1977). The BCS then describes breakdowns according to potential problems, including phonological, lexical, content rejection, pragmatic, nonverbal, incomplete, and low volume errors.

For the purpose of this study, children's phonological breakdowns were transcribed phonetically using the conventions of the International Phonetic Association (IPA, 1999). Children's productions resulting in phonological breakdowns were then described according to the error types. Possible errors included the following: unintelligible (i.e., reduplicated CV syllables that do not resemble adult words), sound additions or deletions, contextual errors (i.e., assimilation and reduplication), syllable errors, vowel errors, and unusual errors (i.e., initial consonant deletion, /h/ replacement) that are not characteristic of typical speech development.

Reliability

Each breakdown was transcribed by the first author according to IPA conventions. A second judge independently transcribed 20% of the data. Point-by-point inter-judge agreement was 82% for the phonological breakdowns.

RESULTS

The SLI group had a total of 123 phonological breakdowns. The majority of phonological breakdowns resulted from unintelligible speech, harmony and reduplication, and sound substitutions and deletions. The remaining phonological breakdowns were from syllable additions or deletions, vowel errors, and unusual error patterns. The frequencies of phonological breakdown types are provided in Table 1. The three most common phonological breakdowns will be discussed in detail in the following sections.

TABLE 1
Frequency of phonological breakdown types for children with SLI.

Error Type	Total Number	Range
Unintelligible	53	3-9
Subst/deletion	30	0-9
Harmony	25	0-8
Unusual errors	5	0-4
Syllable changes	5	0-2
Vowel changes	5	0-2

Note. subst/deletion = sound substitutions and deletions.

Unintelligible Breakdowns

Each child experienced at least three or more phonological breakdowns due to unintelligible utterances. Example 1 describes a phonological breakdown resulting from an unintelligible production. Here, Jimmy and his mother were playing with playdough and Jimmy responded to his mother's question with the unintelligible production, [pitɑ'keɪt]. His mother signaled a breakdown by asking the clarification request, "Hmm?" Jimmy did not repair his breakdown, and rather than asking for clarification again, Jimmy's mother continued the conversation by questioning his activity.

Example 1:
Child: {Tries to get playdough out of the container}.
Mom: What are we gonna make?
Child: [ə'tɪs]
Child: [pitɑ'keɪt]   [UNINTELLIGIBLE].
Mom: Hmm [CLARIFICATION REQUEST]?
Child: {Plays with playdough already on the table}.
Mom: Are you gonna use your tools?
Child: No.
         [no]

Sound Substitution and Deletion Breakdowns

The second most common phonological breakdown occurred when children produced sound substitutions and/or deletions that made their utterances difficult to understand. In Example 2, Mary had several sound substitutions and deletions in her production of "the big crack," including [d] for [θ] in "the," omission of

[g] in "big," and cluster reduction of [kr] to [k]. Mary's mother asked the neutral clarification request, "What?" to signal a breakdown. Mary's response to her mother's clarification request resulted in a looped phonological breakdown where her attempted repair resulted in a subsequent breakdown, identified by her mother's second clarification request, "A big crack?" Mary repaired the breakdown with "Yes" and the conversation continued.

Example 2:
Child: The big crack [SUBSTITUTION & DELETION].
           [deɪbə'kæk]
Mom: What [CLARIFICATION REQUEST]?
Child: A big crack [SUBSTITUTION & DELETION].
           [əbɪgkæk]
Mom: A big crack [CLARIFICATION REQUEST]?
Child: Yes.
           [jɛs]
Mom: Yeah.

Harmony and Reduplication Breakdowns

Harmony (i.e. articulation of one phonological unit is influenced by another unit in the same word of phrase) and reduplication (i.e. one syllable of a word is repeated) resulted in the third most frequent type of phonological breakdowns. As illustrated in Example 3, Johnny's production of [t] in "cut" harmonized with the [k] resulting in [tʌt]. His mother's clarification request identified the breakdown and asked Johnny for confirmation that he was saying "cut."

Example 3:
Mom: And then what are we gonna do with it [= playdough]?
Child: I cut it {making cutting motion} [HARMONY].
           [aɪ'tʌt:eɪ]
Mom: Cut [CLARIFICATION REQUEST]?
Child: Yeah.
           [jæ]
Mom: Why?

DISCUSSION

Analysis of phonological breakdowns highlighted the types of speech production errors that limited communicative competence in children with developmental speech and language disorders. This study identified the important relationship between intelligibility and successful communication. The SLI group experienced almost half of their breakdowns from unintelligible utterances, many of which resembled babbling (i.e., reduplicated CV syllables). Findings also indicated that mothers had difficulty understanding children with SLI because their productions contained within-word and between-word harmony and reduplication. Phonological breakdowns from harmony and reduplication errors accounted for approximately one-fifth of this group's total communication failures during connected speech. These findings extend earlier research on the phonological characteristics of children with SLI by indicating that context-related errors impair successful communication of children with SLI.

Clinically, findings highlight the need to assess children's phonological skills during connected speech in order to evaluate the effects of harmony and intelligibility past the word level. Although sound substitution and deletion errors and syllable-related errors, will occur in children's productions on single word articulation tests, harmony across words, a common type of phonological breakdown in connected speech, will not occur in citation form. Similarly, unintelligible productions resulting in the greatest number of phonological breakdowns for the SLI group in this study would not be evident from articulation tests since the intended production is known at the outset. In summary, two of the primary error types that reduced communicative competence in the current sample of children are generally not measured on single-word articulation tests. These findings support Morrison and Shriberg's (1992) argument for the use of conversational speech sampling to assess children's phonological skills.

ACKNOWLEDGMENTS

This study was funded in part from a 1998 Graduate Student Scholarship from the American Speech-Language-Hearing Association and NIH (NIDCD, F32-DC00419-01; NICHD, RO3-HD37586).

REFERENCES

American Speech-Language-Hearing Association (1990). Guidelines for screening hearing impairment and middle ear disorders. *Asha, 32(Suppl. 2)*, 17-24.

Burgemeister, B., Blum, L., & Lorge, I. (1972). *The Columbia Mental Maturity Scale.* New York: Harcourt Brace Jovanovich.

Catts, H., & Jensen, P. (1983). Speech timing of phonologically disordered children: Voicing contrasts of initial and final stop consonants. *Journal of Speech and Hearing Research, 26*, 501-510.

Chiat, S. (1989). The relation between prosodic structure, syllabification and segmental realization: Evidence from a child with fricative stopping. *Clinical Linguistics & Phonetics, 5*, 329-337.

Dunn, L., & Dunn, L. (1997). *Peabody picture vocabulary test (Third Edition).* Circle Pines, MN: American Guidance Service.

Farwell, C. (1972). A note on the production of fricatives in linguistically deviant children. *Papers and Reports on Child Language Development, 4*, 93-101.

Fey, M. (1985). Articulation and phonology: Inextricable constructs in speech pathology. *Human Communication, 9*, 7-16.

Fey, M. E., Warr-Leeper, G., Webber, S. A., & Disher, L. M. (1988). Repairing children's repairs: Evaluation and facilitation of children's clarification requests and responses. *Topics in Language Disorders, 8*, 63-84.

Gallagher, T. M. (1981). Contingent query sentences with adult-child discourse. *Journal of Child Language, 8*, 51-82.

Garvey, G. (1977). The contingent query: A dependent act in conversation. In M. Lewis & L. A. Rosenblum (Eds.), *Interaction, conversation, and the development of language* (pp. 63-93). New York: Wiley.

Goldman, R., & Fristoe, M. (1986). *Goldman-Fristoe test of articulation.* Circle Pines, MN: American Guidance Service.

Grunwell, P. (1992). Assessment of child phonology in the clinical context. In C. Ferguson, L. Menn, & C. Stoel-Gammon (Eds.), *Phonological development: Models, research, implications* (pp. 457-483). Timonium, MD: York.

International Phonetics Association (1999). *Handbook of the International Phonetic Association.* Cambridge, UK: Cambridge University Press.

Leonard, L. B. (1982). Phonological deficits in children with developmental language impairment. *Brain and Language, 16*, 73-86.

Leonard, L. B. (1985). Unusual and subtle phonological behavior in the speech of phonologically disordered children. *Journal of Speech and Hearing Disorders, 50*, 4-13.

Leonard, L. B. (1998). *Children with specific language impairment.* Cambridge, MA: MIT Press.

Leonard, L. B. (1973). The nature of deviant articulation. *Journal of Speech and Hearing Disorders, 38,* 156-161.

Leonard, L. B., & Brown, B. (1984). The nature and boundaries of phonologic categories: A case study of an unusual phonologic pattern in a language-impaired child. *Journal of Speech and Hearing Disorders, 49,* 215-224.

Leonard, L. B., Camarata, S., Schwartz, R., Chapman, K., & Messick, C. (1985). Homonymy and the voiced-voiceless distinction in the speech of children with specific language impairment. *Journal of Speech and Hearing Research, 28,* 419-428.

Lowe, R. (1996). *Phonology: Assessment and intervention applications in speech pathology.* Baltimore: Williams & Wilkins.

Miller, J. F., & Chapman, R. (1981). The relation between age and mean length of utterance in morphemes. *Journal of Speech and Hearing Research, 24,* 154-161.

Miller, J. F., & Chapman, R. S. (1991*). SALT: A Computer program for the systematic analysis of language transcripts.* Computer Software. Madison: University of Wisconsin.

Morrison, J. A., & Shriberg, L. D. (1992). Articulation testing versus conversational speech sampling. *Journal of Speech and Hearing Research, 35,* 259-273.

Ninio, A., & Snow, C. E. (1996). *Pragmatic development: Essays in developmental science.* Boulder, CO: Westview.

Shriberg, L., & Kwiatkowski, J. (1982). Phonological disorders III. A procedure for assessing severity of involvement. *Journal of Speech and Hearing Disorders, 47,* 256-270.

Shriberg, L., Tomblin, B., & McSweeny, J. L. (1999). Prevalence of speech delay in 6-year-old children with comorbidity with language impairment. *Journal of Speech, Language and Hearing Research, 42,* 1461-1481.

Yont, K. M. (1999). The source of conversational breakdowns in children with specific language impairment and children with typical language development. Unpublished doctoral thesis, Pennsylvania State University, University Park, PA.

Yont, K. M., Hewitt, L. E., & Miccio, A. W. (2000). A coding system for describing conversational breakdowns in preschool children. *American Journal of Speech Language Pathology, 9,* 300-309.

14

Phonological Saliency and Phonological Acquisition by Putonghua Speaking Children: A Cross-Populational Study

Li Wei, Zhu Hua and Barbara Dodd

Zhu & Dodd (2000) proposed a concept of phonological saliency in their explanation of the order of acquisition of different syllable components by Putonghua-speaking children. Phonological saliency is a syllable-based, language-specific concept. It is affected by a combination of several factors, including the status of the component in the syllable structure (a compulsory component is more salient than an optional one), the capacity of a component in differentiating lexical meaning of a syllable (a component which is more capable of distinguishing lexical information is more salient than one which carries less lexical information), and the number of permissible choices within a component in the syllable structure (the more permissible choices a component has, the less salient it is).

Using data from a cross-sectional study of normally developing Putonghua-speaking children aged 1;6-4;6, Zhu & Dodd (2000) suggested that syllable components with higher phonological saliency should be acquired earlier and are less likely to be subject to speech disorders and hearing impairment than syllable components with lower phonological saliency. This chapter will further investigate this hypothesis using data from a cross-populational study comparing the acquisition of syllable components by three groups of children: normally developing children, children with speech disorders and children with hearing impairment. It is believed that a cross-populational perspective, together with a cross-linguistic perspective, is crucial in identifying 'developmental universals' and providing answers to some major theoretical questions about language acquisition (Zhu, 2000).

The chapter begins with a brief discussion of Putonghua phonology and a hypothesis of the saliency of different syllable components. The three studies of normally developing children, children with speech disorders and children with hearing impairment are then presented and discussed. A general discussion of the findings concludes the chapter.

PUTONGHUA PHONOLOGY

Putonghua, literally 'common speech', is the language variety which has been promoted by the mainland Chinese government since the 1950s. It is a standardized language, based on the phonological and grammatical system of *Beifang* varieties of Chinese (which is often referred to as Mandarin in the English-speaking world), and is widely used in the mass media and taught in schools.

In a Putonghua syllable, the onset and coda are optional and the vowel in the nucleus is compulsory. The onset can be one of 21 consonants and the coda can only be one of the two consonants, /n/ and /ŋ/. /ŋ/ can only occur in coda. There are 22 vowels and four lexical tones in Putonghua. Differences in tones can change the meaning of morphemes. High level tones are register tones and the other three are contour tones which are a combination of two or more basic tones (Katamba, 1989).

According to the definition of phonological saliency (Zhu & Dodd, 2000), tones have the highest saliency in Putonghua: it is compulsory for every syllable; change of tones would change lexical meaning; and there are only four alternative choices. Syllable-initial consonants have the lowest saliency of the four syllable components: their presence is optional (not all the syllables have syllable-initial consonants); and there are 21 syllable-initial phonemes. Vowels are compulsory syllable components. However, the relatively large number of options (21 in total including simple vowels, diphthongs and triphthongs) lowers their saliency. Although there are only two syllable-final consonants, their saliency is undermined by their optional presence in the syllable structure. Briefly, the saliency ranking of the syllable components of Putonghua (from the highest to the lowest) is tone, syllable-final consonant/vowel, and syllable-initial consonant.

STUDY 1: LONGITUDINAL STUDY OF NORMALLY DEVELOPING CHILDREN

Participants

Four children (referred to as J.J., Z.J., H.Y., and Z.W.) in Beijing took part in a one-year-long longitudinal study. All of the children were healthy and had no hearing impairment according to their medical records. Their motor development was reported to be within normal range. The children were the only child in the family. All the parents were Putonghua speakers. The subject information is summarized in Table 1.

TABLE 1
Subject information.

	Sex	Age range	Age of four word point	Total number of tokens in the data
J.J.	girl	1;1.15-2;0.15	1;2	947
Z.J.	boy	1;0-2;0.15	1;4	683
H.Y.	boy	0;10.15-2;0.15	1;2	890
Z.W.	girl	1;2-1;8	1;2.15	432

Note. Four word point is defined by Vihman (1996) as the approximate beginning of lexical use.

Data collection took place every 15 days. In each data collection session, the mothers were asked to talk with the children while playing games together. They were also asked to repeat the children's words when they could so that the target/adult forms were recorded on tape for ease of transcription by the non-participating researcher later. The conversation was recorded using a Sony professional micro-recorder.

A maximum of 50 tokens from each session were transcribed using the International Phonetic Alphabet (IPA). Inter-transcriber reliability (on 10% of the samples) for syllable-initial word-initial, syllable-initial within-word, syllable-final word-final, and syllable-final within-word consonants was 94.3%, 92.9%, 98.5% and 98.1%, respectively. Imitated productions from the children were marked and included in the data analysis, following Ferguson & Farwell's arguments (1975). The target words the children were attempting were identified either on the basis of the mother's repetition of the children's vocalizations or the contexts, using the criteria proposed by Vihman and McCune (1994).

Results

The age of emergence and stabilization of vowels and consonants. Table 2 lists the age at which the children were able to produce a vowel phonologically correctly for the first time (i.e. emergence). Despite individual differences, some patterns were identifiable in the development of vowels in the children. For example, among the simple vowels, the central low vowel /ɐ/ and back high vowel /u/ were the earliest to emerge in the four children: as early as 1;2 in two children; the retroflex vowel /ɚ/ and the back vowel /o/ seemed to be the last simple vowels to emerge in the children's output (as late as 1;9 in one child, and two children did not use the sound in their utterances).

TABLE 2
Age of emergence of vowels (in years, months, days).

Vowels	J.J.	Z.J.	H.Y.	Z.W.
i	1;3.0	1;4.0	1;5.0	1;2.15
y	1;3.15	1;7.0	1;8.15	1;6.0
u	1;2.15	1;4.0	1;2.0	1;3.0
ɤ	1;5.15	1;9.0	1;2.0	1;2.15
o	1;7.15	1;9.0	?	1;7.15
ɐ	1;2.0	1;4.0	1;2.0	1;2.15
ɚ	1;7.15	1;7.0	?	?
ae	1;5.15	1;8.0	1;4.15	1;5.15
ɑo	1;4.0	1;7.0	1;3.0	1;5.0
ei	1;2.15	1;7.0	1;2.0	1;3.0
oʊ	1;3.0	1;8.0	1;5.0	1;4.15
ia	1;3.15	1;8.0	1;4.0	1;3.15
iɛ	1;3.15	1;8.15	1;2.15	1;2.15
ua	1;5.15	1;7.15	1;2.15	1;3.15
uo	1;7.15	1;9.15	1;8.0	1;5.0
yɛ	1;10.0	?	?	1;6.15
iɑo	1;3.15	1;6.15	1;6.15	1;5.15
ioʊ	1;3.15	1;4.15	1;5.15	1;3.15
uae	1;6.15	1;9.15	1;5.15	1;6.0
uei	1;4.15	1;8.0	1;6.0	1;3.15

Note. '?' means no examples in data

TABLE 3
Age of emergence of consonants.

Age	J.J.	Z.J.	H.Y.	Z.W.
1;2			m	m
1;2.15	k, ŋ		p	t, n-
1;3	p		t	
1;3.15	t, m			s, x
1;4		t		p
14.15	n-, -n	ŋ	ŋ	ŋ
1;5	tɕ	p	l	ʂ
1;5.15	tʰ, x, ɕ		n-	ɕ, tʂ, ts, -n
1;6	f			f, l
1;6.15	ts	m, n-		k, tɕ
1;7	s, tsʰ	s	k	
1;7.15	pʰ, l, ɹ			
1;8		tɕ, -n	pʰ, tʰ, s, x, tɕ, -n	
1;8.15		x, ts	ɕ	No data
1;9		k, ɹ		No data
1;9.15		l	f	No data
1;10	ʂ	tʂ	kʰ	No data
1;10.15	tʂ	f	tsʰ	No data
1;11		tʰ	ʂ, tʂ	No data
1;11.15		ɕ	ts, tɕʰ	No data
2;0	tʂʰ			No data
2:0.15				No data
Missing sounds	kʰ, tɕʰ	pʰ, kʰ, ʂ, tɕʰ, tsʰ, tʂʰ	ɹ, tʂʰ	pʰ, tʰ, kʰ, ɹ, tɕʰ, tʂʰ, tsʰ

Note. '-n' = syllable-final consonant /n/; 'n-'= syllable-initial consonant /n/.

Tables 3 and 4 show the age of emergence and stabilization of consonants in the children. If a sound occurred in a child's realization of a meaning unit, the sound would be considered as 'emerged' irrespective of whether it was the correct target. A sound was 'stabilized' when the child produced the sound phonologically correctly on at least two of three opportunities. By the end of the data collection (J.J., Z.J., & H.Y. were 24 months old and Z.W. was 20 months old), syllable-initial consonants /p, t, m/ and syllable-final consonants /n, ŋ/ have stabilized in the speech of all the children.

TABLE 4
Age of stabilization of consonants.

Age	J.J.	Z.J.	H.Y.	Z.W.
1;2				
1;2.15				
1;3				
1;3.15				t
1;4				
14.15	m, ŋ			ŋ
1;5				m
1;5.15				-n
1;6		p		
1;6.15	-n	t		p, k
1;7		m		
1;7.15				
1;8	p, t	-n, ŋ	m	
1;8.15				No data
1;9		n-	t, -n, ŋ	No data
1;9.15				No data
1;10				No data
1;10.15	ɕ		l, tɕ	No data
1;11				No data
1;11.15				No data
2:0			p	No data
2:0.15				No data
Missing sounds	pʰ, tʰ, k, kʰ, n-, f, s, x, ʂ, l, ɻ, tɕ, tɕʰ, tʂ, tʂʰ, ts, tsʰ	pʰ, tʰ, k, kʰ, f, s, x, ʂ, l, ɻ, tɕ, tɕʰ, ɕ, tʂ, tʂʰ, ts, tsʰ	pʰ, tʰ, k, kʰ, n-, f, s, x, ʂ, ɻ, tɕʰ, ɕ, tʂ, tʂʰ, ts, tsʰ	pʰ, tʰ, kʰ, n-, f, s, x, ʂ, l, ɻ, tɕ, tɕʰ, ɕ, tʂ, tʂʰ, ts, tsʰ

Note. '-n' = syllable-final consonant /n/; 'n-'= syllable-initial consonant /n/.

The age of emergence and stabilization of tones. Table 5 summarizes the age at which the four Putonghua tones emerged in the children's speech. A tone was considered to have emerged when a child could produce it at least once either in his/her spontaneous speech or in imitation. In terms of emergence, high level and high falling tones were the earliest and they both existed in all the children's speech data collected at the time when the children began to produce first words (four-word point). Rising tones existed in two children's first words (Z.J. & Z.W.), yet they emerged about one month later than high level and high falling tones in the other two children. Falling-rising tones were the last to emerge in all the four children.

TABLE 5
Age of emergence of tones (in years; months. days).

	J.J.	*Z.J.*	*H.Y.*	*Z.W.*
High level tone	1;2*	1;4*	1;2*	1;2.15*
Rising tone	1;3	1;4*	1;3	1;2.15*
Falling-rising tone	1;4	1;7	1;5	1;4.15
High falling tone	1;2*	1;4*	1;2*	1;2.15*

Note. '*' marks the first session when the child uttered a recognizable meaningful word.

Table 6 summarizes the age of stabilization derived using 66.7% criterion (where there were two occurrences, both must be correct; or two correct out of three occurrences). It was clear that high level tones were the first to be stabilized, and high falling tones second, in the speech of all the children. There were variations in the order of stabilization of rising and falling-rising tones among the children. Falling-rising tones were stabilized earlier than rising tones in two children, at the same time as rising tones in another child and later than rising tones in yet another child.

TABLE 6
Age of stabilization of tones using 66.7% criterion.

	J.J.	**Z.J.**	**H.Y.**	**Z.W.**
High level tone	1;4	1;5.15	1;2.15	1;2.15
Rising tone	1;7	1;8.15	1;8	1;6
Falling-rising tone	1;6.15	1;9.15	1;8	1;4.15
High falling tone	1;4.15	1;7	1;4	1;4.15

Summary

The longitudinal study of four children between the ages of one and two years found that tonal acquisition was completed earlier than syllable-final consonants and vowels, which were completed earlier than syllable-initial consonants. In addition, order of emergence and stabilization of four lexical tones was identified: in terms of emergence, high level and high falling tones emerged first, followed by rising tones. Falling-rising tones were the last to emerge. In terms of stabilization, high level tones were stabilized first, followed by high falling tones. Rising and falling-rising tones were the last to stabilize.

STUDY 2: CASE STUDIES OF CHILDREN WITH DEVELOPMENTAL SPEECH DISORDERS

Participants

Thirty-three children (9 girls and 24 boys) aged 2;8–7;6 were referred by their teachers during a pilot survey of developmental speech disorders in Putonghua-speaking children in Beijing. Three screening tests were given prior to inclusion in the study: pure tone audiometry, oromotor examination (Ozanne, 1992), and Visual Motor Integration Test (Beery, 1989). All the children were acquiring Putonghua as their first language. None of the children had siblings. The subject distribution over the age bands were (M: boys; F: girls):

2;7-3:0: 1 M;	3;1-3;6: 2 M;	3;7-4;0: 5 M + 3 F;
4;1-4;6: 10 M + 2 F;	4;7-5;0: 1 M+2 F;	5;1-5;6: 3 M;
5;7-6;0: 1 F;	6;1-6;6: 1 F;	6;7-7;0: 1 M;
7;1-7;6: 1 F.		

The children were assessed individually in a quiet room at their nurseries or schools, using picture-naming and picture-description tasks (for details of the tests and the normative data, see Zhu & Dodd, 2000). Each child was first asked to name the objects or actions in 44 pictures, three times, and then to describe what was happening in five pictures. The 44 lexical items covered all the consonants, vowels and tones in Putonghua phonology. The children's speech was audiotaped using a Sony professional micro-recorder. The speech sample from the picture-naming task was phonetically transcribed. Inter-transcriber reliability (on 18.5% of the data) for syllable-initial word-initial, syllable-initial within-word, syllable-final word-final, and syllable-final within-word consonants was higher than 96%.

Results

PPE (Percentage of Phonemes in Error; the number of times of phonemes produced in error / total number of phonemes in the sample ×100%) was used to compare children's production on tones, syllable-initial consonants, syllable-final consonants and vowels. Table 7 summarizes PPEs of the four syllable components in each child's production. Despite the diversity of error types, the Putonghua-speaking children with speech disorders seldom made tonal errors. Statistical analysis indicated that there were significant differences between the children's performance with four syllable components (ANOVA: $F(3,29) = 2.9717, p < 0.05$).

One child, aged 3;7, with the highest PPEs for syllable-initial consonants (0.64), syllable-final consonants (0.64), and vowels (0.22) among all the children, presented an interesting case. He had very restricted phonetic and phonemic inventories: 11 phones (/tʰ, k, kʰ, pʰ, s, tɕʰ, ʂ, tʂ, tʂʰ, ts, tsʰ/) were missing from his phonetic inventory (i.e. all the sounds produced at least once in the speech sample, irrespective of whether they were the target) and 15 phonemes (/tʰ, x, ɕ, k, kʰ, pʰ, l, s, tɕ, tɕʰ, ʂ, tʂ, tʂʰ, ts, tsʰ/) were missing from his phonemic inventory (i.e. all the sounds produced both phonetically and phonologically correctly on at least two of three opportunities). His syllable structure was restricted with V or CV being the predominant shape. There were frequent occurrences of reduplication in his production: he tended to substitute [tia], [tɕia] or [tɕɐ] for a large number of different syllables (eg [tia] /tʌŋ/; [tia] /tsʰuaŋ/; [tɕia tɕɐ]/tɕʰyn tsi/). Assimilation was frequent in his speech too: adjacent syllables shared the same initial consonant and sometimes the same vowel (eg [tia tiao] /ɕiaŋ tɕiao/; [nia nia] /nan xan/; [tʂʌ tʂiaŋ] /tsae tɕiɛn/). Inconsistent productions of the same words on different occasions were also evident. For example, /ɕin/ realized as [iŋ], [tia], and [tin]. However, the child had very few errors with the tones. Even if the target phoneme sequences were frequently replaced with his favorite templates, which sometimes shared few features in common with the targets, the original tones of the target syllables were retained in his speech.

Summary

This study of children with speech disorders found that tones were least likely to be subject to disruption during phonological acquisition. In contrast, most of the errors made by Putonghua-speaking children with speech disorders involved syllable-initial consonants.

STUDY 3: CASE STUDY OF A CHILD WITH SEVERE PRELINGUAL HEARING IMPAIRMENT

Participant

The child, referred to as ZL, had a severe bilateral prelingual hearing loss, using American National Standards Institute (ANSI, 1989) classification criterion. Unaided pure tone averages of thresholds at 500KHz, 1KHz, and 2KHz were 75 dB in the right ear and 107 dB in the left ear. Aided levels were 54 dB in the right ear and 83 dB in the left ear. Born in Beijing, ZL was the only child in the family. His mother and father were university clerks and monolingual Putonghua speakers.

TABLE 7
PPEs of the four syllable components.

Age	PPE			
	Syllable-initial consonants	Syllable-final consonants	Vowels	Tones
2;8	0.58	0.09	0.04	0
3;11	0.18	0.27	0.04	0
3;11	0.39	0	0.03	0
3;11	0.43	0.05	0.10	0
3;2	0.19	0.22	0.06	0.03
3;6	0.16	0.13	0.01	0
3;7	0.39	0.09	0.03	0.01
3;7	0.64	0.64	0.22	0.03
3;8	0.28	0.18	0.03	0
4;0	0.14	0.09	0.01	0
4;0	0.29	0	0.01	0
4;1	0.18	0.05	0	0
4;1	0.09	0	0.01	0
4;2	0.13	0	0.01	0
4;2	0.25	0.05	0.01	0
4;2	0.13	0.09	0.01	0.06
4;3	0.19	0.05	0.06	0
4;3	0.18	0.55	0.04	0
4;3	0.08	0.14	0.04	0
4;4	0.19	0.05	0.01	0
4;6	0.28	0.09	0	0
4;7	0.16	0	0.03	0
4;7	0.07	0	0.01	0
4;8	0.29	0.23	0.08	0
5;0	0.05	0.23	0.04	0
5;2	0.18	0.05	0	0
5;3	0.11	0.05	0.01	0
5;6	0.09	0.05	0	0
5;6	0.11	0	0	0
5;7	0.09	0	0	0
6;1	0.05	0	0	0
6;7	0.07	0.05	0	0
7;6	0.02	0	0	0
Mean	0.2018	0.1055	0.0285	0.0039
SD	0.1470	0.1479	0.0425	0.0125

The possible cause for ZL's hearing impairment was maternal infection during pregnancy. He also had a middle ear infection at the age of 6 months. He had been wearing binaural hearing aids since he was one year old. He had regular check-ups and his hearing remained in a stable condition. ZL was acquiring Putonghua as his first language and attended a mainstream kindergarten, seven hours a day, five days a week. According to the parental and school reports, his cognitive development was within normal range. There were no abnormalities in oral structure as assessed by an oromotor examination (Ozanne, 1992), or learning problems as assessed by Visual Motor Integration test (Beery, 1989).

ZL was assessed in a quiet room at the kindergarten, using the same picture-naming and description task as in the study of children with speech disorders. The boy was assessed at the age of 3;5, 3;9, 4;1, and 4;5, following the same procedure. The speech sample collected was transcribed using the IPA by two native Putonghua-speaking linguists. Inter-transcriber reliability on the child's speech sample collected at the age of 3;5 was 92.1%, 90.1%, 98.2%, 98.4%, 98.2% and 100% for syllable-initial word-initial consonants, syllable-initial within-word consonants, syllable-final word-final consonants, syllable-final within-word consonants, vowels, and prosodic features such as tones, weak stress and rhotacization, respectively.

Results

Over the observation period, ZL's syntactic ability (MLUs were 4.9, 5.4, 5.9 and 6.1 at the age of 3;5, 3;9, 4;1 and 4;5) showed a slow but steady increase. The analysis of ZL's single word speech showed that he had complete syllable-final consonant (2 in total) and vowel repertoires (22 in total). His acquisition of tones was within normal range. However, he had difficulties with syllable-initial consonants. Table 8 lists ZL's phonetic and phonemic inventories identified in his single word speech sample at each assessment. He had an almost complete phonetic inventory by the end of the observation period, though there were some phones in his speech which did not belong to Putonghua phonology. In contrast, his phonemic inventory was underdeveloped. His phonemic inventory did not show any sign of growth over the observation period. For example, while 90% of the children aged 3;7–4;0 in the normative data would have mastered 12 phonemes, ZL had only 7 phonemes in his inventory when assessed at the age of 3;9.

TABLE 8

ZL's phonetic and phonemic inventories at the age of 3;5, 3;9, 4;1 and 4;5.

Age	Phonetic inventory	Phonemic inventory
3;5	t, tʰ, m, n, k, kʰ, f, x, l, ɹ, ɕ, tɕ, tɕʰ, s, ts, ʂ, tʂ, tʂʰ, ð*	t, tʰ, m, n, k, kʰ, f, x, ɹ, ɕ, tɕ
3;9	t, m, n, pʰ, k, f, x, l, ɹ, ɕ, tɕ, tɕʰ, s, ts, ʂ, ɵ*, ð*	t, tʰ, m, n, f, x, ɹ
4;1	t, tʰ, m, n, p, pʰ, k, kʰ, f, x, l, ɹ, ɕ, tɕ, tɕʰ, s, ts, tʂʰ, g*	t, m, n, pʰ, x, ɹ, tɕʰ
4;5	t, tʰ, m, n, p, pʰ, k, kʰ, f, x, l, ɹ, ɕ, tɕ, tɕʰ, s, ts, tʂʰ, ʂ, tʂʰ	t, tʰ, m, n, pʰ, kʰ, f, x, l, ɹ

Note. Phones marked by * are not legal in Putonghua.

ZL's PPEs for syllable-initial consonant, syllable-final consonant, vowel and tone were summarized in Table 9. Because some phonemes (e.g. /ɕ, tɕ/) which the child was able to use accurately at the age of 3;5 'disappeared' in his subsequent three assessments, his PPEs (except PPE for tone), as a measure of inaccurate realization of phonemes, increased over time, while the normally developing hearing children tended to eliminate errors over the same period of time (Zhu & Dodd, 2000).

TABLE 9

ZL's PPEs at the age of 3;5, 3;9, 4;1 and 4;5

Age	PPE			
	Syllable-initial consonants	Syllable-final consonants	Vowels	Tones
3;5	0.35	0.09	0.01	0
3;9	0.53	0	0	0.01
4;1	0.55	0.18	0.03	0
4;5	0.54	0	0.07	0

Summary

The longitudinal study of a child with severe prelingual hearing impairment showed that despite hearing impairment, the boy had little difficulty acquiring tones. He had complete syllable-final consonant and vowel repertoires, while his syllable-initial consonant inventory was far from complete.

GENERAL DISCUSSION

Research findings comparing the acquisition of various syllable components from three studies were reported in this paper. It was found that different populations of Putonghua-speaking children showed similar sensitivity to the structure of the phonological system they were acquiring. It provided support for Zhu & Dodd's (2000) hypothesis that the phonological acquisition patterns across different populations of Putonghua-speaking children were influenced by the saliency value of syllable components.

The notion of phonological saliency accounts well for the acquisition of tones which have the highest saliency value. Evidence arising from the three studies reported here and the normative study reported in Zhu & Dodd (2000) included:

- Tonal acquisition was completed earlier than that of syllable-initial consonants, syllable-final consonants, and vowels in normally developing Putonghua-speaking children as shown both in the normative study (Zhu & Dodd, 2000) and the longitudinal study reported here.
- Tones were resistant to impairment during the process of phonological acquisition, as the study of 33 Putonghua-speaking children with developmental speech disorders showed.
- The effect of hearing loss on tonal acquisition was minimal as the longitudinal study on a child with prelingual severe hearing impairment showed.

In comparison, syllable-final consonants, being an optional component in a Putonghua syllable, have a lower saliency value than tones, but higher saliency value than syllable-initial consonants. Specific acquisitional patterns associated with syllable-final consonants were:

- The phonetic acquisition of syllable-final consonants was completed by the age of two (as found in the longitudinal study), while that of syllable-initial consonants was not completed until 4;6 for 90% of the children (as found in the normative study).
- Syllable-final consonants were less likely to be subject to impairment than syllable-initial consonants: statistically fewer errors were

made at syllable-final position than at syllable-initial position by Putonghua-speaking children with speech disorders.

- The child with hearing impairment had a complete syllable-final consonant repertoire while his syllable-initial inventory was far from complete.

Compared with syllable-initial consonants, vowels have a higher saliency value, since they are a compulsory syllable component. The saliency value of vowels was reflected in their acquisitional patterns:

- The vowels emerged early in the children's production, between the age of 1;0–2;0. The proportions of vowel errors in the total number of speech errors in each age group were significantly less than that of syllable-initial consonants as found in the normative data.
- The vowels were more resistant to impairment than syllable-initial consonants. With the exception of one child, all of the Putonghua-speaking children with speech disorders in the study made very few errors with vowels.
- The child with hearing impairment had little difficulty in acquiring vowels.

In general, the cross-populational study confirmed Zhu & Dodd's (2000) hypothesis that syllable components with higher phonological saliency (e.g. tones) are acquired earlier and are less likely to be subject to speech disorders and hearing impairment than syllable components with lower phonological saliency (e.g. syllable-initial consonants).

However, it must be pointed out that the phonological acquisition patterns of children speaking a particular language might be influenced by a combination of several factors. For example, apart from its high phonological saliency value, several other factors could also contribute to the earlier acquisition of tones. Among these possible factors are:

- the perceptual saliency of prosodic features (Quigley & Paul, 1984);
- the relative ease in physiologically producing tonal contrasts as opposed to segmental contrasts (Allen & Hawkins, 1980);
- the less complexity of contrasts and rules involved in acquiring prosodic features as opposed to that of segmental contrasts (Vihman, 1996).

For more detailed discussions on these factors, see Zhu (2000) and Zhu, Li, & Dodd (in press).

REFERENCES

Allen, G. D., & Hawkins, S. (1980). Phonological rhythm: Definition and development. In G. H. Yeni-Komshian, J. Kavanagh & C. Ferguson (Eds.), *Child phonology: Vol 1 production* . New York: Academic.

American National Standards Institute (1989). *Specifications for audiometers (ANSI S3.6-1989)*. New York: Acoustical Society of America.

Beery, K. (1989). *The Beery-Buktenica developmental test of visual-motor integration*. Cleveland: Modern Curriculum Press.

Ferguson, C. A., & Farwell, C. (1975). Words and sounds in early language acquisition. *Language, 51*, 419-439.

Katamba, F. (1989) *An introduction to phonology*. London: Longman.

Ozanne, A. (1992). Normative data for sequenced oral movements and movements in context for children aged three to five years. *Australian Journal of Human Communication Disorders, 20*, 47-63.

Quigley, P., & Paul, P. (1984). *Language and deafness*. San Diego: College-Hill Press.

Vihman, M. M. (1996). *Phonological development*. Oxford: Blackwell.

Vihman, M. M., & McCune, L. (1994). When is a word a word? *Journal of Child Language, 21*, 517-542

Zhu Hua (2000). Phonological development and disorder of Putonghua (Modern standard Chinese)-speaking children. Unpublished Ph.D thesis, University of Newcastle upon Tyne.

Zhu Hua, & Dodd, B. (2000). The phonological acquisition of Putonghua (Modern Standard Chinese). *Journal of Child Language, 27*, 3-42.

Zhu Hua, Li Wei, & Dodd B. (In press). The acquisition of suprasegmental phonology by Putonghua (Modern Standard Chinese) Speaking children. In *Proceedings of the VIIIth IASCL Congress*. Boston, MA: Cascadilla.

15

Typological Description of the Normal Acquisition of Consonant Clusters

Sharynne McLeod, Jan van Doorn and Vicki A. Reed

Consonant clusters provide a microcosm for the study of the systemic and structural (phonotactic) components of speech. However, few attempts to describe the normal acquisition of consonant clusters have examined both structural and systemic components and the interrelationship between these two aspects. For example, studies primarily focusing on the systemic components of speech include those documenting the age of acquisition of consonant clusters (e.g., Olmsted, 1971; Smit, Hand, Frelinger, Bernthal & Bird, 1990; Templin, 1957). Studies focusing on the structural (phonotactic) components primarily describe the phonological processes that occur; most commonly cluster reduction and cluster simplification[1] (e.g. Grunwell, 1987; Shriberg & Kwiatkowski, 1980; Watson & Scukanec, 1997). Systemic analyses tend to provide extremely detailed information, to the extent that universal statements are difficult to glean, while structural analyses tend to provide information that is so inclusive that many subtleties of development are hidden. Ingram (1976) stated with regard to the cluster reduction process, "data like this show the points of acquisition of the clusters, but not the stages that occur between the first attempts at clusters and final correct production" (Ingram, 1976, p. 32).

An alternative approach is to use a typological framework to describe consonant cluster production. A typological approach provides a hierarchy of realization types to accommodate all possible non-adult productions of a consonant cluster. Typological descriptions of consonant clusters go beyond the broad categories of phonological process descriptors but they do not include so

---

[1] 'Cluster reduction' is defined as the deletion of one or more elements in the consonant cluster, whereas 'cluster simplification' is the replacement of any or all of the consonants within the cluster while the syllable shape is retained (cf. Grunwell, 1987).

much phonetic detail that patterns become difficult to discern. Some typological analyses (e.g., Chin & Dinnsen, 1992) also provide a framework for describing the interrelationship between the systemic and structural components of children's realizations of consonant clusters.

Typological Descriptions of Consonant Clusters

Typologies suitable for describing consonant cluster production have been developed by Greenlee (1974) and Chin and Dinnsen (1992). Greenlee (1974) described three stages and numerous 'subprocesses' in the development of stop + liquid consonant clusters. Her work was extended by a number of researchers to describe the development of two-element word-initial consonant clusters (e.g. Catts & Kamhi, 1984; Elbert & McReynolds, 1979). Chin and Dinnsen (1992) profiled realizations of two-element word-initial stop and word-initial fricative consonant clusters according to 17 types. They aimed to ensure that every realization type of fricative cluster and stop cluster was included in their typology and they used different codes for stop versus fricative clusters. The typologies of Greenlee (1974) and Chin and Dinnsen (1992) were modified by McLeod, van Doorn and Reed (1997) and applied to two-element clusters relevant to the Australian context. Each typology was extended by incorporating the effect of syllable position and constituent type on children's realizations of consonant clusters. It was intended that these typologies would provide insight into children's realizations which extended beyond the commonly used phonological descriptors of cluster reduction and cluster simplification.

Modification of the Greenlee (1974) Typology. McLeod et al. (1997) developed a six-stage typology based on Greenlee (1974) by retaining Elbert and McReynolds' (1979) four stages and adding two of Greenlee's subprocesses: epenthesis (e.g., [səpun] for *spoon*) and metathesis (e.g., [maks] for *mask*). These two subprocesses were selected as they were possible realizations for the production of every group of consonant clusters. Greenlee's (1974) velar-dental interchange, for example, was not included as it pertained only to clusters containing velars. Thus the six-stage typology was: (1) Null realization, (2) One-element realization, (3) Two-element realization (where at least one element is not matched to the adult target), (4) Epenthesis, (5) Metathesis, (6) Correct (matches with the adult target).

Modification of the Chin and Dinnsen (1992) Typology. Chin and Dinnsen's typology was modified by McLeod et al. (1997) so that it could be applied to all groups of two-element consonant clusters in all word positions. Table 1 shows the modified 12-point typology. The new typology used nomenclature that was appropriate for any type of consonant cluster, not just fricative or stop clusters.

It also included additional categories to account for metathesis and for the different types of epenthesis, which were not included by Chin and Dinnsen.

TABLE 1

Typology of two-element cluster realizations (adapted from Chin & Dinnsen, 1992)

Stage	Realization code	Typology	Word-initial example skip /skɪp/	Word-final example task /task/
Null	1	$C_1C_2 = 0$	[ɪp]	[ta]
One element	2	$C_1C_2 = C_1$	[sɪp]	[tas]
	3	$C_1C_2 = C_2$	[kɪp]	[tak]
	4	$C_1C_2 = x$	[tɪp]	[tat]
Two elements	5	$C_1C_2 = C_1x$	[stɪp]	[tast]
	6	$C_1C_2 = xC_2$	[θkɪp]	[taθk]
	7	$C_1C_2 = xy$	[θtɪp]	[taθt]
Epenthesis	8	$C_1C_2 = C_1VC_2$	[səkɪp]	[tasək]
	9	other epenthesis	[sətɪp]	[tasət]
Metathesis	10	$C_1C_2 = C_2C_1$	[ksɪp]	[taks]
	11	other metathesis	[kθɪp]	[takθ]
Correct	12	$C_1C_2 = C_1C_2$	[skɪp]	[task]

Note. Elements to the left of the equal sign represent the adult realization of the target clusters; those to the right represent the child's realization. C_1 = the first element of the consonant cluster; C_2 = the second element of the consonant cluster; 0 = a null realization; V = an epenthetic vowel; x, y = any phoneme not within the target realization of the cluster.

Previous Research Using the Modified Typologies. McLeod et al. (1997) applied the modified typologies to speech samples collected from children with impaired speech, using a comprehensive single-word task that was controlled for the number and type of consonant clusters. The modified typologies were useful for identifying differences in realization types depending on the constituents of the consonant cluster, number of elements and word position. For example, null realizations occurred for word-final clusters but not word-initial clusters (see Table 2).

Even though the typologies contained only a limited number of stages, individual subjects could not be classified into just one stage at any one time. Extensive individual variation was apparent on every measure. The two typologies proved promising for capturing variation in realizations of consonant clusters by children with speech impairment, and thus providing useful information beyond that of "cluster reduction" and "cluster simplification".

TABLE 2
Speech-impaired subjects' realizations of consonant clusters according to
Greenlee's typology (data from McLeod et al., 1997).

Realization	Initial stop	Initial fricative	Final fricative +stop	Final nasal
Null realization	0.0%	0.0%	11.3%	3.4%
One element	25.8%	36.1%	30.0%	20.9%
Two elements	47.1%	43.1%	31.6%	34.6%
Epenthesis	5.1%	2.1%	0.0%	0.0%
Metathesis	0.0%	0.0%	11.9%	0.0%
Correct	22.0%	18.6%	15.6%	41.1%

Note. The quoted figures are a percentage of the total number of realizations for each group of consonant clusters.

Aims of the Research

The main aim of the research was to describe normally developing two-year-olds' realizations of consonant clusters using the typologies of Greenlee (1974) and Chin and Dinnsen (1992), as modified by McLeod et al. (1997). A second purpose was to ascertain whether consonant clusters were realized differently depending on constituent features and word position. Finally, the findings of the present investigation were compared with those from the children with speech impairment (from McLeod et al., 1997).

METHOD

Sixteen normally developing Australian children, aged 2;0 to 2;11 at the first observation, were the subjects for the longitudinal investigation. Each potential subject was assessed by a speech pathologist, audiologist and psychologist to determine that they had normal expressive language (Miller, 1981), receptive language (Reynell & Huntley, 1985), oromusculature (Robbins & Klee, 1987), hearing (tympanogram, pure tone) and cognition (Griffiths, 1984). Their phonological skills were assessed via the analysis of a 100-utterance sample using PROPH+ (Long, Fey & Channell, 1999). Each subject had normal phonetic inventories, cluster production and word shapes and percentage of consonants correct (PCC; mean = 68.2) when their results were compared with Dodd (1995), Dyson (1988) and Stoel-Gammon (1987; see McLeod, 1999 for individualized subject data). All of the subjects spoke Australian English as their first language and came from families from a cross section of socioeconomic status groupings (Daniel, 1983).

Six observations were made at monthly intervals. During each observation naturalistic connected speech samples were elicited through play with toys with names and attributes containing consonant clusters (e.g. <u>cl</u>ock, elepha<u>nt</u>, <u>fr</u>og, <u>bl</u>ocks, toy <u>st</u>ove, <u>pl</u>ate, dri<u>nk</u>, and <u>sp</u>oon; see McLeod, 1997). The first author engaged in self-talk, parallel talk and prompting to elicit speech as the subjects played. Every word produced by the subjects that contained a word-initial or word-final consonant cluster was transcribed by the first author using narrow transcription. There was no attempt to limit the number of productions of each word.

Subjects' speech was recorded onto audiotape via a radio lapel microphone. Speech was transcribed online and checked using audiotape recordings. Two experienced speech-language pathologists independently transcribed ten percent of the data. Inter-judge percent agreement on 2865 data points revealed agreement of .845 for narrow transcription. The range of agreement from individual subjects was 75.4% to 88.2%. In cases of disagreement, the first judge's transcription was used for analysis.

Data Analysis

Typological analyses were carried out on the 96 (16 subjects x 6 observations) elicited spontaneous speech samples that were rich with attempts at consonant clusters. Realizations based on narrow transcription were analyzed. Consonant clusters which were created due to the addition of a morpheme (e.g., /ts/ in *cats*) were excluded from the analysis because it was difficult to determine whether their realization was due to the subjects' morphological or phonological development. At each monthly observation, the subjects produced between 19 and 139 word tokens in which the target word contained a consonant cluster (mean = 76.9; SD = 29.2), giving a subset of 6167 words for analysis. The majority of attempted consonant clusters (82%) occurred in the word-initial position.

Although the spontaneous speech samples provided many examples of consonant clusters, not every consonant cluster group was produced by every subject on every occasion. Therefore, only two-element clusters were analyzed and productions were categorized into the following subgroups: word-initial fricative clusters, word-initial stop clusters and word-final clusters. Two changes were made to accommodate the variable number of productions of words containing consonant clusters from each spontaneous speech sample. Firstly, the realizations were converted to percent occurrence instead of raw numbers (as in McLeod et al., 1997; see Table 3 for the number of productions). Secondly, a post-hoc limit was placed on the number of occurrences permitted of a realization type, because of the potential for bias created by transcribing all productions of words in the spontaneous speech task. Only the first five occurrences of any production were counted. For example, during observation 4, subject 1 produced fifteen words with a target word-initial /bl/ cluster, where

/bl/ was produced as [bw] ten times, [b] three times, [b$_x$w] once and [w] once. All occurrences of [b], [b$_x$w] and [w] were included, but only the first five occurrences of [bw].

TABLE 3
Number of realizations of each subgroup of consonant clusters across all subjects and all observations.

	Total	Mean/ observation	Minimum/ observation	Maximum/ observation
Word-initial stop clusters	3543	36.9	14	62
Word-initial fricative clusters	1498	15.6	5	38
Word-final stop clusters	1126	11.7	0	29

Note. The zero in the final row occurred for the youngest subjects only: subject 1, observation 1 and subject 2, observations 1, 2 and 5.

RESULTS

The results were considered by initially collapsing all data for all subjects to report group characteristics, then by considering individual subject data.

Analysis Using the Modified Greenlee (1974) Typology

Group Data. Overall, the subjects showed few differences in their production of consonant clusters depending on the word position and constituents within the consonant clusters. The majority of productions were either incorrect two-element realizations or correct realizations; there were few instances of null realizations, epenthesis or metathesis (see Table 4). The most common realization for word-initial stop clusters (43.0%) was a two-element realization where at least one element was not matched to the adult target (e.g., [pw] for /pl/). Correct productions were the most common realization for word-initial fricative cluster realizations (38.5%) and word-final clusters (48.9%).

Individual Subject Data. The younger subjects (notably subjects 1, 2, 3, 4, 5, and 12) initially produced one-element realizations and as time progressed they added two-element realizations (see Appendices A through D). All produced at least a few correct consonant clusters by the final observations. Null realizations were produced primarily by the younger subjects, but not exclusively. The older subjects commenced with a range of realizations; most produced one-element, two-element, epenthesis and correct realizations on the first observation. The majority of their realizations were two-element or correct. This trend continued over the six months of observations, generally with an increase in the prevalence of correct realizations.

TABLE 4
Subjects' realizations of consonant clusters according to the modified Greenlee typology.

Realizations	Initial stop	Initial fricative	Final	Overall
Null realization	0.1%	0.1%	0.5%	0.2%
One element	27.7%	26.1%	29.6%	27.7%
Two elements	43.0%	33.7%	24.1%	37.5%
Epenthesis	4.8%	1.3%	0.2%	3.1%
Metathesis	0.0%	0.1%	0.3%	0.0%
Correct	24.3%	38.5%	48.9%	31.5%

Note. The quoted figures are a percentage of the total number of realizations for each group of consonant clusters.

Word-Initial Stop Cluster Realizations. Word-initial stop cluster realizations accounted for over half of the words with consonant clusters in the adult target produced in the spontaneous speech task. The majority of the subjects demonstrated a shift over time from predominantly producing one-element realizations, to progressively producing more two-element and then correct realizations. However, subjects did not always demonstrate a linear progression from one-element to two-element to correct realizations. An example of a reverse progression was shown by subject 15 for two-element word-initial stop clusters. At observation 1, she had 41.9% one-element realizations and 45.2% correct realizations; by observation 6 she had 23.6% one-element realizations, 50.9% two-element realizations and 23.6% correct realizations. Although there was a decrease in the number of one-element realizations, there was also a decrease in the percentage of correct realizations.

Only two subjects produced null realizations in their attempts at words containing stop clusters: observation 1 for subject 4 (1 example) and observation 3 for subject 1 (3 examples). When null realizations occurred, they did not necessarily coincide with predominantly one-element realizations. On the contrary, null realizations occurred at any point along the progression of data collection.

Epenthesis occurred for all 16 subjects on at least one monthly observation in their attempts to produce words containing two-element stop consonant clusters. For example, subject 4 realized approximately 20% of the words with epenthesis during observations 5 and 6. Epenthesis occurred more for stop clusters than for any other group of consonant clusters.

It was rare for a subject within one observation to realise word-initial stop consonant clusters in only one of Greenlee's stages. It was possible to confidently classify observations into one stage for four subjects only (subject 1, observation 1; subject 2, observation 1; subject 3, observation 3; subject 12, observation 1). In each case, these subjects produced one-element realizations only.

Word-Initial Fricative Cluster Realizations. Two-element word-initial fricative clusters were more likely than stop clusters to be produced correctly. In general, however, subjects' realizations were similar to those of stop consonant clusters (see Table 4).

Word-Final Cluster Realizations. There were fewer instances of word-final consonant clusters than word-initial consonant clusters (see Table 3), but when they occurred, they were more likely to be produced correctly than any other group of consonant clusters (see Table 4). Each subject tended to have concurrent examples of one-element, two element and correct realizations at each observation.

Analysis Using the Modified Chin and Dinnsen (1992) Typology

Group Data. The data were analyzed according to token-prevalence (cf. McLeod et al., 1997) and Table 5 shows the realization types for each two-element cluster. For all cluster groups the most common realization type was the correct realization of C_1C_2 (type 12; stop = 24.3%; fricative = 38.6%; final = 45.4%). The two next most common realizations of word-initial stop clusters were a two-element realization with the first element correct (type 5 [C_1x] - 22.3%) and a one-element realization (type 2 [C_1] - 14.9%) (see Table 5). The next most common realizations of word-initial fricative clusters were a two-element realization with the second element correct (type 6 [xC_2] - 22.6%) and a one-element incorrect realization (type 4 [x] - 12.9%) (see Table 5). These realizations were also the most common for word-initial fricative clusters found by McLeod et al. (1997). The common realizations of word-final clusters were the same as the word-initial stop clusters: a two-element realization with the first element correct (type 5 [C_1x] - 16.1%) and a one-element realization (type 2 [C_1] - 14.7%) (see Table 5).

Individual Subject Data. Nine of the twelve types were produced by almost every subject (see Appendix A). The three types that were rarely (if ever) produced were null realizations (type 1) and the two forms of metathesis (types 10 and 11). Two subjects had no realizations of type 8 epenthesis (subjects 2 and 12). The youngest subjects predominantly realized their consonant clusters as type 2 ($C_1C_2 = C_1$), type 4 ($C_1C_2 = x$) and type 5 ($C_1C_2 = C_1x$). The majority of the older subjects (subjects 6, 7, 8, 9, 10, 11, 13, 15, 16) predominantly realized their consonant clusters as type 12 (correct). Appendices A to D provide individual data for each group of consonant clusters. Appendix B provides individual data for word-initial fricative clusters, Appendix C provides data for word-initial stop clusters and Appendix D provides data for word-final clusters.

TABLE 5
Token-prevalence of each realization type for two-element consonant clusters.

Type	Typology	Initial stop	Initial fricative	Final	Overall
1	$C_1C_2 = 0$	0.1%	0.1%	0.5%	0.2%
2	$C_1C_2 = C_1$	14.9%	10.8%	14.7%	13.9%
3	$C_1C_2 = C_2$	0.9%	2.5%	10.3%	3.0%
4	$C_1C_2 = x$	11.9%	12.9%	4.6%	10.8%
5	$C_1C_2 = C_1x$	22.3%	6.8%	16.1%	17.4%
6	$C_1C_2 = xC_2$	7.8%	22.6%	6.7%	11.3%
7	$C_1C_2 = xy$	12.9%	4.5%	1.3%	8.7%
8	$C_1C_2 = C_1VC_2$	2.5%	0.9%	0.0%	1.7%
9	other epenthesis	2.3%	0.4%	0.2%	1.4%
10	$C_1C_2 = C_2C_1$	0.0%	0.0%	0.1%	0.0%
11	other metathesis	0.0%	0.1%	0.2%	0.0%
12	$C_1C_2 = C_1C_2$	24.3%	38.6%	45.4%	31.5%
	Total number	3543	1498	1126	6170

Note. Elements to the left of the equals sign represent the adult realization of the target clusters; those to the right represent the child's realization. C_1 = the first element of a two-element consonant cluster; C_2 = the second element of a two-element consonant cluster; 0 = a null realization; x, y = any phoneme not within the target realization of the cluster.

DISCUSSION

Categorization of the data showed that children who are normally developing do not realize consonant clusters only as the term cluster reduction would suggest. The majority of realizations for each category of consonant clusters contained two elements (see Table 4), and were not reduced clusters. The data also showed that two-element realizations which contained non-matches with the adult target were common amongst the subjects (see Appendices B, C and D). These findings suggest that the terms cluster reduction and cluster simplification could be replaced by a more comprehensive set of typological descriptors of children's realizations of consonant clusters.

Each stage of development of consonant clusters based on Greenlee (1974) was apparent in the normally developing subjects. The subjects exhibited null, one-element, two-element and correct realizations. The subjects also exhibited some of the subprocesses described by Greenlee, such as epenthesis. However, not all these realizations were evidenced for each category of consonant clusters. Greenlee's stages, while useful for documenting the development of consonant clusters, could not be used to classify individual subjects into a particular stage.

There were few subjects who produced every consonant cluster as the same type. None of the subjects produced only null realizations and a few produced only one-element types. The data from the present investigation support the use of Greenlee's stages as a more comprehensive method for describing children's realizations of consonant clusters than the phonological processes of cluster reduction and cluster simplification. However, Greenlee's stages do not appear to be the ideal method of classification, since most of the subjects' realizations of consonant clusters could not be described by a discrete stage. Subjects showed considerable within- and between-subject variability. These findings further demonstrated that children are not homogeneous in learning phonology (Dodd, Leahy & Hambly, 1989; Ferguson, 1989; Vihman & Greenlee, 1987).

The typology of realizations based on the work of Chin and Dinnsen (1992) provided a means for analyzing the interrelationship between the structural and systemic components for the realizations of consonant clusters. Almost every one of the most common realization types for all categories of consonant cluster included a phoneme that was a non-match with the adult target (i.e., x, y or both). This occurred in one- and two-element realizations of the consonant clusters. For example, 10.8% of realizations were of the form $C_1C_2 = x$ and 17.4% of realizations were of the form $C_1C_2 = C_1x$. One limitation of typological analyses is that the actual production of the non-adult realization is not accessible. For example, it is unknown if $C_1C_2 = x$ is due to coalescence, velar fronting, interdentalization, gliding, or another possibility.

Impact of Features and Word Position on Realization of Clusters

The second aim of the investigation was to ascertain whether or not realizations of consonant clusters depended on constituent features and word position. Word-initial stop clusters were realized differently from word-initial fricative and word-final clusters. For example, a correct production of a word-final consonant cluster was more likely than a correct production in word-initial position (see Table 4). A further example is that a common realization of word-initial fricative clusters (22.6%) was type 6 - xC_2; a two-element realization with the fricative element realized as a non-adult production and the second element correct (see Table 5). Non-adult production of fricatives in young children has been documented by Smit (1993). In contrast, one of the most common realizations of the initial stop clusters (22.3%) was type 5 - C_1x; a two-element realization with the first element correct and a non-adult production of the second element (typically a liquid; see Table 5). Difficulty producing the liquids /l/ and /r/ also has been documented by Smit (1993).

Normal and Impaired Realizations of Consonant Clusters

The findings of the present investigation were compared with those from the children with speech impairment (McLeod et al., 1997). The stages of development of consonant clusters based on Greenlee (1974) were apparent in both McLeod et al. (1997) and the present research. Two areas of difference were the occurrence of null realizations and epenthesis. For the children with normally developing speech null realizations in small numbers occurred across all three groups of clusters; both in word-initial and word-final positions. Only six of the 16 subjects produced one or more null realizations; subject 1 produced five (see Appendix A). Null realizations occurred predominantly in the younger of the two-year-old subjects, but not exclusively. The results provide additional examples to the rare finding of null realizations in normally developing children (see also Chervela, 1981; Greenlee, 1974; Stemberger, 1989). Null realizations also occurred infrequently in the speech-impaired subjects described by McLeod et al. (1997). Seven of the 40 subjects produced null realizations. However, in contrast to the normally developing children, the children with speech impairment produced null realizations for word-final clusters only.

The normally developing two-year-old subjects exhibited epenthesis in word-initial and word-final consonant clusters (see Appendix A). Epenthesis has been found to occur in word-initial consonant clusters for normally developing two-year-olds (Bortolini & Leonard, 1991; Dyson & Paden, 1983; Higgs, 1968) but has not previously been examined in the word-final position. In contrast, for the children with speech impairment in the study of McLeod et al. (1997), epenthesis occurred in each group of word-initial consonant clusters but there were no instances of epenthesis for any word-final clusters.

CONCLUSION

Typological analysis of phonetically transcribed speech revealed patterns of speech production in children, beyond the categories found in phonological processes descriptions. Two typologies based on Greenlee (1974) and Chin and Dinnsen (1992) were found to be appropriate for describing the acquisition of clusters by normally developing children. These typologies showed that clusters were realized in different typological categories depending on constituent features and word position. When the findings of the present investigation were compared with those from children with speech impairment (McLeod et al., 1997), differences were found between the two groups with respect to the word position of clusters where null realizations and epenthesis occurred.

ACKNOWLEDGMENTS

This chapter presents a portion of work from a doctoral dissertation by the first author. The research was supported by grants from The University of Sydney

Research Awards and the Charles Sturt University PhD Write-up Award Scheme. The authors wish to thank Elise Baker, Sally Hooper, Johanna Keene, Simone Stuchbury, Timothy Hewitt, Kerrie Lee, and the subjects and their families for their assistance in the conduct of this research.

REFERENCES

Bortolini, U., & Leonard, L. B. (1991). The speech of phonologically disordered children acquiring Italian. *Clinical Linguistics and Phonetics, 5*, 1-12.

Catts, H. W., & Kamhi, A. G. (1984). Simplification of /s/ + stop consonant clusters: A developmental perspective. *Journal of Speech and Hearing Research, 27*, 556-561.

Chervela, N. (1981). Medial consonant cluster acquisition by Telugu children. *Journal of Child Language, 8*, 63-73.

Chin, S. B., & Dinnsen, D. A. (1992). Consonant clusters in disordered speech: Constraints and correspondence patterns. *Journal of Child Language, 19*, 259-285.

Daniel, A. (1983). *Power, privilege and prestige: Occupations in Australia.* Melbourne: Longman Cheshire.

Dodd, B. (1995). Children's acquisition of phonology. In B. Dodd (Ed.), *Differential diagnosis and treatment of speech disordered children* (pp. 21-48). London: Whurr.

Dodd, B., Leahy, J., & Hambly, G. (1989). Phonological disorders in children: Underlying cognitive deficits. *British Journal of Developmental Psychology, 7*, 55-71.

Dyson, A. T. (1988). Phonetic inventories of 2- and 3- year-old children. *Journal of Speech and Hearing Disorders, 53*, 89-93.

Dyson, A. T., & Paden, E. P. (1983). Some phonological acquisition strategies used by two-year-olds. *Journal of Childhood Communication Disorders, 7*, 6-18.

Elbert, M., & McReynolds, L. V. (1979). Aspects of phonological acquisition during articulation training. *Journal of Speech and Hearing Disorders, 64*, 459-471.

Ferguson, C. A. (1989). Individual differences in language learning. In M. L. Rice & R. L. Schiefelbusch (Eds.), *The teachability of language* (pp. 187-198). Baltimore, WA: Brookes.

Greenlee, M. (1974). Interacting processes in the child's acquisition of stop-liquid clusters. *Papers and Reports on Child Language Disorders, Stanford University, 7*, 85-100.

Griffiths, R. (1984). *Griffiths mental development scales.* Amersham: Association for Research in Infant and Child Development.

Grunwell, P. (1987). *Clinical phonology* (2nd ed.). London: Croom Helm.

Higgs, J. A. W. (1968). The phonetic development of word initial /s/ plus stop clusters in a group of young children. *British Journal of Disorders of Communication, 3,* 130-138.

Ingram, D. (1976). *Phonological disability in children.* New York: Elsevier.

Long, S. H., Fey, M. E., & Channell, R. W. (1998). *Computerized profiling (MS-DOS version 9.0).* Cleveland, OH: Case Western Reserve University.

McLeod, S. (1997). Sampling consonant clusters: Four procedures designed for Australian children. *Australian Communication Quarterly, Autumn,* 9-12.

McLeod, S. (1999). Children's acquisition of consonant clusters. Unpublished doctoral dissertation, The University of Sydney.

McLeod, S., van Doorn, J., & Reed, V. A. (1997). Realizations of consonant clusters by children with phonological impairment. *Clinical Linguistics and Phonetics, 11,* 85-113.

Miller, J. F. (1981). Procedures for analysing free-speech samples: Syntax and semantics. In J. F. Miller (Ed.), *Assessing language production in children: Experimental procedures* (pp. 21-72). Austin, TX: Pro-Ed.

Olmsted, D. (1971). *Out of the mouth of babes: Earliest stages in language learning.* The Hague: Mouton.

Reynell, J., & Huntley, M. (1984). *Reynell developmental language scales.* Windsor, UK: NFER-Nelson.

Robbins, J., & Klee, T. (1987). Clinical assessment of oropharyngeal motor development in young children. *Journal of Speech and Hearing Disorders, 52,* 271-277.

Shriberg, L., & Kwiatkowski, J. (1980). *Natural process analysis.* New York: John Wiley.

Smit, A. B. (1993). Phonologic error distributions in the Iowa-Nebraska articulation norms project: Word-initial consonant clusters. *Journal of Speech and Hearing Research, 36,* 931-947.

Smit, A. B., Hand, L., Freilinger, J. J., Bernthal, J. E., & Bird, A. (1990). The Iowa articulation norms project and its Nebraska replication. *Journal of Speech and Hearing Disorders, 55,* 779-798.

Stemberger, J. P. (1989). Speech errors in early child language production. *Journal of Memory and Language, 28,* 164-188.

Stoel-Gammon, C. (1987). Phonological skills of 2-year-olds. *Language, Speech, and Hearing Services in Schools, 18,* 323-329.

Templin, M. (1957). *Certain language skills in children (Monograph Series No. 26).* Minneapolis: University of Minnesota, The Institute of Child Welfare.

Vihman, M. M., & Greenlee, M. (1987). Individual differences in phonological development: Ages one and three years. *Journal of Speech and Hearing Research, 30,* 503-521.

Watson, M. M., & Scukanec, G. P. (1997). Phonological changes in the speech of two-year olds: A longitudinal investigation. *Infant-Toddler Intervention, 7,* 67-77.

APPENDIX A
Overall occurrence of each of the twelve realization types

Subj	T1*	T2	T3	T4	T5	T6	T7	T8	T9	T10	T11	T12
1	5	57	3	38	73	3	22	1	2	0	0	44
2	0	77	17	73	14	3	21	0	5	0	0	6
3	0	120	15	37	34	3	11	7	1	0	0	31
4	2	121	18	45	51	2	16	3	11	0	0	27
5	1	70	30	106	28	68	33	3	6	0	0	66
6	1	41	6	11	83	14	37	4	10	1	1	138
7	0	39	10	12	98	30	52	12	4	0	0	220
8	2	53	26	59	99	88	64	7	8	0	1	103
9	0	29	2	12	90	91	39	3	1	0	0	256
10	0	81	4	25	70	13	16	13	4	0	0	178
11	0	13	4	16	7	54	3	8	3	0	1	172
12	1	58	9	134	118	50	91	0	13	0	0	35
13	0	14	17	5	46	50	36	8	2	0	0	218
14	0	19	4	15	141	104	61	2	7	0	0	125
15	0	37	14	54	83	85	30	14	4	0	0	103
16	0	26	6	27	38	42	6	17	8	0	0	221
Tota	12	855	185	669	107	700	538	102	89	1	3	1943

APPENDIX B
Typological distribution of two-element word-initial fricative cluster realizations

Subj	T1*	T2	T3	T4	T5	T6	T7	T8	T9	T10	T11	T12
1	0	16	3	15	8	0	4	0	0	0	0	30
2	0	17	13	20	0	0	4	0	1	0	0	2
3	0	25	1	12	2	2	0	2	0	0	0	11
4	0	40	6	15	7	1	3	1	0	0	0	8
5	1	10	6	20	2	43	5	1	0	0	0	7
6	0	7	0	2	12	3	1	0	0	0	0	56
7	0	1	0	1	17	4	4	2	0	0	0	73
8	0	11	4	29	6	68	8	5	2	0	0	12
9	0	5	0	2	10	40	2	0	0	0	0	56
10	0	10	0	6	3	3	2	1	0	0	0	84
11	0	1	0	0	1	4	0	1	0	0	1	64
12	0	2	0	61	6	29	15	0	0	0	0	2
13	0	6	3	2	12	0	2	0	0	0	0	70
14	0	3	0	4	9	70	9	0	2	0	0	18
15	0	3	1	3	5	66	7	0	0	0	0	12
16	0	5	0	1	2	5	1	0	1	0	0	73
Total	1	162	37	193	102	338	67	13	6	0	1	578

* T_1 = Type 1, T_2 = Type 2, etc (see Table 1 for details).

APPENDIX C

Typological distribution of two-element word-initial stop cluster realizations

Subj	T1*	T2	T3	T4	T5	T6	T7	T8	T9	T10	T11	T12
1	3	35	0	22	63	3	18	1	2	0	0	5
2	0	57	1	53	14	3	17	0	4	0	0	3
3	0	89	0	23	27	0	10	5	1	0	0	6
4	1	61	0	28	29	0	13	2	11	0	0	1
5	0	53	15	83	5	25	27	2	6	0	0	30
6	0	19	0	8	59	11	36	4	10	0	0	47
7	0	11	1	10	70	23	47	10	4	0	0	90
8	0	29	2	13	69	11	55	2	5	0	0	66
9	0	10	0	6	70	37	37	3	1	0	0	139
10	0	55	1	18	63	7	14	12	4	0	0	41
11	0	5	2	16	2	45	1	7	3	0	0	84
12	1	54	0	63	86	0	73	0	12	0	0	5
13	0	3	4	3	28	49	34	8	2	0	0	96
14	0	7	1	6	115	13	52	2	5	0	0	78
15	0	29	0	45	60	14	19	14	4	0	0	61
16	0	12	5	25	30	36	5	17	7	0	0	108
Total	5	529	32	422	790	277	458	89	81	0	0	860

APPENDIX D

Typological distribution of two-element word-final cluster realizations

Subj	T1*	T2	T3	T4	T5	T6	T7	T8	T9	T10	T11	T12
1	2	6	0	1	2	0	0	0	0	0	0	9
2	0	3	3	0	0	0	0	0	0	0	0	1
3	0	6	14	2	5	1	3	0	0	0	0	14
4	1	20	12	2	15	1	0	0	0	0	0	18
5	0	7	9	3	21	0	1	0	0	0	0	34
6	1	15	6	1	12	0	0	0	0	1	1	35
7	0	27	9	1	11	3	1	0	0	0	0	57
8	2	13	20	15	24	9	1	0	1	0	1	26
9	0	14	2	4	10	4	0	0	0	0	0	61
10	0	16	3	1	4	3	0	0	0	0	0	53
11	0	7	2	0	4	5	2	0	0	0	0	24
12	0	2	9	10	26	21	3	0	1	0	0	28
13	0	5	10	0	6	1	0	0	0	0	0	52
14	0	9	3	5	17	21	0	0	0	0	0	29
15	0	6	13	6	18	5	4	0	0	0	0	30
16	0	9	1	1	6	1	0	0	0	0	0	40
Tota	6	165	116	52	181	75	15	0	2	1	2	511

* T_1 = Type 1, T_2 = Type 2, etc.

16

Effects of Oral Language on Sound Segmentation Skills: Crosslinguistic Evidence

Elena Zaretsky

The ability to segment sounds, or phonological awareness[1], is considered to be an essential skill for reading acquisition. Phonological awareness refers to the ability to consciously think about a spoken word in terms of sublexical elements such as syllables, onsets and rimes, and phonemes, and to manipulate these elements in a range of metaphonological tasks, from rhyme recognition to phonemic analysis. Learning to read and write in a language that employs an alphabetic orthography requires that novices come to understand the way that the components of spoken language are represented by the orthographic system in question.

Research since the 1980s has found phonological awareness to be a significant predictor of success in early reading (Liberman, 1971; Blachman, 1983; Bradley & Bryant, 1983; Treiman & Baron, 1983; see Share & Stanovich, 1995, for a recent review). One of the most common aspects of these studies is the relationship between the acquisition of alphabetical literacy and the development of phonological awareness (Ehri, 1979, Morais, Cary, Algeria & Bertelson, 1979, Morais, Bertelson, Cary & Alegria, 1986; see Catts, 1989, for review). That is, preschoolers who show good sound segmentation skills tend to become good readers, whereas children who show poor skills in this area are likely to become less proficient readers (Goswami & Bryant, 1990; Wimmer, Landerl, Linortner & Hummer, 1992). As the evidence in the field of reading acquisition suggests, the relation between sound segmentation skills and reading abilities in alphabetic orthography is bi-directional, whereas phonological awareness is enhanced by the exposure to print (see Catts, 1989 for review) while at the same time influencing reading proficiency (Daneman & Stanton, 1991).

---

[1] The terms 'sound segmentation skills' and 'phonological awareness' are used interchangeably.

Developmentally, larger sublexical units, such as syllables, are easier to recognize than onsets and rimes and individual phonemes. English-speaking children develop awareness of syllables as a first step, and a majority of pre-readers are able to manipulate these units and can be very sensitive to sound similarities and differences (Treiman, 1985a; Treiman & Baron, 1981). Within the onset and rime category, complex onsets are more difficult to segment than simple ones, because it implies manipulation of "subsegments", i.e. segmenting /s/, which is just a phoneme representing the initial part of complex onset, from 'sled' is harder for younger children than segmenting /t/, which is both a phoneme and a whole onset, from 'top'. Difficulties with cluster onsets are apparent in written as well as oral tasks (Bruck & Treiman, 1990).

Influence of the relationship between phonology and orthography (opaque vs. transparent) on the development of phonological awareness after the beginning of written instruction was investigated in a cross-linguistic study with English- and Italian-speaking children (Cossu, Shankweiler, Liberman, Katz & Tola, 1988). Italian children performed considerably better in tasks requiring counting syllables and phonemes. This was attributed to the open syllabic structure of the Italian language. It has been postulated that learning to read and write in a transparent writing system facilitates the acquisition of literacy skills (Treiman, 1992; Oney & Durgunoglu, 1996).

One factor that may influence the development of sound segmentation skills, but which has not been fully explored, is the phonological structure of the spoken language itself. Cossu et al., (1988), provided some evidence that the characteristics of the particular language that children hear might play a role, judging by the performance of Italian-speaking children. Italian speakers as young as 4 years of age performed much better than English-speaking American children on syllable and phoneme segmentation tasks, presumably because of the simpler syllabic structure of Italian. This factor is very important in understanding the contribution of oral language for later success in literacy development, given the findings showing that phonemic segmentation is very difficult for English-speaking children younger than 6 or 7 years of age (Ehri, 1979).

Caravolas and Bruck (1993) addressed the issue of oral and written language influences on sound segmentation skills by comparing the phonological skills of English- and Czech-speaking preschoolers, kindergarteners and first-graders. The tasks of segmenting complex and simple onsets were given in oral and written modalities, where appropriate. Czech and English differ considerably in the composition and use of complex onsets. In Czech, 26 consonants yield 258 different consonant clusters with fewer position restraints within complex onsets, whereas English has a complex vowel system (12 to 19 vowels, 5 to 8 diphthongs) and is governed by very strong phonotactic constraints. Caravolas and Bruck (1993) hypothesized that Czech children would attend better to complex elements within the language structure and thereby heighten their segmentation abilities. Their English-speaking peers may be more inclined to perceive complex consonant clusters as indivisible units, since there are fewer possible permutations. The results reported by Caravolas and Bruck revealed that English-speaking children develop the ability to manipulate whole onsets by the age of 4, and by age 5, show no difficulty with these units. However, their awareness of parts of the onsets is relatively poor and continues to lag behind, even when formal reading instruction has begun. Their Czech counterparts seem to develop awareness of both types of onsets starting at age 4, finding them to present the same degree of difficulty. By kindergarten, they can manipulate complex onsets without difficulty, demonstrating mastery of both linguistic units by grade one.

The intent of the present study was to replicate and extend the results of Caravolas and Bruck (1993), by comparing English- and Russian-speaking children's sound segmentation skills. In doing so, our aim was to look at the influence of the oral structure of language only. If Caravolas and Bruck's hypothesis was correct, the same outcome in the performance of sound segmentation tasks should be found comparing Russian- and English-speaking children, given the many similarities found in the linguistic structures of Russian and Czech.

Like Czech, Russian employs a transparent orthography and is rich in complex onsets, although Russian employs only 21 consonants with distinct orthographic representations, compared to 24 in English. However, these 21 consonants produce 33 sounds depending on palatization[2] (12 can be both hard and soft and 9 remain unchanged). The presence of prefixes greatly increases possible complex clusters, allowing up to 4 segments in the initial position: (/vz/+/gl/+/janul/=/**vzgl**-janul/, i.e. "looked upon", /vs/+/krik/=/**vskrik**/, i.e. "sudden surprised cry"). In addition, the same letter/sound combinations are interchangeable in the initial position (/**glup-lgun**/, /**vriet-rvjet**/).

Unlike English, the Russian vowel system is relatively simple: It employs 10 vowels, which can be divided into 5 basic ones, i.e. /a/, /o/, /e/, /i/, /u/, and 5 corresponding complex ones. These are represented as a distinct single grapheme in the alphabetic system, but a complex phoneme with the addition of /j/ sound before the original, basic one.

Given this information, and based on previous research, we hypothesized that if the structure of spoken language influences the development of phonological awareness, Russian-speaking pre-readers should show higher awareness of the individual phonemes in complex onsets than their English-speaking peers.

---

[2] Palatization of consonants in the Russian language depends on the following vowel, (/mor/ -'death' in Old Russian has hard /r/, but /mor'e/ -'sea' has soft /r/), as well as on the use of 'myahky znak' (soft sign) after the consonant in the middle and final position, i.e. /redko/ ('seldom') vs. /red'ka/ ('black radish'), /mel/ ('chalk') vs. /mel'/ ('shallow water').

METHOD

To test this hypothesis, participants were given a battery of oral tasks that involved making judgments based on auditory information: similarity of complex (CCV) and simple (CVC) onsets of monosyllabic nonwords (*Same–Different*), identification of the first sound in monosyllabic words (*Sound Isolation*), and deleting the first phoneme of the monosyllabic word (*Phoneme Deletion*). Russian and English versions were constructed for each task and all the children were administered both versions. Relative performance of Russian- and English-speaking children on complex and simple onset items in both versions was compared. According to our hypothesis, two outcomes were anticipated: 1) Russian speakers should perform better than English speakers on tasks requiring segmentation of complex onsets, regardless of the task version, and 2) there should be a greater discrepancy between the number of correct CCV and CVC items among English speakers, regardless of the version of the task.

Participants

Thirty Russian- and English-speaking monolingual preschoolers (15 in each group) from day-care centers in the Greater Boston area participated in the study. All of the children came from comparable middle-class homes. Russian children came from families of recent immigrants who were educated professionals and enjoyed middle-class status in Russia. The language spoken at home was strictly Russian. (Russian parents tend to preserve their native language, firmly believing that English will be acquired without difficulty as soon as the child enters regular school.)

Mean age of the participants in months was 59.2 for Russian-speakers and 57.8 for English-speakers (range from 47 to 76 months). Each language group was further divided into two subgroups, referred to as Younger and Older, adding a maturational dimension to our sample. The Younger group had a mean age of 52 months for both groups. The Older group had a mean age of 64 months for English speakers and 68 months for Russian speakers.

Only pre-readers were included in the study: If a child was able to read three out of 10 basic words in his native language, he was excluded from the study. Structural analysis of Russian-speaking children's abilities to communicate in English revealed linear, "telegraphic" utterances with few or no morphological inflections. Therefore, these children were considered monolingual.

All children were administered the Peabody Picture Vocabulary Test-Revised (PPVT-R, form L). The items on the test were administered in Russian to Russian-speaking subjects. Both groups performed in a very similar way (Mean SS = 113 for Russian-speakers and Mean SS = 114 for English speakers).

Procedures

All children were given three oral tasks created in parallel forms in Russian and English: *Same–Different* (identifying the initial consonant as being the same or different in a pair), *Sound Isolation* (identifying the initial consonant only for simple or complex onsets), and *Phoneme Deletion* (identifying the initial consonant, removing it and saying what is left of the word). In each task, the material consisted of monosyllabic nonsense words equally divided into target items containing complex and simple onsets. Onsets of stimuli were balanced across categories for relative frequency in each language. The Russian version used 34 different clusters, compared with 22 in English. The Russian version contained 17 language-specific clusters, whereas the English version had three. The rest of the sample contained clusters possible in both languages. All the children were administered both versions (native and foreign).

Each child had a warm up time with a puppet and sample words to assure full understanding of the procedure and was tested individually. For the *Same–Different* task the children were instructed to listen carefully to two 'funny' words and say if they sound the same or different in the beginning. *Sound Isolation* task required a child to listen to the word and repeat the first sound only. *Phoneme Deletion* task required the child to listen to the word, repeat the word, say the first sound only, and than say the word without the first sound.

Tasks and order of presentation. The *Same–Different* task consisted of 20 CCVC and 20 CVCC pairs of nonwords. Half of the CCVC pairs shared the first consonant of the complex onset (/gliz/-/grof/) and half did not (/flep/-/drok/). The same was true for CVCC pairs (/silp/-/serk/; /borg/-/nist/). Therefore, Same pairs shared the onset or the first consonant of the onset, and Different pairs did not share any parts of the onset. The resulting 40 pairs were divided into two 20-items blocks consisting of 5 pairs each of Same CCVC and CVCC nonsense words, and 5 pairs each of Different CCVC and CVCC nonsense words. The order was randomized and blocks administered on separate days. The same procedure applied to both versions of the tests and the order of the version administration was randomized as well.

The *Sound Isolation* task consisted of 10 CCV and 10 CVC items. There was no foreign or native version. The same consonants of CCV items occurred in different positions on the CVC items (/dor/-/dro/). Although there were no versions, in some instances the CVC combination was possible in both languages, but the CCV combination of the same letters was possible only in Russian (/mur/-/mru/). The order of the items was randomized for presentation.

The *Phoneme Deletion* task consisted of 16 monosyllabic nonsense words based on phonotactic constraints of both languages and divided into Russian and English versions. Each version consisted of 8 items: 4 CVCC and 4 CCVC.

Each child received 2 tests on the same day: Block I (or II) of the *Same–Different* task and *Sound Isolation* task on one day, and the remaining Block and *Phoneme Deletion* task on the other.

RESULTS

Accuracy scores from the *Same–Different* task were submitted to the initial 5-way analysis of variance (ANOVA) with Language (Russian vs. English), Age (younger vs. older), Version (native vs. foreign), Onset (complex vs. simple), and Decision (same vs. different) as factors. Only the main effect of onset type (complex vs. simple), was found to be significant, where collapsed results in both linguistic groups of children showed a better performance on complex onsets [F (1,26) = 5.429, p < 0.05], with M = 77.9% for complex and M = 73.3% for simple onsets. This result was surprising because we had postulated an advantage for Russian children only in performance on complex onsets.

The 2-way interaction of Age and Onset types, which approached significance [F (1,26) = 3.080, p = 0.091], provided an idea of the pattern of performance that influenced the main effect of Onset type. It was within the younger group that a clear preference for complex over simple onsets was seen (M = 77.3% vs. 69.5%). The older group performed with near equal proficiency on both (M = 78.6% for complex 77.7% for simple onsets). The preference for complex onsets in general was consistent with the results of the main effect of onset type. (But, as we will note in the discussion, performance of the younger group may have been influenced by the greater perceptual salience of complex phonological entities, rather than by language-specific features.) Mastery of both types of onsets might be attributed to linguistic capability as the child matures.

A significant interaction was found between the task Version and Decision [F (1,26) = 5.650, p < 0.05]. This showed an advantage of Different over Same items in the foreign condition (M = 80.2% vs. M = 68.8%) and a very slight one in the same direction in the native condition (M = 78.3% vs. M = 75.2%). Thus, it may be postulated that perhaps the discrimination of different onsets is carried out at an acoustic or phonetic level, whereas reliable performance on the same trials depend on abstract categorical (e.g. phonemic) influences.

A 3-way interaction between Age, Version and Decision proved to be the most significant [F (1,26) = 9.600, p < 0.005]. Younger children showed very different sized effects in Same and Different tasks: They were more successful with Same items in the native condition (M = 78.1% vs. M = 71.9%), but with Different items in the foreign condition (M = 77.8% vs. M = 65.9%). Older children were consistently better on Different items regardless of version. These results could be interpreted as follows: The effect of the acoustical familiarity of the same-sounding clusters in the native condition made the younger group show preference for these items, but by the same token, acoustical differences made them more attentive to the unfamiliar sounds in the foreign condition. As to the older group's better results in Different items, it could be indicative of the fact that different items have inherent acoustic characteristics that 5 to 6 year olds with a certain degree of meta-linguistic skills can discriminate with ease (Table 1).

TABLE 1
Same-Different task: percentage correct by age, version and decision.

Test Version	Age	Same	Different
Native	Young	78.1	71.9
Foreign	Old	65.9	77.8
Native	Young	71.8	85.7
Foreign	Old	72.1	82.9

A three-way analysis of variance was carried out for the *Sound Isolation* task with Language, Age and Onset types as factors. Only the main effect of age approached significance [F (1,26) = 3.006, p = 0.095]. As expected, the older group was marginally superior, displaying an accuracy rate of M = 62.5% as compared to M = 53.6%. We interpreted it as a maturation factor.

Of most interest to us was a significant interaction between the Onset type and native Language of the subjects [F (1,26) = 7.27, p < 0.02]. This predicted interaction showed that Russian-speaking children, as a group, scored significantly higher on CCV than on CVC items, whereas English-speaking children showed the opposite pattern of performance. This finding supports Caravolas and Bruck's (1993) hypothesis that language structure does affect the development of phonological awareness, i.e. manipulation of complex onsets is easier for children whose oral language input is more varied in complex onset combinations

A three-way interaction between Language, Age, and Onset type approached significance [F (1,26) = 3.776, p = 0.063]. This result reflects the most interesting trend among language groups in their performance. It is within the younger group of children that we see the strongest inclination to show a language-dependent performance advantage. With the same pattern of performance as mentioned above (see Table 2), younger children showed more discrepancies in their performance on complex (English speakers) or simple onsets (Russian speakers), whereas older children in both language groups showed better competence (meta-linguistic skills) and, therefore, compatible results.

TABLE 2
Sound isolation task: percentage correct by language, age and onset type.

Language	Age	Onset Type Complex (CCV)	Simple (CVC)
English	Combined	73.3	87.3
	Young	65.0	86.3
	Old	82.9	88.6
Russian	Combined	83.3	78.7
	Young	78.8	68.8
	Old	88.6	90.0

The *Phoneme Deletion* task could not be submitted to an analysis of variance because a number of subjects in each group failed to perform the task, although it was administered to all the children. Seven out of 15 Russian-speakers were able to respond and as a group they did better on the foreign than the native version (32.75% vs. 24.75% correct). However, they had more success with CCV than CVC items (38.5% vs. 19%). Eleven out of 15 English speaking children were able to perform this task. For this group the native version was somewhat easier to process (51% vs. 48.5%). Of interest is the fact that the majority of Russian speakers, even the ones who could not perform this task, could still identify (say) the initial consonant within consonant clusters. English speakers were more inclined to give undivided complex onsets as an answer, supporting our hypothesis that complex onsets are more difficult to manipulate for English-speaking children (Fig.1).

DISCUSSION

The primary purpose of this study was to investigate the influence of oral language structure on the development of phonological awareness. In contrasting the Russian and English languages, our focus, like that of Caravolas and Bruck (1993), was on the effects that differences in phonological inventory, frequency and variety of complex onsets in languages (Czech vs. English and Russian vs. English, respectively) have on the native speakers' awareness of these items.

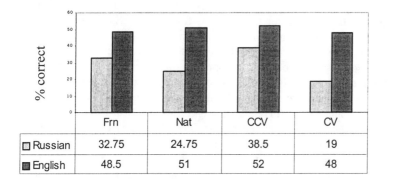

	Frn	Nat	CCV	CV
Russian	32.75	24.75	38.5	19
English	48.5	51	52	48

FIG.1 Phoneme deletion task by version and onset type.

Our hypothesis that language structure in the form of oral language input plays a role in the development of sound segmentation skills has been supported by the results of the *Sound Isolation* task. As was predicted, Russian-speaking children performed better on complex onsets, whereas English-speaking children were more comfortable with simple onsets, which is within the structure of that language. Moreover, the overall phonemic awareness of Russian speakers showed up in comparable performances on both types of onset, whereas English speakers' performance on simple onsets was dramatically better, especially among younger children.

The *Sound Isolation* task suggested a developmental trend in the acquisition of phonological awareness. It seems that by the age of 4, as our groups' performance indicated, English speakers begin to develop the ability to manipulate simple onsets and by age 5 they show no difficulties manipulating these units. This is consistent with Caravolas and Bruck's hypothesis. And although complex onsets continue to be more difficult for young English speakers to manipulate, by age 5 the difference in the percentage of correct responses begins to shrink. In contrast, Russian speakers are better at manipulating complex onsets by age 4, but by age 5 there is no difference between their performances on both types of onsets. This suggests that perhaps they begin to develop these skills in tandem, rather than strictly one after the other. Caravolas and Bruck (1993) came to the same conclusion regarding the performance of Czech children on similar tasks.

The *Phoneme Deletion* task, although very poorly performed by both groups, especially by the Russian speakers, deserves a special look and consideration in terms of to what degree the structure of a given language influences the development of metaphonological abilities in pre-readers. As we saw, version played a large role in the ability of children to delete the initial phoneme and to say what remains of the word. Caravolas and Bruck (1993), provided a possible explanation for the better performance of English-speaking children on this task which can be applied to our study as well. Inherently, syllabic structure differences between the English and Russian (or Czech) languages may allow English speakers to approach these items as an onset and rime. And by removing the onset, be it complex or simple, many English words are left with rimes that represent another legal word, (i.e. /b-at/, /br-at/, /b-rat/, /s-it/, /sl-it/, /s-lit/) and so on (Treiman's suggestion to Bruck by personal communication). Russian word structure does not allow this division. The syllables are built around vowels with the consonants bound by the vowel's gravity, to a point where a consonant will be added to the next syllable, rather than make a previous one a closed syllable, (i.e. /re-da-ktor/ (editor), rather than /re-dak-tor/). These phonotactic constraints are imposed over the morphological units within the words: Prefixes, suffixes and even roots are pulled apart by the syllabic division described above (Modern Russian Language, 4th Ed., 1984)

As to the pattern of performance that showed a clear preference for complex onsets in the *Same–Different* task for both linguistic groups, especially in the foreign condition, it raises certain questions as to the kind of processes that are involved in carrying out the judgment on this task: meta-phonological skills or temporal processing? If it is the latter, then the results can be explained by acoustic/phonetic perception on a global, non-analytical level of awareness (Morais, 1991), therefore making it a categorization task on the basis of the initial phoneme. This holds especially true when a preliterate child is faced with the phonotactic constraints of the native language. By the same token, it could affect decision making when the same child hears a stimulus made up within the constraints of a foreign language. Therefore, this particular task should be considered a "phonological awareness" task with some reservations, especially if we are looking for cross-linguistic evidence in the development of sound segmentation skills.

The fact that age played a role in the performance of both linguistic groups, allowing the older ones to be equally proficient (near, but not at ceiling) on simple and complex onset items, suggests that there might be a window of time when phonemic segmentation skills begin to develop and transform from internal ability to meta-linguistic skill.

In conclusion, our results support the hypothesis that the structure of the language that children are learning to speak affects their ability to perceive and manipulate the components of syllabic structure. This was demonstrated by significant differences between Russian- and English-speaking children's abilities to manipulate complex and simple onsets on a variety of phonological awareness tasks. It would be of interest to further explore and understand the basis of between-language differences and the way they heighten children's awareness of the elements these languages comprise.

REFERENCES

Blachman, B. A. (1983). Are we assessing the linguistic factors critical in early reading? *Annals of Dyslexia, 33*, 91-109.

Bradley, L., & Bryant, P. E. (1983). Categorizing sounds and learning to read a causal connection. *Nature, 301*, 419-421.

Bruck, M., & Treiman, R. (1990). Phonological awareness and spelling in normal children and dyslexics: The case of initial consonant clusters. *Journal of Experimental Child Psychology, 50*, 156-178.

Caravolas, M., & Bruck, M. (1993). The effect of oral and written language input on children's phonological awareness: a cross-linguistic study. *Journal of Experimental Child Psychology, 55*, 1-130.

Catts, H. W. (1989). Phonological processing deficits and reading disabilities. In A. G. Kamhi & H. W. Catts (Eds.), *Reading disabilities: A developmental language perspective* (pp. 101-132). Boston: Allyn & Bacon.

Cossu, G., Shankweiler, D., Liberman, I. Y., Katz, L. E., & Tola, G. (1988). Awareness of phonological segments and reading ability in Italian children. *Applied Psycholinguistics, 9*, 1-16.

Daneman, M., & Stainton, M. (1991). Phonological recoding in silent reading. *Journal of Experimental Psychology: Learning, Memory, and Cognition, 17*, 618-632.

Dunn, L. M., & Dunn, L. M. (1961). *Peabody picture vocabulary test-revised.* American Guidance Service.

Ehri, L. C. (1979). Linguistic insight: Threshold of reading acquisition. In T. G. Waller & G. E. MacKinnon (Eds.), *Reading research: Advances in theory and practice* (Vol. 1, pp. 63-114). New York: Academic Press.

Goswami, U., & Bryant, P. E. (1990). *Phonological skills and learning to read.* Hillsdale, NJ: Lawrence Erlbaum Associates.

Liberman, I. Y. (1971). Basic research in speech and lateralization of language: Some implications for reading disability. *Bulletin of the Orton Society, 21*, 71-87.

Morais, J. (1991). Constraints on the Development of Phonemic Awareness. In S. Bradley & D. Shankweiler (Eds.), *Phonological processes in literacy: A tribute to Isabella Y. Liberman.* Hillsdale, NJ: Lawrence Erlbaum Associates.

Morais, J., Bertelson, P., Cary, L., & Alegria, J. (1986). Literacy training and speech segmentation. *Cognition, 24*, 45-64.

Morais, J., Cary, L., Alegria, J., & Bertelson, P. (1979). Does awareness of speech as a sequence of phones arise spontaneously? *Cognition, 7*, 323-331.

Oney, B., & Durgunoglu, A. Y. (1996). Beginning to Read in Turkish: A Phonologically Transparent Orthography. *Applied Psycholinguistics, 18*, 1.

Rosental, D. E. (1984). *Modern Russian language: Lexicon, phraseology, phonetics, orthoepics, graphemes, orthography, word formation, morphology and syntax.* Moscow: Fourth Edition Editor

Share, D., & Stanovich, K. (1995). Cognitive processes in early reading development: Accommodating individual differences into a model of acquisition. *Issues in Education.*

Treiman, R. (1985a). Onsets and rimes as units of spoken syllables: evidence from children. *Journal of Experimental Psychology, 39*, 161-181.

Treiman, R. A. (1992). Children's spelling errors on syllable-initial consonant clusters. *Journal of Educational Psychology, 83*, 346-360.

Treiman, R., & Baron, J. (1981). Segmental analysis ability: Development and relation to reading ability. In G. E. MacKinnon & T. G. Waller (Eds.), *Reading research: Advances in theory and practice* (Vol. 3, pp. 159-198). New York: Academic Press.

Treiman, R., & Baron, J. (1983). Phonemic analysis training helps children benefit from spelling-sound rules. *Memory and Cognition, 11*, 382-389.

Wimmer, H., Landerl, K., Linortner, R., & Hummer, P. (1992). The relationship of phonemic awareness to reading acquisition: More consequence than precondition but still important. *Cognition, 40*, 219-249.

17

Onset Clusters and the Sonority Sequencing Principle in Spanish: A Treatment Efficacy Study

Raquel T. Anderson

Treatment efficacy has been a fruitful area of research in child phonology (Gierut, Morrisette, Hughes & Rowland, 1996). Linguistic models of phonological acquisition, structure, and change have been used to predict system level changes in children undergoing treatment for functional (i.e. nonorganic) phonological disorders. Most of the research has focused on establishing treatment paradigms that result in more ample changes to the child's phonological system. One area that has received particular attention is the notion of markedness (Elbert, Dinnsen & Powell, 1984; Gierut et al., 1996). Markedness is best explained by universal patterns of use across languages. It usually refers to the relative complexity of a feature or segment, as compared to other features or segments. Unmarked features or segments are usually acquired before more marked features. They are also more frequently occurring across languages. Implicational universals are particularly relevant to the notion of markedness. In phonology, they indicate that the presence of certain sound classes or segments imply that other sound classes or segments are also present in the language (Elbert et al., 1984; Gierut et al., 1996). For example, the presence of fricatives in a language implies the presence of stops, but the presence of stops does not imply fricatives.

Using markedness as a guide for choosing treatment targets, various studies have supported the notion that treating more marked sounds, because these imply presence of other sounds, will result in more changes to the child's developing phonological system. Examples of such treatment paradigms include teaching voiced obstruents and not voiceless obstruents (McReynolds & Jetzke, 1986), and fricatives instead of stops (Dinnsen & Elbert, 1984). In both studies, teaching an unmarked form resulted in generalizations across classes, and syllable positions, whereas teaching the more unmarked form resulted in only within category changes.

Markedness principles have also been used when targeting onset clusters. For example, in a study by Elbert et al. (1984), children with phonological disorders were taught clusters that varied on relative markedness: fricative + liquid versus stops + liquid clusters. For children who did not show knowledge of both types of clusters, generalization across cluster types was obtained when the more marked cluster - fricative + liquid - was targeted during treatment.

More recently, Gierut (1999) has applied a model of markedness for onset clusters to establish treatment targets that may result in greater generalization. This model is based on Clements' (1990) description of sonority values across syllable constituents. In the scheme described by Gierut (1999), the values for the consonant classes are as follows: (1) glides, (2) liquids, (3) nasals, (4) voiced fricatives, (5) voiceless fricatives, (6) voiced stops, and (7) voiceless stops. The relative sonority difference between the two consonants that constitute the onset cluster are obtained by subtracting the smaller value from the larger value. This difference is used to place the cluster at a particular level, which corresponds to its relative markedness. Smaller differences result in more marked onset clusters. For example, a cluster such as [bw] has a sonority value of 5 (b = 6, w =1; 6 - 1 = 5), whereas [fl] has a value of 3 (f = 5, l = 2; 5 - 2 = 3), [fl] being thus more marked than [bw]. Applying this scheme, Gierut (1999) presents evidence that targeting more marked onset clusters results in significant changes to the child's phonological system. In various single subject treatment studies where clusters with differing sonority values were chosen for training, children who were taught a more marked cluster on the sonority hierarchy demonstrated greater generalization across cluster classes.

Although most studies with English-speaking children confirm the value of using markedness principles for choosing treatment targets, this pattern has been slow to emerge in treatment studies with other language groups. A case in point is Spanish. The treatment research on phonological training with Spanish-speaking children is arguably limited, and has not addressed the important issue of generalization (cf. Goldstein, 1996). This investigation, thus, focuses on the application of the markedness concept in the intervention provided to a Spanish-speaking child with a functional phonological disorder. In particular, the sonority sequencing hierarchy for onset clusters described by Gierut (1999) was used as a template for choosing intervention targets in Spanish. The main goal then, was to examine if the teaching of more marked sequences would result in generalized learning across all onset cluster classes.

METHOD

The Participant

J.C., a Colombian Spanish-speaking girl with functional articulation problems, participated in the study. At the beginning of the investigation, she was 3;2 years of age. Parental concern indicated that J.C. was not producing many of the sounds in Spanish and her speech was often unintelligible. In addition, the parents reported that her productive skills in Spanish were poor, as compared to other children her age. Speech and language assessment in Spanish confirmed the parents' observations. J.C. presented with a significant delay in phonological development with depressed skills in expressive language. Results from the McArthur Communicative Development Inventory (Spanish) (Jackson-Maldonado, Bates & Thal, 1992), indicated difficulties in the use of verbs and verbal inflection, as well as in the use of pronominal forms. Because of her significant phonological deficits, assessment of the use of functional categories (i.e. verb inflection) was difficult. Receptive skills, as assessed via informal means and parental reports, were deemed to be age appropriate. A hearing screening at 20 dB revealed normal hearing acuity bilaterally. Oral motor structure was also adequate for speech.

A Spanish single word phonological probe consisting of 88 items was administered. Each singleton consonant was tested at least three times in all syllable positions in which the sound typically occurs in Spanish. A variety of onset clusters were also targeted. A summary of the child's phonetic inventory for singletons is presented in Table 1. A sound was considered to be part of the child's phonetic inventory if it was produced at least twice in the sample. As can be noted, J.C. produced fricatives, nasals, glides, stops, and liquids. Missing from her inventory were the following Spanish sounds for the child's particular dialect: [ɾ, r, h, g]. In addition, the Spanish spirant allophones of the voiced stops were not produced. Non target productions included mainly place and manner errors. There was only one instance where an onset cluster was produced correctly (i.e. [sj]). Phonetic analysis revealed production of two other onset clusters (i.e., [fw, gj]). Onset clusters were reduced to one element (e.g., [k/kɾ, f/fɾ]). J.C.'s main syllable shape was CV. Although produced, frequent omission of final consonants was also evidenced (i.e. 39% incidence). Singletons in all other positions were not omitted, with the exception of [h].

At the time of the research, J.C. was enrolled in the clinic's language based preschool program. This preschool includes children who are English speakers and who have typical language skills, English-speaking children with language disorders, and children who are learning English as a second language. J.C. participated as a second language learner. In addition to attending this

TABLE 1
J.C.'s initial phonetic inventory.

Manner	Sound
Plosive	p b t d k
Nasal	m n
Fricative	f s ʒ
Liquid	l
Glide	w j

preschool, J.C. also attended an English-speaking preschool in the community. During the initial stages of the investigation, J.C. had limited English skills. During the final stages, J.C. was more proficient in the language, but was still considered, from parental and school report, more fluent in Spanish.

Establishing Markedness in Spanish Onset Clusters

Identification of the relative markedness of Spanish onset clusters was based on the sonority sequencing hierarchy (Gierut, 1999). Specifically, each consonant in the cluster was assigned a particular number within a scale that indicates relative sonority, from most sonorous to least sonorous. Following this procedure, Spanish onset clusters were categorized in terms of degree of markedness. This categorization scheme is presented in Table 2. Included in this scheme are consonant sequences with a glide as its second element. Although the identification of obstruent + glide sequences as true clusters in Spanish is subject to debate (Barrutía & Schwegler, 1994; Harris, 1983), these were included for two main reasons. First, they have been analyzed as clusters in English research (Chin & Dinnsen, 1992; Gierut, 1999), and the child who participated in the present study had difficulty producing these, in addition to the other permissible sequences (i.e. liquid clusters). Least marked clusters are those with higher sonority scores and most marked clusters have the lowest scores. As can be observed, in Spanish, the consonant sequence with the lowest sonority value, and thus most marked, is a liquid + glide combination, whereas the least marked sequence is that of a voiceless stop + glide.

Procedures

Because onset clusters were evidently problematic for J.C., and because she had a reduced syllabic inventory, treatment was developed   that focused on increasing syllable complexity. The intervention was designed to address the issue of generalization; that is, the particular onset cluster that should be targeted so as to obtain the greatest change in the child's phonological system. Following previous research (e.g. Elbert et al., 1984; Gierut, 1999), treatment

TABLE 2
Sonority Sequencing Principle hierarchy for Spanish onset clusters.

Level	Onset clusters	Example
Level 1	liquid + glide	rweða, familja
Level 2	voiced fricative + liquid	aβɾe
	nasal + glide	nweβe
Level 3	voiceless fricative + liquid	fɾesa
	voiced fricative + glide	dʒuβja
Level 4	voiced stop + liquid	blaŋko
	voiceless fricative + glide	fjesta
Level 5	voiceless stop + liquid	pɾimo
	voiced stop + glide	bweno
Level 6	voiceless stop + glide	pjano

targets chosen were those that were the most marked. Based on this categorization scheme, the clusters targeted for intervention were [lw] and [lj].

A single-subject treatment design was followed. Prior to the beginning of treatment, a baseline probe was administered where the child's imitative production of ten words at each sonority level was gathered. Therapy began after the initial probe was completed. These probes were readministered every four weeks. Care was taken to use words that were similar in length and syllable shape across all sonority levels. A non-targeted sound was also probed following the procedures used for assessing production of onset clusters. The sound chosen was the singleton [ɾ] in intervocalic position. This sound was chosen because it was not in J.C.'s initial phonetic inventory and it was not the focus of the established training protocol. Treatment was conducted once a week for 45 minutes. J.C. was seen for a total of 24 treatment sessions. The first 12 sessions targeted the production of [lj] and [lw] at the syllable level (e.g., [lje, lwa]). The last 12 sessions focused on the production of these clusters in initial position in bisyllabic (CCVCV and CVCCV) nonsense words (e.g., [ljepe], [palja]). After each set of sessions, the initial 88 word phonological probe was readministered to the child. To evaluate maintenance of acquired skill, a probe was also given to the child six weeks post treatment. This probe consisted of the same items used during the four-week period assessment for generalization. All probes were targeted using imitation.

Treatment procedures consisted of various strategies for the correct production of the target onset clusters. Because the focus of the investigation was on the efficacy of choosing a particular target for intervention, and not a particular treatment paradigm, the procedures used across sessions were varied and focused on both motor and linguistic aspects of sound production. Activities included drills and minimal pair tasks where the child's production of the target cluster was contrasted with its correct production. Both types of procedures were incorporated in all sessions. During the sessions that focused on the production of liquid + glide clusters in nonsense words, the invented words were paired with objects and human figures. Objects were also paired with the child's production, so as to be able to use minimal pair contrasts as a strategy during intervention. The parents were also provided with activities that focused on the production of the target onset clusters. These paralleled those that were followed in the therapy sessions. All sessions were conducted in Spanish by a graduate clinician with good Spanish speaking skills.

Reliability

All productions obtained using probes were transcribed by the graduate clinician and the investigator, who is a native Spanish-speaker. Reliability was gathered for the identification of onset clusters. For all probes, there was an 87% point-by-point agreement for the identification of clusters within the sample.

RESULTS

Probes

Results from the 4-week probe data are presented in Fig. 1. Initial baseline data indicated that the child failed to produce onset clusters across all levels. After treatment was initiated, there was an increase in correct production of onset clusters. This increase did not occur immediately after initiation of treatment, and was not evidenced across all levels. The most significant and earlier gains were noted in the production of level 6 onset clusters. The level that evidenced the smallest gains was level 1, which was targeted during intervention. The major gains were noted after the first 12-week intervention period, where an increase in correct production for all sonority levels was observed. The largest gains were noted during the last 4-week probe session, which occurred immediately after treatment had been completed. Correct production varied from as low as 30% (level 1) to as high as 90% (level 6). In contrast to the use of onset clusters, correct production of [ɾ] in intervocalic position did not increase significantly during treatment, as noted in J.C.'s production of this sound during probes. By the fourth probe session, the child produced [ɾ] correctly on one occasion. This pattern was maintained throughout the remaining probes. Correct production was limited to the same word across all sessions, specifically [naɾis].

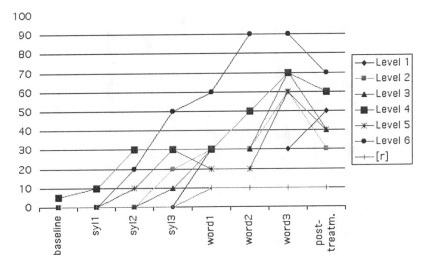

FIG. 1 Production of onset clusters by sonority hierarchy.

Results from the 6-week post-treatment probe session are also presented in Fig. 1. As can be observed, all levels, with the exception of level 1, demonstrated a decrease in accuracy of production. Accuracy levels varied form 70% (level 6) to 30% (level 2). Nevertheless, J.C.'s correct productions during this session were higher than what was noted during baseline and the four initial 4-week probes. Level 1 production increased from 30% during the last treatment probe to 50% accuracy during the post-treatment probe. No change was observed in the child's production of [ɾ].

Error Patterns

To address changes in the production of onset clusters, the child's nontarget productions were analyzed. Of particular interest was to note changes in production of the target clusters that evidenced a movement toward more complex syllable shapes. Based on previous studies on cluster development (Chin & Dinnsen, 1992; McLeod, Van Doorn & Reed, 1997; Smit, 1993), five types of nontarget responses were identified. These include: (1) cluster omission (isa/brisa), 2) cluster reduction (b/br), 3) consonant + glide production (bjaŋko/blaŋko), 4) epenthesis (bʌlaŋko/blaŋko), and (5) same level substitution (blisa/brisa – level 4/level 4). In addition, following research by Chin and Dinnsen (1992) on children's use of coalescence in the production of clusters, all instances of cluster reduction were further analyzed

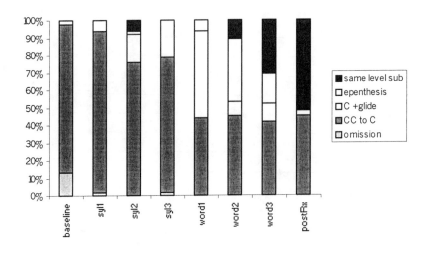

FIG. 2 Type of error across probes.

for presence of this process. Results of the error analyses are summarized in Fig. 2.

During initial baseline and the following three 4-week probes, the most common non-target response was one that changed the structure of the syllable, mainly cluster reduction. The incidence of this type of error ranged from 85% (baseline) to 77% at the third probe. Most of the cluster reduction errors resulted in the use of one of the elements or with a common substitution in the use of the element in singleton productions. Few productions were instances of coalescence. These occurred during the first three probe periods, and were noted in the production of some [w] sequences, where the glide's place of articulation merged with the manner of articulation of the other consonant (e.g. m/nw, p/kw). Omission of cluster, which also reduces syllable complexity, was uncommon, the highest incidence (13%) noted during initial baseline. Marked differences in error productions were observed during the last three 4-week probes, as well as during post-treatment baseline. During the fourth treatment probe, J.C. began to produce many of the target clusters as a consonant + glide sequence. Although this pattern began to emerge during the third 4-week probe, it became more apparent at this time. Fifty percent of her nontarget responses were of this type. Use of epenthesis began to emerge as well. During the last two 4-week probes, J.C. evidenced an increase in the use of another error pattern: same level substitutions. This consisted primarily of [l] for [ɾ] substitution. At the time when the last probe was administered, 36% of J.C.'s nontarget responses were of this type. Post-treatment probes demonstrated the changes in nontarget responses more dramatically. Although cluster reduction was still present, the incidence of same level substitutions was higher than any other error.   Fifty-two percent of all nontarget responses consisted of the use of an onset cluster from the same sonority level.

Other Analyses

To further study changes in J.C.'s production of onset clusters, production patterns noted during the three single word testing procedures (i.e. initial assessment, mid treatment assessment, post-treatment assessment) were analyzed.   Accuracy of production of onset clusters and type of nontarget response were identified for all three testing sessions. Results from the initial single word production showed that only three onset clusters were produced, where only one corresponded to the actual target. These clusters corresponded to levels 4 and 5 in the sonority hierarchy.   At this time, 95% of nontarget responses were cluster reductions.   When J.C. was tested after the initial 12-week treatment sessions, she continued to demonstrate 95% incidence of cluster reduction. Two onset clusters were produced correctly (i.e., [pj, fw]). Although clusters were still infrequent in the child's single word sample, an increase in the presence of onset clusters was noted. Phonetic analysis revealed at least one instance of a cluster from each sonority level in J.C.'s corpora. Single word production testing conducted after treatment was completed and revealed that significant changes had occurred. Percent accuracy in the production of onset clusters increased to 35%.   As in the previous testing, all sonority levels were represented. Unlike the previous testing, correct production of these was also noted. Analysis of nontarget responses showed a change in error patterns.   Incidence of cluster reduction dropped to 44%, and other errors such as the use of epenthesis (24%), and substitution of same level cluster (33%) emerged. These two patterns were not present in the previous two single word samples.

DISCUSSION

Our investigation sought to explore the application of markedness principles in the treatment of phonological disorders in a Spanish-speaking child.   In particular, the sonority sequencing hierarchy was used as a guide for identifying onset clusters for treatment. The most marked consonant sequence in Spanish was thus targeted for intervention. The data suggest that this strategy resulted in significant changes to the child's phonological system.   The changes were noted in J.C.'s error pattern and in the production of onset clusters across untreated classes.   The data are thus in accord with previous research that has identified relative markedness as an important variable to consider when choosing treatment targets that result in major changes to the child's phonological system. Of course, such principles need to be applied considering the target adult phonological system, in the present case Spanish.

Treatment for J.C. focused on teaching the most marked onset cluster in Spanish, which, according to the sonority sequencing principle, is a liquid + glide sequence. Although traditionally onset clusters in Spanish have been described as containing a consonant + liquid (Goldstein & Iglesias, 1996a, 1996b; Harris, 1983), consonant + glide combinations were included as clusters, as the child evidenced limited use of glides within that context. Prior to treatment, the child's use of onset clusters was minimal. Clusters in her phonetic inventory were few and these were of a lower markedness value than the one targeted during intervention. As treatment progressed, the productive use of onset clusters across the sonority hierarchy was noted. Thus, focusing the most marked cluster not only resulted in the emergence of these forms in her speech, but in the production of a variety of onset clusters not targeted during treatment. Because other aspects of the child's system did not undergo significant changes, as for example the use of the liquid [r], suggests that the changes on onset cluster production were the result of the established treatment, and not other factors such as maturation.

Perhaps more telling of treatment effects were the child's incorrect productions of onset clusters, and the changes that these underwent as therapy progressed. During the initial probes, J.C.'s errors consisted mainly of reducing the cluster to a singleton. Probes collected during the latter part of the treatment suggested that the child was beginning to incorporate clusters, across all markedness levels, in her phonological system. These errors were not unlike those reported previously in children with both typical and atypical phonologies who are learning English (Chin & Dinnsen, 1992; McLeod et al., 1997; Smit, 1993) and who are learning Spanish (Anderson & Smith, 1987, Goldstein & Iglesias, 1996a). The patterns, though, attest to the influence the treatment paradigm was having on her use of clusters.

When J.C. began to evidence more consistent use of onset clusters in her inventory, these were exclusively obstruent + glide clusters. Although [l] was part of her phonetic inventory, consonant + [l] clusters were not present. The onset cluster that was targeted during intervention consisted of a liquid-glide combination. It is plausible that this initially constrained the child's onset cluster system in such a manner that liquids could only appear as the initial segments. Although liquid gliding was not evidenced in her use of singletons, it was observed in her realizations of [l] and [r] clusters, a pattern that is not typical in Spanish speaking children (Anderson & Smith, 1987, Goldstein & Iglesias, 1996a). Later probes indicate the emergence of clusters where the second element was a liquid, thus indicating that the child was further restructuring her system. During the final probes, these clusters were consistently produced with a liquid as the second element. Thus, the changes in error patterns noted throughout treatment attest to the influence the treatment target had on the child's developing system.

The results, then, of the present investigation support the use of linguistic principles when choosing intervention targets for phonologically impaired children from different language backgrounds. The changes in error patterns and the inclusion of onset clusters from various sonority levels indicate that targeting the most marked cluster in the language resulted in the child's reorganization of her phonological system, at least for onset clusters. Although the non-target responses do suggest that treatment effected the changes, it is not known if treating other onset clusters would result in similar patterns. Future studies should include more than one child, as the relative markedness of the targeted cluster can thus be manipulated across each child. This, in turn, can provide a more complete picture of how markedness impacts phonological change in the Spanish-speaking child.

REFERENCES

Anderson, R. T., & Smith, B. L. (1987). Phonological development of two-year old monolingual Spanish-speaking children. *Journal of Child Language, 14,* 57-78.

Barrutía, R., & Schwegler, A. (1994). *Fonética y fonología españolas* (Spanish phonetics and phonology). New York: Wiley.

Chin, S. V., & Dinnsen, D. A. (1992). Consonant clusters in disordered Speech: Constraints and correspondence patterns. *Journal of Child Language, 19,* 259-285.

Clements, G. N. (1990). The role of the sonority cycle in core syllabification. In J. Kingston & M. E. Beckman (Eds.), *Papers in laboratory phonology I: Between the grammar and physics of speech* (pp. 283-333). New York: Cambridge University Press.

Dinnsen, D. A., & Elbert. M. (1984). On the relationship between phonology and learning. In M. Elbert, D. A. Dinnsen & G. Weismer (Eds.), *Phonological theory and the misarticulating child* (ASHA Monographs No. 22, pp. 59-68). Rockville, MD: American Speech-Language-Hearing Association.

Elbert, M., Dinnsen, D. A., & Powell, T. W. (1984). On the prediction of phonologic generalization learning patterns. *Journal of Speech and Hearing Disorders, 49,* 309-317.

Gierut, J. A. (1999). Syllable onsets: Clusters and adjuncts in acquisition. *Journal of Speech, Language, and Hearing Research, 42,* 708-726.

Gierut, J. A., Morrisette, M. L., Hughes, M. T., & Rowland, S. (1996). Phonological treatment efficacy and developmental norms. *Language, Speech, and Hearing Services in Schools, 27,* 215-230.

Goldstein, B. A. (1996). The role of stimulability in the assessment and treatment of Spanish-speaking children. *Journal of Communication Disorders, 29,* 299-314.

Goldstein, B. A., & Iglesias, A. (1996a). Phonological patterns innormally developing Spanish-speaking 3- and 4-year olds of Puerto Rican descent. *Language, Speech, and Hearing Services in Schools, 27,* 82-90.

Goldstein, B. A., & Iglesias, A. (1996b). Phonological patterns in Puerto Rican Spanish-speaking children with phonological disorders. *Journal of Communication Disorders, 29,* 367-387.

Harris, J. W. (1983). *Syllable structure and stress in Spanish.* Cambridge, MA: MIT Press.

Jackson-Maldonado, D., Bates, E., & Thal, D. (1992). *Fundación MacArthur: Inventario del Desarrollo de Habilidades Comunicativas* (MacArthur Communicative Development Inventory). San Diego: University of California, Center for Research in Language.

McLeod, S., Van Doorn, J., & Reed, V. A. (1997). Realizations of consonant clusters by children with phonological impairment. *Clinical Linguistics and Phonetics, 11,* 85-114.

McReynolds, L. V., & Jetzke, E. (1986). Articulation generalization of voiced-voiceless sounds in hearing-impaired children. *Journal of Speech and Hearing Disorders, 51,* 348-355.

Smit, A. B. (1993). Phonologic error distributions in the Iowa-Nebraska Norms Project: Word-initial consonant clusters. *Journal of Speech and Hearing Research, 36,* 931-947.

18

The Realization of English Liquids in Impaired Speech: A Perceptual and Instrumental Study

Barry Heselwood and Sara Howard

This chapter discusses five speakers with unusual realizations of the English liquid consonants, /l/ and /r/, who form part of a larger group currently being studied. Perceptual and instrumental evidence is presented to illustrate the different articulatory strategies adopted by these speakers. They maintain phonological contrasts by using realizations which are atypical, but which relate to adult normal realizations in consistent and perceptually-driven ways.

/l/ AND /r/ IN ENGLISH: PHONETICS AND PHONOLOGY

Phonotactic Distribution of /l/ and /r/

In the phonology of English the liquids have highly restricted and predictable contexts. In syllable onsets, /l/ and /r/ must occur adjacent to the nucleus. Where the onset consists of a consonant cluster, /l/ can cluster with six different obstruents: /p, b, k, g, f, s/; and /r/ with nine: /p, b, t, d, k, g, f, θ, ʃ/ (Gimson, 1980). In syllable codas, the requirement for /l/ and /r/ to occur next to the nucleus applies again. Both /l/ and /r/ are vocalized in some accents of English, but in accents where they are not, if they co-occur (for example, in *farl* /faːrl/), /r/ is adjacent to the nucleus. Vocalized /l/ varies, depending on accent, between a mid-close back and close back vowel and may or may not be rounded; in accents where /r/ is vocalized there is typically a mid-central vowel but again accents can vary, e.g. in Tyneside English it is low-central. In nonvocalizing accents, approximant realizations of both /l/ and /r/ may occur as the nucleus in unstressed syllables: *bottle* ['bɒtl̩] *letter* [lɛtɹ̩]. If we look at the position of /l/

and /r/ in the sonority hierarchy (Goldsmith, 1990), we observe that the liquids come between glides and nasals, with /r/ being more sonorous than /l/. This may help to explain /r/'s greater clustering potential, its precedence over /l/ in nucleus-adjacency in codas, and the fact that /r/-vocalization is generally more widespread than /l/-vocalization in accents of English.

Articulatory Properties of /l/ and /r/

The liquids, /l/ and /r/, form part of the broader class of approximants and are what Ball and Rahilly (1999) refer to as "non-semi-vowel approximants" or "prolongable approximants", in contrast with, for example, the glides /w/ and /j/, which are classed as momentary or nonprolongable and in which the movement to and/or from the articulatory stricture is an essential part of the sound. In most accents in British English, both /l/ and /r/ involve the tip/blade of the tongue in a stricture at or near to the alveolar ridge.

British English /l/ typically involves a stricture of complete closure between the tip and/or blade of the tongue and the alveolar ridge, with one or both sides of the tongue lowered to permit lateral escape of air. This is in contrast to alveolar stop segments, such as /t/, /d/ and /n/, where a complete bilateral lingual seal, continuous with the anterior alveolar seal, is necessary to prevent oral air escape during the hold phase. Articulatory overshoot in /l/ production may, therefore, result in an alveolar stop. Fig. 1 shows an electropalatographic recording of the lingualpalatal contact patterns for the two phonetic variants of /l/ in a Near RP production of *Liverpool* ['lʲɪvəpuɬ].

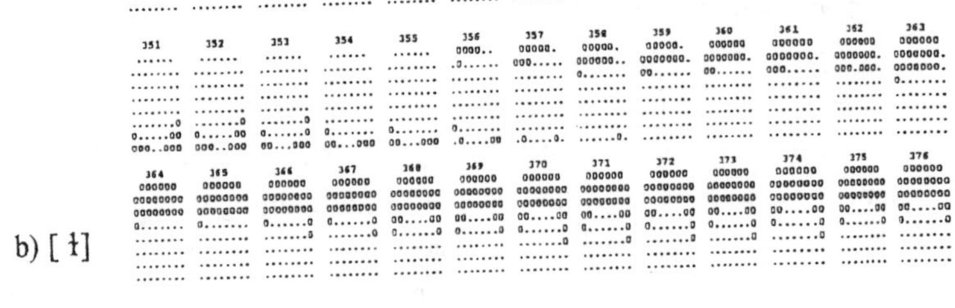

FIG. 1 Lingualpalatal contact patterns for clear and dark allophones of /l/ in *Liverpool*.

Different phonetic contexts appear to produce considerable realizational variation for /l/. For example, there is more extensive lateral contact where /l/ occurs adjacent to high front vowels, but this does not extend as far back as for the alveolar stops. Dent (1984) suggested that in certain consonantal contexts (e.g. adjacent to /s/), perceptually acceptable realizations of /l/ may not have complete central alveolar closure.

The most common variants of British English /r/ require that the tip/blade of the tongue is raised toward the rear of the alveolar ridge, but that it does not make contact in the midline. The centre of the tongue is lowered, creating some sulcalization behind the tip/blade stricture. Typically the only lingualpalatal contact is between the lateral margins of the tongue and the rear molars or the gums at the rear of the oral cavity. Fig. 2 shows lingualpalatal contact patterns for prevocalic /r/ in Near RP realizations of *rabbit* ['ɹæbɪt] and *parrot* ['pæɹət].

As with /l/, /r/ displays considerable intra- and inter-speaker variation. The amount of voicing and friction present may relate to particular phonetic contexts (see below), but will also reflect inter-speaker differences. The degree to which individual speakers retroflex their tongue tip also varies, as does the amount of labialization present.

Acoustic Properties of /l/ and /r/

Both the alveolar lateral approximant [l] and the postalveolar median approximant [ɹ] involve side-chambers off the main glottis-to-lips acoustic path (Stevens, 1998). In [l] the side-chamber is supralaminal, between the superior surface of the tongue and the hard palate. For [ɹ] the side-chamber is mainly sublaminal, between the inferior surface of the tongue and the floor of the mouth, enlarged anteriorly by lip protrusion; there may also be side-chamber effects due to sulcalization.

The effect of both side-chambers is to introduce a zero into the spectrum; for /l/ this creates a resonance in the F4 region while attenuating F2, for /r/ the resonance is in the lower F2 region with higher formants suppressed (Stevens,

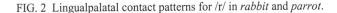

FIG. 2 Lingualpalatal contact patterns for /r/ in *rabbit* and *parrot*.

1998). A significant distinguishing factor for /l/ and /r/ is that typically, /r/ has F3 values which are approximately 1 kHz lower than F3 values for /l/. These resonance differences can be seen as chromatic contrasts of light and dark respectively (Kelly and Local, 1986). Voiceless analogues of these resonances occur when /l/ and /r/ follow voiceless plosives in syllable onsets (Fig. 3).

In relation to other sound classes, Fujimura and Erickson (1997) noted that liquids show relatively rapid spectral shifts, compared with glides, at the juncture with adjacent vowels. Kent and Read (1992) commented that these spectral changes are more rapid for /l/ than for /r/. The general pattern is that /l/ exhibits a long F1 steady state with short transitions, whereas /r/ has a short F1 steady state and longer transitions, but not as long as for glides. /l/ shows some significant acoustic similarities with /n/ (its neighbor in the sonority hierarchy), including suppression of energy in the F2 region and a sudden spectral shift at the juncture with adjacent vowels, but has a higher F1 than is typically associated with nasals (Fig. 4). /l/ also shows affinities of light resonance with /j/, marked by concentration of energy in the region between 3–4 kHz. /r/, however, shows an acoustic affinity with /w/: as well as suppression of energy in the F2 region, they display a gradual spectral shift at the juncture with vowels, and a concentration of energy in the lower part of the spectrum, leading to a dark resonance.

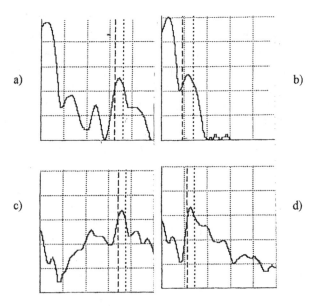

FIG. 3 Spectral peaks in voiced [l] (a), voiced [ɹ] (b), voiceless [l̥] (c), and voiceless [ɹ̥] (d). For the /l/, peaks are around 3500 Hz, and around 1200 Hz for the /r/.

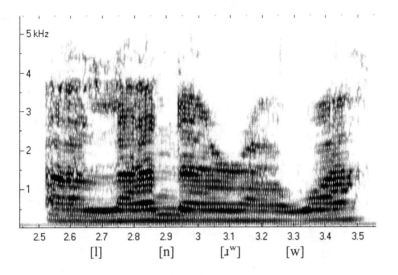

FIG. 4 Rapid ([l] and [n]) vs. slow ([ɹ] and [w]) spectral shifts at the juncture with adjacent vowels.

Realizational Forms (Allophones of /l/ and /r/)

Kent and Read (1992) and Ladefoged and Maddieson (1996) commented on the rich allophonic and sociophonetic variation of realizations of /l/ and /r/ in British and American English. Ladefoged and Maddieson (1996, p. 235) observed, for example, that "We can exemplify nearly all the different forms of rhotics we have been discussing by reference to this one language." For the lateral /l/, there is a major division in many English accents world-wide between light and dark variants. Light (or clear) /l/ may have some palatalization (Gimson, 1980) and in many accents, including Near RP, it occurs in syllable onsets. Dark /l/ is a velarized variant which occurs in nuclei and codas, the same contexts which are affected in some accents by vocalization. The distribution of light and dark /l/ is, however, different in other accents of English. For example, Wells (1982) noted that Irish English uses a light /l/ in all contexts, and Watt and Milroy (1999) observed the same pattern in Newcastle in Northern England; speakers from North Wales and Scotland will tend to do the reverse, having dark /l/ throughout. Wells (1982, p. 370) suggested that some Northern English accents may use "a middle kind of /l/ in all environments". Mathisen (1999) noted gender differences in light/dark /l/ distribution in an urban accent in Midlands English. Outside the British Isles similar patterns can be observed: Australian and Canadian English have dark /l/ in all contexts, whereas English accents of the Indian subcontinent and South Africa typically use light /l/ throughout, as do many British-born speakers of Pakistani origin (Heselwood & McChrystal, 2000).

English /r/ is notable for a wide range of possible realizations, according both to context and to regional accent. Near RP generally uses a slightly retroflexed postalveolar approximant with significant labialization. A labiodental approximant, [ʋ], is noted as becoming more common in younger speakers in England (Trudgill, 1999; Foulkes & Docherty, 2000). However, it is notable that other variants of /r/ are obstruents: the alveolar tap, [ɾ], found in older speakers of Received Pronunciation, in many Scottish accents, and in some urban accents of the North of England; the alveolar trill, [r], which still occurs in the speech of many Scottish English speakers and in Afrikaans English, an apico-postalveolar fricative, found in some contexts in Irish English and South African English (Wells, 1982). Apico-postalveolar friction also occurs for /r/ when it is devoiced, as is the case when it occurs after a voiceless plosive in many accents of British English. Both /r/ and /l/ have extensive coarticulatory effects, particularly on preceding vowels, beginning up to 1000ms in advance of the liquid segment (Heid & Hawkins, 2000) and have an important perceptual role (West, 2000). Wells (1982) notes a tendency for certain groups of vowels to neutralize perceptually preceding /r/ and/or /l/ in different accents of English.

NORMAL AND ATYPICAL DEVELOPMENT OF [l] AND [ɹ] IN CHILDREN'S SPEECH

/l/ and /r/ develop rather late in English-speaking children and this seems to be true of liquids in other languages, for example, the trilled /r/ in Spanish (Carballo & Mendoza, 2000) and Polish (Łobacz, 2000). Common patterns of development have been suggested, both for children learning a particular language, such as English, and also to some extent cross-linguistically. These patterns relate to:

    a) Perceptual/sensory factors
    b) Articulatory/production factors
    c) The phonological system of the ambient language

Common Patterns in Near RP

The most common patterns in Near RP that are also found in other variants of British and American English (see Edwards, 1973; Grunwell, 1982), are gliding of /l/ to [j] and /r/ to [w] in onsets, and vocalization of /l/ in codas. However, other less common patterns have also been reported for normal speech development in British and American English, including stopping, frication, and nasalization (see, e.g. Vihman, 1996), all of which have also been found cross-linguistically for the class of liquids discussed next.

Perceptual/Sensory Factors Affecting Liquid Development

Gliding appears to relate to features of acoustic/auditory similarity between [l] and [j], and between [ɹ] and [w]. Both temporal and spectral factors appear to be involved (Slawinski and Fitzgerald, 1998). The categorical discrimination of /r/ versus /w/, for example, develops only gradually, and in the early stages children appear to categorize many tokens of /r/ in the /w/ category. Children who have delayed or atypical development of liquids seem to find it particularly difficult to discriminate between normal and misarticulated tokens of /r/ in the speech of others, (Hoffman, Stager & Daniloff, 1983), and in their own speech (Shuster, 1998).

Production/Articulatory Factors Affecting Liquid Development

/l/ and /r/ are articulations which, in most variants in English, involve the tip and blade of the tongue, and Gibbon (1999) pointed out that precise tip/blade movement is a particularly challenging task for young children. The coarticulatory demands of the lingual and labial aspects of [ɹ] are also apparently troublesome in early speech development. Oller and Warren (cited in Oller & Kelly, 1974) suggested that in early attempts at producing a postalveolar approximant [ɹ], young children appear to be able to achieve the necessary raising of the tongue dorsum towards the palate, but are unable to produce the corequisite liprounding, achieving only a slight but insufficient protrusion of the lips. Hoffman, Shuckers and Daniloff (1989), in explaining the late development of liquids and their tendency toward misarticulation, also comment on the articulatory difficulties involved. Gliding appears to be at least in part motivated by a strategy of moving the articulation away from the tip/blade of the tongue to the lips and the tongue dorsum. Westbury, Hashi and Lindstrom (1995, p. 56) capture the likely relationship between perceptual and articulatory factors in atypical realizations of the liquids, and stress the importance of evaluating such realizations both from the speaker's and the listener's perspectives, when they say, of /r/, "Speakers must achieve an acoustic result their listeners will accept as /r/."

Subperceptual Differences in Liquid Development

In fact, a number of instrumental studies have shown that for some children, where the process of gliding appears to result in identical realizations of /l/ and /j/, or /r/ and /w/, subtle but consistent acoustic differences between each pair can be identified (McCleod & Isaac, 1995; Hoffman, Stager & Daniloff, 1983). Chaney (1988), compared the realization of liquids and glides across three groups of children: children with normal /w/, /r/, /j/ and /l/; children with developmental substitutions which were appropriate for their age (/r/ → [w] or, less often, [j]; /l/ → [j]); and older children with delayed development of these sounds, where /r/ and /l/ were both realized as [w]. Chaney's analysis showed that where the two latter groups realized /w/, /r/, and /l/ perceptually as [w], these realizations were not differentiable acoustically, either spectrally or temporally, but that this [w] was acoustically differentiable from the /w/ produced by the group of children with normal articulations.

Crosslinguistic Differences in Liquid Development

The different realizations of /l/ and /r/ produced by young children seem to be also motivated by the phonology of the language they are developing. Whereas gliding is attested as a widespread process cross-linguistically, there are differences related to particular languages. For example, English and Dutch children (who both have labial approximant articulations in their native languages) frequently glide /r/ to [w]. Swedish and Turkish children (whose native sound system does not contain a labial approximant) do not do this. Instead, /r/ is often realized as [l] (Kopkalli-Yavuz & Topbas, 1998). Edwards (1973) notes that in the speech of young French children /r/ is much more likely to be produced as [j] or even deleted in onset position, which again seems to reflect the child's ambient sound system.

ATYPICAL LIQUIDS IN IMPAIRED SPEECH: FIVE SINGLE CASES

Case One: Bill

Bill is a 72-year-old male from West Yorkshire in Northern England. He presented with acquired apraxia of speech which included unusual and markedly consistent realizations of liquids, particularly in syllable onset positions. In this context both /l/ and /r/ are devoiced and are preceded by a homorganic devoiced stop. Fig. 5 shows the acoustic data for Bill's pronunciation of *leaf* as [d̥l̥if] and *rake* as [d̥ɹ̥eɪk]. The intrusive stop may be functioning as an articulatory anchor for the tongue-gesture required for the liquid. The syllable onset in each case then conforms more closely to the sonority principle (see e.g. Buckingham, 1989).

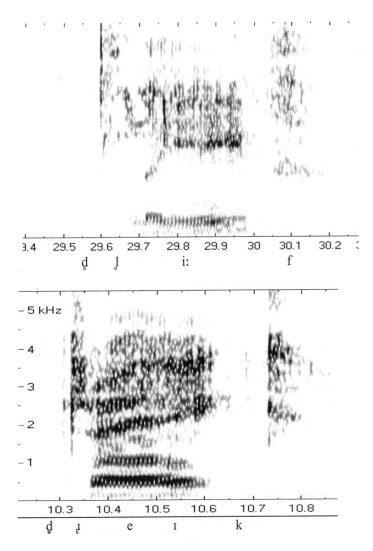

FIG. 5 Spectrograms of *leaf* (upper) and *rake* (lower) with abrupt onsets due to preceding homorganic plosive. Speaker: 72-yr-old male with CVA.

Case Two: Alison

Alison is aged 4 years and 4 months, is from West Yorkshire, and has a developmental speech disorder. Of particular interest to this study are her unusual realizations of onset clusters containing liquids. Normally, in such prevocalic consonant clusters, the realizations of liquids, where they are atypical, vary according to the place of articulation of the plosive member of the cluster.

With Alison's unusual cluster realizations, we see the reverse pattern. Thus in plosive + /r/ clusters, the plosive harmonizes with the labiality of /r/, which in turn, is realized appropriately long and fortis, or short and lenis, producing items such as *crash* [pfʷːas] and *grass* [b̥ɣ̥ʷas]; (see Fig. 6).

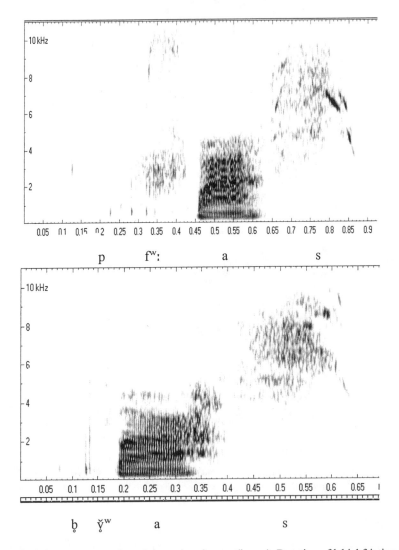

FIG. 6 Spectrograms of *crash* (upper) and *grass* (lower). Duration of labial friction in realization of /r/ correlates with voicing feature of the initial target plosive. Plosive harmonizes with the labiality of the /r/. Speaker: 4-year, 4-month-old girl with developmental speech disorder.

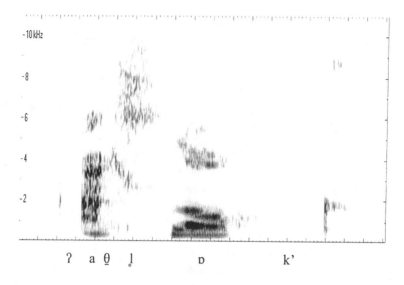

FIG. 7 Spectrogram of *a clock*. Realization of plosive harmonizes with the alveolar /l/.
Speaker: same as Fig. 6.

In plosive + /l/ clusters, the same pattern emerges. An example is Alison's production of *a clock* as [ʔa θ̟lɒk']; (see Fig. 7). The alveolar realization of the plosive element as [θ̟] harmonizes with the alveolar realization of /l/.

Case Three: Rebecca

Rebecca is a 10-year-old girl from South Yorkshire, with a history of developmental speech disorder who received speech and language therapy between ages three and five. Her accent is that of Near RP. She had normal language development and no history of hearing impairment or other disability. At age 10 she presented with a lateralized sibilant fricative system (Howard, 1994, 1995), which combined with a general tendency to realize alveolars as dentals. Where normal developmental patterns might predict that /r/ would be realized as [w], and /l/ as [j], in Rebecca's speech neither pattern was in evidence, but both /l/ and /r/ were realized in an atypical manner, which was perceptually intrusive in her spontaneous speech. /l/ was realized as a dental lateral approximant, as might have been predicted in relation to her general tendency to advance tip/blade articulations. Less usual was her realization of /r/ as an inter-dental lateral approximant. Thus, /l/ → [l̪] and /r/ → [l̟]. For /l/ → [l̪] EPG data reveals that there is considerable lingualpalatal contact in the

```
        153      154      155      156      157      158         159      160      161      162      163      164
                                                                                                            .....0
       000000   000000   000000   000000   000000   000000      000000   000000   000000   000000   ..0000  .....0
      0000000  0000000  0000000  0000000  0000000  0000000     00000000 00000000 00000000 00000000 00000000 00000000
      00...000 00...000 00...000 00...000 00...000 00...000    00...000 00..0000 00000000 00000000 00000000 000000.0
      0.....00 0.....00 0.....00 0.....00 0......00 0......00   0......00 0......00 0......00 0......00 .00...00 000.0000
      .......0 .......0 .......0 .......0 .......0 .......0     .......0  .......0  .......0  .......0  .......0 .........
      ........ ........ ........ ........ ........ ........     ........  ........  ........  ........  ........ .........
      ........ ........ ........ ........ ........ ........     ........  ........  ........  ........  ........ .........
```

FIG. 8 Lingualpalatal contact patterns for a dental realization of /l/. Speaker: 10-year-old girl with developmental speech disorder.

alveolar region of the palate (Fig. 8). In fact, the patterns look similar to those for a normal speaker producing /l/ (see Fig. 1). In this case, however, they form only a part of the complete lingual stricture of central approximation. An advancement of the tongue tip onto the rear of the front teeth, which is clearly visible to the eye, indicates that the EPG patterns show only the posterior part of an unusually broad contact pattern that spans the dental and alveolar regions, finally retracting to alveolar in its release phase. In contrast, the EPG data for /r/ → [l] (Fig. 9) reveal only fragmentary lingualpalatal contact in the anterior region of the palate, consistent with the rearmost portion of the lingualdental gesture. Lateral contact is achieved by the blade of the tongue forming a central closure against the upper incisors, with the tip of the tongue protruding visibly through the upper and lower front teeth. Thus, although the auditory perceptual distinction is lost from the listener's perspective, careful visual observation of the articulations and recourse to the EPG data together reveal an intention to be phonologically contrastive from the speaker's perspective.

Case Four: Derek

Derek is a 29-year-old male from West Yorkshire with Down Syndrome and dysfluent speech (Heselwood, 1997). His realizations of the liquids /l/ and /r/ vary according to whether his speech is fluent. In periods of fluent speech /l/, in common with other coronal sonorants /j/ and /n/, is realized appropriately and thus the three segments are distinct in articulatory, perceptual and phonological terms. /r/ is sometimes realized appropriately, but sometimes /r/ → [j], so that the /r/ - /j/ contrast is only variably present in Derek's fluent speech.

In his dysfluent speech, however, all of these segments /j/, /r/, /l/, and /n/ – which occupy a continuous section of the sonority hierarchy – share the same unusual realization [ŋ͡ɫ], with articulatory and perceptual differences lost. Thus, for example, Derek's realization of the place–name Leeds /liːdz/ is [ŋ͡ɫidʒ]. This very unusual realization of the target liquid, /l/, can be explained by looking at what happens to Derek's vocal organs during periods of dyfluency: as he

```
  236      237      238      239      240      241      242      243      244      245      246      247
 oo....   oo...o  oo...o  oo...o  oo...o  oo...o  oo...o  o....o  o....o  o.....   .......  .....
 oo.....  oo.....o oo.....o oo.....o oo.....o o.....o o.......o o.....o o.....o o.......o .......  ......
 o....... o....... o....... o....... o....... o....... o....... o....... o.......  .......  .......  .......
 ........ ........ ........ ........ ........ ........ ........ ........ ........ ........ ........ ........
 ........ ........ ........ ........ ........ ........ ........ ........ ........ ........ ........ ........
 .......o .......o .......o ........ ........ .......o .......o .......o ........, .......o .......o .......o
 o.......o o.......o o.......o .......o .......o .......o .......o .......o .......o .......o .......o o......o
```

FIG. 9 Lingualpalatal contact patterns for an interdental realization of /r/.
Speaker: same as Fig. 8.

attempts to initiate an utterance in this condition, a complete closure takes place between the back of the tongue and the soft palate. In this state, it is suggested that the only way that he can achieve the desired coronal aspect of the target articulation is by producing a click, on a velaric ingressive airstream. At the same time, he meets the requirements of relative sonority for the segment by producing a velar nasal, on a pulmonic egressive airstream behind the dorsovelar closure.

Case Five: Danny

Danny is a 13-year-old boy from South Yorkshire with a history of a cleft of the soft palate related to Pierre Robin sequence (Shprintzen, 1992). As part of the early medical management of this condition, Danny had a long-term tracheostomy from age four months to age one year and nine months, and has a history of delayed language development and impaired speech production involving phonatory, articulatory and phonological aspects of his speech development (Howard, 1998). Danny has specific physical difficulties in achieving range and accuracy of tongue-tip elevation that relate to his medical condition. In his speech, in syllable onsets, /l/ is typically realized as [j], and /r/ as [w] or [ʊ]. In syllable codas, /l/ vocalizes to [ʊ]. (In common with the other speakers reported in this chapter, Danny's accent is nonrhotic, so /r/ does not appear in coda position.)

These atypical realizations of the liquids are variants which could be satisfactorily explained, at an earlier developmental stage, as corresponding to the normal process of gliding of liquids. However, it would be inappropriate and misleading to describe them in this case merely as the result of a severe phonological delay. Rather, they can be seen as compensatory articulations which, given Danny's specific lingual movement restrictions, obviate the need to elevate the tongue-tip by displacing the articulations to other articulators (the tongue dorsum for /l/ → [j] and the lips (and tongue dorsum) for /r/ → [ʊ] or [w]; (cf. Hoffmann, Shuckers & Daniloff, 1989). Fig. 10 shows Danny's lingualpalatal contact patterns for /l/ → [j], clearly identifying the way he raises both lateral margins of the tongue to make contact with the lateral margins of the palate, although failing to raise the tongue tip or blade to achieve the central anterior closure required for /l/.

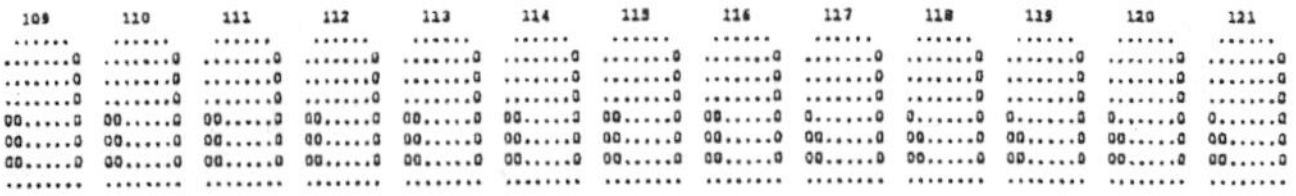

FIG. 10 Lingualpalatal contact patterns for /l/ → [j]. Speaker: 13-year-old boy with Pierre Robin sequence.

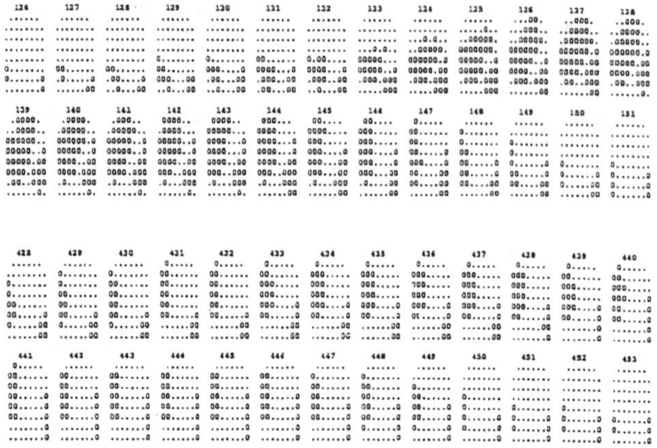

FIG. 11 Lingualpalatal contact patterns of attempts to copy a visual prompt for /l/. Speaker: same as Fig. 10

Danny's specific articulatory difficulties with /l/ are further revealed when he is asked to copy a visual prompt of normal lingualpalatal contact patterns for /l/; (see Fig. 11). Despite clearly understanding the nature of the task and genuinely attempting to match the model provided, he can only produce fragmentary, distorted patterns of contact in the alveolar region, particularly if by attempting to meet the articulatory requirement of lowering one or both lateral margins of the tongue at the same time as raising the tip, he deprives himself of the lateral lingual bracing which may facilitate tip raising. His anterior contacts in the data shown in Fig. 11 are only achieved by trapping the tongue-tip interdentally and then attemping elevation behind this constriction, which necessarily involves tongue dorsum strictures rather than those of the tip and blade of the tongue.

CONCLUSION

Realizations of /r/ seem to be more varied than those for /l/, which may be due to the presence of a secondary articulation in [ɹʷ], the principal allophone, motivating bilabial and labiodental realizations. In all the unusual realizations of liquids described in this chapter it is possible to identify component features that link the impaired realization to the normal realization. Each individual speaker devises his/her own way around the problems that prevent normal production but their routes appear to be guided by knowledge of the phonetic structure of normal realizations. For example, Bill copies the place of articulation of the target into his 'anchoring' stop; Alison opposes [labial] to [alveolar] in her plosive+/r/ and plosive+/l/ clusters; Rebecca may also be attempting a labial-alveolar contrast for /r/-/l/, but with a gesture towards a linguolabial articulation for /r/; Derek cannot maintain a perceptual contrast between the liquids in his dysfluent mode but does manage to replicate gross place of articulation information by initiating a velaric ingressive airstream alongside a pulmonic egressive one; Danny, like Alison and Rebecca, found his own way to oppose [labial] to [alveolar] for the /r/-/l/ distinction.

The sounds that we find useful to put into the category of liquids, and those realizations which we find in developing or disordered speech, seem to be related by a network of relationships which shift between ones anchored in the production domain and ones anchored in the perceptual domain. As Lindau (1985) pointed out in relation to 'r' sounds, they form a Wittgensteinian family resemblance set, rather than a set with a single defining property. Speakers with certain kinds of disorders appear to be actively extending these sets by creating idiosyncratic allophones of /r/ and /l/. The intriguing thing about them is that they do make phonetic sense and indicate that their production is driven by a sophisticated process of phonetic analysis and equivalence mapping, that is, creating something believed to be in some sense equivalent to the unobtainable target.

REFERENCES

Ball, M. J., & Rahilly, J. (1999). *Phonetics: the science of speech.* London: Edward Arnold.

Buckingham, H. (1989). Phonological paraphasia. In C. Code (Ed.), *Characteristics of aphasia.* London: Taylor & Francis.

Carballo, G., & Mendoza, E. (2000). Acoustic characteristics of trill productions by groups of Spanish children with specific language impairment. *Clinical Linguistics & Phonetics, 14,* 587-601.

Chaney, R. M. (1988). Acoustic analysis of correct and misarticulated semivowels. *Journal of Speech and Hearing Research, 31,* 275-287.

Dent, H. (1984). Coarticulated devoicing in English laterals. *Speech Research Laboratory Work in Progress, 4, University of Reading,* 111-134.

Edwards, M. L. (1973). The acquisition of liquids. *Working Papers in Linguistics, 15,* Ohio State University, 1-54.

Foulkes, P. & Docherty, G. J. (2000). Another chapter in the story of /r/: 'labiodental' variants in British English. *Journal of Sociolinguistics, 4,* 30-59.

Fujimura, O., & Erickson, D. (1997). Acoustic phonetics. In W. J. Hardcastle & J. Laver (Eds.), *The handbook of phonetic sciences* (pp. 65-115). Oxford: Blackwell.

Grunwell, P. (1982). *Clinical phonology.* London: Croom Helm.

Gibbon, F. (1999). Undifferentiated lingual gestures in children with articulation/phonological disorders. *Journal of Speech, Language & Hearing Research, 42,* 382-397.

Gimson, A. C. (1980). *An introduction to the pronunciation of English* (3rd ed.). London: Arnold.

Goldsmith, J. (1990). *Autosegmental and metrical phonology.* Oxford: Blackwell.

Heid, S., & Hawkins, S. (2000). An acoustical study of long domain /r/ and /l/ coarticulation. Written paper presented at the *British Association of Academic Phoneticians Colloquium,* University of Glasgow, April 3-6.

Heselwood, B. (1997). A case of nasal clicks for target sonorants: a feature geometry account. *Clinical Linguistics & Phonetics, 11,* 43-61.

Heselwood, B., & McChrystal, L. (2000). Gender, accent features and voicing in Punjabi-English bilingual children. *Leeds Working Papers in Linguistics & Phonetics, 8.*

Hoffman, P. R., Stager, S., & Daniloff, R. G. (1983). Perception and production of misarticulated /r/. *Journal of Speech and Hearing Disorders, 48,* 210-215.

Hoffman, P. R., Shuckers, G., & Daniloff, R. G. (1989). *Children's phonetic disorders.* Boston: College-Hill Press.

Howard, S. J. (1994). Phonetic reorganisation following articulation therapy: an EPG study. In R. Aulanko & A.-M. Korpijaakko-Huuhka (Eds.), *Proceedings of the 3rd ICPLA congress* (pp. 67-74), Helsinki.

Howard, S. J. (1995). Intransigent articulation disorder: using electropalatography to assess and remediate misarticulated fricatives. In M. R. Perkins & S. J. Howard (Eds.), *Case studies in clinical linguistics* (pp. 39-64). London: Whurr.

Howard, S. J. (1998). A perceptual and electropalatographic case study of Pierre Robin sequence. In W. Ziegler & K. Deger (Eds.), *Clinical phonetics and linguistics* (pp. 157-164). London: Whurr.

Kent, R., & Read, C. (1992). *The acoustic analysis of speech.* San Diego: Singular.

Kelly, J., & Local, J. (1986). Long-domain resonance patterns in English. *International conference on speech input/output: Techniques and applications* (pp. 304-309). Conference publication no. 258. London: Institution of Electrical Engineers.

Kopkalli-Yavuz, H., & Topbas, S. (1998). Phonological processes of Turkish phonologically disordered children: Language specific or universal? In W. Ziegler & K. Deger (Eds.), *Clinical phonetics and linguistics* (pp. 88-97). London: Whurr.

Ladefoged, P., & Maddieson, I. (1996). *Sounds of the world's languages.* London: Blackwell.

Lindau, M. (1985). The story of /r/. In V. Fromkin (Ed.), *Phonetic Linguistics* (pp. 157-168). Orlando: Academic Press.

Łobacz, P. (2000). The Polish rhotic. A preliminary study in acoustic variability and invariance. *Speech and Language Technology, 4,* 85-101.

Mathisen, A. G. (1999). Sandwell, West Midlands: ambiguous perspectives on gender patterns and models of change. In P. Foulkes & G. Docherty (Eds.), *Urban voices* (pp. 107-123). London: Arnold.

McLeod, S., & Isaac, K. (1995). Use of spectrographic analyses to evaluate the efficacy of phonological intervention. *Clinical Linguistics & Phonetics, 9,* 229-234.

Oller, D. K., & Kelly, C. A. (1974). Phonological substitution processes of a hard-of-hearing child. *Journal of Speech and Hearing Disorders, 39,* 65-74.

Shprintzen, R. J. (1992). The implications of the diagnosis of Pierre Robin sequence. *Cleft Palate - Craniofacial Journal, 29,* 205-209.

Shuster, L. I. (1998). The perception of correctly and incorrectly produced /r/. *Journal of Speech, Language and Hearing Disorders, 41,* 941-950.

Slawinski, E., & Fitzgerald, L. (1998). Perceptual development of the categorization of the /r-w/ contrast in normal children. *Journal of Phonetics, 26,* 27-43.

Stevens, K. N. (1998). *Acoustic phonetics.* Cambridge, MA: MIT Press.

Trudgill, P. (1999). Norwich: endogenous and exogenous linguistic change. In P. Foulkes & G. Docherty (Eds.), *Urban voices* (pp. 124-140). London: Arnold.

Vihman, M. M. (1996). *Phonological development.* London: Blackwell.

Watt, D., & Milroy, L. (1999). Pattern of variation and change in three Newcastle vowels: is this dialect levelling? In P. Foulkes & G. Docherty (Eds.), *Urban voices* (pp. 25-46). London: Arnold

Wells, J. C. (1982). *Accents of English* (Vols. 1-3). Cambridge: Cambridge University Press.

West, P. (2000). Perception of distributed coarticulatory properties of English /l/ and /r/. *Journal of Phonetics, 27,* 405-425.

Westbury, J., Hashi, M., & Lindstrom, M. J. (1995). Differences among speakers in articulation of American English /r/: an X-ray microbeam study. In *Proceedings of the XIIIth international congress of phonetic sciences* (Vol. 4, pp. 50-57). Stockholm.

19

Vocal Development in the Human Infant: Functions and Phonetics

John L. Locke

This chapter concerns the vocal behavior, particularly the babbling, of the human infant. I will ask why the human infant engages in this behavior, and what doing so might conceivably foretell about later developments of speech and language, including developmental disorders.

To understand the vocal behaviors of the infant, we must look at the biological context within which infants develop. The newly born human is helplessly unable to take care of itself. Left to its own devices, it will die within a few days of birth. With round-the-clock feeding and protection the neonate is likely to live, with some reasonable prospect that it will transmit the parental genes that supported its care in infancy. A great deal of caregiving is influenced by the infant's own behaviors, including its *vocalizations*. This suggests that the mechanisms responsible for care-eliciting vocal behaviors have also been naturally selected.

I will propose here that in evolutionary history (1) the sounds of babbling encouraged parental care, thus natural selection of the supporting vocal-motor activity; and (2) the movements of babbling predated and influenced the shape of speech when vocal languages appeared.

WHAT IS BABBLING?

Babbling refers to mandibular oscillations that occur during phonation. There may or may not be many movements of the intraoral articulators. With no more than passive bunching of the apical portion of the tongue, raising and lowering the jaw while vocalizing yields sounds like [jaja] or [dada]. If the tongue is flattened, the resulting labial contact yields [wawa] or [baba]. If the laryngeal action is suppressed or the velum lowered, the same activity produces sounds like [nana], [mama], [papa], and [tata]. With the slightest tongue movement the repertoire expands rapidly, but most babbling involves no more than a half-dozen sound-movements.

While crying occurs throughout the first year of life, babbling usually doesn't begin until 7–10 months. Then, it usually continues for a year or more, overlapping indistinguishably with words. The overlap is indistinguishable for a reason – many of *our* syllables are made of the same sounds as *theirs*.

Infants who are retarded, premature, or from impoverished homes begin to babble at about the same time, and do so in much the same way, as other infants (cf. Oller, 2000). Even damage to the linguistic areas of the left cerebral hemisphere does little to throw babbling off course (Marchman, Miller & Bates, 1991). Being so hardy, one assumes that babbling produces benefits, both in the long-term and the short-term. Let's take a look, first, at some short-term benefits – in effect, the immediate causes of babbling. These may be broken down into auditory factors and motor factors.

Auditory Factors

By applying strict acoustic and quantitative criteria, Oller and Eilers (1988) were able to demonstrate that deaf infants typically do not begin to babble "on time." Most do not begin until at least 11 months of age, and many do not begin until many months later. One might suppose that this merely reflects reduced vocalization by the deaf but there is evidence that congenitally deaf infants vocalize at least as often as hearing infants and possibly even more often. Ray Kent and his associates (Kent, Osberger, Netsell & Hustedde, 1987) studied twin boys, one who was severely hearing impaired, the other normally hearing. They found that the deaf infant vocalized more often than his hearing twin did. The deaf infant followed by Kim Oller and his team (Oller, Eilers, Bull & Carney, 1985) averaged about 30% more vocalizations than the eleven hearing infants in the study did. If these infants are typical, the congenitally deaf have ample opportunity to produce syllables.

Limited to these findings, one might be tempting to conclude that infants babble for the sound, but there are several problems with such a conclusion. The first, which we discussed previously, is the possibility that deaf infants vocalize as frequently as their hearing peers. If audibility is a factor, why does it selectively affect syllabic but not other forms of vocalization? The second problem is that the deaf do eventually babble, just begin to do so later than other infants. The third problem, as we see next, is that deaf and hearing infants rhythmically operate their jaw whether it makes a noise or not.

Motor Factors

Richard Meier and his colleagues at the University of Texas have found that infants often carry out jaw openings and closings silently (Meier, McGarvin,

Zakia & Willerman, 1997). Periods of peak activity of these "jaw wags" occurred between seven and nine months for three deaf infants, slightly later for the one hearing infant in their study. Most of the wags consisted of one or two cycles, the equivalent of [da] and [dada], with far fewer three-cycle openings and closings.

This study did not determine whether the deaf produce as many jaw wags as the hearing, but it does complicate the conclusion that infants babble only for the sound. What, then, is to be made of the fact that in many cultures infants seem to enjoy various kinds of noisemakers? If self-produced sound is the attraction of rattles, why not activate the vocal tract and achieve similar effects?

Several years ago, my colleagues and I put into the hands of 60 infants of different ages a normal rattle and a rattle that had been silenced (Locke, Bekken, McMinn-Larson & Wein, 1995). We recorded more shakes per second when the rattle was placed in the right than the left hand, and there was a sharp increase in shakes per second during the period in which babbling began, regardless of whether the rattle made a noise or not. We also obtained a weak advantage for the audible over the silent rattle. In a later study by Ejiri (1998), a more significant audibility effect was obtained.

These and other studies suggest that just as babbling begins, infants increase their output of audible limb movements in a repetitive and rhythmic fashion, with preferential control by mechanisms that are situated in the left cerebral hemisphere. Since speech involves an audible series of movements that are preferentially controlled by mechanisms in the left cerebral hemisphere, one can see neurophysiological reasons why there might be relationship between babbling and speaking. It made sense, then, when research by Kim Oller's group revealed an additional relationship between canonical babbling and hand banging. Both hand banging and babbling are slightly early in premature infants, with age adjusted for shorter gestation period, and slightly late in Down syndrome infants (Cobo-Lewis, Oller, Lynch & Levine, 1996; Eilers, Oller, Levine, Basinger, Lynch & Urbano, 1993).

The rhythmic mandibular behaviors that precede and phase into speech may not be uniquely vocal or phonetic. And yet these movements, rendered audibly, are treated by listeners as lexical items. The reason is not terribly mysterious. Parents say similar things, e.g., *mama, papa, dada, bye-bye, pee-pee*, especially when addressing the infant. With no more to learn than a few associations between sound and meaning, the receptive infant can move seamlessly from babble into speech, and this is exactly what most of them do.

FUNCTION

What about the function of babbling? It seems reasonable to suppose that in evolutionary history babbling encouraged parental care. If babbling performed such a function, it would have been submitted to the processes of natural selection. As we will see, this proposal bears similarities to speculation that male songbirds are selected for mating on the basis of the quality of their song (Nottebohm, 1975).

The proposal that babbling facilitates care receives some indirect support from observations of a species that has no linguistic capability. Snowdon and Elowson and their colleagues at the University of Wisconsin have reported that pygmy marmoset infants produce babble-like sounds. These sounds contain elements that also occur in adult vocalization, but they are certainly not analogous to human infant babbling, which is highly stereotyped, with few audibly different movements.

The relevant finding is that dependent pygmy marmoset infants produce babble-like sounds more often than independent ones; and that, after issuing these sounds, infants are more likely to be picked up or cared for (Elowson, Snowdon & Lazaro-Perea, 1998a, 1998b; Snowdon, Elowson & Roush, 1997). That is, babbling appears to work as a signal that elicits care.

There is a further connection between mandibular movements and affiliation in the grooming practices of adult primates. Grooming is a behavior that has less to do with style or nutrition than social relationships. It's an important way to reveal friendly dispositions. Interestingly, grooming is frequently preceded and accompanied by mandibular oscillations rendered audibly. These lip- and tonguesmacking sounds appear to operate as affiliative signals (perhaps ritualized from intention movements associated with manual grooming).

What about lipsmacking in infant monkeys? If audible oscillations of the mandible are calls for care, there ought to be a fair amount of lipsmacking in the young. Kenney, Mason and Hill (1979) found a high incidence of lipsmacking during the early infancy of caged monkeys, which declined with age and independence. If babbling works similarly in our own species, there ought to be more babbling when infants are alone. Data from Jones and Moss (1971), and from Delack (1976), indicate that throughout the first year of life, infants vocalize more often when alone than when in the presence of their mother. Delack's data reveal a relative increase in solitary vocalization at about 4.5 months, just before babbling usually begins, and a sharp rise at about 33 to 38 weeks, when approximately ninety percent of typically developing infants begin to babble.

Regardless of whether infants babble in order to affiliate or not, there is at least one hint that babbling may actually serve that end. Kathleen Bloom and her colleagues have reported that infants who produce a high rate of syllables per utterance are adjudged, from audiotapes, to be more pleasant, friendly, and likeable than infants who use simpler forms of vocalization (Bloom & Lo, 1990; Bloom, D'Odorico & Beaumont, 1993). I would propose that, other things being equal, babblers are more likely than other infants to be approached, picked up or touched, spoken to, and offered other forms of care.

There are at least two reasons for thinking this might be so. The first reason is that crying often produces the opposite effect: inconsolable crying can lead to neglect and abuse, including shaken-baby syndrome. In terms of a functional account, it is interesting to note that disabled infants have a different cry from healthy ones, one that is far harder to tolerate, and that disabled infants are nearly twice as likely to be abused than normally developing infants. Consider the following facts:

1. Infants who are unusually ill tend to cry more often than healthy infants do (cf. Furlow, 1997; Lummaa, Vuorisalo, Barr & Lehtonen, 1998).

2. The crying of infants who are in pain, or have various physical conditions, is higher in pitch than the wails of healthy infants, and tends to sound different (Bisping, Steingrueber, Oltmann & Wenk, 1990; Frodi & Senchak, 1990; Zeskind & Collins, 1987; Zeskind & Lester, 1978).

3. The crying of sick infants is also more aversive to the ear. This may be one reason why abnormally developing infants, especially those with physical and mental disabilities, are abused more than healthy infants (Sobsey, Randall & Paårrila, 1997).

4. Crying is frequently implicated in "shaken baby syndrome" (Becker, Liersch, Tautz, Schlueter & Andler, 1998; Dykes, 1986), and appears to be the "primary reason for aggression" toward children under the age of two years (Norman, 1983).

Incidentally, the greater abuse of disabled children includes those with communicative disabilities: in one study, the rate of *pre-existing* language and hearing problems in a large population of abused children was double that of a nonabused control sample (Sullivan & Knutson, 1998). As for the mechanisms involved, experiments indicate that the sight and sound of infant crying typically alters physiological measures in adult observers, particularly cardiac and skin conductance indices of stress-induced arousal (Donovan & Leavitt, 1985; Murray, 1985). Crying also produces psychological effects such as frustration and aggression. One notes evidence that nonabusive mothers experienced blood pressure increases to videotapes of crying infants but blood pressure decreases to tapes of smiling infants (Frodi & Lamb, 1980). If babbling works at all like smiling, the sound of it ought to lower blood pressure.

I suggest that babblers are, for various reasons, more healthy (and more nearly on developmental schedule) than other infants, and that they may be more likely than others to achieve an autonomous level of functioning –something that would have interested our hominid ancestors – and more complex forms of language, something that interests modern humans.

One reason for proposing a link to autonomy is the resemblance of babbling to other forms of play. Unlike crying, babbling has no obvious signaling function and appears to be done preferentially by infants who are rested, fed, and relaxed – circumstances that favor play in the young of all species (cf. Locke, 1993). Infants who babble often and cry rarely are likely to be considered less noxious than infants with the opposite pattern, and as we saw earlier, are likely to be more enjoyable than infants who do not babble.

Onset of Babbling and Words

Infants who fail to babble, or are delayed in the onset of babbling, may learn words slowly or get off to a late start in doing so. The first to notice this was Carol Stoel-Gammon (1989), who found that nested in a larger sample of 34 children were two participants whose early phonetic development was atypical. One child produced few canonical syllables from nine to 21 months. The other had an unusual pattern of sound preferences in its babbling. Compared to peers, the words of both subjects at 24 months were produced with a more limited phonetic repertoire and with simpler syllable shapes.

With different populations and modes of analysis, congruent findings were provided by two other studies. Whitehurst and his colleagues (Whitehurst, Smith, Fischel, Arnold & Lonigan, 1991) found that the ratio of consonants to vowels was the single strongest predictor of subsequent language development. Jensen and his colleagues in Denmark (Jensen, Boggild-Andersen, Schmidt, Ankerhus & Hansen, 1988) longitudinally followed a number of infants who were or were not at risk for developmental delay (based on Apgar scores, birthweight, and presence or absence of neonatal cerebral symptoms). During the first year, participants who were judged to be at risk produced significantly fewer consonant-like sounds and reduplicated syllables than normal children. In addition, some five years later, a much higher proportion of the at risk children also scored below age level on a language test.

Recently, Kim Oller and his colleagues found that infants who begin to babble after 10 to 12 months evince far more developmental problems, including sensory, cognitive, and linguistic disorders, than infants who begin to babble earlier (Oller, Eilers, Neal & Cobo-Lewis, 1998). Among infants in a high-risk population (as indexed by low birthweight and socioeconomic standing, and exposure to illness or drugs), late babblers had significantly lower expressive vocabulary scores at 18, 24, and 30 months than those who began to babble on time (Oller, Eilers, Neal & Schwartz, 1999). Receptive vocabulary scores were slightly lower at 18 months, but not at 24 months, suggesting that late babbling may relate more closely to production than perception, as one might suppose.

Links between the onset of babbling and measures of sensory, motor, and cognitive function suggest that mandibular oscillations, rendered audibly, may be tied to the rate of development, or the integrity, of the infant's central nervous system. Connections between babbling and speech more specifically suggest that to understand the form of early words one needs to look at the phonetic patterns of babbling. As we will see below, analyses of babbling are in fact related to the shape of words, but not just the words of children.

PHONETICS

At one time, scholars thought that babbling involved a wide range of sounds – even all the sounds that occur in the world's languages, or that can be made by a human vocal tract – seemingly produced randomly. Now it is known that the actual sounds made by infants are rather limited. In a study of the sounds produced spontaneously by nine to 18-month-old American infants recorded in their homes, my colleagues and I found that the first four sounds in frequency ([d,b,n,t]) make up over 50% of all consonant-like sounds (Locke, Hodgson, Macaruso, Roberts, Lambrecht-Smith & Guttentag, 1997).

In previous work I have pointed out that high frequency sounds such as these are less likely than lower-frequency sounds to need attention in the clinic. Indeed, they tend to serve as substitutes for rarer sounds. In this connection, it is logical to ask if the appearance of [t] in places where one would expect a /tʃ/ is best regarded as a substitution of /t/ for /tʃ/ or an over-extension of [t] that happens to involve /tʃ/ (cf. Locke, 1980).

Fig. 1 indicates that the sounds babbled most frequently are produced more accurately by English-learning 2-year-olds, and appear more often in the languages of the world, than other sounds. The four bilabial consonants of English are shown in circles; coronals articulated in a similar manner appear in boxes. Together, these items comprise about 60 to 80% of all consonant-like sounds in the babbling of preverbal infants. Note the high frequency, in percent, of the labials (except /p/, which requires momentary interruption of laryngeal vibration) in children's speech and established languages. The coronals are about as frequent in archived languages but take longer to acquire. Fricative (F), affricate (A), and liquid (L) consonants, shown in ovals, are rarely babbled and are found at a reduced frequency in both children's speech and the languages of the world.

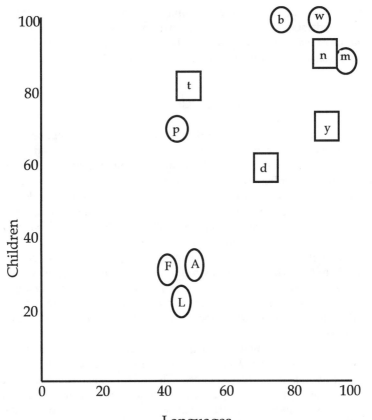

FIG. 1 Relationship between articulatory accuracy, in children, and penetrance, in languages, for labial and coronal consonants as well as fricatives, affricates, and liquids (after Locke, 2000).

Clearly, there are many phonetic patterns in babble that correspond to what happens in speech.   For example, babble is made up mainly of single consonants, with few clusters, and there are entire languages that have no clusters but none that lacks single sounds. Babble also is characterized by CV syllables, with few, if any VC syllables, and there are languages that have no final consonants but all languages have initial ones.

It has also been discovered that infants also produce *sequences* of sounds that commonly occur in established languages.   In the babbled syllables of prelexical infants and the speech of very young children, consonants and vowels tend to travel together.   When the tongue tip is positioned for a consonant-like sound, the positioning tends to carry-over into the following vowel (Davis & MacNeilage, 1990, 1994; MacNeilage & Davis, 2000; Stoel-Gammon, 1983).

In the infant vocalization study described earlier (Locke et al., 1997), tabulations were made of all the syllables in which alveolars preceded front vowels, labials preceded mid-vowels, and velars preceded back vowels. These sums were then divided by the total frequency with which segments of these places of articulation preceded all vowels.

Fig. 2 shows the distribution. In the labial and velar distributions, note the regular progression whereby back vowels exceed mid vowels, which exceed front vowels. In the alveolar distributions, the pattern is reversed. It appears that the tongue movement associated with consonant-like sounds like /d/ dragged the vowel along with it, making [di] syllables more frequent than [da] or [du] syllables. If, in development, this effect continued at an abnormally high rate, one might wonder if the child were fully phonological, since phonologies involve phonemes – single segments – and when the vowel goes with the consonant it looks more like a syllable-based system.

Some years ago, I pointed to an "anterior-to-posterior progression" in the utterances of children and the vocabularies of English and French (Locke, 1983). Lip-to-tongue words like "pat" and "mad" surpassed reverse-order items like "tap" and "dam." MacNeilage and Davis (2000) now report that this labial-coronal effect occurs in several other languages on which relevant statistics are available. The front-to-back effect that is evident in babbling anticipates the "fronting" effect in children's speech, which occurs mainly when velar consonants appear in word-initial position (Locke, 1983). Clearly, the human mouth doesn't like these movement sequences.

CONCLUDING REMARKS

I conclude with a few thoughts about the biology and basic phonetic science of babbling. From a *developmental* perspective, I think we have to assume that when infants babble, they are *not* practicing the movements that will be needed for speech. Seven-month-olds cannot be assumed to know which movements speech requires. What they *are* doing, I think, is exercising an inherited system of vocal-motor play behaviors that benefited previous generations of infants by attracting prospective care-givers, just as that signaling system will benefit them. Iverson and Thelen (1999) have argued that these behaviors are very tightly linked to manual behaviors – they're part of an integrated system of expressive behaviors.

In babbling, infants may be revealing something our prelinguistic ancestors would have cared about – physical and, perhaps, emotional health – and, at the same time, a neuromaturational readiness for behavior that additionally concerns us modern humans – speech. Moreover, in nurturant homes, many babbling infants will get a great deal of sympathetic vocal behavior from caregivers, who typically respond with the closest lexical equivalents to the sounds of babble.

Veneziano (1988) has shown that these contingent responses facilitate the
development of expressive vocabulary. Thus babbling may lead to social
engagement at a higher and more interesting level, complete with new
opportunities for meshing.

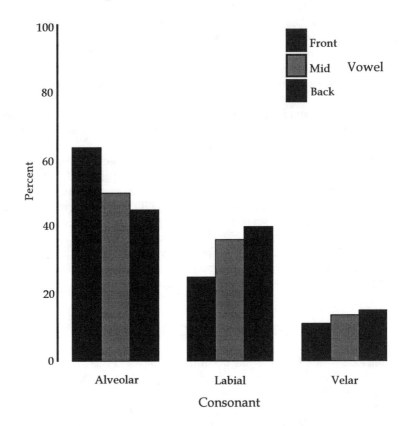

FIG. 2   Consonant-vowel co-occurrence patterns in the babbling of
American English infants.

From a basic *biolinguistic* perspective, I think it is clear that by concerning
ourselves with babbling we can add to our understandings of the sound-making
capacity of our young and ourselves, thus improve upon current understandings
of human language. From a *clinical* standpoint, studies of vocal behavior enable
us to fulfil an important clinical goal, for if there are ostensibly normal infants
who fail to babble, or are delayed in the onset of babbling, we may be able to
find out what's wrong before precious developmental time slips away.

REFERENCES

Becker, J. C., Liersch, R., Tautz, C., Schlueter, B., & Andler, W. (1998). Shaken baby syndrome: Report on four pairs of twins. *Child Abuse & Neglect, 22,* 931-937.

Bisping, R., Steingrueber, J., Oltmann, M., & Wenk, C. (1990). Adults' tolerance of cries: An experimental investigation of acoustic features. *Child Development, 61,* 1218-1229.

Bloom, K., & Lo, E. (1990). Adult perceptions of vocalizing infants. *Infant Behavior and Development, 13,* 209-219.

Bloom, K., D'Odorico, L., & Beaumont, S. (1993). Adult preferences for syllabic vocalizations: Generalizations to parity and native language. *Infant Behavior and Development, 16,* 109-120.

Cobo-Lewis, A. B., Oller, D. K., Lynch, M. P., & Levine, S. L. (1996). Relations of motor and vocal milestones in typically developing infants and infants with Down syndrome. *American Journal on Mental Retardation, 100,* 456-467.

Davis, B. L., & MacNeilage, P. F. (1990). Acquisition of correct vowel production: a quantitative case study. *Journal of Speech and Hearing Research, 33,* 16-27.

Davis, B. L., & MacNeilage, P. F. (1994) Organization of babbling: a case study. *Language and Speech, 37,* 341-355.

Delack, J. B. (1976). Aspects of infant speech development in the first year of life. *Canadian Journal of Linguistics, 21,* 17-37.

Donovan, W. L., & Leavitt, L. A. (1985). Physiology and behavior: parents' response to the infant cry. In B. M. Lester & C. F. Z. Boukydis (Eds.), *Infant crying: theoretical and research perspectives* (pp. 241-261). New York: Plenum Press.

Donovan, W. L., Leavitt, L. A., & Balling, J. D. (1978). Maternal physiological response to infant signals. *Psychophysiology, 15,* 68-74.

Dykes, L. J. (1986). The whiplash shaken baby syndrome: What has been learned? *Child Abuse & Neglect, 10,* 211-221.

Eilers, R. E., Oller, D. K., Levine, S., Basinger, D., Lynch, M. P., & Urbano, R. (1993). The role of prematurity and socioeconomic status in the onset of canonical babbling in infants. *Infant Behavior and Development, 16,* 297-315.

Ejiri, K. (1998). Relationship between rhythmic behavior and canonical babbling in infant vocal development. *Phonetica, 55,* 226-237.

Elowson, A. M., Snowdon, C. T., & Lazaro-Perea, C. (1998a). "Babbling" and social context in infant monkeys: Parallels to human infants. *Trends in Cognitive Sciences, 2,* 31-37.

Elowson, A. M., Snowdon, C. T., & Lazaro-Perea, C. (1998b). Infant "babbling" in a nonhuman primate: Complex vocal sequences with repeated call types. *Behaviour, 135,* 643-664.

Frodi, A. M., & Lamb, M. E. (1980). Child abusers' responses to infant smiles and cries. *Child Development, 51,* 238-241.

Frodi, A., & Senchak, M. (1990). Verbal and behavioral responsiveness to the cries of atypical infants. *Child Development, 61,* 76-84.

Furlow, F. B. (1997). Human neonatal cry quality as an honest signal of fitness. *Evolution and Human Behavior, 18,* 175-193.

Iverson, J. M., & Thelen, E. (1999). Hand, mouth and brain: The dynamic emergence of speech and gesture. *Journal of Consciousness Studies, 6,* 19-40.

Jensen, T. S. Boggild-Andersen, B., Schmidt, J., Ankerhus, J., & Hansen, E. (1988). Perinatal risk factors and first-year vocalizations: Influence on preschool language and motor performance. *Developmental Medicine and Child Neurology, 30,* 153-161.

Jones, S. J., & Moss, H. A. (1971). Age, state, and maternal behavior associated with infant vocalizations. *Child Development, 42,* 1039-1051.

Kenney, M. D., Mason, W. A., & Hill, S. D. (1979). Effects of age, objects, and visual experience on affective responses of rhesus monkeys to strangers. *Developmental Psychology, 15,* 176-184.

Kent, R. D., Osberger, M. J., Netsell, R., & Hustedde, C. G. (1987). Phonetic development in identical twins differing in auditory function. *Journal of Speech and Hearing Disorders, 52,* 64-75.

Locke, J. L. (1980). The prediction of child speech errors: Implications for a theory of acquisition. In G. Yeni-Komshian, J. F. Kavanagh & C. Ferguson (Eds), *Child phonology, Volume 2: Production* (pp. 193-209). New York: Academic Press.

Locke, J. L. (1983). *Phonological acquisition and change.* New York: Academic Press.

Locke, J. L. (1993). *The child's path to spoken language.* Cambridge, MA: Harvard University Press.

Locke, J.L. (2000). Movement patterns in spoken language. *Science, 288,* 449-450.

Locke, J. L., Bekken, K. E., McMinn-Larson, L., & Wein, D. (1995). Emergent control of manual and vocal-motor activity in relation to the development of speech. *Brain and Language, 51,* 498-508.

Locke, J. L., Hodgson, J., Macaruso, P., Roberts, J., Lambrecht-Smith, S., & Guttentag, C. (1997). The development of developmental dyslexia. In C. Hulme & M. Snowling (Eds.), *Dyslexia: biological bases, identification and intervention* (pp. 72-96). London: Whurr Publishers.

Locke, J. L., & Pearson, D. M. (1990). Linguistic significance of babbling: Evidence from a tracheostomized infant. *Journal of Child Language, 17,* 1-16.

Luumaa, V., Vuorisalo, T., Barr, R. G., & Lehtonen, L. (1998). Why cry? Adaptive significance of intensive crying in human infants. *Evolution and Human Behavior, 19,* 193-202.

MacNeilage. P. F., & Davis, B. L. (2000). On the origin of internal structure of word forms. *Science, 288,* 527-531.

Mann, J. (1992). Nurturance or negligence: Maternal psychology and behavioral preference among preterm twins. In J. H Barkow, L. Cosmides & J. Tooby (Eds.), *The adapted mind: Evolutionary psychology and the creation of culture* (pp. 367-390). Oxford: Oxford University Press.

Marchman, V. A., Miller, R., & Bates, E. A. (1991). Babble and first words in children with focal brain injury. *Applied Psycholinguistics, 12,* 1-22.

Meier, R. P., McGarvin, L., Zakia, R. A. E., & Willerman, R. (1997). Silent mandibular oscillations in vocal babbling. *Phonetica, 54,* 153-171.

Murray, A. D. (1985). Aversiveness is in the mind of the beholder: Perception of infant crying by adults. In B. M. Lester & C. F. Z. Boukydis (Eds.), *Infant crying: Theoretical and research perspectives* (pp. 217-239). New York: Plenum Press.

Norman, L. E. (1983). Child abuse. *Clinics in Laboratory Medicine, 3,* 321-342.

Nottebohm, F. (1975). A zoologist's view of some language phenomena with particular emphasis on vocal learning. In E. H Lenneberg & E. Lenneberg (Eds.), *Foundations of language development: A multidisciplinary approach.* Volume 1 (pp. 61-103). New York: Academic Press.

Oller, D. K. (2000). *The emergence of the speech capacity.* Mahwah, NJ: Lawrence Erlbaum Associates.

Oller, D. K., & Eilers, R. E. (1988). The role of audition in infant babbling. *Child Development, 59,* 441-449.

Oller, D. K., Eilers, R., Bull, D., & Carney, A. (1985). Prespeech vocalizations of a deaf infant: A comparison with normal metaphonological development. *Journal of Speech and Hearing Research, 28,* 47-63.

Oller, D. K., Eilers, R. E., Neal, A. R., & Cobo-Lewis, A. B. (1998). Late onset canonical babbling: A possible early marker of abnormal development. *American Journal on Mental Retardation, 103,* 249-263.

Oller, D. K., Eilers, R. E., Neal, A. R., & Schwartz, H. K. (1999). Precursors to speech in infancy: The prediction of speech and language disorders. *Journal of Communication Disorders, 32,* 223-245.

Oller, D. K., Eilers, R. E., Steffens, M. L., Lynch, M. P., & Urbano, R. (1994). Speech-like vocalizations in infancy: An evaluation of potential risk factors. *Journal of Child Language, 21,* 33-58.

Snowdon, C. T., Elowson, A. M., & Roush, R. S. (1997). Social influences on vocal development in New World primates. In C.T. Snowdon & M. Hausberger (Eds.), *Social influences on vocal development* (pp. 234-248). Cambridge: Cambridge University Press.

Sobsey, D., Randall, W., & Parrila, R. K. (1997). Gender differences in abused children with and without disabilities. *Child Abuse & Neglect, 21,* 707-720.

Stoel-Gammon, C. (1983). Constraints on consonant-vowel sequences in early words. *Journal of Child Language, 10*, 455-457.

Stoel-Gammon, C. (1989). Prespeech and early speech development of two late talkers. *First Language, 9*, 207-224.

Sullivan, P. M., & Knutson, J. F. (1998). The association between child maltreatment and disabilities in a hospital-based epidemiological study. *Child Abuse & Neglect, 22*, 271-288.

Veneziano, E. (1988). Vocal-verbal interaction and the construction of early lexical knowledge. In M. D. Smith & J. L. Locke (Eds.), *The emergent lexicon: the child's development of a linguistic vocabulary* (pp. 110-147). New York: Academic Press.

Whitehurst, G. J., Smith, M., Fischel, J. E., Arnold, D. S., & Lonigan, C. J. (1991). The continuity of babble and speech in children with specific language delay. *Journal of Speech and Hearing Research, 34*, 1121-1129.

Zeskind, P. S., & Collins, V. (1987). Pitch of infant crying and caregiver responses in a natural setting. *Infant Behavior and Development, 10*, 501-504.

20

Speech Motor Subprocesses in DAS Studied with a Bite-Block

Lian Nijland, Ben Maassen and Sjoeke van der Meulen

The speech of children with Developmental Apraxia of Speech (DAS) is characterized by low intelligibility due to a large number of consonantal errors. The origin of the speech problems in children with DAS can be localized somewhere in the transition from a 'phonological code' into 'articulo-motor output'.

In earlier studies we tried to find evidence of a deviance in planning or in motor programming of speech (Nijland, Maassen & Van der Meulen, 1999a; Nijland, Maassen, Van der Meulen & Bellaar 1999b; Nijland et al., submitted). Results of these studies showed that both planning and programming were disturbed in DAS. Evidence suggesting deviant phonetic *planning* was found in a study in which we manipulated the place of syllable boundary in an otherwise unchanging context. The absence of systematic durational patterns in the speech of children with DAS was interpreted as a problem in phonetic planning. However, it remained unclear whether the primary problem was on a segmental or prosodic level. The main evidence suggesting a *programming* problem lay in the inconsistency of repeated utterances. Because the issue of planning versus programming remained unresolved, with the suggestion of involvement of both, we are investigating the stages of speech production from programming to execution, with a view to unraveling whether the deviance lies with planning or with programming.

In their speech production model, Levelt and Wheeldon (1994) proposed an articulatory network as the last stage of speech production in which the exact execution of the articulators is calculated. Browman and Goldstein (1997) suggested that the input to the last stage of speech production is the 'articulatory gesture'. This gesture only defines the task of the articulators (the result of the articulatory movement) and not the exact way to accomplish this task. For example, one of the tasks in producing the consonant /p/ is 'lip closure'. The execution can consist of movements of the mandibular, the lower lip, both lips, or combinations of these articulators. The exact information must be specified in the last stage of speech production, the articulatory network. At this stage it is also possible to compensate articulatory movements, enabling a speaker, for example, to clench a pipe between the teeth while producing intelligible speech.

The aim of this study was to investigate the ability of normally speaking children (NS) and children with DAS to compensate their articulation when the mandible is fixed by a bite-block clenched between the teeth. Various studies have investigated compensation for a bite-block, in normal and disturbed speech, resulting in diverse conclusions. Some studies (e.g. Baum & Katz, 1988; Edwards, 1992; Lindblom, Lubker & Gay, 1979) concluded that normally speaking adults and children were equally able to compensate for a bite-block, whereas other studies (e.g. Smith & McLean-Muse, 1987) concluded that children were not able to completely compensate for a bite-block. De Jarnette (1988) investigated compensation for a bite-block in normally speaking and articulatory disordered children. The articulatory disordered children showed limited flexibility in compensation as compared to adults and normally speaking children. Baum, Kim, and Katz (1997) found substantial but incomplete compensation in three subject groups, consisting of non-fluent and fluent aphasics, and normal control subjects. They suggested that any deficit in speech motor programming demonstrated by the non-fluent aphasics did not affect their compensatory abilities. This led them to conclude that compensatory abilities are processed at a later stage of speech production.

In this study we investigated the question whether children with DAS show a disturbance at the motor programming level of speech production. For this, the ability to compensate a bite-block manipulation was studied in normally speaking children, in order to assess reference data, and in children with DAS. Differential results between normally speaking children and children with DAS could be interpreted as evidence of a disturbance at the motor programming level in DAS. After all, if children with DAS show the same effects of the manipulation as normally speaking children do, they presumably have similar compensatory abilities and thus do not display a problem at the motor programming level. However, if children with DAS show different effects to the bite-block condition compared with normally speaking children, this must be caused by a problem at the level of motor programming or execution.

METHOD

Participants

Participants were five children with DAS and five normally speaking children, between the ages of 5;0 and 6;10 years. All children were native speakers of Dutch and they were taken from a group of 19 children with DAS and 19 normally speaking children (matched for sex, age, and dialect), who participated in the project of which this study was a part. The children with DAS were 'clear' cases selected from special schools for children with speech and language disorders according to the clinical criteria described by Hall, Jordan and Robin (1993) and Thoonen, Maassen, Wit, Gabreëls and Schreuder (1996). The following further criteria were also adopted: no hearing problems, no comprehension problems, no organic disorders in the orofacial area, no gross motor disturbances or dysarthria, and at least average non-verbal intelligence. Only five children (together with their matched counterparts among the normally speaking children) were selected for this study because not all the children with DAS were able to talk with a bite-block, mostly due to high mouth sensitivity.

Speech Material

The stimulus-set consisted of two-word utterances, in which the relevant part was [əCV] where C = /b,d,x,s/ and V = /a,i,u/ (henceforth 'schwa', 'consonant' and 'V2', respectively). These bisyllabic utterances were spoken within the carrier phrase *hé ... weer* (*hey ... again*) both with bite-block and without it. Each item was repeated six times and the utterances were spoken in random order.

Acoustic Analyses

The speech samples were digitized at 25 kHz and the relevant sections were spliced out, using the Kay Elemetrics Computerized Speech Lab analysis system. The second formant (F2) trajectory through the utterance was used as a measure of coarticulation. For this, markers were set at the onset and offset of each segment. By using these markers the F2 values were obtained at six locations: at schwa-midpoint and schwa-offset, in the consonant, and in V2 at transition onset, transition end and vowel-midpoint (see Fig. 1).

In the voiced sections of the signal (i.e. schwa and V2) the formant values (with corresponding bandwidths) were obtained using pitch-synchronous LPC analyses followed by the root-solving procedure. An LPC analysis at location was performed in the consonant. In the fricatives (/s/ and /x/) this was done with a window of 20 ms centered at 20 ms before offset; in the plosives (/b/ and /d/) a window of 20 ms was centered at the plosive burst.

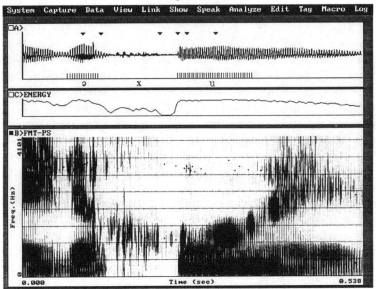

FIG. 1 Example of the analysis used to extract F2 values: oscillogram, energy-window and spectrogram.

Subsequently, F2 ratios were calculated from F2 values by dividing the F2 values in /i/-utterances by the F2 values in /u/-utterances. This was done in order to make a better comparison between the individual children. By using the calculation of F2 ratios we can correct for systematic differences between speakers (due to anatomical variation). These ratios can be interpreted as a measure of the distinction between the utterances, and thus can be used as a measure of coarticulation. A ratio of 1 means that the formant frequencies of both utterance-types are equal, whereas the higher the ratio is above 1 the more distinction there is between the utterances.

Segment durations were measured using markers that were placed at the onset and offset of each segment.

The statistical analyses used in this study were all non-parametric tests, since the homogeneity criteria for parametrical tests could not be satisfied. The significant results are all at a level of $p < 0.05$, unless indicated differently.

RESULTS

F2 Measurements

The interpretation of coarticulation from F2 ratios (a ratio of more than 1 means an influence of the upcoming vowel) is easier than from the second formant trajectories (where a distinction between second formant values of different utterances indicates coarticulation). Because of this (and due to space limitations), the second formant values themselves are not given here in figures; only the statistical results are reported. After this, the coarticulation and bite-block effects will be discussed using F2 ratios.

The effect of bite-block on the F2 values was different in the two groups. In the normally speaking children, the F2 values measured in the schwa (mid and end) were significantly higher due to the bite-block (Wilcoxon Signed Ranks Test in 'mid schwa': $Z = -2.93$, $p < 0.01$; 'end schwa': $Z = -3.66$, $p < 0.001$). In contrast, children with DAS had significantly lower F2 values in the middle of the schwa, caused by the bite-block ($Z = -2.04$). Furthermore, they showed significantly lower formant values measured at transition onset in V2 and at mid V2 ('transition onset': $Z = -2.44$; 'mid V2': $Z = -2.74$, $p < 0.01$].

F2 Ratios. Figs. 2 and 3 display the F2 ratios of the normally speaking children and the children with DAS. Since the largest distinction in utterance-types is found in a comparison of the /i/-utterances (highest F2 values) with the /u/-utterances (lowest F2 values), we show the F2 ratios of /i/ divided by /u/. The broken lines represent the ratios in the condition without bite-block, the solid lines in the condition with bite-block.

High F2 ratios at the location 'mid V2' indicate that there is a large distinction between vowels. Of course, high ratios here were expected, demonstrating that different vowels are characterized by different F2s. Earlier in the utterance the ratios indicate the extent of anticipatory coarticulation of the vowel (V2) on the preceding consonant and schwa: the higher the ratio, the more anticipatory coarticulation there is. The F2-ratio curves in Fig. 2 and 3 show differential coarticulatory effects through the utterances of the two groups. In both conditions, with and without bite-block, the ratios of the normally speaking children were higher throughout the utterance than those of the children with DAS. Children with DAS showed less anticipatory coarticulation and less distinction between the different vowels compared to normally speaking children. In the condition without bite-block the groups differed significantly ($p < 0.01$) at 'end schwa' ($Z = -2.84$), 'transition onset' ($Z = -3.12$), 'transition end' ($Z = -3.46$), and 'mid V2' ($Z = -3.15$). In the bite-block condition, we see a slightly different pattern. In this condition significant differences between the groups were found at 'mid schwa' ($Z = -2.13$), 'end schwa' ($Z = -3.21$), 'consonant' [$Z = 2.32$], and 'transition end' ($Z = -2.05$). Thus, due to the bite-block, the difference between the groups disappeared at 'transition onset' and 'mid V2', but they became larger at the locations 'mid schwa' and 'consonant'. This indicates that the two groups reacted differently to the bite-block.

The results of the statistical tests comparing the F2 ratios in the two conditions (with and without bite-block), within each group, corroborated this

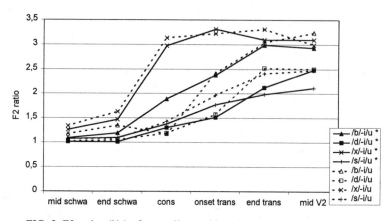

FIG. 2   F2 ratios (i/u) of normally speaking children without bite-block (broken lines) and with bite-block (solid lines).

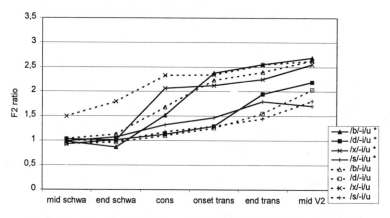

FIG. 3   F2 ratios (i/u) of children with DAS without bite-block (broken lines) and with bite-block (solid lines).

finding. Although the ratios seem to be smaller in the condition with bite-block, normally speaking children did not show a significant effect of bite-block on the F2 ratios. In contrast to this, the children with DAS showed significantly higher ratios at 'transition end' ($Z = -2.07$) and 'mid V2' ($Z = -2.17$). The slightly smaller ratios in the schwa due to the bite-block did not reach significance.

TABLE 1

Mean segment durations in ms (standard deviations in brackets) of the DAS and the normally speaking (NS) groups.

Group	+/-BB	Schwa	Consonant	V2	Total
DAS	-BB	72 (35)	206 (108)	230 (66)	508 (141)
	+BB	73 (36)	254 (156)	213 (81)	520 (160)
NS	-BB	50 (21)	138 (34)	139 (35)	327 (39)
	+BB	42 (24)	165 (48)	168 (41)	372 (52)

Note. -BB = without bite-block and +BB = with bite-block.

Durations

The mean durations of the segments (with standard deviations) are displayed in Table 1. The total durations show that children with DAS had longer durations than normally speaking children, in both conditions. Furthermore, the segment durations were significantly longer, and more variable, in the utterances of children with DAS than in those of normally speaking children, again in both conditions.

In normally speaking children, the bite-block condition led to a significant increase in total utterance duration ($Z = -5.68$, $p < 0.001$) and in the consonant and V2 segments (consonant: $Z = -6.27$, V2: $Z = -5.78$; $p < 0.001$). However, the duration of the schwa was significantly shorter ($Z = -2.20$). In the case of children with DAS, no effect was found on total utterance duration, nor in the duration of schwa. Only the duration of the consonant was significantly longer in the bite-block condition ($Z = -3.65$, $p < 0.001$) and the duration of V2 was actually shorter in the bite-block condition [$Z = -2.74$, $p < 0.01$].

DISCUSSION

Children with DAS did show differential effects to the bite-block manipulation compared to normally speaking children, which suggests a problem in the final stages of speech production.

Although in the normally speaking children significantly higher formant values were found in the schwa due to the bite-block, no significant bite-block effect emerged in the ratios. Thus, the bite-block did not affect the extent of anticipatory coarticulation in these children. Children with DAS demonstrated lower F2 values in the schwa, at the onset of the transition in the vowel, and at mid V2. And, in these children a bite-block effect did emerge in the F2 ratios, namely in an increase of distinction between the vowels. Thus, children with DAS were actually helped by the bite-block in making more distinction between the vowels, which led to more 'normal' F2 ratios. Nevertheless, the articulatory patterns still showed aberrance in children with DAS compared to normally speaking children.

Differential effects of the bite-block manipulation were also found in the durational measures. Although the durations of children with DAS are longer in both conditions, the effect of bite-block on durations was different in the two groups. In normally speaking children, articulation with a bite-block led to longer total utterance durations, and longer durations of consonant and V2. These longer consonant and V2 durations were slightly compensated by shorter durations of schwa. However, in children with DAS, a longer duration was only found in the consonant. These children did display an effect of bite-block on V2 duration, but it was the reverse of the effect found in normally speaking children.

In summary, normally speaking children can compensate for a bite-block in the spatial domain of the articulatory movements. Children with DAS were helped by the bite-block in making more spatial distinctions between the vowels. In the temporal domain neither normally speaking children nor children with DAS were able to compensate for the bite-block. However, the effects were different in the two groups. In normally speaking children this incomplete compensation in the temporal domain could be an effect of immature automation in the stages from programming speech to the execution. It has been suggested that children with DAS have problems in motor programming (Nijland et al., submitted), leading to longer durations. Apparently, this motor programming problem interacts with motor execution, leading to deviant compensatory patterns in the temporal domain.

ACKNOWLEDGMENTS

The Netherlands Organization for Scientific Research (NWO) and the Hersenstichting Nederland are gratefully acknowledged for funding this project. This research was conducted while the first author was supported by a grant from the Foundation for Behavioral and Educational Sciences of NWO (575-56-084) and of the Hersenstichting Nederland (7F99.06) awarded to the second and third authors. We also thank Rody Aldenhoven for her work on the bite-block data.

REFERENCES

Baum, S. R., & Katz, W. F. (1988). Acoustic analysis of compensatory articulation in children. *Journal of Acoustical Society of America, 84,* 1662-1668.

Baum, S. R., Kim, J. A., & Katz, W. F. (1997). Compensation for jaw fixation by aphasic patients. *Brain and Language, 56,* 354-376.

Browman, C. P., & Goldstein, L. (1997). The gestural phonology model. In W. Hulstijn, H. F. M. Peters, & P. H. H. M. Van Lieshout (Eds.), *Speech production: Motor control, brain research and fluency disorders* (pp. 57-71). Amsterdam: Elsevier Science.

De Jarnette, G. (1988). Formant frequencies (F1, F2) of jaw-free versus jaw-fixed vowels in normal and articulatory disordered children. *Perceptual and Motor Skills, 67,* 963-971.

Edwards, J. (1992). Compensatory speech motor abilities in normal and phonologically disordered children. *Journal of Phonetics, 20,* 189-207.

Hall, P. K., Jordan, L. S. & Robin, D. A. (1993). *Developmental Apraxia of Speech.* Austin, TX: Pro-ed.

Levelt, W. J. M., & Wheeldon, L. (1994). Do speakers have a mental syllabary? *Cognition, 50,* 239-269.

Lindblom, B., Lubker, J., & Gay, T. (1979). Formant frequencies of some fixed-mandible vowels and a model of speech motor programming by predictive simulation. *Journal of Phonetics, 7,* 147-161.

Nijland, L., Maassen, B., & Van der Meulen, Sj. (1999a). Use of syllables by children with developmental apraxia of speech. In J.J. Ohala, Y. Hasegawa, M. Ohala, D. Granville & A.C. Bailey (Eds.). *Proceedings of the 14th International Conference of Phonetic Sciences,* Vol. 3 (pp. 1921-1923). Berkeley, CA: University of California Linguistics Department.

Nijland, L., Maassen, B., Van der Meulen, Sj., & Bellaar, M. (1999b). Acoustic analyses to assess the underlying deficit in children with developmental apraxia of speech (DAS). *Proceedings of the International Association of Logopedics and Phoniatrics, 24th Congress, II,* 626-629.

Nijland, L., Maassen, B., Van der Meulen, Sj., Gabreëls, F., Kraaimaat, F. W., & Schreuder, R. (submitted). Coarticulation patterns in children with developmental apraxia of speech.

Smith, B. L., & McLean-Muse, A. (1987). Effects of rate and bite block manipulations on kinematic characteristics of children's speech. *Journal of the Acoustical Society of America, 81,* 747-754.

Thoonen, G., Maassen, B., Wit, J., Gabreëls, F., & Schreuder, R. (1996). The integrated use of maximum performance tasks in differential diagnostic evaluations among children with motor speech disorders. *Clinical Linguistics and Phonetics, 10*, 311-336.

21

Spectral Contrast Sensitivity of Lateralized /s/ Spectra Produced by High School Lateralizers

Judith Oxley, Raymond Daniloff, Gordon Schuckers[1] and M. Irene
Stephens

Eleven /s/-lateralizing kindergarten children were followed for two years during kindergarten and first grade, and their fricatives analyzed perceptually. Their kindergarten misarticulations occurred only on /s/ or, at most, one other sound. The present authors were intrigued when it was discovered that eight of 11 original lateralizing kindergarteners, who were now in 10th grade in a local high school, were still lateralizing /s/. Five of the eight consented to be reassessed. Each had received 4–5 years or more of conventional speech therapy after they had not spontaneously overcome lisping in first grade. For four of the five subjects, acoustic measures of lateralization had decreased, and for one, increased (Stephens et al., 1999a; Stephens, Lu, Kao, Khavazadeh & Daniloff, 1999b). Spectral moments for the five subjects revealed context sensitivity that was highly idiosyncratic across speakers and contexts and that had changed over time. We speculated that different spectral measures might yield fresh insight into context sensitivity, thus yielding information that might be used profitably for conventional articulatory treatment. These children represented the "discrete" misarticulators noted by Gibbon, Hardcastle, and Dent (1995), and would therefore be likely to profit from EPG training.

---

[1] Sadly, since completion of this investigation our colleague Gordon Schuckers passed away.

METHOD

The five teenage, lateralizing participants were recorded as they read the list of 40 sentences containing /s/ in the various contexts used for the first study (Stephens et al., 1999a). The contexts studied, /sp, st, sl, ps, ts, ks, ls, si, su, sʌ/, were repeated three times. A GW Soundscope system was used to produce 14-coefficient LPC spectra made at the midpoint of each lateralized /s/. The following series of seven spectral measures was recorded:

1. Energy Balance (EB). The dB value of average spectrum level of the 4000-10,000 Hz band minus the dB value of the average spectrum level of the 0-4000 Hz band.

2. Ideal Spectral Peaks (ISP). Presence or absence of strong peaks at 4000 and 8000 Hz +/- 750 Hz, respectively.

3. High Frequency Band (HFB). Frequency of Highest Pole minus frequency of Lowest Pole in 4000-8000 Hz range.

4. Full Frequency Band (FFB). Frequency of Highest Pole minus Lowest Pole in 0-10,000 Hz band.

5. HFB/FFB Ratio.

6. Number of Higher Resonances (NHR). NHR in 4000-10,000 Hz band.

7. Number of Lower Resonances (NLR). NLR in 0-4000 Hz band.

All poles utilized were no more than 10 dB less intense than the strongest pole frequency in the spectrum. Complete data sets (i.e. three repetitions, per subject, of targets over all seven contexts) were collected from all available participants. However, data on two of the five participants were contaminated by ambient noise in the school setting. Thus, statistical analyses were limited to data from three participants.

RESULTS

Table 1 lists the average (over all seven measures) rank of each context (there were two /sl/ contexts) for three participants. The scores for spectral rank reflect combined strong lateralization and relatively weaker coarticulatory influences on the fricative sound. A low average numerical rank-score presumably reflects less lateralization, while a high score reflects more. Ideally, nonlateralized spectra would reflect a rank of one, and strong lateralized fricatives, a rank of 12. The nearly 2.3:1 ratio across contexts suggests that the measures used are context sensitive. The question is which of the seven spectral measures has highest score across the 12 phonetic contexts studied, while displaying the smallest Coefficients of Variation made on different speakers, repetitions, and contexts. The Coefficient of Variation, V, measures the spread of a set of data as a proportion of its mean and may be expressed as a percentage (Maxwell & Satake, 1997). A V-value was computed for each measure in each context, repetition, and speaker. Collapsed across speakers and repetitions, the average CV was 35% (range 21 to 73%).

TABLE 1
Averaged ranks of seven spectral measures of lateralized /s/ spectra based on three speakers, three repetitions, and 12 phonetic contexts.

Averaged rank	Context
3.79	sk
4.40	st
4.50	ls
4.70	sl^2
5.20	sl^1
6.40	sp
7.10	ps
7.40	si
7.70	su
8.60	ks
8.70	ts
8.90	sʌ

Fig. 1 presents the mean rank across contexts for the average of all seven spectral measures. Notice that FFB (7), HFB (6), EB (5), and ISP (4) ranked highest, being least variable (smallest range of values). Thus the measures that were the least variable were FFB, HFB, and EB.

Fig. 2 presents the percentage of instances in which each of the seven spectral scores (for 12 phonetic contexts, three speakers, and three repetitions) produced V-values less than or equal to 20%. The highest ranked measures (smallest V-values) were FFB (7), HFB (6), NHR (5), HFR (4), and EB (3). Combining rank values for both types of analysis, it was found that FFB (14), HFB (12), and EB (8) were the three highest jointly ranked spectral measures: they combined low context variability with reasonably low V-values. They reflect stable and context-sensitive estimates of fricative lateralization.

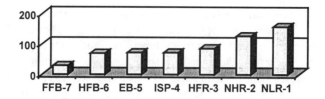

FIG. 1 Range of averaged spectral scores in percentages, where a high rank (7) reflects a measure that is least labile across phonetic contexts.

Each of the seven ranked spectral measures was correlated with the measure expected to be most discriminating with regard to acoustic lateralization, EB. All correlations were positive and substantial in size, but none achieved significance at even the $p < 0.05$ level, probably because of too many tied-rank scores and too few degrees of freedom.

Table 2 presents the results of a Chi Square analysis of the facilitative/non-facilitative contexts. Three contexts, /sk, st, and ls/, were found to be significantly facilitating, according to analysis of data averaged over all three participants. Separate analyses were conducted for each individual participant's data. The top three contexts were found to be significantly facilitative for two subjects. For individuals, all facilitating contexts were consonant clusters. The three least facilitative contexts were, on average, significantly non-facilitative. For two participants, /Cs/ and /sV/ were significantly non-facilitative.

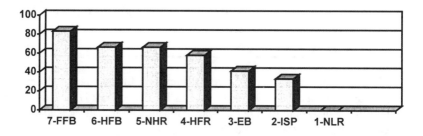

FIG. 2 Rank ordering of each of the spectral measures according to the percentage of instances accounted for by Average Coefficients of Variation less than or equal to 20%.

TABLE 2
X^2 $_{2df}$ tests of facilitation and non-facilitation of /s/-like production.

Source	Three most facilitative contexts	Three least facilitative contexts.
Mean Data	$X^2 = 6.19, p \leq 0.05$	$X^2 = 6.86, p \leq 0.05$
Participant 1	$X^2 = 5.99, p \leq 0.05$	$X^2 = 2.31, p > 0.05$ ns
Participant 2	$X^2 = 8.37, p \leq 0.05$	$X^2 = 8.59, p \leq 0.05$
Participant 3	$X^2 = 1.23, p > 0.05$ ns	$X^2 = 1.02, p > 0.05$ ns

DISCUSSION

The three measures (EB, HFB, HFB/FFB) revealed sufficiently low Coefficients of Variation, and sufficient range of context sensitivity, to serve as useful indices of context-sensitive lateralization of /s/. All reflected whether higher frequency noise and power bandwidths predominated in the lateralized spectrum. Our results show that certain phonetic contexts, such as /st/, /sk/ and /ls/, favor production of acoustically less lateralized /s/ spectra, and changes in articulatory gestures for lateral /s/. No ready explanation offers itself for why /ls/ contexts would facilitate less lateral /s/-frication. One explanation could be that /l/ may exhibit velar or alveolar productions that would not be noted in a standard articulatory screening. Second, it could be that the juxtaposition of the two phonemes resulted in greater perceptual differentiation, resulting in better grooving. Third, tongue-alveolar contact prior to /s/ production may have facilitated better tongue placement and central grooving for the /s/ offset, by means of a perseveratory coarticulation effect.

EPG context sensitivity for /s/ misarticulations has been reported by Gibbon (1999), Dagenais (1995), and Gibbon, Hardcastle, and Moore (1990). Gibbon (1999) observed that appropriate tip/blade placement accompanied by raised tongue-blade edges (i.e. a spoon-shaped posture), which spatially anchors blade and tip, are vital to appropriate stops, as well as later acquisition of centrally grooved sibilants.

Gibbon, citing the EPG work of the Edinburgh research team and others, speculates that many misarticulators of /s/ and /ɹ/ persist in infantile, undifferentiated shaping of the tongue tip and blade. The more severe, multiply misarticulating children exhibit particularly significant motoric disorganization. It is important to note McNutt's (1977) study of teenaged misarticulators of /s/ and /ɹ/. Factor analyses revealed at least four subgroups with differing factor weights accorded to sensory, motor, and perceptual measures. Some had a sensory basis, whereas others had motoric, perceptual, or mixed bases.

The older children observed in our study appeared to be discrete misarticulators in kindergarten, most having only /s/, and in a few cases, an /ɹ/ as a co-occurring misarticulation. It is important to notice that not only did these children persist for nearly a decade with all other phonemes appropriately articulated, but they were vocally averse to public speech, and conversation with anyone but their familiars (Stephens et al., 1999a, b). They were also justifiably frustrated about ineffective therapy.

In conclusion, our data suggest that contextually sensitive co-production can move even the lateralized /s/ spectrum about rather substantially, as revealed by three spectral measures with potential clinical utility. We may conclude, based on observations of Winitz (1975), that children characterized as "discrete" misarticulators (Gibbon, 1999) may profit from context-sensitive clinical retraining procedures, which include ear-training, to extinguish acquired perceptual similarity between normal and lateral /s/, with use of phonetic context to set up and enhance central grooving and a more spoon-shaped tongue. In a forthcoming study we will present data on seven elementary school-age children who achieved normal /s/ production in 3 months or less while undergoing treatment based on use of these facilitating techniques, without the need for additional equipment, such as the EPG.

REFERENCES

Dagenais, P. A. (1995). Electropalatography in the treatment of articulation/ phonological disorders. *Journal of Communication Disorders, 28,* 303-329.

Gibbon, F. (1999). Undifferentiated lingual gestures in children with articulatory/phonological disorders. *Journal of Speech, Language and Hearing Research, 42,* 382-397.

Gibbon, F., Hardcastle, W., & Dent, H. (1995). A study of obstruent sounds in school-aged children with speech disorders using electropalatography. *European Journal of Disorders of Communication, 30,* 213-225.

Gibbon, F., Hardcastle, W., & Moore, H. A. (1990). Modifying abnormal tongue patterns in an older child using electropalatography. *Child Language Teaching and Therapy, 6,* 227-245.

Maxwell, D. L., & Satake, E. (1997). *Research and statistical methods in communication disorders.* Baltimore, MD: Williams and Wilkins.

McNutt, J. (1977). Oral sensory and motor behaviors of children with /s/ or /r/ misarticulation. *Journal Speech and Hearing Research, 20,* 694-703.

Stephens, M. I., Lu, F., Khavazadeh, L, Kruger, C., Kao, K., Daniloff, R., & Schuckers, G. (1999a). Context sensitivity of lateralized /s/: A developmental study. In, J. J. Ohala, Y. Hasegawa, M. Ohala, D. Granville & A. C. Bailey (Eds.), *Proceedings of the 14th Congress of Phonetic Sciences,* (pp. 815-817).

Berkeley: University of California Press.

Stephens, M. I., Lu, F., Kao, K., Khavazadeh, L., & Daniloff, R. (1999b). Fishing for the past: Remains of early lateralization of /s/. In J. Ohala (Ed.), *Proceedings of the 14th Congress of Phonetic Sciences*, (pp. 819-821). Berkeley: University of California Press.

Winitz, H. (1975). *Articulatory acquisition and behavior*. Englewood Cliffs, NJ: Prentice Hall.

22

Speech Errors in Japanese

Haruko Miyakoda

Speech errors are a fruitful source of information about language. They provide evidence concerning language storage and processing. However, most past studies have been concerned with English and other European languages. There are few studies that have dealt with other languages.

This chapter analyzes speech errors in Japanese. The material forming the basis of this study is a collection of 298 spontaneous speech errors in spoken Japanese. We attempt to find out whether the generalizations claimed for speech errors in English also apply to Japanese. Specifically, we concern ourselves with the following questions:

1. What types of speech errors are observed? Do anticipations outnumber perseverations and transpositions, as in English?
2. Which features are involved in errors?
3. What is the interaction between the syllable structure of a language and the speech errors observed?

Of particular interest to us is question 3. In English speech errors, it has been claimed that onsets interact with onsets, nuclei with nuclei. This implies that syllable structure plays an important role in analyzing the data for speech errors. We will see how syllable structure affects the pattern of errors observed for Japanese, a language that has a different structure from English.

This chapter is organized as follows. First, we analyze the Japanese data by comparing the results with those reported for English speech errors. The three aspects that we will focus on are: error types, distinctive features, and syllable structure. Discussion and conclusion follow. For our analysis of the errors we divide the speakers by age into the four groups shown in Table 1.

TABLE 1
The four groups used in the study.

Group	Age	Number of errors collected
A	3-6 years old	84
B	10-16 years old	26
C	20-29 years old	95
D	30-55 years old	93

DATA ANALYSIS

Error Types

In English, there are three basic types of speech errors: perseverations, anticipations, and transpositions. Anticipations are errors where the influencing syllable is in the part of the utterance that is still unspoken. Perseverations are errors where the influencing syllable has already been spoken. Transposition errors involve two elements being exchanged. Laubstein (1987), using a sample of 559 English speech errors, gives examples of each type, as shown in (1).

(1)   *Perseverations*
      practice teaching > practice preaching
      quadruple > quadwuple

      Anticipations
      grapefruit flavor > grapefluit flavor
      Did he play for the Redwings > Did he play for the wedwings

      Transpositions
      Lloyd Moseby > Lloyz Modeby, It hurts Tate > It turts hate

                                                    (Laubstein, 1987, p. 343)

In Japanese, these three types of speech errors are also observed. Examples are given in (2).

(2)   *Perseverations*
      i ra Q sja i ma se > i ra Q sja i sja se   'to welcome'

      Anticipations
      go mei wa ku > go mei ka ku   'to cause trouble'

Transpositions
ga N ba Q te ne > ba N ga Q te ne   'good luck'

There is, however, a difference in the rate of their occurrence. In English, it is claimed that anticipation errors outnumber the other two types (Cutler, 1982; Nakao, 1996). In Japanese, there is a general tendency for transpositions to outnumber anticipations. If we compare the adult data with those of children, both anticipation and transposition errors are observed to occur often in adults, but in child phonology, there is a strong tendency for transpositions to take place. In Table 2, the occurrence rate of these three error types are summarized according to the four age groups.

TABLE 2
Speech errors according to each age group.

	Group A	Group B	Group C	Group D
Perseverations	2 (2.3%)	3 (11.5%)	2 (2.1%)	12 (12.9%)
Anticipations	2 (2.3%)	2 (7.6%)	7 (7.3%)	18 (19.3%)
Transpositions	21 (25%)	4 (15.3%)	21 (22%)	9 (9.6%)

Distinctive Features and Speech Errors

It has often been noted that the feature [coronal] has a special status. The coronals are the most frequent consonants in languages. In terms of acquisition, coronals with labials are the first consonants acquired by children. These frequency and acquisition facts have lead researchers to claim that coronals are the most neutral, unmarked consonants (Paradis & Prunet, 1991, p. 1). Let us see if this also holds true for Japanese.

Table 3 shows that a high percentage of errors involved [coronal]: of the 96 consonant substitutions, only seven did not involve [coronal].

TABLE 3
The correlation between [coronal] and speech errors.

Features involved	Group A	Group B	Group C	Group D
[+cor] > [-cor]	20(58.8%)	3 (37.5%)	18 (56.2%)	12 (54.5%)
[-cor] > [+cor]	9 (26.5%)	2 (25%)	6 (18.8%)	4 (18.2%)
[+cor] > [+cor]	5 (14.7%)	1 (12.5%)	4 (12.5%)	5 (4.6%)
[-cor] > [-cor]	0 (0%)	2 (25%)	4 (12.5%)	1 (4.6%)

A point worth noting is that *all* the errors attested in the child group involved this feature. Our findings suggest that in Japanese, as in English, [coronal] is the most unmarked feature.

A closer examination of the data shows that the features violated the most in speech errors differ among the groups. Jaeger (1992) claimed that in English, [place] is violated the most, with [continuant], [fricative], [voice], and [nasal] following. For adults, [place] is violated the most, and the least likely to be involved is [nasal]. However, there is a major difference between these two groups concerning the position of [voice] in the hierarchy: for adults the [voice] feature is the second most violated, while for children, it is second to last in the scale (see 3, below).

(3)   CHILD: Place > Continuant > Fricative > Voice > Nasal
       ADULT: Place > Voice > Stop > Fricative+Approximate > Nasal

In Japanese, as in English, [place] is violated the most in all four groups. As shown in (4), however, in all age groups, [voice] is one of the features least likely to be violated in Japanese, in contrast to the pattern seen in the English adult hierarchy, where [voice] follows [place] in being the feature most violated.

(4)   Group A: Place > Continuant > Resonant > Nasal > Voice, Consonantal
       Group B: Place > Continuant, Resonant, Nasal, Voice > Consonantal
       Group C: Place > Continuant > Resonant, Nasal, Voice > Consonantal
       Group D: Place > Resonant > Continuant > Voice > Nasal > Consonantal

Syllable Structure and Speech Errors

Researchers including Laubstein (1987) have claimed that the most common types of speech errors are those where a consonant interacts with another consonant, and a vowel segment is exchanged with, or substituted for another vowel. The examples from English in (5) illustrate this:

(5)   C > C   left hemisphere > heft lemisphere

                Rolling pin > rolling pill

       V > V   the boy bows > the bay bows

                Bev and Bill > Biv and Bell

                                    (Laubstein, 1987, p. 343)

This is also true of Japanese. As the examples in (6) show, a consonant is exchanged with another consonant, a vowel with another vowel. Furthermore, a CV syllable (or mora) may be exchanged with another CV.

(6)   C > C   se ba N go u > se ga N bo u   'uniform number'

      V > V   ke Q ka N > ke Q ko N   'blood vessel'

      CV > CV   ta ra ko su pa > ta ra su ko pa 'cod roe spaghetti'

However, there are exceptions, and these involve the moraic phonemes. Examples are given in (7).

(7)   V > C   ke i za i te ki > ke N za N te ki   'economical'

      CV > Q   o ku sa N > o Q sa N   'madame'

      C > V   ra N ki N gu > ra i ki N gu   'ranking'

In the case of moraic phonemes, consonants can be replaced by vowels, and vice versa. This is allowed, just as long as they interact within their 'own kind'. The four types of moraic phonemes are summarized in (8):

(8)   a.   the moraic nasal (N), occupying the coda position of the syllable
      b.   the moraic obstruent (Q), which is the first half of a geminate consonant
      c.   the second half of diphthongal vowel sequences
      d.   the second half of long vowels

Where there is an interaction between a consonant and a vowel, it is between a moraic nasal or obstruent and the second half of a long vowel or diphthong.

Let us next turn to the status of the onset in speech errors. Fudge (1987) reported that in English speech errors, the nucleus and the coda exhibit a cohesiveness. The errors suggest that the relationship between the nucleus and the coda is closer than that between the nucleus and the onset, that is, a split is assumed between the onset and the rhyme. Davis (1989) has also claimed the special status of the onset in inducing speech errors. Examples are shown below in (12):

(12)   left hemisphere > heft lemisphere
           Roman Jakobson > Yoman Rakobson

                                              (Davis, 1989, p. 212)

Let us see if the same tendency can be seen in Japanese speech errors. There are five different types of errors attested in onset position: substitution (SUB), palatalization (PAL), deletion (DEL), insertion (INS), and transposition (TRANS). The rate of occurrence of each is summarized in Table 4.

TABLE 4
Errors occurring in onset position.

SUB	PAL	DEL	INS	TRANS
96 (32.2%)	48 (16.1%)	11 (3.6%)	3 (1%)	4 (1.3%)

Of the 298 errors, 162 involved the onset (54.3%). Just as in English, we find that onsets are often involved in speech errors in Japanese.

The internal structure of the syllable in Japanese is considered to have the structure as in (13a) (Kubozono, 1989, p. 254).

(13)

If we compare the structure in (13a) with the 'Germanic' type of syllable structure in (13b), there is a significant difference in how the consonantal and vocalic elements are grouped. In English, as mentioned earlier, the break is assumed to be between the onset and the nucleus; the nucleus forms a constituent (rhyme) with the following consonantal element. In Japanese, however, there is cohesiveness between the onset and the nucleus rather than between the nucleus and the coda. The onset–nucleus cluster and the moraic phoneme in coda position are both assigned the same status within the syllable – they each are attached to a mora node.

In a language such as English where the break is assumed to exist between the onset and the nucleus, it is not particularly surprising that errors involving just onsets to occur. However, our data has shown that even in Japanese, a language that considers the onset-nucleus to be a single constituent, the onset has a special status in inducing errors.

DISCUSSION

The analysis of Japanese speech errors has shown that there are common characteristics observed for both English and Japanese errors. For example, in both languages, [place] is the feature most violated. Regardless of the difference in syllable structure, there was a strong tendency for errors to occur in onsets in both English and Japanese. However, there are differences between the two languages. For example, in Japanese, transpositions outnumber anticipations and perseverations, whereas in English, anticipations are attested more than the other two types. What is so striking about the Japanese transposition errors is that not only do consonants and vowels interact with one another, but the consonant plus the vowel as a whole transpose. How can we account for this uniqueness? One way is to focus on the influence of orthography, since the majority of the letters in the Kana syllabary consist of combinations of a consonant and a vowel.

Influence of Orthography

Although most phonologists work under the assumption that a language "is the same no matter what system of writing may be used to record it" (Bloomfield, 1933, p. 21), the error patterns attested in Japanese suggest that the influence of orthography cannot be ignored. For example, as mentioned previously, transposition errors occur frequently in Japanese, with the CV cluster being transposed as a whole. This might be attributed to the influence of the kana spelling system.

In Japanese, the syllabary is composed basically of 48 letters, of which five correspond to vowels, one to the moraic nasal, and the rest to a combination of a consonant and a vowel. The Hiragana syllabary is given in Table 5.

Table 5
Hiragana syllabary

あ	か	さ	た	な	は	ま	や	ら	わ
a	ka	sa	ta	na	ha	ma	ya	ra	wa
い	き	し	ち	に	ひ	み	ゐ	り	を
i	ki	si	ti	ni	hi	mi	yi	ri	wo
う	く	す	つ	ぬ	ふ	む	ゆ	る	ん
u	ku	su	tu	nu	hu	mu	yu	ru	N
え	け	せ	て	ね	へ	め	ゑ	れ	
e	ke	se	te	ne	he	me	ye	re	
お	こ	そ	と	の	ほ	も	よ	ろ	
o	ko	so	to	no	ho	mo	yo	ro	

Evidence in favor of the view that orthography has influence on the errors can be found in the pattern observed for transposition errors: the consonant and the vowel as a whole transpose. Since the majority of the kana letters fail to 'isolate' the individual sounds of the language, there may be a closer relationship between the consonants and vowels in Japanese compared to other languages. For example, let us consider the transposition errors in (14):

(14)

de ga ra shi > de ga shi ra   '(the tea leaves) are already used'
he ko ta re ru > he ta ko re ru   'be tired out'
to u mo ro ko shi > to u mo ko ro shi 'corn'

If we convert the symbols into kana as in (15), we find that transposition occurs between two kana letters that are adjacent to one another:

(15)   でがらし > でがしら
            へこたれる > へたこれる
            とうもろこし > とうもころし

The representation based on kana better accounts for why a consonant and a vowel transpose as a whole. The problem with this approach, however, is that it fails to account for why young children who have not yet acquired the writing system still make the same CV transposition errors (e.g. te re bi > te bi re 'television'). Clearly the errors are not solely influenced by the writing system.

The feature [voice] is another aspect implying the influence of the writing system on the errors. Recall that this feature followed [place] in being one of the most violated features in the adult phonology of English. However, in Japanese, it did not play an active part. This may be due to the influence of the basic kana syllabary.

The letters shown in Table 5 represent either voiced elements (i.e. vowels, nasals, glides) or combinations of a voiceless consonant plus a vowel. The combinations of a voiced consonant and a vowel are shown in the writing system by adding the diacritic ' ゛ ' to the corresponding voiceless counterpart (e.g. た > だ 'ta > da', さ > ざ 'sa > za'). The addition of the diacritic can be interpreted as depicting the 'marked' status of the voiced sounds. Since the letters can clearly be grouped into the voiceless and the voiced based on whether this diacritic is used, this might account for why there are few errors concerning this feature.

On the other hand, here again even children who have not yet acquired the writing system make few errors concerning [voice]. This, of course, might reflect the fact that in child phonology, there is a universal tendency for young children not to have a voicing distinction in obstruent phonemes, and that leads to a much lower possibility of their violating the voicing distinction than adults (Jaeger, 1992, p. 203).

However, Noda (1995), citing a study by Ohwada, reported that two-year-old children can pronounce /p/, /b/, /t/, /d/ with more than 90% accuracy. So it seems that Japanese children do have a voicing distinction at an early age and that orthography has little to do with the errors observed. Perhaps [voice] is more important in Japanese than in English, hence fewer errors involve this feature. If so, how can this 'importance' be accounted for theoretically?

Status of the Moraic Phonemes

Recall that in Japanese, the moraic phonemes display a unique behavior in that consonants and vowels within this group can interact with one another. This clearly indicates the highly marked characteristic of these phonemes. Another aspect worthy of note is that speech errors taken from child data suggest that the moraic phonemes are either deleted or simply ignored. For example, in our data, we observed a three-year-old child make the speech errors in (16).

(16) mi ka N > [mi:]   'tangerine'

     me gu mi > [mi:mi]   'Megumi (female name)'

This child was unable to pronounce [mikan], and produced the form [mi:]. However the same child, in pronouncing a word with regular CV sequences, does recognize that there are three 'parts' within the word and pronounces [megumi] as [mi:mi]. Possibly the child has not yet acquired the moraic phoneme, and was not able to recognize that it differed from the unmarked CV pattern. This is indirect evidence that the moraic phonemes are acquired later than the regular CV mora.

     This raises the following question: if moraic phonemes have a unique status within the language, and are also acquired later, does this have anything to do with the fact that adults rarely mix up regular CVs with these moraic phonemes in speech errors? Furthermore, is there a way to account for the difference between the two groups within a theoretical framework? Hua and Dodd (2000) claim that the concept of phonological saliency can account for the order of phonological acquisition in Putonghua (Modern Standard Chinese). The same concept might shed light on why Japanese speech errors occur as they do.

Phonological Saliency

Although there is no agreement on the definition of phonological saliency, the factors that determine and affect saliency can be summarized as in (17):

(17)
     a. The status of a component in the syllable structure, especially whether it is compulsory or optional (a compulsory component being more salient than an optional one).
     b. The capacity of a component to differentiate the lexical meaning of a syllable; (a component which is more capable of distinguishing lexical information being more salient).
     c. The number of permissible choices within a component in the syllable

structure (the fewer the choices the higher the saliency).

(cf. Hua & Dodd, 2000, p. 34)

In the case of Putonghua, tones were acquired earlier than syllable final consonants and vowels, which were in turn acquired earlier than syllable initial consonants. This ordering is accounted for on the basis of the three factors given in (17): tone is acquired earlier because it has the highest 'saliency' in Putonghua, being compulsory for every syllable (cf. 17a); a change of tone would lead to the change in lexical meaning (cf. 17b); and there are only four alternative choices (compared to 21 syllable initial phonemes, 21 monophthongs, diphthongs and triphthongs) (cf. 17c).

Following tone, came the acquisition of syllable final consonants and vowels (mainly monophthongs). The syllable initial consonants were acquired last. This can be attributed to two factors: first, in terms of the number of permissible choices, there are only two syllable final consonants compared to 21 syllable initial consonants; second, while vowels occupy compulsory positions within the syllable, syllable initial consonants occupy the optional position. Based on the claims given in (17b) and (17c), syllable final consonants are considered to be more salient, and therefore, are acquired earlier.

Hua and Dodd (2000) emphasize that phonological saliency is a language-specific phenomenon. The saliency level of a particular phonological feature is determined by its role within the phonological system of a given language. In the case of Japanese, moraic phonemes can only occupy the position within the syllable that is optional, whereas the regular (C)Vs occupy the compulsory position. This difference leads to the less salient status of the moraic phonemes within the phonological system. Because moraic phonemes are less salient, they are acquired later. It may be postulated that this difference in saliency discriminates the moraic phonemes with regular CVs in such a way that interaction rarely occurs between these two groups.

In terms of speech errors, it might be claimed that the less salient components have a greater tendency to become involved in errors. As mentioned above, the reason why [voice] errors occur less in Japanese than in English can be attributed to the fact that [voice] (or rather [-voice]) has a more 'important' status in Japanese (recall that the basic kana syllabary is composed of just the voiceless consonants). In terms of saliency, we can claim that this 'importance' can be measured in terms of the number of permissible choices for voiced and voiceless consonants, respectively. For Japanese, the only place within the syllable where there is the voicing distinction is in the onset. Here, the number of permissible choices for voiceless is five (/k/, /s/, /t/, /c/, /p/), whereas for voiced the number increases to 10 (/g/, /z/, /d/, /n/, /h/, /m/, /j/, /w/, /r/, /b/). Because there are only five options, the voiceless consonants are considered more salient, thus preventing the confusion of voiced with voiceless.

Although we have attempted to account for the Japanese errors based on saliency, the concept of saliency itself together with its implications must, of course, be explored further. There might be a language-specific ranking constraint among the factors determining saliency, or there might be other aspects that should be added to the criteria. These we leave for future research.

CONCLUSION

Let us summarize the characteristics of Japanese speech errors based on the three questions posited at the beginning of this chapter:

1. Do anticipations outnumber perseverations and transpositions in Japanese? In adult phonology, both anticipation and transposition errors occur but in child phonology, transposition errors stand out as being the most common error type.

2. Do most errors involve the feature [coronal]? Yes. However, unlike English, the [voice] feature does not have a role in errors in Japanese.

3. What is the interaction between the syllable structure of a language and the speech errors observed? Regardless of structure, there is a strong tendency for errors to occur in onsets in both English and Japanese. Also, the Japanese errors reflect the unique distributional pattern of moraic phonemes. Generally, consonants interact with consonants, vowels with vowels. However, in the case of moraic phonemes, consonants interact with vowels.

Although influence of orthography can be claimed on the grounds that the majority of the kana letters consists of a combination of a consonant and a vowel, it cannot account for why errors occur in young children who have not yet acquired knowledge of the writing system.

Close observation of the transposition errors, however, suggests the writing system of the language might influence the errors, at least in some cases. This is evident when errors involving two or more moras are considered, as in (18).

(18) a.　　満員御礼　　　　　　御礼満員
　　　　　　 ma N i N o N re i　 > o N re i ma N i N 'Full house- thanks'

　　　　　　助六　　　　　　六助
　　　　　　su ke ro ku >　 ro ku su ke　　　　　'Rokusuke (male name)'

　　 b. ライセンス　　　センライス
　　　　　　 ra i se N su >　 se N ra i su　　　　　'license'

This type of error often involves words depicted in Chinese characters (cf. 18a), or foreign loan words (cf. 18b). These examples all seem to suggest the need to reconsider the relationship between orthography and speech errors. It might be that the writing system has more influence on how Japanese speakers process and store language information compared to other languages.

REFERENCES

Bloomfield, L. (1933). *Language*. New York: Holt.

Cutler, A. C. (1982). *Slips of the tongue*. The Hague: Mouton.

Davis, S. (1989). On a non-argument for the rhyme. *Journal of Linguistics, 25,* 211-217.

Fudge, E. (1987). Branching structure within the syllable. *Journal of Linguistics, 23,* 359-377.

Hua, Z., & Dodd B. (2000). The phonological acquisition of Putonghua. *Journal of Child Language, 27,* 3-42.

Jaeger, J. (1992). Phonetic features in young children's slips of the tongue. *Language and Speech, 35,* 189-205.

Kubozono, H. (1989). The mora and syllable structure in Japanese: Evidence from speech errors. *Language and Speech, 32,* 249-278.

Laubstein, A. S. (1987). Syllable structure: the speech error evidence. *Canadian Journal of Linguistics, 32,* 339-363.

Nakao, T. (1996). *Onin ni okeru tsujiteki fuhen* (Diachronic universals). Tokyo: Liber Press.

Noda, U. (1995). *Nyuyoji no kotoba* (Language of infants). Tokyo: Dai Nippon Tosho.

Paradis, C. & Prunet. J. F. (1991) *Phonetics and phonology: The special status of coronals*. New York: Academic Press.

23

Segment Production in Mono-, Di- and Polysyllabic Words in Children Aged 3;0 to 7;11

Deborah G. H. James, Jan van Doorn and Sharynne McLeod

Polysyllabic words (PSWs), that is, words of three or more syllables, make up a significant proportion of young children's lexicons. Vihman (1996) reported a range from 2% to 27% in children aged 1;0 to 2;0 years from different linguistic backgrounds. Calculations based on Klein's (1981) study indicated an average of 24% of PSWs (predominantly monomorphemic) in the lexicons of five children speaking American English in an age range of 20 to 24 months. However, few tests of speech in citation form include this proportion of PSWs. For example, the proportion of PSWs in The Fisher-Logemann Test of Articulation Competence (Fisher & Logemann, 1971) is 4.5% (5 PSWs). The proportion within The Goldman-Fristoe Test of Articulation (Goldman & Fristoe, 1969) is 9% (4 PSWs). The proportion within the Smit-Hand Articulation and Phonology Evaluation (Smit & Hand, 1997) is 3.8% (3 PSWs). The proportion in the Articulation Survey (Atkin & Fisher, 1996) is 7.6% (5 PSWs). Even the word corpus developed by Grunwell (1987) to account for medial sounds occurring in either syllable-initial or syllable-final position only contains 7% PSWs (14 PSWs). Furthermore, most of the normative data about speech in citation form have been developed from word corpora dominated by monosyllabic words (MSWs) and disyllabic words (DSWs) not PSWs (Ingram, 1976). For example, the American normative data about consonants developed by Smit, Hand, Freilinger, Bernthal and Bird (1990) were developed from a protocol of 81 words, three of which were PSWs. Australian data developed by Kilminster and Laird (1978) and Chirlian and Sharpley (1982) were based on a protocol of 59 words, four of which were PSWs. The normative data developed by Arlt and Goodban (1976) were developed from a protocol of 48 words, one of which was a PSW. The normative data for the Edinburgh Articulation Test (Anthony, Bogle, Ingram & McIsaac, 1971) were developed from 41 words, four of which were PSWs. If the inclusion of significant numbers of PSWs in the normative data results in different, possibly lower norms, then children's speech skills may be overestimated when using tests containing few PSWs.

There are several reasons why significant numbers of PSWs should be included in speech tests. First, as PSWs are present in children's earliest lexicons (Ingram, 1976; Jaeger, 1997; Pater, 1997; Priestly, 1977; Salidis & Johnson, 1997; Smith, 1973) and make up about 20% of their lexicons (Klein, 1981), they should be routinely sampled to ensure validity. Second, the production of PSWs draws more heavily on skills to sequence and juxtapose sounds, syllables and linguistic stress than MSWs and DSWs. Consequently, their inclusion in tests improves construct validity because they include a wider range of phonological constituents than MSWs and DSWs. They better account for current concerns in modern phonology about syllable structure, such as onsets, rimes, codas and edge-based factors (Borowski, 1989; Kehoe & Stoel-Gammon, 1997). Their inclusion also allows for the consideration of prominence and linguistic stress as well as the interaction between stress, syllabic structure and segmental effects (Kehoe & Stoel-Gammon, 1997). Third, poor PSW production is a characteristic of children with speech impairment and literacy difficulties (Katz, 1986; Ozanne, 1995). Significantly, for some children, speech impairment is only apparent in renditions of PSWs, not in renditions of MSWs and DSWs (Gillon & Dodd, 1993; Katz, 1986). If testing protocols do not include PSWs, then speech impairment confined to PSWs may not be identified. Fourthly, evidence is accumulating that PSW production is a sensitive indicator of speech and language impairment in children (Lewis, Freebairn & Taylor, 2000), a predictor of speech impairment in adulthood and a predictor of later literacy problems (Felsenfeld, Broen & McGue, 1992; Lewis & Freebairn, 1992; Stackhouse & Wells, 1997). Finally, consonants produced in PSWs appear more vulnerable to change than do the same consonants spoken in MSWs and DSWs (Ingram, Christensen, Veach & Webster, 1980). This latter finding implied that when sampling speech, attention must be paid to the syntagmatic aspects of phonemes as well as the paradigmatic aspects. PSW production elicits some of these syntagmatic aspects of phonemes. The finding of Ingram et al. (1980) also implied that the application of the current norms may pose some difficulties in determining the status of children's speech because they are mostly derived from MSWs and DSWs, not PSWs.

James et al (2001) proposed that norms derived from a corpus of words that contained a significant number of PSWs in addition to MSWs and DSWs would yield different norms than those norms derived from a corpus dominated by MSWs and DSWs. To examine this, they used a test that included 39 PSWs, 23% of the speech sample. They reported significant age effects on percentage of consonants correct (PCC) and percentage of vowels correct (PVC) in 283 children ranging in age from 3;0 to 7;11 years. Vowel production appeared to stabilize at five and consonant production appeared to stabilize at six. This age for vowel stabilization is later than usually reported as there is widespread agreement that vowels are acquired by three years of age (Bernthal & Bankson, 1998; Smit, Hand, Freilinger, Bernthal & Bird, 1990; Vihman, 1998). The later age of acquisition of phonemes was attributed to the use of a greater number of PSWs in the test.

The aim of this study was to determine more precisely the effect of the number of syllables in a word on the accuracy of consonant production as measured by percentage of consonants correct (PCC). Specifically, PCC was calculated separately for three groups of words: MSWs, DSWs and PSWs. It was expected that PCC would be lowest for PSWs and highest for MSWs. Given the clinical usefulness of PSW production, more normative information is required to delimit the normal variation of PSW production; this work contributes to the definition of these parameters. The work presented here is one part of the larger project of developing a new test for assessing children's speech in citation form and the accompanying normative data.

METHOD

Participants

A total of 354 South Australian children ranging in age from 3;0 to 7;11 years participated in this study with 283 of them meeting the selection criteria. All children 4;0 years or more were randomly sampled from all preschools and schools in South Australia. The sample was stratified to ensure it matched the South Australian demography for rural and urban location and socioeconomic status. The three-year-old children were solicited through a variety of sources. Children included in the study were considered normal speakers and judged to be progressing normally at preschool or school by their teachers. The teachers reported that they did not have a disability or a speech pathology, used English as their main language and had normal hearing, expressive language and nonverbal intellectual skills. The details of the children are displayed in Table 1 and further detail is provided in James et al. (2001).

Procedure

The participant's parents completed a questionnaire that elicited biographical and other information in relation to the children's health, hearing, vision, speech and school progress. The children were assessed either in the university clinic, their child care center, preschool, or school. To be included in the study, the children had to have proven normal hearing, normal expressive language and

TABLE 1
Distribution of children by age and gender.

Age range	Age (months)			Girls	Boys	Total
	Mean	SD	Range			
3;0-3;11	42.4	3.7	36-47	10	9	19
4;0-4;11	55.1	3.0	48-59	22	23	45
5;0-5;11	65.1	3.9	60-71	29	30	59
6;0-6;11	77.6	3.3	72-83	42	44	86
7;0-7;11	88.9	3.3	84-95	43	31	74
Total				146	137	283

normal nonverbal intellectual skills. The children age four and above had their hearing screened at 25dB at 500, 1000, 2000 and 4000 Hz. As screening audiometry is unreliable for children under four (J. Boswell, personal communication, April 17, 1997), hearing for the three-year-olds was screened via parental questionnaire. Expressive language was examined through a discourse task of telling a story from a single picture stimulus. Stories were rated for their developmental level using *The binary decision tree* described by Westby (1992). Each child's story had to reach the appropriate developmental level as defined by Westby. The storytelling skills of the school-age children were reported in James (1999). For the children age five and over, nonverbal skills were measured using the using Raven's Colored Progressive Matrices (Raven, J. C., Court, & Raven, J., 1990). For children aged three and four years the Picture Similarities subtest of the Differential Ability Scales (Elliott, 1990) was used. Children had to achieve a score equivalent to, or above, the 25th percentile on either test to be included in the study.

The speech test, Assessment of Children's Articulation and Phonology (ACAP; James, in press-a, in press-b, 2001) was administered. The full form of the test, containing 166 words, was administered to the children aged four and older. The screening version of the test, which contained 82 words, was administered to the three-year-old children. Both forms of the test repeatedly sample all the phonemes, both consonants and vowels, in all word positions in MSWs, DSWs and PSWs where the phonotactic shapes and the stress of the syllables varied. The full form of the test contained 71 MSWs, of which three are polymorphemic (such as *toys* and *eyes*), 56 DSWs with eight compound words (such as *football*), and nine polymorphemic words, and 39 PSWs five of which are compound words and five are polymorphemic words. The screening version of the test contained 34 MSWs, 28 DSWs (of which four are compound words and three are polymorphemic words), and 20 PSWs (of which five are compound words and three are polymorphemic words).

Spontaneous naming of each picture was sought and children were prompted according to a predetermined schedule with imitation used as the last resort. All speech samples were recorded digitally and mouth-to-microphone distance was constant.

Analysis

The speech corpus was transcribed by the first author, using diacritics where necessary, and entered into the *PROPH+* component of *Computerized profiling* (Long & Fey, 1993–1995) which provides relational and independent analyses of speech. The transcription file created by *PROPH+* for each participant was separated into three subfiles based on the number of syllables in the words. Thus there was one file for the MSWs, another for the DSWs and another for the PSWs. The *PROPH+* analysis was conducted on each of these subfiles.

The relational analysis of the revised PCC is reported. PCC is the total number of accurate consonants said expressed as a percentage of the total number of consonants in the sample.

PROPH+ eliminates from its analysis all renditions of words where there is a mismatch in the number of syllables to the target word. This means that words that children either added syllables to or deleted syllables from were omitted from the analysis. As these patterns of syllable deletion and addition have been reported in the literature for normally developing children (e.g. Young, 1991), the PCC was varied to allow for their inclusion. Thus, the additional consonants were added into the calculations for the PCC derived by *PROPH+* to yield revised PCC scores. These additions were made as described by James et al. (2001). The mean number of additional consonants added to the numerator and denominator of the PCC formula for each group of words is displayed in Table 2.

The mean PCC scores for MSWs, DSWs and PSWs derived from *PROPH+* were compared with the revised mean PCC scores using paired samples t-tests. Whereas significant differences were found for all three pairs, the absolute differences in each of the means was less than 1%. The result for the comparison of the PCC and the revised PCC for MSWs was $t(282) = 7.36, p < 0.001$.

TABLE 2
Mean number of additional consonants that children said correctly in the rejected words and the mean additional consonants in the rejected words.

	Mean additional consonants correct added to the numerator		Mean additional consonants added to the denominator	
	Mean (SD)	Range	Mean (SD)	Range
MSWs	0.49 (1.1)	0-9	0.83 (1.78)	0-13
DSWs	1.67 (2.42)	0-11	2.12 (3.10)	0-13
PSWs	8.12 (9.18)	0-50	10.93 (13.36)	0-76

The result for the comparison of the PCC and the revised PCC for DSWs was $t(282) = 3.53$, $p < 0.001$. The result for the comparison of the PCC and the revised PCC for PSWs was $t(282) = 7.45$, $p < 0.001$. Given the results were significant, the revised PCC scores are presented.

The data were analysed using a two-way ANOVA with repeated measures. The within-participant factor was the number of syllables and the between-participant factor was age. As an interaction effect was found, the syllable number effect within each age group was determined.

Reliability

Two qualified speech pathologists independently transcribed 10% of the data. The average point-to-point agreement for the data for the school-aged children was 88%. Differences were resolved through agreement. For the preschool-aged children, the point-to-point agreement for all phonemes was 93.2%; 92% for all consonants and 95% for all vowels.

RESULTS

The younger children had lower PCC scores than the older children. Overall, the total mean PCC score for MSWs was higher than the total mean PCC score for the DSWs and the total mean score for the PSWs. The total mean PCC score for DSWs was also higher than the total mean PCC score for the PSWs. The mean PCC scores for MSWs, DSWs and PSWs for each group are displayed in Fig. 1.

FIG. 1 Mean PCC scores.

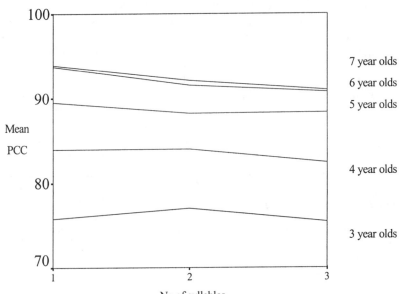

No of syllables

The means, standard deviations and the ranges for the PCC for MSWs, DSWs and PSWs are displayed in Table 3. Inspection of this table shows that whilst the overall trends held for the five-, six- and seven-year-old children, they did not hold for the younger children. For the three- and four-year-old children, the mean PCC scores for the DSWs were higher than the mean PCC scores for both the MSWs and PSWs. For these children the mean PCC scores for MSWs were higher than the mean PCC scores for PSWs.

A two-way ANOVA with repeated measures showed an age effect $F(4, 278) = 62.03$, $p < 0.001$, a syllable number effect $F(2, 556) = 19.48$, $p < 0.001$ and an interaction effect $F(8,556)$, $p < 0.001$.

Post hoc analysis using a Scheffé adjustment for the between subject variable of age indicated that all the pair-wise comparisons were significant except for the six- and seven-year-old children. Post hoc analysis of the syllable number effect using the Scheffé adjustment indicated there were no significant syllable number effects for the three- and four-year-old children. For the five-year-old children there was a significant syllable number effect only between the MSWs and DSWs. There were no significant differences between the MSWs and PSWs nor the DSWs and PSWs. For the six- and seven-year-old children, there were significant syllable number effects. There were significant differences between the MSWs and DSWs, the DSWs and PSWs and the MSWs and PSWs.

DISCUSSION

Significant age and syllable number effects indicates that children are still mastering aspects of consonant production up to age 7;11 years. The PCC increased with age until the age group 6;0 to 6;11 (mean age 6;6 years) for all words regardless of the numbers of syllables in words. Additionally, even

TABLE 3
Mean PCC scores for mono-, di- and polysyllabic words.

Age	MSWs		DSWs		PSWs	
	Mean (SD)	Range	Mean (SD)	Range	Mean (SD)	Range
3	76.77 (10.80)	51-97	77.29 (8.48)	60-91	76.41 (6.97)	63-85
4	83.97 (7.62)	65-97	84.01 (5.89)	72-96	82.45 (5.59)	66-93
5	89.54 (7.27)	68-98	88.24 (5.61)	72-96	88.36 (6.06)	71-95
6	93.74 (3.97)	81-100	91.57 (3.97)	76-100	90.76 (3.73)	79-99
7	93.93 (4.66)	79-99	92.12 (3.83)	79-97	90.99 (4.11)	75-97
Total	90.22 (7.98)	51-100	88.86 (6.55)	60-100	88.03 (6.97)	63-99

though there was no age effect between the six- and seven-year age groups, there were significant differences in the performance of those children in the productions of PSWs compared with DSWs and MSWs as indicated by the syllable number effect.

These results imply that up to the age of six years, children are still acquiring control over the paradigmatic aspects of consonants. The significant age effect and the pair-wise comparisons indicated this. All the pair-wise comparisons were significant up to this age, whereas the pair-wise comparison between the six- and seven-year-olds was not. This lack of significance suggests that control of the paradigmatic aspect of consonants said in citation form has reached maturity by 6;11 years. This pattern of consonant development is consistent with the trend reported in the literature that children are still acquiring consonants up to age nine (Chirlian & Sharpley, 1982; Kilminster & Laird, 1978; Smit et al., 1990). However, this finding that development continues with the paradigmatic aspects of consonants until age six, is probably more robust than the findings of the more traditional studies of segment acquisition, such as those conducted by the above mentioned researchers, for three reasons. First, the accuracy of every consonant spoken was considered in this study whereas in the traditional studies, only a sample of the consonants spoken was considered. For example, in the work by Smit et al. (1990), only the accuracy of word-final /r/ was considered in the word *spider*; the consonant cluster, /sp/, was ignored as was the consonant /d/. Likewise in the word *snake*, only the /sn/ cluster was considered not the /k/. Second, each consonant was repeatedly sampled in each word position whereas in the traditional studies generally only one production of each consonant in each word position was recorded. Third, in this study, the number of words spoken and, therefore, the number of sounds produced, was greater than in the other studies. In this study, the children named 166 words whereas in the study by Smit et al. (1990), participants named 80 words. In the studies by Kilminster and Laird (1978) and Chirlian and Sharpley (1982) 59 words were elicited from each subject. Repeated sampling of phonemes is more likely to capture the variability and variations in speech production.

These results also imply that up to the age of 7;11 years, children are still acquiring control over the syntagmatic aspects of consonants. This continued refinement of the consonants is indicated by the significant syllable number and interaction effects observed for these older age groups. The overall syllable number effect is qualified by the age effect and the syllable number effect does not become significant until age five. There are two possible interpretations of these patterns. First, the syllable number effect may simply have been masked by the variability in the data for the younger children. Alternatively, the patterns may imply that there are qualitative differences in the development of speech that become evident from age five. The implication of the latter interpretation is that the key developmental achievement up until age five is gaining control over the paradigmatic aspects of consonants. From age five there is a qualitative shift from the paradigmatic aspects of consonant development to the syntagmatic aspects. This shift increases in strength at age six and remains at this level until 7;11 years, at least, which is the limit of the present data set. This shift is supported by the fact that at five years of age the syllable number effect was only apparent between the MSWs and DSWs. At ages six and seven there were significant differences between the MSWs and DSWs, the DSWs and PSWs and the MSWs and PSWs. Such qualitative shifts in the focus of speech development are consistent with other reports. For example, Netsell (1981) suggested such shifts in his model of motor speech development and Vihman (1996) noted that at approximately age three, children's focus of learning shifts from whole words to segments.

Words with varying syllable numbers, stress and phonotactic shapes were all represented in the corpus used in the present study. Thus, it was concluded that these features differentially affected the children's ability to produce accurate consonants. The results implied that, over the age range of 3;0 to 7;11 years, children are refining the preprogramming skills required to sequence and juxtapose sounds, syllables and linguistic stress such that the output is faithful to accepted production of the target word. The results also imply that there are two overlapping stages of speech development within this age range. In the first stage, the focus of development is refining the paradigmatic aspects of consonants and appears to be complete by age six. In the second stage, the focus of development is the syntagmatic aspects of consonants and becomes apparent at five-years-old and continues to at least seven-years-old. The fact that the variability in this second stage is mostly confined to the syllable numbers points to the need to gain control over the sequencing aspects demanded by PSWs. This notion is consistent with the third stage of Netsell's (1981) model of motor speech development when the focus is on achieving adult-like timing through the development of anticipatory coarticulatory skills.

These findings of mastering aspects of consonant production up to the age of 7;11 years have significant clinical implications. Sampling some aspects of the syntagmatic aspects of consonants can be measured by asking children to name words of differing syllable numbers. Yet tests of phonology typically include MSWs and DSWs, not PSWs. For children age five years and over, the syntagmatic aspects of consonant production may not be captured with such sampling tools. Furthermore, their production on the shorter words will probably be perfect giving the illusion of adequate, or age appropriate, speech when this may not be the case. It is recommended that speech testing of children five years or more must include significant numbers of PSWs.

ACKNOWLEDGMENTS

This research was supported by a grant from the South Australian Channel 7 Children's Research Foundation. The authors gratefully acknowledge the assistance of the child-care center directors, the preschool directors and school principals, and most importantly, the parents and the children. The authors wish to acknowledge the contributions of Wendy Ferguson, the research assistant, Paul McCormack for work on the inter-rater reliability, Lincoln Turner for data preparation and Willem van Steenbrugge for general advice. The authors also wish to thank James Scobbie for his comments on an earlier draft of this chapter. This chapter is based on a portion of the first author's work toward a PhD at The University of Sydney, which is supervised by the remaining authors.

REFERENCES

Anthony, A., Bogle, D., Ingram, T.T.S., & McIsaac, M. (1971). *Edinburgh articulation test.* Edinburgh: Churchill Livingstone.

Arlt, P. B., & Goodban, M. T. (1976). A comparative study of articulation acquisition as based on a study of 240 normals, aged three to six. *Language, Speech, and Hearing Services in Schools, 7,* 173-180.

Atkin, N., & Fisher, J. (1996). *Articulation survey.* Melbourne: Royal Children's Hospital.

Bernthal, J. E., & Bankson, N. W. (Eds.). (1998). *Articulation and phonological disorders* (4th ed.). Needham Heights, MA: Allyn & Bacon.

Borowski, T. (1989). Structure preservation and the syllable coda in English. *Natural* Language *and Linguistic Theory, 7,* 145-166.

Chirlian, N. S., & Sharpley, C. F. (1982). Children's articulation development: Some regional differences. *Australian Journal of Human Communication Disorders, 10,* 23-30.

Elliott, C. D. (1990). *Differential ability scales* (U.S. adaption ed.). San Antonio, TX: The Psychological Corporation.

Felsenfeld, S., Broen, P. A., & McGue, M. (1992). A 28-year follow-up of adults with a history of moderate phonological disorder: Linguistic and personality results. *Journal of Speech and Hearing Research, 35,* 1114-1125.

Fisher, H., & Logemann, J. (1971). *The Fisher-Logemann test of articulation competence.* Boston, MA: Houghton-Mifflin.

Gillon, G., & Dodd, B. (1993). The phonological, syntactic and semantic skills of children with specific reading disability. *Australian Journal of Human Communication Disorders, 21,* 86-102.

Goldman, R., & Fristoe, M. (1969). *Goldman-Fristoe test of articulation.* Circle Pines, MN: American Guidance Service.

Grunwell, P. (1987). *PACS pictures language elicitation materials.* Windsor, UK: NFER-Nelson.

Halliday, M.A.K. (1985). *An introduction to functional grammar.* London: Edward Arnold.

Ingram, D. (1976). *Phonological disability in children.* London: Edward Arnold.

Ingram, D., Christensen, L., Veach, S., & Webster, B. (1980). The acquisition of word-initial fricatives and affricates in English between 2 and 6 years. In G. Y. Yeni-Komshian, J. F. Kavanagh & C. Ferguson (Eds.), *Child phonology* (Vol. 1; pp. 169-192). New York: Academic Press.

Jaeger, J. J. (1997). How to say "Grandma": The problem of developing phonological representations. *First Language, 17,* 1-29.

James, D.G.H. (1999). Children's story telling skills in the age range of 5 to 7 years. In S. McLeod & L. McAllister (Eds.), *Towards 2000:Embracing change, challenge and choice. Proceedings of the 1999 Speech Pathology Australia National Conference* (pp. 102-109). Melbourne: Speech Pathology Australia.

James, D.G.H. (in press-a). The use of phonological processes in Australian children aged 2 to 7;11 years. *Advances in Speech Language Pathology.*

James, D.G.H. (in press-b). An item analysis of words for an articulation and phonological test for children aged 2 to 7 years. *Clinical Linguistics & Phonetics.*

James, D.G.H. (2001). *Assessment of children's articulation and phonology.* Manuscript in preparation. Flinders University of South Australia.

James, D.G.H., Ferguson, W. A., McCormack, P. F., Butcher, A. R., Chiveralls, K., & Russell, A. (2001). A new assessment of Australian English speech development in the age range 3;0-7;11 years and some normative information. Manuscript in preparation, Flinders University of South Australia.

Katz, R. B. (1986). Phonological deficits in children with reading disability: Evidence from an object naming task. *Cognition, 22,* 225-257.

Kehoe, M., & Stoel-Gammon, C. (1997). The acquisition of prosodic structure: An investigation of current accounts of children's prosodic development. *Language, 73,* 113-144.

Kilminster, M. E., & Laird, E. M. (1978). Articulation development in children aged three to nine years. *Australian Journal of Human Communication Disorders, 6,* 23-30.

Klein, H. B. (1981). Productive strategies for the pronunciation of early polysyllabic lexical items. *Journal of Speech and Hearing Research, 24,* 389-405.

Lewis, B. A., & Freebairn, L. (1992). Residual effects of preschool phonology disorders in grade school, adolescence and adulthood. *Journal of Speech and Hearing Research, 35,* 819-831.

Lewis, B. A., Freebairn, L., & Taylor, H. G. (2000). Follow-up of children with early expressive phonology disorders. *Journal of Learning Disabilities, 33,* 433-444.

Long, S. H., & Fey, M. E. (1993-1995). *Computerized profiling* (2nd ed.). San Antonio, TX: The Psychological Corporation.

Netsell, R. (1981). The acquisition of speech motor control: A perspective with directions for research. In R. Stark (Ed.), *Language behaviour in infancy and early childhood* (pp. 128-156). North Holland, NY: Elsevier.

Ozanne, A. (1995). The search for developmental verbal dyspraxia. In B. Dodd (Ed.), *Differential diagnosis and treatment of children with speech disorder* (pp. 91-124). London: Whurr.

Pater, J. (1997). Minimal violation and phonological development. *Language Acquisition, 6,* 201-253.

Priestly, T.M.S. (1977). One idiosyncratic strategy in the acquisition of phonology. *Journal of Child Language, 4,* 45-65.

Raven, J. C., Court, J. H., & Raven, J. (1990). *Manual for Raven's colored progressive matrices: Section 2.* Oxford: Oxford Psychologists Press.

Salidis, J., & Johnson, J. S. (1997). The production of minimal words: A longitudinal case study of phonological development. *Language Acquisition, 6,* 1-36.

Smit, A. B., Hand, L., Freilinger, J. J., Bernthal, J. E., & Bird, A. (1990). The Iowa articulation norms project and its Nebraska replication. *Journal of Speech and Hearing Disorders, 55,* 779-798.

Smit, A. B., & Hand, L. S. (1997). *Smit-Hand articulation and phonology evaluation.* Los Angeles, CA: Western Psychological Services.

Smith, R. V. (1973). *The acquisition of phonology.* Cambridge: Cambridge University Press.

Stackhouse, J., & Wells, B. (1997). *Children's speech and literacy difficulties.* London: Whurr.

Vihman, M. M. (1996). *Phonological development.* Oxford: Blackwell.

Vihman, M. M. (1998). Later phonological development. In J. E. Bernthal & N. W. Bankson (Eds.), *Articulation and phonological disorders* (4th ed., pp. 113-147). Needham Heights, MA: Allyn and Bacon.

Westby, C. (1992). Narrative analysis. *Best Practices in School Speech-Language Pathology: Descriptive/nonstandardized Language Assessment, 2,* 53-63.

Young, E. C. (1991). An analysis of young children's ability to produce multisyllabic words. *Clinical Linguistics & Phonetics, 5,* 297-316.

24

Features of Impaired Tongue Control in Children with Phonological Disorder

Fiona E. Gibbon

A central issue in phonological disorder is whether the basis of the disorder is impaired speech motor control, a linguistic deficit, or immature perceptual strategies. This chapter presents physiological speech data from children with phonological disorder (PD) that suggest that impaired tongue control in the spatial domain is not only more widespread in this group, but is also more centrally involved in the articulation difficulties experienced by these children. The discussion centers on evidence from studies that have recorded articulatory data from children with PD using the technique of electropalatography (EPG). Three phenomena interpreted as reflecting impaired motor control are discussed in this chapter: the widespread occurrence of gestures involving EPG spatial distortions; covert contrasts; and the unreliability of identifying normal articulatory skills from transcription-based analyses.

PHONOLOGICAL DISORDER

Children with phonological disorder (PD) have speech difficulties in the absence of identifiable organic pathology. Investigating underlying deficits in these children is highly relevant for making a diagnosis, planning therapy and estimating prognosis. Impaired speech motor control is often ruled out as a central component in children with PD based on evidence from various sources. For example, children with PD often demonstrate ability to produce sounds correctly under some conditions, despite failing to use the same sounds consistently in their speech. This is similar to the "puzzle" phenomenon described by Smith (1973), whereby his typically developing son Amahl produced the word *puddle* as [pʌgəl], and *puzzle* as [pʌdəl]. In other words, Amahl was "unable to produce a particular sound or sound sequence in the correct place, but [was] perfectly capable of producing it as his interpretation of something else" (p. 4). Smith interpreted Amahl's ability to produce sounds in certain contexts as evidence that articulatory difficulties alone were insufficient to account for speech errors. Since the 1970s, puzzles have been noted to occur extensively in the speech of children, including those with PD. Like Smith, others have used evidence of puzzles to claim that articulatory difficulties alone are insufficient to explain speech errors observed to occur in PD (e.g. Grunwell, 1981; Leonard, 1995).

Further evidence against motor-based accounts of PD comes from research (e.g. Shriberg & Kwiatkowski, 1988) which showed that speech errors of distortion, which are thought to reflect motor-based difficulties, are relatively rare in PD. Shriberg and Kwiatkowski (1988) argued that because the majority of children with PD show predominantly phonological errors (i.e. omissions and substitutions), the underlying deficit is accurately judged as one of linguistic impairment.

Evidence of correct productions in some contexts (Smith's puzzles) and the rarity of distortions have been used to rule out impaired speech motor control as a central component in the speech of children with PD. Other studies used instrumental procedures to investigate speech motor control abilities directly. Such studies have focused largely on timing and variability of speech gestures (e.g. Catts & Jensen, 1983; Henry, 1990; Waters, 1992). Such studies have investigated features such as vowel duration, consonant closure duration, and voice onset time. Some studies show that children with PD have slower segment durations than typically developing children (Catts & Jensen, 1983; Waters, 1992; Weismer & Elbert, 1982). Although studies of speech timing and variability suggested speech motor control may be a contributory factor to the speech disorder in some children with PD, the evidence has not yet been proven sufficient to explain the range or severity of perceptual speech characteristics observed to occur in many children with PD. Furthermore, there is little evidence of impaired speech motor control in the spatial domain, due largely to methodological difficulties in recording physiological data in young children.

EPG Data from Children with PD

The technique of EPG provides an opportunity to investigate speech motor control of the tongue in children with PD. EPG records details of the location and timing of tongue contacts with the hard palate during speech (Hardcastle, Gibbon, & Jones, 1991; Hardcastle & Gibbon, 1997). Tongue palate contact is registered in normal speakers' productions of sounds such as /t/, /d/, /n/, /k/, /g/, /s/, /z/, /l/, /ʃ/, /tʃ/, /dʒ/, /j/, and /ŋ/. In terms of speech motor control, EPG is a valuable technique for measuring aspects of control, such as speed of articulation, spatial (i.e. positional) accuracy of articulation, timing of tongue apex/tongue body movements, lingual coarticulation, and consistency of articulatory movement. Speech data from approximately 20 children with PD have been reported in the literature, including studies reporting EPG characteristics of common phonological processes, such as velar fronting (Friel, 1998), alveolar backing (Dagenais, 1995; Gibbon, 1990; Gibbon et al., 1993; Hardcastle & Morgan, 1982; Gibbon, Stewart, Hardcastle & Crampin, 1999), final consonant deletion (Dagenais, 1995; Hardcastle & Morgan, 1982), and cluster reduction (Dagenais, 1995; Hardcastle & Morgan, 1982). EPG patterns associated with phonetic distortions (e.g. so-called lateral lisps) have also been reported in a number of studies (e.g. Dagenais, 1995; Dagenais, Critz-Crosby & Adams, 1994; Gibbon & Hardcastle, 1987; Gibbon, Hardcastle & Dent, 1995; Gibbon, Hardcastle & Moore, 1990).

EPG SPATIAL DISTORTIONS

Spatial distortions are EPG patterns where the configuration of contacted electrodes is unlike that seen in normal speakers. If the whole palate is contacted during production of /s/ or /t/, for example, then this is considered a spatial distortion. The next section discusses undifferentiated gestures, which are interpreted as reflecting a specific impairment of motor control in the spatial domain.

Undifferentiated Lingual Gestures

One type of EPG spatial distortion involves undifferentiated lingual gestures UGs (Gibbon, 1999). UGs are defined as EPG patterns that have, at maximum constriction, contact in the midsagittal anterior region of the palate occurring simultaneously with midsagittal contact in the posterior region. The EPG configuration involved in UGs suggests that the tongue tip/blade and tongue body are active simultaneously. This undifferentiated tongue apex and tongue body action results in increased contact across the palate. The finding that the occurrence of UGs tends to occur with reduced tongue palate shape repertoires suggests a fundamental motor constraint, that is, the basic control mechanism that allows the tongue apex, lateral margins and tongue body systems to operate relatively independently has not yet developed. Kent (1983) suggested that during the early stages of speech development, articulators operate according to the "everything moves at once principle" whereby sets of articulatory gestures are produced in a largely synchronous manner. UGs would seem to be a good example of this type of immature speech motor control.

A further feature of UGs noted by Gibbon (1999) is that these gestures are associated with positional variability. Gibbon noted that UGs often had one place of articulation (e.g. alveolar) at onset, and a different place of articulation (e.g. velar) at release. The change in placement from onset to release is referred to as "articulatory drift". The change in placement at onset and release gives rise to conflicting placement cues, which is one explanation for the perceptual variability of placement recorded for many children with PD (Grunwell, 1981). The pivotal point about the spatial distortions that involve UGs and associated articulatory drift is that they occur during productions transcribed as correct, and during productions judged as phonological errors of substitution. A common assumption is that correct productions and phonological substitutions do not involve articulatory distortions, a finding that is not supported by the EPG evidence from UGs (Gibbon 1999). Leonard (1995) stated that "if speech sound difficulties were due principally to errors of articulatory accuracy, distortions … should represent a much higher percentage of the errors observed" (p. 575). But, the EPG evidence of UGs shows that spatial distortions in the form of UGs are common in the speech of children with PD, with more than 70% of children investigated producing them (Gibbon 1999).

COVERT CONTRAST

In research published in 1971, Kornfeld reported spectrographic evidence from children with typical speech development who were using the phonological process of cluster reduction. The purpose was to compare the children's cluster production in words like *truck*, *play*, and *ski* with singleton consonants in similar contexts such as *tuck*, *pay*, *lay*, *see*, and *key*. Kornfeld found that children's productions of *grass* and *glass* were homphonous to adult listeners and both targets were transcribed as [gwas]. Although homophonous, the spectrographic analysis of the utterances showed differences in F2 locus and duration of the glide segment between the [w] in the target word *grass* when compared with the [w] in the target word *glass*. Kornfeld concluded, "adults do not always perceive distinctions that children make" (p. 462), and that adult listeners are biased to hear children's speech in terms of the distinctions present in the target system. In other words, a biased adult may judge as neutralized two acoustically or articulatorily distinct phonological categories produced by a child. This phenomenon has come to be known as covert contrast (Hewlett, 1988).

Since Kornfeld's (1971) study, researchers have investigated the phenomenon of covert contrast in the speech of children with PD, and it has become evident that covert contrast is widespread in both normal and abnormal child speech. The majority of studies have used acoustic analysis to detect covert contrast, but studies using EPG have also been used (see Tables 1 and 2).

Although the interpretation of covert contrast is controversial, many view their presence as indicating phonetic level rather than phonological difficulties. Kent's (1997) view is that covert contrast cannot be explained in any way "except by attributing it to faulty phonetic implementation" (p. 265). Sell, Harding, and Grunwell (1994) agreed with Kent's view, stating if an

TABLE 1
EPG studies showing covert contrast in the speech of children with PD.

References	Process	Comment
Hardcastle & Morgan (1982)	Cluster reduction	EPG patterns showed more forward and more overall contact for clusters than singletons
Gibbon (1990); Gibbon et al. (1999)	Alveolar backing	EPG patterns had more lateral and alveolar contact for alveolar than velar targets
Friel (1998)	Velar fronting	More lateral and alveolar EPG contact for alveolar than velar targets
Gibbon et al. (1995)	Lateralization	EPG contact more retracted for /ʃ/ than for /s/ targets

articulatory distinction between phoneme classes exists (such as occurs in covert contrast), then the child appreciates the need to signal a phonological contrast, and "the speech difficulty is phonetic in nature" (p. 8).

UNRELIABILITY OF PUZZLES

Impaired motor control is often ruled out on the grounds that children show evidence of puzzles. Samples of child speech often display variability, in that sounds or sound classes are produced apparently correctly in some contexts, but as errors in other contexts. EPG data from studies (e.g. E. described in Gibbon et al., 1993) question the assumption that perceptually correct productions are always produced as normal articulations, however, E. (Gibbon et al., 1993) was heard to have perceptually variable realizations of /t/ and /d/ targets: incorrect velar/palatal substitutions in some contexts, but correct alveolars in other contexts. Despite perceptual variability, and contrary to expectations from the listener judgements, E.'s EPG patterns showed gross articulatory errors not only during perceptual errors but also during perceptually correct realizations. Similar findings are reported from other studies (Hardcastle & Morgan, 1982; Dagenais et al., 1994).

The EPG data from E. (Gibbon et al., 1993) suggests that impaired speech motor control should not be ruled out on the basis of the occurrence of puzzles (Smith, 1973). In the case of *puzzle* and *puddle*, it could have been that Amahl produced abnormal articulations (such as UGs) for both /d/ and /z/ targets in these words. The gesture for /d/ in *puddle* (heard as [g] in [pʌgəl]) involving predominantly velar contact at closure and release, and the gesture for /z/ in *puzzle* (heard as [d] in [pʌdəl]) involving predominantly contact in the alveolar region during these phases. Perhaps Amahl was not "perfectly capable" of a normal articulation for /d/ in any context.

TABLE 2
Acoustic studies showing covert contrast in the speech of children with PD.

References	Process	Comment
Maxwell & Weismer (1982); Gierut & Dinnsen (1986); Forrest & Rockman (1988); Tyler, Edwards & Saxman (1990); Tyler, Figurski & Langsdale (1993); Tyler & Saxman (1991)	Voicing of stops	Targets distinguished by VOT, closure duration and voicing during closure
Hoffman, Stager & Daniloff (1983); Chaney (1988)	Gliding	Targets distinguished by onset frequencies of F1, F2, F3; duration of [r], [w], and following vowel; and amplitude of consonant
Tyler et al. (1990); Tyler et al. (1993); Forrest, Weismer, Hodge, Dinnsen & Elbert (1990)	Velar fronting	Targets distinguished by VOT, spectral moments and locus equations
Daniloff, Wilcox & Stephens (1980); Baum & McNutt (1990)	Dentalization	Targets distinguished by mean duration, amplitude, and centroid measures of frication noise of /s/, /θ/ targets
Tyler (1995)	Fricative stopping	Targets distinguished by VOT
McLeod & Isaac (1995)	Liquid replacement	/l/ and /j/ targets distinguished by formant frequency, consonant duration and intensity
Gibbon et al. (1999); Weismer (1984)	Cluster reduction	Obstruent interval duration, VOT and spectral tilt distinguish reduced clusters from singletons
Weismer, Dinnsen & Elbert (1981); Weismer (1984); Riley, Hoffman & Damico (1986); Camarata & Erwin (1988); Tyler & McOmber (1999)	Final consonant deletion	Targets distinguished by vowel duration, peak and F_0; intensity.

According to Smith, Amahl produced puzzles with "completely regular rules" (p. 4). So why should closure and/or release phases be different for /d/ and /z/ targets? It is speculation, but it could be that Amahl produced alveolar stops in a similar way to E. (Gibbon et al., 1993), whose alveolar gestures involved a movement from velar to alveolar during the closure phase. In addition, the longer the closure phase of E.'s gestures, the more likely the occurrence of an alveolar release. If Amah's /z/ targets had a longer duration than /d/ targets, this could increase the likelihood of an alveolar release, and hence, increase the chance of an alveolar percept for these targets. Although Amahl's actual articulation during *puzzle* and *puddle* can never be known, the EPG data suggest a motor-based mechanism that could be responsible for the puzzle phenomenon.

CONCLUSION

The EPG evidence suggests that speech motor control in the spatial domain is more common in PD than transcription based studies indicate. Furthermore, the EPG evidence leads us to question common assumptions made in the past about articulation and its control, when the evidence is based solely on transcription. Future research must address whether the aspects of abnormal spatial control described here occur in young PD children and typically developing children. Research at the physiological level is being conducted using techniques other than EPG with very young typically developing children (e.g. Smith & Goffman, 1998; Ruark & Moore, 1997). The procedures adopted in these studies could be used to investigate speech motor control in young children with PD.

With a greater physiological database of articulatory characteristics of speech in children with PD, it is likely that more attention will be paid to the interface between phonetics and phonology and theories such as articulatory phonology and dynamic systems (see the work of Goodell & Studdert-Kennedy, 1993). Articulatory phonology theory sees speech development and breakdown in terms of the ability to build up gestural scores (Kent, 1997). In terms of tongue control, for example, the development of adult-like gestural scores might involve learning independent control of tongue regions, learning to phase and scale tongue gestures (Kent, 1997), and learning how to coordinate tongue movements in time with other articulators such as the velum, lips, and larynx.

REFERENCES

Baum, S. R., & McNutt, J. C. (1990). An acoustic analysis of frontal misarticulation of /s/ in children. *Journal of Phonetics, 18*, 51-64

Camarata, S. M., & Erwin, L. (1988). Rule invention in the acquisition of morphology revisited: A case of transparent semantic mapping. *Journal of Speech and Hearing Research, 31*, 425-431.

Catts, H. W., & Jensen, P. J. (1983). Speech timing of phonologically disordered children: Voicing contrast of initial and final stop consonants. *Journal of Speech and Hearing Research, 26*, 501-510.

Chaney, C. (1988). Acoustic analysis of correct and misarticulated semivowels. *Journal of Speech and Hearing Research, 31*, 275-287.

Dagenais, P. A. (1995). Electropalatography in the treatment of articulation/phonological disorders. *Journal of Communication Disorders, 28*, 303-329.

Dagenais, P. A., Critz-Crosby, P., & Adams, J. B. (1994). Defining and remediating persistent lateral lisps in children using electropalatography: Preliminary findings. *American Journal of Speech-Language Pathology, 3*, 67-76.

Daniloff, R. G., Wilcox, K., & Stephens, M. I. (1980). An acoustic-articulatory description of children's defective /s/ productions. *Journal of Communication Disorders, 13*, 347-363.

Forrest, K., Weismer, G., Hodge, M., Dinnsen, D. A., & Elbert, M. (1990). Statistical analysis of word-initial /k/ and /t/ produced by normal and phonologically disordered children. *Clinical Linguistics and Phonetics, 4*, 327-340.

Forrest, K., & Rockman, B. K. (1988). Acoustic and perceptual analysis of word-initial stop consonants in phonologically disordered children. *Journal of Speech and Hearing Research, 31*, 449-459.

Friel, S. (1998). When is a /k/ not a /k/? EPG as a diagnostic and therapeutic tool for abnormal velar stops. *International Journal of Language and Communication Disorders, 33* (suppl.), 439-444.

Gierut, J. A., & Dinnsen, D. A. (1986). On word-initial voicing: converging sources of evidence in phonologically disordered speech. *Language and Speech, 29*, 97-114.

Gibbon, F. (1990). Lingual activity in two speech-disordered children's attempts to produce velar and alveolar stop consonants: evidence from electropalatographic (EPG) data. *British Journal of Disorders of Communication, 25*, 329-340.

Gibbon, F. E. (1999). Undifferentiated lingual gestures in children with articulation/phonological disorders. *Journal of Speech, Language, and Hearing Research, 42*, 382-397.

Gibbon, F., Dent, H., & Hardcastle, W. (1993). Diagnosis and therapy of abnormal alveolar stops in a speech-disordered child using electropalatography. *Clinical Linguistics and Phonetics, 7*, 247-267.

Gibbon, F., & Hardcastle, W. (1987). Articulatory description and treatment of "lateral /s/" using electropalatography: A case study. *British Journal of Disorders of Communication, 22*, 203-217.

Gibbon, F., Hardcastle, B., & Dent, H. (1995). A study of obstruent sounds in school age children with speech disorders using electropalatography. *European Journal of Disorders of Communication, 30*, 213-225.

Gibbon, F., Hardcastle W., & Moore, A. (1990). Modifying abnormal tongue patterns in an older child using electropalatography. *Child Language Teaching and Therapy, 6*, 227-245.

Gibbon, F., & Scobbie, J. M. (1997). Covert contrasts in children with phonological disorder. *Australian Communication Quarterly. Autumn 1997*, 13-16.

Gibbon, F., Stewart, F., Hardcastle, W. J., & Crampin, L. (1999). Widening access to electropalatography for children with persistent sound system disorders. *American Journal of Speech-Language Pathology, 8*, 319-334.

Goodell, E. W., & Studdert-Kennedy, M. (1993). Acoustic evidence for the development of gestural coordination in the speech of 2-year-olds: A longitudinal study. *Journal of Speech and Hearing Research, 36*, 707-727.

Grunwell, P. (1981). *The nature of phonological disability in children*. London: Academic Press.

Hardcastle, W. J., & Gibbon, F. (1997). Electropalatography and its clinical applications. In M. J. Ball & C. Code (Eds.), *Instrumental clinical phonetics* (pp. 149-193). London: Whurr Publishers.

Hardcastle, W. J., Gibbon, F. E., & Jones, W. (1991). Visual display of tongue-palate contact: Electropalatography in the assessment and remediation of speech disorders. *British Journal of Disorders of Communication, 26*, 41-74.

Hardcastle, W. J., & Morgan, R. A. (1982). An instrumental investigation of articulation disorders in children. *British Journal of Disorders of Communication, 17*, 47-65.

Henry, C. (1990). The development of oral diadochokinesia and non-linguistic rhythmic skills in normal and speech disordered young children. *Clinical Linguistics and Phonetics, 4*, 121-137.

Hewlett, N. (1988). Acoustic properties of /k/ and /t/ in normal and phonologically disordered speech. *Clinical Linguistics and Phonetics, 2*, 29-45.

Hoffman, P. R., Stager, S., & Daniloff, R. G. (1983). Perception and production of misarticulated /r/. *Journal of Speech and Hearing Disorders, 48*, 210-215.

Kent, R. (1983). The segmental organization of speech. In P. F. MacNeilage (Ed.), *The production of speech* (pp. 57-90). New York: Springer Verlag.

Kent, R. D. (1997). Gestural phonology: Basic concepts and applications in speech-language pathology. In M. J. Ball & R. D. Kent (Eds.), *The new phonologies: Developments in clinical linguistics* (pp 247-268). London: Singular Press.

Kornfeld, J. R. (1971). Theoretical issues in child phonology. *Papers of the 7th Regional Meeting, Chicago Linguistic Society,* 454-468.

Leonard, L. B. (1995). Phonological impairment. In P. Fletcher & B. MacWhinney (Eds.), *The handbook of child language* (pp. 573-602). Oxford: Blackwell.

Maxwell, E. M., & Weismer, G. (1982). The contribution of phonological, acoustic, and perceptual techniques to the characterization of a misarticulating child's voice contrast for stops. *Applied Psycholinguistics, 3,* 29-43.

McLeod, S., & Isaac, K. (1995). Use of spectrographic analyses to evaluate the efficacy of phonological intervention. *Clinical Linguistics and Phonetics, 9,* 229-234.

Riley, K., Hoffman, P. R., & Damico, S. K. (1986). The effects of conflicting cues on the perception of misarticulations. *Journal of Phonetics, 13,* 481-487.

Ruark, J. L., & Moore, C. A. (1997). Coordination of lip muscle activity by 2-year-old children during speech and nonspeech tasks. *Journal of Speech, Language, and Hearing Research, 40,* 1373-1385.

Sell, D., Harding, A., & Grunwell, P. (1994). A screening assessment of cleft palate speech (Great Ormond Street Speech Assessment). *European Journal of Disorders of Communication, 29,* 1-15.

Shriberg, L. D., & Kwiatkowski, J. (1988). A follow-up study of children with phonologic disorders of unknown origin. *Journal of Speech and Hearing Disorders, 53,* 144-155.

Smith, N. V. (1973). *The acquisition of phonology: A case study.* Cambridge: Cambridge University Press.

Smith, A. & Goffman, L. (1998). Stability and patterning of speech movement sequences in children and adults. *Journal of Speech, Language, and Hearing Research, 41,* 18-30.

Tyler, A. A. (1995). Durational analysis of stridency errors in children with phonological impairment. *Clinical Linguistics and Phonetics, 9,* 211-228.

Tyler, A. A., Edwards, M. L., & Saxman, J. H. (1990). Acoustic validation of phonological knowledge and its relationship to treatment. *Journal of Speech and Hearing Disorders, 55,* 251-261.

Tyler, A. A., Figurski, G. R., & Langsdale, T. (1993). Relationships between acoustically determined knowledge of stop place and voicing contrasts and phonological treatment progress. *Journal of Speech and Hearing Research, 36,* 746-759.

Tyler, A. A., & McOmber, L. S. (1999). Examining phonological-morphological interactions with converging sources of evidence. *Clinical Linguistics and Phonetics, 13,* 131-156.

Tyler, A. A., & Saxman, J. H. (1991). Initial voicing contrast acquisition in normal and phonologically disordered children. *Applied Psycholinguistics, 12*, 453-480

Waters, D. (1992). An investigation of motor control for speech in phonologically delayed children, normally developing children and adults. Unpublished PhD thesis, Queen Margaret College, Edinburgh.

Weismer, G. (1984). Acoustic analysis strategies for the refinement of phonological analysis. In M. Elbert, D. A. Dinnsen & G. Weismer (Eds.), *Phonological theory and the misarticulating child. ASHA Monographs,* (Vol. 22, pp. 30-52). Rockville, MD: American Speech and Hearing Association.

Weismer, G., & Elbert, M. (1982). Temporal characteristics of "functionally" misarticulated /s/ in four- to six-year-old children. *Journal of Speech and Hearing Research, 25*, 275-287.

Weismer, G., Dinnsen, D., & Elbert, M. (1981). A study of the voicing distinction associated with omitted, word-final stops. *Journal of Speech and Hearing Disorders, 46*, 320-327.

25

Phonemic Integrity and Contrastiveness in Developmental Apraxia of Speech

Harvey M. Sussman, Thomas P. Marquardt, Jadine Doyle
and Heather Knapp

The speech and language deficits of children diagnosed with Developmental Apraxia of Speech (DAS) have been found to span three levels of language structure: input processing, organizational processing, and output processing (Shriberg, Aram, & Kwiatkowski, 1997). The goal of our research program in DAS is to uncover an underlying core deficit that can parsimoniously account for much of the varied behavioral symptomatology of this disorder. Our initial working hypothesis is that DAS primarily involves an impoverishment in the neural representation, and hence functional operation, of phonological categories. Most researchers agree that DAS is a neurologically based disorder, but to date, documented neurological hard signs are not readily evident. In our view, DAS is a developmental neural dysmorphology involving brain tissue that, in the normal brain, subserves the formation of phonemically structured equivalence classes that function as the basic building blocks of a child's emerging phonological system. Without a well-formed neural representation of the contrastive segmental entities of a language's sound system, acquisition of normal articulation, morphology, prosody, and syntactic structure can be severely compromised. By focusing our inquiry on the higher order linguistic abstraction of the phonetic category, we can (a) utilize experimentally matched studies investigating categorical integrity for both speech production and perception, and (b) investigate a language entity (the phonetic category) that lies at the core of the organizational level of language structure. The production and perception studies presented next should be viewed primarily as a work in progress, as to date our DAS participant population is relatively small, precluding statistical analysis.

ACOUSTIC ANALYSIS OF CV PRODUCTION IN DAS

Voiced stop consonants (/bdg/) varying along a place of articulation dimension (labial, alveolar, velar) were chosen for this initial analysis because of their long-standing history in speech perception as the ultimate litmus test for invariance seekers (Liberman & Mattingly, 1985). Stop consonants best illustrate coarticulation as different vowel-contexts create variability in the consonant-vowel signal that seemingly precludes a direct and transparent acoustic-auditory account for the perception of these sounds. The acoustic structure of stop + vowel productions was assessed by using locus equations. Locus equations are linear regressions of the frequency of the F2 transition sampled at its onset on the frequency of F2 as measured in the middle of the following vowel. These frequency coordinates are measured for a single consonant coarticulated with a wide range of vowels. The onset frequency of F2 is plotted along the ordinate and F2 in the vowel nucleus is plotted along the abscissa. When these (x, y) frequency coordinates (in Hz) of the onset and offset of the second resonance (F2) are plotted for a stop place category, for example [d] as in "deet, dit, debt, date, dat, dot, dut, doot, daught, dote," the data points tightly cluster in a positively correlated distribution that is nicely fit by a linear regression line, the 'locus equation.' Its form is F2 onset = k x F2 vowel + c, where k and c are constants, slope and y-intercept (Lindblom, 1963). Locus equations are ideally suited for studying speech production capabilities in children diagnosed as DAS because (a) locus equation slopes have been consistently found, in normal speakers, to vary as a direct function of place of articulation, and (b) they exhibit a signature linear form characterized by tight clustering of coordinates about the regression line. Therefore they can serve as a phonetic benchmark with which to quantitatively assess departure from a normal articulatory/acoustic form.

Participant Description and Experimental Procedures

Production data were gathered from five DAS children and three normal age-matched controls. Participants ranged from 5:6 to 6:9 years in age. The clinical diagnosis of DAS was determined from a detailed clinical assessment of speech and language that included: phonological analyses of various speech samples, peripheral oral exams, and administration of clinical tests like the Goldman-Fristoe Test of Articulation (Goldman & Fristoe, 1986), Peabody Picture Vocabulary Test (Dunn & Dunn, 1981), and the Screening Test for Developmental Apraxia of Speech (Blakeley, 1980). Scores on tests of receptive vocabulary were at least at the 45th percentile for both DAS and normal participants; percentile scores for articulation were in the 5th percentile or less for the DAS participants; articulation percentile scores were greater than 50th percentile for normal participants. Based on the weighted scores from the

Screening Test of Developmental Apraxia of Speech the probability of correct assignment to the DAS diagnostic category was more than 99% for the DAS subjects and less than 1% for the normal subjects.

CV tokens were elicited from each child by having them imitate words spoken by one of the investigators (JD). The child's utterances were recorded using a high quality microphone fed to an analog tape recorder. After sampling at 10kHz and filtering, the speech signal was analyzed using the MacSpeech Lab software system on an Apple MacIntosh computer. Measurement and analysis procedures followed protocols well established in previous locus equation studies (Sussman, McCaffery, & Matthews, 1991; Sussman, Hoemeke, & Ahmed, 1993; Sussman, Fruchter, & Cable, 1995; Sussman, Bessell, Dalston, & Majors, 1997). Representative locus equation scatterplots for a normal speaker (age 6:7) relative to a DAS subject (6:8) are illustrated in Fig. 1.   The scatterplots for each stop place category are shown across each row, with the normal child on the left and the DAS child on the right. There are two important aspects of the locus equation plots to notice. First, the slope value for each place of articulation, and second, the tightness of the clustering of the data points around the regression line (the linearity of the distribution). Locus equation slopes are directly related to extent of coarticulation, with higher slopes indicating greater amounts of coarticulatory influence of the vowel onto the preceding stop (Krull, 1989). Customarily, labials have relatively high slopes (> .70), alveolars have the lowest/flattest slopes (.25 to 50), and velars have the steepest slopes (> .80). In addition, velar scatterplots usually show two separate allophonic groupings corresponding to velars produced before front vowels and velars preceding back vowels. Looking first at the labial functions (top row) it can be seen that the normal speaker's /bV/ productions had a slope of .78, which is identical to the adult norm (Sussman et al., 1991), whereas the DAS speaker had a lower slope of .65.   This isn't particularly abnormal except when compared to the alveolars: labial slopes are *always* higher than alveolars. The /dV/ slope for the DAS child, however, was .73 relative to .47 in the normal child.   This fact indicates that in terms of articulation, the DAS child was moving his tongue apex to different stop occlusion locations on the alveolar ridge depending on vowel contexts, rather than the typical articulatory strategy of a fairly steady occlusion location for /d/ across varying vowel contexts. Alveolar productions should reflect the least coarticulated interaction between C and V of all stops. For the DAS child the velar slope did not differ relative to the alveolar slope (/d/ = .73; /g/ = .75), whereas the normal child had a large contrast between alveolar/velar categories (/d/ = .47; /g/ = .85). Turning to the linear form of the scatterplots, the distributions are considerably less linear in the output of the DAS speaker. Quantifying this impression, the standard error of estimate (SE) was used to determine the average distance (in Hz) of each point from the regression line.

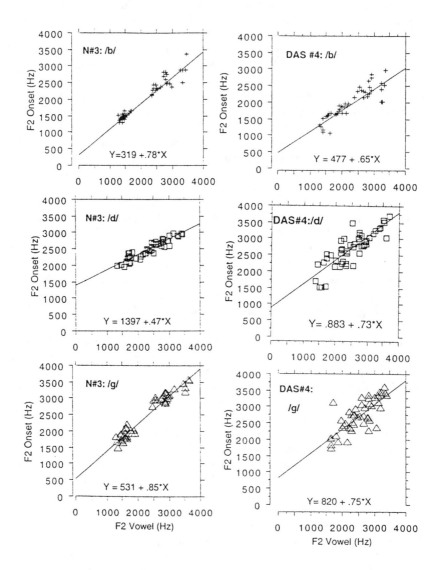

FIG.1 Locus equation scatterplots for normal speaker (N #3) and a speaker with DAS (DAS #4). Slopes and y-intercepts are indicated for /bV/, /dV/ and /gV/ utterances.

The SEs for /b/, /d/, and /g/ for the normal child were 140 Hz, 100 Hz, and 155 Hz, respectively; in sharp contrast the SEs for the DAS child were 213 Hz, 286 Hz, and 308 Hz. In a cross- linguistic study involving normal adult speakers, highly linear locus equation plots were found to be a linguistic universal (Sussman et al., 1993).

Phonological Distances Separating Stop Place Categories

Locus equation parameters, slope and y-intercept, can also be used to quantify the relative phonological distances separating the three stop place categories. Fig. 2 shows the total Euclidean distance (ED) between /b/-/d/-/g/ categories for the two speakers discussed previously.

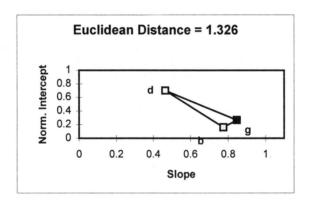

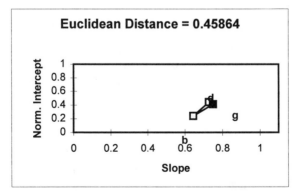

FIG. 2 Euclidean distances separating stop place coordinates for a normal speaker (top), and a speaker with Developmental Apraxia of Speech (bottom).

ED is calculated as the perimeter of a triangle formed by connecting the three slope/y-intercept coordinates. The normal child shows widely spaced categorical coordinates with an ED of 1.326; the DAS child has closely spaced stop place categories with an ED of only .45864. The DAS child fails to contrast coarticulation levels across stop place categories and produces /bdg/ categories that are close neighbors in acoustic space. Looking at group means (three normal children and five DAS speakers), the mean ED separating stop place categories was 1.678 for the normal group and 0.6319 for the DAS group.

Additional locus equation parameters were examined to characterize production differences across the two speaking groups. R^2 indicates the extent of variability accounted for by the regression function, and the standard error of estimate is a measure of the "goodness of fit" of the regression function (i.e. it indicates the average frequency distance of each coordinate from the regression function).

Table 1 below summarizes these parameters. R^2 values were approximately .16 higher for the normal speakers across the three stop categories, and the standard error of estimate was 90 Hz smaller across stop place categories for the normal speakers in relation to the DAS speakers.   In summary, all three indices of production, based on locus equation analyses, indicate fairly robust deficiencies in DAS speakers relative to normal age-matched controls.

TABLE 1

Summary of R^2 values and standard error of estimate
for normal and DAS speakers.

	R-squared			Standard Error		
	b	*d*	*g*	*b*	*d*	*g*
Norm #1	0.96	0.79	0.96	134	134	169
Norm #2	0.95	0.87	0.92	163	138	227
Norm #3	0.94	0.88	0.95	140	100	155
mean	0.95	0.85	0.94	146	124	184
DAS #1	0.77	0.71	0.84	194	263	256
DAS #2	0.79	0.64	0.73	173	256	261
DAS #3	0.71	0.61	0.55	222	316	232
DAS #4	0.79	0.71	0.62	213	286	308
DAS #5	0.87	0.87	0.94	215	236	197
Mean	0.79	0.71	0.74	203	271	251

Locus equation scatterplots are less linear in DAS (as quantified by SEs), less differentiated in contrastive slope values across stop place (as shown by smaller EDs), and less able to predict F2 onsets, using F2 vowel (as shown by lower R^2 values).

PERCEPTUAL ANALYSIS OF CVs IN DAS

If DAS involves an impoverished neural representation of phonemic categories then we should expect to see deficits in basic perception abilities such as consistency in labeling stimuli that vary along a physical continuum from /b/-to-/d/-to-/g/. Our intent in examining the perceptual abilities of DAS speakers was to arrive at a quantifiable measure of the "perceptual distance" separating the three stop place categories. In this way, we would have a matched comparison of 'categorical separability' measured for both production and perception. In the identification experiment, participants used two responses to sort two sets of seven auditory stimuli into categories: one seven item continuum ranged from /b/-to-/d/; a second seven item continuum ranged from /d/-to-/g/. The stimuli were C[a] syllables in which C was resynthesized to vary along a continuum from /b/ to /d/ and from /d/ to /g/. Upon listening to a stimulus, the participants identified the consonant of the token as either /b/, /d/, or /g/. Our goal was to compare the perceptual sensitivity of normal and DAS subjects to physical changes in the stimuli, both pairwise and along the continuum.

Procedures

Resynthesized stimuli were used in this experiment. A clear [da] was recorded from a male speaker (TM). This signal was analyzed by pitch synchronous LPC (autocorrelation analysis) with a pre-emphasis factor of 0.95 by using the Analysis/Synthesis Lab, resynthesis module of the Kay CSL. Continua were then created by manipulation of the LPC parameters with the same de-emphasis factor. F2 and F3 onsets were set to a value and then linearly smoothed to the formant midpoint. All transitions were 54 msec in duration. F1 was constant at 406 Hz. Stimuli were randomized and transferred to a DAT tape for playback via a speaker. Participants were seated at a small table in a quiet therapy room of the University of Texas Speech and Hearing Center. To acquaint the child with the task several practice trials were first administered. The first phase consisted of non speech sounds: a high tone (500 Hz), a low tone (100 Hz), and white noise. After hearing each item, the child indicated whether they heard a high pitched, low pitched, or noise sound. Following this, there were six trials of /ba-da/ exemplars followed by six trials of /da-ga/ exemplars. The child simply pointed to the letters B, D, and G, printed in both upper and lower case, with appropriate pictures (e.g., "boy", "dog," and "girl"). When performance reached a criterion of > 75 % correct labeling, the experimental trials started. In each series (b-d and d-g), every stimulus item was randomly repeated 12 times with a 4-sec inter stimulus interval. Labeling curves were derived from the percent identifications of each stimulus along each 7-item continuum. We then used z transformations to convert percent identification for a given stimulus item to a z-score, a standard deviation unit. Macmillan and Creelman (1991) have shown that d' (from signal detection theory) can be calculated as the difference in z-scores between a stimulus and its adjacent neighbor along the continuum:

$$d' = z\,(\%\ \text{identification item x}) - z\,(\%\ \text{identification item x+1})$$

A large value of d' indicates a large perceptual difference between adjacent stimuli, and a small d' value reflects a small perceptual distance. When there is no perceptual difference between adjacent stimuli (the subject thinks the two stimuli sound the same), d' will be zero. Perceptual sensitivity along the continuum can also be measured cumulatively, by keeping a running total of d's derived from adjacent z-scores. The cumulative d' is equivalent to the sensitivity distance between any stimulus and the endpoint stimulus. When cumulative d' is plotted against stimulus number, a picture of the sensitivity of the participant to systematic stimuli changes emerges. The resulting function compares the physical and psychological spacing of the stimuli, and its slope tells us how rapidly the perceptual effect grows with stimulus value, i.e., how sensitive the listener is to systematic stimulus changes.

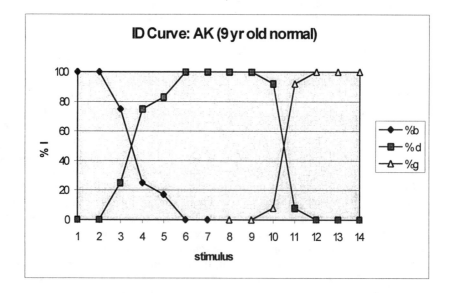

FIG 3. Identification curve for labial, alveolar and velar stops for a normal 9-year-old male.

Comparisons of any two cumulative d' scores along the continuum reveal the perceptual distance between those stimuli.

Labeling Data and d' Transformations

Fig. 3 shows a representative labeling curve for a normal child, aged 9 years, to serve as a comparison to three DAS children that were administered the identification test. AK's boundaries were sharply defined and very similar to adult identification curves. Figs. 4 to 6 show identification curves for three DAS speakers: GJ (age 8); JS (age 11); and DL (age 12). Looking first at GJ, it can be seen that the labial-alveolar boundary is extremely sharp, but the alveolar-velar boundary is abnormal. Velar tokens were inconsistently labeled with stimulus items 11, 12 and 13 equivocating between /d/ and /g/ when they should all have been clear /g/s. DAS speaker JS showed an unusual labial-alveolar boundary, with a normal alveolar-velar crossover.   For example, stimulus #3 was labeled as /b/ only 63% of the time relative to stimulus #4, which was labeled a /b/ 88% of the time. Stimulus #3 is a better exemplar of /b/ (closer to labial endpoint) than stimulus #4, which was often identified as a /d/ by other participants. DAS speaker DL also exhibited an abnormal identification pattern with a normal labial-alveolar boundary, but a highly unusual alveolar-velar boundary.   DL did not identify any velar stimuli as 100% /g/ until the endpoint item (#14). In contrast, normal age-matched controls typically labeled items #12, 13 and 14 as /g/ 100% of the time.

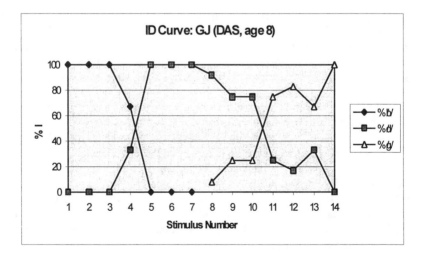

FIG. 4 Identification curves for labial, alveolar, velar stops for an 8-year-old male with Developmental Apraxia of Speech.

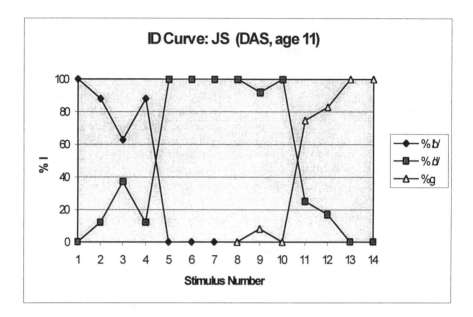

FIG. 5 Identification curves for labial, alveolar, and velar stops for an 11-year-old male with Developmental Apraxia of Speech

To gain a more quantifiable perspective on these ID functions, cumulative d' plots were derived from the z-scores of the percent identification scores shown above. In each figure, the phoneme pair revealing deficits for the DAS speaker is compared to normal speaker AK. The first cumulative d' comparison is shown in Fig. 7 between the /d/-/g/ boundary of the DAS participant

GJ relative to that of normal subject AK. The slope of the cumulative d' function indicates how sensitive the listener is to systematic step changes in the stimulus continuum. AK's sharply rising function has a slope of 1.32 compared to a considerably flatter slope of .64 for GJ. GJ's function did not start at zero for stimulus #1 as it should have and did not reach the maximum ceiling of 6.18 for stimulus #7 as it should have. What this means is that GJ did not hear the initial two items (#1 versus #2) as identical allophones of /d/, whereas AK labeled these as being the same (cumulative d' = 0). At the other end of the continuum, AK labeled items #4, #5 and #6 as identical /g/s and thus detected no difference among the /g/ allophones; GJ heard these items as being different and never reached a steady asymptotic level indicating no detectable differences between these within category allophones.

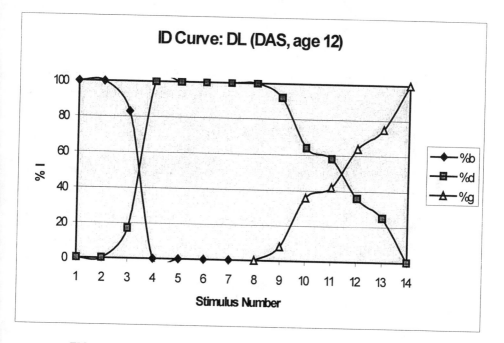

FIG. 6 Identification curves for labial, alveolar, velar stops for a 12 year-old male with Developmental Apraxia of Speech.

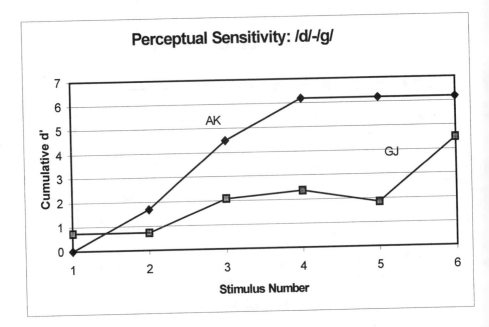

FIG. 7 Cumulative d' curves for alveolar-velar stops comparing a normal speaker (AK) to a speaker with Developmental Apraxia of Speech (GJ).

In Fig. 8 AK's /b/-/d/ boundary is shown relative to JS's /b/-/d/ boundary. The slope for AK was 1.214 and the slope for JS was 1.02. In addition, JS showed a cumulative d' of nearly 2.0 for the comparison of stimulus #1 versus # 2. This same comparison showed a cumulative d' = 0 for AK as they were both within category /b/ allophones. JS's function also showed a drop in perceptual sensitivity for stimulus #3 indicating a lessening of perceptual sensitivity between that item and the end-point — item #3 was heard as less /b/-like than item #4, which was counter to normal perceptual behavior.

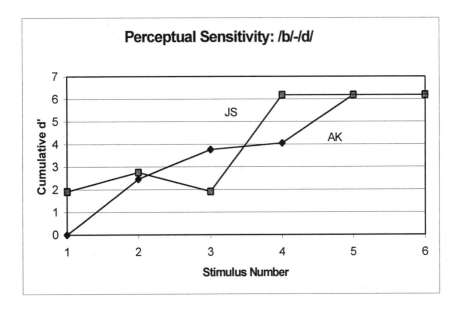

FIG. 8 Cumulative d' curves for labial-alveolar stops comparing a normal speaker (AK) to a speaker with Developmental Apraxia of Speech (JS).

FIG. 9 shows the cumulative d' between AK's /d-g/ boundary in relation to DL's /d-g/ boundary. Again, the perceptual sensitivity function is steep (slope = 1.32) for AK and relatively flat for DL (slope = .77). In addition, DL did not identify the #1 and #2 pair equivalently (allophones of /d/) as AK did. The perceptual changes between adjacent items along the continuum for DL were small, rather than sharp and abrupt and ending in a steady /g/ identification for the last three within-category stimulus pairs.

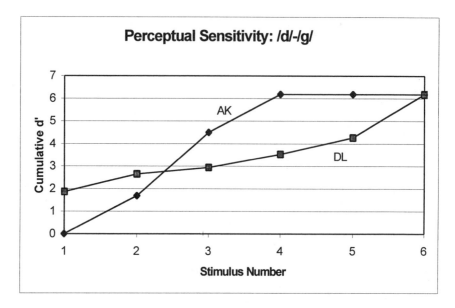

FIG. 9 Cumulative d' curves for alveolar-velar stops comparing a normal speaker (AK) to a speaker with Developmental Apraxia of Speech (DL).

Summary and Conclusions

Both the production and perception studies revealed deficits in children diagnosed with DAS in relation to normal controls. Locus equation form was markedly less linear for DAS speakers. Moreover, acoustic contrasts across stop place categories were less well differentiated, resulting in relatively closely spaced category coordinates (slope/y-intercept), and thus smaller EDs separating stop place categories. The lack of contrastive slope values as a function of stop place indicates that DAS children do not adequately adjust coarticulation levels in their production of CV utterances. Labial + vowel utterances should reveal high levels of anticipatory coarticulation (indicated by steep locus equation slopes) because the tongue shape for the upcoming vowel should already be in position when the labial occlusion is formed; alveolar + vowel utterances should reflect minimal degrees of coarticulation (indicated by flatter slopes) as the tongue occlusion position should be relatively unchanging across varied vowel contexts; velar + vowel utterances should reflect high levels of anticipatory coarticulation for velars preceding back vowels; and very flat slopes for velars preceding front vowels. These coarticulatory adjustments must be learned because articulatory motor skills during language acquisition.

Identification functions clearly indicated faulty phonetic boundaries between specific stop place categories in all DAS speakers examined thus far (N = 3). This finding is counter to that reported by Groenen, Maassen, Crul, and Thoonen (1996) who reported deficits only in discrimination abilities, not identification, in DAS in relation to normal age-matched participants. A cumulative d' analysis allowed us to quantify the perceptual sensitivity of each participant to physical changes along the continuum. The less steep slopes of the cumulative d' functions for the DAS children relative to the control subject indicated a considerably diminished perceptual sensitivity to the systematic changes in the stimuli. The DAS children also showed equivocation in labeling within-category stimuli and less abrupt shifts at phonetic boundaries, especially the alveolar-velar cross-over. Taken together, the results for both production and perception indicate a more fragile control of categorical entities in DAS speakers. Although these results are only preliminary, they do lend support to the notion that a core deficit of DAS could very well be a neural-based inability to establish well formed phonetic categories. There are two basic requirements needed to establish well-formed contrastive phonetic categories: (1) sensitivity at phonetic boundaries, combined with (2) the ability to ignore or generalize across (within category) allophonic variations. Neurophysiological studies have documented the concept of 'tolerance limits' in neuronal responses to stimulus features such as horizontal "edge detectors" in pigeons (Maturana & Frenk, 1963). Specific retinal cells tolerated different extents of variation from the horizontal (e.g., 10-15 degrees) and maintained a consistent firing response despite small differences in the input signal. Similarly, in speech perception, there needs to be functional neuronal operations that maintain categorical consistency in the face of non-phonemic physical variation. Listeners must learn to tolerate (or ignore) allophonic variation while showing acute sensitivity to the quantal change-overs at phoneme boundaries. These are complementary operations that are both needed to establish well-formed categorical representations that can mediate phonological intent in production as well as the foundation for perceptual decoding. It is our contention that the neural substrates responsible for such basic functions is maldeveloped in children with DAS.

REFERENCES

Blakeley, R. (1980). *Screening test for developmental apraxia of speech*. OR: Tigard, CC Publications.

Dunn, L. M. & Dunn, L. M. (1981). *Peabody picture vocabulary test-revised.* Circle Pines, MN: American Guidance Service.

Goldman, R., & Fristoe, M. (1969). *Goldman-Fristoe Test of Articulation.* Circle Pines, MN: American Guidance Service.

Groenen, P., Maassen, B., Crul, T.,& Thoonen, G. (1996). The specific relation between perception and production errors for place of articulation in Developmental Apraxia of Speech. *Journal of Speech and Hearing Research, 39,* 468–482.

Krull, D. (1989). Second formant locus patterns and consonant-vowel coarticulation in spontaneous speech. Phonetic Experimental Research, Institute of Linguistics, University of Stockholm, *(PERILUS)10,* 87–108.

Liberman, A., & Mattingly, I. (1985). The motor theory of speech perception: revised. *Cognition, 21,* 1–36.

Lindblom, B. (1963). *On vowel reduction.* Report No. 29, Speech Transmission Laboratory. The Royal Institute of Technology, Sweden.

Macmillan, N. A., & Creelman, C.D. (1991). *Detection theory: A user's guide.* Cambridge University Press, UK.

Maturana, H. R., & Frenk, S. (1963). Directional movement and horizontal edge detectors in the pigeon retina. *Science, 142,* 977–979.

Shriberg, L., Aram, D., & Kwiatkowski, J. (1997). Developmental apraxia of speech: I. Descriptive and theoretical perspectives. *Journal of Speech Language, and Hearing Research, 40,* 273–285.

Sussman, H. M., Bessell, N., Dalston, E., & Majors, T. (1997). An investigation of stop place of articulation as a function of syllable position: A locus equation perspective. *Journal of the Acoustical Society of America, 101,* 2826–2838.

Sussman, H. M., Fruchter, D., & Cable, A. (1995). Locus equations derived from compensatory articulation. *Journal of the Acoustical Society of America, 97,* 3112–3124.

Sussman, H. M., Hoemeke, K., & Ahmed, F. (1993). A cross-linguistic investigation of locus equations as a relationally invariant descriptor for place of articulation. *Journal of the Acoustical Society of America, 94,* 1256–1268.

Sussman, H. M., Mccaffrey, H., & Mattthews, S.A. (1991). An investigation of locus equations as a source of relational invariance for stop place categorization. *Journal of the Acoustical Society of America, 90,* 13091325.

26

Voice Onset Time in Normal Speakers of a German Dialect: Effects of Age, Gender and Verbal Material

Gabriele Scharf and Harald Masur

Voice onset time (VOT) is defined as the time span between release of oral constriction and beginning of periodic vocal fold vibration in the production of stop-vowel sequences. In most languages, including German, VOT plays a primary role in the distinction between voiced and voiceless plosives (Lisker & Abramson, 1964; Jessen, 1998). In most of these languages, the VOT values for voiced and unvoiced stops are produced in discrete duration ranges that correspond to the voicing categories. Even though boundaries between the contrasting categories along the continuum of VOT vary from language to language it is claimed that the VOT categories "voiced" and "unvoiced" are separated by a range of times in which no production occurs (Auzou et al., 2000, p. 137). We will call this the 'illegal range'. Lisker and Abramson (1967) qualify that claim by saying that it is true for initial stops in citation forms of words whereas in running speech the separation might be less sharp.

Although VOT is the most relevant acoustic parameter of voicing, additional acoustic features provide voicing information such as presence, absence and intensity of fricative noise during the oral release, duration of the burst release (Auzou et al., 2000, p. 132), F0 after release (Whalen, Abramson, Lisker & Mody, 1993) and formant transitions (Stevens & Klatt, 1974; Pind, 1991).

VOT is an important factor of speech motor timing control and is influenced by various linguistic factors such as speech rate, phonological context and word length (Lisker & Abramson, 1967). It has been assumed that extralinguistic factors such as emotional status, experimental situation, speaking style and degree of dialectal features might influence VOT production (e.g. Decoster & Debruyne, 1997, p. 278), but evidence is sparse. The influences of age and gender on VOT production in normal speakers are still unanswered questions, too.

With respect to the influence of age, there are contradictory results. Benjamin (1982) observed a general reduction of VOT with increasing age. Sweeting and Baken (1982), Morris and Brown (1994) and Petrosino, Colcord, Kurcz and Yonker (1993) reported similar mean VOT values across age groups but increasing variability around the mean in the older subjects. Decoster and Debruyne (1997) in their longitudinal study, however, report substantially longer VOT values in the same speakers following a 30 year interval.

With respect to gender differences in VOT production relatively few data are available (Ryalls, Zipprer & Baldauff, 1997; Sweeting & Baken, 1982; Swartz, 1992; Whiteside & Irving, 1998). Although Sweeting and Baken (1982) reported no significant sex differences in the VOT of labial stops, Swartz (1992) found a significant VOT difference between men and women for alveolar stops in words embedded in phrases. Whiteside and Irving (1998) described a significant larger VOT voicing contrast in female than in male speakers due to longer VOT values for voiceless plosives and shorter values for voiced plosives. These authors attributed this not only to anatomical and physiological differences in the vocal tracts of men and women but also to idiosyncratic differences and a more "careful style of speech" in the female participants than in the males.

VOT has also been measured in patients with various neurogenic speech and language disorders such as different types of aphasia and dysarthria to help differentiate their phonemic and phonetic error patterns (Baum & Ryan, 1993; Blumstein, Cooper, Zurif & Caramazza, 1977; Blumstein, Cooper, Goodglass, Statlender & Gottlieb, 1980). Blumstein et al. (1980) described characteristic error patterns of VOT in different aphasic syndromes and different types of dysarthria. For example, Broca's aphasics presented a continuum of VOT values with overlap between the two voicing categories whereas Wernicke's aphasics maintained a bimodal VOT distribution but showed VOT values for voiced stops in the range of the voiceless and vice versa. Although the interpretation of these error patterns in terms of phonetic or phonemic disturbances is still a matter of discussion (Walsh, 1983; Auzou et al., 2000), VOT has been established as an important parameter in the investigation of speech motor and language disorders.

However, neither for English nor for German have normative data been published that would verify the clinical benefit of this parameter. Bender, Dogil and Mayer (1992) provide some preliminary data for German, but more data, about the VOT production in different German dialects (Braun, 1996), about age and gender effects and about the strength and stability of the VOT contrast of voicing are urgently needed.

It is the purpose of the present study to provide a corpus of normative VOT data in German that allows an adequate comparison with clinical data. Since absolute VOT values and ranges say litte about the strength of the phonemic voicing contrast, different contrast measures are calculated in addition to means and ranges. Possible effects of age, gender and verbal material on VOT duration and on the bimodal distribution of the voiced and unvoiced categories are investigated. The robustness of VOT as phonetic–phonological timing parameter and as diagnostic criterion to differentiate between normal and pathological speech is discussed.

METHOD

Participants

Forty speakers born and brought up in the same dialectal region (*Pfälzisch*) in southwest Germany, the palatinate, took part in the study. The group consisted of patients with orthopedic lesions and staff members. None had any neurological or speech disorders. They were divided into 4 groups with 10 speakers each with respect to gender (Male, Female) and age (Young, Old; see Table 1).

TABLE 1
Experimental groups.

Younger Males	Younger Females
n = 10	n = 10
Range: 23 – 39 years	Range: 22 – 41 years
Mean: 30.9 years	Mean: 32.4 years

Older Males	Older Females
n = 10	n = 10
Range: 54 – 80 years	Range: 51 – 80 years
Mean: 65.9 years	Mean: 66.7 years

Material

Voiced and unvoiced plosives with different places of articulation and following vowel /a/, [pa – ba; ta – da; ka – ga], were produced in word initial position as part of:

(i)   single words: »Panther – Banken, tanken – danken, Karten – Garten«
                    (panther–banks, to tank up– to thank, cards– garden)
(ii) the same words, embedded in the carrier phrase:
                    »Du hast doch ___ gesagt« *(You did say ___)*
(iii) minimal pairs which were nonwords, embedded in the same target
      sentence:
      »pammen – bammen, tammen – dammen, kammen – gammen«

Since the verbal material has been selected with the comparison with clinical data in mind, we used 6 highly frequent, concrete, single word nouns and verbs which were likely to be easily produced by aphasic and dysarthric subjects. Target words embedded in a carrier phrase were designed to show whether there is a difference between citation forms and connected speech. The voiceless fricative preceding the target consonant allows reliable detection of the articulatory closure phase on the one hand and of the voicing onset on the other hand. Finally, in order to exclude lexical effects and because there are not six German words which are identical except for the initial plosive, nonsense words constituting three exact minimal pairs were also used.

The single words and sentences were presented visually, written with large bold letters, as well as auditorily, on a tape spoken by one male speaker in a standard German accent.[1] Each item was repeated 8 times in random order, leading to 3 x 48 = 144 items (single words, sentences) per speaker.

Data Acquisition

The participants produced the test items at a comfortable speech rate and amplitude. Recordings were made in a soundproofed room. The acoustic and the laryngographic (EGG) signal of the speakers' productions were recorded synchronically. Articulatory release was labeled manually in the oscillographic record and voice onset was likewise marked in the laryngographic record. VOT was then calculated as difference between these two time points (Fig. 1).

---

[1]This speaker was recorded producing several repetitions of each target word and nonword. One of each item, with average voice onset time, was then selected and later embedded in the carrier phrase which was the same for all sentences.

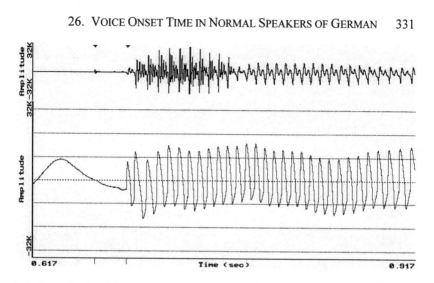

FIG. 1 Acoustic signal (upper panel) and laryngographic signal (EGG, lower panel) of the syllable [ga]. Note the two time marks on the top for burst and voice onset.

In contrast to VOT measurements usually obtained exclusively from the acoustic signal (see Auzou et al., 2000, for a review) this two-channel method reflects the interarticulatory coordination between oral articulator (identified from the acoustic signal) and larynx (EGG) which is involved in VOT production, and was therefore the preferred method in this study.

In some cases incomplete articulatory closures or harsh voice quality lead to difficulties in the localization of bursts and voice onsets. In the case of double bursts, measurements were taken from the start of the first burst. In the case of voice interruptions or abrupt changes of voice quality in the beginning of the vowel, the first voice onset was taken if the voice interruption or irregularity was not longer than 1 or 2 glottal pulses. If the voice interruption was longer than that the test item was excluded from the study. Errors due to technical problems, ambiguous or missing bursts and ambiguous voice onset were excluded from the data.

Analysis

In addition to minimum, maximum, mean, range and standard deviation of VOT duration the following measures of VOT contrast between unvoiced and voiced plosives were calculated: mean difference (C1), a rough measure of the strength of the contrast, mean difference divided by the standard deviation (C2), indicating the intraspeaker stability of the VOT contrast and, thirdly, the difference between the VOT minimum of the voiceless plosives and the VOT maximum of the voiced plosives (C3). The latter defines the 'illegal range' which separates the VOT ranges of voiced and unvoiced plosives (see Table 2). These three parameters were designed to represent three different aspects of the VOT voicing contrast.

TABLE 2
Parameters of VOT Contrast.

Aspect of VOT contrast:	Parameter:	Definition:
Strength of contrast	C1	Mean unvoiced – Mean voiced
Stability of contrast	C2	C1/(Standard deviation unvoiced + Standard deviation voiced)
Illegal range	C3	Minimum unvoiced – Maximum voiced

Statistical analysis included Multivariate Analyses of Variance (MANOVA's) with the factors place of articulation and voicing as well as gender, age, and material.

RESULTS

Fig. 2 shows the VOT values of each speaker in the four experimental group productions of the single words with [da] – [ta] contrast, serving as an example of the VOT contrast pattern in the various experimental conditions. You see the ranges of voiced (left) and unvoiced (right) VOT values with mean marks.

VOT duration ranges from short voicing lags for voiced consonants to long voicing lags for unvoiced consonants, velar plosives showing longer durations than alveolars and alveolars, in turn, longer values than labials. Negative VOT associated with voice onset preceding articulatory release was observed on only one occasion and was therefore assumed not to be characteristic of the dialect of palatinate.

As can be seen in the [da] – [ta] example there was generally a clear VOT contrast between voiced and unvoiced counterparts. However, there were some speakers (e.g. younger male speakers No. 3 and 5, and older male speaker No. 7 in Fig. 2) who showed no clear contrast but even an overlap between VOT values of voiced and unvoiced plosives. Such cases were found in all age and gender groups and in different experimental conditions (different consonantal contexts, words in sentences, nonwords in sentences). Although this study does not include a detailed perceptual analysis of the VOT productions, an informal judgement revealed clear perceptible voicing contrasts in all speakers.

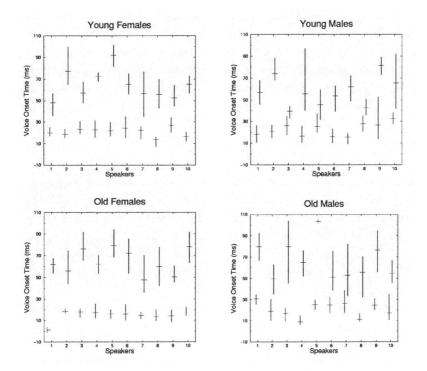

FIG. 2 VOT ranges and means for all speakers in the single words 'danken', *thank*, (the lower bars in each panel) and 'tanken', *tank* (upper bars).

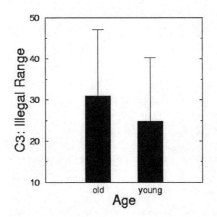

FIG. 3 Illegal range (group means with standard deviation) in the two age groups.

Age

The older speakers showed a tendency to produce shorter VOT duration for voiced consonants and longer VOT duration for unvoiced consonants as compared to the younger speakers, which resulted in larger VOT voicing contrasts with respect to mean difference and illegal range in the older subjects.

Fig. 3 shows the illegal range in both age groups. Table 3 gives an overview of the statistical results of the three different contrast measures.

TABLE 3
Effects of age on VOT contrasts with the statistical parameters of significance value
(p) and F-value (df = 1).

Contrast parameter	Definition	Effect	p	F
Strength of contrast (C1)	Mean Difference	old > young	0.001	10.570
Stability of contrast (C2)	C1 / Standard deviation	old > young	0.081	3.057
Illegal range (C3)	Min unvoiced – Max voiced	old > young	0.000	12.874

Gender

Female speakers in our corpus showed the tendency to produce shorter VOT duration for voiced consonants and longer VOT duration for unvoiced consonants in comparison to the male speakers. This pattern resulted in significantly larger VOT contrasts in female than in male speakers (Fig. 4, Table 4).

Verbal Material

Verbal material had an effect on VOT production. Whereas nonwords in sentences and single words showed only a slight tendency to longer VOT duration in comparison to words embedded in sentences (p = 0.508, F = 0.678, df = 2), significant differences were found with respect to the standard deviation which was larger in single word productions than in words and nonwords embedded in a carrier sentence (p = 0.006, F = 5.199, df = 2). That is, the single words were produced with higher intraspeaker variability which might be caused by a more careful speech style.

The VOT contrasts, however, were found to be largest for the nonwords in sentences, followed by the words in sentences, with the single words showing the smallest voicing contrast (see Table 5 and Fig. 5).

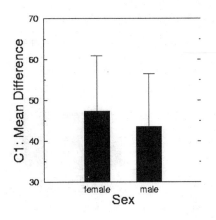

FIG. 4 Mean difference (group means with standard deviation) in the two gender groups.

TABLE 4:
Effects of gender on VOT contrasts with the statistical parameters of significance value (*p*) and F-value (df=1).

Contrast parameter	Definition	Effect	p	F
Strength of contrast (C1)	Mean Difference	female > male	0.008	7.225
Stability of contrast (C2)	C1 / Standard deviation	female > male	0.001	12.351
Illegal range (C3)	Min unvoiced – Max voiced	female > male	0.000	13.059

TABLE 5
Effects of verbal material on VOT contrasts (ENW = Embedded Nonwords, EW = Embedded Words, SW = Single Words) with the statistical parameters of significance value (*p*) and F-value (df=2).

Contrast parameter	Effect	p	F
Strength of contrast (C1)	ENW > EW > SW	0.000	21.059
Stability of contrast (C2)	ENW > EW > SW	0.000	16.461
Illegal range (C3)	ENW > EW > SW	0.000	24.718

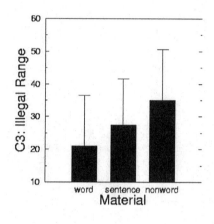

FIG. 5 Illegal range (group means with standard deviation) in the different verbal materials: single words, words embedded in sentences and embedded nonwords.

DISCUSSION

The data reported here have demonstrated that not only VOT duration but also strength and stability of the VOT voicing contrast were all highly influenced by the age and gender of the speaker as well as by verbal material and context: We make the following conclusions:

(1) In general, there was no significant age effect with respect to VOT duration and standard deviation That is, the older speakers produced VOT values in similar ranges and with similar variability to the younger speakers. In addition, the older speakers separated the VOT ranges of voiced and unvoiced plosives more clearly than the younger speakers. This result is surprising in the light of some previous studies that reported weaker VOT contrasts in older speakers.

(2) There was a clear gender effect on the VOT contrast with the female speakers presenting a stronger voicing contrast than the male speakers. This result held not only for single words but was also true for nonwords and words in carrier sentences. It goes beyond the findings in Whiteside and Irving (1988) who observed larger VOT contrasts in women only in the single word context. Looking for an explanation for this clear gender effect leads us, like Whiteside and Irving (1988), to the assumption that females might articulate more carefully than male speakers.

(3) Verbal material showed a highly significant effect on the variability of

VOT values on the one hand and on strength and stability of the VOT voicing contrast on the other hand. Single word productions showed a higher intraspeaker variability of VOT durations than target items embedded in a carrier sentence. Therefore, the extraction of VOT values from sentence productions might provide more reliable information about the speech timing control mechanism in a speaker. Even if embedded in a carrier phrase the nonwords seemed to 'force' the normal speakers to produce larger VOT contrasts than the lexical items (single words, words in sentences). That is why the nonword condition is of special interest in the investigation of the VOT voicing contrast – in normal and in pathological speech production.

(4) There were some instances of very small illegal ranges or even overlapping VOT ranges of voiced and unvoiced categories in some of the speakers and in different experimental conditions. Therefore, it should be emphasized that overlapping VOT ranges are characteristic not only of pathological speech but also of normal speakers. Furthermore, it should be noted that, in contrast to observations of Lisker and Abramson (1967), the VOT overlaps occurred not only in sentence productions but also in the elicited single word productions (Fig. 2). However, one shouldn't infer a general German VOT pattern from these observations since the present data were obtained exclusively from speakers of the dialect of the palatinate. Therefore this might be a specific property of the *Pfälzischer* dialect. Comparative dialect studies are needed to confirm this assumption.

The lack of a VOT contrast in some of the normal speakers of course does not mean that these speakers didn't realize a voicing contrast at all. Perceptually there was a noticeable voicing contrast in the acoustic signal. Therefore, obviously the dialect of palatinate allows the use of other voicing features than VOT. Fundamental frequency, intensity of fricative noise and other acoustic features are possible candidates. The question of which particular combination of features was used by our participants was outside the scope of the study reported here and will be investigated in the near future. Combined production and perception studies will play an important role in this kind of research.

Some additional factors presumably influenced VOT production in the normal speakers of the present study: The different speakers spoke with different degrees of dialect influence and different degrees of naturalness in the experimental situation. These factors might be of relevance for future research.

The results from this corpus of 40 healthy speakers of the southwestern German *Pfälzischer* dialect raise questions about the robustness of VOT as the most relevant acoustic correlate of voicing. More work with large corpora of normative VOT data is needed in order to test the relevance of VOT as a diagnostic criterion to differentiate between normal and pathological speech.

REFERENCES

Auzou, P., Özsancak, C., Morris, R. J., Jan, M., Eustache, F. & Hannequin, D. (2000). Voice onset time in aphasia, apraxia of speech and dysarthria: A review. *Clinical Linguistics and Phonetics, 14*, 131 – 150.

Baum, S. R. & Ryan, L. (1993). Rate of speech effects in aphasia. Voice onset time. *Brain and Language, 44*, 431-445.

Bender, A., Dogil, G. & Mayer, J. (1992). Computerunterstützte Diagnostik und Therapie der neurogenen Lautstörungen: Elektrolaryngographie. In V.M. Roth (Ed.), *Computer in der Sprachtherapie. Neue WEGE* (pp. 125-134). Tuebingen: Gunter Narr Verlag.

Benjamin, B. J. (1982). Phonological performance in gerontological speech. *Journal of Psycholinguistic Research, 11*, 159-167.

Blumstein, S. E., Cooper, W. E., Goodglass, H., Statlender, S. & Gottlieb, J. (1980). Production deficits in aphasia: A voice onset time analysis. *Brain & Language, 9*, 153-170.

Blumstein, S. E., Cooper, W. E., Zurif, E. B. & Caramazza, A. (1977). The perception and production of voice-onset time in aphasia. *Neuropsychologia, 15*, 371-383.

Braun, A. (1996). Zur regionalen Distribution von VOT im Deutschen. In Braun, A. (Ed.), *Untersuchungen zu Stimme und Sprache* (pp. 19-32). Stuttgart: Franz Steiner Verlag.

Decoster, W. & Debruyne, F. (1997). Changes in spectral measures and voice-onset time with age: A cross-sectional and a longitudinal study. *Folia Phoniatrica et Logopaedica, 49*, 269-280.

Jessen, M. (1998). *Phonetics and phonology of tense and lax obstruents in German.* Amsterdam: Benjamins.

Lisker, L. & Abramson, A. S. (1964). A cross-language study of voicing in initial stops: Acoustical measurements. *Word, 20*, 384-422.

Lisker, L. & Abramson, A. S. (1967). Some effects of context on voice onset time in English stops. *Language and Speech, 10*, 1-28.

Morris, R. J. & Brown, W. S. (1994). Age-related differences in speech variability among women. *Journal of Communication Disorders, 27*, 49-64.

Petrosino, L., Colcord, R. D., Kurcz, K. B. & Yonker, R. J. (1993). Voice onset time of velar stop productions in aged speakers. *Perceptual and Motor Skills, 76*, 83 – 88.

Pind, J. (1991). The role of F1 in the perception of voice onset time and voice offset time. *Journal of the Acoustic Society of America, 106*, 434-437.

Ryalls, J., Zipprer, A. & Baldauff, P. (1997). A preliminary investigation of the effects of gender and race on voice onset time. *Journal of Speech, Language and Hearing Research, 40*, 642-645.

Stevens, K. N. & Klatt, D. H. (1974). Role of formant transitions in the voiced-voiceless distinction for stops. *Journal of the Acoustical Society of America*, *55*, 653-659.

Swartz, B.L. (1992). Gender differences in voice onset time. *Perceptual and Motor Skills*, *75*, 983-992.

Sweeting, P. M. & Baken, R. J. (1982). Voice onset time in a normal-aged population. *Journal of Speech and Hearing Research*, *25*, 129-134.

Till, J. A. & Stivers, D. K. (1981). Instrumentation and validity for direct-readout voice onset time measurement. *Journal of Communication Disorders*, *14*, 507 – 512.

Walsh, T. (1983). Voice-Onset Time as a clue to the nature of Broca speech errors. *Brain and Language*, *19*, 357-363.

Whalen, D. H., Abramson, A. S., Lisker, L. & Mody, M. (1993). F0 gives voicing information even with unambigious voice onset times. *Journal of the Acoustic Society of America*, *93*, 2152-2159.

Whiteside, S. P. & Irving, C. J. (1988). Speaker sex differences in voice onset time: A study of isolated word production. *Perceptual and Motor Skills*, *86*, 651 – 654.

27

Voice Onset Time Patterns in Bilingual Phonological Development

Mehmet Yavas

Language skills in bilinguals have almost always been appraised in terms of monolingual standards, and research is in large part conducted in terms of the bilingual's individual and separate languages. This is due to the belief that the bilingual has (or should have) two separate and isolable language competencies, and that in each system the bilingual is comparable to a monolingual in that language (Grosjean, 1992). Although normative data from both languages are important, for a truly reliable assessment, data on normal development of the bilingual who may have a unique and specific linguistic configuration is needed. This pilot study examines the development of VOT patterns in Spanish–English bilingual children. Spanish and English differ in their VOT values for stop consonants. English voiceless stops /p, t, k/ at the beginning of a stressed syllable have long lag VOT (aspirated), whereas Spanish voiceless stops have coincident and short lag VOT (unaspirated). The reason for choosing to study VOT patterns is due to the fact that global foreign accent is significantly correlated with VOT production in stop consonants by non-native speakers (Flege, 1992). The question dealt with here is whether participants produce the stops in an authentic manner in the two languages involved or deviate from this by showing "compromise" values of VOT. To date, studies on bilinguals have provided an ambiguous set of findings. Some studies have shown evidence that bilinguals use a single set of compromised phonetic representations in both languages (Caramazza et al., 1973; Flege & Eefting, 1987; Hazan & Boukalia, 1993; Obler, 1982; Raphael et al., 1995; Schmidt & Flege, 1996; Williams, 1977), whereas others have shown evidence of separate representations for each language (Flege, 1991; Mack, 1989; Schmidt & Flege, 1996). The question asked here is an important one, as it pertains to a rather controversial area. If the measurements obtained from the bilinguals do not match those of monolinguals in the two respective languages, it may be argued that intervention is justified simply because this is similar to the situation in second/foreign language learning where remediation is not controversial. Another issue related to this is that if there is the influence of one language over the other, which language is influencing the production of the other language?

VOICELESS STOPS IN ENGLISH AND SPANISH

Although English and Spanish have voiceless stops /p, t, k/ in their inventories, in initial position, stops in the two languages differ in terms of the timing of the beginning of vocal cord vibration. In Spanish voiceless stops, vocal cord vibration begins shortly after the release of the closure (short lag, i.e. unaspirated), while in English voiceless aspirated stops, it begins after a longer time interval (long lag, i.e. aspirated). The lag values, which are the duration of time interval by which the onset of periodic pulsing follows the release, are variable from speaker to speaker within a language but norms have been fairly well established.

Table 1 is from the seminal study by Lisker and Abramson (1964):

TABLE 1
VOT values in English and Spanish voiceless stops.

	English		Spanish	
	Mean VOT (ms)	*VOT range (ms)*	*Mean VOT (ms)*	*VOT range (ms)*
/p/	58	20 - 120	4	0 - 15
/t/	70	30 - 105	9	0 - 15
/k/	80	50 - 135	29	15 - 55

In regard to acquisition patterns, studies show that in English, children predominantly produce short lag stops earlier, but the acquisition of short versus long lag contrast is generally accomplished by age 2 (Macken & Barton, 1979). The same researchers found the early production of short lag stops in Spanish, as in the English data, but the Spanish "lead" (voiced stops) versus "lag" contrast did not develop as early as the English contrast (Macken & Barton, 1980). The early productions of short lag stops may be accounted for because of their easier articulatory gestures in comparison to the other two types ("lead" and "long lag"); voicing lead requires more muscle gestures than those needed for short voicing lag because it requires mechanisms external to the larynx to sustain an adequate transglottal pressure drop during the closure. Also, consonants with long lag require more carefully controlled timing between the oral stop and laryngeal closure.

Combining these with backgrounds as Spanish monolinguals until age 5, we can hypothesize that if there is an influence of one language over the other, Spanish would be more likely to influence English.

PARTICIPANTS

Participants of the study are 10 bilingual 2nd graders (5 male and 5 female), who attended a Miami, FL elementary school in a lower-middle class neighborhood. All children fit the description of consecutive bilingual in that they were monolingual in Spanish until age 5; their English learning began in kindergarten. From then on instruction was all in English. At the time of testing, the children were in the middle of their second grade, thus were in the third year of their schooling. Their home language continues to be Spanish with their relatives, parents, and grandparents. However, frequent use of English and/or code mixing is observed among siblings and among friends. The availability of English and Spanish TV channels also gives children the opportunity to move back and forth between the two languages. Another enhancing factor in their bilingualism is their age – they have not reached a point where shyness or intimidation would hamper their capacity for language acquisition. Finally, one should mention the predominance of Spanish in South Florida; unlike in other parts of the United States (e.g. Texas, Arizona, Southern California), Spanish does not have a secondary status; rather, it enjoys equal footing with English.

PROCEDURE

Participants were asked to repeat 15 sentences (see Appendix). These sentences were of two different types: entirely English (5 sentences; e.g. "Put the picture on the table"), and mixed (10 sentences that are endemic among bilinguals, e.g. "Pon el papel on the table" or "Put the tuna en la caja"). These yielded nine opportunities for English /p, t, k/ (3 opportunities for each) in entirely English sentences. In the mixed sentences, there were three opportunities for each English stop and two opportunities for each Spanish stop. The sentences were given to children orally by a bilingual teacher (VOT values of her productions were checked and found to be within monolingual norms). In dealing with bilinguals, one of the difficulties is putting them into one language mode or another. To establish a particular language set, researchers give instructions in one language or another, or engage the bilingual in conversation in a particular language. The attempt to *activate* one language and *deactivate* the other is not guaranteed, but is thought to be helpful especially if the bilingual is not aware that the experimenter is interested in his/her bilingualism. For this reason, the two different types of data examined here were collected at different times. In preparing the test items, we did not pay special attention to whether they occurred sentence initially or not, as this was claimed to be a non-factor (Lisker & Abramson, 1964). However, we did control the number of syllables, since the literature shows that switching from monosyllabic to disyllabic words makes a significant difference in VOT values (VOT in disyllabics is generally 8% to 10% shorter than in monosyllabics; Klatt, 1975). Our words were chosen from disyllabic vocabulary items with penultimate stress. Also, we chose the test items with /p, t, k/ of English with vowels of different heights, as the literature reveals that VOT is generally 15% longer before high vowels than before low vowels (Klatt, 1975).

Participants' production of entirely monolingual English and mixed sentences with stops of different places of articulation were recorded; VOT values were measured spectrographically by a DSP-Sona-Graph (Kay Elemetrics, Model 5500). VOT intervals from the beginning of the release burst to the onset of voicing were measured; this refers to the interval between the start of the energy "burst" representing the release of an articulatory constriction, and the first of the regularly spaced vertical striations representing the vocal cord vibration. The instant of release is defined as the point where the spectrogram shows an abrupt spectral change representing the transient noise burst. Interjudge and intrajudge reliability were assessed by reexamining randomly selected 30 tokens. Both interjudge and intrajudge agreements within 8 ms were above 92%.

RESULTS AND DISCUSSION

The results of the measurements are shown in Table 2. Looking at the results one observes that S2 is the worst and S7 is the best in terms of hitting the expected values and differentiating the two systems. Although S7 is perfectly within monolingual VOT values for /p, t, k/, the measurements from S2 do not show any indication that she has differentiation between the two systems; the values for English targets are lower than the minimum expected for all three places of articulation, and the values for Spanish are higher for bilabial and alveolar targets. Although S2's VOT seems to be in the range for the Spanish velar target, the fact that the value is so close to what she produced for English /k/, it is not convincing that S2 separated the two systems for this place of articulation either. Next to S7, S3, S4, and S8 are the ones that seem to have successfully separated the two systems with reasonable VOT values, although their English bilabials are at the lower end of the acceptable range, S4's Spanish alveolar is slightly higher than the highest in the non-native Spanish data. S5 and

TABLE 2
VOT values (in milliseconds) for English and Spanish /p, t, k/.

	S1	S2	S3	S4	S5	S6	S7	S8	S9	S10
					/p/					
English	27	18	25	26	20	20	38	25	28	31
Spanish	13	16	12	11	16	13	7	9	14	10
					/t/					
English	29	28	48	57	28	28	59	55	28	29
Spanish	20	22	13	16	25	19	13	12	16	18
					/k/					
English	51	36	66	78	50	60	79	71	78	60
Spanish	35	31	25	29	28	34	25	28	32	50

Note. Average values from the 3 tokens of each English stop and 2 tokens from each Spanish stop.

S6 show a somewhat similar behavior in that their only successful separation of the two systems is at the velar place of articulation. Both participants reveal lower than acceptable VOTs for English alveolar and bilabial.

In addition, S5 has higher than acceptable VOT for the Spanish /p/. The results of S1 and S9 point to the same direction; both participants seem to differentiate bilabial and velar places of articulation, although failing to do so at the alveolar targets in both languages (low VOT for English, high VOT for Spanish /t/). Finally, S10 is the only participant who differentiated in bilabial stops, but failed to do so in the separation of the alveolars and velars. In alveolars his VOT is low for English, and high for Spanish. As for /k/, although his VOT for English is fine (60ms), his Spanish /k/ with 50ms VOT is unusually high.

If we analyze the data in a place by place fashion, we can conclude the following. For bilabials, two participants (S2 and S5) showed failure in both languages; one participant (S6) was unsuccessful only for English. Alveolar place of articulation was the greatest source of problems for several participants; six (S1, S2, S5, S6, S9, S10) failed to make the distinction in the two languages. This was due to their lower than expected VOTs for English and higher than expected VOTs for Spanish. One other (S4) had the problem only for Spanish /t/

by revealing higher VOT than expected. Velars were the most successful targets. Only two subjects (S2 with English, S10 with Spanish) revealed unusual VOTs.

Although the results revealed a great deal of individual variation, the following generalizations can be derived from the study:

1. There was no effect of gender with the exception of English /k/. Males (S6-S10) had longer lag VOTs (all longer than 60 ms, 3/5 over 70 ms). Females (S1-S5): only 2 of 5 age 60 (one age over 70). This is not entirely unheard of. Swartz (1992) found a significant effect of gender in VOT productions of alveolar stops in monolingual speakers of English.

2. /i/ and /u/ (high vowels) resulted in (an average of 10% to 12%) longer lag than did nonhigh vowels for preceding stops, regardless of place of articulation. This conclusion was valid for 7 out of 10 participants. This is consistent with the conclusions of Klatt, 1975; Weismer, 1979; Flege, 1991; and Thornburg and Ryalls 1998.

3. As expected, overall longer lag was found when the place of articulation moved from bilabial to alveolar to velar. This is also in accordance with Lisker and Abramson, 1964; Zlatin, 1974; and Volaitis and Miller, 1992.

4. Velars were produced more accurately than the other places of articulation. However, one participant (S10) revealed greater VOT distinction between the two languages in bilabials; this was contrary to expectations.

5. Differences in the VOT for English stops between monolingual and mixed sentences were never greater than 10 milliseconds in all participants. Because of this, and because of the small sample, no statistical tests were performed.

Earlier we said that the expectations were such that, if there is influence of one language over the other, the expected direction would be from Spanish to English. This was due to the fact that subjects spoke only Spanish until age 5, and that the short lag stops /p, t, k/ (the ones in Spanish) are articulatorily less complex than the long lag stops that are found in English. The results do not confirm such a tendency. The bilabials of S6 and velars of S2 may be used as evidence for Spanish influencing English in bringing down the VOTs of the English productions. The opposite can be said for the alveolar productions of S4 and velar productions of S10 where we can claim the high VOTs for Spanish targets were due to English influence. Beyond these, the examples of unsuccessful productions and thus insufficient (monolingual-like) separations between the two phonological systems (bilabials of S2 and S5, alveolars of S1, S2, S5, S6, S9, and S10) all point to a direction of mutual influence of the two languages on each other. It is interesting to note that in all cases in which the productions were not within the monolinguals' standards in either language, the VOT values were never reversed from the expected direction. That is, although the English VOTs were lower than expected and the Spanish VOTs were higher than expected, the VOTs were always higher in the English productions than the Spanish. This supports the view that although a bilingual speaker does not have the same phonetic production as a monolingual, he or she still makes a distinction between the two languages.

We conclude that this pilot project supports the heterogeneity of bilinguals. While some in that group would reveal similar, or almost identical, linguistic configuration to monolinguals, several others might have unique, specific linguistic patterns. What remains observable, however, is the systematic behavior of treating the systems differently, although this may not be revealed phonetically in an identical way by monolinguals of English and Spanish.

APPENDIX

English sentences

1. Put the *picture* on the *table.*
2. Put the *carrot* near the *package.*
3. Put the *ticket* in the *pocket.*
4. Put the *tuna* in the *cooler.*
5. Put the *kettle* on the *table.*

Mixed sentences

1. Put the *package* en el *carro.*
2. Pon el *papel* on the *table.*
3. Put the *kettle* en la *tabla.*
4. Pon el *queso* in the *cooler.*
5. Put the *cooler* en el *carro.*
6. Put the *tuna* en la *caja.*
7. Put the *paper* en el *taxi.*
8. Put the *ticket* en la *caja.*
9. Pon el *pato* near the *carrot.*
10. Put the *picture* en el *taxi.*

REFERENCES

Caramazza, A., Yeni-Komshian, G. H., Zurif, E. B., & Carbone, E. (1973). The acquisition of a new phonological contrast: The case of stop consonants in French and English bilinguals. *Journal of the Acoustical Society of America, 54,* 421-428.

Flege, J. E. (1992). Speech learning in a second language. In C. A. Ferguson, L. Menn & C. Stoel-Gammon (Eds.) *Phonological development: Models, research, implications* (pp. 565-603). Timonium, MD: York Press.

Flege, J. E. (1991). Age of learning affects the authenticity of voice onset time in stop consonants produced in a second language. *Journal of the Acoustical Society of America, 89*, 395-411.

Flege, J. E., & Eefting, W. (1987). Production and perception of stops by native Spanish speakers. *Journal of Phonetics, 15*, 67-83.

Grosjean, F. (1992). Another view of bilingualism. In R. J. Harris (Ed.) *Cognitive processing in bilinguals* (pp. 51-62). Elsevier.

Hazan, V. L., & Boulakia, G. (1993). Perception and production of a voicing contrast by French-English bilinguals. *Language and Speech, 36*, 17-38.

Klatt, D. (1975). VOT, frication, and aspiration in word-initial consonant clusters. In R. J. Baken & R. G. Daniloff (Eds.) *Readings in the clinical spectrography of speech.* San Diego, CA: Singular Publishing Group.

Lisker, L., & Abramson, A. (1964). A cross-language study of voicing in initial stops: Acoustical measurements. In R. J. Baken & R. G. Daniloff (Eds.) *Readings in the clinical spectrography of speech.* San Diego, CA: Singular Publishing Group.

Mack, M. (1989). Consonant and vowel perception and production: Early English-French bilingual and English monolinguals. *Perception and Psychophysics, 46*, 187-200.

Macken, M., & Barton, D. (1980). The acquisition of voicing contrast in Spanish: A phonological study of word-initial stop consonants. *Journal of Child Language, 7*, 433-458.

Macken, M., & Barton, D. (1979). The acquisition of voicing contrast in English: A study of voice onset time in word-initial stop consonants. *Journal of Child Language, 7*, 41-74.

Obler, L. K. (1982). The parsimonious bilingual. In L. K. Obler & L. Menn (Eds.) *Exceptional language and linguistics* (pp. 339-346). New York: Academic Press.

Raphael, L. J., Tobin, Y., Faber, A., Most, T., Kollia, H. B., & Millstein, D. (1995). Intermediate values of voice onset time. In R. Bell-Berti (Ed.) *Producing speech: Contemporary issues* (pp. 117-128). New York: American Institute for Physics Press.

Volaitis, L. E., & Miller, J. L. (1992). Phonetic prototypes: influence of place of articulation and speaking rate on the internal structure of voicing categories, *Journal of the Acoustical Society of America, 92*, 723-735.

Schmidt, A. M., & Flege, J. E. (1996). Speaking rate effects on stops produced by Spanish/English bilinguals. *Phonetica, 53*, 162-179.

Swartz, B. L. (1992). Gender differences in voice onset time. *Perceptual and Motor Skills, 75*, 983-992.

Thornburg, D., & Ryalls, J. H. (1998). Voice onset time in Spanish-English bilinguals: Early versus late learners of English. *Journal of Communication Disorders, 31*, 215-229.

Weismer, G. (1979). Sensitivity of VOT measures to certain segmental features in speech production. *Journal of Phonetics, 7*, 197-204.

Williams, L. (1977). The perception of stop consonant voicing by Spanish-English bilinguals. *Perception and Psychophysics, 21*, 289-297.

Zlatin, M. A. (1974). Voicing contrast: Perceptual and productive VOT characteristics of adults. *Journal of the Acoustical Society of America, 56*, 981-994.

28

Quantitative Aspects of Glossectomy Speech Production

Tim Bressmann, Tara Whitehill, Robert Sader,
Nabil Samman and Phil Hoole

Intelligible speech following the partial or total loss of the tongue has historically been perceived as a divine miracle and has inspired theological debate (Twisleton, 1873). Today, although glossectomy speech is no longer seen as a heavenly wonder, the functional consequences of ablative tongue surgery are still a mystery.

A high percentage of tumors of the tongue can be treated successfully by surgical resection and (if necessary) by adjuvant radiation therapy. However, while surgical therapy may save a patient's life, it can also affect basic functions such as eating, swallowing, speech, and social encounters. The location and the extent of a tumor resection are obviously directly related to the location and the size of the tumor. The affected tissue must be resected with a safety margin of approximately one centimeter in order to reduce the risk of a reoccurence. Although there are well-established medical protocols regarding the extent of the resection, there are no surgical guidelines as to how the defect should be closed or reconstructed. A defect can be closed locally by suturing the surrounding tongue tissue, it can be left open to heal, or it can be closed with a local or free flap. Each method may have advantages and disadvantages regarding the functional results, but to date, surgeons do not have empirical criteria or controlled phonetic outcome measures to guide their decisions. Another current shortcoming is a lack of appropriate documentation. Given the complex anatomical structure of the tongue, it is quite difficult for anyone other than the surgeon to infer, from surgical notes, exactly what part of the tongue has been affected during an operation and how the reconstruction was performed. Consequently, there is much variation in patients regarding the functional outcomes for speech and swallowing. We may find near-normal speech in a patient with very extensive surgery, and largely unintelligible speech in another patient who had more limited surgery.

A study by Massengill, Maxwell, and Pickrell (1970) was one of the first systematic approaches to explore the speech characteristics of the glossectomee. A number of studies since have investigated glossectomy speech, although many studies relied on small patient numbers (Greven, Meijer & Tiwari, 1994) or were merely anecdotal in nature (Dworkin, 1982). Generally, it is assumed that the sheer amount of tissue removed may be a strong indicator of the resulting problems (Rentschler & Mann, 1980). The site of the resection is another crucial factor (Logemann et al., 1993). In contrast, a recent retrospective survey of 60 patients identified the technique of reconstruction as the single most important factor, followed by the extent of the defect (Konstantinovic & Dimic, 1998). Lesion localization did not have a significant impact, according to the results from their study.

A number of studies have explored the benefits of different techniques of reconstruction (e.g. Michiwaki, Schmelzeisen, Hacki & Michi, 1992; Jacobson, Franssen, Fliss, Birt & Gilbert, 1995) or examined rehabilitation by speech therapy (Skelly, 1973) or prosthodontic rehabilitation (Leonard & Gillis, 1990). The negative influence of radiation therapy on saliva production and swallowing has also been examined (Pauloski, Rademaker, Logemann & Colangelo, 1998). Of particular interest is the dynamic analysis of tongue movements in order to determine the postoperative range of tongue mobility. Imai and Michi (1992) demonstrated how this could be done using electropalatography, whereas Schliephake, Schmelzeisen, Schonweiler, Schneller, and Altenbernd (1998) favored dynamic imaging of sagittal movement using ultrasound. Heller, Levy, and Sciubba (1991) demonstrated that tongue mobility can be assessed indirectly by measuring diadochokinetic rate.

The postoperative articulation behaviour of glossectomees has also been investigated using acoustic analysis of vowel sounds (Georgian, Logemann & Fisher, 1982; Morrish, 1984). In the nine patients who underwent reconstruction with pectoralis major myocutaneous flaps, Knuuttila, Pukander, Maatta, Pakarinem, and Vilkman (1999) observed a drop of the first vowel formant of /a/ and a raising of the second vowel formant of /i/. They were able to demonstrate a statistical relationship between acoustic changes and the extent of the reconstruction. Similarily, the 14 patients studied by Perrier, Savariaux, Lebeau, and Magana (1999) demonstrated a reduced ability to achieve extreme articulatory positions during the production of sustained vowels and in coordinating their articulatory movements in consonant-to-vowel transition phases.

METHOD

The aim of this study was two-fold:
(1) To devise and test a graphic mapping protocol for the accurate documentation of lingual resection and reconstruction.
(2) To analyze the pre- and postoperative speech performance of glossectomy patients with regard to simple quantitative aspects of speech, such as speech tempo, and a number of articulatory distortions. These measures may be used as indicators of the individual speech ability in relation to the postoperative defect as documented by the surgical mapping procedure.

Operation Mapping Procedure

Mackenzie-Beck et al. (1998) developed a graphic surgical mapping protocol. The protocol requires the surgeon to sketch the exact location and extent of the lingual defect during or immediately after an operation. Because the drawings from the protocol represent the same anatomical structures in the sagittal, frontal and transversal plane, three-dimensional information can be obtained from the protocol.

The mapping procedure was modified for the purposes of this study. The same four anatomical drawings from the Mackenzie-Beck et al. (1998) study were used representing the structures in the oral cavity and the pharynx. Surgeons were asked to draw the defect on one sheet and the technique of reconstruction on a seperate sheet so that information about the reconstruction technique could be recovered.

Next, a scoring system was developed to evaluate the protocols. The scoring system was based on a simplified version of the model of functional tongue segments proposed by Stone (1990) and Stone and Lundberg (1996). Based on data from x-ray microbeam and ultrasound, Stone (1990) suggested that the tongue can be segmented into four functional segments along the sagittal plane (apical, middle, dorsal and posterior), and two median and four lateral functional segments along the frontal plane that moved independently from each other. The evaluation of the mapping protocol was done using acetate overlays with the segmentation lines (see Fig. 1). A simple coding system was used to document how a given defect in one of the segments had been reconstructed by the surgeon. Unaffected segments were coded with 0, defects which had been closed locally were coded with -1 and defects which had been closed using a flap were coded with 1. A total score of the overall number of affected segments was also calculated.

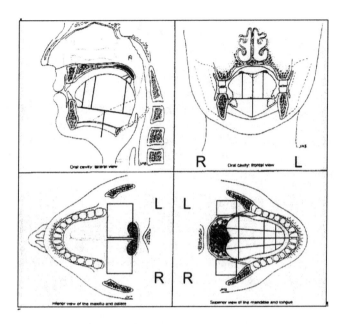

FIG. 1 The surgical mapping protocol (Mackenzie-Beck et al. 1998) with a superimposed segmentation grid based on Stone & Lundberg (1996).

Patients

Pre- and postoperative speech performance was evaluated in 10 patients (8 males and 2 females) with carcinomas of the tongue and adjacent oral structures. The mean age was 51 years (median 56 years, SD 8.83 years). Four patients had tumors confined to the anterior portions of the tongue and/or floor of the mouth, and the tumor was in a posterior location in two cases. In four patients, the side of the tongue was affected. Table 1 summarizes the tumor locations of individual patients and their surgery mapping scores.

Recording Procedure

For this study, we used the Modular Diagnostic System (MODIAS) developed by Merk and Ziegler (1999). The MODIAS has been programmed to run in the MATLAB environment on a PC. Recordings were made with a AKG 420 C headset condensator microphone amplified with a Behringer Ultragain 2000 linedriver. The mouth-to-microphone distance was adjusted to be within a distance of 5 to 10 cm for all patients. Analog to digital signal conversion, at a rate of 22.05 kHz with a resolution of 16 bits, was achieved with a generic

TABLE 1
Description of the patient group.

Patient #	Age	Sex	Tumor location	Affected segments with local closure	Affected segments with flap closure	Overall number of affected segments
1	60	M	left lateral tongue	-11	0	11
2	57	M	anterior floor of mouth, bilateral	-6	0	6
3	56	M	right lateral tongue	-2	0	2
4	46	M	left posterior tongue	-2	1	3
5	40	M	right lateral tongue	-5	0	5
6	56	F	left lateral tongue	-4	6	10
7	59	F	anterior floor of the mouth, left	-3	8	11
8	36	M	right posterior tongue	-7	0	7
9	57	M	anterior floor of the mouth, left	-6	0	6
10	43	M	anterior floor of the mouth, bilateral	-10	0	10

SoundBlaster Vibra 16 soundboard. The recordings were made in a quiet environment.

Two of the MODIAS modules were used in this study. In the module "Rapid Syllable Repetition", the patients repeated six sequences of syllables as fast as possible for a duration of four to five seconds. Four of these sequences are simple patterns (/bababa.../, /dadada.../, /gagaga.../, /nanana.../) and two are alternating patterns (/bada.../, /dana.../). The MODIAS module "Sentence Repetition" has three ensembles of eight sentences, each with different target words (two-syllabic without consonant clusters, two-syllabic with consonant clusters, and three-syllabic). The carrier sentence always has the form "Ute kann die TARGET bekommen" (Ute can get the TARGET). In this study, only the ensemble of eight two-syllable words with consonant clusters (Pflanze, Katze, Kränze, etc.) was used.

Data Processing and Analysis

In both MODIAS modules, energy models of the syllable repetitions or sentences are calculated and syllable centers and boundaries are automatically identified. Each model was checked for accuracy of segmentation, and if necessary, corrections were made manually. During the segmentation, each sentence recording was played back at least two times, one time in normal play back mode and one time in syllable-by-syllable mode. If articulatory distortions were present, the process was repeated until the affected segment had been identified accurately and a marker was placed into the energy model.

Outcome Measures

The speech rate in syllables per second was calculated from the syllable repetitions and sentences as an indicator of the post-operative efficiency of articulation. For the sentences, the total time needed to repeat the sentence and the mean syllable duration were also calculated. Additionally, the number of articulatory distortions in the sentences was counted for the separate syllables.

RESULTS

Rapid Syllable Repetition Rate

All rapid syllable repetition tasks were analyzed separately for pre- and postoperative performance. An overview of the results is given in Table 2. The data were analyzed using a simple multifactor design ANOVA with the mean hz-rate as the dependent factor, the time of the recording (presurgical versus post-surgical) as the grouping factor and the syllable repetition subset as

TABLE 2
Results for the rapid syllable repetition rates before and after the operation.

	pre-OP		post-OP		
Item	mean hz-rate	SD	mean hz-rate	SD	t-test
baba	5.98	1.00	5.86	0.78	n.s.
dada	6.47	0.84	5.73	0.99	n.s. ($p \leq 0.09$)
gaga	5.91	1.15	5.20	1.12	n.s.
bada	7.00	1.18	6.22	0.88	n.s.
nana	6.30	1.24	5.71	1.09	n.s.
dana	6.64	0.74	5.73	0.67	*($p \leq 0.02$)
Total	6.38	1.06	5.74	0.95	*($p \leq 0.002$)

Note. Non-significant results for the independent sample t-tests are indicated by 'n.s.'.

the co-variate. There was a significant main effect for the factor "time of the recording" (pre- vs. post-operative) ($p = 0.002$). However, no significant main effect was obtained for the co-variate itmes. To identify possible sources of the significant differences more clearly, t-tests (independent samples) were calculated for the six different syllable repetition subsets. Significant results could only be found for the item /dana/ ($p \le 0.02$), all other comparisons were not significant. A tendency toward significant differences was found for the item /dada/ ($p \le 0.09$).

To correlate the functional outcomes to the results from the surgical mapping, a Spearman rank-order correlation coefficient was computed. A weak negative correlation was found between the total number of affected functional segments and the syllable repetition rate ($r \le 0.3618$, $p \le 0.005$). A t-test revealed that the patients with local defect closure had significantly faster syllable repetition rates than the patients with flaps ($p \le 0.001$).

Speech Tempo for Sentence Repetition

The sentence repetition tasks were collapsed for each patient in order to facilitate data analysis. Table 3 gives a summary of the results. Single factor ANOVAs showed the differences between the subjects' pre- and postoperative performances were highly significant ($F \le 0.001$) in all cases. Postoperatively, the mean rate of syllables per second was significantly lower, whereas the mean syllable duration and the mean total time increased significantly. To correlate the functional outcomes to the results from the surgical mapping, a Spearman rank-order correlation coefficient was computed. A weak negative correlation was found between the mean number of syllables per second and the total number of affected segments ($r \le -0.2299$, $p \le 0.001$). A t-test revealed that the patients with local defect closure had a significantly higher rate of syllables per second than the patients with flaps ($p \le 0.001$).

TABLE 3

Results for the sentence repetition task before and after the operation.

	pre-OP		post-OP		
Item	*mean*	*SD*	*mean*	*SD*	*ANOVA*
mean syllable duration in ms	202.02	32.48	234.87	49.29	$F \le 0.001$
total time in ms	1822.2	296.0	2122.6	444.5	$F \le 0.001$
mean Hz rate	5.05	0.73	4.41	0.82	$F \le 0.001$

Distribution of Articulatory Distortions

Articulatory distortions in the eight sentences were marked by the first author during the segmentation process. Before the operation, no articulatory distortions were noted, and all 720 segmented syllables were judged to be correct. Following the partial glossectomy operation, a total of 107 (14.9%) segmented syllables were judged to be distorted. All distortions were presumed to result from articulatory undershoot due to reduced tongue motility after the glossectomy surgery.

The majority (66% or 61.7%) of the ariculatory errors were made in two positions: on the third syllable (the /k/ in "kann") in 33 instances and on the sixth sylable (carrying the medial alveolar consonant cluster of the target word) in another 33 instances.

Patients whose tongue defects had been reconstructed by means of a flap showed a lower mean number of articulatory errors (mean 1.52 errors, SD = 1.2) than the patients reconstructed locally. Statistical comparison with the Mann-Whitney U-test showed that this difference was significant ($p \leq 0.001$).

A Spearman rank order correlation coefficient was calculated to establish the relation between the surgical mapping and the number of articulatory errors. There was only a very weak correlation of the number of articulatory errors and the overall extent of the defect ($r \leq 0.146$, $p \leq 0.2$). The Mann-Whitney U-test revealed that the patients with local defect closure made significantly more articulatory errors than the patients with flaps ($p \leq 0.001$).

DISCUSSION

Tentative as it is, our quantitative mapping and scoring sytem gives some interesting information for the small, heterogeneous patient group studied. We found that the mean speech rate in rapid syllable repetition and sentence repetition was more affected in the patients with flap closure than in those with local defect closure. Alternately, although apparently speaking more slowly, patients with flap reconstruction made significantly less articulatory errors in the sentence repetition task than patients with local defect closure. Given the small patient sample, further studies must confirm this interesting dissociation before any causal explanation can be attempted.

It is also interesting to note that the statistical differences were related more to the type of the defect reconstruction than the defect size. Again, given the limitations of the small patient sample, this may be taken as a confirmation of the results of Konstantinovic and Dimic (1998), who found that the type of reconstruction was more important for functional outcome than the defect size. This hypothesis must be confirmed by findings from larger patient groups.

CONCLUSION

Given the unique anatomical structure of the tongue, it is difficult to classify the exact effects of glossectomy surgery on this organ. A grid system based on a functional segmentation from Stone's (1990) model is certainly reasonably simple and practical. The results from our study show that such a system can be used in a clinical context and that interesting information can be gained from the mapping protocol. Further studies must confirm the findings from this pilot study. Hopefully, future larger scale studies will allow the use of more sophisticated statistical analysis in order to identify the lingual segments whose structural integrity is most critical to speech, and if the segment is affected, which reconstructive technique is best for restoring this integrity. Eventually, this knowledge may lead to an improvement in patient management so optimum functional outcomes can be achieved for every patient.

ACKNOWLEDGMENT

We would like to gratefully acknowledge that this project was funded by a Germany-Hong Kong Joint Research Grant from the German Academic Research Service (Deutscher Akademischer Auslandsdienst, DAAD) and the Hong Kong Research Grants Council (RGC). Previous collaboration had been funded by a Hochschulsonderprogramm 3 stipend by the DAAD to the first author.

REFERENCES

Dworkin, J. P. (1982). Glossectomy: A case report. *Archives of Physical Medicine and Rehabilitation, 63,* 182-183.

Georgian, D. A., Logemann, J. A., & Fisher, H. B. (1982). Compensatory articulation patterns of a surgically treated oral cancer patient. *Journal of Speech and Hearing Disorders, 47,* 154-159.

Greven, A. J., Meijer, M. F., & Tiwari, R. M. (1994). Articulation after total glossectomy: a clinical study of speech in six patients. *European Journal of Disorders of Communication, 29,* 85-93.

Heller, K. S., Levy, J., & Sciubba, J. J. (1991). Speech patterns following partial glossectomy for small tumors of the tongue. *Head and Neck, 13,* 340-343.

Imai, S., & Michi, K. (1992). Articulatory function after resection of the tongue and floor of the mouth: palatometric and perceptual evaluation. *Journal of Speech and Hearing Research, 35,* 68-78.

Jacobson, M. C., Franssen, E., Fliss, D. M., Birt, B. D., & Gilbert R. W. (1995). Free forearm flap in oral reconstruction: Functional outcome. *Archives of Otolaryngology, Head and Neck Surgery, 121,* 959-964.

Knuuttila, H., Pukander, J., Maatta, T., Pakarinen, L., & Vilkman, E. (1999). Speech articulation after subtotal glossectomy and reconstruction with a myocutaneous flap. *Acta Otolaryngologica, 119,* 621-626.

Konstantinovic, V. S., & Dimic, N. D. (1998). Articulatory function and tongue mobility after surgery followed by radiotherapy for tongue and floor of the mouth cancer patients. *British Journal of Plastic Surgery, 51,* 589-593.

Leonard, R. J., & Gillis, R. (1990). Differential effects of speech prostheses in glossectomized patients. *Journal of Prosthetic Dentistry, 64,* 701-708.

Logemann, J. A., Pauloski, B. R., Rademaker, A. W., McConnel, F. M., Heiser, M. A., Cardinale, S., Shedd, D., Stein, D., Beery, Q., Johnson, J., & Baker, T. (1993). Speech and swallow function after tonsil/base of tongue resection with primary closure. *Journal of Speech and Hearing Research, 36,* 918-926.

Mackenzie-Beck, J., Wrench, A., Jackson, M., Soutar, D., Robertson, A., Laver, J. (1998). Surgical mapping and phonetic analysis in intra-oral cancer. In W. Ziegler & K. Deger (Eds), *Clinical phonetics and linguistics* (pp. 481-492). London: Whurr.

Massengill, R. Jr, Maxwell, S., & Pickrell, K. (1970). An analysis of articulation following partial and total glossectomy. *Journal of Speech and Hearing Disorders, 35,* 170-173.

Merk, M., & Ziegler, W. (1999). MODIAS: A PC-based system for routine analysis of neurogenic speech disorders. In B. Maassen & P. Groenen (Eds), *Pathologies of speech and language* (pp. 315-321). London: Whurr.

Michiwaki, Y., Schmelzeisen, R., Hacki, T., & Michi, K. (1992). Articulatory function in glossectomized patients with immediate reconstruction using a free jejunum flap. *Journal of Craniomaxillofacial Surgery, 20,* 203-210.

Morrish, L. (1984). Compensatory vowel articulation of the glossectomee: Acoustic and videofluoroscopic evidence. *British Journal of Disorders of Communication, 19,* 125-134.

Pauloski, B. R., Rademaker, A. W., Logemann, J. A., & Colangelo, L. A. (1998). Speech and swallowing in irradiated and nonirradiated postsurgical oral cancer patients. *Otolaryngology - Head and Neck Surgery, 118,* 616-624.

Perrier, P., Savariaux, C., Lebeau, J., & Magana, G. (1999). Speech production after tongue surgery and tongue reconstruction. *Proceedings of the XIVth International Congress of Phonetic Sciences* (pp. 1805-1808). San Francisco.

Rentschler, G. J., & Mann, M. B. (1980). The effects of glossectomy on intelligibility of speech and oral perceptual discrimination. *Journal of Oral Surgery, 38,* 348-354.

Schliephake, H., Schmelzeisen, R., Schonweiler, R., Schneller, T., & Altenbernd, C. (1998). Speech, deglutition and life quality after intraoral tumour resection. A prospective study. *International Journal of Oral and Maxillofacial Surgery, 27,* 99-105.

Skelly, M. (1973). *Glossectomee speech rehabilitation.* Springfield, IL: Thomas.

Stone, M. (1990). A three-dimensional model of tongue movement based on ultrasound and x-ray microbeam data. *Journal of the Acoustical Society of America, 87,* 2207-2217.

Stone, M., & Lundberg, A. (1996). Three-dimensional tongue surface shapes of English consonants and vowels. *Journal of the Acoustical Society of America, 99,* 3728-3737.

Twisleton, E. (1873). *The tongue: Not essential to speech; with illustrations of the power of speech in the African confessors.* London: Murray.

29

Acceptability and Intelligibility of Moderately Dysarthric Speech by Four Types of Listeners

Paul A. Dagenais and Amy F. Wilson

When communication breakdowns occur, there may be problems of competency that involve the speaker, the listener or both. Traditionally, when the speaker has a motor speech disorder, it is the speaker who is considered the sole source of the communication difficulty. This is the premise behind the development of assessment procedures such as the word and sentence intelligibility measures of the Assessment of Intelligibility of Dysarthric Speech (AIDS; Yorkston & Beukelman, 1981) and phonetic intelligibility testing (Kent, Weismer, Kent, & Rosenbek, 1989). Changes in impaired speaker performance usually are cited as the major influence in communicative success. For example, reducing a speaker's rate has been reported as being the single most powerful variable for increasing the intelligibility of dysarthric speech (Yorkston, Dowden, & Beukelman, 1992). Duffy (1995) stated that reducing speech rate improves speaker intelligibility by allowing more time for articulatory precision (a full range of motion) and coordination as well as improved linguistic phrasing. However, the communicative success of an interaction may not depend just on the speaker, but also on the listener. Different listening strategies may be needed depending on a speaker's abilities (Lindblom, 1990; Weismer & Martin, 1992).

As summarized by Liss, Spitzer, Caviness, Adler and Edwards (1998), listeners may modify their perceptual strategies when faced with the impoverished acoustic signals produced by dysarthric speakers. Liss et al. (1998) reported that listeners made errors in word boundary judgments of hypokinetic speech because the speakers did not produce the stress patterns that the listeners anticipated. When listeners are required to shift their strategies in order to understand impaired speech, the shift may be reflected in the perceived ease with which impaired speech is understood. This could result in negative responses to the impaired speaker. For example, Most, Weisel and Avivit (1996) found that when inexperienced listeners were presented with speech by children with hearing impairments, the children's cognitive competence and personalities were rated poorly. This contrasted sharply with experienced listeners who showed no difference in the ratings of children with and without hearing loss.

This study is a follow up to earlier work (Dagenais, Garcia, & Watts, 1998; Dagenais, Watts, Turnage, & Kennedy, 1999) in an investigation of listener characteristics on the intelligibility and acceptability of impaired speech. The term acceptability was used as a best-fit criterion when comparing its definition to bizarreness, naturalness, or normalcy as summarized by Southwood and Weismer (1993). For acceptability, the listeners were not required to process the content in an utterance but to rate its presentation without defining the rationale for their ratings. They were specifically asked, "How would you rate this person's speaking skills?" Thus, it was hoped that a contrast could be obtained between an objective measure of speech abilities (intelligibility) and a subjective measure (acceptability).

In the previous studies, young adults, older adults, and experienced speech–language pathologists listened to sentences spoken by normal older adults and older adults with either mild or moderate dysarthria. When comparing intelligibility and acceptability results for speakers with mild dysarthria, acceptability ratings were similar for all groups of listeners. Although the female speaker with dysarthria was rated as being more intelligible than the unimpaired male speaker, her acceptability was much lower than his. The speech–language pathologists provided higher intelligibility scores, but appeared equally critical of speaker quality. As there appeared to be a ceiling effect due to the mildness of the speech deficits, further studies were warranted using speakers with moderate speech impairments. The current study presents the results of using four types of listeners (young normal, older normal, listeners with dysarthria, and speech–language pathologists) to rate four speakers for intelligibility and acceptability of spoken sentences. Specifically, the current study added a group of listeners with dysarthric speech who did not have disabilities such as aphasia that would exclude them from being viable listeners. Unfortunately, the listeners with dysarthria in this study were able to complete only the subjective ratings of acceptability due to writing difficulties. However, it was reasoned that using this group might result in new insight into the possibility of a perceptual component which impacts the speech capabilities of those with dysarthria. It was suggested that if the listeners with dysarthria were to provide different acceptability scores (higher or lower), then it might suggest that speakers with dysarthria produce poor quality speech because it requires less effort, or they cannot detect differences between good or bad speech. Should a perceptual component be revealed by studies such as this, there could be repercussions on the efficacy of dysarthria therapy.

METHOD

Participants

Four speakers participated in the study: a woman (age 72) with dysarthria as a result of multiple brainstem strokes, a man (age 74) with dysarthria as a result of a right CVA, and age- and gender-matched controls (female aged 71 and male aged 76) with no neurologic deficits. All speakers were raised in the Southeastern region of the United States. The woman with dysarthria presented with monopitch, slow rate, slight hypernasality, imprecise articulation, and a coarse voice. The man with dysarthria used an excessive rate and exhibited hypernasality and imprecise articulation. Three experienced listeners provided intelligibility ratings for each speaker using the sentence portion of the Assessment of Intelligibility of Dysarthric Speech (AIDS; Yorkston & Beukelman, 1981). Averaged ratings are reported in Table 1.

The listeners consisted of four groups, 10 normal young adults, age range 19 to 30 years, 10 normal older adults, age range 61 to 71 years, 10 speech-language pathologists (SLPs) with a minimum of 2 years experience working with patients who have dysarthria, and 10 older adults with dysarthria, aged 63 to 87. The group of listeners with dysarthria consisted of seven people who had had left hemisphere strokes, two with right hemisphere strokes and one with amyotrophic lateral sclerosis (ALS). These listeners exhibited normal (greater than 90%) ability to follow auditory comprehension and verbal expression tasks. All listeners in all groups passed a hearing screening test for 1000, 2000 and 4000 Hz at 25 dB HL.

TABLE 1

Intelligibility rating as percent correct for all speakers determined with the sentences portion of the AIDS. Results were averaged across three experienced listeners.

Participant	Percent Correct
Normal female	100
Normal male	100
Female with dysarthria	67
Male with dysarthria	56

Procedures

Speakers were audiorecorded reading sentences from the AIDS. Digital files were created for each sentence utilizing Computer Speech Laboratory (CSL, Kay Elemetrics Corp.) using a sampling rate of 20 kHz. One sentence was randomly selected from word lengths 6 through 12, one per speaker resulting in 28 items (7 sentences × 4 speakers). Two randomly ordered audio master tapes were created which included 7 repeated items for reliability (total 35 items). Each item was recorded twice with a 3-second interstimulus interval between items and a 2-second interstimulus interval between repetitions. Test items were presented to listeners with headphones adjusted for most comfortable listening level. The young normal, older normal and SLP groups had two tasks:

1. After they heard a stimulus the first time, they rated the speaker's speaking skills using a 9-point equal-interval scale from terrible through excellent. They were specifically asked "How would you rate this person's speaking skills?"
2. After they heard the sentence the second time, listeners orthographically transcribed the sentence they heard. Written sentences were scored for percent correctly identified words.

The listeners with dysarthria did not complete the intelligibility component due to writing difficulties. They listened to the sentences twice then rated them for acceptability.

Reliability

Reliability measures were undertaken by having all listeners rescore 7 of the 28 items presented. Thus, the young adults, older adults and the SLPs provided reliability data for intelligibility and acceptability ratings while the older adults with dysarthria provided reliability data for the acceptability measures only. Reliability was determined by exact word agreement for intelligibility or exact agreement of acceptability rating. Results are presented in Table 2. As can be seen in the table, intelligibility ratings were higher than acceptability, probably due to the methods for obtaining scores (objective vs. subjective). It should be noted however, that the speakers with dysarthria had a noticeably lower score than the other groups for acceptability.

TABLE 2

Reliability scores reported as percent agreement for intelligibility and acceptability rating for four types of listeners.

Group	Intelligibility	Acceptability
Young Adults	80.9	71.4
Older Adults	71.4	61.9
Speech–Language Pathologists	80.9	66.6
Speakers with dysarthria	- -	45.0

RESULTS

Intelligibility scores for the four speakers across the three listener groups are reported in Table 3 and Fig. 1. The intelligibility scores for the two normal speakers showed near ceiling effects with the older adult listeners having slightly lower scores. For the two speakers with dysarthria, the scores provided by the SLPs were the highest followed by the young normal group then the older normal group.

TABLE 3
Intelligibility ratings (Mean, SD) for four speakers by three groups of listeners.

Rating Groups	Normal Female	Normal Male	Female With Dysarthria	Male With Dysarthria
Young adults	98.2 (1.9)	98.7 (1.9)	57.3 (11.8)	24.0 (7.6)
Older adults	92.8 (5.6)	93.7 (1.1)	37.3 (12.3)	14.3 (8.9)
Speech–Language Pathologists (SLPs)	96.4 (2.7)	98.9 (2.5)	73.2 (5.6)	32.7 (8.8)

A two-way ANOVA (Listener Group × Speaker) indicated significant differences between Listener Groups ($F(2,27)$ = 7.6, $p < 0.01$) and Speakers ($F(3,81)$ 697.7, $p < 0.01$). There was also a significant interaction ($F(3,81)$ 3.7, $p < 0.01$). Subsequent one-way ANOVAs for each Group revealed that normal speakers performed similarly and had significantly higher scores than the woman with dysarthria, who had significantly better scores than the man with dysarthria ($p < 0.01$). Subsequent one-way ANOVAs for each Speaker revealed no differences between listener groups for normal speakers ($p > 0.05$). For the speakers with dysarthria, the SLPs obtained significantly higher scores ($p < 0.01$) than the other two groups who did not differ from one another.

Acceptability scores are reported in Table 4 and Fig. 2. Acceptability ratings broadly corresponded with the intelligibility ratings. The SLPs and listeners with dysarthria rated the normal speakers more poorly than did the other two listener groups. All listener groups rated the speakers with dysarthria similarly. These speakers received notably lower ratings than the normal speakers, with the woman with dysarthria receiving slightly higher scores than the man with dysarthria.

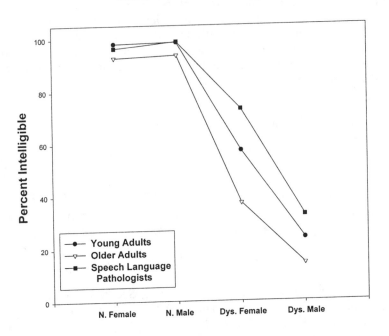

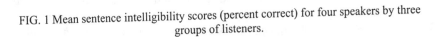

FIG. 1 Mean sentence intelligibility scores (percent correct) for four speakers by three groups of listeners.

One-way ANOVAs for each Speaker revealed that for the normal female and male speakers, the young and older normal listeners rated these speakers similarly and with significantly higher ratings ($p < 0.05$) than the SLPs and the dysarthric listeners who did not differ. There were no differences for the impaired speakers.

A correlational analysis was used to assess for possible relationships between Intelligibility and Acceptability for the young, older and SLP groups. Positive, significant correlations were found (range $r = 0.82$ to 0.93; $p < 0.01$).

TABLE 4
Acceptability ratings, scale 1–9 (SD) for four speakers by four groups of listeners.

Rating Groups	Normal Female	Normal Male	Female with Dysarthria	Male with Dysarthria
Young adults	8.3 (0.6)	8.5 (0.7)	2.8 (0.9)	1.9 (0.4)
Older adults	8.1 (0.8)	8.4 (0.5)	2.9 (0.6)	2.2 (0.6)
Speech–Language Pathologists (SLPs)	7.4 (1.2)	7.3 (1.2)	2.4 (1.1)	1.9 (0.6)
Listeners with Dysarthria	7.3 (0.6)	7.1 (1.0)	2.8 (1.0)	2.3 (0.9)

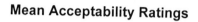

Mean Acceptability Ratings

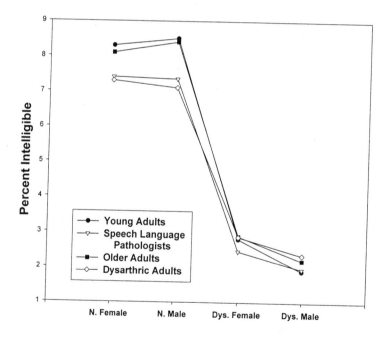

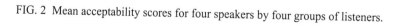

FIG. 2 Mean acceptability scores for four speakers by four groups of listeners.

DISCUSSION

Results from this study indicated that the normal speakers were significantly more intelligible and received significantly higher acceptability ratings than did the speakers with dysarthria. There appeared to be a ceiling effect for the intelligibility ratings of the normal speakers. For the speakers with dysarthria, the SLPs obtained significantly higher intelligibility scores compared to the other two groups. This finding supports earlier findings that the intelligibility ratings of the impaired speakers provided by SLPs were higher than ratings provided by untrained, younger and older adult listeners. As impaired speakers generally associate with older adults, intelligibility scores determined with this older population might be a better determinant of the clinical efficacy of treatment.

All groups rated the acceptability of the speakers with dysarthria similarly. In contrast, the SLPs and the listeners with dysarthria were significantly more critical of the normal speakers who had near-perfect intelligibility, giving these speakers lower acceptability ratings. This is difficult to explain. Listeners were not informed about the medical status of the speakers. The SLPs and the listeners with dysarthria may have presumed that all the speakers were impaired. Thus all the speakers (impaired and unimpaired) were judged to be deserving of less than highly acceptable ratings. These listeners also may have been critical of the speakers due to their perceived age. That is, the vocal qualities (e.g., timbre, rate, prosody) that the normal, older speakers presented were rated as being somewhat unacceptable. Overall, the discrepancies in acceptability ratings by the different listener groups suggested that trained listeners (the SLP group) and the impaired listeners may have different constructs than the untrained listeners as to the limits for acceptable speech. It is also possible that the SLPs and the impaired listener groups had similar constructs with each other. That is, because the SLP group dealt with impaired speakers as part of their caseload, they assumed all speakers were impaired. Similarly, all the impaired listeners had been exposed to therapy, and as such, may have assumed that they were being asked to rate others in similar situations to their own. Additionally, because both groups had been involved in the therapy process, they may have been more critical than the untrained listeners.

The intelligibility scores strongly correlated with the acceptability scores. In contrast, the earlier study with mildly impaired speakers showed no correlation (Dagenais, Garcia & Watts, 1998). This suggested that, as impairment increases, the correspondence between what listeners can understand (objective assessment) and what they prefer to listen to (subjective assessment) becomes stronger. Further work is needed to assess which characteristics of dysarthric speech are most disconcerting to listeners. Factors such as poor vocal quality and limited suprasegmental control (e.g., rate, stress, intonation) may be found to have a negative impact on the speaker who produces segmental information effectively.

Reliability measures showed that the impaired listeners were the least reliable rating acceptability of the four groups. This may suggest that these listeners had more difficulty than the other listeners in evaluating the quality of speech. It could also suggest that they did not retain overall quality concepts regarding the speakers despite the fact there were just four speakers presented.

Finally, the results of this study showed that the four listener groups rated the impaired speakers similarly with regard to acceptability. Within the limits of the current study, this suggested that the listeners with dysarthria did not have any overt perceptual processing differences or difficulties in completing this task. As such, there does not appear to be a perceptual component involved in the production of the poor quality speech by this group. Alternately, if there are perceptual deficits that contribute to the production of dysarthric speech, this study failed to expose them. Further studies will evaluate the possibility that when speakers with dysarthria are recorded while speaking under degraded listening conditions, their intelligibility and acceptability may suffer in contrast to the speech produced by unimpaired speakers.

REFERENCES

Dagenais, P. A., Garcia, J. M., & Watts, C. R. (1998). Acceptability and intelligibility of mildly dysarthric speech by different listeners. In M. P. Cannito, K. M. Yorkston & D. R. Beukelman (Eds.), *Neuromotor speech disorders: Nature, assessment, and treatment* (pp. 229-239). Baltimore, MD: Brookes.

Dagenais, P. A., Watts, C. R., Turnage, L. M., & Kennedy, S. (1999). Intelligibility and acceptability of moderately dysarthric speech by three types of listeners. *Journal of Medical Speech Language Pathology, 7,* 91-96.

Duffy, J. R. (1995). *Motor speech disorders. Substrates, differential diagnosis, and management.* St. Louis: Mosby.

Kent, R. D., Weismer, G., Kent, J. F., & Rosenbek, J. C. (1989). Toward phonetic intelligibility testing in dysarthria. *Journal of Speech and Hearing Disorders, 54,* 482-499.

Lindblom, B. (1990). On the communication process: Speaker-listener interaction and the development of speech. *AAC Augmentative and Alternative Communication, 6,* 220-230.

Liss, J. M., Spitzer, S., Caviness, J. N., Adler, C., & Edwards, B. (1998). Syllable strength and lexical boundary decisions in the perception of hypokinetic dysarthric speech. *Journal of the Acoustical Society of America, 104,* 2457-2466.

Most, T., Weisel, A., & Avivit, L. (1996). Speech intelligibility and evaluation of personal qualities by experienced and inexperienced listeners. *Volta Review, 98,* 181-190.

Southwood, M. H., & Weismer, G. (1993). Listener judgments of the bizarreness, acceptability, naturalness and normalcy of dysarthria associated with amyotrophic lateral sclerosis. *Journal of Medical Speech-Language Pathology, 1,* 151-161.

Weismer, G., & Martin, R. E. (1992). Acoustic and perceptual approaches to the study of intelligibility. In R. Kent (Ed.), *Intelligibility in speech disorders: Theory, measurement and management* (pp. 68–118). Philadelphia: John Benjamins.

Yorkston, K., & Beukelman, D. (1981). *Assessment of intelligibility of dysarthric speech.* Austin, TX: Pro-Ed.

Yorkston, K., Dowden, P., & Beukelman, D. (1992). Intelligibility measurement as a tool in the clinical management of dysarthric speakers. In R. D. Kent (Ed.), *Intelligibility in speech disorders: Theory, measurement and management* (pp. 265-285). Philadelphia: John Benjamins.

30

The Use of Prosody in Interaction: Observations from a Case Study of a Norwegian Speaker with a Non-Fluent Type of Aphasia

Marianne Lind

In this chapter, we analyze the use and function of pitch variation in utterances by a participant with a non-fluent (Broca) type of aphasia in spontaneous verbal interaction. The analysis is focused around the following topics: (a) the use of prosody to contextualize direct reported speech, (b) the use of prosody to contextualize single-word utterances as requests and responses, respectively, and (c) the use of prosody to demarcate functional-grammatical units within longer contributions.

Prosody refers to "non-verbal dimensions of speech which have the syllable as their minimal domain and which can be related to the auditory parameters of loudness, duration and pitch" (Couper-Kuhlen, 1996, p. 369). In this study, prosodic devices are understood as contextualization cues, that is, "'empirically detectable signs' which *cue* conversational interpretation by evoking interpretative schemata or frames" (Couper-Kuhlen & Selting, 1996, p. 13; cf. Gumperz, 1982, 1992). Furthermore, in line with an interactional approach to prosody, it is assumed that prosodic functions derive from the situated use of language to accomplish interactional goals. Hence, no *a priori* correspondence is assumed between particular prosodic configurations and for instance specific grammatical sentence types.

Aspects of Prosody and Intonation with an Emphasis on Norwegian

In Norwegian, variation in pitch has a function on the lexical level as well as on the utterance level. On the lexical level, pitch variation on accented syllables gives a tonal opposition which is used to distinguish between the lexical meanings of words (cf. e.g. Fretheim, 1984; Moen & Sundet, 1996). The variation in pitch on the syllable(s) following the accented syllable is not part of the lexical tonal distinction, but belongs to the domain of utterance intonation. Intonational pitch variation serves different, but complementary, functions. It can have grammatical functions (e.g. signaling different kinds of syntactic and semantic borders within an utterance, or generating information structure within an utterance), pragmatic functions (e.g. signaling whether an utterance is to be understood as a question or as a statement), attitudinal functions (e.g. signaling how a speaker feels about a given proposition), and discursive and interactional functions (e.g. signaling potential exchange of speaking turns) (cf. Cruttenden, 1997; Nilsen, 1989; Schegloff, 1998).

A model has been developed to account for the prosodic system of East Norwegian and its role in assigning information structure to utterances (Fretheim, 1987, 1988; Fretheim & Nilsen, 1988, 1989; Nilsen, 1989, 1992). In the latest version of this model (Nilsen, 1992), a distinction is made between units at three levels: (a) the tonal foot, (b) the intonational phrase, and (c) the intonational utterance. The tonal foot is the basic unit, and it is demarcated by accented syllables. That is, each tonal foot starts with an accented syllable and includes all syllables up to the next accented syllable. Tonal feet are either focal, i.e. ending in a sharp rise in pitch, or non-focal, i.e. ending in an even or only moderately rising pitch. Following the fundamental frequency maximum point in the focal foot, there may be a more or less pronounced falling tone or no downward pitch movement at all. These are referred to as a falling terminal tone and a rising (or non-falling) terminal tone, respectively.

A focal foot signals the end of the intonational phrase. There may also be post-focal tonal feet added to the intonational phrase. These are extrametrical in relation to the preceding intonational phrase, and they are hierarchically dominated by the intonational utterance. Intonational utterances, then, consist of minimally one and maximally two intonational phrases with a possible "tail" of extrametrical, postfocal feet directly dominated by the intonational utterance node.

Prosody and Language Impairment

A growing number of studies have been conducted on the production and comprehension of different aspects of prosody (lexical and clausal, linguistic and affective) in population groups with different types of language impairment (different types of aphasia as well as right hemisphere damage; cf. Baum & Pell, 1997; Danly & Shapiro, 1982; Gandour, Petty & Dardarananda, 1989; Moen & Sundet, 1996, 1999; Pell & Baum, 1997; Ryalls & Behrens, 1988). As for patients with a Broca-type of aphasia, impaired as well as intact aspects of prosody are attested. Several studies point to the lack of continuity in the speech (slower tempo, smaller units of speech programming) as an important factor explaining the perception of Broca-aphasic speech as dysprosodic. However, most studies have used experimental data (reading tests, repetitions etc.); less is known about how prosody is used by language impaired speakers in spontaneous interaction, which is the topic of this study.

Data and Methodology

The data are taken from a data set of three audio- and video-recorded spontaneous interactions (with a total duration of approximately 2.5 hours) between an aphasic participant and different non-aphasic participants. The aphasic participant is a Norwegian man – "Aksel" – in his mid-fifties, who has suffered from a severe, non-fluent (Broca) type of aphasia since 1992. The recordings of the conversations were made 5-6 years post onset.

Aksel's verbal production is severely limited, lexically as well as grammatically. His vocabulary is dominated by a small set of interjections and set phrases, and only a minor portion of the words he uses is content words. His utterances are short – often consisting of single words – and consequently there is a severely reduced variety of sentence and phrase structures (Lind, 1998, in progress; Simonsen & Lind, this volume). Like other non-fluent aphasic speakers, Aksel makes quite extensive use of direct reported speech, sound effects and expressions of exclamation (Menn, O'Connor, Obler & Holland, 1995). His speech tempo is reduced, although each word is not pronounced particularly slowly. In an experimental study of prosody, his performance was not unimpaired (Moen, 2000).

The present study aims at a description of some aspects of the use and function of pitch variation in Aksel's utterances in spontaneous interaction. Pitch is here measured acoustically as variation in fundamental frequency.[1] The functions of pitch variation are analyzed using a conversation-analytic approach, in which one seeks to validate the analytical categories (grounded in the data themselves) by demonstrating the participants' orientation to them (cf. e.g. ten Have, 1999; Pomerantz & Fehr, 1997).

---

[1]The analysis was performed with *Signalyze 3.12* on a Macintosh computer. I thank Professor Inger Moen for her assistance with this analysis.

THE USE OF PROSODY TO CONTEXTUALIZE
DIRECT REPORTED SPEECH

Direct reported speech is a form of reflexive use of language in which (at least) two speech contexts are evoked in one speech situation, and there is a co-referential relation between the deictic reference points of these two speech contexts. In addition to deictic retention, different types of cues (syntactic, lexical, prosodic and non-verbal) are used to contextualize utterances as direct reported speech (cf. e.g., Coulmas, 1986; Eriksson, 1997; Holt, 1996; Lucy, 1993).

Direct reported speech is not uncommon in the speech of individuals with a non-fluent type of aphasia, but it may be contextualized in other ways than in "normal" interaction (Wilkinson, 2000). For instance, aphasic speakers often omit some or all of the grammatical devices that are normally used to tie the direct reported speech utterance to the preceding discourse (Menn, O'Connor, Obler & Holland, 1995). This is the case with Aksel, who produces direct reported speech-utterances without using verbal deixis or lexical indicators. Instead he uses a combination of other verbal and non-verbal cues, including prosody.

The prosodic feature which Aksel uses to distinguish between non-reported and reported utterances is an abrupt leap in pitch or, in other words, a high onset on the reported utterance(s), (Couper-Kuhlen, 1998b), as seen in Fig. 1.[2] Aksel first refers to a person named *Heidi*, then presents an utterance which is constructed so as to give the impression that the words are Heidi's, spoken in her own voice. Aksel's pronunciation of the proper name ends fairly low (at 93 Hz), and the direct reported speech-utterance starts much higher (at 125 Hz).

This type of leap is found even when the whole direct reported speech sequence is temporarily interrupted by a side-sequence, as in Fig. 2. The pronunciation of the referring expression introducing the "speaker" in the reported speech context (*Anne*) ends fairly low (at 97 Hz). There is a side-sequence (lines 2 through 9 in the transcription) partly dealing with who the proper noun *Anne* refers to, and partly containing signals of preparation for a contribution, before the direct reported speech utterance is presented (line 10). This utterance starts fairly high (at 177 Hz).

---

[2] Values for fundamental frequency (in hertz (Hz)) are given on the vertical axis in each figure. The horizontal axis is a time line.

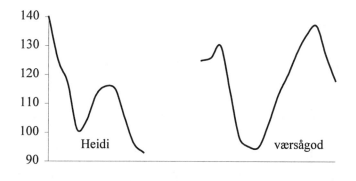

Aksel: Heidi .. (0.4) værsågod   *Heidi .. (0.4) here you are*[3]

FIG. 1 Pitch contour of a direct reported speech sequence.

---

[3] The transcriptions follow a simplified version of the system developed by Du Bois, Schuetze-Coburn, Cumming, and Paolino (1993). Verbal utterances are transcribed (more or less) orthographically; pauses are measured with *Signalyze 3.12*. The translations are meant to capture the content of the original, without aiming for idiomatic English.

..	a pause of less than 0.2 seconds
.. (N)	a pause between 0.2 and 0.9 seconds
... (N)	a pause of 1.0 seconds or more
.em., .em=. etc.	filled pauses
=	lengthening
[xx] [[xx]]	overlaps
[xx] [[xx]]	
<h xx h>	uttered on inhalation
(clears throat), (laughter)	non-verbal

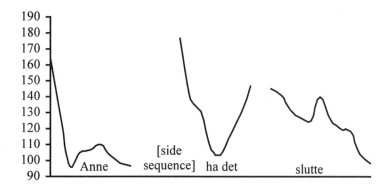

FIG. 2 Pitch contour of a direct reported speech-sequence with a side-sequence.

1	Aksel:	Anne	Anne
2	Non-aphasic:	.. (0.8) er det	.. (0.8) is that the
3		fysioterapeuten	physiotherapist
4	Aksel:	.. (0.8) ja	.. (0.8) yes
5		.. (0.8) .em=.	.. (0.8) .em=.
6		... (5.0)	... (5.0)
7	Non-aphasic:	(latter)	(laughter)
8	Aksel:	.. (0.5) .em=.	.. (0.5) .em=.
9		... (1.4) .em=.	... (1.4) .em=.
10		... (1.3) ha det	... (1.3) bye bye
11		.. (0.2) slutte	.. (0.2) quit

This kind of abrupt leap in pitch is not found in other, comparable contexts in the data. Fig. 3 shows the pitch contour of the utterance *fint ... (1.0) hun flink* ('fine ... (1.0) she clever'), which on a segmental level is not structurally unlike the direct reported speech sequence in Fig. 1: there is first one word, then a short pause, and finally one or two words. In the example in Fig. 3 there is no leap between the end-point of the first word (at 114 Hz) and the beginning of the last words (at 109 Hz).

It seems then, that Aksel uses an abrupt leap in pitch as a contextualization cue to set off an utterance as direct reported speech. As other studies have shown (cf. e.g., Couper-Kuhlen, 1998a; Günthner, 1998; Klewitz & Couper-Kuhlen, 1999) a variety of prosodic and other voice quality features are used in "normal" interaction as contextualization cues of direct reported speech. The main point is that the features employed are clearly distinguishable from those used to index the current speaker's own voice. There should be a departure from a local prosodic norm. In Figs. 1 and 2 the leap in pitch constitutes such a departure from the norm (the latter being exemplified in Fig. 3).

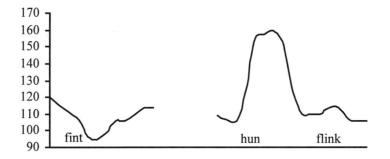

FIG. 3 Pitch contour of a normal (i.e. non-direct reported speech) sequence

THE USE OF PROSODY TO CONTEXTUALIZE SINGLE-WORD UTTERANCES AS REQUESTS AND RESPONSES

Like other severely agrammatic aphasic speakers, Aksel produces a lot of single-word utterances (cf. Klippi, 1996, on uninflected single-word turns in aphasic interaction). These utterances fulfil different functions; they may for instance function as responses and as requests. In these two functions single-word utterances seem to be contextualized prosodically in different ways by Aksel. As responses, single-word utterances are pronounced with a falling terminal pitch contour, whereas they are pronounced with a rising (or a non-falling) terminal pitch contour when they function as requests, as the pitch contours in Figs. 4 and 5 illustrate. The utterance in Fig. 4 is Aksel's response to a yes/no question (lines 1and 2 in the transcription) to which, however, more than a simple 'yes' or 'no' may be expected. The affirmative *ja* ('yes'; line 4) is somewhat lengthened and pronounced with a rise, indicating some sort of continuation. The more substantial part of the response is presented in the form of a single noun (line 6) pronounced with a distinctly falling terminal pitch contour. In Fig. 5, Aksel makes a request for information in the form of a return question (line 6) which is pronounced with a distinct rise in the terminal pitch contour.

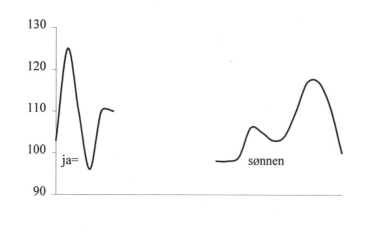

1	Non-aphasic:	.. (0.7) er det noen som driver	.. *(0.7) is there somebody*
2		den gården	*running that farm*
3	Aksel:	... (1.0) .eh.	*... (1.0) .eh.*
4		.. (0.7) ja=	*.. (0.7) yes=*
5	Non-aphasic:	... (1.3) (kremt)	*... (1.3) (throat clearing)*
6	Aksel:	.. (0.5) .ehm. .. sønnen	*.. (0.5) .ehm. .. the son*
7	Non-aphasic:	... (1.2) javel	*... (1.2) yes I see*

FIG. 4 Pitch contour of a single-word utterance as a response

In the sequences illustrated in Figs. 4 and 5, the non-aphasic participant orients to the relevant single-word utterances by Aksel as a response and a request, respectively. Evidence for this is found in the relevant next turns by the non-aphasic participants, which in Fig. 4 is a minimal third turn contribution (line 7), and in Fig. 5 a response to Aksel's request (line 7).

Fretheim and Nilsen (1989) have analyzed the functions of terminal rises (non-falls) and terminal falls in non-aphasic Norwegian, and they conclude that terminal rises imply openness and non-finality, whereas terminal falls imply finality and conclusiveness. Aksel's use of the distinction between rising and falling terminal pitches thus fits well with the description of non-aphasic Norwegian.

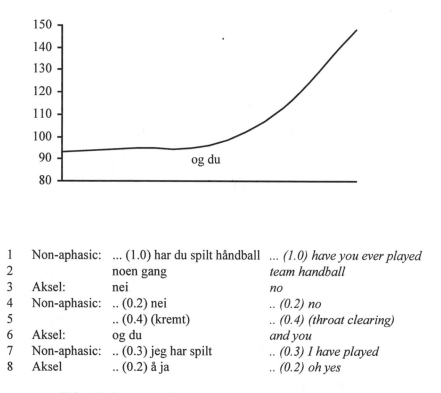

1	Non-aphasic:	... (1.0) har du spilt håndball	... *(1.0) have you ever played*
2		noen gang	*team handball*
3	Aksel:	nei	*no*
4	Non-aphasic:	.. (0.2) nei	*.. (0.2) no*
5		.. (0.4) (kremt)	*.. (0.4) (throat clearing)*
6	Aksel:	og du	*and you*
7	Non-aphasic:	.. (0.3) jeg har spilt	*.. (0.3) I have played*
8	Aksel	.. (0.2) å ja	*.. (0.2) oh yes*

FIG. 5 Pitch contour of a single-word utterance as a request

THE USE OF PROSODY TO DEMARCATE FUNCTIONAL-GRAMMATICAL UNITS WITHIN LONGER CONTRIBUTIONS

There are few extended phrases or longer grammatical constructions in Aksel's speech production in interaction. He does, however, occasionally make longer contributions. These generally consist of successions of very short utterances (one or two words) which are linked prosodically.

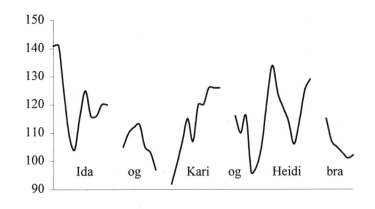

1	Non-aphasic:	... (1.4) men= .. (0.4) dem	*... (1.4) but= .. (0.4) they*
2		forstår deg ganske [godt]	*understand you fairly [well]*
3	Aksel:	[ja] ja	*[yes] yes*
4	Non-aphasic:	.. ja .. (0.4) [[mm]]	*.. yes .. (0.4) [[mm]]*
5	Aksel:	[[<h ja h>]]	*[[<h yes h>]]*
6	Non-aphasic:	.. (0.2) så du treng ikke --	*.. (0.2) so you don't have to --*
7	Aksel:	nei	*no*
8	Non-aphasic:	.. nei	*.. no*
9	Aksel:	.. [<h nei h>]	*.. [<h no h>]*
10	Non-aphasic:	.. [<h nei h>]	*.. [<h no h>]*
11	Aksel:	.. (0.2) Ida	*.. (0.2) Ida*
12	Non-aphasic:	.. (0.2) ja	*.. (0.2) yes*
13	Aksel:	.. (0.4) og .. Kari	*.. (0.4) and .. Kari*
14	Non-aphasic:	.. mm	*.. mm*
15	Aksel:	.. og Heidi	*.. and Heidi*
16	Non-aphasic:	.. (0.2) ja	*.. (0.2) yes*
17	Aksel:	.. bra	*.. good*
18	Non-aphasic:	.. (0.5) ja	*.. (0.5) yes*
19		.. (0.8) ja men det er fint	*.. (0.8) yes but that's good*

FIG. 6 Pitch contour of a longer contribution.

Aksel uses a form of "list" intonation to signal whether an utterance is an early/middle or a final part of a contribution, respectively. Non-final parts of a contribution are pronounced with a rise at the end of the word, whereas the final part of the contribution is pronounced with a fall. Fig. 6 illustrates this form of "list" intonation. The proper nouns *Ida, Kari* and *Heidi* are all pronounced with a rise at the end, signaling that they are part of a contribution that is not yet complete. The completion is signaled by a fall on the word *bra* ('good'). As long as Aksel's contributions are prosodically marked as non-final, the non-aphasic participant contributes only back-channel utterances (lines 12, 14 and 16), but when Aksel has marked an utterance prosodically as final, the non-aphasic participant provides a more substantial contribution in the form of an evaluation (lines 18-19). Thus, the non-aphasic participant evidently orients to the single utterances as parts of a larger contribution.

In Fig. 6, the single utterances Aksel produces may be interpreted as belonging to one syntactic clause in which the proper nouns constitute the theme (or topic) whereas the final utterance of the contribution (the evaluative adverb *bra* ('good')) constitutes the rheme (or comment; Halliday, 1985). Longer contributions may, however, also consist of a complex of clauses that are related paratactically or hypotactically. Fig. 7 gives the pitch contours of the single utterances of a clausal complex consisting of two "clauses" that are related through parataxis.

The two 'clauses' – *Heidi Tyskland* ('Germany') and *Kari hjem* ('home') – have similar prosodic structures: a rise on the thematic constituents (*Heidi* and *Kari*) and a fall on the rhematic constituents (*Tyskland*, 'Germany' and *hjem*, 'home'). As in Fig. 6, non-final utterances are marked by a rising contour, whereas final utterances are marked by a falling contour. The variation in pitch thus serves to delimit constituents at different structural levels, within the "clause" as well as above the clause level. This use of continuation rises by aphasic speakers – even extensively at minor syntactic boundaries – has also been attested by Danly and Shapiro (1982).

The fall on the final utterance of a longer contribution may be replaced by a rise when the whole contribution functions as a request, as illustrated in Fig. 8. There is a terminal rise in pitch on all the substantial utterances of Aksel's contribution, even on the last one (*klokka* ('o'clock')), which is repeated once, probably due to a lack of response by the non-aphasic participant (cf. the 1.5 second pause, line 10). In the repetition the pitch is raised even higher, thus more clearly signaling that this is the final component of a longer contribution functioning as a request. The formulation by the non-aphasic participant in lines 11and 12 shows that the contribution is indeed interpreted as a request.

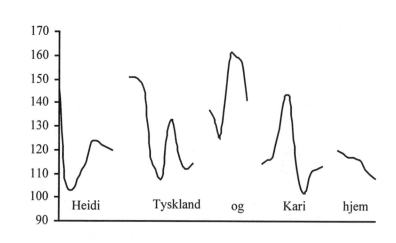

	1	Non-aphasic:	bor de hjemme da	*do they live at home then*
	2	Aksel:	... (1.2) .eh=.	*... (1.2) .eh=.*
	3		.. (0.5) Heidi	*.. (0.5) Heidi*
	4	Non-aphasic:	.. (0.2) ja	*.. (0.2) yes*
	5	Aksel:	.. (0.6) .eh=. Tyskland	*.. (0.6) .eh=. Germany*
	6	Non-aphasic:	.. (0.2) jaha	*.. (0.2) oh yes*
	7	Aksel:	.. (0.8) og=	*.. (0.8) and=*
	8		.. (0.9) Kari	*.. (0.9) Kari*
	9		.. (0.4) hjem	*.. (0.4) home*
10		Non-aphasic:	.. (0.3) javel	*.. (0.3) yes I see*

FIG. 7 Pitch contour of a longer clausal complex.

PROSODIC ANALYSIS AND
THE SPEECH PLANNING PROCESS

As the contours in Figs. 6 through 8 show, variation in pitch seems to be an efficient way for Aksel to express syntactical relations in his utterances. The use of pitch variation to signal the differential status of the single-word utterances within the longer contributions thus indicates that Aksel is at some level able to plan for more than one lexical unit at a time.

However, there is also evidence in the data that some aspects of the speech planning process are fairly short-range. In the longer contributions, nearly every word is accented, thus contributing to a high number of tonal feet in the utterances.

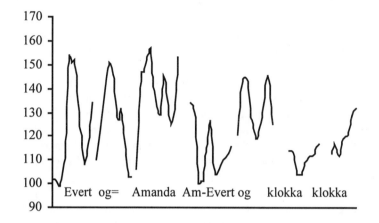

FIG. 8 Pitch contour of a longer contribution functioning as a request

1	Aksel:	.. du=	.. *you=*
2		Evert	*Evert*
3	Non-aphasic:	.. (0.2) ja	*.. (0.2) yes*
4	Aksel:	og Amanda	*and Amanda*
5	Non-aphasic:	.. (0.4) ja	*.. (0.4) yes*
6	Aksel:	... (2.6) .eh=.	*... (2.6) .eh=.*
7		... (1.1) Am- Evert	*... (1.1) Am- Evert*
8		.. (0.4) og .eh=.	*.. (0.4) and .eh=.*
9		.. (0.6) klokka	*.. (0.6) o'clock*
10		... (1.5) klokka	*... (1.5) o'clock*
11	Non-aphasic:	.. (0.7) når de var her	*.. (0.7) when they were here*
12		[mener] ˈdu	*[you] mean*
13	Aksel:	[ja]	*[yes]*
14		.. ja akkurat	*.. yes exactly*

In (i) and (ii), below, the utterances in Fig. 6 and Fig. 7 are analyzed within the model for East Norwegian intonation described in the initial part of this chapter.

(i) $_{IU}(_{IP}(_{F}(IDA))$ .. $_{IP}(og\ _{F}(HEIDI))$ .. $_{IP}(og\ _{F}(KARI))$ .. $_{F}(bra))$ L%
        Ida and Heidi and Kari good

(ii) $_{IU}(_{IP}(_F(HEIDI))$ .. $_F(tyskland))$ L% .. $_{IU}(_F(og))$ .. $_{IP}(_F(KARI))$ .. $_F(hjem))$ L%
        Heidi Germany and Kari home

(Capital letters indicate focal accent. IU means *intonational utterance*, IP means *intonational phrase*, and F is *tonal foot.* L% indicates a *falling terminal tone.* Two full stops indicate pauses in the utterance.)

Firstly, we may note that intonational utterances in Aksel's spontaneous speech may contain more than the postulated maximum of two intonational phrases, indicating a more extensive segmentation (shorter stretches of speech planning) than in "normal" speech production. Secondly, we may note that even a conjunction like *og* ('and') is accented in certain utterances (cf. ii). This utterance is a paratactic construction which in non-aphasic Norwegian could very likely be realized with a focal rise on the first IU (i.e. with a rise on *Tyskland*) and a post-focal fall on the second IU (i.e. with a fall on *hjem*) (Fretheim & Nilsen, 1988). The overall contour covering both of the IUs would then be a focal rise and a post-focal fall. In Aksel's version, this overall contour is instead realized on each of the two IUs, also indicating a shorter stretch of speech planning than in a non-aphasic case. The realization of the conjunction *og* ('and') as a separate tonal foot pronounced at a slightly higher level than the rest of the words in the whole utterance, may be a way of signaling that even though the first IU is presented as if it is final (with a post-focal fall), this IU does not constitute the whole contribution. There is more to follow.

The extensive segmentation of utterances in smaller prosodic units in Aksel's speech can be the result of relying heavily on one type of intonational patterning, viz. the "list" intonation, in which each member in the list has equal relevance, hence receives equal prosodic prominence (i.e. is accentuated). It can also, however, be the result of a slower speech tempo (cf. the pauses after nearly every lexical unit in the utterances), or of a combination of the two.

In addition to this extensive segmentation, there is evidence in the data that Aksel uses the syllable as a primary unit for accentuation to a greater extent than non-aphasic speakers do. This explains the great number of "ups and downs" in the pitch contours in the figures. The pitch contour of the word *sønnen* ('the son') in Fig. 4 illustrates this clearly. Instead of one peak within the word, there are two peaks, indicating separate accentuations on each of the syllables.

CONCLUDING REMARKS

The data analyzed in this chapter illustrate some of the ways in which a non-fluent aphasic speaker uses prosody – here limited to variation in pitch – in spontaneous verbal interaction as a resource for communication. Pitch variation is used as a contextualization cue pragmatically (in direct reported speech) as well as grammatically (in responses, requests and longer contributions constituted by single-word utterances). In this there are no qualitative differences between this aphasic speaker and non-aphasic speakers. The data indicate that the aphasic participant is, at least on some level, able to plan for more than one lexical unit at a time, even though there is also evidence that some aspects of his speech planning are managed with relatively short segments.

This chapter has reported preliminary observations from one case, and there is obviously need for further research on different aspects of prosody in aphasic interaction, for instance concerning how other interactional tasks, such as turn-transition, repair and word-searches, are managed prosodically. Given the extensive individual differences among aphasic speakers (even those with similar types of aphasia), which include prosody (Moen, 2000), analyses of other cases may reveal rather different uses of this resource for communication.

REFERENCES

Baum, S. R., & Pell, M. D. (1997). Production of affective and linguistic prosody by brain-damaged patients. *Aphasiology, 11,* 177-198.

Coulmas, F. (Ed.). (1986). *Direct and indirect speech.* Berlin: Mouton de Gruyter.

Couper-Kuhlen, E. (1996). The prosody of repetition: on quoting and mimicry. In E. Couper-Kuhlen & M. Selting (Eds.), *Prosody in conversation* (pp. 366-405). Cambridge: Cambridge University Press.

Couper-Kuhlen, E. (1998a). Coherent voicing. On prosody in conversational reported speech. *InLiSt – Interaction and Linguistic Structures, 1.* URL: <http://inlist.uni-konstanz.de/issues/1>.

Couper-Kuhlen, E. (1998b). On high onsets and their absence in conversational interaction. *InLiSt – Interaction and Linguistic Structures, 8.* URL: <http://inlist.uni-konstanz.de/issues/8>.

Couper-Kuhlen, E., & Selting, M. (1996). Towards an interactional perspective on prosody and a prosodic perspective on interaction. In E. Couper-Kuhlen & M. Selting (Eds.), *Prosody in conversation* (pp. 11-56). Cambridge: Cambridge University Press.

Cruttenden, A. (1997). *Intonation* (2nd ed.). Cambridge: Cambridge University Press.

Danly, M., & Shapiro, B. (1982). Speech prosody in Broca's aphasia. *Brain and Language, 16,* 171-190.

Du Bois, J. W., Schuetze-Coburn, S., Cumming, S., & Paolino, D. (1993). Outline of discourse transcription. In J. A. Edwards & M. D. Lampert

(Eds.), *Talking data. Transcription and coding in discourse research* (pp. 45-87). Hillsdale, New Jersey: Lawrence Erlbaum Associates.

Eriksson, M. (1997). *Ungdomars berättande. En studie i struktur och interaktion.* Doctoral thesis, University of Uppsala, Sweden.

Fretheim, T. (1984). What is accent and what is stress in East Norwegian sentence prosody? *Working Papers in Linguistics, 2,* 28-63. University of Trondheim, Norway.

Fretheim, T. (1987). Pragmatics and intonation. In J. Verschueren & M. Bertuccelli-Papi (Eds.), *The pragmatic perspective* (pp. 395-420). Amsterdam: John Benjamins.

Fretheim, T. (1988). Intonational phrases and syntactic focus domains. *Working Papers in Linguistics,6,* 125-151. University of Trondheim, Norway.

Fretheim, T., & Nilsen, R. A. (1988). Alternativspørsmål: opp som en løve, ned som en skinnfell. *Norsk Lingvistisk Tidsskrift, 1/2,* 89-104.

Fretheim, T., & Nilsen, R. A. (1989). Terminal rise and rise-fall tunes in East Norwegian intonation. *Nordic Journal of Linguistics, 12,* 155-181.

Gandour, J., Petty, S. H., & Dardarananda, R. (1989). Dysprosody in Broca's aphasia: a case study. *Brain and Language, 37,* 232-257.

Gumperz, J. J. (1982). *Discourse strategies.* Cambridge: Cambridge University Press.

Gumperz, J. J. (1992). Contextualization revisited. In P. Auer & A. di Luzio (Eds.), *The contextualization of language* (pp. 39-53). Amsterdam & Philadelphia: John Benjamins.

Günthner, S. (1998). Polyphony and the layering of voices in reported dialogues. An analysis of the use of prosodic devices in everyday reported speech. *InLiSt - Interaction and Linguistic Structures, 3.* URL: <http://inlist.uni-konstanz.de/issues/3>

Halliday, M. A. K. (1985). *An introduction to functional grammar.* London: Edward Arnold.

ten Have, P. (1999). *Doing conversation analysis. A practical guide.* London: SAGE Publications.

Holt, E. (1996). Reporting on talk: the use of direct reported speech in conversation. *Research on Language and Social Interaction, 29,* 219-245.

Klewitz, G., & Couper-Kuhlen, E. (1999). Quote - unquote? The role of prosody in the contextualization of reported speech sequences. *InLiSt - Interaction and Linguistic Structures, 12.* URL: <http://inlist.uni-konstanz.de/issues/12>

Klippi, A. (1996). *Conversation as an achievement in aphasics.* Helsinki: SKS.

Lind, M. (1998): Hva innnebærer det å delta i en samtale? Et eksempel fra en samtale mellom en afasirammet og en ikke-afasirammet deltaker. In J. T. Faarlund, B. Mæhlum & T. Nordgård (Eds.), *MONS 7, Utvalde artiklar frå det 7. Møtet om Norsk Språk i Trondheim 1997* (pp. 131-153). Oslo: Novus.

Lind, M. (In progress). Conversational cooperation: The establishment of reference and displacement in aphasic interaction. Doctoral thesis. Department of Linguistics. University of Oslo.

Lucy, J. A. (Ed.) (1993). *Reflexive language. Reported speech and metapragmatics.* Cambridge: Cambridge University Press.

Menn, L., O'Connor, M., Obler, L. K. & Holland, A. (1995). *Non-fluent aphasia in a multilingual world.* Amsterdam & Philadelphia: John Benjamins.

Moen, I. (2000). Prosody in the speech of Norwegian brain damaged patients: An acoustic investigation of the speech of patients with left hemisphere damage and patients with right hemisphere damage. Paper presented at The VIIIth Meeting of the International Clinical Phonetics & Linguistics Association, Edinburgh, August, 2000.

Moen, I., & Sundet, K. (1996). Production and perception of word tones (pitch accents) in patients with left and right hemisphere damage. *Brain and Language, 53,* 267-281.

Moen, I., & Sundet, K. (1999). An acoustic investigation of pitch accent contrasts in the speech of a Norwegian patient with a left-hemisphere lesion (Broca's aphasia). In B. Maassen & P. Groenen (Eds.), *Pathologies of speech and language. Advances in clinical phonetics and linguistics* (pp. 221-228). London: Whurr Publishers.

Nilsen, R. A. (1989). On prosodically marked information structure in spoken Norwegian. *Working Papers in Linguistics, 7,* 1-101. University of Trondheim, Norway.

Nilsen, R. A. (1992). *Intonasjon i interaksjon – sentrale spørsmål i norsk intonologi.* Doctoral thesis. University of Trondheim, Norway.

Pell, M. D., & Baum, S. R. (1997). Unilateral brain damage, prosodic comprehension deficits, and the acoustic cues to prosody. *Brain and Language, 57,* 195-214.

Pomerantz, A., & Fehr, B. J. (1997). Conversation analysis: An approach to the study of social action as sense making practices. In T. A. van Dijk (Ed.), *Discourse as social interaction* (pp. 64-91). London: Sage Publications.

Ryalls, J. H., & Behrens, S. J. (1988). An overview of changes in fundamental frequency associated with cortical insult. *Aphasiology, 2,* 107-115.

Schegloff, E. A. (1998). Reflections on studying prosody in talk-in-interaction. *Language and Speech, 41,* 235-263.

Simonsen, H. G., & Lind, M. (this volume): Past Tense in a Norwegian Broca's Aphasic.

Wilkinson, R. (2000). The use of direct reported speech and mime in speakers with aphasia in conversation. Paper presented at The 7th International Pragmatics Conference, Budapest, July 2000.

31

Learning to Apprehend Phonetic Structure from the Speech Signal: The Hows and Whys

Susan Nittrouer

Ever since the technology was developed to make spectrograms, it has been known that the acoustic signal of speech does not consist of strings of physical segments that correspond to the strings of psychological segments perceived by competent speaker/listeners of a language (Joos, 1948). For this reason, much research during the latter half of the twentieth century was focused on discovering and cataloging the shards of acoustic information that correspond to these psychological segments (i.e., phonemes). The model of speech perception implicit to that work was that specific settings of isolable acoustic properties (or "cues") define each phonemic category, even though temporal slices cannot be found to correspond to these units. Unfortunately, this line of investigation has largely failed to explain how it is that listeners derive phonemic strings from the acoustic speech signal.

Just before the turn of the century, many speech researchers turned away from the view of speech perception underlying that experimental approach. In its place has emerged the notion that speech perception involves integrating several kinds of acoustic information to derive phonetic structure. According to this view, the perceiver can integrate information from across the temporal and spectral domains of the signal to make judgments about the phonetic structure represented therein. The listener is no longer seen as a passive receiver of the information needed to pluck segments from the signal. Instead, the speech perceiver is viewed as active, knowing where in the signal to turn for information, even depending on context, and knowing how much weight to assign to each of the extracted properties. Furthermore, the end-product of the process is no longer seen as necessarily being a string of phonemes, picked off one at a time, but rather as larger linguistic units (syllables or words). Of course phonetic structure is integral to these larger units, and skilled language users know how to extricate that structure. The focus of investigation in the Speech Perception Laboratory at Boys Town National Research Hospital has been on discovering how children learn to do this: derive phonetic structure from an acoustic signal that lacks any invariant correlates. This chapter reviews that work.

Working Model of Speech Perception

Fig. 1 illustrates the model of speech perception that has served as the foundation for much of the work to be reported here. This model should be interpreted as a heuristic only, supporting the empirical work being undertaken. It is not proposed as a model of actual physiological or psychological processes. The basic components of this model are (1) a component that recognizes auditory properties; (2) a component that assigns weighting functions to those properties; and (3) a component that combines these weighted properties to derive linguistic units. The model is deliberately vague about the linguistic units derived from the speech perception process because research continues to investigate that question. As suggested previously, the approach taken here is that adults listening to their native language likely derive whole syllables or words, from which they can extract phonetic structure. For other listeners (such as children and adults listening to a language other than their native language), the ability to extract phonetic structure is likely not as good. Work in the Speech Perception Laboratory has focused largely on the middle component, the one that assigns weighting functions to auditory properties. Our working hypothesis has come to be known as the Developmental Weighting Shift (DWS), and suggests that the weighting of speech-relevant acoustic properties is modified as a consequence of early experience with a native language. Furthermore, it is hypothesized that the end-product is a set of perceptual weighting strategies for speech that most accurately and efficiently provide for the recognition of phonetic structure in that language.

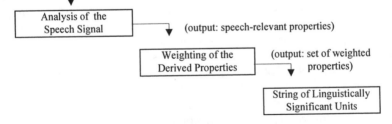

FIG. 1 Working model of speech perception.

RELEVANT STUDIES

General Procedures

When speech perception research was based on the notion that isolated acoustic correlates of phonemic categories could be identified, the basic procedure was to vary one acoustic property along a continuum, and measure changes in phonetic judgments. With the shift in the underlying model to one in which several auditory properties are integrated by the listener to derive phonetic structure, procedures have changed accordingly. Currently, investigations of the perceptual weighting strategies for speech perception involve manipulations of more than one acoustic property at a time. Usually, one property is manipulated along a continuum, going from a setting appropriate for one phonemic judgment to a setting appropriate for another phonemic judgment. Another property is manipulated dichotomously, set for one or the other phonemic judgment. The resulting stimuli (i.e., every level of the continuously varied property paired with each level of the dichotomously varied property) are played for listeners multiple times. The listener's task is to make a binary choice labeling decision. Results are plotted as the proportion (or percentage) of one category label (the Y axis) given at each level of the continuously varied property (the X axis), for both settings of the dichotomously varied property.

Example.   Frequently used stimuli in our laboratory are fricative-vowel syllables. Synthetic fricative noises are created, with a single pole varying in frequency from 2.2 kHz (appropriate for /ʃ/) to 3.8 kHz (appropriate for /s/), along a nine-step continuum. These noises are stable over time, and are on the order of 150 to 200 ms long (depending on the experiment). Vocalic portions can be synthetic or natural, taken from a speaker saying /ʃ/-vowel and /s/-vowel. Whether synthetic or natural, the dichotomously manipulated property of interest is that formant transitions are appropriate for syllable-initial /ʃ/ or /s/. In most experiments, two vowels are used: one rounded and one non-rounded, both English. The resulting 36 stimuli (nine noises x four vowel portions) are presented to listeners ten times each, in blocks of 18 (each vowel presented separately). Results are plotted as the percent 's' responses, at each level of the fricative noise, for each vowel context separately. Such a plot from one adult listener is shown in Fig. 2. Generally speaking, the weight assigned to the continuously varied property (i.e., the one represented on the X-axis, which in this case was the fricative noise spectrum) can be estimated from the steepness of the functions: the steeper the function, the more weight that was assigned to the noise spectrum. The weight assigned to the dichotomously varied property (i.e., the one represented by different functions, which in this case was whether the vocalic portion had formant transitions appropriate for a syllable-initial /ʃ/ or /s/) can be gleaned from the separation in functions: the more separated the functions, the more weight that was assigned to the formant transitions.

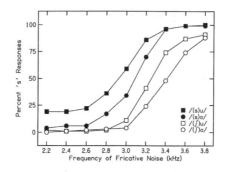

FIG. 2 Results of a typical labeling experiment.

Differences in Perceptual Weighting Strategies Across Languages

Probably because adults are so much easier to work with than children, we understand much more about how adults weight auditory properties in speech perception than we understand about how children do. The most exciting finding in this area is the well-replicated fact that these weighting strategies differ depending on the native language of the adult. Strange (1995) provides an excellent survey of that work.

Example. Crowther and Mann (1994) investigated the weight assigned to two acoustic properties that affect judgments of voicing for syllable-final stops in English: duration of the vocalic portion and frequency of the first formant (F1) at voicing offset. In English, the vocalic portion is longer preceding voiced final stops than preceding voiceless final stops. In all languages, F1 is lower in frequency at voicing offset before voiced than before voiceless final stops. Accordingly, Crowther and Mann constructed synthetic versions of 'pot' and 'pod' that varied in vocalic duration (the continuously varied property) and in F1-offset frequency (the dichotomously varied property). These stimuli were played for adults whose native language was either English or Arabic. The voicing-related vocalic length difference does not exist in Arabic. Mean functions for each group are shown in Fig. 3. The primary finding of this experiment was that the functions for listeners whose native language was Arabic are much more shallow than those of the native-English listeners. Thus we conclude that the Arabic listeners did not weight vocalic length as much as the English listeners in their decisions of syllable-final stop voicing. There is no apparent difference in the separation between functions, and so we conclude that listeners in both groups weighted the frequency of F1 at voicing offset to similar extents.

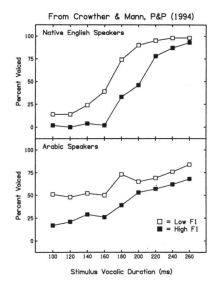

FIG. 3 Results of a 'pod' versus 'pot' labeling experiment. (From Crowther & Mann, 1994. Reprinted with permission.)

Developmental Changes in Perceptual Weighting Strategies

The cross-linguistic results indicate that some learning must be involved in acquiring the most appropriate and efficient weighting strategies for speech perception. If either these strategies remained the same across the lifespan or changed due to biologically driven developmental effects, we would not expect differences in strategies across languages. Work in the Speech Perception Laboratory has tracked developmental changes in these strategies. Fricative-vowel syllables of the sort already described have served as stimuli in several studies. Typical results can be seen in Fig. 4, from Nittrouer (1992). Here we see mean functions for adult listeners and for listeners between the ages of 3 years, 5 months and 3 years, 11 months. The functions of these 3-year-olds are shallower and more separated depending on whether formant transitions are appropriate for a preceding /ʃ/ or /s/. Thus we conclude that 3-year-olds weighted the fricative-noise spectrum less and formant transitions more than adults in their decisions of syllable-initial fricatives. This kind of result has been found in several other experiments using similar stimuli. Furthermore, a developmental trend has been observed in the data: as children get older, labeling functions become steeper and less separated.

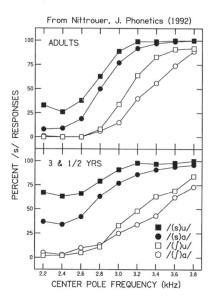

FIG. 4 Results of a '/s/-vowel' versus '/ʃ/-vowel' labeling experiment. (From Nittrouer, 1992. Reprinted with permission.)

General Auditory Development Does not Explain Changes in Speech Perception

As a result of the cross-linguistic and developmental results we are able to say with some certainty that perceptual weighting strategies for speech change as a child gets older. Because each language has its own set of optimal strategies, it seems likely that these changes arise from experience with a language, rather than from more general sorts of experiences (such as general auditory experience). Nonetheless, we specifically tested this alternative hypothesis, that age-related differences in general auditory abilities account for developmental shifts in perceptual weighting strategies for speech. Specifically we asked if the developmental changes in weighting strategies for fricative-vowel syllables could be accounted for by developmental changes in general auditory sensitivity. The most obvious question was whether children fail to use the fricative-noise spectrum to the same extent as adults because they are not as sensitive to changes in stable spectra, i.e., they have larger frequency difference limens (DLs). Of course, a corollary of that position must be that children are more sensitive than adults to changes in frequency glides because children weighted the formant transitions more in their fricative decisions. Fig. 5 illustrates the kind of hypothetical age differences in auditory sensitivity that would need to exist, if general auditory sensitivity accounted for age-related differences in perceptual weighting strategies for speech. On the left, we see that children would have larger DLs for the static property (i.e., the time-invariant spectra), and on the right, we see that children would have smaller DLs for the dynamic property (i.e., formant transitions). Of course, it may be that children never have smaller DLs than adults, either because they are truly less sensitive to all acoustic change or because they must be more certain of their decision to respond that they heard a change. In either case, we might expect larger measured DLs for children than for adults, but perceptual weighting strategies that reflect relative sensitivities for each group: adults would show greater sensitivity to changes in stable spectra than to changes in frequency glides, and children would show greater sensitivity to changes in frequency glides than to changes in stable spectra. This hypothetical situation is illustrated in Fig. 6, which shows children demonstrating larger DLs than adults for both sorts of properties, but within-group differences across properties matching the predictions just offered: that is, children showing larger DLs for the stable property than for the dynamic property and adults showing the opposite pattern. Empirical data supporting the hypothetical situations in Fig. 5 or 6 are needed to support the suggestion that the developmental shifts in perceptual weighting strategies for fricative-vowel syllables are explained by general auditory abilities.

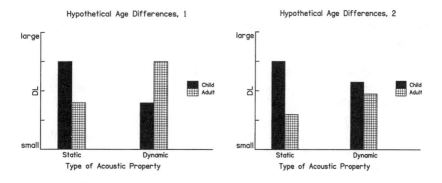

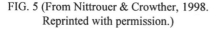

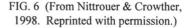

FIG. 5 (From Nittrouer & Crowther, 1998. Reprinted with permission.)

FIG. 6 (From Nittrouer & Crowther, 1998. Reprinted with permission.)

Nittrouer and Crowther (1998) tested these hypotheses using three-component sinewave complexes, 150 ms long. A go/no-go task was used in which a comparison stimulus was embedded in ongoing presentations of a standard stimulus, and the listener had to press a button when this change was heard. For the static condition, the middle sinewave varied in frequency across the entire stimulus in the comparison stimuli. For the dynamic condition, the first 50 ms of the middle sinewave consisted of a falling glide with different starting frequencies. An adaptive procedure was used to estimate DLs, defined as the 71% points on the psychometric functions. Fig. 7 shows the estimated DLs for children (i.e., 5- and 7-year-olds) and adults, and reveals that neither of the hypothetical situations illustrated in Fig. 5 and Fig. 6 was found. Similar results were reported by Nittrouer (1996a) when stable noise spectra were used for the static condition, therefore mimicking fricative noises more closely.

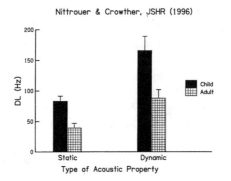

FIG. 7 Results of a discrimination task. (From Nittrouer & Crowther, 1998. Reprinted with permission.)

Evidence that Developmental Shifts in Weighting Strategies Arise from Language Experience

The result described above discounted the possibility that age-related changes in general auditory abilities explain changes in weighting strategies for decisions about syllable-initial fricatives. In fact, we know of no result bolstering the position that developmental changes in general auditory abilities can account for a specific change in strategies for listening to speech, a situation that should not be surprising. Any differences in auditory sensitivity between young children and adults that have been reported from laboratory studies tend to be trivial, with 'trivial' defined as less than we would expect to find for normal-hearing adults listening in laboratory conditions versus in typical listening conditions. On the other hand, the differences in settings of acoustic properties typically associated with differences in phonemic categories are not trivial, and differences in several acoustic properties distinguish phonemic categories. This situation is exactly what would be needed for phonetic perception to proceed in the real world. Consequently, work in the Speech Perception Laboratory has focused on understanding the linguistic underpinnings of developmental changes in perceptual weighting strategies for speech. Specifically, we have tested the hypothesis that it is early language experience that affects the development of mature weighting strategies for speech perception. To achieve this goal, we examined differences in weighting strategies for same-age children presumed to vary in the amount of language experience they have had. In addition, we tested the related hypothesis that optimal weighting strategies for speech perception facilitate the recovery of phonetic structure from the speech signal by examining the phonological processing abilities of these children.

8-Year-olds' Results. To obtain groups of children presumed to vary in the amount of language experience they have had, children with early, chronic histories of otitis media with effusion (OME) and children living in conditions of low socio-economic status (low-SES) served as participants. It was presumed that children with early, chronic histories of OME would effectively have diminished language experience due to periods of raised auditory thresholds at younger ages. Children living in conditions of low SES were presumed to have diminished language experience because several investigators have documented that the amount and kind of parental language input differs for these children from that of middle-class children (e.g., Hart & Risley, 1995). A group of children experiencing both early, chronic OME and low-SES also participated, as did a control group that consisted of children experiencing neither condition. Children in all four groups had normal hearing and speech articulation. Table 1 shows mean scores for the four groups on three measures. The metric of socio-economic status was obtained by rating both the highest educational level and the job status of the primary income earner in the household on eight-point scales, and then multiplying the two scores together. Thus, the highest SES score possible was 64, obtained by university professors, attorneys, and such. Nonverbal ability was estimated using the Coloured Progressive Matrices, the children's version of Raven's Progressive Matrices (Raven, 1975). Verbal IQ was estimated using the Peabody Picture Vocabulary Test-Revised (PPVT-R) (Dunn & Dunn, 1981).

To evaluate the weighting strategies of these children for speech stimuli, the fricative-vowel stimuli described above (from Nittrouer, 1992) were presented using the same labeling paradigm. Fig. 8 from Nittrouer (1996b) shows mean labeling functions for each of the four groups. Children with histories of early, chronic OME, living in conditions of low SES, or suffering both conditions, showed functions that were shallower and more separated than those of children in the control group. Thus it was concluded that children in the experimental groups weighted the fricative noise spectra less and formant transitions more than children in the control group. These perceptual weighting strategies are typical of younger language users. This result suggests that these conditions (which diminish the amount of language experience a child has) may delay the development of mature perceptual weighting strategies for speech.

TABLE 1
8-year-olds (cf. Nittrouer, 1996b).

	Control n = 12	OM n = 12	Low-SES n = 12	Both n = 5
SES Metric	39 (17)	35 (19)	6 (5)	4 (1)
Nonverbal Ability (%)	79 (22)	91 (11)	65 (24)	50 (29)
Verbal IQ (St. Score)	104 (15)	102 (14)	90 (6)	90 (12)

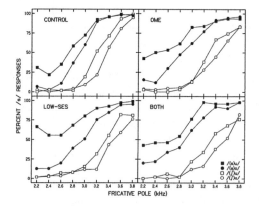

FIG. 8 Results of a '/s/-vowel' versus '/ʃ/-vowel' labeling task. (From Nittrouer, 1996b. Reprinted with permission.)

The next step was to evaluate whether group differences would also be found in children's abilities to access phonetic structure. To achieve this goal, two tests specifically of phonetic awareness (i.e., the ability to recognize and manipulate phonetic segments) were used. The phoneme deletion task required the child to remove a phonetic segment from a nonword, and produce the resulting word (e.g., /pɪnt/ without the /t/ is /pɪn/). The pig-Latin task required the child to move the first segment of a word to the end of the word, and combine it with the rime /eɪ/ (e.g., pig Latin for 'boat' is 'oat-bay'). There were 38 items on the phoneme-deletion task, and 30 items on the pig-Latin task.

Mean percent correct for each task for each group is given on Fig. 9, and reveals that children in the control group were better on both tasks of phonetic awareness than children in any of the experimental groups.   Within the experimental groups, however, mean scores for the OME group were not as poor as mean scores for the low-SES or both groups.

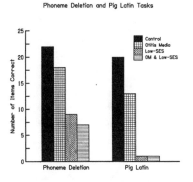

Phoneme Deletion and Pig Latin Tasks

FIG. 9 Results of phonetic awareness tasks.

5-Year-olds' Results. A similar experimental paradigm was used with 5-year-olds, with and without significant histories of OME. As with 8-year-olds, these children had normal hearing and speech articulation. Table 2 shows mean results for several independent measures. Here, mean numbers of separate OME episodes before the age of 3 years are given. Mean annual family incomes are also given, in the tens of thousands. Estimates of nonverbal IQ were obtained with these children using the Block Design subtest of the Wechsler Preschool and Primary Scale of Intelligence-Revised (WPPSI-R) (Wechsler, 1989). This scale has a mean of 10 and a standard deviation of 3. As with 8-year-olds, the PPVT-R was used to estimate verbal IQ.

TABLE 2
5-year-olds with history of OME, and control participants.

	Control (n = 13)	*OME* (n = 13)
Age (Months)	65	65
# Infections < 3 Yrs.	1.5	10.4
SES Metric	37	30
Mean Income	3.8	4.2
Nonverbal IQ Est.	11.5	11.2
Verbal IQ Est.	112	108

The fricative-vowel stimuli already described were used with these 5-year-olds to evaluate their perceptual weighting strategies for speech. These results are shown in Fig. 10, which indicates that the children with histories of early, chronic OME had shallower functions and functions more widely separated (depending on formant transitions) than children in the control group.

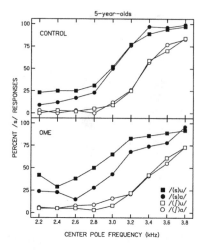

FIG. 10 Results of a '/s/-vowel' versus '/ʃ/-vowel' labeling task.

Phonetic awareness abilities were evaluated in these 5-year-olds using a task in which the child had to pick the word (out of three) that began with the same 'sound' as a target word. Results for this task are shown in Fig. 11. Chance performance is represented here with the dashed line. As can be seen, 5-year-olds who experienced frequent episodes of OME before the age of 3 years could not select the word with the same initial sound with above-chance accuracy.

To compare speech perception results for 8- and 5-year-olds with and without histories of early, chronic OME, two metrics were used. Slopes of the labeling functions were given as changes in probit units (essentially z scores) per kilohertz of change in fricative-noise spectrum. The separations in labeling functions (depending on formant transitions) were given in distance between the functions with formant transitions appropriate for /ʃ/ or /s/, for /ɑ/ and /u/ separately. These distances are measured at the 50% point on the labeling functions (i.e., at the phoneme boundaries), and are given in Hertz of fricative noise. Table 3 gives mean slopes for each group, averaged across the four syllable types, as well as mean difference in phoneme boundaries. The striking aspect of this table is that even by 8 years of age, children with histories of early, chronic OME were not demonstrating perceptual weighting strategies similar to those of 5-year-olds without such histories. This is strong evidence for the notion that deficits in early language experience have long lasting effects on the development of speech perception strategies.

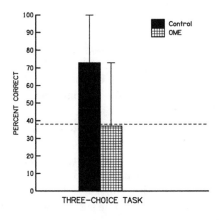

FIG. 11 Results of phonetic awareness tasks.

TABLE 3
Comparison of 8- and 5-year-olds.

Mean slope, across all syllable types

	8-ctl	5-ctl	8-OME	5-OME
Slope	3.89	3.03	2.70	1.71
	(0.98)	(1.41)	(1.03)	(0.53)

Mean difference in phoneme boundaries

	8-ctl	5-ctl	8-OME	5-OME
/ʃɑ/-/sɑ/	462	488	620	634
	(134)	(284)	(223)	(352)
/ʃu/-/su/	610	708	942	1013
	(462)	(480)	(515)	(516)

SUMMARY

The studies described in this chapter have shown that speech perception changes through childhood. The weights assigned to the various acoustic properties of the speech signal change, and the final strategies are language-specific. Also, these studies reveal that the developmental changes described are related to early language experience, rather than to some general developmental change in the auditory system. Finally, evidence is provided that these changes in speech perception are related, in the same participants, to changes in abilities to access phonetic structure.

REFERENCES

Crowther, C. S., & Mann, V. A. (1994). Use of vocalic cues to consonant voicing and native language background: The influence of experimental design. *Perception & Psychophysics, 55*, 513-525.

Dunn, L. M., & Dunn, L. M. (1981). *Peabody picture vocabulary test-revised.* Circle Pines, MN: American Guidance.

Hart, B., & Risley, T. R. (1995). *Meaningful differences in the everyday experiences of young American children.* Baltimore: Brookes.

Joos, M. (1948). Acoustic phonetics. *Language, 48* (Suppl. 2), 1-136.

Nittrouer, S. (1992). Age-related differences in perceptual effects of formant transitions within syllables and across syllable boundaries. *Journal of Phonetics, 20*, 1-32.

Nittrouer, S. (1996a). Discriminability and perceptual weighting of some acoustic cues to speech perception by 3-year-olds. *Journal of Speech and Hearing Research, 39*, 278-297.

Nittrouer, S. (1996b). The relation between speech perception and phonemic awareness: Evidence from low-SES children and children with chronic OM. *Journal of Speech and Hearing Research, 39*, 1059-1070.

Nittrouer, S., & Crowther, C. S. (1998). Examining the role of auditory sensitivity in the developmental weighting shift. *Journal of Speech, Language, and Hearing Research, 41*, 809-818.

Raven, J. C. (1975). *Coloured progressive matrices.* London: H.K. Lewis.

Strange, W. (Ed.). (1995). *Speech perception and linguistic experience: Issues in cross-language research.* Baltimore: York Press.

Wechsler, D. (1989). *Wechsler preschool and primary scale of intelligence* (2nd ed.). San Antonio, TX: Harcourt Brace Janovich.

32

Intelligibility and Acceptability in Speakers with Cleft Palate

Tara Whitehill and Joyce C. Chun

Speech disorders associated with cleft palate include disorders of resonance, such as hypernasality, as well as disorders of articulation or phonology (Bzoch, 1997; McWilliams, Morris & Shelton, 1990). Such problems may result in reduced speech intelligibility, reduced speech acceptability, or both. Witzel (1995) defined speech intelligibility as "how well a listener understands [speech]" and acceptability as "...the subjective impression of the pleasingness of speech" (p. 147). It is important to differentiate between reduced intelligibility and reduced acceptability, both theoretically and because they may have different management implications. A determination of the components contributing to reduced speech intelligibility and acceptability may increase our understanding of cleft palate speech, and serve to guide intervention.

Whitehill (2001) recently conducted a critical review of intelligibility studies in the cleft palate literature, surveying the period 1960-1998. Four main findings from the literature review are summarized here: First, there was much confusion between global terms of speech performance such as intelligibility, acceptability, naturalness, severity, and proficiency. Confusion between such terms was clearly identified in over 20% of the 57 studies reviewed. In addition, few studies provided clear definitions of the terms used in the investigations.

Second, the validity of the methods used to evaluate intelligibility was frequently questionable. For example, almost 50% of the studies reviewed used interval scaling, which is no longer considered a valid method for the measurement of speech intelligibility (Schiavetti, 1992). As illustrated by Schiavetti (1992), experimental evidence has shown that, when listeners attempt to partition speech intelligibility into equal intervals, there is a tendency to subdivide the lower end of the continuum into smaller intervals than the upper end (Schiavetti, 1992). Using the framework suggested by Stevens (1975), speech intelligibility has therefore been defined by Schiavetti (1992) and others as a "prothetic" continuum, in contrast to "metathetic" continua, such as pitch, which can be easily partitioned into equal intervals (Schiavetti, 1992). Orthographic transcription, multiple-choice, and direct magnitude estimation have been recommended as valid procedures for the evaluation of intelligibility (Schiavetti, 1992). In the literature review cited, an additional 16% of the studies used a gross estimate of speech intelligibility, and in 9% of the studies, the method was not specified.

A third finding from the literature review was that there was poor reporting of inter-rater and intra-rater reliability. Almost 50% of the reviewed studies included no information about reliability.

Finally, the review indicated that there has been little attempt to increase our understanding of intelligibility deficits in this population using procedures such as statistical modeling or analysis.

AIMS OF THE STUDY

The current study was a small-scale pilot study, which aimed to address some of the shortcomings of earlier studies, and to illustrate how further studies might also address these needs. An additional aim of the study was to provide a model for further explanatory studies of intelligibility and acceptability in speakers with cleft palate.

More specifically, this study aimed to examine the relationship between intelligibility and acceptability, and the relative contributions of nasality and articulatory accuracy to each, in a group of speakers with repaired cleft palate. With the operational definitions we employed, we predicted that there would be a strong correlation between intelligibility (percentage accuracy at the single-word level, based on a multiple-choice task), and articulatory accuracy (percentage of phonemes transcribed as correct, from a single-word list), and a strong correlation between acceptability and nasality (both based on perceptual judgement by a panel of listeners on an equal-appearing-interval scale).

METHOD

Participants

The speakers were 20 Cantonese-speaking children with repaired cleft palate. There were 8 males and 12 females. Age ranged from 5 years, 1 month to 15 years, 4 months (mean age was 9;0 years). All the speakers were recruited from the Cleft Lip and Palate Centre, Prince Philip Dental Hospital, University of Hong Kong. All the children had been identified as hypernasal during speech-language screening, and were referred for videonasopharyngoscopy evaluation of velopharyngeal status as well as Nasometer evaluation of nasalance. The speakers had normal hearing and no cleft-related syndrome. Speakers with concomitant hyponasality were eliminated from the study in an effort to restrict the scope of the study. All speakers had primary repair of the palate between 12 and 18 months.

The listeners were three native-Cantonese speakers with normal hearing. They were qualified speech-language therapists but were 'nonexperts', in orofacial or resonance disorders. This was thought to best reflect the clinical reality of Hong Kong, where most clinicians treating speakers with cleft palate are nonexperts. A training session was provided for the listeners that focussed on the judgement of resonance. Speech samples from an audiotape (McWilliams & Philips, 1990) were used for the training; Chun & Whitehill (in press) provides further details of the training session.

Materials

The *Cantonese Single-Word Intelligibility Test* (*CSIT*, Whitehill, 1998) was used for the evaluation of intelligibility. This is a 75-item multiple-choice, single-word task. The *CSIT* is similar in both purpose and administration to the intelligibility test developed by Kent and colleagues (Kent, Weismer, Kent & Rosenbek, 1989) and to a lesser extent, that developed by Ziegler and colleagues (Ziegler, Hartmann & von Cramon, 1988). In brief, the listener hears a word produced by one of the speakers and is presented with four written words. The listener must select the character which most resembles the word heard. For each item, three foils differ from the target word, each by one phonetic contrast. The *CSIT* was originally developed for speakers with dysarthria, and the contrasts were thus selected on the basis of errors known to occur in Cantonese speakers with dysarthria (Whitehill & Ciocca, 2000a). However, most of the contrasts were also determined to be problematic for speakers with cleft palate (e.g. place of articulation of stops and fricatives, stop versus nasal, stop versus fricative and affricate; see Chun, 1999 for further details). Intelligibility was defined as the percentage of words correctly identified. The 75 target words of the *CSIT* were also used for the evaluation of articulation.

For the evaluation of nasality, two sets of sentences were used, hereafter referred to as 'oral sentences' and 'nasal sentences'. The five oral sentences contained no nasal consonants; the five nasal sentences were heavily loaded with nasal consonants. The sentences were developed and routinely used for the evaluation of nasalance and nasality in Cantonese speakers (Chun & Whitehill, in press; Whitehill, 2001). The same sets of sentences were used for the evaluation of acceptability.

Procedures

Speech data were collected in a quiet room using a Sony 241 minidisk player, a Bruel and Kjaer low noise unidirectional microphone (Model 4003), and a preamplifier (Bruel & Kjaer Type 2812). The microphone was positioned at a mouth-to-microphone distance of 10 cm. The stimuli were randomized (within each set of materials) before presentation to the speakers. All speech tasks were done as a repetition task, due to the young age of some of the participants, who were unable to read fluently.

The target words of the *CSIT* were low-pass filtered at 22 kHz and digitized at a sampling rate of 44.1 kHz, using a DigiDesign Audiomedia II DSP card on a Macintosh PowerMac computer. Each word was stored as a separate file for the intelligibility listening task.

The listening tasks were conducted in a quiet room, using Sennheiser HD 545 headphones. Listening tasks were administered individually, with each task performed on a different day. Stimuli were randomized within each task, before presentation. Written instructions were provided to the listeners for each task.

The stimuli for the intelligibility task were presented to listeners using a previously designed computer program (Whitehill & Ciocca, 2000b). In addition to randomization of stimuli across speakers and target words, the characters were randomized in terms of the position of the target word on the computer screen. Responses were tallied by the computer program, giving a percentage correct word identification.

For nasality, the sets of sentences were randomized across speaker and condition (oral v. nasal). After hearing each set of five sentences, the listener was asked to make a perceptual judgement of nasality using a 7-point, equal-appearing interval scale (1 = normal and 7 = severe; McWilliams & Philips, 1990).

The procedures for acceptability were similar to those for nasality. That is, after hearing a set of five sentences, the listener was asked to make a perceptual judgement of acceptability, using a 7-point, equal-appearing interval scale. A written definition was provided for acceptability, based on the definitions used by Dagenais, Garcia and Watts (1998) and Southwood (1990). Specifically, listeners were asked "How would you rate this person's speaking skills? Indicate your judgement by circling a number from the 7-point scale provided. A rating of 1 represents acceptable speech, a rating of 7 represents unacceptable speech".

Southwood and Weismer (1993) demonstrated that acceptability is a metathetic continuum, and that interval scaling can thus validly be used to measure acceptability. At the time of this study, there had been no systematic investigation of the validity of interval scaling for the measurement of hypernasality. However, interval scaling is the most commonly practiced method for assessing hypernasality (McWilliams et al., 1990).

For the evaluation of articulation, the 75 target words of the *CSIT* were phonetically transcribed by the second author, a native Cantonese speaker trained in IPA transcription, using narrow phonetic transcription. Twenty percent of the data were retranscribed by the second author, and transcribed by the first author, for reliability. Articulation proficiency was defined as the percentage of words transcribed as correct. (There were no tone errors in the sample.)

Reliability

The inter-judge and intra-judge reliabilities of all four measures are shown in Table 1. Reliability of the oral and nasal sentences were calculated separately. Inter-judge reliability, calculated using Cronbach's alpha, was between 0.75 and 0.79 for acceptability and intelligibility, and about 0.90 for nasality. Intra-judge reliability, calculated using Pearson's r, was above 0.98 for all three measures. For articulation, both inter-judge and intra-judge reliability, calculated on a point-to-point basis, were above 90%.

TABLE 1
Reliability.

		Inter-judge *Cronbach's Alpha*	*Intra-judge* *Pearson's*
Nasality	(oral sentences)	0.91	> 0.98
	(nasal sentences)	0.90	> 0.98
Acceptability	(oral sentences)	0.75	> 0.98
	(nasal sentences)	0.76	> 0.98
Intelligibility		0.79	> 0.98
Articulation		91%*	93%*

*Calculated on a point-by-point basis.

RESULTS

Table 2 shows the range and average (for intelligibility and articulation, the mean, and for acceptability and nasality, the median) for each of the four speech measures. Intelligibility ranged from 76.4 to 97.8%, with a mean of 91%. Acceptability ranged from 1 to 7 for the oral sentences and 2 to 7 for the nasal sentences; the median was just over 4 for both sets of sentences. There was also a wide range of scores for nasality; the median was 3.8 for the oral sentences and 4.1 for the nasal sentences. Finally, articulation proficiency ranged from 81.9 to 100%, with a mean of 96%.

TABLE 2
Descriptive statistics for intelligibility, acceptability, nasality and articulation.

	Range	Average
Intelligibility (% single words correct)	76.4 – 97. 8	91.0
Acceptability (oral)	1–7	4.18
(7-point scale) (nasal)	2–7	4.15
Nasality (oral)	1.7– 6.7	3.8
(7-point scale) (nasal)	1.3–7	4.1
Articulation (% phonemes correct)	81.9–100	95.9

The relationships between intelligibility, acceptability, articulation proficiency, and nasality were examined using Pearson's product-moment correlations. Fig. 1 shows the correlations between the four measures. There was a moderate correlation between the two 'global' speech measures, intelligibility and acceptability, for both the nasal and the oral sentences ($r = 0.61$, $p < 0.001$, and $r = 0.56$, $p < 0.005$, respectively). As predicted, there was a strong correlation between articulation and intelligibility ($r = 0.77$, $p < 0.001$). There was a strong correlation between nasality and acceptability ($r = 0.78$, $p < 0.001$, and 0.75, $p < 0.001$, for oral and nasal sentences, respectively) also as predicted. The correlation between articulation and acceptability was significant, but weaker than that for articulation and intelligibility ($r = 0.56$ $p < 0.01$, for oral sentences and $r = 0.64$, $p < 0.005$, for nasal sentences). The correlation between nasality and intelligibility was not significant ($p > 0.05$).

DISCUSSION

Although there have been a number of investigations of intelligibility in speakers with cleft palate (see McWilliams et al., 1990 for a review), there have been limitations associated with many of these studies, as identified by Whitehill (in press). In addition, there has been little exploration of the relationship between intelligibility and acceptability in speakers with cleft palate, such as has taken place for speakers with dysarthria (e.g., Dagenais et al., 1998; Dagenais, Watts, Turnage & Kennedy, 1999; Southwood, 1990).

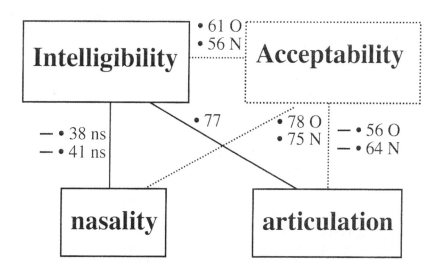

FIG. 1 Correlations between intelligibility, acceptability, nasality and articulation (O = oral sentences; N = nasal sentences; ns = non-significant; all other correlations were significant at the $p < 0.01$ level).

In this small-scale study, we attempted to overcome some of the problems associated with previous studies of intelligibility in speakers with cleft palate. First, a clear differentiation was made between intelligibility and acceptability, as indicated by the operational definitions employed, and the relation between these two measures was investigated. Second, we used a method for evaluating intelligibility (a single-word, multiple-choice task) which is considered to be valid (Schiavetti, 1992). Third, both inter-judge and intra-judge reliability were calculated and reported (as reported previously, more than 50% of the studies reviewed by Whitehill, in press, had failed to do so). Finally, we illustrated how contributors to intelligibility and acceptability can begin to be determined.

Due to the constraints of service delivery in Hong Kong, nonexpert listeners were used for the listening tasks. The high inter-judge and intra-judge agreements obtained were at least partially attributed to the training session we provided, particularly those for nasality, a dimension notoriously unreliable for naïve or nonexpert listeners (McWilliams et al., 1990).

Although there was a range of articulation proficiency in this group of speakers, overall, both articulation and intelligibility were relatively mildly affected. It would be valuable to include speakers with more severely affected articulation in future studies.

The results of this small-scale study supported the belief that intelligibility and acceptability are related, but not identical measures. Similar findings have been reported by Dagenais, et al. (1999) and Southwood (1990) for speakers with dysarthria.

For the purposes of this study, intelligibility was defined as the percentage of single words correctly identified. As predicted, there was a strong correlation between intelligibility and the percentage of phonemes transcribed as correct, our measure of articulation proficiency. This strong correlation was not surprising, given the operational definition of intelligibility used in this study, which was heavily dependent on the ability of listeners to employ minimal phonetic contrasts to extract meaning. In contrast, the correlation between intelligibility and nasality was non-significant. Although hypernasality may reduce speech acceptability or naturalness, we would not expect hypernasality to have a detrimental effect on intelligibility, unless it was so severe as to lead to changes in phonemic contrasts (e.g. /t/ → [n]).

Our results showed a strong correlation between nasality and acceptability. Although hypernasality may not affect speech intelligibility, it can of course be distracting or rated as unacceptable by listeners. Reduced articulatory proficiency also had a detrimental effect on acceptability, as might be expected, although the correlation was not as strong as that between articulation and intelligibility ($r = 0.56$ and 0.64, v. 0.77).

In this study, we examined the impact of only two factors, nasality and articulation, on intelligibility and acceptability. A further determination of variables contributing to reduced intelligibility and acceptability in speakers with cleft palate is strongly encouraged. Determination of such variables would provide evidence-based guidelines for clinical intervention. For example, a clinician would have support for prioritizing certain targets for intervention, if it is known that those targets make the strongest contribution to reductions in intelligibility or acceptability. Or, a clinician might chose to target those variables that have the strongest impact on intelligibility first, reserving targets which may increase acceptability until such time as the client is able to make him or herself understood to daily communication partners.

The relationship between instrumental and perceptual measures is already well established for several components of cleft palate speech (Kuehn & Moller, 2000). Instrumental as well as perceptually-based measures should be considered for explanatory models of intelligibility and acceptability (see, for example, Fletcher, 1978, who predicted speech intelligibility in a group of speakers with cleft palate using ten physiological variables, resulting in an R^2 of 0.81).

Fig. 2 illustrates how the scope of investigation of this small-scale, pilot study could be extended to include other perceptual and instrumental variables in an explanatory model of intelligibility and acceptability for speakers with cleft palate. In the current study, only simple correlations were employed to investigate relationships between 'global' and 'contributing' speech variables in speakers with repaired cleft palate. Future, larger-scale studies could employ methods such as stepwise multiple regression (e.g. Kent et al., 1989; Whitehill

& Ciocca, 2000b) or structural equation modeling (e.g. Shriberg, Friel-Patti, Flipsen & Brown, 2000) to better explain reductions in intelligibility and acceptability in this population. Speech signal manipulations such as those employed by Maasen and Povel (1985) in their study of speakers with hearing impairment would be another fruitful future approach.

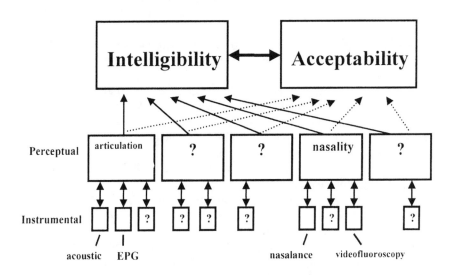

FIG. 2 Explanatory model of intelligibility and acceptability in cleft palate.

REFERENCES

Bzoch, K. R. (Ed.). (1997). *Communicative disorders related to cleft lip and palate* (4th ed.). Austin, TX: Pro-Ed.

Chun, C. J. (1999). *The relationship between nasalance, nasality and intelligibility of Cantonese children with cleft palate*. Unpublished undergraduate thesis, University of Hong Kong.

Chun, C. J., & Whitehill, T. L. (in press). The relationship between nasalance and nasality in Cantonese children with cleft palate. *Asia Pacific Journal of Speech, Language and Hearing*.

Dagenais, P. A., Garcia, J. M., & Watts, C. R. (1998). Acceptability and intelligibility of mildly dysarthric speech by different listeners. In M. P. Cannito, K. M. Yorkston & D. R. Beukelman (Eds.), *Neuromotor speech disorders: Nature, assessment, and management* (pp. 229–239). Baltimore, MD: Paul H. Brooks.

Dagenais, P. A., Watts, C. R., Turnage, L. M., & Kennedy, S. (1999). Intelligibility and acceptability of moderately dysarthric speech by three types of listeners. *Journal of Medical Speech-Language Pathology, 7*, 91–96.

Fletcher, S. G. (1978). Diagnosing speech disorders from cleft palate. New York: Grune & Stratton.

Kent, R. D., Weismer, G., Kent, J. F., & Rosenbek, J. C. (1989). Toward phonetic intelligibility testing in dysarthria. *Journal of Speech and Hearing Disorders, 54*, 482–499.

Kuehn, D. P., & Moller, K. T. (2000). Speech and language issues in the cleft palate population: The state of the art. *Cleft Palate-Craniofacial Journal, 37*, 348–35.

Maasen, B., & Povel, D. J. (1985). The effect of segmental and suprasegmental corrections on the intelligibility of deaf speech. *Journal of the Acoustical Society of America, 78*, 877–886.

McWilliams, B. J., & Philips, B. J. (1990). *Velopharyngeal incompetence: An Audio Seminar.* Philadelphia, PA: B. C. Decker, Inc.

McWilliams, B. J., Morris, H. L., & Shelton, R. S. (1990). *Cleft palate speech* (2nd ed.). Philadelphia, PA: B. C. Decker, Inc.

Schiavetti, N. (1992). Scaling procedures for the measurement of speech intelligibility. In R. D. Kent (Ed.). *Intelligibility in speech disorders* (pp. 11–34). Amsterdam: John Benjamins.

Shriberg, L. D., Friel-Patti, S., Flipsen, P. Jr., & Brown, R. L. (2000). Otitis media, fluctuating hearing loss, and speech-language outcomes: A preliminary structural equation model. *Journal of Speech, Language, and Hearing Research, 43*, 100–120.

Southwood, M. H. (1990). A term by any other name: Bizarreness, acceptability, naturalness and normalcy judgments of speakers with amyotrophic lateral sclerosis. Unpublished doctoral dissertation, University of Wisconsin, Madison.

Southwood, M. H., & Weismer, G. (1993). Listener judgments of the bizarreness, acceptability, naturalness and normalcy of the dysarthria associated with amyotrophic lateral sclerosis. *Journal of Medical Speech-Language Pathology, 1*, 151–161.

Stevens, S. S. (1975). *Psychophysics*. New York: Wiley.

Whitehill, T. L. (1998). *Speech intelligibility in Cantonese speakers with congenital dysarthria.* Unpublished doctoral dissertation, University of Hong Kong.

Whitehill, T. L. (2001). Nasalance measures in Cantonese-speaking women. *Cleft Palate-Craniofacial Journal, 38*, 119–125.

Whitehill, T. L. (in press). Assessing intelligibility in speakers with cleft palate: A critical review of the literature. *Cleft Palate-Craniofacial Journal.*

Whitehill, T. L., & Ciocca, V. (2000a). Speech errors in Cantonese speaking adults with cerebral palsy. *Clinical Linguistics and Phonetics, 14*, 111–130.

Whitehill, T. L., & Ciocca, V. (2000b). Perceptual-phonetic predictors of single-word intelligibility: A study of Cantonese dysarthria. *Journal of Speech,Language, and Hearing Research, 43*, 1451–1465

Witzel, M. A. (1995). Communicative impairment associated with clefting. In R. J. Shprintzen & J. Bardach (Eds.), *Cleft palate speech management: A multidisciplinary approach* (pp. 137–166), St Louis, MO: Mosby.

Ziegler, W., Hartmann, E., & von Cramon, D. (1988). Word identification testing in the diagnostic evaluation of dysarthric speech. *Clinical Linguistics and Phonetics, 2*, 291–308.

NOTES

Parts of this study were based on an undergraduate dissertation conducted by the second author, under the supervision of the first author. An earlier version of this study was presented at the 4th Asian Pacific Cleft Lip & Palate Conference, Fukuoka, Japan, September, 1999.

33

Voicing Contrasts and the Deaf: Production and Perception Issues

Sandra Madureira, Luisa Barzaghi and Beatriz Mendes

In this chapter we are interested in considering production in direct relation to perception. According to Whalen (1999, p. 1257) the relationship between production and perception "has received little direct experimentation and the vast majority of production studies have no measurement of the perceptual effects, except for a check by the experimenter that the category produced was the one intended". This is not the case with our study, which used spectrographic analysis to investigate the production of stop consonants by a hearing-impaired participant and the perception of these consonants by a group of participants who acted as judges.

Two measures, VOT and closure duration, were made on word-initial stops occurring at the beginning of stressed syllables in a corpus recorded by the hearing-impaired participant and by a normal-hearing participant who acted as control. Considering the results of our study with respect to the normal-hearing participants' perception of stops as produced by the hearing-impaired participant meant taking into account the nature of the articulatory gestures produced, the acoustic output and the resulting auditory effects of these gestures.

METHOD

Corpus and Recording Procedures

The experimental data consisted of six high-frequency, two-syllable minimal pairs *pata* ('duck'), *bata* ('gown'; 'to strike'), *tata* ('great grandmother'), *data* ('date'), *cata* ('to get') and *gata* ('cat'), inserted in a carrier sentence *Diga* _____ *baixinho* ('Say _____ in a soft way'). The words all had the structure CVCV where 'V' was /a/ and the stress fell on the first vowel. This stress pattern, known as paroxyton, was chosen because it is the most frequent stress pattern in Brazilian Portuguese (Albano, Moreira, Aquino, Silva & Kakinohara, 1995). Brazilian Portuguese has six stop consonants differing from each other by place of articulation and voicing contrast.

TABLE 1
Portuguese stop consonant sounds.

	Bilabial	Dentoalveolar	Velar
Unvoiced	/p/	/t/	/k/
Voiceless	/b/	/d/	/g/

The data were recorded in a sound treated studio. The sentences in each of the ten lists were presented in random order. The participants were seated in front of the microphone and the sentences were presented on cards through the acoustically isolated window of the booth. The recording was made on DAT tape, TCD-D8 Sony, with Audio Technica (ATM 25) microphone, 600 ohms impedance, placed 10 cm from the speaker's mouth. Ten repetitions of the six sentences, by each participant, were recorded. The recordings were digitized by means of the CSL, model 4300B, from Kay Elemetrics, at a 22 kHz sampling rate and analyzed using the MultiSpeech software from Kay Elemetrics. The data were stored in a sampled file on computer for listening and analysis.

Participants

The participants of both the production and the perception experiments were native speakers of Brazilian Portuguese from São Paulo, Brazil. The perception task was carried out by sixty normal-hearing undergraduate students who were not familiar with hearing-impaired speech. One of the participants of the production task was a normal-hearing 35-year-old woman with modal vocal quality (Laver, 1980) and no history of articulatory disorders. The other was a hearing-impaired female participant, 16 years old, with bilateral sensorineural hearing loss, severe in the right ear and profound in the left, acquired at the age of 18 months as a consequence of meningitis. She has worn a hearing aid and has been following an oral approach rehabilitation program at Derdic[1] – PUC/SP

---

[1]Derdic is a division of Pontifícia Universidade Católica de São Paulo (PUC/SP) whose mission is offering clinical and educational assistance to people with hearing, voice or language disorders.

since she was two years old. At the time of the recording, she was attending Grade 7 of a regular school. Her pure tone thresholds are given in Table 2.

TABLE 2
Hearing-impaired participant: pure tone thresholds.

	250Hz	500Hz	1000Hz	2000Hz	3000Hz	4000Hz	6000Hz	8000Hz
RE	90dB	90dB	100dB	80dB	75dB	80dB	120dB↓	100dB↓
LE	90dB	110dB	120dB	120dB↓	120dB↓	120dB↓	120dB↓	100dB↓
HA	-	55dB	50dB	40dB	45dB	50dB	-	-

Note. RE stands for right ear, LE for left ear and HA for hearing-aided.

Perception Task Procedures

Six sentence tokens (all the sentences of the fifth repetition of the data set, recorded by the hearing-impaired participant) were presented in random order to the 60 students through head phones connected to a computer. The intensity was adjusted to the most comfortable level for each participant. The participants were told to write down what they heard even if it didn't sound like a familiar word.

Spectrographic Analysis Procedures

Two measurements were made on the initial stops of the experimental words: VOT (voice onset time) and closure duration. Among the various cues[2] to voicing in word-initial stops, VOT was chosen for this investigation, since the voicing categories of Brazilian Portuguese stops are based on the timing events of laryngeal and supralaryngeal gestures (Behlau, 1986; Levy, 1993; Rocca, 1999). Duration of closure was measured since voiceless stop closures in Brazilian Portuguese follow the trend of a great number of languages in being longer than their voiced counterparts (Barbosa, 1999).

The recordings were analyzed using a preemphasis of 0.98, an analysis size of 75 points and a Hanning window. VOT was measured from the release to the start of voicing (Lisker & Abramson, 1964). The voicing starting point was considered to be where at least the first two formants were energized. Closure duration was measured from both spectrograms and waveforms, using both visual and auditory cues, with the waveform cursors being linked to the those on the spectrograms. Positive and negative VOT were measured for the normal-hearing productions. Examples of wide band spectrograms of [pa] (a) and [ba] (b) as pronounced by the normal-hearing participant can be seen in Fig.1.

---

[2]Shimizu (1996) presents a good review of the literature.

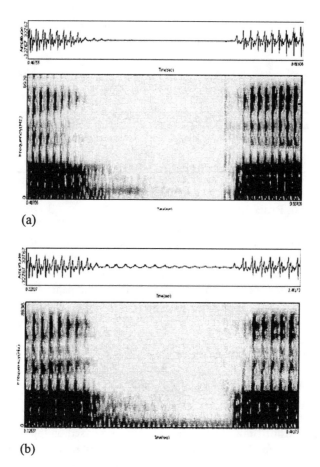

FIG. 1 Examples of wide band spectrograms of [pa] (a) and [ba] (b), as pronounced by the normal-hearing participant.

No voicing lead (voicing lead being characteristic of voiced stop consonants in Brazilian Portuguese) was observed in the wide band spectrograms of the stops produced by the hearing-impaired participant. Inspection of these spectrograms revealed that the release of the stop was preceded by a silent gap that, in turn, was preceded by a voice bar. This voice bar followed the final vowel of the word before the stop consonant under analysis. Three measurements were made from the hearing-impaired productions: duration of the voice bar preceding the silent gap, duration of the silent gap preceding the release and the interval from the release to the onset of voicing (positive VOT). Examples of wide band spectrograms of [pa] (a) and

[ba] (b) as pronounced by the hearing-impaired participant are shown in Fig. 2.

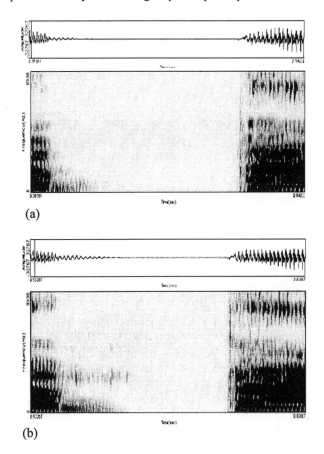

(a)

(b)

FIG. 2 Examples of wide band spectrograms of [pa] (a) and [ba] (b) as pronounced by
the hearing-impaired participant.

RESULTS

The perception task revealed that the hearing-impaired pronunciations of /b/, /d/
and /g/ were almost always identified as voiceless. The word *gata* (cat) was
never correctly identified. The voiced bilabial and the voiced dentoalveolar were
better identified than the voiced velar. The voiceless consonants /p/ and /k/
were correctly identified, but the listeners had difficulty in identifying both /t/
and /d/. Voiceless bilabial and voiceless velar stops obtained the best scores in

the perception task. Voiceless dentoalveolar stops were poorly identified. It is worth noting that manner of articulation was not troublesome: only eight out of 360 words were identified incorrectly with respect to manner. The results of the perception task are summarized in Table 3.

TABLE 3
Perception task results showing the distribution of the responses.

Stimuli→ ↓Responses	Pata	Bata	Tata	Data	Cata	Gata
Pata	**51**	46	10	5	7	3
Bata	4	**4**	4	2	1	1
Tata	0	2	**31**	34	0	1
Data	0	1	5	**7**	1	0
Cata	3	7	8	8	**50**	55
Gata	0	0	0	0	1	**0**
Other	2	0	2	4	0	0
Total	60	60	60	60	60	60

As the voicing contrast in the deaf speaker's productions proved troublesome, we were interested in how VOT measures of the stops produced by the deaf participant differed from those of the normal-hearing participant. The results of the VOT measures of stops as pronounced by the normal-hearing participant show that voiced stops exhibit negative VOT values, bilabials showing the highest negative values and velars the lowest ones. Voiceless stops had positive VOT values, as would be expected in Brazilian Portuguese (Behlau, 1986; Rocca, 1999), velars exhibiting the highest positive values and bilabials the lowest, again as expected. Statistically significant differences ($p < 0.01$) were found between the VOT values of /b/, /d/ and /g/ by the hearing-impaired participant and the normal-hearing participant. While VOT values in the stops produced by the normal-hearing participant vary according to the place of articulation, for the hearing-impaired participant VOT values for bilabials and dentoalveolars partially overlap (see Table 4 and Fig. 3).

The hearing-impaired participant had no negative VOT values. Positive VOT values were on average slightly higher in voiceless stops than in voiced stops, though this difference was not significant (see Fig. 4). There was no significant difference in VOT between /b/ as pronounced by the hearing-impaired participant and /p/ as pronounced by the normal-hearing participant. However /d/ and /g/ as pronounced by the hearing-impaired participant differed significantly ($p < 0.05$) in VOT from (respectively) /t/ and /k/ as pronounced by the normal- hearing participant.

TABLE 4
Mean VOT values (in ms) of Brazilian Portuguese stop consonants
for the normal- hearing (n. h.) and the hearing-impaired (h. i.) participants.

	Pata	Bata	Tata	Data	Cata	Gata
	mean	mean	mean	mean	mean	mean
	(SD)	(SD)	(SD)	(SD)	(SD)	(SD)
n.h.	11	-90	19	-77	32	-66
	(3)	(7)	(2)	(6)	(5)	(6)
h.i.	13	12	15	14	37	35
	(2)	(3)	(5)	(3)	(5)	(4)

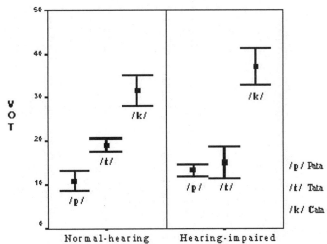

FIG. 3 VOT values (in ms) of /p, t, k/ for the normal-hearing and hearing-impaired
participants, bracketed by standard deviations.

Table 5 shows means and standard deviations of the durations of the voice bar (1), the silent gap (2) and the positive VOT values (3) for all the stops by the hearing-impaired participant. Voiceless bilabial and velar duration values for (1) are smaller than those of their voiced counterparts. No such difference was found for dentoalveolars. However, the period of voicing in (1) was longer for dentoalveolars than for bilabials and velars and their total duration was also longer. Voiceless bilabial, dentoalveolar and velar duration values for (2) are higher than those of their voiced counterparts. The difference between the voiced and voiceless velar stop consonant was found to be significant for (2).

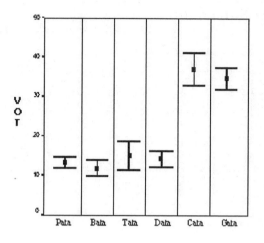

FIG. 4 VOT (in ms) of /p, t, k/ and /b, d, g/ for the hearing-impaired participant.

TABLE 5
Mean durations (in ms) of the voice bar (1), the silent gap (2) and the
positive VOT (3) in stops by the hearing-impaired participant.

	Pata (1)	Pata (2)	Pata (3)	Bata (1)	Bata (2)	Bata (3)
mean	26	163	13	31	152	12
SD	12	29	2	12	14	3

	Tata (1)	Tata (2)	Tata (3)	Data (1)	Data (2)	Data (3)
mean	36	167	15	35	164	14
SD	14	10	5	12	10	3

	Cata (1)	Cata (2)	Cata (3)	Gata (1)	Gata (2)	Gata (3)
mean	16	157	37	19	144	35
SD	3	31	6	4	25	4

Stop closure durations for the normal hearing-participant followed the general trend indicated in the phonetic literature, that is, higher values were obtained for voiceless stops than for voiced stops ($p < 0.001$; see Table 6).

TABLE 6

Mean stop closure durations (in ms) for stops by the normal-hearing participant.

	Pata	Bata	Tata	Data	Cata	Gata
mean	118	99	120	93	115	83
SD	5	6	7	5	8	6

Differences in stop closure duration between voiced and voiceless stops are smaller in the hearing-impaired participant's productions than in the normal-hearing participant's productions. The difference is statistically significant for the velar minimal pair ($p < 0.05$), but not for the bilabial and dentoalveolar minimal pairs (see Table 7).

TABLE 7

Average duration values (in ms) for stop consonant sounds as produced by the hearing-impaired participant

	Pata	Bata	Tata	Data	Cata	Gata
mean	202	195	218	213	210*	198*
SD	26	11	16	13	26	25

Note. * means significant voiced-voiceless difference

In general, all stop closures produced by the hearing-impaired participant were longer than those by the normal-hearing participant ($p < 0.001$). Furthermore, the hearing-impaired participant's were more variable, as can be seen in Fig. 5, which shows the median closure duration of each stop (horizontal bar), bracketed by the highest and lowest values, with the box showing the inter-quartile range.

In summary, no statistically significant differences in VOT values were found between /p/~/b/; /p/~/t/; /b/~/d/; /t/~/d/; /k/~/g/ in the hearing-impaired participant's productions of stop consonants. Statistically significant differences were found between /p/~/k/; /t/~/k/; /d/~/g/; /b/~/g/. Measurements of VOT and stop closures in the initial stops produced by the hearing-impaired revealed four interesting facts: overlapping of bilabial and dentoalveolar VOT values; absence of voicing lead; greater dispersion of the distribution of VOT values and longer closures.

DISCUSSION

The results of the perception and production tasks are congruent in two respects: 1) extremely poor discrimination by the judges between voiceless and voiced

stops and absence of contrasts between positive and negative VOT in the
hearing impaired participant's productions and 2) excellent discrimination
between bilabials and velars by the judges and distinct VOT length in the
hearing-impaired participant's production of front (bilabials and dentoalveolars)
and back (velar) stop consonants.

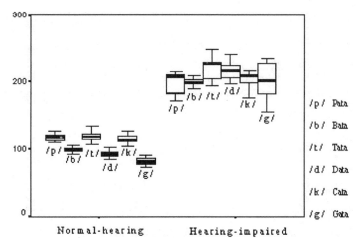

FIG. 5 Median closure durations (in ms) of the stops by the hearing-impaired participant
and the normal-hearing participant.

Dentoalveolars posed a lot of difficulties as expected, since, from the acoustic
point of view, they are characterized by high frequency spectral dominance
(troublesome for the hearing-impaired) and, from a physiological point of view,
they require more precise actions of the tip and blade of the tongue. The
dispersion in the identification of dentoalveolars can be thought of not only in
terms of production and auditory constraints but also in terms of linguistic
constraints. The adjustment of the tip of the tongue is more difficult to make and
there is little tolerance, since a lot of contrasts in Brazilian Portuguese depend
on the degree of constriction in the dentoalveolar region.

Bilabials were well identified in the perception task. Bilabial gestures are
easy to imitate because of their visual cues and are not usually difficult for
hearing-impaired participants. They are also characterized by low frequency
spectral dominance.

The least dispersion found in the results of the perception tasks in terms of
identifying the place of articulation of velar stops can be thought of as reflecting
acoustic, physiological and linguistic constraints. Acoustically, velar sounds are
characterized by mid-frequency spectral dominance. From the point of view of
articulation, actions of the body of the tongue (dorsum) are easier to produce

than those of the tip and blade of the tongue. From the linguistic point of view, there are few velar consonants in Portuguese. In CV syllable initial position, there are only two contrasting velar sounds: /k/ and /g/. However, it has eleven sounds contrasting in the labial/dentoalveolar region: /p/, /b/, /t/ ,/d/ , /n/, /l/, /s/, /z/, /f/, /v/, and /r/.

Difficulty in coordinating articulatory gestures is made evident by inspection of the average duration of the stop sounds as produced by the hearing-impaired participant. In her productions, dentoalveolars were much longer than velars and bilabials. This is not the case with the normal hearing participant either in this study and in the one by Barbosa (1999; see Table 8).

TABLE 8
Average duration and standard deviation (in ms) of the closure phase of stops
in Brazilian Portuguese for a normal-hearing participant (Barbosa, 1999).

	Bilabial	Dentoalveolar	Velar
Unvoiced	/p/ 120 (20)	/t/ 113 (20)	/k/ 121 (21)
Voiced	/b/ 86 (17)	/d/ 71 (17)	/g/ 67 (16)

The results of the perception task reflect the complexity of coordinating the different articulatory gestures. The velar points of articulation were 106 times correctly identified, the bilabials 105 and the dentoalveolars 77 times, out of 120. As far as discrimination of voiced segments is concerned, the results showed that the hearing-impaired participant's pronunciations of /g/ were always identified as voiceless. Her pronunciations of /d/ and /b/ were identified as voiced seven and four times respectively. The fact that no /g/ sound was identified as voiced by the judges is intriguing. From the production point of view, it is more difficult to set the vocal folds vibrating before velars than before front sounds because the passage of airflow is halted nearer to the folds. Differences in duration of the voice bar preceding the silent gap in the stops produced by the hearing-impaired participant (32 ms for /d/, 28 ms for /b/ and 17 ms for /g/) are congruent with the physiological constraints mentioned previously. The misidentification of /g/ as a voiceless sound, compared to the slightly better discrimination of /b/ and /d/, can be tentatively interpreted as reflecting the differences in duration values of the voice bar before the silent gap.

Spectrographic inspection of the data in our study has shown that the hearing-impaired participant tries to differentiate between voiced and voiceless segments but in a way that differs from the normal hearing participant and consequently fails in getting the sounds she produces discriminated.

ACKNOWLEDGMENTS

Thanks are given to the participants of the study, to Yara de Castro for the Statistics, to Mario Fontes, Ernesto Foscai, Mario Augusto de Souza Fontes, Maurício Alexandre de Souza Campos and Eduardo Kawanishi for their technical support in the Phonetics Laboratory (LIAC) at Pontifícia Universidade Católica de São Paulo, to CEFAC for the use of CSL, to Plinio Barbosa, Aglael Gama Rossi, Marcelo Marcelino Rosa and Ellen Osborn for their assistance and to an anonymous reviewer for helpful suggestions.

REFERENCES

Albano, E., Moreira, A., Aquino, P., Silva, A., & Kakinohara, R. (1995). Segment frequency and word structure in Brazilian Portuguese. *Proceedings of the 13th International Congress of Phonetic Sciences,* Stockholm, *3*, 346-349.

Behlau, M. S. (1986). *Análise do Tempo de Início da Sonorização na Discriminação de Sons Plosivos do Português.* Unpublished doctoral dissertation, Escola Paulista de Medicina (UFESP), São Paulo.

Barbosa, P. (1999). Revelar a estrutura rítmica de uma língua construindo máquinas falantes: pela integração de ciência e tecnologia de fala. In: E. Scarpa (Ed.), *Estudos de prosódia* (pp. 21-52). Campinas: Editora da Unicamp.

Laver, J. (1980). *The Phonetic Description of Voice Quality.* Cambridge, UK: Cambridge University Press.

Levy, I. P. (1993). Para além da Nau dos Insensatos *Português.* Unpublished doctoral dissertation, University of Campinas (UNICAMP), Campinas.

Lisker, L., & Abramson, A. S. (1964). A cross-language study of voicing in initial stops: Acoustic measurements. *Word, 20*, 384-422.

Rocca, P. D. A. (1999). Some characteristics of VOT in stops produced by speakers of English and Portuguese. *Proceedings of the 14th International Congress of Phonetic Sciences.* San Francisco. (Vol. 2; pp. 1425-1428).

Shimizu, K. (1996). *A cross-language study of voicing contrasts of stop consonants in Asian languages.* Tokyo: Seibido Publishing.

Whalen, D. H. (1999). Three lines of evidence for direct links between production and perception in speech. In J. J. Ohala, Y. Hasegawa, M. Ohala, D. Granville & A.C. Bailey (Eds.).*Proceedings of the 14th International Conference of Phonetic Sciences,* San Francisco. (Vol. 2; pp. 1257-1260).

34

Otitis Media and the Acquisition of Consonants

Adele W. Miccio, Kristine M. Yont, Heather L. Clemons
and Lynne Vernon-Feagans

Otitis media (OM) is one of the most common childhood diseases and frequently results in a fluctuating mild-to-moderate conductive hearing loss (Paradise et al., 1997). Children in day care are also exposed daily to high levels of background noise (Painter & Frank, 1999). The combination of these factors places children in day care at high risk for not obtaining the auditory–verbal experience necessary for acquiring speech normally (Vernon-Feagans, Manlove & Volling, 1996).

Findings of previous studies have not always yielded significant differences between children with chronic otitis media (COM) and those who are non-chronic (NOM), possibly due to measurement limitations (Schwartz, Mody & Petinou, 1997). Most studies of the effects of otitis media on consonant development have been retrospective or cross-sectional and based on general indices of correctly produced consonants (Roberts & Clarke-Klein, 1994). Some young children with OM are limited in the amount and/or diversity of their babbling inventories (Luloff, Menyuk & Teele, 1991; Miccio, Yont, Davie & Vernon-Feagans, 1999; Robb, Psak & Pang-Ching, 1993; Yont, Miccio & Vernon-Feagans, 1999). In addition, children with OM may have delayed onset of meaningful speech (Miccio et al., 1999; Yont et al., 1999). Some children with OM continue to produce a reduced number of initial consonants at two years of age (Abraham, Wallace & Gravel, 1996) and are less intelligible at three years of age (Shriberg, Friel-Patti, Flipsen & Brown, 2000). Additionally, phonetic limitations may be associated with limited lexical (Mirak & Rescorla, 1998; Rvachew, Slawinski, Williams & Green, 1999; Yont et al., 1999), syntactic (Wallace, Gravel, Schwartz & Ruben, 1996), and/or pragmatic (Yont, Snow & Vernon-Feagans, in press) acquisition.

To provide data that is sensitive to the effects of COM, there is a need for longitudinal investigations of individuals using repeated measures. These methods may distinguish between children who compensate for OM-related phonologic constraints and those who continue on a downward spiral to later language problems. The objective of this study is to examine prospectively and longitudinally the relationship among COM, hearing acuity and the range and the types of consonants produced by infants and toddlers in day care. This chapter describes preliminary results from a subset of children whose developing phonologies are representative of the different patterns of phonological acquisition observed over a two year period.

METHOD

Participants

Ten children who entered the Penn State Child Development Center during the first year of life participated in this study. These children were selected because they were enrolled in day care for a minimum of 20 hours per week. Additionally, all children were Caucasian and from two-parent dual income families. Health status prior to enrollment in the study was determined by parent questionnaire. With the exception of histories of OM, all participants were healthy. Hearing was evaluated at the time of entrance to the study and annually thereafter unless a positive diagnosis occurred. A nurse practitioner assessed middle ear function weekly by pneumatic otoscopy and immittance audiometry. To be classified as COM, children had positive diagnoses of OM a minimum of 30% of the time.

Procedure

Speech sampling occurred in a playroom adjacent to the children's day care. Samples were videotaped during a 30-minute play routine approximately every two weeks. Children wore a small lavaliere microphone connected to a wireless FM transmitter and linked to an FM receiver. Audio signals were recorded onto a hifi audio channel of a videotape simultaneously with the video signal.

Transcription and Analysis

Samples were glossed and transcribed phonetically using Logical International Phonetic Programs (LIPP; Oller & Delgado, 1999). Analyses completed from the transcribed data were the number of true consonants (not a glottal or a glide) in babbling and in meaningful speech (Stoel-Gammon, 1989), the complexity of babbling (babbling levels, Stoel-Gammon, 1989), and the phonetic complexity of meaningful speech (phonetic levels, Dinnsen, Chin, Elbert & Powell, 1990).

RESULTS

Of the ten children participating in this longitudinal study, three were NOM throughout the study and demonstrated multiple paths to the adult phonological system. Two children were COM throughout the study. They had elevated hearing levels and atypical phonetic development that included continuous use of non-English sounds across time. Of the five remaining children, three had COM during the first year of life and two had COM during the second year of life. The three children affected during the first year of life had more atypical speech characteristics than children not affected until the second year. The consonant systems of children affected during the second year experienced a growth plateau or regression during bouts of OM and one also used non-English speech sounds. Speech characteristics of four boys, representative of these patterns, are discussed next.

Participant 2: Chronic

P2 was classified as COM throughout the study. This child did not begin to babble until the second year of life and the onset of canonical babble coincided with a period of wellness. This child was nearly two years of age at the onset of meaningful speech, also coincidental with a period of wellness. Throughout the study, declines in the amount of vocalizations co-occurred with elevated hearing levels. During a severe bout after age 2;0, P2 ceased to produce an earlier acquired /s/. PE tubes were inserted bilaterally at age 2;4. Directly following tube placement, the amount and diversity of meaningful speech increased sharply and babbling decreased. This child's general speech characteristics were described as "hard to understand" and he produced non-English fricatives, particularly velars. Although the growth of the phonological system was delayed, all phonetic inventories were lawful (Dinnsen et al., 1990; Stoel-Gammon, 1985).

Participant 3: Non-chronic

P3 demonstrated typical phonological development. Glides and labial and anterior stops and nasals occurred first, followed by members of the fricative, affricate, and liquid manner classes. As meaningful speech increased, babbling decreased. Generally speaking, his learning curve was not affected by intermittent bouts of OM. Overall, his speech was characterized as following a normal developmental hierarchy of acquisition with occasional plateaus that corresponded to episodes of OM.

Participant 6: Early Chronic

P6 was diagnosed with COM during the first year of life. In addition to stops and nasals, his early consonant inventories included non-English fricatives and trills. At age 18 months, PE tubes were inserted bilaterally. After tube placement, there was an immediate improvement in hearing acuity and a sharp rise in the number of consonants produced. In addition, the number of canonical and variegated babbles increased. Unlike P2 however, no decrease in the quantity of babbled utterances occurred, despite an increase in the number of English consonants used meaningfully. P6 acquired English fricatives and affricates but also continued to use lateral and velar fricatives and alveolar trills following tube placement.

Participant 9: Later Chronic

P9 experienced bouts of OM early in the first year of life but did not meet the criteria for COM until the second year of life. Onset of babbling occurred at about eight months of age and the onset of meaningful speech occurred at about 14 months of age. This child's consonant inventory, however, increased slowly with plateaus over as much as two to three months in time. In addition, the inventory was atypical. Speech production contained consistent use of glottals as syllable onsets. In addition to stops and nasals, this child's phonology was characterized by bilabial and velar fricatives, and sounds with alternative airstream mechanisms (e.g. dental clicks used in CV syllables). Early episodes of OM may have compromised phonological learning despite the low occurrence of the disease until the second year of life.

CONCLUSION

Both chronicity of OM and the amount of hearing loss negatively affect phonological acquisition. In this study, children with COM produced non-English consonants and were less intelligible than children classified as NOM. The children with the earliest diagnoses of OM produced the most unusual sounds (e.g. clicks) and/or were more likely to have unlawful phonetic inventories (Dinnsen et al., 1990; Stoel-Gammon, 1985) that persisted across time. Although young children in Stoel-Gammon's (1985) study of early consonant acquisition also produced non-English consonants, productions were temporary and were not seen consistently across time in any individual. Children in this study, however, continued to produce non-English sounds in babbling and early words and across multiple time samples.

Previous studies of consonant acquisition have yielded mixed results. Methodological differences may explain why more severe phonetic problems were observed in these children than in other studies. In this study, the status of the ears was diagnosed weekly, regardless of overt symptoms. Consequently, a number of cases of "silent OM" were discovered. In previous studies, children's ear status was assessed in a number of ways ranging from monthly observations to observations whenever parents brought their children to the clinic with overt symptoms of illness. Consequently, children with "silent COM" may have been presumed to be free of otitis media. In addition, the definitions of COM vary widely across studies. In our study, a 30% cut-off was used. In other studies, other percentages of occurrence or number of episodes were used. Finally, many studies, especially those with a large number of participants, are cross-sectional. As a result, observation of individual children's speech production in relation to their hearing and OM status is difficult. This study reports data on individual children followed for two years from their entrance to day care. Results support the hypothesis of a relationship among the chronicity of OM, hearing acuity, and consonant development. Continued study of early phonological acquisition of infants and toddlers with otitis media may assist in the early identification of children at risk for subsequent problems learning language.

ACKNOWLEDGMENTS

The assistance of Heather Brown and Abram Falek with data analysis is appreciated. This study was funded in part by grants from the National Institutes of Health-National Institute of Child Health and Human Development (RO3-HD37586 and RO1-HD131540) and the National Institute on Deafness and other Communication Disorders (F32-DC00419).

REFERENCES

Abraham, S., Wallace, I. F., & Gravel, J. S. (1996). Early otitis media and phonologic development at age 2 years. *Laryngoscope, 106*, 727-732.

Dinnsen, D. A., Chin, S. B., Elbert, M., & Powell, T. W. (1990). Some constraints on functionally disordered phonologies: Phonetic inventories and phonotactics. *Journal of Speech and Hearing Research, 33*, 28-37.

Luloff, A., Menyuk, P., & Teele, D. (1991). Effects of persistent otitis media on the speech sound repertoire of infants. In D. J. Lim, C. D. Bluestone, J. O. Klein & J. D. Nelson (Eds.), *Recent advances in otitis media* (pp. 431-433). Philadelphia: Decker Periodicals.

Miccio, A. W., Yont, K. M., Davie, J., & Vernon-Feagans, L. (1999). Continuity in the acquisition of consonants by toddlers with chronic otitis media. In J. J. Ohala, Y. Hasegawa, M. Ohala, D. Granville & A. C. Bailey

(Eds.), *Proceedings of the 14th International Conference of Phonetic Sciences*, Vol. 1 (pp. 827-830). Berkeley, CA: University of California Linguistics Department.

Mirak, J., & Rescorla, L. (1998). Phonetic skills and vocabulary size in late talkers: Concurrent and predictive relationships. *Applied Psycholinguistics, 19*, 1-17.

Oller, K., & Delgado, R. (1999). Logical International Phonetic Programs (LIPP) Version 2.02 for Windows. Miami, FL: Intelligent Hearing Systems.

Painter, S., & Frank, T. (1999). *Ambient noise levels in infant/toddler rooms in daycare centers.* Poster presented at the American Academy of Audiology, Miami, FL.

Paradise, J. L., Rocketter, H. E., Colborn, K., Bernard, B. S., Smith, C. G., Kurs-Lasky, M., & Janosky, J. E. (1997). Otitis media in 2253 Pittsburgh-area infants: Prevalence and risk factors during the first two years of life. *Pediatrics, 99*, 318-333.

Robb, M. P., Psak, J. L., & Pang-Ching, G. K. (1993). Chronic otitis media and early speech development: A case study. *International Journal of Pediatric Otorhinolaryngology, 26*, 117-127.

Roberts, J. E., & Clarke-Klein, S. (1994). Otitis media. In J. E. Bernthal & N. W. Bankson (Eds.), *Child phonology: Characteristics, assessment, and intervention with special populations* (pp. 182-198). New York: Thieme.

Rvachew, S., Slawinski, E. B., Williams, M., & Green, C. L. (1999). The impact of early onset otitis media on babbling and early language development. *Journal of the Acoustical Society of America, 105*, 467-475.

Schwartz, R. G., Mody, M., & Petinou, K. (1997). Phonological acquisition and otitis media: Speech perception and speech production. In J. E. Roberts, I. F. Wallace & F. W. Henderson (Eds.), *Otitis media in young children: Medical, developmental, and educational considerations* (pp. 109-131). Baltimore, MD: Paul H. Brookes Publishing Co.

Shriberg, L. D., Friel-Patti, S., Flipsen, P.,& Brown, R. L. (2000). Otitis media, fluctuant hearing loss, and speech-language outcomes: A preliminary structural equation model. *Journal of Speech, Language, and Hearing Research, 43*, 100-120.

Stoel-Gammon, C. (1985). Phonetic inventories, 15-24 months: A longitudinal study. *Journal of Speech and Hearing Research, 28*, 505-512.

Stoel-Gammon, C. (1989). Prespeech and early speech development of two late talkers. *First Language, 9*, 307-224.

Vernon-Feagans, L., Manlove, E. E., & Volling, B. L. (1996). Otitis media and the social behavior of day-care-attending children. *Child Development, 67*, 1528-1539.

Wallace, I. F., Gravel, J. S., Schwartz, R. G., & Ruben, R. J. (1996). Otitis media, communication style of primary caregivers, and language skills of 2 year olds: A preliminary report. *Developmental and Behavioral Pediatrics, 17*, 27-35.

Yont, K. M., Miccio, A. W., & Vernon-Feagans, L. (1999). Children with chronic otitis media: The relationship between babbling and the onset of meaningful speech. In J. J. Ohala, Y. Hasegawa, M. Ohala, D. Granville, & A .C. Bailey (Eds.), *Proceedings of the 14th International Conference of Phonetic Sciences, 3*, 2181-2184. Berkeley, CA: University of California Linguistics Department.

Yont, K. M., Snow, C. E., & Vernon-Feagans, L. (In press). Early communicative intents in 12-month-old children with and without chronic otitis media. *First Language.*

35

The Voice of Polypoid Vocal Folds before and after Surgery

Smiljka Štajner-Katušic, Damir Horga and Sanja Krapinec

The vibratory or phonating surface of the vocal folds is a complex layered structure. The presence of pathological changes to the vocal folds will cause deterioration of voice quality due to mechanical properties of the vibrating structures as well as due to the aerodynamic factors of phonation in the glottis. Benign growths and pseudotumors of the vocal folds can influence the functional properties of the different structures for voice production (Milinović, 1996). Repeated trauma from vocal misuse or overuse frequently leads to the development of nodules, polyps or cysts. In nodules and polyps there is an abnormal pattern of fibronectin deposition within the superficial layer of the *lamina propria*. In addition, the basement membrane zone of the overlying mucosa is thickened in nodules and thinned in polyps (Bastian, 1996; Courey, Garret & Ossoff, 1997; Wendler, 1997).

A primary phonomicrosurgical principle in glottal surgery is to maximally preserve the vocal folds' layered microstructure. Following this principle, the flexible oscillation of the musculomembranous mucosa can be achieved. Selection of instrumentation for a variety of laryngeal pathologies in an effort to achieve good voice function is very important. It has been found that using cold instruments alone is generally better suited for the resection of superficial and/or smaller vocal lesions, rather than laser treatment, because of the greater surgical precision which can be achieved (Zeitels, 1996).

The medial microflap technique was used in our microsurgical approach so that vocal fold structure was maximally preserved.

METHOD

The aim of the investigation reported in this chapter was to evaluate the acoustic parameters of the voice before and after surgical removal of a vocal fold polyp.

Participants and Phoniatric Treatment

Participants in this investigation were 10 male and 10 female patients who visited the Phoniatric Clinic because of breathiness. For all patients a polyp of one vocal fold was diagnosed. The complex phoniatric tests were performed before surgery and the complete phoniatric anamnesis and voice status were recorded. After indirect laryngoscopy, laryngovideostroboscopy was performed on each patient. In the preoperative procedure subjective voice analysis was made according to the HRB schema, namely: H - hoarseness, R - roughness and B - breathiness (Wendler, 1993). Surgery was made under general endotracheal anaesthesia by means of laryngomicroscopy and phonosurgery. All the surgical interventions were performed by the same phonosurgeon. The operation was based on the principles of contemporary phonosurgery, aiming at maximally preserving the phonatory bridge of the vocal fold.

After surgery, during the early postoperative period, the patients were treated by inhalations. During the first seven postoperative days maximal voice rest was recommended. After surgery, all patients were satisfied with the results of the treatment and with their voice quality except two patients who had a prolonged recovery period because of vocal fold inflammation.

Speech Material

Participants were recorded twice: once before surgery and again one month later. The recording was made on a CD player in a sound-proof booth with the microphone at 30 cm from the patient's mouth. The patients read a short tale (The Sun and the Wind) and they pronounced a sustained vowel /a/.

Clinical Variables

During laryngomicroscopy the distance of the polyp from the anterior commissure, the width of the polyp base and the size of the polyp were measured. The duration of the patients' voice problems and their smoking status were recorded. Table 1 shows measures of clinical variables for male and female participants.

TABLE 1
Clinical variables.

Variable	Males	Females
Right vocal fold polyp	n = 7	n = 5
Left vocal fold polyp	n = 3	n = 5
Distance from the anterior commisure	3–8 mm	3–10 mm
Width of the polyp base	2–5 mm	2–4 mm
Size of the polyp	4–8 mm	4–7 mm
Subjective estim. of voice quality	H1R0B2 – H2R0B3	H1R0B1 – H2R0B3
Duration of breathiness	2 – 12 months	3 – 24 months
Smokers	n = 4	n = 6
Nonsmokers	n = 6	n = 4
Diagnosis	Nodules teleangiectaticus	Nodules teleangiectaticus

Measurement of Acoustic Variables

Acoustic variables were measured by means of the *Multi Dimensional Voice Program* (MDVP) on two seconds of sustained phonation of /a/. Though all the parameters were calculated, in this chapter only the variables representing certain voice qualities are reported. These are detailed in Table 2.

Long Term Average Spectrum (LTAS)

LTAS was calculated from the rendition of the tale *The Sun and the Wind* (duration of about 1 minute) by using the AGOS program (Stamenković, Bakran, Miletić & Tancig, 1990). The calculated frequency range was 70-10000 Hz.

RESULTS

Pre- and Post-operative Results

The significance of the difference in the average values of the chosen variables for preoperative and postoperative phonation was tested by means of a paired samples t-test. The results are shown in Table 3 and Fig. 1. In all variables except F0 the difference is statistically significant showing the improvement in voice quality.

TABLE 2
Acoustic variables.

Fundamental frequency	F0	Average fundamental frequency for all extracted pitch periods.
Frequency perturbation	Jita	Absolute jitter gives an evaluation of the period-to-period variability of the pitch period within the analyzed voice sample.
	Jitt	Jitter percent gives an evaluation of the variability of the pitch period within the analyzed voice sample.
Amplitude perturbation	ShdB	Shimmer in dB gives an evaluation of the period-to-period variability of the peak-to-peak amplitude within the analyzed voice sample.
	Shim	Shimmer percent of the peak-to-peak amplitude within the analyzed voice sample.
Harmonic-to-noise relationships	HNR	Harmonic-to-noise ratio gives an average ratio of energy of the non-harmonic components in the range 1500–3000 Hz to the harmonic components in the range 70–4500 Hz. It is a general evaluation of the noise presence in the analyzed signal (such as amplitude and frequency variations, turbulence noise, sub-harmonic components and/or voice breaks).
	VTI	Voice turbulence index is an average ratio of the spectral non-harmonic high frequency energy in the range 2800 to 5800 Hz in the regions of the signal where the influence of frequency and amplitude variations, voice breaks and sub-harmonic components are minimal. VTI measures the relative energy level of high frequency noise. It mostly correlates with the turbulence created by incomplete or loose adduction of the vocal folds.
Voice irregularity	DUV	Degree of voicelessness is an estimated relative evaluation of non-harmonic areas (where F0 cannot be detected in the voice sample).
	DVB	Degree of voice breaks shows in percentage the ratio of total length of voicelessness to the length of the complete sample.

In the variable F0 the mean voice pitch was higher in postoperative phonation, particularly for the male patients (male: preop. 131.1 Hz, postop. 139.5 Hz; female: preop. 208.6 Hz, postop. 211.3 Hz). Although this difference was not statistically significant it suggested that the polyp influenced the general phonatory behavior of the vocal folds.

The comparison of mean values of the other acoustic variables with the normal voice values showed that the preoperative voice was in the pathological region. After surgery, however, its quality was so improved that the values of normal voice were reached. The variables HNR measuring the noise components in the higher frequency region (1500 to 4500 Hz) and VTI measuring the voice turbulence index already in the preoperative state were within the range (though at the limit) of the normal voice. Variable DVB, measuring the degree of voice breaks, did not show up as a statistically significant improvement in postoperative voice, although the change in this parameter was such that its values reached the normal range.

TABLE 3

Means (M), standard deviations before surgery (s1) and after surgery (s2), correlation (r) between pre- and post-operative values, paired samples t-test (t), significance (p) and threshold values for normal voice (norm).

| | preop | | postop | | | | | |
	M1	s1	M2	s2	r	t	p	Norm
F_0	169.800	49.000	175.400	57.600	0.823	-0.756	0.459	—
Jita	160.000	160.400	62.300	38.500	-0.152	2.561	0.019	83.200
Jitt	2.549	2.272	1.040	0.730	-0.167	2.707	0.014	1.040
ShdB	0.557	0.515	0.260	0.172	0.127	2.549	0.020	0.350
Shim	6.028	5.651	2.925	1.968	0.154	2.438	0.025	3.810
HNR	0.183	0.000	0.134	0.000	-0.149	2.375	0.028	0.190
VTI	0.057	0.018	0.051	0.012	0.033	1.146	0.266	0.061
DVB	1.238	5.536	0.000	0.000		1.000	0.330	0.000
DUV	10.975	19.848	0.400	1.392	-0.167	2.350	0.030	0.000

In general, it was possible to conclude that postoperative acoustic variables were so improved that their values reached appropriate values for normal voice.

Influence of clinical variables on voice quality. To determine whether clinical variables have any impact on the voice quality variables, six ANOVA analyses were performed, with five voice quality values as dependent variables and each of the clinical variables as independent variables. Also, pre- and post-operative results were treated as another independent variable. The following voice quality variables were used: degree of voicelessness (DUV), shimmer percent (SHIM), average fundamental frequency (F0), jitter percent (JITT) and harmonic-to-noise ratio (HNR). Clinical variables were: sex (SEX, male and female), polyp distance from the anterior commisure (DIST, 3–7 mm and 6–10mm), width of the polyp base (WID, 2 mm and 3–4 mm), size of the polyp (SIZ, 4 mm and 5–8 mm), duration of breathiness (BRE, 2–10 months and 12 to 24 months) and smoking (SMO, smokers and nonsmokers). The significance levels of the ANOVA results are included in Tables 4–9.

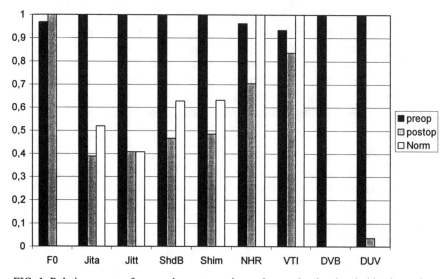

FIG. 1 Relative means of pre- and post-operative and normal voice threshold values of acoustic variables.

In general, male voices were worse than female ones. The difference in degree of voicelessness (DUV) was significant. The distance of the polyp from the anterior commisure (DIST) also had a negative influence on the voice quality as is shown in the values of shimmer (Shim). This variable produced the only statistically significant difference between two groups, defined according to the distance of the polyp from the anterior commisure. On the other hand, the width of the polyp base (WID) and the polyp size (SIZ) itself had no negative influence on the voice quality as far as this sample was concerned. It seems that the very presence of the polyp impairs voice quality regardless of its size or the width of the base. The duration of breathiness (BRE) made a significant change only in fundamental frequency (F0) due to the greater duration of breathiness in women. As far as smoking is concerned (SMO) the significant difference between smokers and nonsmokers was found only in jitter.

Although few significant differences in acoustic variables corresponding to the clinical variables were found, the results of the ANOVA (Tables 4–9) showed tendencies toward the possibility that clinical variables may be important for voice quality. These tendencies have to be tested on a larger sample of participants. The important result of this investigation was that surgery had the same positive effect on the acoustic variables of the voice regardless of the rating of the polyp on the clinical measures.

TABLE 4

Mean values (and significance levels) of pre- and post-operative acoustic variables for sex (M = male, F = female).

	PRE		POST		SIG
	M	F	M	F	
F0	131.12	208.57	139.46	211.32	**0.000**
Jitt	2.89	2.21	0.74	1.33	0.933
Shim	7.66	4.40	2.69	3.16	0.331
HNR	0.21	0.15	0.14	0.13	0.056
DUV	20.51	1.80	0.80	0.00	**0.025**

TABLE 5

Mean values (and significance levels) of pre- and post-operative acoustic variables for the distance of the polyp from the anterior commisure (3–5 mm and 6–10 mm).

	DIST				
	PRE		POST		SIG
	3–5mm	6–10mm	3–5mm	6–10mm	
F0	172.22	167.91	188.02	165.06	0.566
Jitt	1.62	3.31	0.93	1.13	0.061
Shim	3.39	8.18	2.37	3.38	**0.035**
HNR	0.17	0.20	0.13	0.14	0.317
DUV	2.65	17.79	0.22	0.55	0.079

TABLE 6

Mean values (and significance levels) of pre- and post-operative acoustic variables for the width of the polyp base (2 mm and 3–4 mm).

	WID				SIG
	PRE		POST		
	2mm	3–4mm	2mm	3–4mm	
F0	167.44	171.45	166.95	181.02	0.708
Jitt	3.12	2.17	0.99	1.07	0.417
Shim	7.65	4.94	2.93	2.92	0.355
HNR	0.21	0.17	0.13	0.13	0.336
DUV	14.44	8.67	0.75	0.17	0.494

TABLE 7

Mean values (and significance levels) of pre- and post-operative acoustic variables for the size of the polyp (4 mm and 5–8 mm).

	SIZ				SIG
	PRE		POST		
	4mm	5-8mm	4mm	5-8mm	
F0	165.87	174.71	168.07	184.34	0.597
Jitt	2.76	2.30	1.07	0.99	0.610
Shim	7.06	4.77	2.94	2.91	0.425
HNR	0.20	0.16	0.13	0.14	0.269
DUV	15.59	5.33	0.55	0.22	0.241

TABLE 8

Mean values (and significance levels) of pre- and post-operative acoustic variables for breathiness (2–10 months and 12–24 months).

	BRE				SIG
	PRE		POST		
	2–10 mth	12–24 mth	2–10 mth	12–24 mth	
F0*	142.97	202.69	154.92	200.41	**0.017**
Jitt	2.67	2.40	0.87	0.39	0.922
Shim	6.67	5.24	3.21	2.57	0.478
HNR	0.18	0.19	0.14	0.13	0.981
DUV	16.03	4.80	0.73	0.00	0.183

TABLE 9
Mean values (and significance levels) of pre- and post-operative acoustic variables for
smoking (smokers and nonsmokers).

	SMO				SIG
	PRE		POST		
	SMOK	NSMOK	SMOK	NSMOK	
F0	191.58	155.51	187.38	160.74	0.260
Jitt*	3.32	1.61	1.22	0.81	**0.033**
Shim	7.85	3.80	2.39	3.58	0.333
HNR	0.21	0.15	0.13	0.14	0.173
DUV	14.68	6.44	0.00	0.89	0.420

Long-term average spectrum

It is assumed that a speaker's voice quality characteristics are encoded in
sufficiently long samples of speech to be assessed by means of LTAS. The
speech information flow can be divided into two layers: text and voice. The
voice quality of speakers can be expressed as an average value of the spectral
shape of their speech. LTAS is used as a measurement tool in many different
fields of speech research: language differences, speaker identification,
audiology, sociolinguistic research, emotional states, speech and voice
pathology (Horga, 1999; Štajner-Katušić, Krapinec & Horga, 1998).

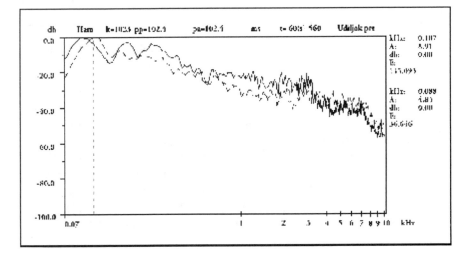

FIG. 2 Preoperative (dotted line) and postoperative (solid line) LTAS curves for the
patient R.U.

In Fig. 2 preoperative and postoperative LTAS curves for the patient R.U. are shown. The averaged preoperative and postoperative LTAS curves were obtained for all participants. The postoperative curve for the whole group was normalized to the preoperative curve represented by the horizontal line (Fig. 3).

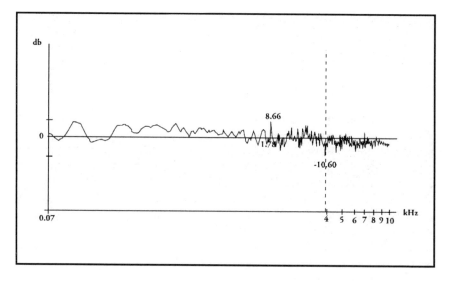

FIG. 3 Postoperative LTAS curve for the whole group normalized to the preoperative LTAS (horizontal line).

Comparison of preoperative and postoperative LTAS curves shows that the overall postoperative F0 is lower, that the frequencies up to 3000 Hz and especially around the F0 for male voices (100 Hz) and female voices (200 Hz) are more intense and that the high frequencies, from 4000 Hz, are weaker compared to the preoperative state. It can be concluded that the part of the spectrum representing voice components is stronger, while the noisy part is weaker, in the postoperative voice compared with the preoperative state.

CONCLUSION

We investigated the influence of medical variables on the acoustic characteristics of the voice and on the subjective estimation of voice quality. Three groups of variables were: 1. *Medical* (the size of the polyp, the distance of the polyp from the anterior commisure and the width of the polyp base on the vocal fold); 2. *Acoustical* (F0, frequency and amplitude perturbation, noise to harmonic relation and voice irregularity) and long-term average spectrum; 3. *Voice quality* (comprising hoarseness, roughness and breathiness).

The results showed significant improvement of voice quality after surgery. In all acoustic variables except F0 the differences were statistically significant.

The long-term average spectrum analysis showed greater sound energy in the frequency regions around the F0 and up to 3000 Hz, improving voice quality.

The estimation of voice quality showed that one month after surgery the hoarseness and roughness disappeared and that first degree breathiness remains in only 30% of cases.

Medial microflap surgery of benign polyps significantly improved voice quality as early as one month after the treatment. Assessed clinical variables for the most part did not participate in the improvement of the voice. LTAS analysis showed a greater sound energy in the frequency regions relevant for improving voice quality.

REFERENCES

Bastian, R. W. (1996). Vocal fold microsurgery in singers. *Journal of Voice, 10*, 389-404.

Courey, M. S., Garrett, C. G. & Ossoff, R.H. (1997). Medial microflap for excision of benign vocal fold lesions. *Laryngoscope, 107*, 340-344.

Horga, D. (1999). The long-term average spectrum as a measure of voice quality in L1 and L2 speakers. In A. Braun (ed.) *Advances in Phonetics. Zeitschrift fur Dialektologie und Linguistik, 106*, 91-97.

Milinović, Z. (1996). Classification of Voice Pathology. *Folia Phoniatrica et Logopaedica, 48*, 301-308.

Stamenković, M., Bakran J., Miletić, M. & Tancig, P. (1990). AGOS-programski sistem za analizu govornog signala. *Zbornik informatička tehnologija u primjenjenoj lingvistici.* Zagreb, 17-22.

Štajner-Katušić, S., Krapinec, S. & Horga, D. (1998). Kakvoća glasa operiranih glasiljki. *3. znanstveni skup Istraživanja govora.* Abstracts. Zagreb, 49.

Wendler, J. (1997). Stimmstörungen. Schwerpunkte der Diagnostik und Therapie. *Laryngo-Rhino-Otologie, 76,* 327-331.

Wendler, J. (1993). *Stroboscopy. Principles and Clinical Application in the Investigation of the Larynx.* Lenzkirch: ATMOS Medizintechnik GmbH & Co.

Zeitels, S. M. (1996). Laser versus cold instruments for microlaryngoscopic surgery. *Laryngoscope, 106,* 545-552.

36

Acoustic Characteristics of the Voice in Young Adult Smokers

Shaheen N. Awan and Catherine L. Knych

Despite current knowledge about the detrimental effects of cigarette smoking, there continues to be a substantial population of smokers throughout the world. As an example, an estimated one-quarter of the adult population in the United States smokes cigarettes (Nelson, Kirkendall & Lawton, 1996). Cigarette smoking is a habit common to men and women alike, however, the gap historically observed between male and female smokers has significantly decreased (Shopland, Hartman, Gibson, Mueller, Kessler & Lynn, 1994). Furthermore, data have been reported which indicate that smoking rates for women working in whitecollar occupations now exceed those of their whitecollar male counterparts (Shopland et al., 1994). In addition, cigarette smoking is not a habit exclusive to adults. Most smokers began smoking as teenagers. In the United States, 82% began smoking before age 18, and despite widespread efforts to educate this group, the prevalence of cigarette smoking among teenagers has been on the rise since 1992 (U.S. Department of Health and Human Services, 1994; 1996).

Effects of Smoking on the Phonatory and Respiratory Systems

It is evident that cigarette smoking may have significant effects on the phonatory and respiratory mechanisms. Because these mechanisms are integral components of the communication mechanism, the effects of smoking are of interest and concern to the speech pathologist. Several key documented effects on the respiratory/phonatory mechanism have been described:

- Smokers are often afflicted with respiratory tract diseases such as pharyngitis, tracheitis, and bronchitis, which leave them susceptible to acute respiratory infections (Burch, 1976). In turn, acute respiratory infections compromise the respiratory system which is needed for voice production.

- Smoking has been related to irritation of the vocal fold mucosa, laryngitis, mucosal thickening, chronic edema, and erythema. In addition, association with the development of a number of precancerous conditions such as hyperkeratosis, leukoplakia, and polypoid degeneration has also been described (Auerbach, Hammond & Garfinkel, 1970; Hirabayashi et al., 1990; Colton & Casper, 1996).
- Of course, cigarette smoking is also a leading risk factor for laryngeal cancer (Auerbach et al., 1970; McKenna, Fornataro-Clerici, McMenamin, and Leonard, 1991).

Effects of Smoking on Acoustic Characteristics of the Voice

Studies of the general effects of cigarette smoking on the acoustic characteristics of the voice are limited. However, several studies have attempted to investigate the effects of smoking on various frequency characteristics of the voice:

1. Gilbert and Weismer (1974) measured the speaking F_0s of 15 smokers and 15 nonsmokers, and found that the F_0s of adult female smokers were significantly lower than those of the nonsmoker group on an oral reading task, but not in spontaneous speech. The authors concluded that a thickening of the vocal folds and the connective tissue as a result of smoking may have been responsible for the lowering of vocal F_0 on the oral reading task.
2. Sorensen and Horii (1982) studied the effects of long-term smoking on fundamental frequency in both male and female participants. A significant difference between the F_0 values was found for the male smokers and nonsmokers in the spontaneous speech and oral reading tasks. Although nonsignificant, similar trends were observed for the female smokers and nonsmokers on these same tasks. The difference in F_0 values for sustained vowel phonation was not significant for smokers and nonsmokers, regardless of gender. Although there was a lack of statistical significance in all measures taken, the authors emphasized that the pre-pathological changes in acoustic measures of the voice signal need to be studied to understand how disease affects the larynx.
3. Murphy and Doyle (1987) speculated that smoking may result in substantial decreases in vocal F_0 because they observed that smoking cessation for as few as 40 hours resulted in an increase in fundamental frequency. Speech and sustained vowel samples of two participants were collected before, during, and after a 40-hour period of smoking cessation. The F_0s of the two participants returned to baseline once they began smoking.
4. Awan and Coy (1992) compared the voice characteristics of 15 young adult female smokers and 15 female nonsmokers (mean ages of 24.7 years and 24.4 years respectively). Results showed the mean speaking fundamental frequency, as well as the maximum fundamental frequency of the smoking

group, to be significantly lower than that of the nonsmoking group. The difference between minimum F_0s of the two groups was not significant. Furthermore, the mean speaking range of the smokers was significantly less than the mean speaking range of the nonsmokers.

5.   Hewlett, Topham, and McMullen (1996) investigated whether average speaking fundamental frequency is lower in smokers than in nonsmokers. The participants were a young group (18 to 24 years) consisting of 20 nonsmokers and 14 smokers versus a middle-aged group (43 to 60 years) consisting of 11 nonsmokers and 13 smokers. Although nonsignificant, results revealed a trend for lower mean speaking F_0s for both age groups within the smokers group when compared to the nonsmokers group.

6.   Hewlett et al. (1996) also compared fundamental frequency ranges of 20 female smokers and 20 female nonsmokers. Whereas the lower limits of the frequency scale of smokers appeared to be similar to those of the nonsmokers, the upper end of the frequency scale was substantially restricted, thereby narrowing the total frequency range.

Although there have been several studies which have investigated the effects of smoking on vocal fundamental frequency, relatively few have included measures related to the periodicity of the phonatory signal. Awan and Coy (1992) compared the voice characteristics of 15 female smokers and 15 female nonsmokers, with mean ages of 24.7 years and 24.4 years respectively. Although no significant difference was revealed between the two groups for measures of jitter and shimmer, measures of harmonic-to-noise ratio for the smoking group were significantly higher than those of the nonsmoking group, although participants in both groups were perceived to have normal vocal quality.

The purpose of this study was to investigate the possible effects of smoking on various objective measures of the voice (including measures of fundamental frequency and periodicity/noise). In addition, the possible differential effects of smoking on gender have not yet been fully investigated. Therefore, this study included an examination of the possible effects of cigarette smoking on the voice in young adult male and female smokers and nonsmokers. It should be noted that the young adult smokers investigated in this study had relatively short smoking histories. It was believed that particular value could be obtained in terms of screening and/or educational potential by investigating those who may be experiencing relatively subtle effects of smoking on the voice.

METHODOLOGY

Participants

Participants were 20 young adult males and 20 young adult females (age 18 to 30 yrs.; total $N = 40$; 10 smokers and 10 nonsmokers per gender group). Primary participant characteristics (means and standard deviations) are presented in Table 1.

All participants had no history of significant injury or trauma to the vocal folds/larynx, no history of hormonal treatments or supplements, and passed a hearing screening at 0.5, 1, 2, and 4 kHz. All participants were judged to have normal voice characteristics (i.e. pitch, loudness, and quality) in reference to their age, gender, and body type.

A smoker was defined as a participant who currently smoked cigarettes and had smoked at least 10 cigarettes per day for at least two years immediately preceding the data collection procedures for this study. The nonsmoking participants were defined as those who (a) had not met the definition of a smoker as used in this study, (b) had not smoked more than 50 cigarettes in one year, and (c) had not smoked more than two cigarettes within a 24-hour period immediately preceding the voice testing conducted in this study.

TABLE 1

Participant characteristics (mean and standard deviation) for the nonsmoking and smoking groups.

	Nonsmoking Males	Smoking Males	Nonsmoking Females	Smoking Females
Age (in yrs.)	24.1 (3.65)	23.4 (2.84)	23.7 (1.85)	23.6 (2.50)
Cigarettes per day	N/A	17.8 (7.25)	N/A	18.0 (7.06)
Duration of smoking habit (in mths.)	N/A	49.8 (33.30)	N/A	61.2 (34.65)

Note. N/A = not applicable; standard deviations are shown in brackets.

Continuous Speech Task

Each participant was asked to read the first paragraph of "The Rainbow Passage" (Fairbanks, 1960) at a comfortable pitch and loudness level. Speech samples were recorded directly into a Pentium-level PC using a SoundBlaster 16 sound card (Creative Labs, Milipitas, CA) at 16-bits of resolution and a sampling rate of 44 kHz. At a later time, the second sentence of the passage was analyzed using the EZVoicePlus™ voice analysis software (VoiceTek

Enterprises, Nescopeck, PA). Each sentence was analyzed for mean F_0 (Hz), pitch sigma (semitones), and speaking F_0 range.

Sustained Vowel Analysis

Each participant was asked to sustain the vowel /ɑ/ for 2 to 3 seconds at a comfortable pitch and loudness. The task was repeated three times with the middle token used for data analysis. Recording specifications were similar to those described for the continuous speech analysis. At a later time, the center one second of the vowel was analyzed using the EZVoicePlus program for the following measures: shimmer (dB); jitter (%), harmonic-to-noise ratio (HNR in dB); and pitch sigma (semitones).

Reliability

Nine subjects (4 nonsmokers and 5 smokers) were retested on all voice measures within two weeks of their original recording session. Table 2 presents mean test–retest results for the various sustained vowel /ɑ/ and continuous speech sample measurements. Absolute test–retest differences were felt to be within acceptable limits for the purposes of this study.

TABLE 2
Intrasubject reliability data for various sustained vowel and continuous speech measurements (N = 9).

Variable	Test	Retest	Absolute Difference	Mean	Pearson's r
Shimmer (/ɑ/)	0.239 dB	0.242 dB	0.003 dB		0.94***
Jitter (/ɑ/)	0.507%	0.478%	0.029%		0.51
HNR (/ɑ/)	17.13 dB	16.69 dB	0.44 dB		0.72*
Pitch Sigma (/ɑ/)	0.228 ST	0.267 ST	0.039 ST		0.16
Range (/ɑ/)	0.606 ST	0.686 ST	0.08 ST		0.08
Mean F_0 (Speech)	176.09 Hz	176.92 Hz	0.83 Hz		0.99***
Pitch Sigma (Speech)	3.36 ST	3.69 ST	0.33 ST		0.88**
Range (Speech)	7.19 ST	8.04 ST	0.85 ST		0.58

Note. ST = Semitones; ***$p < 0.001$; **$p < 0.01$; *$p < 0.05$.

RESULTS

The primary results of sustained vowel and continuous speech analysis indicated the following:

1. Significantly greater shimmer (dB) from sustained vowel samples was observed in the smoking vs. nonsmoking groups ($F = 4.04$; $d.f. = 1,36$; $p < 0.05$: 0.21 dB vs. 0.15 dB).
2. Significantly greater pitch sigma (in semitones) from sustained vowel samples was observed in the female smoking vs. female nonsmoking groups ($F = 5.63$; $d.f. = 1,36$; $p < 0.05$: 0.27 ST vs. 0.21 ST).
3. Significantly greater frequency range (in semitones) from sustained vowel samples in female smoking vs. female nonsmoking groups ($F = 7.00$; $d.f. = 1,36$; $p < 0.05$: 0.73 ST vs. 0.55 ST).
4. Significantly greater pitch sigma (in semitones) from continuous speech samples in smoking vs. nonsmoking groups ($F = 4.29$; $d.f. = 1,36$; $p < 0.05$: 4.58 ST vs. 3.42 ST).

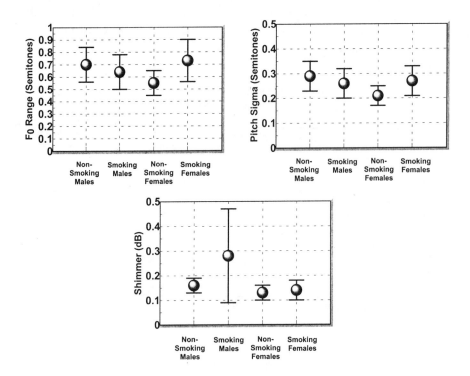

FIG. 1 Results of sustained vowel /ɑ/ analysis for the various male and female nonsmoking versus smoking groups.

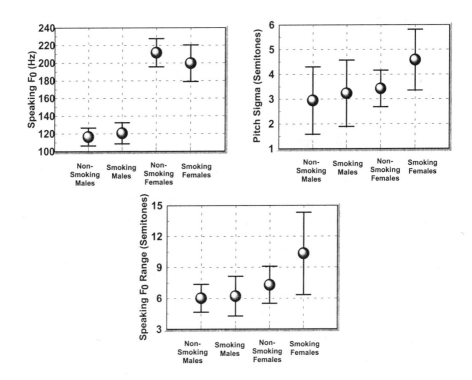

FIG. 2 Results of continuous speech analysis for the various male and female nonsmoking versus smoking groups.

5. No significant differences between smoking groups in terms of speaking fundamental frequency.

6. No significant correlations were observed within the male or female smoking groups or for all smoking participants combined between the various acoustic measures and participant variables of cigarettes smoked per day, months smoking, or estimated total cigarettes smoked.

Figures 1 and 2 show group mean and standard deviations for several of the key acoustic measures conducted in this study.

DISCUSSION

Although all the participants included in this study were perceived as having normal voice characteristics, the results of this study indicate the possible presence of subtle, but significant, effects of smoking on phonatory periodicity and control.

Shimmer

Significantly increased shimmer in the smoking vs. the nonsmoking groups may be due to changes in the vibratory characteristics of the vocal fold mucosa. This result indicates that changes in the periodicity of the vocal signal may occur with relatively short-term smoking and are not observed solely in long-term smokers.

Pitch Sigma and Range

The observation of significantly greater pitch sigma in smoking vs. nonsmoking groups during both continuous speech and sustained vowel productions is indicative of reduced phonatory control over vocal frequency. This reduction in control may be due to tissue changes in the vocal fold mucosa. In addition, increased frequency variability may reflect possible effects of smoking on nervous system control of phonatory behavior.

Effects of Gender

Nonsmoking males and females were observed to differ in terms of pitch sigma and F_0 range in sustained vowel productions consistent with other research which has shown natural gender differences for various acoustic characteristics of the voice. However, no significant differences were observed between male and female smokers on these parameters. It may be that one of the possible effects of smoking is to produce a virilizing effect on the female voice, in which natural acoustic differences between males and females are reduced and in which significant increases in F_0 variability are found in female smokers compared to nonsmokers. If so, the effects of smoking may have some similarity to the effects of aging on the female voice. It has been hypothesized that male and female voices show increased similarity in their acoustic characteristics with advanced aging, particularly in terms of measures of vocal F_0. In addition, both smoking and aging have been associated with vocal fold tissue change and changes in distributed mass (e.g. development of edema). Future research focusing on the possible differential effects of smoking on males vs. females may provide more insight on this matter.

An obvious limitation of this study is that all measures employed were indirect in nature. Future research incorporating direct observation of the larynges may be able to directly relate the presence of laryngeal aberrations (e.g. vocal fold edema; chronic laryngitis and irritation; etc.) with acoustic characteristics of the voice.

CONCLUSIONS

The results of this study indicate that simple acoustic measures of the voice may hold promise as screening and educational tools for use with young adult smokers. With the growing prevalence of smoking in the teenagers and the young adults of this country, it is important that we are able to provide information that may elucidate the detrimental effects of smoking before these effects become permanent, or perhaps, life threatening in nature.

The acoustic methods employed in this study are familiar to speech pathologists engaged in the diagnosis and treatment of voice patients, and therefore, provide simple but effective methods by which speech pathologists may participate in the health care and education of young adult smokers.

REFERENCES

Auerbach, O., Hammond, E. C., & Garfinkel, L. (1970). Histological changes in the larynx in relation to smoking habits. *Cancer, 25,* 92-104.

Awan, S. N., & Coy, K. (1992). The effects of smoking on acoustic characteristics of the female voice. Paper presented at the convention of the American Speech-Language-Hearing Association Convention, San Antonio, TX.

Burch, G. E. (1976). Of smoking and the respiratory tract. *American Heart Journal, 91,* 401-402.

Colton, R. H., & Casper, J. K. (1996). *Understanding voice problems* (2nd ed.). Williams and Wilkins: Baltimore, MD.

Fairbanks, G. (1960). *Voice and articulation drill book* (2nd ed.). New York: Harper and Row.

Gilbert, H. R., & Weismer, G. G. (1974). The effects of smoking on the fundamental frequency of women. *Journal of Linguistic Research, 3,* 225-231.

Hewlett, N., Topham, N., & McMullen, C. (1996). The effects of smoking on the female voice. In M. J. Ball & M. Duckworth (Eds.), *Advances in clinical phonetics* (pp. 227-235). Philadelphia: John Benjamins.

Hirabayashi, H., Koshii, K., Uno, K., Oghaki, H., Nakasone, Y., Fujisawa, T., Shono, N., Hinohara, T., & Hirabayashi, K. (1990). Laryngeal epithelial changes on effects of smoking and drinking. *Auris-Nasus-Larynx (Tokyo), 17,* 105-114.

McKenna, J. P., Fornataro-Clerici, L. M., McMenamin, P. G., & Leonard, R. J. (1991). Laryngeal cancer: Diagnosis, treatment, and speech rehabilitation. *American Family Physician, 44,* 123-129.

Murphy, C. H., & Doyle, P. C. (1987). The effects of cigarette smoking on voice fundamental frequency. *Otolaryngology-Head and Neck Surgery, 97,* 376-380.

Nelson, D. E., Kirkendall, R. S., & Lawton, R. L. (1996). Surveillance for smoking – attributable mortality and years of potential life lost by state. *Mortality and Morbidity Weekly Report, 45,* 1-8.

Shopland, D. R., Hartman, A. M., Gibson, J. T., Mueller, M. D., Kessler, L. G., & Lynn, W. R. (1994). Cigarette smoking among U.S. adults by state and region: Estimates from the current population survey. *Journal of the National Cancer Institute, 88,* 1748-1758.

Sorensen, D., & Horii, Y. (1982). Cigarette smoking and voice fundamental frequency. *Journal of Communication Disorders, 15,* 135-144.

U.S. Department of Health and Human Services (1994). *Preventing tobacco Use among young people: A report of the surgeon general.* Office of Smoking and Health: Rockville, MD.

U.S. Department of Health and Human Services (1996). State-specific prevalence of cigarette smoking – United States 1995. *Mortality and Morbidity Weekly Report, 45,* 961-966.

37

Perceptual, Acoustic and Electroglottographic Analyses of Dysphonia Subsequent to Traumatic Brain Injury

Marion Jaeger, Matthias Fröhlich, Ingo Hertrich,
Hermann Ackermann and Paul-Walter Schönle

More than one third of patients suffering severe traumatic brain injury (TBI) exhibit dysarthria (Gilchrist & Wilkinson, 1979). Besides compromised articulation (Yorkston, Beukelman & Bell, 1988), two thirds of these patients are perceived to be dysphonic to some degree (Theodoros, Murdoch & Chenery, 1994). In the early stage post-injury, voice quality in dysarthric TBI speakers is perceived as mainly weak and breathy, whereas in later stages a harsh and strained-strangled voice quality predominates (Theodoros & Murdoch, 1994; Vogel & von Cramon, 1982). Auditory-perceptual evaluation has been the major clinical approach in diagnosis of voice disorders. In addition, electroglottographic (Theodoros & Murdoch, 1994) and acoustic analyses (Hartmann & von Cramon, 1984) have been performed to determine the nature of the vocal fold vibratory movements as well as the frequency and severity of deviant laryngeal features. However, electroglottographic (EGG) measures yielded rather nonhomogenous profiles of abnormalities (Theodoros & Murdoch, 1994) and most acoustic measures were found to be sensitive to several perceptual dimensions such as roughness and breathiness and, hence, may be ambiguous with respect to the underlying pathophysiological mechanisms, i.e. irregularity of vocal fold oscillations and insufficiency of vocal fold closure (Michaelis, Fröhlich & Strube, 1998). Recently, Michaelis et al. (1998) succeeded in deriving two largely independent parameters from the acoustic signal that are related to distinct perceptual qualities as well as to different modes of vocal tract excitation in organic voice disorders. To test the clinical usefulness of the so-called Goettinger Hoarseness Diagram (GHD) within the domain of neurogenic voice disorders, this study first applied this procedure to dysphonia subsequent to severe TBI and, second, compared these findings to auditory-perceptual ratings, another acoustic analysis program, Multi-Dimensional Voice Program (MDVP), and EGG measures.

METHOD

Participants

Ten male speakers (age 30 to 54 yrs; mean: 39 yrs) with a diagnosis of severe TBI participated in the currrent study. Table I (Appendix) provides the relevant clinical and demographic data. Most patients presented with signs of corticobulbar tract dysfunction at either the cortical and/or brainstem level. Two individuals exhibited additional cerebellar lesions. At the time of investigation, evaluation of spontaneous speech revealed in all patients mildly to severely impaired phonation. In addition, eight speakers (P1, P2, P3, P5, P7, P8, P9, P10) exhibited moderate to severe impairment of speech respirattion (i.e. increased inspiratory rates), moderate to severe hypernasality (not P5), and moderate to severe articulatory disorders as well as reduced intelligibility. All patients were in a late post-injury stage. Ten healthy male individuals (age 20-42 yrs; mean: 35 yrs), members of hospital staff without a history of any neurological or voice disorders, served as control speakers.

Speech Material and Recording

Participants produced the low vowel [ɑː] seven times, extending across a duration of 3 to 4 s each, at a comfortable pitch and loudness level (20 participants × 7 repetitions = 140 vowel productions). Acoustic and EGG signals were simultaneously recorded onto a digital audiotape recorder (Sony DAT TCD-D3) in a sound-treated booth using a high-quality microphone (Beyerdynamic M201 N(C)) and a laryngograph (PCLX Laryngograph Ltd). The mouth-to-microphone distance was approximately 20 cm. EGG electrodes were placed at the level of the upper third of the thyroid lamina, the neckband being firmly fastened to ensure adequate skin contact. Signal recording was monitored with an attached oscillographic display (Oscilloscope Type HM 205-3, HAMEG). Sampling frequency for the acoustic and EGG signals was 50 kHz after anti-aliasing filtering (20 kHz). Analysis relied on segments extending across one second each, starting 0.5 s after vowel onset. For the sake of auditory-perceptual analysis, the same acoustic samples were recorded on an audiotape in randomized order, but blocked by speakers. The productions of 6 randomly selected subjects (3 TBI speakers and 3 controls) were included twice in order to determine intra-rater reliability. Acoustic and EGG signals were analyzed off-line using the Goettinger Hoarseness Diagram (Institute of Physics III at the University of Goettingen, Germany), the Multi-Dimensional Voice

Program (MDVP, Model 5105, Kay Elemetrics, USA), and an EGG processing program (Model 4338, Kay Elemetrics), respectively.

DATA ANALYSIS

Acoustic Analysis using the Goettinger Hoarseness Diagram (GHD)

The GHD separates two largely independent acoustic features related to distinct perceptual qualities (Zwirner, Michaelis, Fröhlich, Strube & Kruse, 1998) and different glottal modes of vocal tract excitation. The first feature, irregularity (IRR), mainly represents a compound of three highly intercorrelated measures addressing different aspects of aperiodicity across a sequence of glottal pulses: 'mean waveform correlation' (MWC)[1], jitter (averaged over three periods), and shimmer (averaged over 15 periods). Noise (NOI), the second parameter, is based on an estimate of 'glottal-to-noise excitation' (GNE)[2] (Michaelis, Gramss & Strube, 1997; Michaelis et al., 1998) and measures additive noise apart from period-to-period irregularity in terms of MWC, jitter, and shimmer. Together with GNE, the latter three measures are entered into a factor analysis to derive two independent main components. For the sake of minimization of an eventual contribution of the GNE to the first factor, the two main components are rotated by 63.9 degrees, and thereafter, define the two axes of the 'hoarseness diagram' (x-axis = IRR; y-axis = NOI). The two measures are rescaled to obtain positive values between 0 and 10 and 0 and 5, respectively (Michaelis et al., 1998). For clinical application, the speakers' data are usually plotted in a two-dimensional diagram as ellipses representing the mean and standard deviation of the two factors, respectively.

---

[1] The MWC is evaluated for every pair of consecutive pitch periods and indicates the overall similarity between the cycles of the time signal.

[2] The procedure is based on the assumption that glottal pulses lead to a synchronous excitation across all frequency bands, leading to high correlation between the intensity envelopes of different bandpass-derivates of the original signal in the absence of further sources of sound energy. In calculating the GNE, the signal is first inverse filtered (Autocorrelation method of 13th order, Hamming window with 30 ms length and 10 ms window shift.) Second, correlation coefficients of the Hilbert envelopes of different filter channels (center frequencies 1.5 to 4.5 kHz shifted in steps of 100 Hz, bandwidth 3 kHz) spaced at least one half of their bandwidth (in order not to confound measures by high correlations due to spectral overlap) are calculated. The maximum correlation coefficient then represents the GNE.

Acoustic Analysis using the Multi-Dimensional Voice Program (MDVP)

On the basis of our correlation data and with regard to parameters used in former studies (Hertrich, Spieker & Ackermann, 1998) only 5 of 33 acoustic parameters calculated by the MDVP were entered into the statistical analysis. These include the following:

Jitter % = period-to-period variability of fundamental frequency in percent

Shim % = variability of peak-to-peak amplitude in percent

NHR = average ratio of energy of the nonharmonic components within the frequency range of 1500-4500 Hz to the harmonic components extending from 70-4500 Hz

SPI = ratio of lower (70-1600 Hz) to higher frequency (1600-4500 Hz) harmonic energy

VTI = average ratio of the spectral non-harmonic high frequency energy (2800-5800 Hz) to harmonic energy in the range 70-4500 Hz

Evaluation of EGG Oscillograms

EGG provides a non-invasive measure of glottal contact area. The relative durations of the various phases of the glottal cycle are widely recognized parameters of voice quality (Houben, Buekers & Kingma, 1992; Orlikoff, 1990; Abberton, Howard & Fourcin, 1989; Gerratt, Hanson & Berke, 1987). Whereas a normal modal voice is characterized by a sharp closing phase due to the Bernouilli effect and a closed phase amounting to approximately 40% to 50% of total glottal cycle (Fig. I, Appendix), the relative durations of the various phases may be changed in pathological voices (Gerratt et al., 1987; Motta, Cesari, Iengo & Motta, 1990; Hertrich & Ackermann, 1995). The 'open quotient' (OQ) relates the open interval to the whole vibration cycle, whereas the 'speed quotient' (SQ) represents the ratio of closing and opening time within the closed phase. Regarding pathological voices, increased OQ and decreased SQ frequently emerge to a prolonged or irregular closing phase and a shortened, or missing, closed phase (Gerratt et al., 1987; Motta et al., 1990, Hertrich & Ackermann, 1995).

Perceptual Ratings

Five certified speech language pathologists independently evaluated the recorded audiotapes in the absence of any knowledge about the speakers. Each vowel was presented twice to the listeners for auditory-perceptual evaluation. Eight dimensions had to be rated: 'strained-strangled'[3], 'rough', 'creaky'[4], and

---

[3] Strained-strangled voice quality is synonymous with tenseness.

[4] Creaky voice corresponds to extremely rough or harsh voice quality.

'breathy' voice quality, 'overall severity' of dysphonia, 'deviation from normal pitch', 'pitch and amplitude fluctuations', and 'nasality'. The latter two perceptual features were included since previous studies frequently observed voice fluctuations in neurogenic disorders (Hertrich & Ackermann, 1995, Hertrich, Lutzenberger, Spieker & Ackermann, 1997; Ackermann & Ziegler, 1994), and hypernasality has been found to be a characteristic feature of TBI-dysarthria (Theodoros, Murdoch & Chenery, 1993) compromising articulation and phonation (Theodoros & Murdoch, 1994; Yorkston et al., 1988). Apart from 'pitch' and 'overall severity', evaluation of the various dimensions relied on a four-point classification scale ('1' = absence of the deviant feature, that is, no disturbance, '2' = just noticeable presence of the dimension, that is, a slight disturbance, '3' = moderate, and '4' = severe disturbance). Pitch was assessed on a 3-point scale ('0' = normal, '1' = above, '-1' = below normal range), and overall severity on a 6-point scale ('1' = normal voice, '6' = severe dysphonia).

Statistical Analysis

As a first step in the analysis, Pearson product-moment correlations were calculated in order to obtain an estimate of the reliability of the ratings and the interdependency of the various parameters. Testing for group differences with respect to the various parameters considered (GHD, MDVP, EGG, and perceptual ratings) relied on MANOVAs after principal component analysis (PCA) for data reduction. Because four groups of variables were considered for analysis, Bonferroni correction of the level of significance had to be performed ($p < 0.05/4$ for the MANOVAs). To further delineate the profiles of voice performance, post-hoc t-tests ($p < 0.05$) were carried out with each single parameter.

RESULTS

Goettinger Hoarseness Diagram

The two GHD parameters, entered simultaneously in a MANOVA, yielded significant inter-group differences ($F[2;17] = 7.12$; $p < 0.01$). Furthermore, t-tests revealed a significantly larger IRR and NOI in the TBI as compared to the control group (Table II, Appendix). This effect was more pronounced with respect to IRR (IRR: 8 out of a total of 10 TBI speakers above the normal range; NOI: 3/10). Furthermore, the TBI patients showed larger intra-subject variability than the control speakers (Fig. 1).

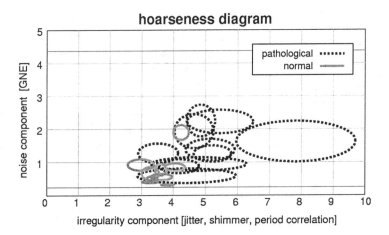

FIG. 1 Goettinger Hoarseness Diagram: Depicted are speakers' means of the two parameters IRR (y-axis) and NOI (x-axis) for the TBI (dotted, black ellipses) and the control group (solid, grey ellipses). The diameters of the ellipses correspond to the respective standard deviations. The grey region in the lower left part of the figure represents the normal range based on 88 normal speakers participating in a study by Michealis et al. (1998).

Multi-Dimensional Voice Program

Because of their extreme aperiodicity, vowel productions of TBI speaker P8 could not be analyzed by means of the MDVP program. Thus, this part of the analysis had to rely on the data from 19 subjects only (9 TBI speakers, 10 controls). PCA of the variables jitter, shimmer, NHR, VTI, and SPI yielded two main factors. The first principal component accounted for 53% of variability, loaded by all five variables, especially shimmer, jitter, and NHR. All three parameters were highly correlated with each other (shimmer/jitter: $r = 0.8788$, $p < 0.001$; shimmer/NHR: $r = 0.6372$, $p < 0.01$; jitter/NHR: $r = 0.4830$, $p < 0.05$). The second component explained 27% of variability, being mainly loaded by SPI without major contributions of the remaining parameters (Table 1). A MANOVA applied to these two components to test for group differences yielded a significant effect ($F[2;16] = 10.06$; $p < 0.01$). Post-hoc t-tests showed significant group differences for the first, but not for the second principal component, as well as for jitter ($p < 0.05$), shimmer ($p < 0.01$), NHR ($p < 0.001$), and VTI ($p < 0.05$) (Table II, Appendix).

TABLE 1

Principal component analysis of the perceptual data and the MDVP parameters.

Perception	Perc-PC1	Perc-PC2	MDVP	MDVP-PC1	MDVP-PC2
EigenValue	3.87	1.39	EigenValue	2.67	1.37
Percent	64.42	23.17	Percent	53.45	27.46
CumPercent	64.42	87.59	CumPercent	53.45	80.92
		E i g e n v e c t o r s			
Strained	0.42	-0.40	Jitter	0.54	0.06
Rough	0.46	0.16	Shimmer	0.58	-0.1
Creaky	0.45	-0.20	NHR	0.29	-0.67
Breathy	0.04	0.83	VTI	0.49	0.1
Nasal	0.41	0.28	SPI	0.24	0.72
Severity	0.50	0.08			

Note. Perc-PC1 and Perc-PC2: First and second principal component derived from the perceptual data. MDVP-PC1 and MDVP-PC2: First and second principal component derived from preselected acoustic features of the Multi-Dimensional Voice Program.

Perceptual Ratings

With the exception of 'deviation from normal pitch' and 'pitch and amplitude fluctuations', all of the perceptual variables considered exhibited fairly good mean inter- and intra-rater reliability (Table 2). Hence, the former two were not considered for statistical analysis. The patients predominantly exhibited strained-strangled, rough, creaky, and hypernasal voices. Mean overall severity of dysphonia amounted to 2.3 (SD = 0.66) in the control and 4.18 (SD = 0.93) in the TBI group. The large standard deviation of the TBI group reflects its heterogenity with respect to perceived voice disorders. Four speakers (P3, P8, P9, P10) were classified as severely disturbed (mean overall severity 4.8, 5.2,

TABLE 2

Mean inter- and intra-rater correlation coefficients.

Perceptual features	Inter-rater correlation	SD	Intra-rater correlation	SD
Strained-strangled	0.56	0.16	0.79	0.14
Rough	0.51	0.25	0.77	0.20
Creaky	0.80	0.07	0.81	0.17
Breathy	0.48	0.20	0.77	0.10
Nasal	0.62	0.16	0.79	0.19
Overall severity	0.78	0.08	0.88	0.05

Note. SD = Standard deviation across pairs of raters for inter-rater and across raters for intra-rater correlations.

5.0, and 5.0, respectively). A single TBI patient (P6) fell into the category "undisturbed" (overall severity 2.2), despite the fact that during conversation, his voice had been considered as mildly to moderately rough and strained-strangled. In retrospect, his speaking mode may have accounted for this impression, since he quite often spoke on residual air and with an intermittent hypernasal voice. PCA yielded two principal components accounting for 64% and 23% of variance, respectively (Table 1). The first component was loaded by all rating dimensions apart from breathiness. The first component might correspond to overall severity of the voice disorder which in this population mainly reflected perceived roughness and hypernasality. Nine subjects of the TBI group achieved higher values than any one of the controls in this regard. The dimensions 'breathiness' and, to a minor degree, nasality, concomitant with an inverse contribution of the features 'strained-strangled' and 'creaky', loaded the second principal component. Only a single TBI speaker (P10) achieved a value above the normal range in this regard. A MANOVA performed with the two principal components derived from the perceptual data yielded a significant group effect $(F[2;17] = 14.63; p < 0.01)$. Post-hoc tests applied to the principal components as well as the underlying original variables showed significant group differences $(p < 0.05)$ both for the first principal component and all perceptual dimensions with the exception of 'breathiness' and 'nasality' (Table II, Appendix).

Correlation of Acoustic and Perceptual Data

The GHD showed a stronger correspondance with the perceptual estimates than the MDVP. First, a highly significant canonical correlation between the two GHD measures and the two principal components derived from the perceptual data emerged. Both the IRR and the NOI parameter showed an inter-relationship with the perceptual severity factor, whereas only the NOI parameter correlated with the second perceptual component, the latter being predominantly loaded by breathiness. Second, canonical correlation between the MDVP factors and the perceptual data failed to reveal any significant effects. As concerns single principal components, only the correlation between MDVP-PC1 and Perc-PC1 achieved significance ($p < 0.01$; Table 3).

EGG Measurements

Group differences with respect to the shape of EGG traces were tested by a MANOVA using the OQ and SQ values. The TBI group did not significantly differ from the control group in this respect ($p > 0.1$). Considering the individual measurements, it is noteworthy, however, that three TBI speakers achieved SQ values exceeding the normal range (Table II, Appendix).

TABLE 3

Correlation of the principal components from the acoustic and perceptual data sets.

	Perc-PC1	Perc-PC2	Canonical Correlation
MDVP-PC1	0.5599*	0.2680	0.6449
MDVP-PC2	-0.0341	0,4252	
GHD-IRR	0.6600**	0.1841	0.8839**
GHD-NOI	0.6588*	0.5679*	

Note. Perc-PC1 and Perc-PC2: First and second principal component of the perceptual features. MDVP-PC1 and MDVP-PC2: First and second principal component of preselected acoustic features of the Multi-Dimensional Voice Program. GHD-IRR and GHD-NOI: the two parameters of the Goettinger Hoarseness Diagram. **$p < 0.001$; *$p < 0.01$

DISCUSSION

Regarding acoustic measures of phonation, the TBI and control speakers could best be differentiated by an increased IRR component (GHD) and enlarged jitter, shimmer, and NHR values (MDVP). Comparison of acoustic and perceptual data showed the first principal component of the MDVP and the IRR-component to be highly correlated with the first principal component of the perceptual ratings. More specifically, NHR values reflected perceived 'strained-strangleness' and 'creakiness', and jitter and shimmer corresponded best with perceived roughness. As expected, the IRR-component correlated highly with both roughness and creakiness (i.e. with irregularity of the vocal fold vibrations). Acoustic and perceptual data, thus, support the notion of laryngeal hypertonicity in most speakers with post-traumatic dysarthrophonia at a late post-injury stage (Morasch, Joussen & Ziegler, 1987). Lesions of the bilateral corticobulbar tract may have caused the laryngeal and pharyngeal musculature to be triggered into hypercontraction by the subglottal airpressure and subsequently caused a strained-strangled and harsh voice (Aronson, 1994).

The EGG parameters considered, i.e. open and speed quotient, failed to differentiate between the control and TBI group. Conceivably, TBI dysphonia is characterized by a rather nonhomogeneous profile of abnormalities. Nevertheless, three (P2, P3, P7) TBI speakers exhibited SQ values above the normal range indicating a longer opening phase most likely due to an enlarged vocal fold resistance and/or a faster closing phase subsequent to increased recoil forces. Indeed, the three TBI speakers with increased SQ values presented with severe ataxic-spastic dysarthrophonia at perceptual evaluation (Table I, Appendix). In accordance with this suggestion Theodoros and Murdoch (1994) found the EGG closing phase to be shortened in patients suffering from post-traumatic speech and voice disorders.

Breathiness was not a salient feature in our TBI group. Only the voice of a single dysarthric speaker was jugded to be breathy above the normal range. This observation is in line with previous studies (Vogel & von Cramon, 1982; Hartmann & von Cramon, 1984) indicating predominant strained-strangled voice quality of various degrees in the late post-injury stage. With regard to acoustic data, SPI did not differentiate between groups. A previous study had found this parameter to contribute to breathiness but not to roughness in Parkinson's dysarthria (Hertrich & Ackermann, 1995). Also the increase of the GHD-NOI component in the TBI group as compared to the control group was due to values above the normal range in three TBI speakers only. In addition, it seems that high SPI and NOI values do not exclusively correspond to increased breathiness, but also to nasality. Only one (P10) of the three TBI speakers (P3, P9, P10) was slightly hypernasal above the normal range and was also perceived as highly breathy (Table II, Appendix).

The EGG parameter OQ was not significantly increased in the TBI group as compared to the control group. Also no significant group differences for the OQ was reported in the TBI subjects studied by Theodoros et al. (1994). Pathophysiologically, an increased OQ indicates an extended open phase or glottal chink (Morasch et al., 1987) adding noise to the speech signal, which in turn would have been perceived as breathiness. In our speakers, breathiness seems to result from irregular and subsequently incomplete vocal fold vibrations and velopharyngeal air leakage.

CONCLUSION

Both the IRR and NOI components showed a significant correlation with perceived overall severity of voice disorder. In addition, NOI was the only acoustic parameter highly correlated with the perceptual dimension breathiness. Regarding the MDVP analysis, only the first main component was significantly correlated with the perceptual ratings. Therefore, the GHD better corresponds to perceptual ratings of post-traumatic dysphonia than MDVP, and therefore, seems to be preferable for the assessment of neurogenic voice disorders. Another advantage was that GHD was superior to MDVP in cases of severely compromised voices because all the parameters of the latter approach depend on the same pitch extraction algorithm which may fail under these conditions.

ACKNOWLEDGMENTS

This study was supported by the Federal Ministry of Education and Research (BMBF, 01 KO 9503).
Tables 2, 3, 4, Table II and Fig. I are reprints from Jaeger, M., Fröhlich, M., Hertrich, I., Ackermann, H., & Schönle, P.W. (2001). Dysphonia subsequent to severe traumatic brain injury: perceptual, acoustic and electroglotto-graphic analyses. *Folia Phoniatrica et Logopaedica*. Permission granted by S. Karger, Basel.

REFERENCES

Abberton, E.R.M., Howard, D. M., & Fourcin, A. J. (1989). Laryngographic assessment of normal voice: A tutorial. *Clinical Linguistics & Phonetics, 3,* 281-296.

Ackermann, H., & Ziegler, W. (1994). Acoustic analysis of vocal instability in cerebellar dysfunctions. *Annals of Otology, Rhinology & Laryngology, 103,* 98-104.

Aronson, E. A. (1994). Laryngeal-phonatory dysfunction in closed-head injury. *Brain Injury, 8,* 663-665.

Gerratt, B. R., Hanson, D. G., & Berke, S. G. (1987). Glottographic measures in individuals with abnormal motor control. In T. Baer, C. Sasaki & K. S. Harris (Eds.), *Laryngeal function in phonation and respiration* (pp. 521-532). Boston: Little, Brown.

Gilchrist, E., & Wilkinson, M. (1979). Some factors determining prognosis in young people with severe head injuries. *Archives of Neurology, 36,* 355-359.

Hartmann, E., & von Cramon, D. (1984). Acoustic measurement of voice quality in central dyphonia. *Journal of Communication Disorders, 17,* 425-440.

Hertrich, I., & Ackermann, H. (1995). Gender-specific vocal dysfunctions in Parkinson's disease: electroglottographic and acoustic analyses. *Annals of Otology, Rhinology & Laryngology, 104,* 197-202.

Hertrich, I., Lutzenberger, W., Spieker, S., & Ackermann, H. (1997). Fractal dimension of sustained vowel productions in neurological dysphonias: An acoustic and electroglottographic analysis. *Journal of the Acoustical Society of America, 102,* 652-654.

Hertrich, I., Spieker, S., & Ackermann, H. (1998). Gender-specific phonatory dysfunctions in disorders of the basal ganglia and the cerebellum: Acoustic and perceptual characteristics. In W. Ziegler & K. Deger (Eds.), *Clinical phonetics and linguistics* (pp. 448-457). London: Whurr.

Houben, G. B., Buekers, R., & Kingma, H. (1992). Characterization of the electroglottographic waveform: A primary study to investigate vocal fold functioning. *Folia Phoniatrica et Logopaedica, 44,* 269-281.

Michaelis, D., Gramss, T., & Strube, H. W. (1997). Glottal-to-noise excitation ratio – a new measure for describing pathological voices. *Acoustica, 83,* 700-706.

Michaelis, D., Fröhlich, M., & Strube H. W. (1998). Selection and combination of acoustic features for the description of pathologic voices. *Journal of the Acoustical Society of America, 103,* 1628-1639.

Morasch, H., Joussen, K., & Ziegler, W. (1987). Central laryngeal motor disorders following severe closed head trauma and cerebrovascular diseases. *Laryngology, Rhinology & Otology, 66,* 214-220 (German).

Motta, G., Cesari, U., Iengo, M., & Motta, G. (1990). Clinical application of electroglottography. *Folia Phoniatrica et Logopaedica, 42,* 111-117.

Orlikoff, R. F. (1990). Assessment of the dynamics of vocal fold contact from the electroglottogram: Data from normal male subjects. *Journal of Speech and Hearing Research, 34,* 1066-1072.

Theodoros, D. G., Murdoch, B. E., & Chenery, H. J. (1993). Hypernasality in dysarthric speakers following severe closed head injury: a perceptual and instrumental analysis. *Brain Injury, 71,* 59-69.

Theodoros, D. G., & Murdoch, B. E. (1994). Laryngeal and phonatory dysfunction in dysarthric speakers following severe closed-head injury. *Brain Injury, 8,* 667-684.

Theodoros, D. G., Murdoch, B. E., & Chenery, H. J. (1994). Perceptual speech characteristics of dysarthric speakers following severe closed head injury. *Brain Injury, 8,* 1101-1124.

Vogel, M., & von Cramon, D. (1982). Dysphonia after traumatic midbrain damage: a follow-up study. *Folia Phoniatrica et Logopaedica, 34,* 150-159.

Yorkston, K. M., Beukelman, D. R., & Bell, K. R. (1988). Traumatic brain injury. In K. M. Yorkston, D. R. Beukelman & K. R. Bell (Eds.), *Clinical management of dysarthric speakers* (pp. 97-109). Boston: Little, Brown.

Zwirner, P., Michaelis, D., Fröhlich, M., Strube, H. W., & Kruse, E. (1998). Korrelationen zwischen perzeptueller Beurteilung von Stimmen nach dem RBH-System und akustischen Parametern. In M. Gross (Ed.), *Aktuelle phoniatrisch-pädaudiologische Aspekte* (pp. 63-67). Heidelberg: Median.

APPENDIX

TABLE 1

Clinical and demographic data of the TBI group.

No	Age	YPI	Lesions	Diagnosis and Aetiology	Evaluation of spontaneous speech: Phonation, respiration, resonance, articulation and intelligibility
1	37	14;5	capsula interna; ventricles; midbrain	moderate spastic-ataxic dysarthrophonia secondary to TBI from car accident	soft phonation, partly strained-strangled voice, pitch rather high, occasional pitch jumps; moderately increased inspiration rate; intermittent hypernasality; fricatives, labials imprecise, frequent reduction of syllables, severely decreased intelligibility
2	42	21;0	no imaging available	moderate spastic-ataxic dysarthrophonia secondary to TBI from car accident	harsh, partly strained-strangled voice, normal pitch; moderately increased inspiration rate; moderately hypernasal; fricatives, plosives, lateral imprecise, moderately decreased intelligibility
3	38	4;9	retrobulbar B; ponto-medullar R; tempo-ro-polar L; fronto-basal L	severe spastic-ataxic dysarthrophonia secondary to TBI from fall in the mountains	severely harsh, strained-strangled voice, pitch rather low, occasional pitch breaks; severely increased inspiration rate; severely hypernasal; imprecise, nasalized, frequently non-identifiable sounds; plosives produced with too much effort; syllabic speech, moderately reduced intelligibility

No	Age	YPI	Lesions	Diagnosis and aetiology	Evaluation of spontaneous speech: Phonation; respiration; resonance; articulation and intelligibility
4	54	27;0	fronto-paramedian R, mild atrophia fronto-parietal B	mild spastic-ataxic dysarthrophonia secondary to TBI from car accident	mildly harsh voice, normal pitch; no respiratory or resonatory deficits; mild articulation disorder for [ʀ] and [ʀ] clusters; intelligibility not impaired
5	41	8;6	midbrain; brainstem secondary to epidural hematoma	moderate spastic-ataxic dysarthrophonia secondary to TBI from fall	severely harsh, strained-strangled, gurgling voice, normal pitch; highly variable, mainly increased inspiration rates; intermittent hypernasality; labials, plosives, fricatives imprecise, intelligibility slightly impaired
6	43	2;4	intra-cerebral; basal ganglia; brainstem	mild spastic-ataxic dysarthrophonia secondary to TBI from car accident	mildly to moderately harsh, strained-strangled voice, normal pitch; while speaking rate slightly increased, inspiration rate close to normal, however, inspiration often audible; intermittent hypernasal; [ʃ] and plosives imprecise, intelligibility not impaired
7	30	1;9	fronto-temporal and fronto-parietal R	severe spastic-ataxic dysarthrophonia secondary to TBI from car accident	moderately harsh, strained-strangled voice, pitch low; moderately increased inspiration rates; severely hypernasal; all sounds nasalized, consonants mostly imprecise; at times blocks and iterations of word-initial labials or vowels, intelligibility severely impaired
8	31	2;10	occipital B, parietal B; cerebellar; pontomes-encephal; basal ganglia L	severe spastic-ataxic dysarthrophonia secondary to TBI from car accident	severely harsh, strained-strangled voice, low pitch; severely increased inspiration rate; severely hypernasal resonance; lengthened sounds, all consonants with nasal emissions, often not recognizable, intelligibility severely reduced, augmented use of spelling device and laptop
9	37	17;0	temporal B; SAB; brainstem	moderate spastic dysarthrophonia secondary to TBI from car accident	moderately harsh, strained-strangled voice, voice decays, pitch lowered; moderately increased inspiration rate; moderately hyper-nasal resonance; plosives imprecise, nasal emission with fricatives; often sustained labialization in clusters, reduction of apical plosive, intelligibility moderately reduced

No	Age	YPI	Lesions	Diagnosis and aetiology	Evaluation of spontaneous speech: Phonation; respiration; resonance; articulation and intelligibility
10	35	4;11	multiple cortical lesions B; brainstem; cerebellum	moderate spastic-ataxic dysarthrophonia secondary to TBI from car accident	moderately harsh, strained-strangled voice, pitch normal; severely increased inspiration rate; severely hypernasal; lengthened sounds, consonant clusters imprecise, reductions of sounds and syllables; nasal emissions; syllabic speech, intelligibility moderately impaired

Note. No: number of patients; age in years; YPI: years post injury; B: bilateral; L: left; R: right; SAB: subarachnoidal bleeding; TBI: traumatic brain injury.

TABLE II

Subject means of principal components and single parameters from all analyses.

	TBI patients										Controls	
MEASURES	1	2	3	4	5	6	7	8	9	10	ξ	SD
GHD-IRR	5.14	3.52	5.45	4.18	4.79	5.21	4.40	7.82	4.64	4.85	3.64	0.43
GHD-NOI	1.38	1.27	2.22	0.88	0.94	1.26	0.59	1.62	1.93	2.25	0.80	0.46
MDVP-PC1	0.75	-0.51	0.60	0.08	1.22	0.99	-0.05	–	0.57	0.57	-0.42	0.29
MDVP-PC2	-0.15	0.05	1.08	-0.58	-0.20	-0.27	0.10	–	-0.50	0.07	0.04	0.42
JITTER	1.75	0.44	1.01	0.58	2.19	1.35	0.83	–	1.19	1.70	0.67	0.33
SHIMMER	7.22	2.54	4.95	4.55	10.9	8.64	2.86	–	7.04	5.75	3.35	1.21
NHR	0.16	0.14	0.18	0.16	0.16	0.19	0.17	–	0.15	0.15	0.13	0.01
VTI	0.05	0.04	0.04	0.06	0.05	0.05	0.04	–	0.06	0.05	0.04	0.01
SPI	14.1	14.3	35.1	10.9	13.7	14.6	13.9	–	15.9	20.7	13.7	5.25
EGG-F0	135	113	114	102	129	107	107	100	94	98	113	19
OQ	51.3	52.2	48.9	51.9	56.6	65.2	56.3	57.1	54.6	62.4	57.1	3.15
SQ	336	488	495	300	323	333	493	408	152	355	381	81
PERC-PC1	0.87	0.39	0.99	0.09	0.22	-0.46	0.41	1.34	1.24	0.63	-0.57	0.35

| | TBI patients | | | | | | | | | | | Controls | |
MEASURES	1	2	3	4	5	6	7	8	9	10	ξ	SD
PERC-PC2	-0.44	0.16	0.16	-0.55	-0.03	0.13	-0.48	-0.07	0.25	1.17	-0.03	0.41
strained	3.2	2.6	2.6	2.8	2.2	1.6	2.8	3,0	3.2	2.0	1.78	0.71
rough	**2.8**	2.0	**2.8**	2.2	**2.6**	2.2	2.2	**3.25**	**3.0**	**3.0**	1.48	0.38
creaky	**3.6**	2.0	**3.4**	2.4	2.4	1.6	**3.0**	**4.0**	**3.6**	1.4	1.28	1.93
breathy	1.2	1.8	1.8	1,0	1.6	1.8	1.0	1.5	2.2	3.2	1.52	0.61
nasal	2.0	**3.0**	**3.2**	1.2	1.6	1.2	2.0	**3.2**	**3.2**	**3.2**	1.58	0.48
severity	**4.6**	**4.0**	**4.8**	3.4	**3.8**	2.2	**3.8**	**5.2**	**5.0**	**5.0**	2.30	0.66

Note. Bold numbers indicate TBI values outside the normal range; bold letters of parameter labels correspond to a significant difference (t-test; $p > 0.05$). – : Missing values; ξ: mean of control group; SD: standard deviation; P1-P10: TBI speakers 1 through 10.

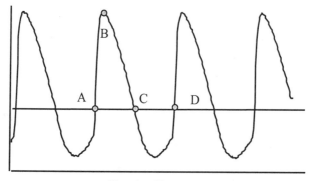

Duration 30 ms

FIG. I Oscillogram of the EGG signal of a normal speaker.
Definition of intervals are based on the zero-crossings (A, C, D) and the peak value (B) of each pitch period. A–B: closing phase, increasing vocal fold contact; B–C: opening phase, decreasing vocal fold contact; A–C: closed phase, vocal fold contact; C–D: open phase, no vocal fold contact.

38

Automatic Estimation of Vocal Harmonics-to-Noise Ratio using Cepstral Analysis

Shaheen N. Awan

Quantification of the relative amount of additive noise in the voice signal is an essential aspect of the diagnostic and therapeutic protocol with voice disordered patients. Traditional methods (jitter, shimmer, and harmonics-to-noise ratio; HNR) of quantifying aperiodicity in the voice may be error prone due to the necessity of accurately identifying cycle boundaries (i.e. 'peaks' or 'zero-crossings'). As an alternative to the aforementioned traditional voice analysis methods, this study attempted to quantify the degree of additive noise using cepstral analysis.

The Cepstral Method

To compute the cepstrum, the following steps are carried out:
1. A Fourier transformation (FFT) is computed for a selected part ('window') of the voice signal
2. The FFT is next converted to the log power spectrum
3. The cepstrum is derived by computing the FFT of the log power spectrum. The cepstrum is then displayed as an amplitude-by-quefrency graph (quefrency is effectively synonymous with period). A prominent 'peak' referred to as the cepstral peak prominence (CPP) characterizes the cepstrum of the voice signal. The CPP occurs at a location that corresponds to the fundamental period of the signal

Of course, the reciprocal of the quefrency is the fundamental frequency. Because the cepstrum is a frequency-domain method, it does not require the identification of cycle boundaries to identify the fundamental period of the voice signal. This is a particular advantage over traditional methods of voice analysis since the cepstral method may be validly applied to even severely perturbed voice signals. Once the fundamental period is identified (via identification of the cepstral peak), a ratio may be calculated between the amplitude of the cepstral peak (i.e. the cepstral peak prominence – CPP) and the background 'noise' of the cepstrum. The relative amplitude of the CPP has been shown to be a strong correlate to perceptual ratings of breathiness (Hillenbrand, Cleveland & Erickson, 1994) and hoarseness (Dejonckere & Wieneke, 1996).

Generally, the cepstral peak prominence has been identified via manual techniques. Hillenbrand et al. (1994) reported that automatic methods of identifying the CPP may show difficulty, particularly with breathy signals. However, Hillenbrand et al. (1994) reported that measures of the cepstral peak amplitude could be used to provide "accurate predictions of breathiness ratings in spite of these errors" (p. 773).

The purpose of this study was to assess the validity of a new algorithm for computing the cepstrum and automatically identifying the cepstral peak prominence (CPP) in synthesized vowels. Once the CPP was identified, an estimate of the harmonics-to-noise ratio (HNR) was also computed.

METHODOLOGY

The cepstral algorithm used in this study is similar to that described by Noll (1967), Baken (1987) and Kent and Read (1992). However, the identification of the cepstral peak prominence is carried out automatically with a peak-picking routine. In addition, prior to peak-picking, the cepstral coefficients are squared to emphasize the cepstral peak. The algorithm discussed herein was written in Visual Basic by the author, and is currently incorporated in the *EZVoicePlus*™ voice analysis software program (VoiceTek Enterprises, Nescopeck, USA).

The algorithm used in this study computes the cepstrum in the following manner:

1. The user selected area of the signal is divided into a successive series of non-overlapping windows. The length of each window is equal to the spectral window length (default 1024 pts.). If the length of the selected sample for analysis is not an integer multiple of the spectral window length, the length of the selected sample is truncated. In this study, 50 cycles of vibration were analyzed for all signals.

2. A Hamming window is applied and the Fourier transformation is computed for each window and stored. The algorithm used in this program is referred to as the discrete Fourier transformation (DFT) and is based on a description by Kassab (1984). The average DFT for the computed series of windows is then computed and displayed.

3. The average DFT is next used to compute the average log power spectrum.

4. The average cepstrum for the selected area is next realized by computing the DFT of the log power spectrum. The cepstrum is graphically displayed.

The algorithm was tested using synthesized vowels at various fundamental frequencies mixed with white noise at various known HNR levels. Vowels were synthesized using a version of the Klatt voice synthesizer at 22 kHz and 16-bits of resolution. Fundamental frequencies extended from 110 Hz to 220 Hz to reflect the range of average speaking fundamental frequencies of adult males and females; formant frequencies for the vowel "ah" [ɑ] were also adjusted to reflect gender differences.

Following vowel synthesis, white noise was added point for point with the synthesized vowels to produce HNRs ranging from 32 to -16 dB in 3 dB steps. The range of HNRs investigated in this study easily encompassed the commonly observed range of normal and disordered HNRs. Because the white noise signals in this study were unmodulated and relatively constant in overall amplitude, the final synthesized signals were consistent with breathy voice samples rather than rough samples, in which characteristics such as phonatory aperiodicity and diplophonia are often key characteristics.

Finally, 50 cycle samples of the synthesized vowels were analyzed using the previously described program which incorporates a simple peak-picking routine to identify the CPP. In this study, cepstral frequencies > 500 Hz were removed from analyses because the fundamental frequencies of the vowel samples were known to not exist in this region and the higher frequencies of the cepstrum are generally reflective of vocal tract resonances rather than phonatory vibration. Figures 1 and 2 provide examples of cepstral analysis for highly periodic vs. relatively aperiodic signals.

The CPP generally occurs at the *quefrency* that corresponds to the dominant *rahmonic* of the signal under analysis. Quefrency (time) can easily be transformed into frequency (in Hz). Therefore, the CPP presents another method by which the fundamental frequency of a signal may be identified. However, the primary importance of the CPP in this study is that a measure of the relative amplitude of this peak has been shown to be a strong predictor of vocal severity and a quantitative measure of the degree of noise within the voice signal. In this study, the two methods used to compute the relative amplitude of the CPP were as follows:

1. CPP/AVG Ratio: The ratio (in dB) of the amplitude of the identified CPP to the average amplitude of the entire cepstrum below the CPP cutoff.

2. CPP/EXP Ratio: The ratio (in dB) of the amplitude of the identified CPP to the expected amplitude at the location of the identified CPP as determined via linear regression. This is based on a technique described by Hillenbrand (1994).

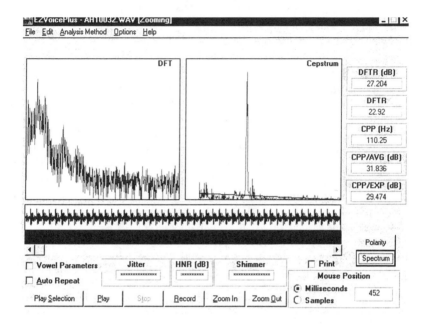

FIG. 1 Discrete Fourier transform (DFT) and cepstrum computed for a 110 Hz synthesized vowel sample mixed with noise to 32 dB HNR. The DFT is an intensity × frequency graph; the cepstrum is an amplitude × quefrency graph (both graphs are automatically scaled within the program). Note the extremely prominent cepstral peak (CPP) in this signal.

RESULTS

A series of Pearson's r correlations were computed between computations of CPP/AVG and CPP/EXP (both in dB) and the expected HNR. For the purposes of this presentation, estimates of HNR via the cepstral method were averaged across test frequencies.

Results showed strong significant correlations between cepstral estimates of HNR and expected HNR (r = 0.93 and 0.96 for CPP/AVG and CPP/EXP, respectively). Further analysis showed that correlations were extremely strong between cepstral estimates of HNR and expected HNR in signals > 2 dB HNR (r = 0.99 for CPP/AVG and CPP/EXP ratios). However, correlations were

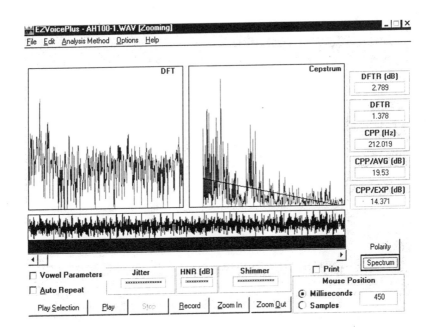

FIG. 2 Discrete Fourier Transform (DFT) and cepstrum computed for a 110 Hz
synthesized vowel sample mixed with noise to -1 dB HNR. Note that the "true" cepstral
peak has been supplanted by higher frequency noise, resulting in failure to accurately
estimate the vocal F_0.

nonsignificant between cepstral estimates and expected HNRs in signals < 2 dB
($r = -0.62$ and 0.10 for CPP/AVG and CPP/EXP, respectively). Figures 3 and 4
display the expected HNRs versus CPP/AVG and CPP/EXP ratios as derived via
cepstral analysis.

DISCUSSION

Traditional methods of quantifying noise in the vocal signal have been
dependent on identifying fundamental frequency from the time-based signal.
The difficulty in identifying cycle boundaries in even marginally perturbed
signals have led some researchers to suggest abandonment of methods such as
jitter and shimmer for quantifying noise in the voice (Bielamowicz, Kreiman,
Gerratt, Dauer & Berke, 1996). Therefore, the fact that cepstral methods of
estimating harmonics-to-noise ratio correlated quite well with expected HNRs

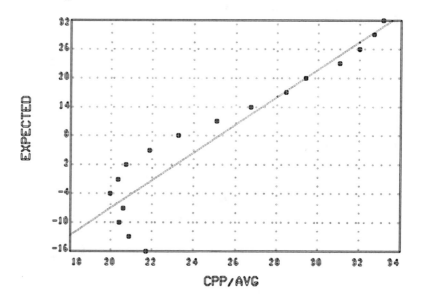

FIG. 3 Plot of expected HNR's vs. the CPP/AVG ratio (both in dB). The linear regression line is also shown ($r = 0.93$, $p < 0.001$).

across a wide range of perturbed signals is highly encouraging for clinical voice analysis, since the cepstral method is not dependent on the identification of cycle-boundaries.

Although the overall findings of this study showed strong correlations between cepstral estimates of HNR and expected HNR levels, results also showed that the automatic cepstral peak identification method used in this study failed for signals < 2 dB HNR. In extremely perturbed signals, the amplitude of the fundamental frequency (as represented by the cepstral peak prominence) is consistently "overshadowed" by some other, usually higher, frequency (see Fig. 4). In these cases, automatic peak-picking methods mistake the higher frequency as the 'true' vocal F_0, with the result being that measures of the relative amplitude of the CPP consistently overestimate the true HNR of the signal. This was most evident in the relation between CPP/AVG vs. expected HNRs for signals < 2 dB HNR in which an inverse correlation was actually observed (i.e. as the signal became more perturbed (HNR decreased), the CPP/AVG ratio actually became greater – the opposite of expectations). It is evident that, for severely perturbed signals, manual selection of the cepstral peak

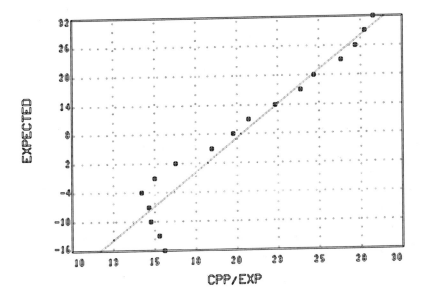

FIG. 4 Plot of expected HNR vs. the CPP/EXP ratio (both in dB). The linear regression line is also shown ($r = 0.96, p < 0.001$).

prominence would probably be more effective than automatic methods. It should be noted, however, that most clinical voice cases present with HNRs much greater than 2 dB, and therefore, the fact that cepstral methods may have difficulty with these types of severe signals may be relatively clinically insignificant.

In conclusion, cepstral methods present a valuable addition to quantitative voice analysis methods (particularly as applied to breathy voice types). Future algorithms may incorporate smoothing and/or weighting of the cepstral coefficients as methods by which more accurate identification of the CPP in severely perturbed signals may be conducted. In addition, future studies using the cepstral method described in this chapter with clinical cases can more clearly ascertain normative versus disordered expectations and investigate the possible relation between cepstral characteristics and perceptual scaling of the severity of quality disturbance in voice disordered patients.

REFERENCES

Baken, R. (1987). *Clinical measurement of speech and voice.* Boston, MA: Little, Brown.

Bielamowicz, S., Kreiman, J., Gerratt, B. R., Dauer, M. S., & Berke, G. S. (1996). Comparison of voice analysis systems for perturbation measurement. *Journal of Speech and Hearing Research, 39,* 126–134.

Dejonckere, P., & Wieneke, G. (1996). Cepstra of normal and pathological voices: Correlation with acoustic, aerodynamic, and perceptual data. In M. Ball & M. Duckworth (Eds.), *Advances in clinical phonetics.* Amsterdam: John Benjamins.

Hillenbrand, J., Cleveland, R., & Erickson, R. (1994). Acoustic correlates of breathy vocal quality. *Journal of Speech and Hearing Research, 37,* 769-778.

Kassab, V. (1984). *Technical basic.* Englewood Cliffs, NJ: Prentice Hall, Inc.

Kent, R., & Read, C. (1992). *The acoustic analysis of speech.* San Diego, CA: Singular Publishing.

Noll, A. M. (1967). Cepstrum pitch determination. *Journal of the Acoustical Society of America, 41,* 293-309.

Author Index

Subject Index

Note: An *f* following a page number denotes a figure; a *t* following a page number denotes a table.